CLYMER®

YAMAHA

KODIAK ATV • 1993-1998

The world's finest publisher of mechanical how-to manuals

PRIMEDIA
Business Directories & Books

P.O. Box 12901, Overland Park, Kansas 66282-2901

FIRST EDITION
First Printing November, 1998
Second Printing August, 2002

Printed in U.S.A.

ISBN: 0-89287-717-0

Library of Congress: 98-72835

TECHNICAL PHOTOGRAPHY: Ed Scott and Ron Wright. Special thanks to Clawson Motorsports, Fresno, California, for their help with this book.

TECHNICAL ILLUSTRATIONS: Mitzi McCarthy and Steve Amos.

WIRING DIAGRAMS: Robert Caldwell.

COVER: Mark Clifford Photography, Los Angeles, California. Yamaha Kodiak courtesy of Apache Yamaha, Phoenix, Arizona.

TOOLS AND EQUIPMENT: K & L Supply Co. at www.klsupply.com.

CONTENTS

QUICK REFERENCE DATA

ATV INFORMATION

MODEL:______________________________ YEAR:______________

VIN NUMBER:______________________________

ENGINE SERIAL NUMBER:______________________________

CARBURETOR SERIAL NUMBER OR I.D. MARK:______________________________

TIRE INFLATION PRESSURE

Year	Front	Rear
1993-1995	3.4-3.3 (17-23)	3.2-3.9 (22-27)
1996-on	3.2-3.9 (22-27)	3.2-3.9 (22-27)

RECOMMENDED LUBRICANTS AND FLUIDS

Engine oil	
Grade	API SE
Viscosity	SAE 10W-30, 10W-40, 20W-40
Final gear oil	SAE 80 API GL-4 hypoid gear oil
Front differential gear oil (4-wheel drive)	SAE 80 API GL-4 hypoid gear oil
Battery refill	Distilled water
Brake fluid	DOT 4

REFILL CAPACITIES

	ml	U.S. quarts	Imp. quarts
Engine oil and transfer oil			
Without oil filter replacement			
Engine oil	2,400	2.5	2.1
Transfer gear oil	300	0.32	0.26
Total engine oil and transfer gear oil	2,700	2.9	2.4
With oil filter replacement			
Total engine oil and transfer gear oil	2,800	3.0	2.5
Engine overhaul total change	3,700	3.9	3.3
Final gear case oil			
Oil change	190	0.20	0.17
Overhaul capacity	240	0.26	0.22
Differential gear case			
Oil change	470	0.50	0.41
Overhaul capacity	500	0.53	0.44

TUNE-UP SPECIFICATIONS

Item	Specification
Carburetor adjustment	
Idle speed	1350-1450 rpm
Pilot air screw (turns out)	2.0
Engine compression	
Standard	920 kPa (131 psi)
Minimum	740 kPa (105 psi)
Maximum	1,020 kPa (145 psi)
Ignition timing	Non-adjustable, see text for procedure
Spark plug	
Type	
Canada and Europe	NGK DR8EA
U.S. and all other	NGK D8EA
Gap	0.6-0.7 mm (0.024-0.028 in.)
Valve clearance (engine cold)	
Intake	0.06-0.10 mm (0.002-0.004 in.)
Exhaust	0.16-0.20 mm (0.06-0.008 in.)

CHAPTER ONE

GENERAL INFORMATION

This detailed, comprehensive manual covers the Yamaha Kodiak ATVs manufactured from 1993-1998. The expert text gives complete information on maintenance, tune-up, repair and overhaul. Hundreds of photos and drawings guide you through every step. The book includes all you need to know to keep your Yamaha running right.

A shop manual is a reference. You want to be able to find information fast. As in all Clymer books, this one is designed with you in mind. All chapters are thumb tabbed. Important items are extensively indexed at the back of the book. All procedures, tables, photos and illustrations in this manual are designed for the reader who may be working on the vehicle or using this manual for the first time. Frequently used specifications and capacities are summarized in the *Quick Reference Data* pages at the front of the book.

Keep the book handy in your tool box or tow vehicle. It will help you better understand how your vehicle runs, lower repair costs and generally improve your satisfaction with the vehicle.

Yamaha uses a letter designation in their serial number to indicate the model year of their vehicles. For example the 1993 model year is designated by a E and the 1998 is K. Refer to **Table 1** at the end of this chapter for the letter-to-year designation information.

Table 1 lists model coverage with engine frame serial numbers.

Table 2 lists general vehicle dimensions.

Table 3 lists vehicle weight.

Table 4 lists conversion factors.

Table 5 lists general torque specifications,

Table 6 lists technical abbreviations.

Table 7 lists metric tap drill sizes.

Table 8 provides decimal and metric equivalents.

Tables 1-8 are at the end of this chapter.

MANUAL ORGANIZATION

All dimensions, specifications and capacities are expressed in metric and U.S. standard units of measure.

This chapter provides general information and discusses equipment and tools useful both for preventive maintenance and troubleshooting.

Chapter Two provides methods and suggestions for quick and accurate diagnosis and repair of problems. Troubleshooting procedures discuss typical symptoms and logical methods to pinpoint the trouble.

Chapter Three explains all periodic lubrication and routine maintenance necessary to keep the Yamaha running well. Chapter Three also includes recommended tune-up procedures, eliminating the need to constantly consult chapters on the various assemblies.

Subsequent chapters describe specific systems such as the engine, clutch, transmission, fuel, exhaust, cooling, suspension and brakes. Each chapter provides disassembly, repair and assembly procedures in simple step-by-step form.

The text indicates procedures that are impractical for the home mechanic. Usually, it is faster and less expensive to take such repairs to a dealership service department or competent repair shop. Specifications concerning a particular system are included at the end of the appropriate chapter.

Some of the procedures in this manual specify special tools. In most cases, the tool is illustrated either in use or alone. Well-equipped mechanics may find they can substitute similar tools already on hand or can fabricate a suitable special tool.

NOTES, CAUTIONS AND WARNINGS

The terms NOTE, CAUTION and WARNING have specific meanings in this manual. A NOTE provides additional information to make a step or procedure easier or clearer. Disregarding a NOTE could cause inconvenience, but would not cause equipment damage or personal injury.

A CAUTION emphasizes areas where equipment damage could result. Disregarding a CAUTION could cause permanent mechanical damage; however, personal injury is unlikely.

A WARNING emphasizes areas where personal injury or even death could result from negligence. Mechanical damage may also occur. WARNINGS *are to be taken seriously*. In some cases, serious injury or death has resulted from disregarding similar warnings.

SAFETY FIRST

Professional mechanics can work for years and never sustain a serious injury. If you observe a few rules of common sense and safety, you can enjoy many safe hours servicing your machine. If you ignore these rules you can injure yourself or someone working nearby, or damage the equipment.

1. *Never* use gasoline or any type of low-flash point solvent to clean parts.

NOTE

Flash point is the lowest temperature at which the vapor of a combustible liquid will ignite momentarily in open air. A solvent with a low flash point will ignite at a lower temperature than one with a high flash point.

2. *Never* smoke or use a torch in the vicinity of flammable liquids or materials.
3. If welding or brazing is required on the machine, remove the fuel tank, carburetor and rear shock to a safe distance, at least 50 ft (15 m) away.
4. Use the proper sized wrenches to avoid damage to fasteners and injury to yourself.
5. When loosening a tight or stuck nut, be guided by what would happen if the wrench slips.
6. When replacing a fastener, make sure to use one with the same measurements and strength as the old one. Incorrect or mismatched fasteners can result in damage to the vehicle and possible personal injury. Avoid fastener kits filled with cheap and poorly made nuts, bolts, washers and cotter pins. Refer to *Fasteners* in this chapter for additional information.
7. Keep all hand and power tools in good condition. Wipe grease and oil off of tools after using them. They are difficult to hold and can cause injury. Replace or repair worn or damaged tools.
8. Keep the work area clean and uncluttered.
9. Wear safety goggles during all operations involving drilling, grinding, the use of a cold chisel, using chemicals, cleaning parts, when using compressed air or *anytime* you feel unsure about the safety of your eyes.
10. Wear the correct type of clothes for the job. Tie long hair up or cover it with a cap so that it can't accidentally fall out where it could be quickly entangled in a tool or a piece of moving equipment .
11. Keep an approved fire extinguisher nearby. Be sure it is rated for gasoline (Class B) and electrical (Class C) fires.
12. When drying bearings or other rotating parts with compressed air, never allow the air jet to rotate the bearing or part. The air jet is capable of rotating them at speeds far in excess of those for which they were designed. The bearing or rotating part is very likely to disintegrate and cause serious injury and

damage. To prevent bearing damage when using compressed air, hold the inner bearing race by hand.

WARNING
The improper use of compressed air is very dangerous. Using compressed air to dust off your clothes, equipment or workbench can cause flying particles to be blown into your eyes or skin. ***Never*** *direct or blow compressed air into your skin or through any body opening (including cuts) as this can cause severe injury or death. Compressed air should be used carefully; never allow children to use or play with compressed air.*

13. Never work on the upper part of the machine while someone is working underneath it.

14. Never carry sharp tools in your pockets.

15. There is always a right and wrong way to use tools. Learn to use them the right way.

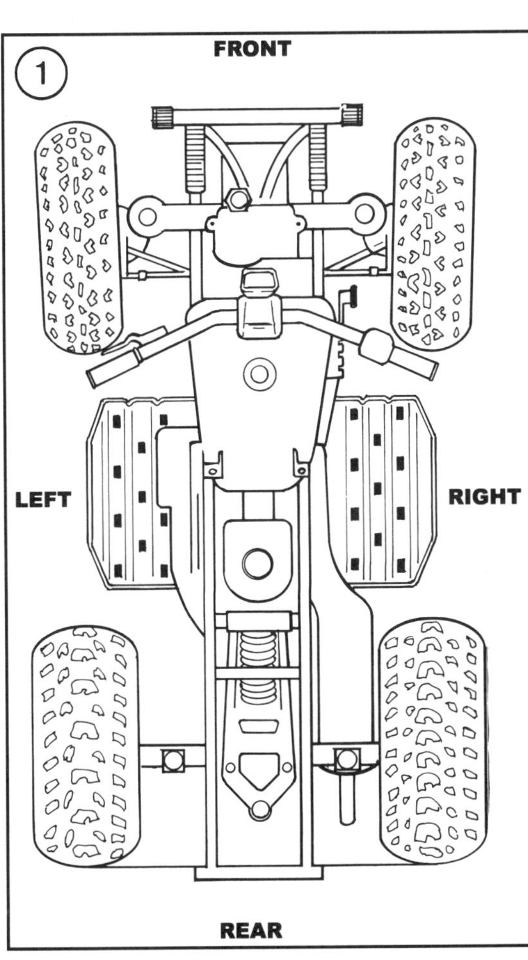

16. Do not start and run the vehicle in an enclosed area. The exhaust gases contain carbon monoxide, a colorless, tasteless and poisonous gas. Carbon monoxide levels build quickly in a small enclosed area and can cause unconsciousness and death in a short time. When it is necessary to start and run the vehicle during a service procedure, always do so outside or in a service area equipped with a ventilating system.

SERVICE HINTS

Most of the service procedures covered are straightforward and can be performed by anyone reasonably handy with tools. However, consider your capabilities carefully before attempting any operation involving major disassembly.

Take your time and do the job right. Do not forget that a newly rebuilt engine must be broken in the same way as a new one. Refer to *Engine Break-In* in Chapter Five.

1. Front, as used in this manual, refers to the front of the vehicle; the front of any component is the end closest to the front of the vehicle. The left- and right-hand sides refer to the position of the parts as viewed by a rider sitting on the seat facing forward. For example, the throttle control is on the right-hand side. These rules are simple, but confusion can cause a major inconvenience during service. See **Figure 1**.

2. Secure the vehicle in a safe manner and apply the parking brake when servicing the engine, clutch or suspension component.

3. Tag all similar internal parts for location and mark all mating parts for position. Record shim number, thickness and alignment when removed. Identify and store small parts in plastic sandwich bags. Seal and label them with masking tape.

4. Place parts from a specific area of the engine (cylinder head, cylinder, clutch, shift mechanism) into plastic boxes to keep them separated.

5. When disassembling transmission shaft assemblies, use an egg flat (the type that restaurants get their eggs in). Set the parts from the shaft in one of the depressions in the same order in which it was removed.

6. Label all electrical wiring and connectors before disconnecting them. Again, do not rely on memory alone.

7. Protect finished surfaces from physical damage or corrosion. Keep gasoline and brake fluid off painted surfaces.

8. Use penetrating oil on frozen or tight bolts, then strike the bolt head a few times with a hammer and punch (use a screwdriver on screws). Avoid the use of heat where possible, as it can warp, melt or affect the temper of parts. Heat also ruins finishes, especially paints and plastics.

9. Unless specified in the procedure, parts should not require unusual force during disassembly or assembly. If a part is difficult to remove or install, find out why before continuing.

10. To prevent small objects and abrasive dust from falling into the engine, cover all openings after exposing them.

11. Read each procedure completely while looking at the actual parts before starting a job. Make sure you thoroughly understand the procedural steps and then follow the procedure, step by step.

12. Recommendations are occasionally made to refer service or maintenance to a Yamaha dealer or a specialist in a particular field. In these cases, the work will be done more quickly and economically than if you performed the job yourself.

13. In procedural steps, the term replace means to discard a defective part and replace with a new or exchange unit. Overhaul means to remove, disassemble, inspect and replace parts as are required to recondition a major system or part.

14. Some operations require the use of a hydraulic press. If you do not own or know how to operate a press, it is wiser to have these operations performed at a shop equipped for such work, rather than to try to do the job yourself with makeshift equipment that may damage your machine.

15. Repairs go much faster and easier if your machine is clean before you begin work. There are many special cleaners on the market, like Bel-Ray Degreaser, for washing the engine and related parts. Follow the manufacturer's directions on the container for the best results. Clean all oily or greasy parts with cleaning solvent as you remove them.

WARNING

Never use gasoline as a cleaning agent. It presents an extreme fire hazard. Be sure to work in a well-ventilated area when using cleaning solvent. Keep a fire extinguisher, rated for gasoline fires, handy in any case.

CAUTION

If you use a car wash to clean your vehicle, do not direct the high pressure water hose at steering bearings, carburetor hoses, suspension components, wheel bearings or electrical components. High pressure water will flush grease out of the bearings or damage the seals.

16. Much of the labor charge for a repair made at a dealership is for the time involved during the removal, disassembly, assembly, and reinstallation of other parts to reach the defective part. It is frequently possible to perform the preliminary operations yourself, then take the defective unit to the dealer for repair at considerable savings.

17. When special tools are required, arrange to get them before you start. It is frustrating and time-consuming to get partly into a job and then be unable to complete it.

18. Make diagrams (or take a Polaroid picture) wherever similar-appearing parts are found. You may think you can remember where everything came from, but mistakes are costly. There is also the possibility that you may be sidetracked and not return to work for days or weeks and the carefully arranged parts may become disturbed.

19. When assembling parts, be sure all shims and washers are installed exactly as they came out.

20. Whenever a rotating part butts against a stationary part, look for a shim or washer. Use new gaskets if there is any doubt about the condition of the old ones. A thin coat of oil on non-pressure type gaskets may help them seal more effectively.

21. Use cold heavy grease to hold small parts in place if they tend to fall out during assembly. However, keep grease and oil away from electrical and brake components.

TORQUE SPECIFICATIONS

The materials used in the manufacture of your Yamaha may be subjected to uneven stresses if the fasteners used to hold the subassemblies are not installed and tightened correctly. Loose or missing fasteners can cause cylinder head warpage, crankcase leaks, premature bearing and seal failure and suspension failure. An accurate torque wrench (described in this chapter) should be used together with the torque specifications listed at the end of most chapters.

Torque specifications throughout this manual are given in Newton-meters (N•m) and foot-pounds (ft.-lb.).

Existing torque wrenches calibrated in meter kilograms can be used by performing a simple conversion. All you have to do is move the decimal point one place to the right; for example, 3.5 mkg = 35 N•m. This conversion is accurate enough for mechanical work even though the exact mathematical conversion is 3.5 mkg = 34.3 N•m.

Refer to **Table 5** for standard torque specifications for various size screws, bolts and nuts not listed in the respective chapter tables. To use the table, first determine the size of the bolt or nut. Use a vernier caliper and measure the inside dimension of the threads of the nut and across the threads for a bolt.

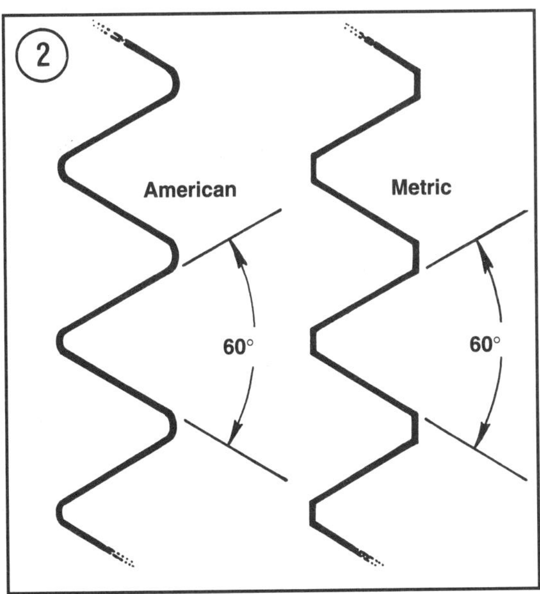

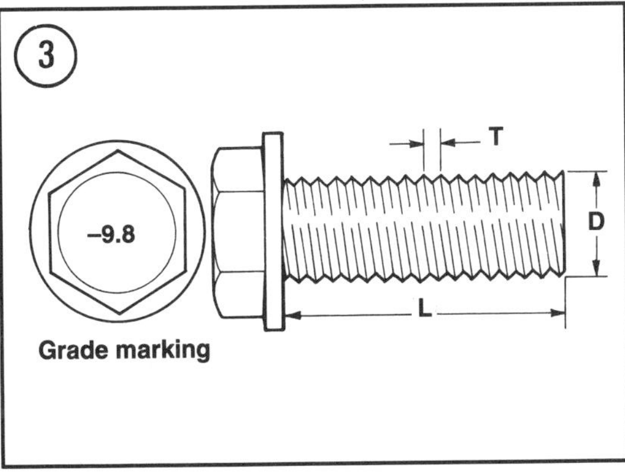

FASTENERS

The materials and designs of the various fasteners used on your Yamaha are not arrived at by chance or accident. Fastener design determines the type of tool required to work the fastener. Fastener material is carefully selected to decrease the possibility of physical failure and ease assembly and maintenance.

Nuts, bolts and screws are manufactured in a wide range of thread patterns. To join 2 fasteners, the diameter and thread size of both parts must be the same.

The best way to tell if 2 fastener threads match is to turn the nut on the bolt (or the bolt into the threaded hole in a piece of equipment) with fingers only. Be sure both pieces are clean. When excessive force is required, check the thread condition on each fastener. If the thread condition is good but the fasteners jam, the threads sizes are different. If necessary, use a thread pitch gauge to determine thread pitch. Yamaha motorcycles and ATVs are manufactured with ISO (International Organization for Standardization) metric fasteners. The threads are cut differently than those of standard U.S. fasteners (**Figure 2**).

Most threads are cut so the fastener must be turned clockwise to tighten it. These are called right-hand threads. Some fasteners have left-hand threads; they must be turned counterclockwise to be tightened. Left-hand threads are used in locations where normal rotation of the equipment would tend to loosen a right-hand threaded fastener.

ISO Metric Screw Threads (Bolts, Nuts and Screws)

ISO (International Organization for Standardization) metric threads come in 3 standard thread sizes: coarse, fine and constant pitch. The ISO coarse pitch is used for almost all common fastener applications. The fine pitch thread is used on certain precision tools and instruments. The constant pitch thread is used mainly on machine parts and not for fasteners. The constant pitch thread, however, is used on all metric thread spark plugs.

Metric fasteners are classified by length (L, **Figure 3**), diameter (D) and distance between thread crests (T). A typical bolt might be identified by the numbers 8 – 1.25 × 130, which indicates that the bolt has a diameter of 8 mm, the distance between thread crests is 1.25 mm and bolt length is 130 mm.

CAUTION
Do not install screws or bolts with a lower strength classification than installed originally by the manufacturer. Doing so may cause engine or equipment failure and possible injury.

Machine Screws

There are many different types of machine screws. **Figure 4** shows a number of screw heads requiring different types of turning tools. Heads are also designed to protrude above the metal (round) or slightly recessed in the metal (counter sunk). See **Figure 5**.

Nuts

Nuts are manufactured in a variety of types and sizes. Most are hexagonal (6-sided) and fit on bolts, screws and studs with the same diameter and pitch. **Figure 6** shows several types of nuts. The common nut is generally used with a lockwasher. Self-locking nuts have a nylon insert which prevents the nut from loosening; no lockwasher is required. Wing nuts are designed for fast removal by hand and are used for convenience in noncritical locations.

To indicate the size of a metric nut, manufacturers specify the diameter of the opening and the thread pitch. This is similar to bolt specifications, but without the length dimension. The measurement across 2 flats on the nut indicates the proper wrench size to be used.

Self-Locking Fasteners

Several types of bolts, screws and nuts incorporate a system that develops an interference between the bolt, screw, nut or tapped hole threads. Interference is achieved in various ways: by distorting threads, coating threads with dry adhesive or nylon, distorting the top of an all-metal nut or using a nylon insert in the center or at the top of a nut.

Self-locking fasteners offer greater holding strength and better vibration resistance than standard fasteners. Some self-locking fasteners can be reused

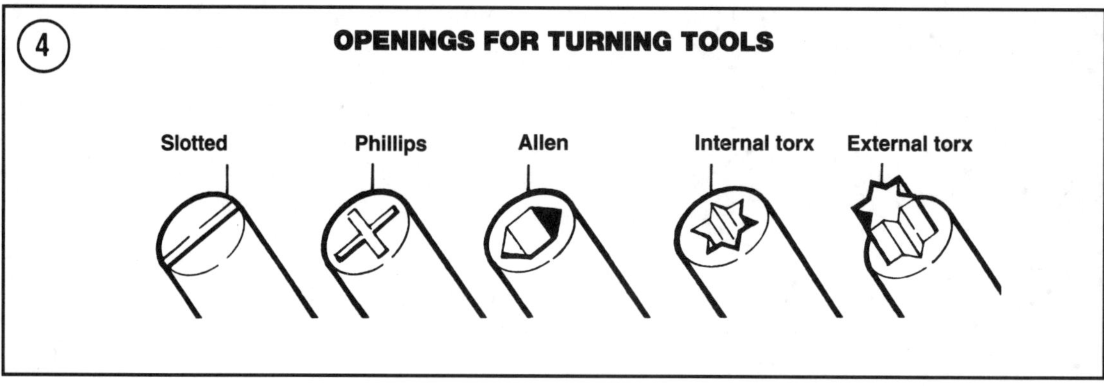

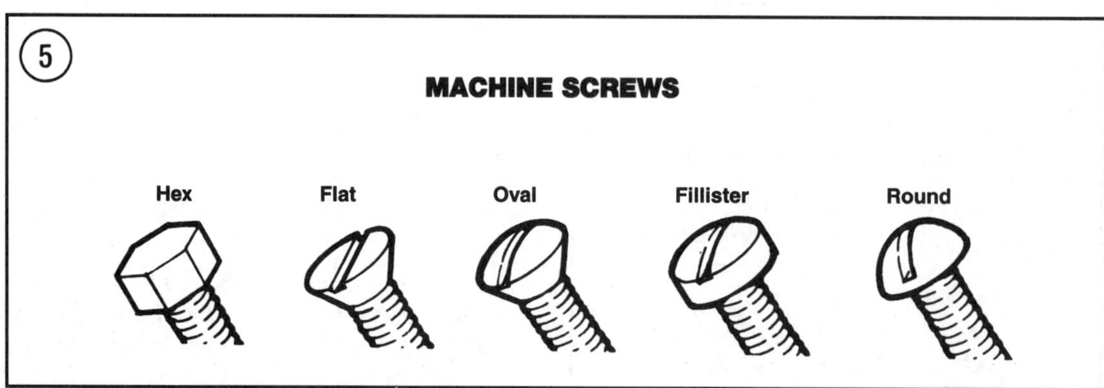

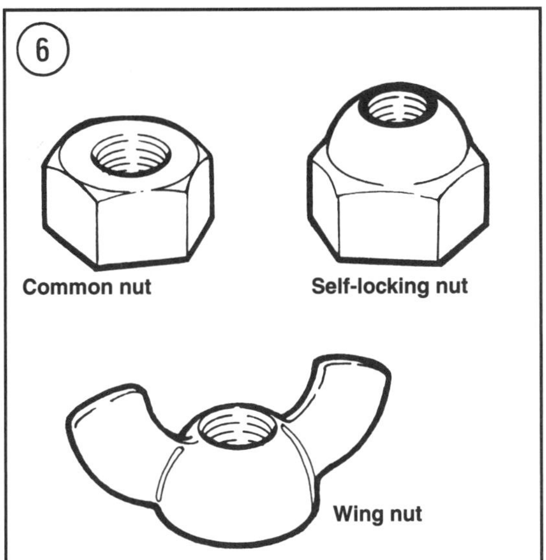

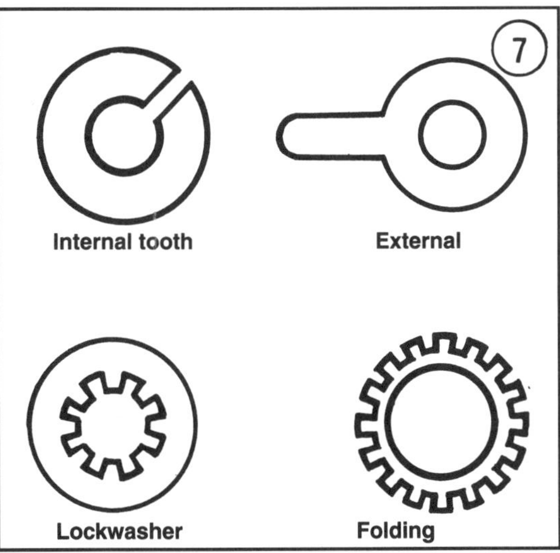

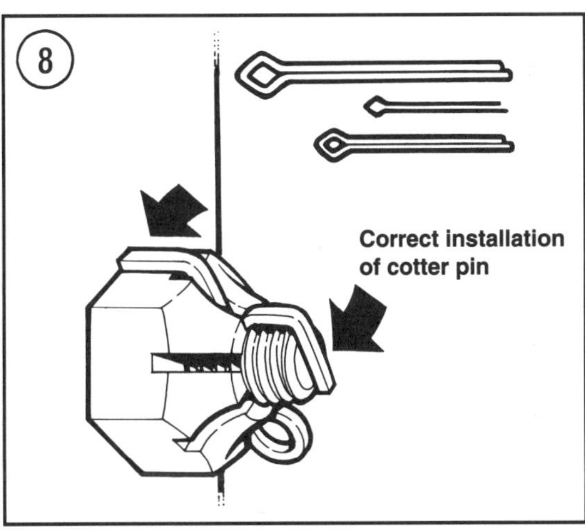

if in good condition. Others, like the nylon insert nut, form an initial locking condition when the nut is first installed. The nylon forms closely to the bolt thread pattern, thus reducing any tendency for the nut to loosen. For greatest safety, discard previously used self-locking fasteners and install new ones during reassembly.

Washers

There are 2 basic types of washers: flat washers and lockwashers. Flat washers are simple discs with a hole to fit a screw or bolt. Lockwashers are designed to prevent a fastener from working loose due to vibration, expansion and contraction. **Figure 7** shows several types of washers. Washers can be used in the following functions:

a. As spacers.
b. To prevent galling or damage of the equipment by the fastener.
c. To help distribute fastener load during tightening.
d. As seals.

Note that flat washers are often used between a lockwasher and a fastener to provide a smooth bearing surface. This allows the fastener to be turned easily with a tool.

NOTE
As much care should be given to the selection and purchase of washers as to bolts, nuts and other fasteners. Beware of washers made of thin and weak materials. These will deform and crush the first time they are used in a high torque application.

Cotter Pins

In certain applications, a fastener must be secured so it cannot possibly loosen. The rear wheel hub on an ATV is one such application. For this purpose, a cotter pin (**Figure 8**) and slotted or castellated nut is often used. To use a cotter pin, first make sure the pin fits snugly, but not too tight. Then, align a slot in the fastener with the hole in the bolt or axle. Insert the cotter pin through the nut and bolt or axle and bend the ends over to secure the cotter pin tightly. If the holes do not align, tighten the nut just enough to obtain the proper alignment. Unless specifically instructed to do so, never loosen the fastener to align the slot and hole. Because the cotter pin is weakened after installation and removal, never reuse a cotter pin. Cotter pins are available in several styles, lengths and diameters. Measure cotter pin length from the bottom of its head to the tip of its shortest prong.

Circlips

Circlips can be internal or external design. They are used to retain items on shafts (external type) or within tubes (internal type). In some applications, circlips of varying thickness' are used to control the end play of assemblies. These are often called selective circlips. Circlips should be replaced during installation, as removal weakens and deforms them.

Two basic styles of circlips are available: machined and stamped circlips. Machined circlips (**Figure 9**) can be installed in either direction (shaft or housing) because both faces are machined, thus creating two sharp edges. Stamped circlips (**Figure 10**) are manufactured with one sharp edge and one rounded edge. When installing stamped circlips in a thrust situation such as transmission shafts, the sharp edge must face away from the part producing the thrust. When installing circlips, observe the following:

a. Compress or expand circlips only enough to install them.
b. After the circlip is installed, make sure it is completely seated in its groove.
c. Transmission circlips become worn with use. For this reason, always use new circlips when reassembling the transmission.

LUBRICANTS

Periodic lubrication helps ensure long life for any type of equipment. The following paragraphs describe the types of lubricants most often used on ATV's. Be sure to follow the manufacturer's recommendations for lubricant types.

Generally all liquid lubricants are called oil. They may be mineral-based (including petroleum bases), natural-based (vegetable and animal bases), synthetic-based or emulsions (mixtures). Grease is an oil to which a thickening base has been added so that the end product is semi-solid. Grease is often classified by the type of thickener added; lithium-soap based grease is commonly used.

Engine Oil

Motorcycle and ATV oil is graded by the American Petroleum Institute (API) and the Society of Automotive Engineers (SAE) in several categories. Oil containers display these ratings on the top or label. API oil grade is indicated by letters; oils for gasoline engines are identified by an S. Yamaha models described in this manual require SE grade oil.

Viscosity is an indication of the oil's thickness. The SAE uses numbers to indicate viscosity; thin oils have low numbers while thick oils have high numbers. A W after the number indicates that the viscosity testing was done at low temperature to simulate cold-weather operation. Engine oils fall into the 5 to 50 range.

Multi-grade oils (for example 10W-40) are less viscous (thinner) at low temperatures and more viscous (thicker) at high temperatures. This allows the oil to perform efficiently across a wide range of engine operating conditions. The lower the number, the easier the engine will start in cold climates. Higher numbers are usually recommended during hot weather operation.

Grease

Greases are graded by the National Lubricating Grease Institute (NLGI). Greases are graded by number according to the consistency of the grease; these range from No. 000 to No. 6, with No. 6 being the most solid. A typical multipurpose grease is NLGI No. 2. For specific applications, equipment manufacturers may require grease with an additive such as molybdenum disulfide (MOS2).

9

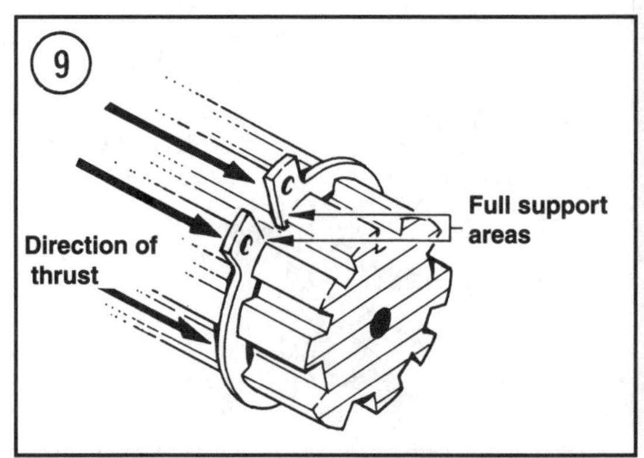

SEALANT, CEMENTS AND CLEANERS

Sealants and Adhesives

Many mating surfaces of an engine require a gasket or seal between them to prevent fluids and gases from passing through the joint. At times, the gasket or seal is installed as is. However, some times a sealer is applied to enhance the sealing capability of the gasket or seal. Note, however, that a sealing compound may be added to the gasket or seal during manufacturing and adding a sealant may cause premature failure of the gasket or seal.

NOTE
If a new gasket leaks, check the 2 mating surfaces for warpage, old gasket residue or cracks. Also check to see if the new gasket was properly installed and if the assembly was tightened correctly.

RTV Sealants

One of the most common sealants is RTV (room temperature vulcanizing) sealant. This sealant hardens (cures) at room temperature over a period of several hours, which allows sufficient time to reposition parts if necessary without damaging the gaskets.

RTV sealant is available in different strengths. For example, while many RTV compounds offer excellent chemical resistance in bonding and sealing applications where oil and water is prevalent, most RTV compounds offers poor chemical resistance to gasoline. Always follow the manufacturer's recommendations when purchasing and using a particular compound.

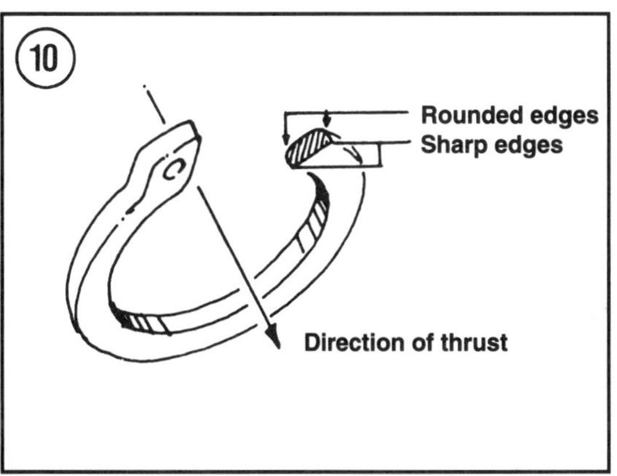

Cleaners and Solvents

Cleaners and solvents are helpful in removing oil, grease and other residue when maintaining and overhauling your vehicle. Before purchasing cleaners and solvents, consider how they will be used and disposed of, particularly if they are not water soluble. Local ordinances may require special procedures for the disposal of certain cleaners and solvents.

WARNING
Some cleaners and solvents are harmful and may be flammable. Follow any safety precautions noted on the container or in the manufacturer's literature. Use petroleum-resistant gloves to protect hands and arms from the harmful effect of cleaners and solvents.

A number of cleaners and solvents are available for servicing your Yamaha. Cleaners designed for ignition contact cleaning are excellent for removing light oil from a part without leaving a residue. Cleaners designed to remove heavy oil and grease residues, called degreasers, contain a solvent that usually must soak for a period of time to be effective. Some degreasers will wash off with water. Ease the removal of stubborn gaskets with a gasket removal compound.

One of the more powerful cleaning solutions is carburetor cleaner. It is designed to dissolve the varnish that may build up in carburetor jets and orifices. A good carburetor cleaner is usually expensive and requires special disposal. Carefully read directions before purchase. Do not immerse nonmetallic parts in a carburetor cleaner.

Gasket Remover

Stubborn gaskets can present a problem during engine service. They can take a long time to remove and there is the added problem of secondary damage occurring to the gasket mating surfaces from the incorrect use of a gasket scraping tool. To remove stubborn gaskets, use a spray gasket remover. Spray gasket remover can be purchased through automotive parts houses. Follow its manufacturer's directions for use.

THREADLOCKING COMPOUND

A threadlocking compound is a fluid applied to fastener threads. After tightening the fastener, the fluid dries to a solid filler between the mating threads, thereby locking the threads in position and preventing the fastener from loosening. Some threadlocking compounds are also useful to help seal against leaks.

Before applying a threadlocking compound, clean the contacting threads with an aerosol electrical contact cleaner. Use only as much threadlocking compound as necessary, depending on the size of the fastener. Excess fluid can work its way into adjoining parts.

Threadlocking compound is available in different strengths, so follow the manufacturer's recommendations when using their particular compound. Two manufacturers of threadlocking compound are ThreeBond of America and the Loctite Corporation. The following threadlocking compounds are recommended for many threadlocking requirements described in this manual:

a. ThreeBond 1342: low strength, frequent repair for small screws and bolts.
b. ThreeBond 1360: medium strength, high temperature.
c. ThreeBond 1333B: medium strength, bearing and stud lock.
d. ThreeBond 1303: high strength, frequent repair.
e. Loctite 242: low strength, frequent repair.
f. Loctite 271: high strength, frequent repair.

There are other quality threadlocking brands on the market.

SERIAL NUMBERS

Yamaha makes frequent changes during a model year, some minor, some relatively major. When you order replaccement parts from the dealer or other parts distributor, always order by frame and engine numbers. The frame serial number is stamped on the left-hand side of the frame horizontal member below the oil filter area (**Figure 11**). The engine number is stamped on a raised pad on the right side of the crankcase (**Figure 12**). The carburetor serial number is on the carburetor body above the float bowl.

Record the numbers and carry them with you when purchasing replacement parts. Compare new parts to old before buying them. If they are not alike, have the parts manager explain the difference to you. **Table 1** lists engine and frame serial numbers for the models covered in this manual. On Kodiak ATVs, the engine and frame numbers are the same.

WARNING LABELS

A number of warning labels have been attached to the Yamaha ATV. These labels contain information that is important to your safety when operating, transporting and storing your vehicle. Refer to your Owner's Manual for a description and location of each label. If a label is missing, order a replacement label from a Yamaha dealership.

BASIC HAND TOOLS

Many of the procedures in this manual can be accomlished with simple hand tools and test equipment familiar to the average home mechanic. Keep your tools clean and in a tool box. Keep them organized with related tools stored together. After using a

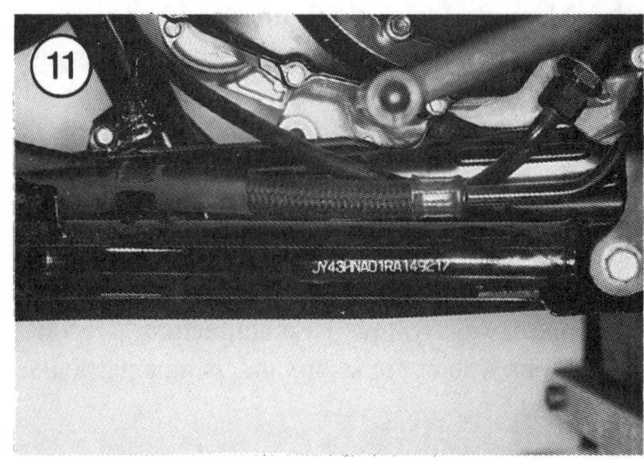

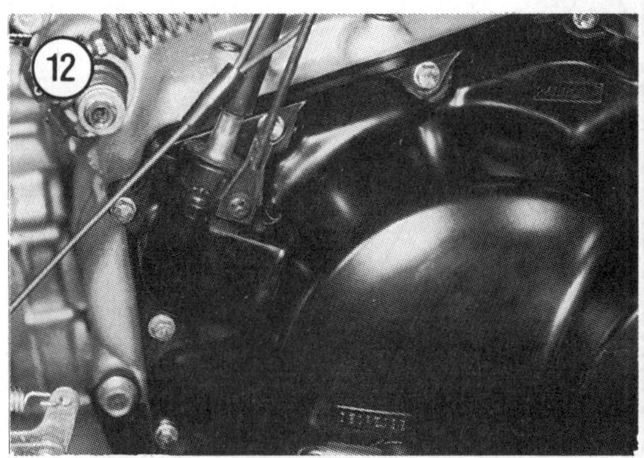

tool, wipe off dirt and grease with a clean cloth and return the tool to its correct place.

Top quality tools are essential. They are also more economical in the long run. If you are now starting to build your tool collection, avoid the advertised specials featured at some parts houses, discount stores and chain drug stores. These are usually poor grade tools that are poorly made and sold cheaply. They are usually made of inferior material, and are thick, heavy and clumsy. Their rough finish makes them difficult to clean and they usually do not last very long. After using these tools, you will probably find the wrenches do not fit the heads of bolts and nuts correctly and damage the fastener.

Quality tools are made of alloy steel and are heat treated for high strength. They are lighter and better balanced than cheap ones. Their surface is smooth, making them a pleasure to work with and easy to clean. The initial cost of good quality tools may be more but they are cheaper in the long run. Do not try to buy everything in all sizes in the beginning; buy a few at a time until you have the necessary tools.

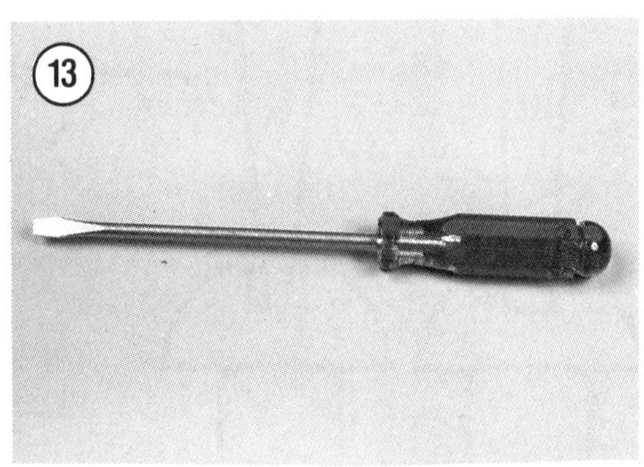

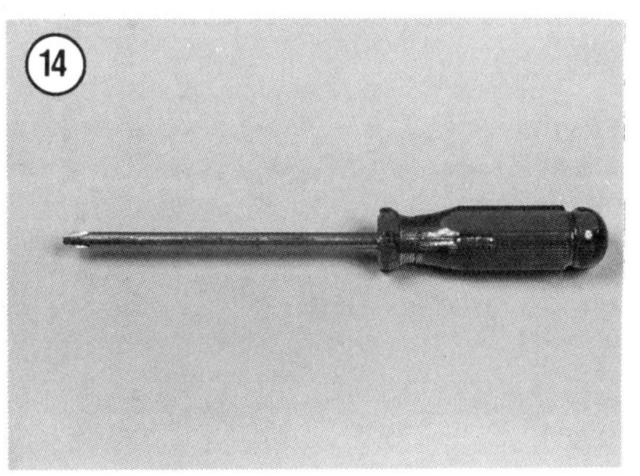

Screwdrivers

The screwdriver is a very basic tool, but if used improperly, it will do more damage than good. The slot on a screw has a definite dimension and shape. A screwdriver must be selected to conform with that shape. Use a small screwdriver for small screws and a large one for large screws; otherwise, the screw head will be damaged.

Two basic types of screwdriver are required: slotted (flat-blade) screwdrivers (**Figure 13**) and Phillips screwdrivers (**Figure 14**).

Screwdrivers are available in sets which often include an assortment of slotted and Phillips blades. If you buy them individually, buy at least the following:

a. Slotted screwdriver—5/16 × 6 in. blade.

b. Slotted screwdriver—3/8 × 12 in. blade.

c. Phillips screwdriver—size 2 tip, 6 in. blade.

d. Phillips screwdriver—size 3 tip, 6 and 10 in. blades.

Use screwdrivers only for driving screws. Never use a screwdriver for prying or chiseling metal. Do not try to remove a Phillips or Allen head screw with a common screwdriver (unless the screw has a combination head that will accept either type); you can damage the head so that even the proper tool will be unable to remove it. Always keep the tip of a common screwdriver in good condition. **Figure 15** shows how to grind the tip to the proper shape if it becomes damaged. Note the symmetrical sides of the tip.

Pliers

Pliers come in a wide range of types and sizes. Pliers are useful for cutting, bending and crimping. Do not use them to cut hardened objects or turn bolts or nuts. **Figure 16** shows several pliers useful in ATV and motorcycle repair, each designed for a specialized function. Combination (slip-joint) pliers are general purpose pliers used mainly for gripping and for bending. Needlenose pliers are used to hold or bend small objects. Adjustable joint pliers can be adjusted quickly to hold various sizes of objects; the jaws remain parallel to grip around objects such as pipe or tubing. There are many more types of pliers.

Locking Pliers

Locking pliers (**Figure 17**) are used to hold objects very tightly like a vise. Locking pliers are available in many types for more specific tasks.

Circlip (Snap ring) Pliers

Circlip pliers (**Figure 18**) are used to remove and install circlips. External pliers (spreading or expanding) are used to remove circlips that fit on the outside of a shaft or similar part. Internal circlips are located inside a tube, gear or housing and require pliers that squeeze the ends of the circlip together so that the circlip can be removed.

WARNING
Circlips can fly off during removal and installation. Always wear safety goggles when removing and installing circlips to prevent eye injury.

Box-end, Open-end and Combination Wrenches

Box-end and open-end wrenches (**Figure 19**) are available in sets or separately in a variety of sizes. The number stamped on open and box-end wrenches refers to the distance between 2 parallel flats of nut or bolt head. Combination wrenches have a box-end wrench on one end and an open-end wrench of the

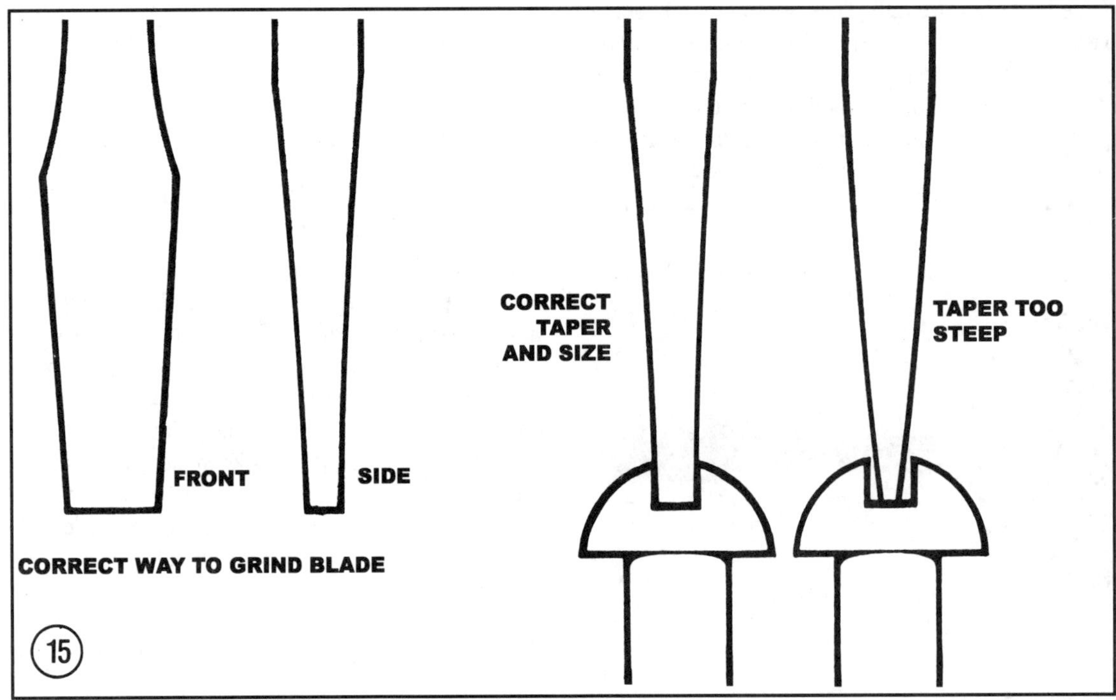

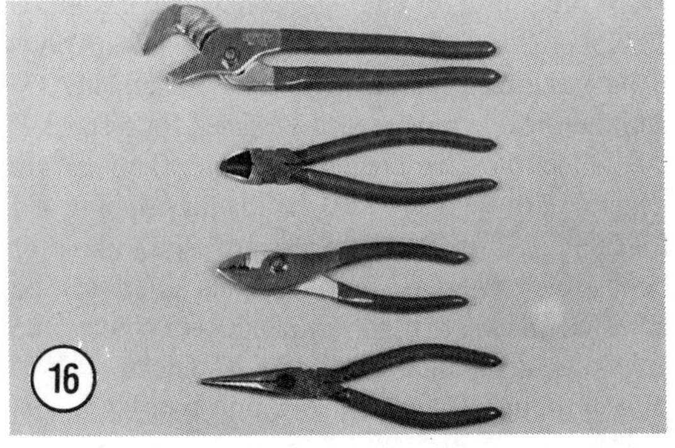

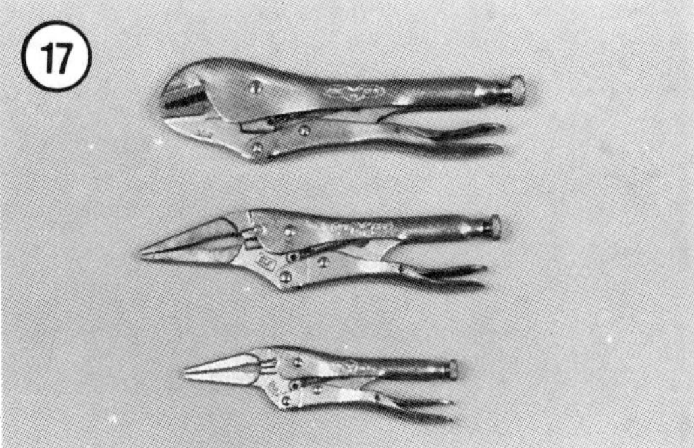

same size on the other end. The wrench size is stamped near the center of combination wrenches.

Open-end wrenches are speedy and work best in areas with limited overhead access. Their wide flat jaws make them unsuitable for situations where the bolt or nut is sunken in a well or close to the edge of a casting. These wrenches only grip on two flats of a fastener so if either the fastener head or the wrench jaws are worn, the wrench may slip off.

Box-end wrenches require clear overhead access to the fastener but can work well in situations where the fastener head is close to another part. They grip on all six edges of a fastener for a very secure grip. Box-end wrenches may be either 6-point or 12-point. The 6-point gives superior holding power and durability but requires a greater swinging radius. The 12-point works better in situations where there is only a small amount of room to turn the wrench.

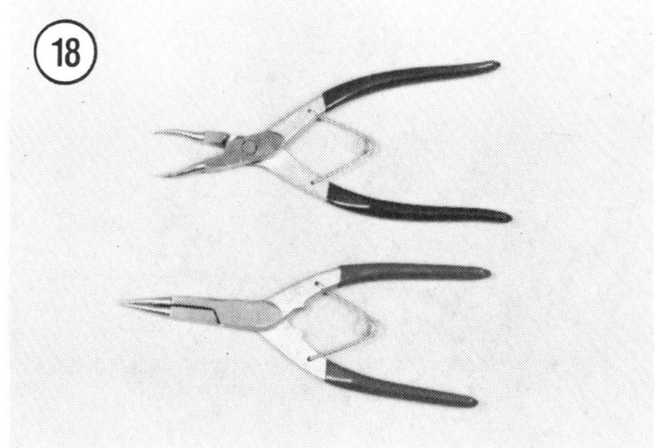

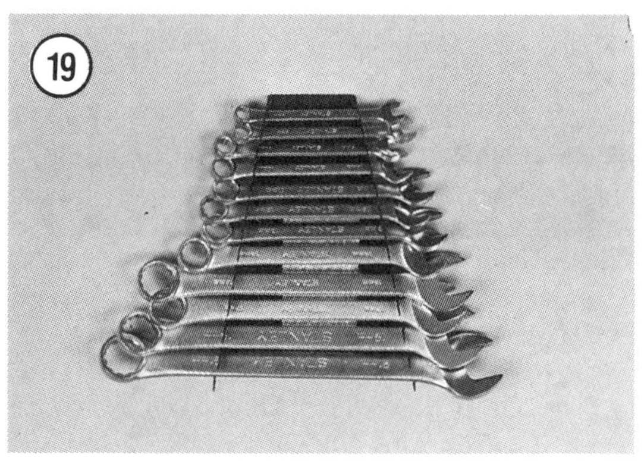

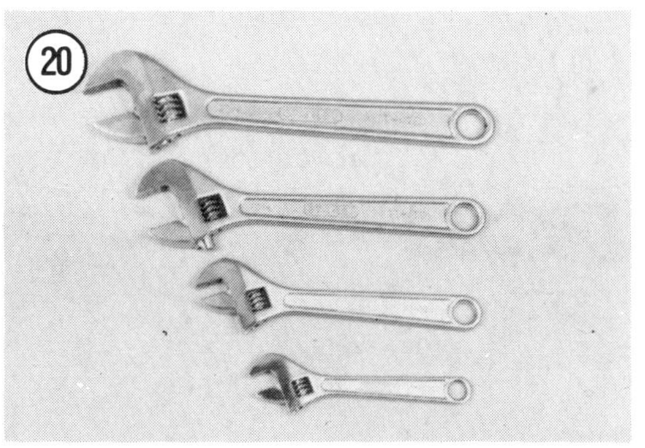

No matter what style of wrench you choose, proper use is important to prevent personal injury. When using any wrench, get in the habit of pulling the wrench toward you. This reduces the risk of injuring your hand if the wrench should slip. If you have to push the wrench away from you to loosen or tighten a fastener, open and push with the palm of your hand. This technique gets your fingers and knuckles out of the way should the wrench slip. Before using a wrench, always consider what could happen if the wrench slips or if the fastener breaks.

Adjustable Wrenches

An adjustable wrench (sometimes called crescent wrench) can be adjusted to fit nearly any nut or bolt head which has clear access around its entire perimeter. Adjustable wrenches (**Figure 20**) are best used as a backup wrench to keep a large nut or bolt from turning while the other end is being loosened or tightened with a proper wrench.

Adjustable wrenches have only two gripping surfaces where one is adjustable. Because of this design makes, adjustable wrenches are directional in how they should be used. The solid jaw must be the one transmitting the force. Applying directional force against the adjustable surface may cause the wrench to slip and round-off the fastener head.

Adjustable wrenches in the 6 to 8 in. and 12 to 14 in. range is recommended for general use.

Socket Wrenches

This type is undoubtedly the fastest, safest and most convenient to use. Sockets which attach to a ratchet handle (**Figure 21**) are available with 6-point or 12-point openings and 1/4, 3/8, 1/2 and 3/4 in. drives. The drive size indicates the size of the square hole which mates with the ratchet handle.

Impact Driver

This tool makes removal of fasteners easy and eliminates damage to bolts and screw slots. Impact drivers and interchangeable bits (**Figure 22**) are available at most large hardware, motorcycle or auto parts stores. Impact sockets can be used with a hand impact driver. Do not use regular hand sockets as they may shatter during impact use.

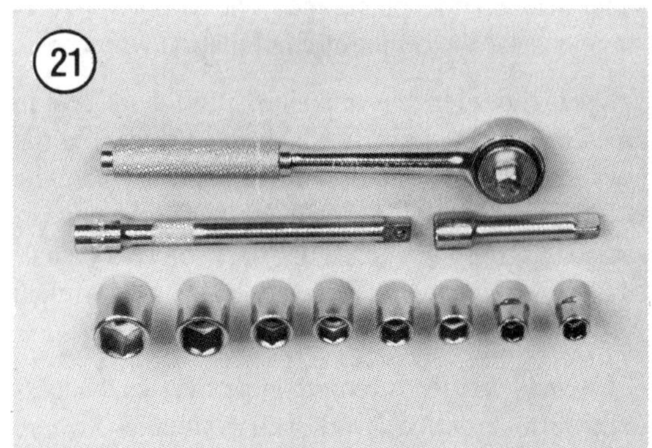
21

Torque Wrench

A torque wrench is used with a socket, torque adapter or similar extension to measure how tightly a nut, bolt or other fastener is installed. They come in a wide price range and with either a 1/4, 3/8 or 1/2 in. square drive. The drive size indicates the size of the square drive which mates with the socket, torque adapter or extension. Popular types are the deflecting beam (A, **Figure 23**), the dial indicator and the audible click (B, **Figure 23**) torque wrenches. As with any series of tools, there are advantages and disadvantages with each type of torque wrench. When choosing a torque wrench, consider its torque range, accuracy rating and price. The torque specifications listed at the end of most chapters in this manual will give you an idea on the range of torque wrench needed to service your Yamaha.

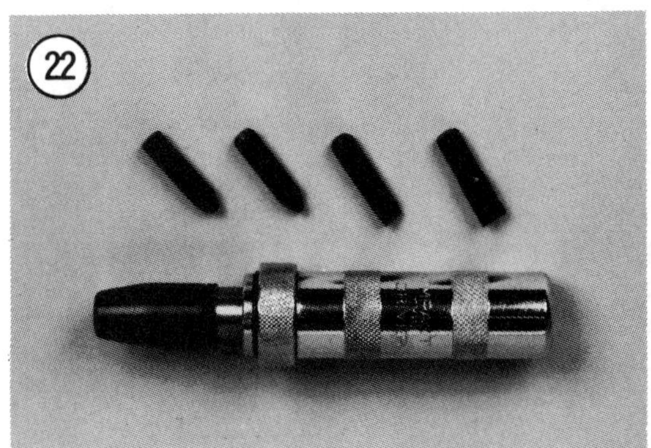
22

Because the torque wrench is a precision tool, do not throw it in with other tools and expect it to remain accurate. Always store a torque wrench in its carrying case or in a padded tool box drawer. All torque wrenches require periodic recalibration. To find out more about this, read the information provided with the torque wrench or write to the manufacturer.

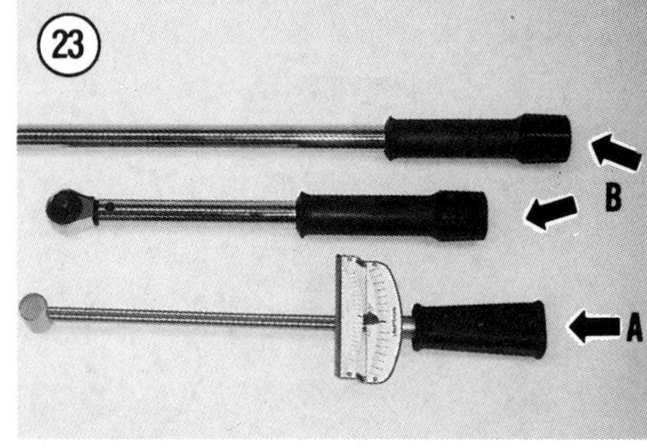

23

Torque Wrench Adapters

Torque adapters and extensions allow you to extend or reduce the reach of your torque wrench. For example, the torque adapter wrench shown in **Figure 24** can be used to extend the length of the torque wrench to tighten fasteners that cannot be reached with a torque wrench and socket. When a torque adapter is used to lengthen or shorten the torque wrench (**Figure 24**), the torque reading on the torque wrench will not be the same amount of torque that is applied to the fastener. Before using a torque adapter in this way, it is necessary to recalibrate the listed torque specification to compensate for the effect of the added torque adapter length. When a torque adapter is set at a right angle on the torque wrench, recalibration is not required (see information and figure below).

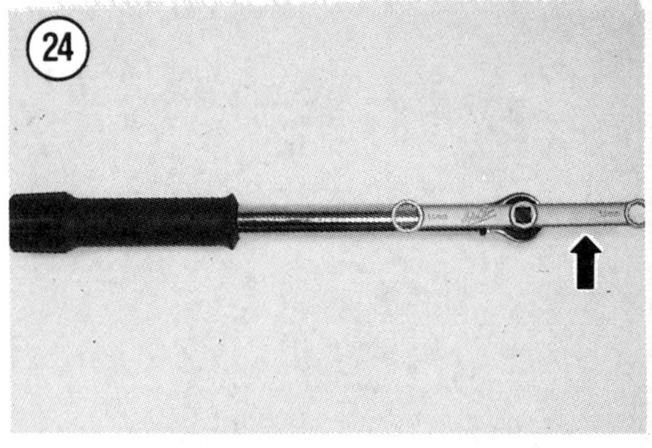
24

To calculate a torque reading when using a torque adapter, it is first necessary to know the lever length of the torque wrench, the length of the adapter from the center of square drive to the center of the nut or bolt, and the actual amount of torque desired at the nut or bolt (**Figure 25**). The formula can be expressed as:

$$TW = \frac{TA \times L}{L + A}$$

TW = This is the torque setting or dial reading to set on the torque wrench when tightening the fastener.

TA = Actual torque setting. This is the torque specification listed in the service manual and will be the actual amount of torque applied to the fastener.

A = This is the length of the adapter from the centerline of the square drive (at the torque wrench) to the centerline of the nut or bolt. If the torque adapter extends straight from the end of the torque wrench (**Figure 26**), the center line of the torque adapter and torque wrench are the same.

However, when the center lines of the torque adapter and torque wrench do not line up, the distance must be measured as shown in **Figure 26**. Also note in **Figure 26** that when the torque adapter is set at a right-angle to the torque wrench, no calculation is needed (the lever length of the torque wrench did not change).

L = This the lever length of your torque wrench. This specification is usually listed in the instruction manual provided with your torque wrench, or you can determine its length by measuring the the distance from the center of the square drive on the torque wrench to the center of the torque wrench handle (**Figure 25**).

Example:

What should the torque wrench preset reading or dial reading be if:

TA = 20 ft.-lb.

A = 3 in.

L = 14 in.

$$TW = \frac{20 \times 14}{14 + 3} = \frac{280}{17} = 16.5 \text{ ft.-lb.}$$

In this example, the recalculated torque value of 16.5 ft.-lb. would be the amount of torque to set on the torque wrench. If using a dial or beam-type torque wrench, torque would be applied until the pointer aligns with the 16.5 ft.-lb. dial reading. When

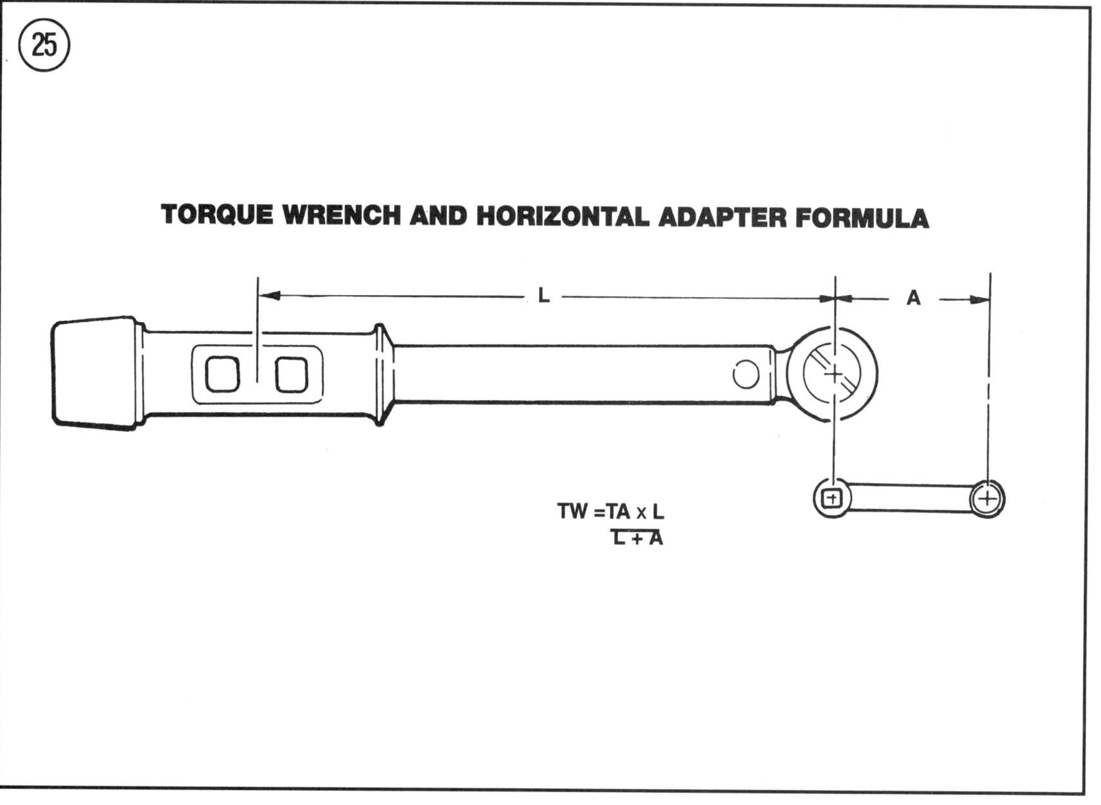

using a click type torque wrench, the micrometer dial would be preset to 16.5 ft.-lb. In all cases, even though the torque wrench dial or preset reading was 16.5 ft.-lb., the fastener will actually be tightened to 20 ft.-lb.

Support Jacks

A support jack is necessary when supporting the ATV with its wheels off the ground. This will be necessary during many steering, brake and suspension service procedures. The K&L MC450 Center Stand (part No. 37-9882 [**Figure 27**]) is an adjustable scissors-type jack that can be ordered through Yamaha dealerships. It is suitable for all of the service procedures described in this manual. A standard floor jack may also be used. However, when using a floor jack, supplement its use with safety stands and/or wooden blocks to prevent the vehicle from falling if the jack slips or loses pressure.

PRECISION MEASURING TOOLS

Measurement is an important part of vehicle and engine service. When performing many of the serv-

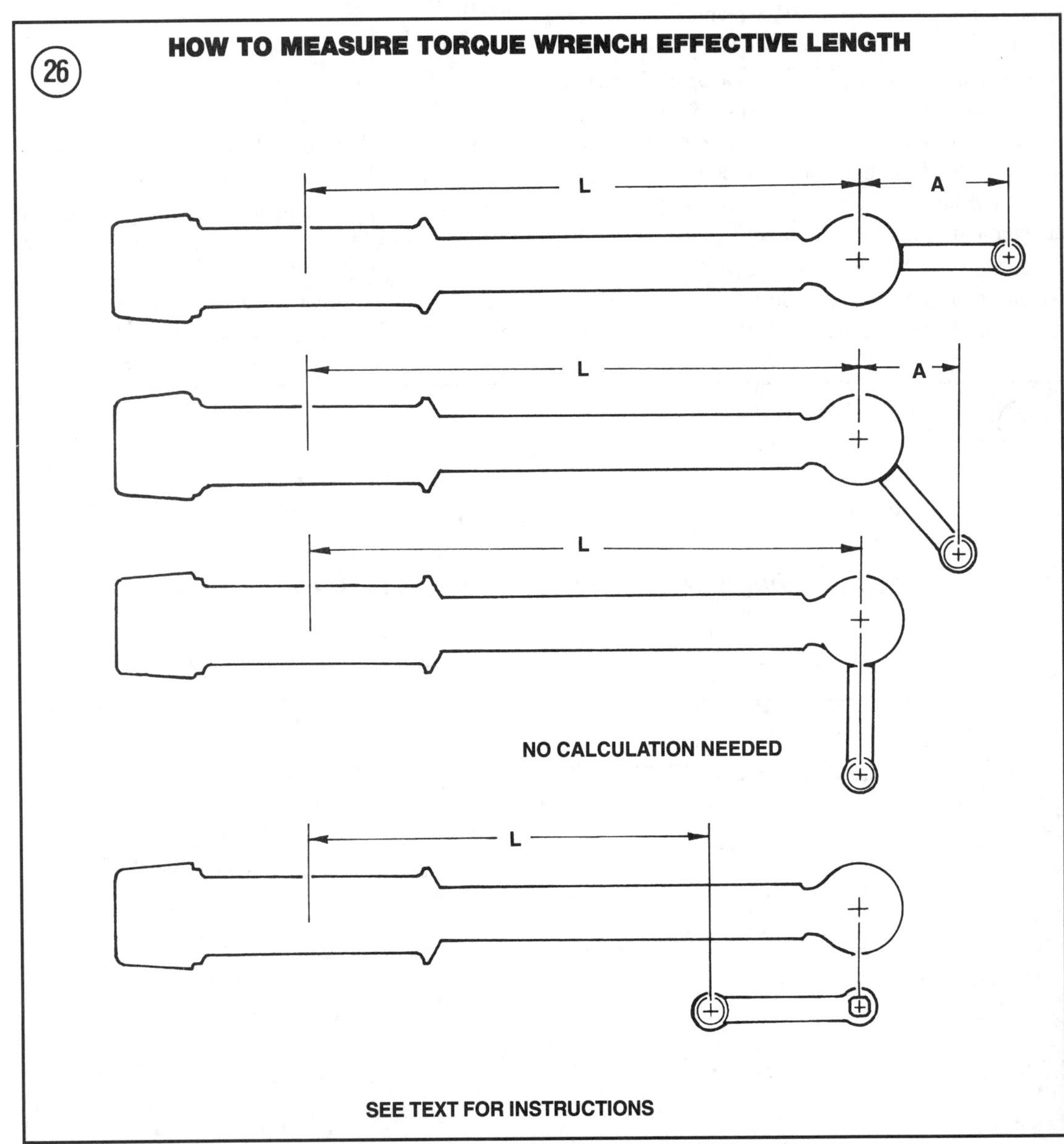

ice procedures in this manual, you will be required to make a number of measurements. These include basic checks such as engine compression and spark plug gap. As you expand your shop work into engine disassembly and service, measurements will be required to determine piston and cylinder bore measurements, crankshaft runout and so on. When making these measurements, the degree of accuracy dictates which tool is required. Precision measuring tools are expensive. If this is your first experience at engine service, it may be advisable to have the checks and measurements made at a dealership. However, as your skills and enthusiasm increase for doing your own service work, you may want to purchase some of these specialized tools. The following is a description of the measuring tools used in this manual.

Feeler Gauge

Feeler gauges are available in sets of various sizes and types (**Figure 28**). The gauge is made of either a piece of a flat or round hardened steel of a specified thickness. Wire (round) ground gauges are used to measure spark plug gap. Flat gauges are used for most other measurements.

27

28

Vernier Caliper, Dial Caliper and Digital Electronic Caliper

These tools (**Figure 29**, typical) read inside, outside and depth measurements. Although a caliper is not as precise as a micrometer, they allow reasonable precision, typically to within 0.025 mm (0.001 in.). These are commonly used when measuring spring length, the thickness of clutch plates, shims and thrust washers, brake lining thickness and bearing bore depth. The caliper jaws must be kept clean and free of burrs to obtain accurate measurements. There are several types of venier calipers available. The standard vernier caliper has a graduated scale on the handle (**Figure 29**) in which the measurements must be calculated. The dial indicator caliper is equipped with a small dial and needle that indicates the measurement reading. The digital electronic caliper uses an LCD display tot show the measurement reading. Because some calipers require calibration, always refer to the manufacturer's instructions when using a new or unfamiliar caliper.

Outside Micrometers

An outside micrometer is a precision tool used to accurately measure parts using the decimal divisions of the inch or meter (**Figure 30**). While there are many types and styles of micrometers, this section describes steps on how to use the outside micrometer. The outside micrometer is the most common type of micrometer used when servicing a motorcycle or ATV.

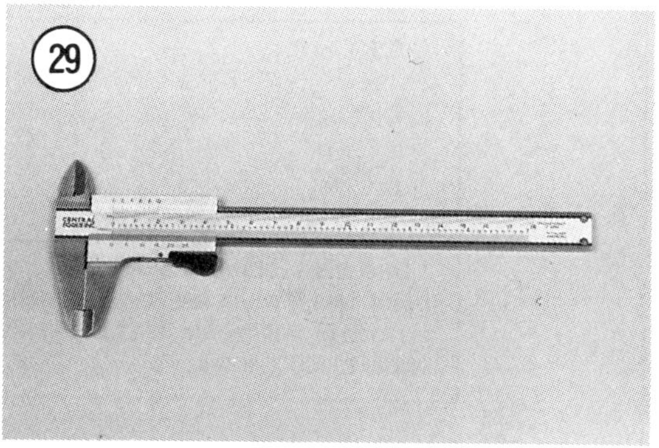

29

Other types of micrometers include the depth micrometer and screw thread micrometer. **Figure 31** illustrates the various parts of an outside micrometer with its part names and markings identified.

Micrometer Range

A micrometer's size indicates the minimum and maximum size of a part that it can measure. The usual sizes are: 0-1 in.(0-25 mm), 1-2 in.(25-50 mm), 2-3 in.(50-75 mm) and 3-4 in.(75-100 mm). These micrometers use fixed anvils.

Some micrometers use the same frame with interchangeable anvils of different lengths. This allows the installation of the correct length anvil for a particular job. For example, a 0-4 in. interchangeable micrometer is equipped with four different length anvils. While purchasing one micrometer to cover a range from 0-4 or 0-6 inches is less expensive, its overall frame size makes it less convenient to use.

How to Read a Micrometer

When reading a micrometer, numbers are taken from different scales and then added together. The following sections describe how to read the standard inch micrometer, the vernier inch micrometer, the standard metric micrometer and the metric vernier micrometer.

Standard inch micrometer

The standard inch type micrometer is accurate to one-thousandth of an inch (0.001 in.). The heart of the micrometer is its spindle screw with 40 threads per inch. Every turn of the thimble will move the spindle 1/40 of an inch or 0.025 in. (to change 1/40 of an inch to a decimal: 1/40 = 0.025 in.).

Before you learn how to read a micrometer, study the markings and part names in **Figure 31**. Turn the micrometer's thimble until its zero mark aligns with the zero mark on the sleeve line. Now turn the thimble counterclockwise and align the next thimble mark with the sleeve line. The micrometer now reads 0.001 in. (one one-thousandth) of an inch. Thus, each thimble mark is equal to 0.001 in. Every fifth thimble mark is numbered to help with reading: 0, 5, 10, 15 and 20.

Reset the micrometer so that the thimble and sleeve line zero marks line up. Then turn the thimble counterclockwise one complete revolution and align the thimble zero mark with the first line in the sleeve line. The micrometer now reads 0.025 in. (twenty-five thousandths) of an inch. Thus, each sleeve line represents 0.025 in.

Now turn the thimble counterclockwise while counting the sleeve line marks. Every fourth mark on the sleeve line is marked with a number ranging from 1 through 9. Manufacturers usually mark the last mark on the sleeve with a 0. This indicates that you have reached the end of the micrometer's measuring range. Each sleeve number represents 0.100 in.

DECIMAL PLACE VALUES*

0.1	Indicates 1/10 (one tenth of an inch or millimeter)
0.01	Indicates 1/100 (one one-hundredth of an inch or millimeter)
0.001	Indicates 1/1,000 (one one-thousandth of an inch or millimeter)

*** This chart represents the values of figures placed to the right of the decimal point. Use it when reading decimals from one-tenth to one one-thousandth of an inch or millimeter. It is not a conversion chart (for example: 0.001 in. is not equal to 0.001 mm).**

For example, the number 1 represents 0.100 in. and the number 9 represents 0.900 in.

When reading a standard inch micrometer, take the following 3 measurements described and add them together. The first two readings are taken from the sleeve. The last reading is taken from the thimble. The sum of the 3 readings will give you the measurement in thousandths of an inch (0.001 in.).

To read a standard inch micrometer, perform the following steps while referring to the example in **Figure 32**.

1. Read the sleeve line to find the largest number visible—each sleeve number mark equals 0.100 in.
2. Count the number of sleeve marks visible between the numbered sleeve mark and the thimble edge—each sleeve mark equals 0.025 in. If there are no visible sleeve marks, continue with Step 3.
3. Read the thimble mark that lines up with the sleeve line—each thimble mark equals 0.001 in.

NOTE
If a thimble mark does not align exactly with the sleeve line but falls between 2 lines, estimate the fraction of decimal amount between the lines. For a more accurate reading, use a vernier inch micrometer.

4. Adding the micrometer readings in Steps 1, 2 and 3 gives the actual measurement.

Vernier inch micrometers

A vernier inch micrometer can accurately measure in ten-thousandths of an inch (0.0001 in.) incre-

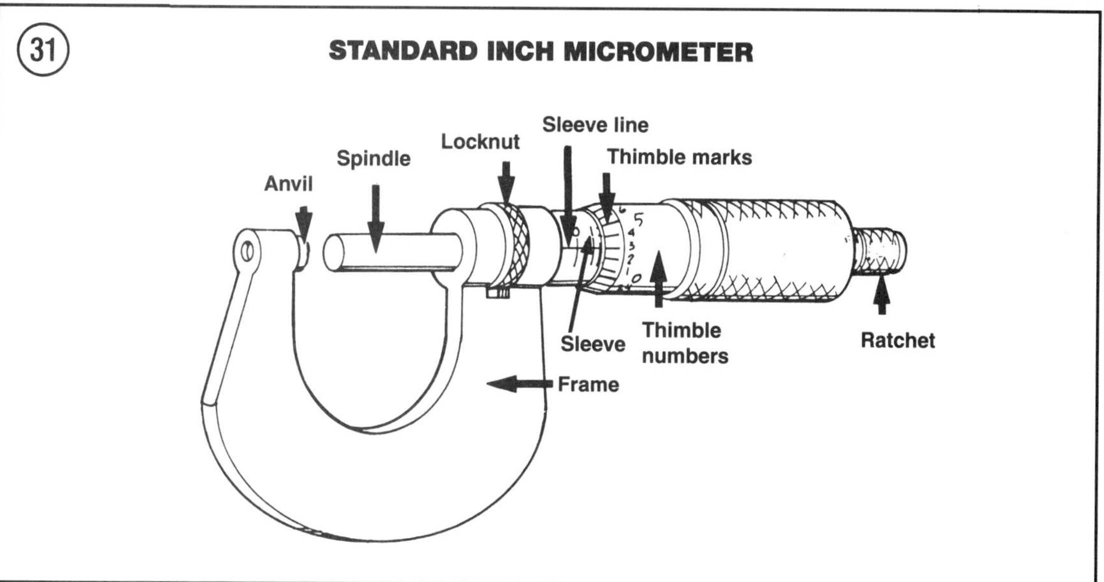

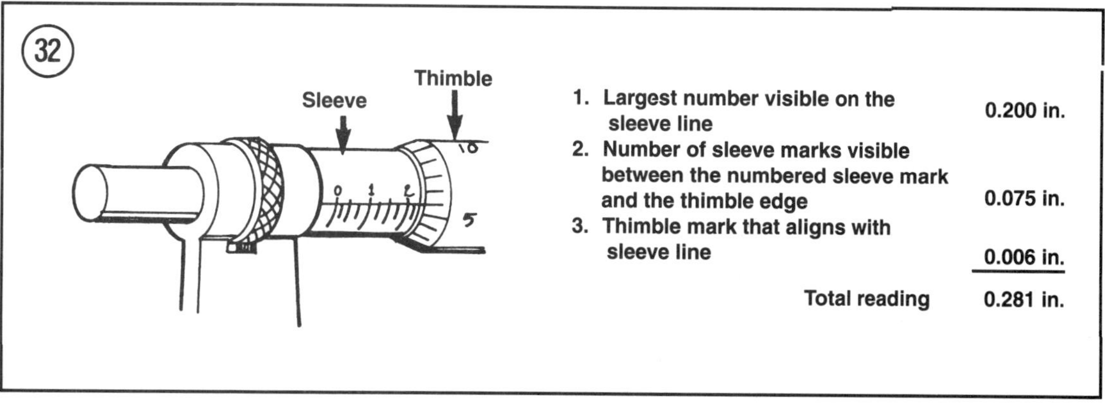

1. Largest number visible on the sleeve line	0.200 in.
2. Number of sleeve marks visible between the numbered sleeve mark and the thimble edge	0.075 in.
3. Thimble mark that aligns with sleeve line	0.006 in.
Total reading	0.281 in.

ments. While it has the same markings as a standard micrometer, a vernier scale scribed on the sleeve (**Figure 33**) makes it unique. The vernier scale consists of eleven equally spaced lines marked 1-9 with a 0 on each end. These lines run parallel on the top of the sleeve where each line is equal to 0.0001 in. Thus, the vernier scale divides a thousandth of an inch (0.001 in.) into ten-thousandths of an inch (0.0001 in.).

To read a vernier inch micrometer, perform the following steps while referring to the example in **Figure 34**.

1. Read the micrometer in the same was as on the standard inch micrometer. This is the initial reading.

2. If a thimble mark aligns exactly with the sleeve line, reading the vernier scale is not necessary. If a thimble mark does not line up exactly with the sleeve line, read the vernier scale in Step 3.

3. Read the vernier scale to find which vernier mark lines up with one thimble mark. The number of that vernier mark is the number of ten-thousandths of an inch to add up to the initial reading taken in Step 1. See Step 4 in **Figure 34**.

Metric micrometers

The metric micrometer is very similar to the standard inch type. The differences are the graduations on the thimble and sleeve as shown in **Figure 35**.

The standard metric micrometer can accurately measure to one one-hundredth of a millimeter (0.01 mm). On the metric micrometer, the spindle screw is ground with a thread pitch of one-half millimeter (0.5 mm). Thus, every turn of the thimble will move the spindle 0.5 mm.

The sleeve line is graduated in millimeters and half millimeters. The marks on the upper side of the sleeve line are equal to 1.00 mm. Every fifth mark above the sleeve line is marked with a number. The actual numbers will depend on the size of the micrometer. For example, on a 0-25 mm micrometer, the sleeve marks are numbered 0, 5, 10, 15, 20 and 25. On a 25-50 mm micrometer, the sleeve marks are numbered 25, 30, 35, 40, 45 and 50. This numbering sequence continues with larger micrometers (50-75 and 75-100). Each mark on the lower side of the sleeve line is equal to 0.50 mm.

The thimble scale is divided into fifty graduations where one graduation is equal to 0.01 mm. Every fifth thimble graduation is numbered to help with reading from 0-45. The thimble edge is used to indicate which sleeve markings to read.

To read a metric micrometer, add the number of millimeters and half-millimeters on the sleeve line to the number of one one-hundredth millimeters on the thimble. To do so, perform the following steps while referring to the example in **Figure 36**.

1. Take the first reading by counting the number of marks visible on the upper sleeve line. Record the reading.

2. Look below the sleeve line to see if a lower mark is visible directly past the upper line mark. If so, add 0.50 to the first reading.

3. Now read the thimble mark that aligns with the sleeve line. Record this reading.

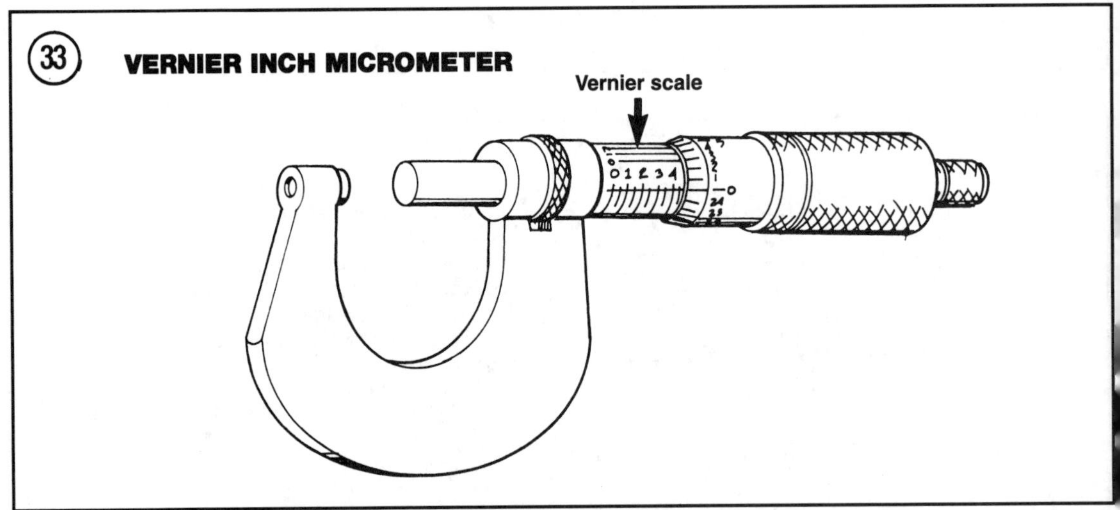

(33) **VERNIER INCH MICROMETER**

(34)

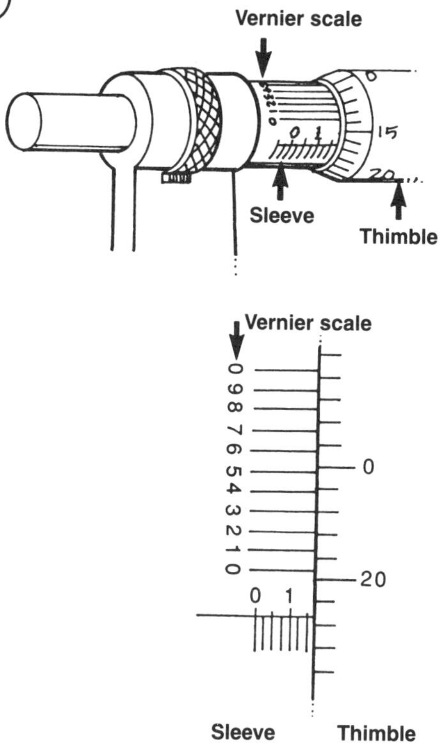

Vernier scale

Sleeve

Thimble

Vernier scale

Sleeve

Thimble

1.	Largest number visible on sleeve line	0.100 in.
2.	Number of sleeve marks visible between the numbered sleeve mark and the thimble edge	0.050 in.
3.	Thimble is between 00.018 and 0.019 in. on the sleeve line	0.018 in.
4.	Vernier line coinciding with thimble line	0.0003 in.
	Total reading	0.1683 in.

(35)

VERNIER METRIC MICROMETER

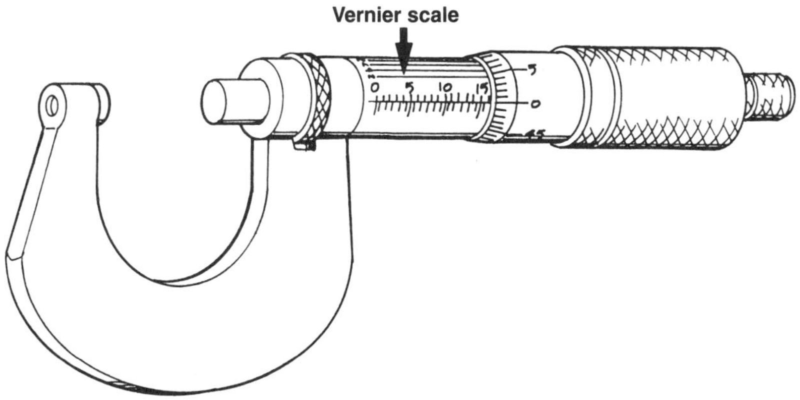

Vernier scale

NOTE
If a thimble mark does not align exactly with the sleeve line but falls between 2 lines, estimate the decimal amount between the lines. For a more accurate reading, use a metric vernier micrometer.

4. Add the micrometer readings in Steps 1, 2 and 3 gives the actual measurement.

Metric vernier micrometers

A metric vernier micrometer is accurate to two thousandths of a millimeter (0.002 mm). While it has the same markings as a standard metric micrometer, a vernier scale scribed on the sleeve (**Figure 37**) makes it unique. The vernier scale consists of five equally spaced lines marked 0, 2, 4, 6 and 8. These lines run parallel on the top of the sleeve where each line is equal to 0.002 mm.

To read a metric vernier micrometer, perform the following steps while referring to the example in **Figure 38**:

1. Read the micrometer in the same way as on the metric standard micrometer. This is the initial reading.
2. If a thimble mark aligns exactly with the sleeve line, reading the vernier scale is not necessary. If a thimble mark does not align exactly with the sleeve line, read the vernier scale in Step 3.
3. Read the vernier scale to find which vernier mark lines up with one thimble mark. The number of that vernier mark is the number of thousandths of a millimeter to add to the initial reading taken in Step 1. See Step 4 in **Figure 38**.

Micrometer Accuracy Check

Before using a micrometer, check its accuracy as follows:

1. Make sure the anvil and spindle faces (**Figure 31**) are clean and dry.
2. To check a 0-1 in. or 0-25 mm micrometer, perform the following:
   a. Turn the thimble until the spindle contacts the anvil. If the micrometer has a ratchet stop, use it to ensure that the proper amount of pressure is applied against the contact surfaces.

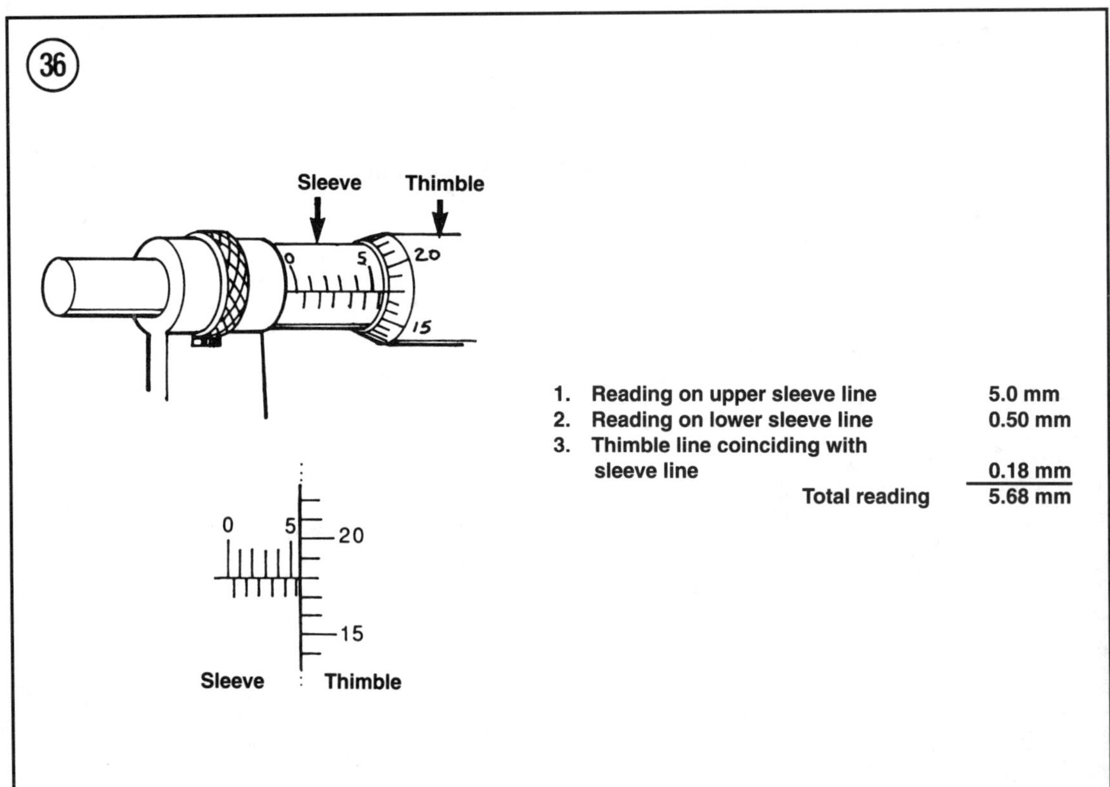

b. Read the micrometer. If the adjustment is correct, the 0 mark on the thimble will align exactly with the 0 mark on the sleeve line. If the 0 marks do not align, the micrometer is out of adjustment

c. To adjust the micrometer, follow the manufacturer's instructions given with the micrometer.

3. To check the accuracy of micrometers above the 1 in. or 25 mm size, perform the following:

a. Manufacturer's usually supply a standard gauge with these micrometers. A standard is a steel block, disc or rod that is ground to an exact size to check the accuracy of the micrometer. For example, a 1-2 in. micrometer is

(37)

STANDARD METRIC MICROMETER

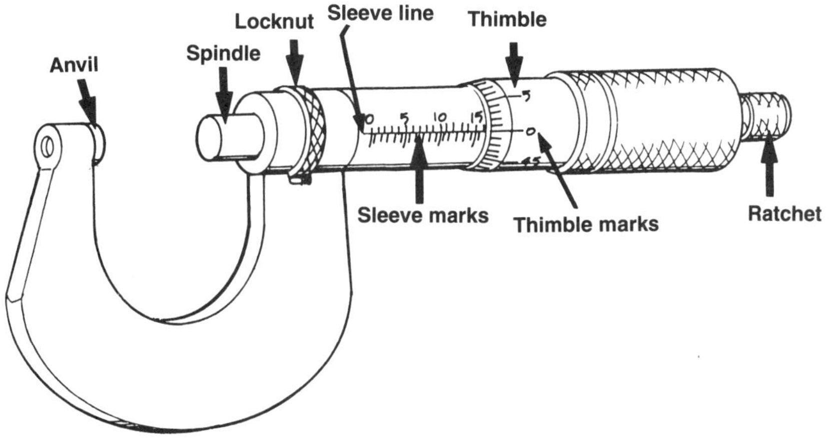

Locknut
Sleeve line
Thimble
Anvil
Spindle
Sleeve marks
Thimble marks
Ratchet

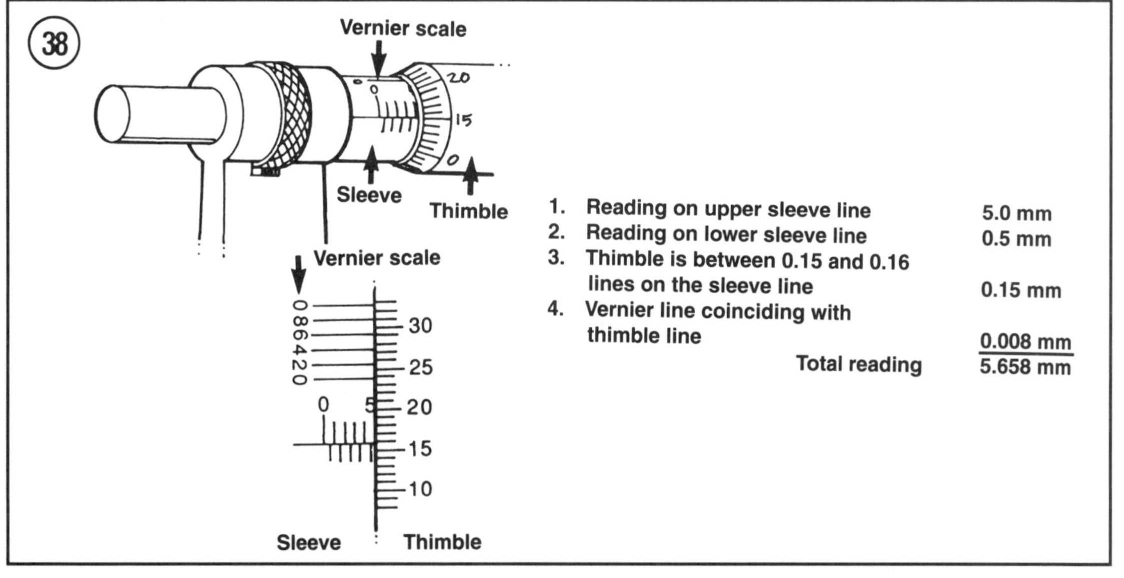

equipped with a 1 inch standard gauge. A 25-50 mm micrometer is equipped with a 25 mm standard gauge.

b. Place the standard gauge between the micrometer's spindle and anvil and measure its outside diameter or length. Read the micrometer. If the adjustment is correct, the 0 mark on the thimble will align exactly with the 0 mark on the sleeve line. If the 0 marks do not align, the micrometer is out of adjustment.

c. To adjust the micrometer, follow the manufacturer's instructions given with the micrometer.

Proper Care of the Micrometer

The micrometer is a precision instrument and must be used correctly and with great care.

1. Store a micrometer in its box or in a protected place where dust, oil, and other debris cannot come in contact with it. Do not store micrometers in a drawer with other tools or hang them on a tool board.
2. When storing a 0-1 in. (0-25 mm) micrometer, turn the thimble so that the spindle and anvil faces do not contact each other. If they do, rust may form on the contact ends or the spindle can be damaged from temperature changes.
3. Do not clean a micrometer with compressed air. Dirt forced into the tool can cause premature damage.
4. Occasionally lubricate the micrometer with a light weight oil to prevent rust and corrosion.
5. Before using a micrometer, check its accuracy. Refer to *Micrometer Accuracy Check* in this section.

Dial Indicator

A dial indicator (**Figure 39**) is a precision tool used to check dimensional variations, of machined parts such as transmission shafts and to check crankshaft runout and end play. For motorcycle and ATV service procedures, select a dial indicator with a continuous dial (**Figure 40**). When using a dial indicator, it must be held securely to ensure accurate measuring results. Various mounts are available for specific measuring requirements.

Cylinder Bore Gauge

The cylinder bore gauge is a very specialized precision tool. The gauge set shown in **Figure 41** is comprised of a dial indicator, handle and a number of different length adapters to adapt the gauge to different bore sizes. The bore gauge is used to make cylinder bore measurements such as bore size, taper and out-of-round. In some cases, an outside mi-

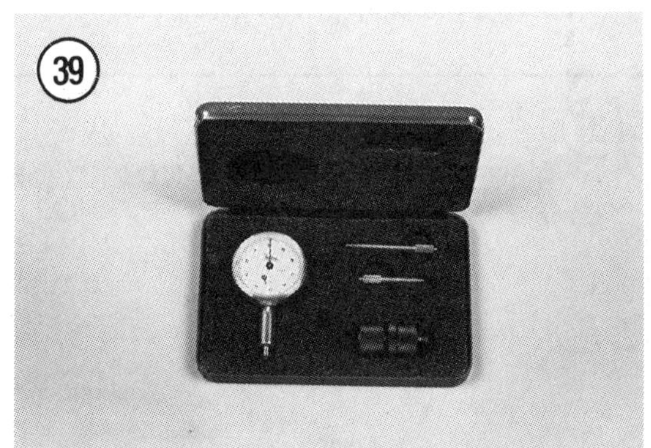
39

40

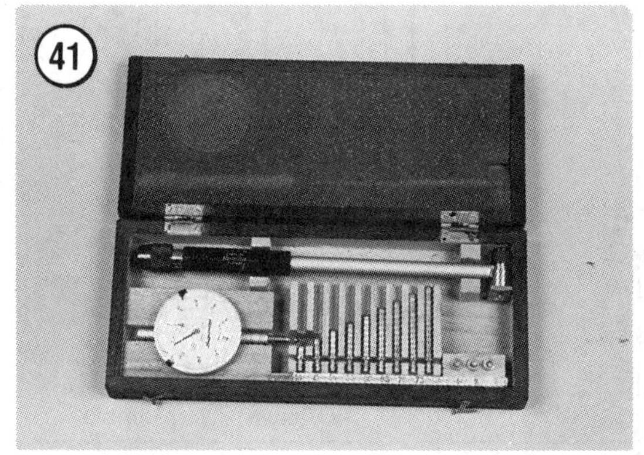
41

crometer must be used to calibrate the bore gauge to a particular bore size.

Select the correct length adapter (A, **Figure 42**) for the size of the bore to be measured. Zero the bore gauge according to its manufacturer's instructions, insert the bore gauge into the cylinder, carefully move it around in the bore to make sure it is centered and that the gauge foot (B, **Figure 42**) is sitting correctly on the bore surface. This is necessary to obtain a correct reading. When using a bore gauge, follow its manufacturer's instructions.

Compression Gauge

An engine with low compression cannot be properly tuned and will not develop full power. A compression gauge (**Figure 43**) measures engine compression. The one shown on the left has a flexible stem with an extension that can allow you to hold it while operating the starter. Open the throttle all the way when checking engine compression. See Chapter Three.

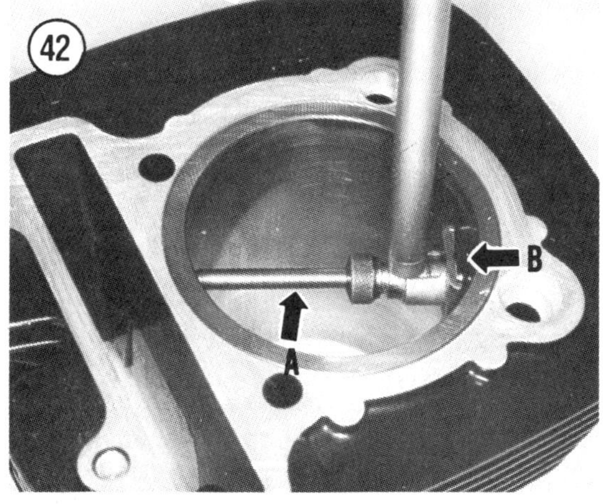

42

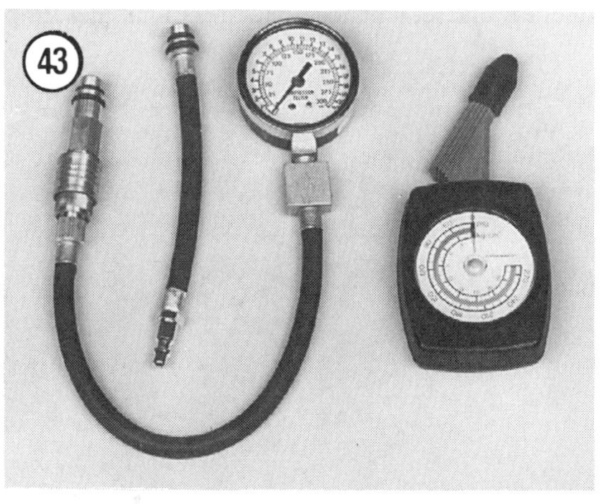

43

Multimeter or VOM

A VOM (Volt and Ohm Meter) is a valuable tool for all electrical system troubleshooting (**Figure 44**). The voltage application is used to indicate the voltage applied or available to various electrical components. The ohmmeter portion of the meter is used to check for continuity, or lack of continuity, and to measure the resistance of a component. Some tests are easily accomplished using meter with a sweeping needle (analog), but other components must be tested using a digital VOM (DVOM).

In some test procedures, the vehicle's manufacturer will instruct you to use their specific test meter due to the internal design of their meter. They will specify that the resistance reading may differ if another type of test meter is used in the test procedure. Such requirements will be noted at the beginning of the electrical test procedure.

To measure voltage

NOTE
Make sure the negative (–) or ground surface being used is clean and free of paint and/or grease. If possible, use an unpainted bolt that is attached directly to the frame.

1. Select the meter voltage range to *one scale higher* than the indicated voltage value of the circuit to be tested.

2. Touch the red test probe to the *positive* (+) end and the black test probe to the *negative* (–), or ground, end of the circuit.

3. Refer to the appropriate procedure in the chapter as to what switch(s) must be either turned ON or OFF within the circuit being tested.

4. With the switch(s) in the correct position, read the position of the needle on the VOLTS or VOLTAGE scale of the meter face, or the digital readout, and refer to the specified voltage listed in the test procedure. Refer to the manufacturer's instruction for any special conditions relating to the meter that you are using.

To calibrate an analog ohmmeter

NOTE
Every time an analog ohmmeter is used to measure resistance it must be calibrated in order to obtain a correct measurement. Most digital ohmmeters are not equipped with a zero ohms adjust feature—when turned on they are automatically set at zero (providing the meter's battery is at full power).

1. Make sure the meter's battery power source is at full power; if its condition is doubtful, install a new battery(s).

2. Make sure the test probes are clean and free of corrosion.

3. Touch the two test probes together and observe the meter needle location on the OHMS scale on the meter face. The needle must be on the 0 mark at the end of the scale.

4. If necessary, rotate the Ohms Adjust knob on the meter in either direction until the needle is directly on the 0 mark on the scale. The meter is now ready for use.

To measure resistance

1. Calibrate the analog meter as previously described.

2. Disconnect the component from the circuit. To obtain an accurate resistance reading, the component or circuit must be isolated.

NOTE
Polarity is usually not important when measuring the resistance of a component. Either test probe can be placed at either terminal of the component.

3. Place the test probe at each end of the component, read the position of the needle on the OHMS scale of the meter face, or the digital readout, and refer to the specified resistance in the test procedure.

4. If the component is not within specification, it should be replaced.

5. If the component is within specification, reinstall it in the circuit.

Continuity test

A continuity test determines the integrity of a circuit. Continuity is indicated by a low resistance reading, usually zero ohms, on the meter. No continuity is indicated by an infinity reading. A broken or open circuit has no continuity, while a complete circuit has continuity. A continuity test is also useful to check components for a short to ground.

1. Calibrate the analog meter as previously described in this section.

2. Place the test probes at each end of the component, or circuit and read the position of the needle on the OHMS scale of the meter face, or digital readout.

3. If there is *continuity (low resistance)* the meter will indicate a certain amount of resistance. In this test the resistance value is not important—all you want to know is if the circuit is complete or not.

4. If there is *no continuity (infinite resistance)* the meter needle will stay at the infinity symbol or the digital readout will indicate infinity.

SPECIAL TOOLS

A few special tools may be required for major service. These are described in the appropriate chapters and are available either from a Yamaha dealership or other manufacturers as indicated.

MECHANIC'S TIPS

Removing Frozen Nuts and Screws

If a fastener rusts and cannot be removed, several methods may be used to loosen it. First, apply penetrating oil such as Liquid Wrench or WD-40 (available at hardware or auto supply stores). Apply it liberally and let it penetrate for 10-15 minutes. Rap

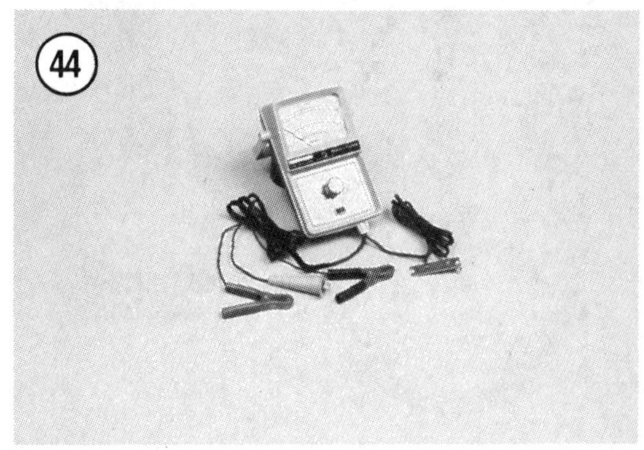

the fastener several times with a small hammer, then try to loosen it with a suitable tool; do not hit or turn it hard enough to cause damage. Reapply the penetrating oil if necessary.

To loosen frozen screws, apply penetrating oil as described, then insert a screwdriver in the slot and rap the top of the screwdriver with a hammer. This may loosen the rust so the screw can be removed. If the screw head is too damaged to use this method, grip the head with locking pliers and twist the screw out.

Avoid applying heat unless specifically instructed, as it may melt, warp or remove the temper from parts.

Removing Broken Screws or Bolts

If the head breaks off a screw or bolt, several methods are available to remove the remaining portion. If a large portion of the fastener projects out, try gripping it with locking pliers. If the projecting portion is too small, file it to fit a wrench or cut a slot in it to fit a screwdriver (**Figure 45**).

If the head breaks off flush, use a screw extractor (**Figure 46**) as follows:

NOTE

In the following step, it is important to drill in the exact center of the broken fastener. This ensures that there will be enough room to install the extractor and that it will be able to grip and lock into the broken fastener correctly. If the hole is drilled off center, the extractor may bite into the threaded hole when installed, further complicating the removal procedure.

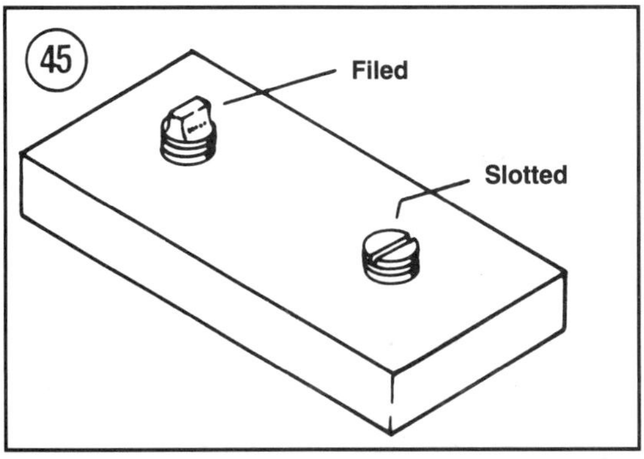

a. Center punch the exact center of the remaining portion of the screw or bolt.

b. Select the correct extractor bit and drill bit for the fastener being removed. Follow the manufacturer's instructions for drill size and hole depth. Then drill a hole into the broken fastener.

c. If the fastener was originally secured with a threadlocking compound, heat the fastener to loosen the sealer bond. Otherwise, spray the fastener with a penetrating oil, such as Liquid Wrench or WD-40, and allow it to penetrate for 10-15 minutes.

d. Tap the tap the extractor into the hole. Back the screw out with a wrench on the extractor.

e. Check the threaded hole for damage and repair if necessary.

Remedying Stripped Threads

Occasionally, fastener threads are damaged during service or repair. Often the threads can be cleaned up by running a tap (for internal threads) or die (for external threads) across the threads. See **Figure 47**. To clean or repair spark plug threads, a spark plug tap can be used.

If an internal thread is damaged, it may be necessary to install a Helicoil or some other type of thread insert. Follow the manufacturer's instructions when installing their insert.

If it is necessary to drill and tap a hole, refer to **Table 7** for metric tap drill sizes.

Studs
Removal/Installation

1. Measure the height of the installed stud so that the new stud can be installed correctly.

2A. If some threads of a stud are damaged, but some remain, you may be able to removed the stud as follows. If there are no usable threads, remove the stud as described in Step 2B.

a. Thread two nuts onto the damaged stud (**Figure 48**), then tighten the nuts against each other so that they are locked.

b. Turn the bottom nut (**Figure 49**) and unscrew the stud.

2B. If the threads on the stud are damaged, remove the stud with a stud remover or with a pair of locking pliers.

3. Clean the threads with solvent or contact cleaner and allow to dry thoroughly.

4. Clean the threaded hole with contact cleaner or solvent and a wire brush. Try to remove as much of the threadlock residue from the hole as possible.

5. Install 2 nuts on the top half of the new stud as in Step 2A. Make sure they are locked securely.

6. Apply a high-strength threadlock to the bottom threads on the new stud.

7. Turn the top nut and thread the new stud in. Install the stud to its correct height position (Step 1) or tighten it to its correct torque specification (see appropriate chapter).

8. Remove the nuts and repeat for each stud as required.

BALL BEARING REPLACEMENT

Ball bearings (**Figure 50**) are used throughout the engine and drive assembly to reduce power loss, heat and noise resulting from friction. Because ball bearings are precision made parts, they must be maintained by proper lubrication and maintenance. If a bearing is damaged, it should be replaced immediately. However, when installing a new bearing, care should be taken to prevent damage to the new bearing.

NOTE

Unless otherwise specified in the service procedure, install bearings with the

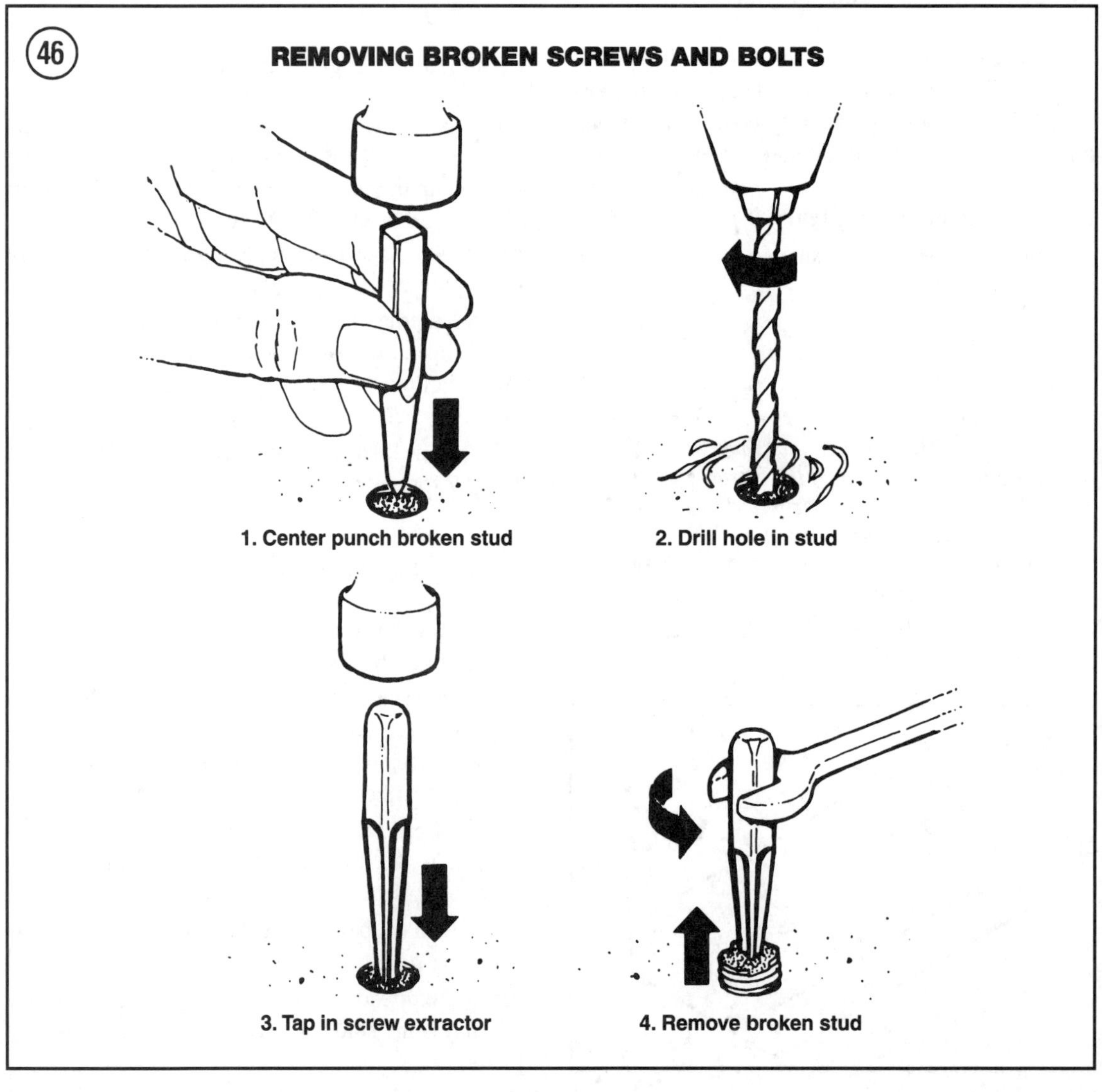

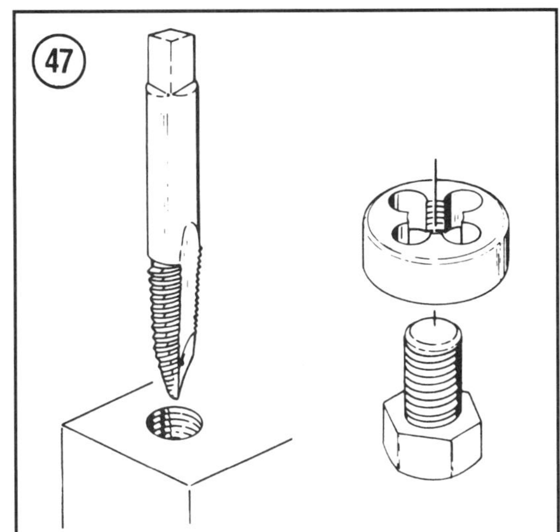
47

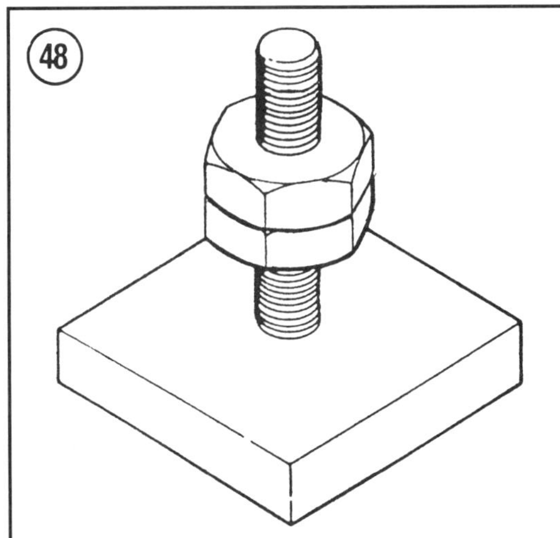
48

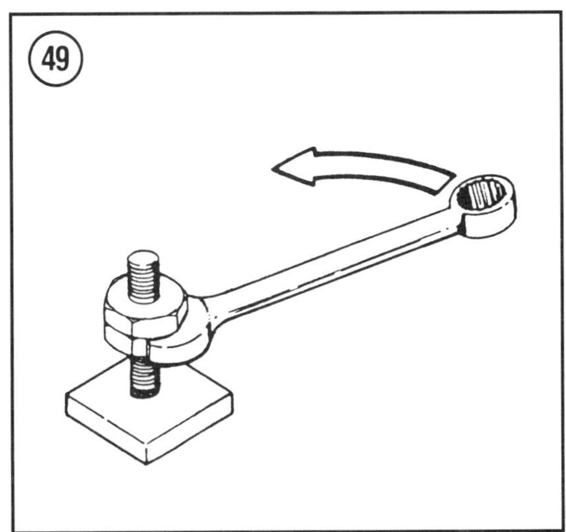
49

manufacturer's mark or number facing outward.

Bearing Removal

While bearings are normally removed only when damaged, there may be times when it is necessary to remove a bearing that is in good condition. However, improper bearing removal will damage the bearing and maybe the shaft or case half. Note the following when removing bearings.

WARNING
Failure to use proper precautions will probably result in damaged parts and may cause personal injury.

1. Before removing the bearings, note the following:
   a. Remove any oil seal(s) that interfere with bearing removal. Refer to *Seals* in this chapter.
   b. When removing more than one bearing, identify the bearings before removing them. Refer to the bearing manufacturer's size code marks on the bearing.
   c. Note and record the direction in which the bearing marks face for proper installation.
   d. Remove any set plates or bearing retainers before removing the bearings.
2. When using a puller to remove a bearing from a shaft, care must be taken so that the shaft is not damaged. Always place a spacer (**Figure 51**) between the end of the shaft and the puller screw. In addition, place the puller arms next to the inner bearing race.
3. When using a hammer to remove a bearing from a shaft, do not strike the hammer directly against the shaft. Instead, support the bearing races with

50

wooden blocks (**Figure 52**) and use a brass or aluminum driver between the hammer and shaft.

4. The ideal method of bearing removal is with a hydraulic press. However, certain procedures must be followed or damage may occur to the bearing or equipment. Note the following when using a press:

a. Always make sure the press is of sufficient capacity to remove the bearing. A 10-12 ton press should be adequate to remove the bearings called out in the manual. However, if overhauling the crankshaft, a 20-30 ton press will be required.

b. Always support the inner and outer bearing races with the proper size wood or aluminum spacer (**Figure 53**). If only the outer race is supported, the balls and/or the inner race will be damaged.

c. Always make sure the press ram (**Figure 53**) aligns with the center of the shaft. If the ram is not centered, it may damage the bearing and/or shaft.

d. The moment the shaft is free of the bearing, it will drop to the floor. Secure or hold the shaft to prevent it from falling.

5. Use a blind bearing remover to remove bearings installed in blind holes (**Figure 54**).

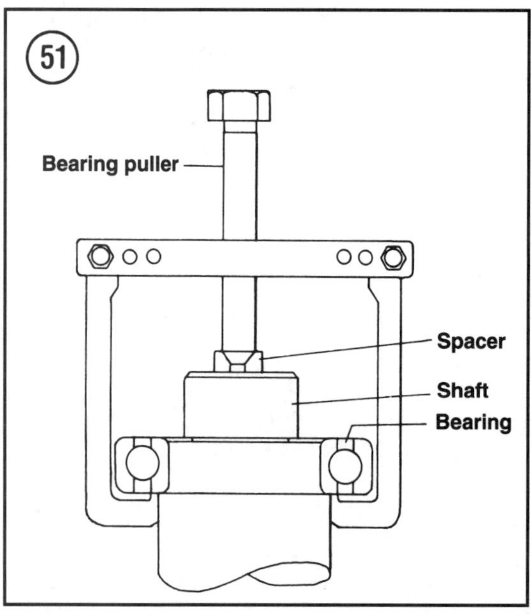

Bearing Installation

1. Before installing the new bearing(s), perform the following:

a. Clean and inspect the bearing bore or shaft.

b. Remove any burrs from the bearing bore or shaft.

c. Compare the old and new bearings to make sure the correct bearing is being installed.

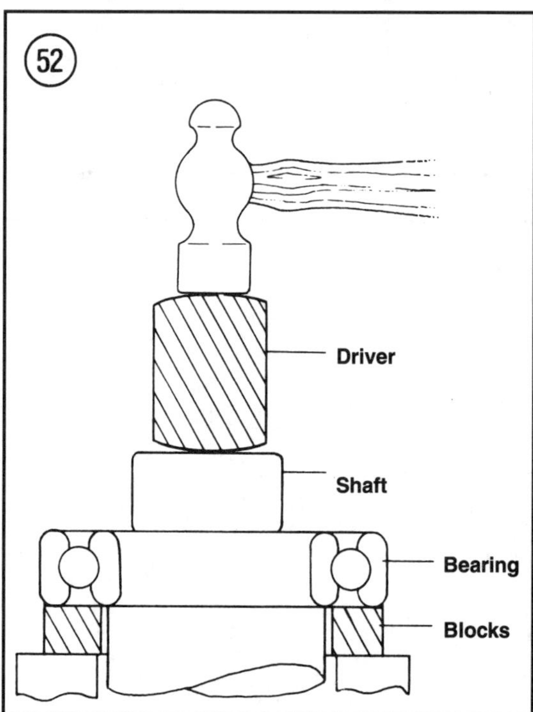

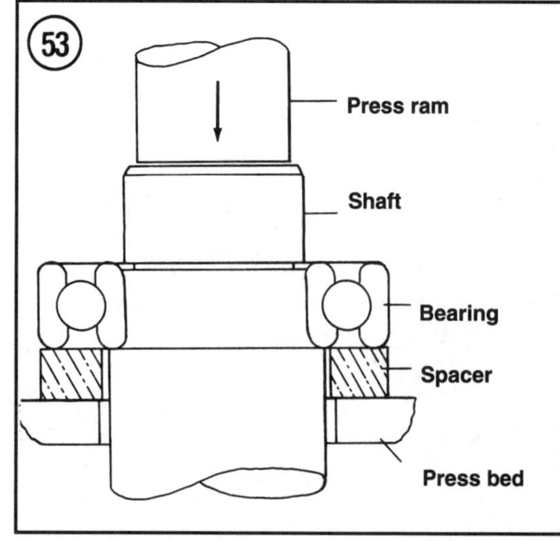

2. When installing a bearing in a housing, apply pressure to the *outer* bearing race (**Figure 55**). When installing a bearing on a shaft, apply pressure to the *inner* bearing race (**Figure 56**).

3. When installing a bearing as described in Step 2, some type of driver will be required. Never strike the bearing directly with a hammer or the bearing will be damaged. When installing a bearing, use a bearing driver, piece of pipe or a driver with a diameter that matches the bearing race. See **Figure 55** and **Figure 56**.

4. Step 2 describes how to install a bearing in a case half and over a shaft. However, when installing a bearing over a shaft and into a housing at the same time, a snug fit will be required for both outer and inner bearing races. In this situation, a spacer must be installed underneath the driver tool so that pressure is applied evenly across both races. See **Figure 57**. If the outer race is not supported as shown in **Figure 57**, the balls will push against the outer bearing track and damage it.

Shrink Fit

1. *Installing a bearing over a shaft*: When a tight fit is required, the bearing inside diameter is smaller than the shaft. In this case, driving the bearing on the shaft using normal methods may cause bearing damage. Instead, heat the bearing before installation.
   a. Secure the shaft so that it is ready for bearing installation.
   b. Clean all residue from the bearing surface of the shaft. Remove burrs with a file or sandpaper.
   c. Fill a suitable pot or beaker with clean mineral oil. Place a thermometer (rated higher than 120° C [248° F]) in the oil. Support the thermometer so that it does not rest on the bottom or side of the pot.
   d. Secure the bearing with a piece of heavy wire bent to hold it in the pot. Hang the bearing in the pot so that it does not touch the bottom or sides of the pot.
   e. Turn the heat on and monitor the thermometer. When the oil temperature rises to approxi-

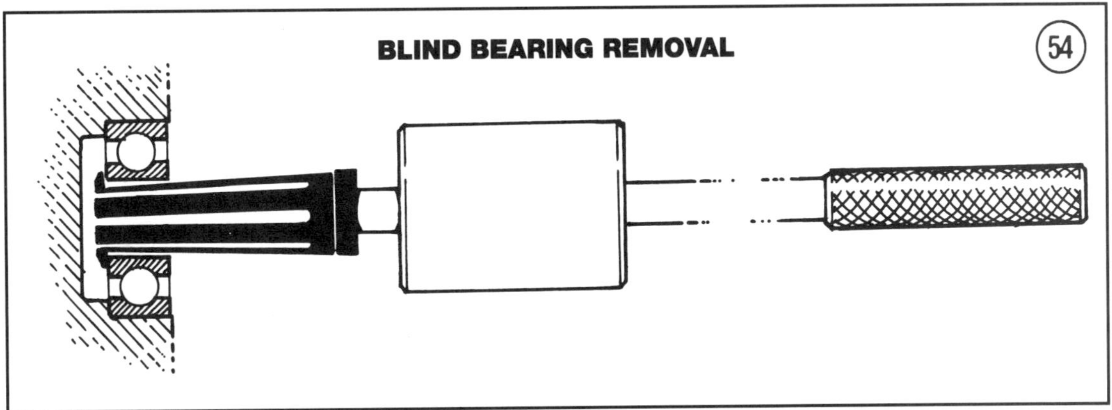
BLIND BEARING REMOVAL
54

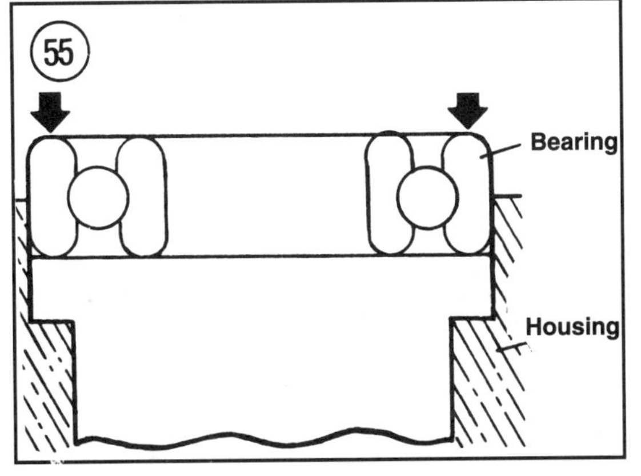

55

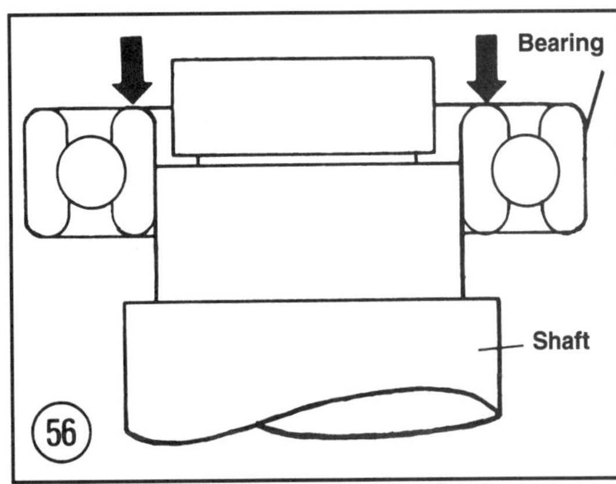

56

mately 120° C (248° F), remove the bearing from the pot and quickly install it. If necessary, place a socket on the inner bearing race and carefully tap the bearing into place. As the bearing chills, it will tighten on the shaft so you must work quickly when installing it. Make sure the bearing is installed all the way.

2. *Installing a bearing in a housing*: Bearings are generally installed in a housing with a slight interference fit. Driving the bearing into the housing may damage the housing or cause bearing damage. Instead, heat the housing before installing the bearing. Note the following:

CAUTION
Before heating the housing in this procedure to remove the bearings, wash the housing thoroughly with detergent and water. Rinse and rewash the housing as required to remove all traces of oil and other chemical deposits.

a. The housing must be heated to approximately 212° F (100° C) in an oven or on a hot plate. An easy way to check that it is at the proper temperature is to place tiny drops of water on the case as it starts to heat up; when they start to sizzle and evaporate immediately, the temperature is correct. Heat only one housing at a time.

CAUTION
Do not heat the housing with a torch (propane or acetylene)—never bring a flame into contact with the bearing or housing. The direct heat will destroy the case hardening of the bearing and is likely to warp the housing.

b. Wearing heavy welding gloves, remove the housing from the oven or hot plate—it is hot.

NOTE
A suitable size socket and extension works well for removing and installing bearings.

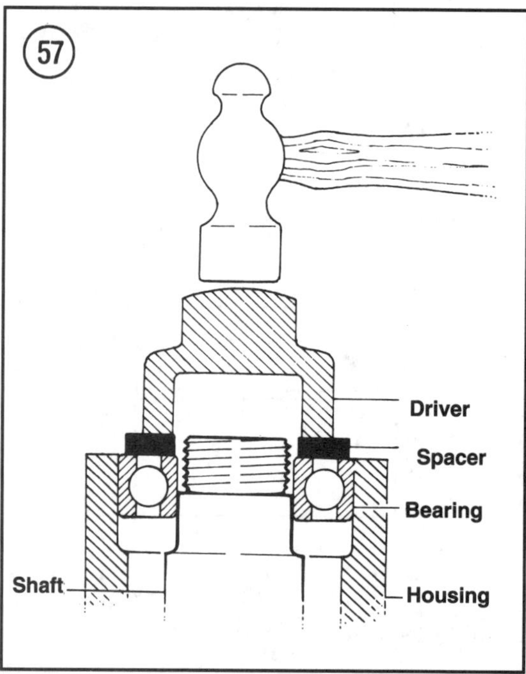

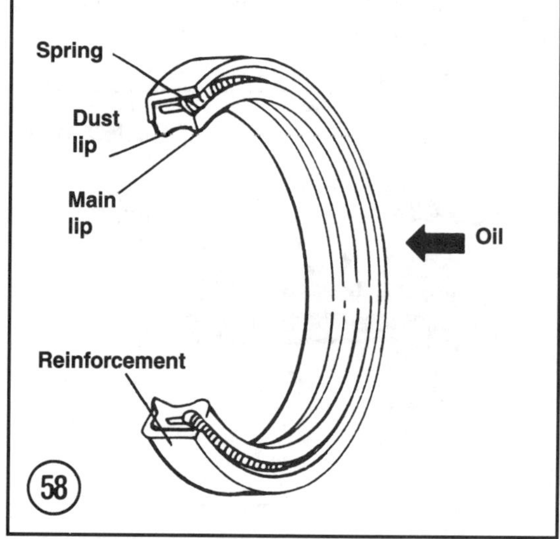

c. Hold the housing with the bearing side down and tap the bearing out. Repeat for all bearings in the housing.

d. Prior to heating the bearing housing, place the new bearing in a freezer, if possible. Chilling a bearing will slightly reduce its outside diameter while the heated bearing housing assembly is slightly larger due to heat expansion. This will make bearing installation much easier.

NOTE
Always install bearings with the manufacturer's mark or number facing outward.

e. While the housing is still hot, install the new bearing(s) into the housing. Install the bearings by hand, if possible. If necessary, lightly tap the bearing(s) into the housing with a socket placed on the outer bearing race (**Figure 55**). Do not install new bearings by driving on the inner bearing race. Install the bearing(s) until it seats completely.

SEALS

Seals (**Figure 58**) are used to contain oil, water, grease or combustion gasses in a housing or shaft. Improper seal removal can damage the housing or shaft. Improper installation of the seal can damage the seal or cause leakage.

1. Prying is generally the easiest and most effective method to remove a seal from a housing. However, always place a rag underneath the pry tool to prevent damage to the housing. See **Figure 59**, typical.

2. Pack the specified grease in the seal lips before installing the seal.

3. While seals are usually installed with the manufacturer's numbers or marks facing out, this is not always the case. In situations where a double sided seal is used, record the markings on the side of the seal that faces out. In some instances, the seal may be marked on both sides; for example, OUTSIDE and INSIDE. Look for these marks and install the seal correctly.

4. Seals can be installed by hand or may require the use of force. When using force, use a bearing driver or socket on the outer portion of the seal, then drive it squarely into its bore. Never install a seal by hitting against the top of the seal with a hammer.

Table 1 ENGINE AND FRAME SERIAL NUMBERS

Model	Engine and Frame Serial Number
1993 YFM400FWE	4GB-000101-on
1994 YFM400FWF	4GB-033101-on
1995 YFM400FWG	4GB-068101-on
1996 YFM400FWH	4SH-000101-on
1997 YFM400FWJ	4SH- *
1998 YFM400FWK	4SH- *

* Serial numbers not listed at the time of publication.

Table 2 GENERAL DIMENSIONS

	mm	in.
Overall length		
1993-1995	1925	75.8
1996-on	1956	77.0
Overall width	1155	45.5
Overall height		
1993-1995	1130	44.5
1996-on	1144	45.0
Seat height	830	32.7
Wheelbase	1210	47.6
Ground clearance (minimum)		
1993-1995	180	7.09
1996-on	215	8.46
Turning radius (minimum)	3500	137.8

Table 3 WEIGHT SPECIFICATIONS

	kg	lb.
Basic weight with oil and fuel tanks full	286	631
Maximum load	200	441

Table 4 CONVERSION TABLES

Multiply	By	To get equivalent of
Length		
Inches	25.4	Millimeter
Inches	2.54	Centimeter
Miles	1.609	Kilometer
Feet	0.3048	Meter
Millimeter	0.03937	Inches
Centimeter	0.3937	Inches
Kilometer	0.6214	Mile
Meter	3.281	Mile
Fluid volume		
U.S. quarts	0.9463	Liters
U.S. gallons	3.785	Liters
U.S. ounces	29.573529	Milliliters
Imperial gallons	4.54609	Liters
Imperial quarts	1.1365	Liters
Liters	0.2641721	U.S. gallons
Liters	1.0566882	U.S. quarts
Liters	33.814023	U.S. ounces
Liters	0.22	Imperial gallons

(continued)

Table 4 CONVERSION TABLES (continued)

Multiply	By	To get equivalent of
Liters	0.8799	Imperial quarts
Milliliters	0.033814	U.S. ounces
Milliliters	1.0	Cubic centimeters
Milliliters	0.001	Liters
Torque		
Foot-pounds	1.3558	Newton-meters
Foot-pounds	0.138255	Meters-kilograms
Inch-pounds	0.11299	Newton-meters
Newton-meters	0.7375622	Foot-pounds
Newton-meters	8.8507	Inch-pounds
Meters-kilograms	7.2330139	Foot-pounds
Volume		
Cubic inches	16.387064	Cubic centimeters
Cubic centimeters	0.0610237	Cubic inches
Temperature		
Fahrenheit	(F-32) × 0.556	Centigrade
Centigrade	(C × 1.8) + 32	Fahrenheit
Weight		
Ounces	28.3495	Grams
Pounds	0.4535924	Kilograms
Grams	0.035274	Ounces
Kilograms	2.2046224	Pounds
Pressure		
Pounds per square inch	0.070307	Kilograms per square centimeter
Kilograms per square centimeter	14.223343	Pounds per square inch
Kilopascals	0.1450	Pounds per square inch
Pounds per square inch	60895	Kilopascals
Speed		
Miles per hour	1.609344	Kilometers per hour
Kilometers per hour	0.6213712	Miles per hour

Table 5 GENERAL TORQUE SPECIFICATIONS

Fastener size or type	N•m	in.-lb.	ft.-lb.
5 mm screw	4	35	–
5 mm bolt and nut	5	44	–
6 mm screw	9	80	–
6 mm bolt and nut	10	88	–
6 mm flange bolt (8 mm head, small flange)	9	80	–
6 mm flange bolt (10 mm head) and nut	12	106	–
8 mm bolt and nut	22	–	16
8 mm flange bolt and nut	27	–	20
10 mm bolt and nut	35	–	25
10 mm flange bolt and nut	40	–	29
12 mm bolt and nut	55	–	40

Table 6 TECHNICAL ABBREVIATIONS

ABDC	After bottom dead center
ATDC	After top dead center
BBDC	Before bottom dead center

(continued)

Table 6 TECHNICAL ABBREVIATIONS

BDC	Bottom dead center
BTDC	Before top dead center
C	Celsius (Centigrade)
cc	Cubic centimeters
CDI	Capacitor discharge ignition
cu. in.	Cubic inches
F	Fahrenheit
ft.-lb.	Foot-pounds
gal.	Gallons
H/A	High altitude
hp	Horsepower
in.	Inches
kg	Kilogram
kg/cm^2	Kilograms per square centimeter
kgm	Kilogram meters
km	Kilometer
L	Liter
m	Meter
MAG	Magneto
ml	Milliliter
mm	Millimeter
N•m	Newton-meters
oz.	Ounce
psi	Pounds per square inch
PTO	Power take off
pt.	Pint
qt.	Quart
rpm	Revolutions per minute

Table 7 METRIC TAP DRILL SIZES

Metric (mm)	Drill size	Decimal equivalent	Nearest fraction
3 × 0.50	No. 39	0.0995	3/32
3 × 0.60	3/32	0.0937	3/32
4 × 0.70	No. 30	0.1285	1/8
4 × 0.75	1/8	0.125	1/8
5 × 0.80	No. 19	0.166	11/64
5 × 0.90	No. 20	0.161	5/32
6 × 1.00	No. 9	0.196	13/64
7 × 1.00	16/64	0.234	15/64
8 × 1.00	J	0.277	9/32
8 × 1.25	17/64	0.265	17/64
9 × 1.00	5/16	0.3125	5/16
9 × 1.25	5/16	0.3125	5/16
10 × 1.25	11/32	0.3437	11/32
10 × 1.50	R	0.339	11/32
11 × 1.50	3/8	0.375	3/8
12 × 1.50	13/32	0.406	13/32
12 × 1.75	13/32	0.406	13/32

Table 8 DECIMAL AND METRIC EQUIVALENTS

Fractions	Decimal in.	Metric mm	Fractions	Decimal in.	Metric mm
1/64	0.015625	0.39688	33/64	0.515625	13.09687
1/32	0.03125	0.79375	17/32	0.53125	13.49375
3/64	0.046875	1.19062	35/64	0.546875	13.89062
1/16	0.0625	1.58750	9/16	0.5625	14.28750
5/64	0.078125	1.98437	37/64	0.578125	14.68437
3/32	0.09375	2.38125	19/32	0.59375	15.08125
7/64	0.109375	2.77812	39/64	0.609375	15.47812
1/8	0.125	3.1750	5/8	0.625	15.87500
9/64	0.140625	3.57187	41/64	0.640625	16.27187
5/32	0.15625	3.96875	21/32	0.65625	16.66875
11/64	0.171875	4.36562	43/64	0.671875	17.06562
3/16	0.1875	4.76250	11/16	0.6875	17.46250
13/64	0.203125	5.15937	45/64	0.703125	17.85937
7/32	0.21875	5.55625	23/32	0.71875	18.25625
15/64	0.234375	5.95312	47/64	0.734375	18.65312
1/4	0.250	6.35000	3/4	0.750	19.05000
17/64	0.265625	6.74687	49/64	0.765625	19.44687
9/32	0.28125	7.14375	25/32	0.78125	19.84375
19/64	0.296875	7.54062	51/64	0.796875	20.24062
5/16	0.3125	7.93750	13/16	0.8125	20.63750
21/64	0.328125	8.33437	53/64	0.828125	21.03437
11/32	0.34375	8.73125	27/32	0.84375	21.43125
23/64	0.359375	9.12812	55/64	0.859375	22.82812
3/8	0.375	9.52500	7/8	0.875	22.22500
25/64	0.390625	9.92187	57/64	0.890625	22.62187
13/32	0.40625	10.31875	29/32	0.90625	23.01875
27/64	0.421875	10.71562	59/64	0.921875	23.41562
7/16	0.4375	11.11250	15/16	0.9375	23.81250
29/64	0.453125	11.50937	61/64	0.953125	24.20937
15/32	0.46875	11.90625	31/32	0.96875	24.60625
31/64	0.484375	12.30312	63/64	0.984375	25.00312
1/2	0.500	12.70000	1	1.00	25.40000

CHAPTER TWO

TROUBLESHOOTING

Diagnosing mechanical and electrical problems is relatively simple if you use an orderly procedure and keep a few basic principles in mind. The first step in any troubleshooting procedure is to define the symptoms closely and then localize the problem. Subsequent steps involve testing and analyzing those areas that could cause the symptoms. A haphazard approach may eventually solve the problem, but it can be very costly in terms of wasted time and unnecessary parts replacement.

Proper lubrication, maintenance and periodic tune-up, as described in Chapter Three, will reduce the necessity for troubleshooting. Even with the best of care, however, all vehicles are prone to problems that will require troubleshooting.

Never assume anything. Do not overlook the obvious. If the engine will not start, the engine stop switch or start switch may be defective or damaged. When trying to start the engine, you may have flooded it.

If the engine suddenly quits, what sound did it make? Consider this and check the easiest, most accessible area first. If the engine sounded as if it ran out of fuel, make sure there is fuel in the tank. If there is fuel in the tank, is it reaching the carburetor? If not, the fuel tank vent hose may be plugged, preventing fuel from flowing from the fuel tank to the carburetor.

If nothing obvious turns up in a quick inspection, look a little further. Learning to recognize and describe symptoms will make repairs easier for you or a mechanic at the shop. Describe problems accurately and fully.

Gather as many symptoms as possible to aid in diagnosis. Note whether the engine lost power gradually or all at once, what color smoke came from the exhaust and so on. Remember that the more complicated a machine is, the easier it is to troubleshoot because symptoms point to specific problems.

After defining the vehicle's symptoms, test and analyze the areas that could cause the problem. Guessing at the cause of a problem may eventually provide the solution, but it can easily lead to frustration, wasted time and a series of expensive, unnecessary parts replacements.

You do not need expensive equipment or complicated test gear to determine whether repairs can be attempted at home. A few simple checks could save a large repair bill and lost time while the machine sits in a dealership service department. On the other hand, be realistic and do not attempt repairs beyond your abilities. Dealership service departments tend to charge heavily for putting together a disassembled engine that may have been abused. Some will not even take on such a job. Use common sense and do not get in over your head.

OPERATING REQUIREMENTS

An engine needs 3 basics to run properly: correct fuel/air mixture, compression and a spark at the right time. If one basic requirement is missing, the engine will not run. Four stroke engine operating principles are described in Chapter Four under *Engine Principles*.

TROUBLESHOOTING INSTRUMENTS

Chapter One lists the instruments needed for the troubleshooting procedures and a detailed instruction on their use.

STARTING THE ENGINE

If your engine refuses to start, frustration can cause you to forget basic starting principles and procedures. The following outline will guide you

through the basic starting procedure. In all cases, make sure there is an adequate supply of fuel in the tank.

A rich air/fuel mixture is required when starting a cold engine. To accomplish this, a separate choke circuit is installed inside the carburetor. The choke circuit is controlled by a hand-operated choke knob (**Figure 1**). To *open* the choke circuit for starting a cold engine, pull the choke knob out. To *close* the choke circuit after the engine is warm or when starting a warm or hot engine, push the choke knob in.

Starting a Cold Engine

1. Shift the transmission into NEUTRAL.
2. Turn the ignition switch to the ON position.
3. Turn the fuel valve (**Figure 2**) to the ON position.
4. Pull the choke knob (**Figure 1**) out to its full ON position.
5. With the throttle completely closed, push the starter button or operate the recoil starter.
6. When the engine starts, work the throttle slightly to keep it running.
7. Idle the engine for approximately one minute or until the throttle responds cleanly, then push the choke knob in to its OFF position. The engine should be sufficiently warmed to prevent stalling.

Starting a Warm or Hot Engine

1. Shift the transmission into NEUTRAL.
2. Turn the ignition switch to the ON position.
3. Turn the fuel valve (**Figure 2**) to the ON position.
4. Make sure the choke knob (**Figure 1**) is in its OFF position (all the way in).
5. Open the throttle slightly and push the starter button or operate the recoil starter.

Starting a Flooded Engine

If the engine is hard to start and there is a strong gasoline smell, the engine is probably flooded. If so, close the choke (**Figure 1**). Then open the throttle all the way and push the starter button or operate the recoil starter until the engine starts. Depending on how badly the engine is flooded, it will generally start after a few attempts. If the engine is flooded badly, you may have to remove the spark plug and dry off its insulator, or install a new plug. When a flooded engine first starts to run, it will initially cough and run slowly as it burns the excess fuel. Then, as this excess fuel is burned, the engine will rev quickly. Release the throttle grip at this point and work it slowly to make sure the engine is running cleanly. Because a flooded engine smokes badly when it first starts to run, start the engine outside and in a well-ventilated area with its muffler pointing away from all objects. Do not start a flooded engine in a garage or other enclosed area.

NOTE

*If the engine refuses to start, check the carburetor overflow hose attached to the fitting at the bottom of the float bowl (**Figure 3**). If fuel is running out of the hose, the float valve is stuck open or leaking, allowing the carburetor to overfill. If this problem exists, remove the carburetor and correct the problem as described in Chapter Eight.*

STARTING DIFFICULTIES

If the engine cranks but is difficult to start, or will not start at all, it does not help to drain the battery. Check for obvious problems even before getting out your tools. Go down the following list step by step. Perform each step while remembering the 3 engine operating requirements described under *Operating Requirements* in this chapter.

If the engine still will not start, refer to the appropriate troubleshooting procedure that follows in this chapter.

1. Is the choke knob in the right position? Pull the choke knob (**Figure 1**) out to its full on position for a cold engine and push it all the way in for a warm or hot engine.
2. Is there fuel in the tank? Fill the tank if necessary. Has it been a while since the engine was run? If in doubt, drain the fuel and fill with a fresh tank full. Check for a clogged fuel tank vent tube (**Figure 4**). Remove the tube from the filler cap, then wipe off one end and blow through it. Remove the filler cap and check for a plugged hose nozzle.

WARNING

Do not use an open flame to check in the tank. A serious explosion is certain to result.

3. Disconnect the fuel line from the carburetor and insert the end of the hose into a clear container. Turn the fuel valve (**Figure 2**) to the ON position and see if fuel flows freely. If fuel does not flow and there is a fuel filter installed in the fuel line, remove the filter and turn the fuel valve on again. If fuel flows, the filter is clogged and must be replaced. If no fuel comes out, the fuel valve may be shut off, blocked by foreign matter, or the fuel cap vent may be plugged. Reconnect the fuel line to the carburetor fitting.
4. If you suspect that the cylinder is flooded, or there is a strong smell of gasoline, open the throttle all the way and push the starter button or operate the recoil starter. If the cylinder is severely flooded (fouled or wet spark plug), remove the spark plug and dry the base and electrode thoroughly with a soft cloth. Reinstall the plug and attempt to start the engine.
5. Check the carburetor overflow hose (**Figure 3**) on the bottom of the float bowl. If fuel is running out of the hose, the float valve is stuck open or leaking. Turn the fuel valve off and tap the carburetor a few times. Then turn on the fuel valve. If fuel continues to run out of the hose, remove and repair the carbu-

retor as described in Chapter Eight. Check the carburetor vent hoses to make sure they are clear. Check the end of the hoses for contamination.

NOTE

If fuel is reaching the carburetor, the fuel system could still be causing a problem. The jets (pilot and main) could be clogged or the air filter could be severely restricted. However, before removing the carburetor, continue with Step 6 to make sure that the ignition provides an adequate spark.

6. Make sure the engine stop switch is operating correctly. Make sure the stop switch wire is not broken or shorted. If necessary, test the engine stop switch as described under *Switches* in Chapter Nine.

NOTE

If you have installed an aftermarket stop switch, check the switch for proper operation. This switch may be causing a no-start condition.

5

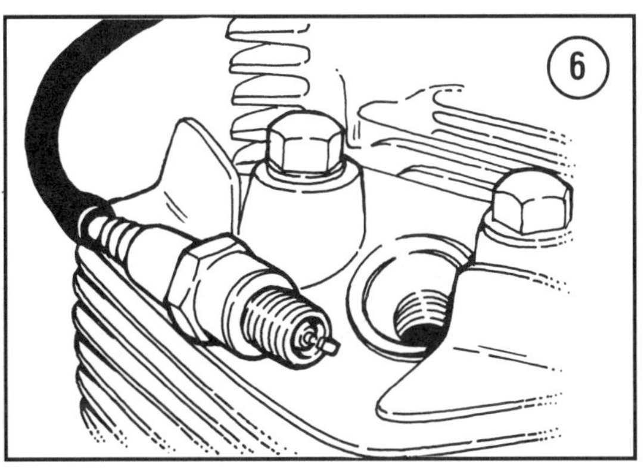

6

7. Is the spark plug high-tension wire and cap on tight (**Figure 5**)? Push it on and slightly rotate it to clean the electrical connection between the spark plug and the wire connector. Push or screw the plug cap into the high-tension wire.

2

NOTE

If the engine will still not start, continue with the following.

8. Perform a spark test as described under *Engine Fails to Start (Spark Test)* in this chapter. If there is a strong spark, perform Step 9. If there is no spark or if the spark is very weak, test the ignition system as described under *Ignition System* in this chapter.

9. Check cylinder compression as follows:

a. Turn the fuel valve (**Figure 2**) off.

b. Remove and ground the spark plug shell against the cylinder head as shown in **Figure 6**.

CAUTION

Grounding the spark plug prevents damage to the ignition system when the engine is cranked.

c. Put your finger tightly over the spark plug hole.

d. Operate the starter, or have an assistant operate the recoil starter. When the piston comes up on the compression stroke, pressure in the cylinder should force your finger from the spark plug hole. If your finger pops off, the cylinder probably has sufficient compression to start the engine.

NOTE

You may still have a compression problem even though it seems good with the previous test. Check engine compression with a compression gauge as described under (ital)Tune-up(ital) in Chapter Three.

Engine Fails to Start (Spark Test)

Perform the following spark test to determine if the ignition system is operating properly. When checking the spark, turn the engine stop switch to RUN and the main switch to ON.

CAUTION
Before removing the spark plug in Step 1, clean all dirt and debris away from the plug base. Dirt that falls into the cylinder will cause rapid engine wear.

1. Disconnect the plug wire and remove the spark plug.

NOTE
*A spark tester (**Figure 7**) is a useful tool for checking the ignition system. This tool is inserted in the spark plug cap and its base is grounded against the cylinder head. Because the tool's air gap is adjustable, it allows you to see and hear the spark while testing the intensity of the spark. A number of different spark testers are available through motorcycle and automotive parts stores. The spark tester shown in **Figure 7** is manufactured by Motion Pro.*

2. If using an adjustable spark tester, set its air gap to 6 mm (0.24 in.).
3. Insert the spark plug (or spark tester) into the plug cap and touch its base against the cylinder head to ground it (**Figure 6**). Position the plug so you can see the electrodes.

CAUTION
Mount the spark plug or spark tester away from the plug hole in the cylinder head so the spark from the plug or tester cannot ignite the gasoline vapor in the cylinder.

4. Turn the engine over with the starter button or operate the recoil starter. A crisp blue spark should be evident across the spark plug electrodes or spark tester terminals.

WARNING
Do not hold or touch the spark plug (or spark checker), wire or connector when making a spark check. A serious electrical shock may result.

5. If the spark is good, check for one or more of the following possible malfunctions:
   a. Obstructed fuel line or fuel filter (if used).
   b. Low compression or engine damage.
   c. Flooded engine.

6. If the spark is weak (white or yellow in color) or if there is no spark, check for one or more of the following conditions:
   a. Fouled or wet spark plug. If you get a spark across a spark tester but not across the original spark plug, the plug is fouled or defective. Repeat the spark test with a new plug.
   b. Loose or damaged spark plug cap connection. Hold the secondary wire and turn the spark plug cap to tighten it. The install the spark plug into the cap and repeat the spark test. If there is still no spark, bypass the plug cap as described in the next step.
   c. Check for a damaged spark plug cap. Hold the secondary wire and unscrew the spark plug cap. Then hold the end of the secondary wire 6 mm (0.24 in.) from the cylinder head as shown in **Figure 8**. Have an assistant crank the engine and repeat the spark test. If there is now a strong spark, the spark plug cap is faulty. Replace the plug cap and repeat the spark test.
   d. Loose or damaged high tension wiring connections (at coil and plug cap).

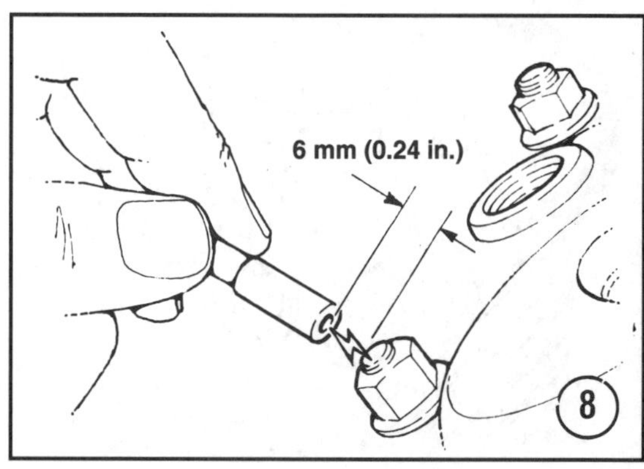

e. Faulty ignition coil or faulty ignition coil ground wire connection.
f. Faulty CDI unit or stator coil(s).
g. Sheared flywheel key.
h. Loose flywheel nut.
i. Loose electrical connections.
j. Dirty electrical connections.

NOTE
If the engine backfires when you attempt to start it, the ignition timing may be incorrect. Because the ignition timing is not adjustable on the Kodiak, incorrect ignition timing can be caused by a loose flywheel, sheared flywheel key, loose pickup coil mounting screws or a damaged or defective ignition system component. Refer to ***Ignition System*** *in this chapter.*

Engine Difficult To Start

The following section groups the 3 main engine operating systems with probable causes of a difficult starting condition.

Electrical System

Yamaha electrical systems are relatively trouble-free. If electrical problems do occur, they can usually be traced to a point in the wiring harness, at the connectors or in one of the switches.

1. *Spark plug*:
   a. Fouled spark plug.
   b. Incorrect spark plug gap.
   c. Incorrect spark plug heat range (too cold). See Chapter Three.
   d. Worn or damaged spark plug electrodes.

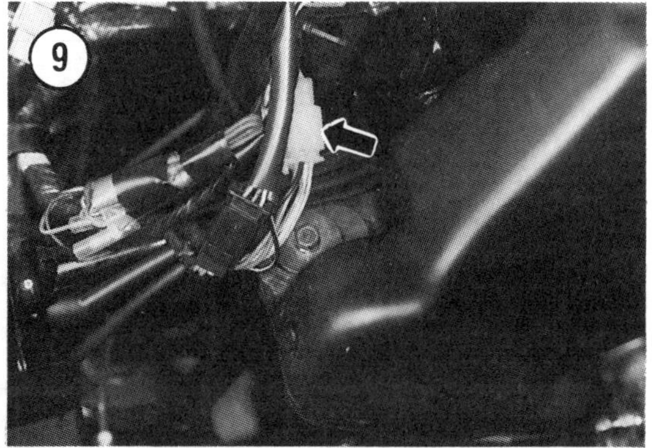

   e. Damaged spark plug.
   f. Damaged spark plug cap or secondary wire.

NOTE
Refer to ***Reading Spark Plugs*** *in Chapter Three for additional information.*

2. *Ignition coil*:
   a. Loose or damaged secondary or primary wires.
   b. Cracked ignition coil body.
   c. Loose or corroded ground wire.
3. *Switches and wiring*:
   a. Dirty or loose fitting terminals.
   b. Damaged wires or connectors (**Figure 9**).
   c. Damaged start switch.
   d. Damaged engine stop switch.
   e. Damaged main switch.
4. *Electrical components*:
   a. Damaged pickup coil.
   b. Damaged CDI unit.
   c. Damaged flywheel Woodruff key.

Fuel System

A contaminated fuel system will cause engine starting and performance related problems. It only takes a small amount of dirt in the fuel valve, fuel line or carburetor to cause problems.

1. *Air filter*:
   a. Clogged air filter element.
   b. Clogged air filter housing.
   c. Leaking or damaged air filter housing-to-carburetor air boot.
2. *Fuel valve*:
   a. Clogged fuel hose.
   b. Clogged fuel valve filter.
3. *Fuel tank*:
   a. No fuel.
   b. Clogged fuel filter.
   c. Clogged fuel tank breather hose (**Figure 4**).
   d. Contaminated fuel.
4. *Carburetor:*
   a. Clogged or damaged choke system.
   b. Clogged main jet.
   c. Clogged pilot jet.
   d. Loose pilot jet or main jet.
   e. Clogged pilot jet air passage.
   f. Incorrect float level.
   g. Leaking or damaged float.
   h. Worn or damaged needle valve.

2

Engine Compression

Check engine compression as described in Chapter Three. To obtain a more accurate gauge of engine wear, perform an engine leak down test. Refer to *Engine Leakdown Test* in this chapter.

1. *Cylinder and cylinder head*:
   a. Loose spark plug.
   b. Missing spark plug gasket.
   c. Leaking cylinder head gasket.
   d. Leaking cylinder base gasket.
   e. Excessively worn or seized piston, piston rings and/or cylinder.
   f. Loose cylinder and/or cylinder head fasteners.
   g. Cylinder head incorrectly installed and/or torqued.
   h. Warped cylinder head.
   i. Defective head gasket.
   j. Defective cylinder base gasket.
   k. Loose cylinder fasteners.
   l. Valve(s) adjusted too tight.
   m. Bent valve.
   n. Worn valve and/or seat.
2. *Piston and piston rings*:
   a. Worn piston rings.
   b. Damaged piston rings.
   c. Piston seizure or piston damage.
3. *Crankcase and crankshaft:*
   a. Seized connecting rod.
   b. Damaged crankcases.
   c. Damaged crankcase seals.

POOR IDLE SPEED PERFORMANCE

If the engine starts but off-idle performance is poor (engine hesitates or misfires), check the following:

1. Clogged or damaged air filter element.
2. *Carburetor*:
   a. Clogged pilot jet.
   b. Loose pilot jet.
   c. Damaged choke system.
   d. Incorrect throttle cable adjustment.
   e. Incorrect carburetor adjustment.
   f. Flooded carburetor (visually check carburetor overflow hose for fuel).
   g. Vacuum piston does not slide smoothly in carburetor bore.
3. *Fuel*:
   a. Water and/or alcohol in fuel.
   b. Old fuel.
4. *Engine*:
   a. Low engine compression.
5. *Electrical system*:
   a. Damaged spark plug.
   b. Damaged ignition coil.
   c. Damaged pickup coil.
   d. Damaged CDI unit.

POOR MEDIUM AND HIGH SPEED PERFORMANCE

Refer to *Engine is Difficult to Start*, then check the following:

1. *Carburetor:*
   a. Incorrect fuel level.
   b. Incorrect jet needle clip position (if adjustable).
   c. Clogged or loose main jet.
2. *Clogged air filter element.*
3. *Other considerations*:
   a. Overheating.
   b. Clutch slippage.
   c. Brake drag.
   d. Engine oil viscosity too high or oil level too high.

ELECTRIC STARTING SYSTEM

This section describes troubleshooting procedures for the electric starting system. A fully charged battery, ohmmeter and jumper cables are required to perform this procedure.

Description

An electric starter motor (**Figure 10**) is used on all models. The starter motor is mounted horizontally at the front of the engine.

The electric starting system requires a fully charged battery to provide the large amount of current required to operate the starter motor. A charge coil (mounted on the stator plate) and a voltage regulator, connected in circuit with the battery, keeps the battery charged while the engine is running. The battery can also be charged externally.

The starting circuit consists of the battery, starter motor, neutral switch, neutral relay, reverse switch, starter relay, starting circuit cut-off relay, CDI unit, main switch and engine stop switch.

The starter relay (**Figure 11**) carries the heavy electrical current to the motor. Depressing the starter switch allows current to flow through the starter relay coil. The starter relay contacts close and allow current to flow from the battery through the starter relay to the starter motor.

The neutral switch and neutral relay are designed to prevent the starter motor from operating if the transmission is in gear. Therefore, the starter motor will only operate if the main switch is ON, the engine stop switch is in the RUN position, the transmission is in NEUTRAL, or in gear with the front brake lever firmly applied, and the select lever (**Figure 12**) is in the forward position.

CAUTION

Do not operate an electric starter motor continuously for more than 5 seconds. Allow the motor to cool for at least 15 seconds between attempts to start the engine.

Troubleshooting

Before troubleshooting the starting circuit, make sure that:

a. The battery is fully charged.
b. The battery cables are the proper size and length. Replace cables that are undersize or damaged.
c. All electrical connections are clean and tight.
d. The wiring harness is in good condition, with no worn or frayed insulation or loose harness sockets.
e. The fuel system is filled with an adequate supply of fresh gasoline.

Starter Troubleshooting

If the starter does not operate, perform the following tests.

When operating the starter switch, turn the engine stop switch to RUN and the main switch to ON.

1. Refer to Chapter Fourteen and remove the following components to access the starting circuit in this procedure:
   a. Seat.
   b. Front fender.
   c. Rear render.
2. First check the 30 amp main fuse. Open the fuse holder and pull the fuse out and visually inspect it. If the fuse is blown, replace it as described under *Fuse* in Chapter Nine. If the main fuse is good, reinstall it, then continue with Step 3.
3. Test the battery as described under *Battery* in Chapter Three. Note the following:
   a. If the battery is fully charged, perform Step 3.

b. If necessary clean and recharge the battery. If the battery is damaged, replace it.

4. Disconnect the electrical connector from the main (key) switch. Test the main switch as described under *Switches* in Chapter Nine. If the main switch is good, continue with Step 5.

5. Disconnect the start switch electrical connectors from the wiring harness. Test the start switch as described under *Switches* in Chapter Nine. Replace the switch if necessary. If the switch is good, perform Step 6.

6. Disconnect the engine stop switch electrical connectors from the wiring harness. Test the engine stop switch as described under *Switches* in Chapter Nine. If the switch is good, perform Step 7.

NOTE

Reconnect all switches before continuing with Step 7.

WARNING

The jumper cable installed in Step 7 must be the same gauge as the battery leads or the jumper cable may overheat. Because the test in Step 7 may cause sparks, perform this test with the vehicle parked away from all flammable fluids.

NOTE

Make sure the transmission is in NEUTRAL before performing Step 7.

7. Momentarily connect a jumper cable between the battery positive (+) cable and the starter motor as shown in **Figure 13**. The starter motor should run when the jumper cable is connected. Disconnect the jumper cable. Note the following:

a. Starter turns: Perform Step 8.
b. Starter does not turn: Remove and test the starter or replace the starter motor as described under ***Electric Starter*** in Chapter Nine.

8. Disconnect the starter relay red/white and blue/white electrical connector. The starter relay is shown in **Figure 11**. Connect a jumper wire between the starter relay red/white terminal and the positive battery cable. Then connect a second jumper wire between the starter relay blue/white terminal and ground as shown in **Figure 14**. When this connection is made, there should be an audible click at the starter relay. Disconnect both jumper wires.

a. Starter relay clicks: perform Step 9.
b. Starter relay does not click: Replace the starter relay as described in Chapter Nine.
c. Reconnect the starter relay connector.

9. Test the starter circuit cut off relay as described in Chapter Nine. If the relay is good, perform Step 10.

10. Test the neutral switch as described under *Switches* in Chapter Nine. If the neutral switch is good, perform Step 11.

11. Test the neutral relay as described in Chapter Nine. If the neutral relay is good, perform Step 12.

12. Test the reverse switch as described under *Switches* in Chapter Nine. If the reverse switch is good, perform Step 13.

13. Test the front brake light switch as described under *Switches* in Chapter Nine. If the switch is good, perform Step 14.

14. If you have not found the starting system problem, recheck the wiring system for dirty or loose terminals or damaged wires. Clean and repair as required. If all of the connectors and wires are in good condition, the CDI unit is probably faulty. Replace the CDI unit as described in Chapter Nine and recheck the starter operation.

NOTE

The CDI unit cannot be tested effectively using conventional equipment. Because starting system problems are most often caused by an open or short circuit or poor wiring connections, replace the CDI unit only if you are certain that all other starting system components are in good condition. The CDI unit is expensive, and once purchased, generally cannot be returned. Therefore, repeat the preceding tests to verify the condition of the starting system before replacing the CDI unit.

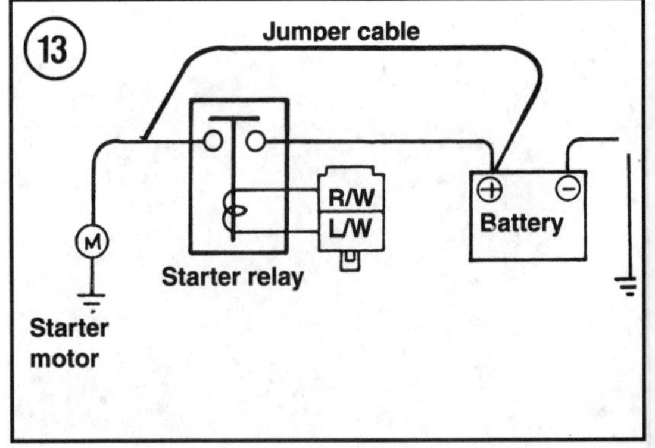

15. Install all parts previously removed. Make sure all of the connectors disconnected during this procedure are free of corrosion and are reconnected properly.

CHARGING SYSTEM

A malfunction in the charging system generally causes the battery to remain undercharged.

Troubleshooting

1. Perform the *Charging System Output Test* described in Chapter Nine. If charging system output is not within specification, check the charging coil resistance as described in Chapter Nine.
   a. Replace the charging coil if its resistance is not within specification.
   b. If charging coil resistance is good, replace the voltage regulator. See Chapter Nine.
2. Repeat the output test to confirm charging system operation.

IGNITION SYSTEM

All models are equipped with a capacitor discharge ignition (CDI) system. This solid state system uses no contact breaker point or other moving parts.

Because of the solid state design, problems with the capacitor discharge system are rare. If a problem occurs, it generally causes a weak spark or no spark at all. An ignition system with a weak spark or no spark is relatively easy to troubleshoot. It is difficult, however, to troubleshoot an ignition system that only malfunctions when the engine is hot or under load.

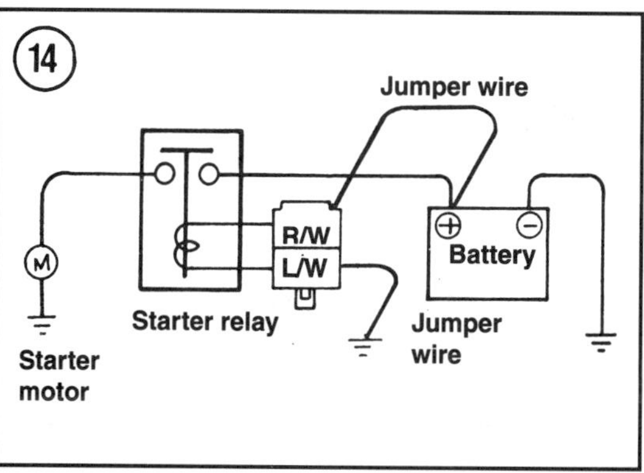

NOTE

If the problem is intermittent, perform the tests with the engine cold, then hot. Then compare the test results.

1. Perform the following ignition spark gap test as follows:

NOTE

If you do not have an adjustable spark tester, perform the spark test as described under ***Engine Fails to Start (Spark Test)*** *in this chapter.*

   a. Disconnect the plug wire.

NOTE

A spark tester is a useful tool to check the ignition system. ***Figure 7*** *shows the Motion Pro Ignition System Tester. The tool's air gap is adjustable, and it allows you to see and hear the spark while testing the intensity of the spark.*

   b. If using an adjustable spark tester, set its air gap distance is 6 mm (0.24 in.).
   c. Insert the spark plug (or spark tester) into the plug cap and touch its base against the cylinder head to ground it (**Figure 7**). Position the tester so you can see its terminals.

CAUTION

If the spark plug is removed from the engine, mount the spark tester away from the plug hole in the cylinder head so that the spark from the tester cannot ignite the gasoline vapors in the cylinder.

   d. Crank the engine over with the starter button or operate the recoil starter. A fat blue spark should be evident across the spark tester terminals.

WARNING

Do not hold the spark tester or connector or a serious electrical shock may result.

   e. If a dark blue spark jumps the gap and is dark blue in color, the ignition system is producing acceptable spark. If the spark does not jump the gap, hold the spark plug cable and twist the plug cap a few times to tighten it. Then recheck the spark gap. If there is still no spark or if a weak yellow or white spark is noted, continue with Step 2.

f. Remove the spark tester from the spark plug cap.

2. Unscrew the spark plug cap from the ignition coil plug wire and hold the end of the wire 6 mm (0.24 in.) from the cylinder head and away from the spark plug hole as shown in **Figure 8**. Have an assistant turn the engine over for you. A fat blue spark should be evident passing from the end of the wire to the cylinder head. Note the following:

a. If there is no spark, perform Step 3.

b. If there is a spark, the plug cap is probably faulty. Test the spark plug cap resistance as described under *Ignition Coil Testing* in Chapter Nine. Replace the spark plug cap and retest.

3. Test the ignition coil secondary and primary resistance as described under *Ignition Coil Testing* in Chapter Nine. Note the following:

a. If the ignition coil is good, perform Step 5.

b. If the ignition coil failed to pass the tests described in Chapter Nine, the ignition coil is probably faulty. However, before replacing the ignition coil, take it to a dealership and have the spark tested using an ignition coil tester. Replace the ignition coil if faulty and retest the ignition system.

4. Test the engine stop switch as described under *Switches* in Chapter Nine. Note the following:

a. If the switch is good, perform Step 5.

b. If the switch failed to pass the test as described in Chapter Nine, the switch is faulty and must be replaced. Replace the switch and retest the ignition system.

5. Test the main switch as described under *Switches* in Chapter Nine. Note the following:

a. If the switch is good, perform Step 6.

b. If the switch failed to pass the test as described in Chapter Nine, the switch is faulty and must be replaced. Replace the switch and retest the ignition system.

6. Test the source coil and pickup coil as described under *Stator Coil Testing* in Chapter Nine. Note the following:

a. If both coils tested good, perform Step 7.

b. If one or both coils tested incorrectly, replace the stator coil assembly and retest the ignition system.

7. If you have not been able to locate the damaged component, check the ignition system wiring harness and connectors. Check for damaged wires or loose, dirty or damaged connectors. If the wiring and connectors are good, the CDI unit is faulty and must be replaced.

NOTE

The CDI unit cannot be tested effectively using conventional equipment. Because ignition system problems are most often caused by an open or short circuit or poor wiring connections, replace the CDI unit only if you are certain that all other ignition system components are in good condition. The CDI unit is expensive, and once purchased, generally cannot be returned. Therefore, repeat the preceding tests to verify the condition of the ignition system before replacing the CDI unit.

8. Install all parts previously removed. Make sure all of the connectors disconnected during this procedure are free of corrosion and are reconnected properly.

LIGHTING SYSTEM

Burnt Bulbs

If the headlight or taillight bulb(s) continually burn out, check for one or more of the following conditions:

a. Incorrect bulb type. See Chapter Nine for the correct replacement bulb types for your model.

b. Damaged battery.

c. Damaged rectifier/regulator.

d. Incorrect grounds.

e. Damaged main switch and/or light switch.

Headlight Operates but is Darker than Normal

Check for one or more of the following conditions:

a. Incorrect bulb type. See Chapter Nine for the correct replacement bulb types for your model.

b. Charging system problem.

c. Accessory load exceeds charging system output. If you have added one or more aftermarket electrical accessories, disconnect each accessory, one at a time. Start the engine and check headlight operation after each accessory is disconnected.

d. Incorrect ground connection.

e. Poor main and/or light switch electrical contacts.

System Troubleshooting

If the taillight and/or taillight do not work, perform the following test procedures.

1. Check for a blown bulb as described in Chapter Nine.
2. Check all of the lighting system connectors and wires for loose or damaged connections.
3. Check the main fuse as described in Chapter Nine. Replace a blown or damaged fuse.
4. Test the battery as described in Chapter Three. Note the following:
   a. If the battery is fully charged, perform Step 5.
   b. If necessary, clean and recharge the battery. If the battery is damaged or won't hold a charge, replace it. If you bought the vehicle used, check the battery to make sure it is the correct size for your model. See *Battery* in Chapter Three.
5. Test the main switch as described in Chapter Nine. If the main switch is good, continue with Step 6.
6. If you have not been able to solve the problem, perform the *Lighting System Check* in this section.

Lighting System Check

Headlight

If the headlights do not come on, perform the following test.

15

1. Remove the headlight bulb (Chapter Nine) and disconnect the headlight socket from the wiring harness. See **Figure 15**, typical.
   a. Connect an ohmmeter across the bulb terminals. The reading should be zero ohms. Replace the bulb if blown.
   b. Connect an ohmmeter between one of the headlight socket terminals and its mating electrical connector. Repeat for the remaining wires and their terminals. Continuity should be noted at each test condition. Repair or replace the headlight socket if no continuity is present.
   c. If both sets of readings were correct, continue with Step 2.
2. Install the headlight bulb into its socket and reconnect the socket back into the wiring harness. Do not install the socket into its headlight housing. The headlight bulb and socket must be connected to the wiring harness when making the following tests.
3. Switch a voltmeter to its DC20V scale. In Step 4 and Step 5, connect the voltmeter leads to the headlight socket electrical connectors with the headlight connector connected to the main wiring harness.
4. Connect the voltmeter positive lead (+) to the headlight connector green lead and the voltmeter negative lead (–) to the headlight connector black lead. Turn the main switch to its ON position and the dimmer switch to its LO position. Note the voltmeter reading:
   a. If the voltmeter reads battery voltage, continue with Step 5.
   b. If the voltmeter does not read battery voltage, check the wiring harness from the main switch to the headlight socket for damage.
5. Turn the main switch to its OFF position. Connect the voltmeter positive lead (+) to the headlight connector yellow lead and the voltmeter negative lead (–) to the headlight connector black lead. Turn the main switch to its ON position and the dimmer switch to its HI position. Note the voltmeter reading:
   a. If the voltmeter reads battery voltage, continue with Step 6.
   b. If the voltmeter does not read battery voltage, check the wiring harness from the main switch to the headlight socket for damage.
6. Turn the main switch to its OFF position and disconnect the voltmeter leads. If the voltmeter read 12 volts for both tests (Step 4 and Step 5), the headlight wiring circuit is good.

Taillight

If the tailight is inoperative, perform the following test.

1.Remove the tailight bulb (Chapter Nine) and disconnect the taillight socket from the wiring harness.

a. Connect an ohmmeter between the bulb terminals. Continuity should be present. Replace the bulb if no continuity is noted.

b. Connect an ohmmeter between one taillight socket terminal and its mating connector. Repeat for the remaining wire/terminal. Continuity should be noted at each test connection. Repair or replace the taillight socket if no continuity is present.

2. Install the taillight bulb into its socket and reconnect the socket into the main wiring harness. The taillight bulb and socket must be connected to the main wiring harness for this test, but do not install the bulb assembly into the taillight housing.

3. Connect a voltmeter positive lead to the blue tailight connector and the negative voltmeter to the black taillight wire (**Figure 16**). Place the main switch to the ON position and the dimmer switch to either HI or LO.

a.If the voltmeter indicates battery voltage, the tailight circuit is operating correctly.

b. If the voltmeter indicates less than battery voltage, inspect the wiring harness between the main switch and taillight for poor connections or damaged wiring.

INDICATOR LIGHT SYSTEM

The indicator light system consists of the NEUTRAL, REVERSE and OIL TEMP indicator lights, switches and relays. The indicator lights are located within the meter assembly mounted on the handlebar. If one or more indicator lights do not work, perform the following test procedure.

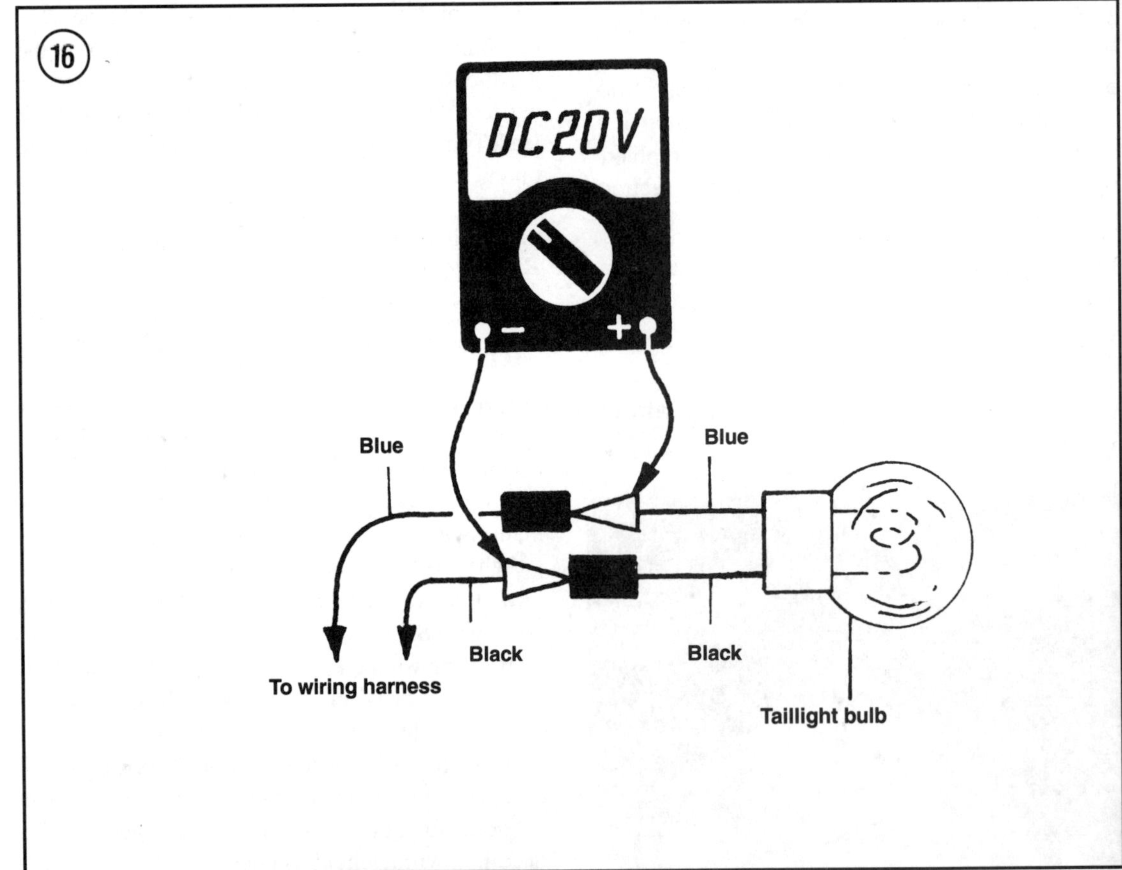

Indicator Lights Testing (Indicator Lights Inoperative)

1. Make sure the indicator bulb is good.
2. Test the appropriate switch as described under *Switches* in Chapter Nine.
3. If the bulb is good and the switch is operating properly, continue with the following steps.
4. *NEUTRAL indicator light*- Perform the following:
   a. Connect a DC voltmeter positive (+) test lead to the brown electrical terminal of the neutral indicator light and the negative (–) test lead to ground.
   b. Turn the ignition switch ON. There should be battery voltage present. If there is no voltage, check the wiring harness from the ignition switch to the neutral indicator bulb socket and repair if necessary.
5. *REVERSE indicator light*: perform the following:
   a. Connect a DC voltmeter positive (+) test lead to the brown electrical terminal of the reverse indicator light and the negative (–) test lead to ground.
   b. Turn the ignition switch ON. There should be battery voltage present. If there is no voltage, check the wiring harness from the ignition switch to the reverse indicator bulb socket and repair if necessary.
6. *OIL TEMP indicator light*: perform the following:
   a. Connect a DC voltmeter positive (+) test lead to the brown electrical terminal of the oil temp indicator light and the negative (–) test lead to ground.
   b. Turn the ignition switch ON. There should be battery voltage present. If there is no voltage, check the wiring harness from the ignition switch to the oil temp indicator bulb socket and repair if necessary.

COOLING SYSTEM TESTING

If the electric cooling fan (**Figure 17**) does not operate, perform the following tests.

1. Check the 30 amp main fuse. Open the fuse holder and pull the fuse out and visually inspect it. If the fuse is blown, replace it as described under *Fuse* in Chapter Nine. If the main fuse is good, reinstall it, then continue with Step 2.
2. Test the battery as described under *Battery* in Chapter Three. Note the following:
   a. If the battery is fully charged, perform Step 3.
   b. If necessary clean and recharge the battery. If the battery is damaged, replace it.
3. Disconnect the electrical connector from the main (key) switch. Test the main switch red and brown wires for continuity as described under *Switches* in Chapter Nine. If the ignition switch is good, continue with Step 4.
4. Test the circuit breaker as described under *Circuit Breaker* in Chapter Nine. Replace the circuit breaker if damaged and retest. If the circuit breaker is good, continue with Step 5.
5. Test the fan motor as described under *Electric Fan Testing* in Chapter Nine. Replace the fan motor if damaged and retest. If the fan motor is good, continue with Step 6.
6. Test the fan motor relay as described under *Relays* in Chapter Nine. Replace the fan motor relay if damaged and retest. If the fan motor relay is good, continue with Step 7.
7. Test the fan motor control unit as described under *Fan Motor Control Unit* in Chapter Nine. Replace the fan motor control unit if damaged and retest. If the fan motor control unit is good, continue with Step 8.
8. Steps 1-7 individually tests all of the cooling system components. If you have not been able to find a problem with one or more of these components, the thermo unit (**Figure 18**) is damaged and must be replaced as described under *Thermo Unit* in Chapter Nine.

FUEL SYSTEM

Many riders automatically assume that the carburetor is at fault if the engine does not run properly.

While fuel system problems are not uncommon, carburetor adjustment is seldom the answer. In many cases, adjusting the carburetor only compounds the problem by making the engine run worse.

When troubleshooting the fuel system, start at the fuel tank and work through the system, reserving the carburetor as the final point. Most fuel system problems result from an empty fuel tank, a plugged fuel filter or fuel valve or sour fuel. Fuel system troubleshooting is covered thoroughly under *Engine Is Difficult To Start, Poor Idle Speed Performance and Poor Medium and High Speed Performance* in this chapter.

The carburetor choke can also present problems. A choke stuck in the OFF position will cause a hard starting problem; one that sticks in the ON position will result in a flooding condition. Check choke operation by moving the choke knob (**Figure 1**) in and out by hand. The choke should move freely without binding or sticking in one position. If necessary, remove the choke as described under *Carburetor Disassembly* in Chapter Eight and inspect its plunger and spring for excessive wear or damage.

ENGINE OVERHEATING

Engine overheating is a serious problem in that it can quickly cause engine seizure and damage. The following section groups 5 main systems with probable causes that can lead to engine overheating.

1. *Ignition system*:
   a. Incorrect spark plug gap.
   b. Incorrect spark plug heat range. See Chapter Three.
   c. Faulty CDI unit/incorrect ignition timing.
2. *Engine compression system*:
   a. Cylinder head gasket leakage.
   b. Heavy carbon buildup in combustion chamber.
3. *Fuel system*:
   a. Carburetor fuel level too low.
   b. Incorrect carburetor adjustment or jetting.
   c. Loose carburetor boot clamps.
   d. Leaking or damaged carburetor-to-air filter housing air boot.
   e. Incorrect air fuel mixture.
4. *Engine load*:
   a. Dragging brake(s).
   b. Damaged drive train components.
   c. Slipping clutch.
   d. Engine oil level too high.
5. *Electric cooling system*: Test the electric cooling system (fan) as described in this chapter.

ENGINE

Preignition

Preignition is the premature burning of fuel and is caused by hot spots in the combustion chamber. The fuel ignites before it is supposed to. Glowing deposits in the combustion chamber, inadequate cooling or an overheated spark plug can all cause preignition. This is first noticed as a power loss but will eventually result in damage to the internal parts of the engine because of higher combustion chamber temperature.

Detonation

Commonly called spark knock or fuel knock, detonation is the violent explosion of fuel in the combustion chamber instead of the controlled burn that occurs during normal combustion. Severe damage can result. Use of low octane gasoline is a common cause of detonation.

Even when using a high octane gasoline, detonation can still occur. Other causes are over-advanced ignition timing, lean fuel mixture at or near full throttle, inadequate engine cooling, or the excessive accumulation of carbon deposits in the combustion chamber (cylinder head and piston crown).

Power Loss

Several factors can cause a lack of power and speed. Look for a clogged air filter or a fouled or damaged spark plug. A piston or cylinder that is galled, incorrect piston clearance or worn or sticky piston rings may be responsible. Look for loose bolts, defective gaskets or leaking machined mating surfaces on the cylinder head, cylinder or crankcase.

Piston Seizure

This is caused by incorrect bore clearance, piston rings with an improper end gap, compression leak, incorrect air fuel mixture, spark plug of the wrong heat range or incorrect ignition timing. Overheating from any cause may result in piston seizure.

Piston Slap

Piston slap is an audible slapping or rattling noise resulting from excessive piston-to-cylinder clearance. If allowed to continue, piston slap will eventually cause the piston skirt to crack and shatter.

To prevent piston slap, clean the air filter element on a regular schedule. If you hear piston slap, disassemble the engine top end and measure the cylinder bore and piston diameter and check for excessive clearance. Replace parts that exceed wear limits or show damage.

ENGINE NOISES

1. *Knocking or pinging during acceleration*—Can be caused by using a lower octane fuel than recommended or a poor grade of fuel. Incorrect carburetor jetting or a spark plug that is too hot can also cause pinging. Refer to *Correct Spark Plug Heat Range* in Chapter Three. Check also for excessive carbon buildup in the combustion chamber or a faulty CDI unit.

2. *Slapping or rattling noises at low speed or during acceleration*—Can be caused by excessive piston-cylinder wall clearance. Check also for a bent connecting rod or worn piston pin and/or piston pin holes in the piston.

3. *Knocking or rapping while decelerating*—Usually caused by excessive rod bearing clearance.

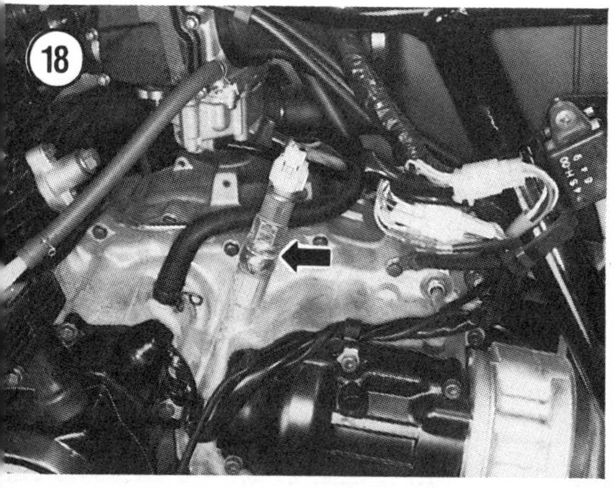

4. *Persistent knocking and vibration or other noise*—Usually caused by worn main bearings. If the main bearings are good, consider the following:
   a. Loose engine mounts.
   b. Cracked frame.
   c. Leaking cylinder head gasket.
   d. Exhaust pipe leakage at cylinder head.
   e. Stuck piston ring(s).
   f. Broken piston ring.
   g. Partial engine seizure.
   h. Excessive connecting rod small end bearing clearance.
   i. Excessive connecting rod big end side clearance.
   j. Excessive crankshaft runout.
   k. Worn or damaged primary drive gear.

5. *Rapid on-off squeal*—Compression leak around cylinder head gasket or spark plug.

ENGINE LEAKDOWN TEST

An engine leakdown test can determine if an engine problem is caused by leaking valves, blown head gasket or broken, worn or stuck piston rings. A cylinder leakage test is performed by applying compressed air to the cylinder and then measuring the percent of leakage. A cylinder leakage tester and an air compressor are required to perform this test (**Figure 19**). Follow the tester manufacturer's directions along with the following information when performing a cylinder leakdown test.

1. Start and run the engine until it reaches normal operating temperature. Then turn the engine off.
2. Remove the air filter assembly as described in Chapter Three. Open and secure the throttle in the wide-open position.
3. Set the piston to TDC on its compression stroke. See *Valve Clearance Check and Adjustment* in Chapter Three.
4. Remove the spark plug.

NOTE
The engine may turn when air pressure is applied to the cylinder. To prevent this from happening, shift the transmission into fifth gear and set the parking brake.

5. Install the leakdown tester into the spark plug hole (**Figure 20**).

6. Make a cylinder leakdown test following the tester manufacturer's instructions. Listen for air leaking while noting the following:

a. Air leaking through the exhaust pipe indicates a leaking exhaust valve.
b. Air leaking through the carburetor indicates a leaking intake valve.
c. Air leaking through the crankcase breather tube indicates worn piston rings.

7. Any cylinder with 10% or more cylinder leakage requires further service.

8. Remove the tester and reinstall the spark plug.

CLUTCH

The most common clutch problems are:

a. Clutch slipping.
b. Clutch dragging.

All clutch service, except adjustment, requires partial engine disassembly to identify and repair the problem. Refer to Chapter Six.

The Kodiak uses 2 clutch assemblies: primary (A, **Figure 21**) and secondary (B, **Figure 21**).

Clutch Slipping

1. *Clutch wear or damage:*
   a. Incorrect clutch lever free play.
   b. Worn clutch shoe (primary clutch).
   c. Loose, weak or damaged clutch spring (primary and secondary).
   b. Worn friction plates (secondary).
   c. Warped steel plates (secondary).
   d. Worn clutch hub and/or clutch housing (secondary).
   f. Incorrectly assembled clutch.
2. *Engine oil*:
   a. Low oil level.
   b. Oil additives.
   c. Low viscosity oil.

Clutch Dragging

1. Clutch wear or damage:
   a. Incorrect clutch adjustment.
   b. Warped steel plates.
   c. Swollen friction plates.
   d. Warped pressure plate.
   e. Incorrect clutch spring tension.
   f. Incorrectly assembled clutch.

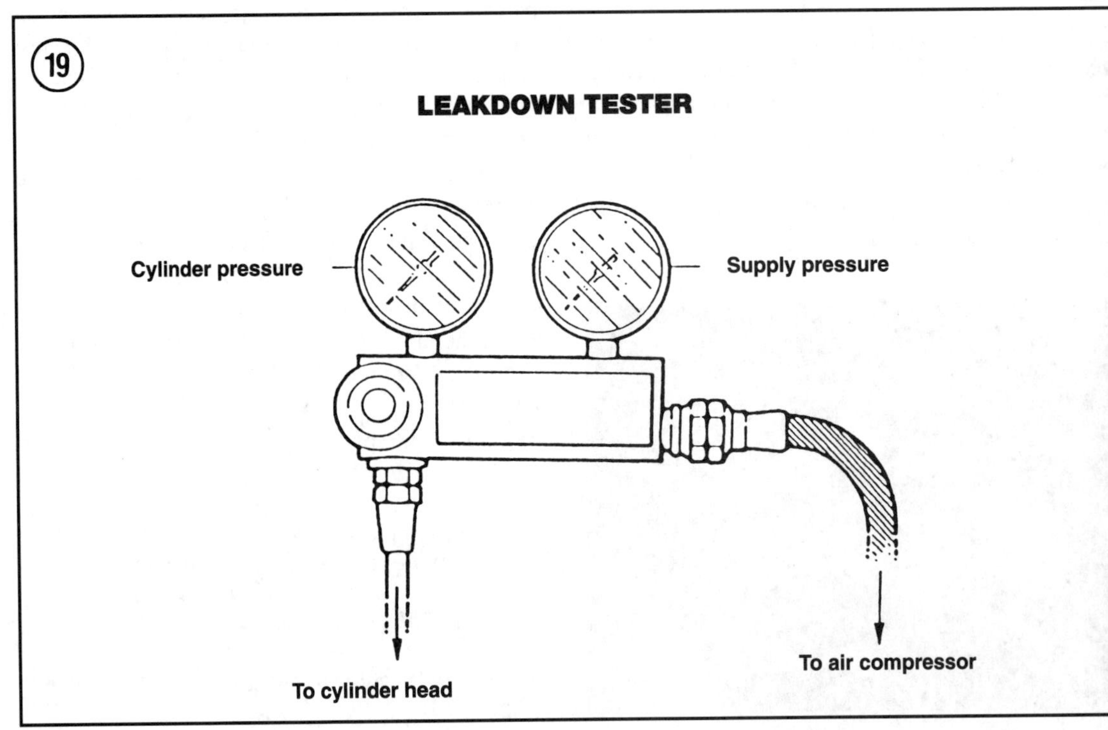

g. Loose clutch nut.
h. Burnt primary driven gear bushing.
i. Damaged clutch boss.
j. Incorrect clutch mechanism adjustment.

2. Engine oil:
   a. Oil level too high.
   b. High viscosity oil.

TRANSMISSION

The most common transmission problems are:

a. Difficult shifting.
b. Gears pop out of mesh.

Transmission symptoms can be hard to distinguish from clutch symptoms. Be sure that the clutch is not causing the trouble before working on the transmission.

Difficult Shifting

If the shift shaft does not move smoothly from one gear to the next, check the following.

1. Shift shaft:
   a. Incorrectly installed shift lever.
   b. Stripped shift lever-to-shift shaft splines.
   c. Bent shift shaft.
   d. Damaged shift shaft return spring.
   e. Damaged shift shaft where it engages the shift drum.
   f. Loose shift return spring pin.
   g. Shift drum positioning lever binding on pivot bolt.
2. Stopper arm:
   a. Seized or damaged stopper arm roller.
   b. Broken stopper arm spring.
   c. Loose stopper arm mounting bolt.
3. Shift drum and shift forks:
   a. Bent shift fork(s).
   b. Damaged shift fork guide pin(s).
   c. Seized shift fork (on shaft).
   d. Broken shift fork or shift fork shaft.
   e. Damaged shift drum groove(s).
   f. Damaged shift drum bearing.

Gears Pop Out Of Mesh

If the transmission shifts into gear but then slips or pops out, check the following:

1. Shift shaft:
   a. Incorrect shift lever position.
   b. Stopper arm fails to move or set properly.
2. Shift drum:
   a. Incorrect thrust play.
   b. Worn or damaged shift drum groove(s).
3. Bent shift fork(s).
4. Transmission:
   a. Worn or damaged gear dogs.
   b. Excessive gear thrust play.
   c. Worn or damaged shaft circlips or thrust washers.

Transmission Overshifts

If the transmission overshifts when shifting up or down, check for a weak or broken shift lever return spring or a weak or broken stopper arm and spring assembly.

2

Inoperative Reverse Gear

If the transmission fails to go into or operate in reverse properly, check the following:

1. Reverse lever:
   a. Incorrect reverse lever adjustment.
   b. Stripped reverse lever-to-reverse shift drum splines.
2. Reverse axle:
   a. Damaged reverse axle pinion gear thrust play.
   b. Excessive reverse axle pinion gear play.
3. Counter axle:
   a. Damaged counter axle gear bearings or shaft.
4. Reverse shift drum and fork:
   a. Damaged reverse shift drum groove.
   b. Bent reverse shift fork.

DRIVE TRAIN TROUBLESHOOTING

Noise is usually the first thing to draw attention to drive train problems. It is not always easy to diagnose the trouble by determining the source of the noise and the operating conditions that produce it.

Some clues as to the cause of the trouble may be gained by noting whether the noise is a hum, growl or knock; whether it is produced when the vehicle is accelerating under load or coasting; and whether it is heard when the vehicle is going straight or making a turn.

Drive train service procedures are covered in Chapter Eleven (front) and Chapter Twelve (rear).

NOTE

Improperly diagnosed noises can lead to rapid and severe drive train wear and damage. If you are not familiar with the operation and repair of the front and rear final drive assembly, refer troubleshooting to a qualified Yamaha mechanic.

Noise During Acceleration

This can result from insufficient lubricant, incorrect tooth contact between the drive gear and drive pinion, damaged bearings or damaged gears. A rolling rumble that increases with wheel speed and not from engine or transmission speed indicates a damaged wheel bearing. When troubleshooting this problem, drive the vehicle on a flat and smooth road surface.

Noise During Coasting

This can be caused by incorrect backlash between the drive gear and drive pinion gear.

Noise During a Turn

This is generally caused by loose or worn wheel or axle bearings, pinion gears that are too tight on their shafts, or a damaged drive shaft.

Driveline "Clunk" When Shifting From Forward Into Reverse, or Reverse Into Forward

This noise is usually caused by an idle speed that is too high or insufficient lubrication. Other possible causes include loose or damaged engine mounting bolts, excessive backlash in the transmission or worn drive shaft components.

Other Noises

A steady or intermittent whining noise that varies with engine speed may be caused by a worn, cracked or damaged gear. If the noise started after the front differential or final drive unit was rebuilt, suspect too-little gear lash. This condition prevents normal tooth contact between the gears. If ignored, rapid tooth wear will occur and the noise will become more like a growl. This condition should be corrected as soon as the noise is heard to prevent damage to the gears.

Oil Inspection

Drain the gearcase oil (Chapter Three) into a clean container. Wipe a small amount of oil on a finger and rub the finger and thumb together. Check for the presence of metallic particles. Also check the drain bolt for metal particles. While a small amount of particles in the oil is normal, an abnormal amount of debris is an indication of bearing or gear damage.

HANDLING

Poor handling will reduce overall performance and may cause you to crash. If you are experiencing poor handling, check the following items:

1. If the handlebars are hard to turn, check for the following:
   a. Low tire pressure.
   b. Incorrect throttle cable routing.
   c. Incorrect kill switch routing.
   d. Bent steering shaft.
2. If there is excessive handlebar shake or vibration, check for the following:
   a. Loose or damaged handlebar clamps.
   b. Incorrect handlebar clamp installation.
   c. Bent or cracked handlebar.
   d. Worn wheel bearing(s).
   e. Dry rotted tire(s).
   f. Severely worn front tire(s).
   g. Damaged rim(s).
   h. Loose, missing or broken engine mount bolts and mounts.
   i. Cracked frame, especially at the steering head.
   j. Incorrect tire pressure for prevailing riding conditions.
   k. Incorrect shock absorber adjustment.
   l. Damaged shock absorber damper rod.
   m. Leaking shock absorber damper housing.
   n. Sagged shock spring(s).
   o. Loose or damaged shock mount bolts.
3. If the rear suspension is too soft, check for the following:
   a. Incorrect shock absorber adjustment.
   b. Damaged shock absorber damper rod.
   c. Leaking shock absorber damper housing.
   d. Sagged shock spring.
   e. Loose or damaged shock mount bolts.
4. If the rear suspension is too hard, check for the following:
   a. Incorrect shock absorber adjustment.
   b. Rear tire pressure too high.
   c. Incorrect shock absorber adjustment.
   d. Damaged shock absorber damper rod.
   e. Leaking shock absorber damper housing.
   f. Sagged shock spring.
   g. Loose or damaged shock mount bolts.
5. Frame—check the following:
   a. Damaged frame.
   b. Cracked or broken engine mount brackets.

FRAME NOISE

Noises traced to the frame or suspension are usually caused by loose, worn or damaged parts. Various noises that are related to the frame are listed below:

1. Disc brake noise—A screeching sound during braking is the most common disc brake noise. Some other disc brake associated noises can be caused by:
   a. Glazed brake pad surface.
   b. Severely worn brake linings or pads.
   c. Warped brake discs (models so equipped).
2. Front or rear shock absorber noise—Check for the following:
   a. Loose shock absorber mounting bolts.
   b. Cracked or broken shock spring(s).
   c. Damaged shock absorber(s).
3. Some other frame associated noises can be caused by:
   a. Cracked or broken frame.
   b. Broken swing arm or shock linkage.
   c. Loose engine mounting bolts.
   d. Damaged steering shaft bearings.
   e. Loose mounting bracket(s).

BRAKES

The drum brake units are critical to riding performance and safety. Inspect the brakes frequently and repair any problem immediately. When replacing or refilling the drum brake fluid, use only DOT 3 or DOT 4 brake fluid from a sealed container. See Chapter Thirteen for additional information on brake fluid selection and drum brake service.

Front Drum Brake Troubleshooting

If the front drum brakes are not working properly, check for one or more of the following conditions:

a. Incorrect front brake adjustment.
b. Air in brake line.
c. Brake fluid level too low.
d. Loose brake hose banjo bolts. Brake fluid is leaking out.
e. Loose or damaged brake hose or line.
f. Worn or damaged brake drum.
g. Worn or damaged brake linings.
h. Oil on brake drum or brake lining surfaces.
i. Worn or damaged wheel cylinder(s).
j. Weak or damaged brake return springs.

Rear Drum Brake Troubleshooting

If the rear drum brake is not working properly, check for one or more of the following conditions:

a. Incorrect rear brake adjustment.

b. Incorrect brake cam lever position.

c. Worn or damaged brake drum.

d. Worn or damaged brake linings.

e. Oil on brake drum or brake lining surfaces.

f. Worn or damaged wheel cylinder(s).

g. Weak or damaged brake return springs.

CHAPTER THREE

LUBRICATION, MAINTENANCE AND TUNE-UP

This chapter explains lubrication, maintenance and tune-up procedures required for the Kodiak models covered in this book.

Table 1 lists the factory recommended maintenance and lubrication schedule.

Table 2 lists tire inflation specifications.

Table 3 lists battery capacity.

Table 4 lists battery state of charge.

Table 5 lists recommended lubricants and fluids.

Table 6 lists recommended oil capacity.

Table 7 lists maintenance and tune-up torque specifications.

Table 8 lists tune-up specifications.

Tables 1-8 are at the end of this chapter.

PRE-RIDE CHECK LIST

Perform the following checks before the first ride of the day. All of these checks are described in this chapter. If a component requires service, refer to the appropriate section.

At the end of each riding day, clean the vehicle thoroughly and inspect it carefully. Then give it a good general lubrication and make any adjustments necessary.

1. Inspect all fuel lines and fittings for leakage.
2. Make sure the fuel tank is full of fresh gasoline.
3. Make sure the engine oil level is correct.
4. Check the throttle operation for proper operation. Open the throttle all the way and release it. The throttle should close quickly with no binding or roughness. Repeat this step with the handlebar facing straight ahead and at both full lock positions.
5. Check that the brake levers operate properly with no binding. Replace any broken lever. Check the lever housings for damage.
6. Inspect the front and rear suspension. Make sure they have a good solid feel with no looseness. Turn the handlebar from side to side to check steering play. Service the steering assembly if excessive play is noted. Make sure the handlebar cables do not bind.
7. Check the brake fluid level in the front master cylinder reservoir. Add DOT 3 or DOT 4 brake fluid if necessary.
8. Check the parking brake operation and adjust if necessary.
9. Check the front differential and the final drive unit oil level. Top off if necessary.
10. Check tire pressure as listed in **Table 2**.
11. Check the exhaust system for looseness or damage.
12. Check the tightness of all fasteners, especially engine, steering and suspension mounting hardware.
13. Make sure the headlight and taillight work.
14. Start the engine, then stop it with the engine stop switch. If the engine stop switch does not work

properly, test the switch as described under *Switches* in Chapter Nine.

MAINTENANCE SCHEDULE

Table 1 is a factory maintenance schedule. Strict adherence to this schedule will help ensure long service from your vehicle. Perform the services more often if operating the vehicle commercially and in dusty or other harsh conditions.

Most of the services shown in **Table 1** are described in this chapter. However, some procedures which require more than minor disassembly or adjustment are covered elsewhere in the appropriate chapter and are so indicated.

TIRES AND WHEELS

Tire Pressure

Check and adjust tire pressure to maintain the smoothness of the tire, ensure good traction and handling and to get the maximum life from the tire. A simple, accurate gauge (**Figure 1**) can be purchased for a few dollars and should be carried in your tool box. The appropriate tire pressures are listed in **Table 2**. Check tire pressure when the tires are cold.

NOTE
*The tire pressure specifications listed in **Table 2** are for the original equipment tires. If you have installed aftermarket tires, follow the tire pressure recommened specified by the tire manufacturer.*

WARNING
Always inflate both tire sets (front and rear) to the correct air pressure. If the vehicle is run with unequal air pressures, the vehicle will run toward one side, causing poor handling.

CAUTION
Do not overinflate the stock tires as they can be permanently distorted and damaged.

Tire Inspection

The tires take a lot of punishment due to the variety of terrain they are subjected to. Inspect them daily for excessive wear, cuts, abrasions or punctures. If you find a nail or other object in the tire, mark its location with a light crayon before removing it. Service the tire as described in Chapter Ten.

To gauge tire wear, inspect the height of the tread knobs. If the average tread knob height measures 3 mm (0.12 in.) or less (**Figure 2**), replace the tire as described in Chapter Ten.

WARNING
Do not ride your vehicle with damaged or excessively worn tires. Tires in these conditions can cause you to lose control. Replace damaged or severely worn tires immediately.

Rim Inspection

Inspect the wheel rims (**Figure 3**) for damage. Rim damage may be sufficient to cause an air leak and could indicate that the wheel is out of alignment. Improper wheel alignment can cause rapid tire wear and result in an unsafe riding condition.

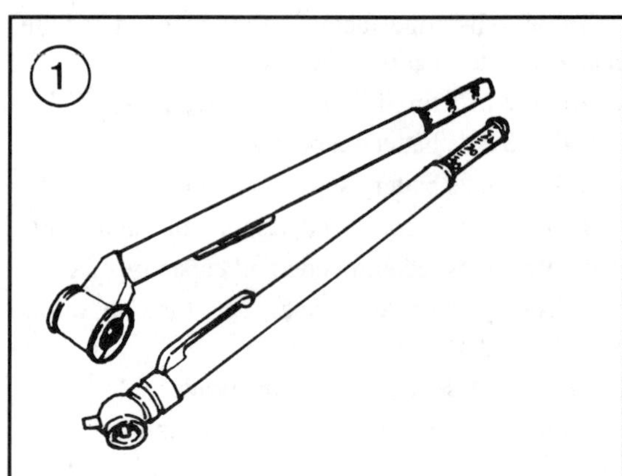

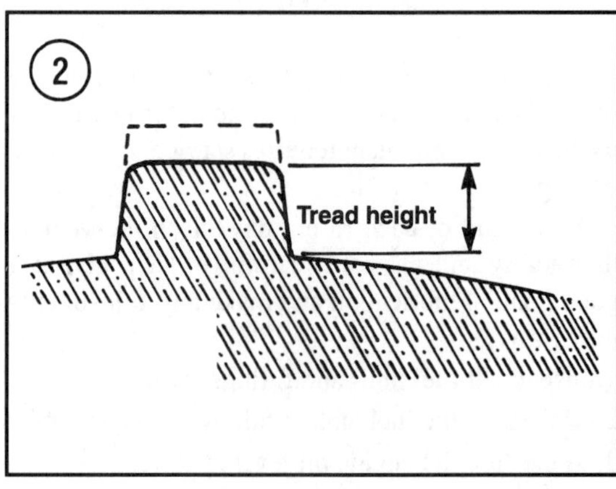

Make sure the lug nuts (**Figure 4**) are tightened securely on each wheel. Tighten the lug nuts as specified in **Table 7**.

BATTERY

The battery is an important component in the electrical system, yet most electrical system troubles can be traced to battery neglect. In addition to checking and correcting the battery electrolyte level (1993-1995) on a weekly basis, the battery should be cleaned and inspected at periodic intervals.

Battery Application

A standard battery (**Figure 5**) is used on all 1993-1995 models. This type of battery is equipped with removable filling caps that allow water to be added to the battery to maintain its electrolyte level within the upper and lower marks on the batter case.

A maintenance-free battery (**Figure 6**) is used on all 1996 and later models. This battery is sealed at the time of service and does not require additional water. Do not try to remove the sealing caps or the battery may be damaged.

NOTE

Because a maintenance-free battery requires a higher voltage charging system, do not replace a maintenance-free battery with a standard battery. Always make sure you replace the battery with its correct type and designated capacity. ***Refer to Table 3****.*

Safety Precautions

When working with a battery, use extreme care to avoid spilling or splashing the electrolyte. This solution contains sulfuric acid, which can ruin clothing and cause serious chemical skin burns. If any electrolyte is spilled or splashed on clothing or skin, immediately neutralize with a solution of baking soda and water, then flush with an abundance of clean water.

WARNING

Electrolyte splashed into the eyes is extremely harmful and painful. Always wear safety glasses when servicing the battery. If you get electrolyte in your eyes, call a physician immediately and force your eyes open and flood them with cool, clean water for approximately 15 minutes.

When electrolyte is spilled or splashed onto a finished surface, neutralize it with a baking soda and water solution. Then rinse the area with clean water.

While batteries are being charged, highly explosive hydrogen gas forms in each cell. Some of this gas escapes through filler cap openings and may form an explosive atmosphere in and around the battery. This condition can persist for several hours. Sparks, an open flame or a lighted cigarette can ignite the gas, causing an explosion and possible serious personal injury.

Note the following precautions to prevent an explosion:

1. Do not allow anyone to smoke or permit any open flame near any battery being charged or which has been recently charged.

2. Do not disconnect live circuits from battery terminals since a spark usually occurs when a live circuit is broken.

3. Take care when connecting or disconnecting any battery charger. Be sure the ignition switch is in the OFF position before making or breaking connections. Poor connections are a common cause of electrical arcs which cause explosions.

4. Keep children and pets away from charging equipment and batteries.

Battery Connections

On all models covered in this manual, the negative (–) side of the battery is grounded. When removing the battery, disconnect the negative (–) cable first, then the positive (+) cable. This minimizes the chance of a tool shorting to ground when disconnecting the battery positive cable.

WARNING

When performing the following procedures, protect your eyes, skin and clothing. If electrolyte gets into your eyes, flush your eyes thoroughly with clean water and get prompt medical attention.

Electrolyte Level Check (Standard Battery)

1. The electrolyte level should be maintained between the 2 marks on the battery case (**Figure 7**).

2. If the electrolyte level is low, remove the battery from the frame as described in this chapter. Do not add water while the battery is still in the frame as any spilled water along with electrolyte will flow onto the frame resulting in corrosion.

3. Make sure all cell caps are tightened securely.

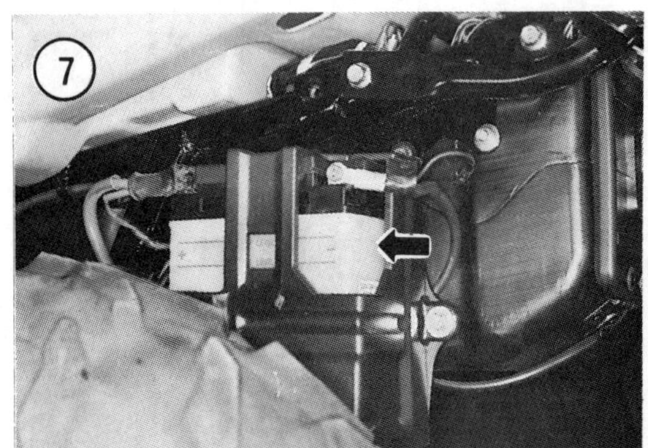

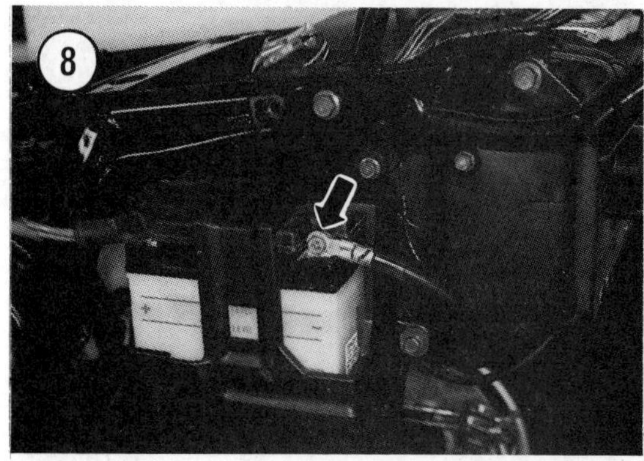

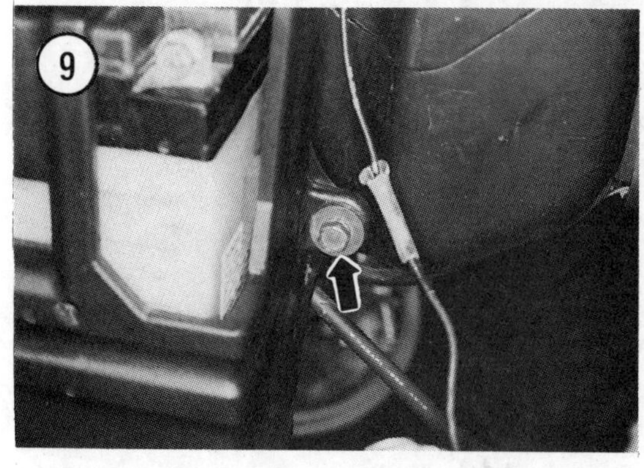

Battery Removal (Standard Battery)

NOTE
The battery can be removed with the rear fender in place by removing the rear wheel but the working room is very limited. Remove whatever component is your preference.

1A. Remove the rear carrier rack and fender (Chapter Fourteen).

1B. Remove the left rear wheel (Chapter Twelve).

2. Use a stiff whisk broom or brush and thoroughly clean any dirt and debris from the top of the battery before removing any parts or connectors.

3. Disconnect the negative (–) battery cable from the battery (**Figure 8**).

4. Unbolt the battery holder (**Figure 9**) and slide it toward the rear and off the battery box.

5. Disconnect the positive (+) battery cable from the battery (A, **Figure 10**).

6. Disconnect the battery vent hose (B, **Figure 10**) from the battery. Leave the vent hose routed through the frame.

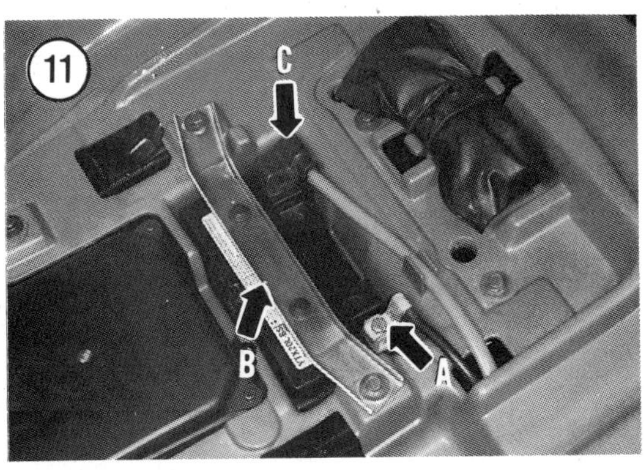

WARNING
When performing the following procedure, protect your eyes, skin and clothing. If electrolyte gets into your eyes, flush your eyes thoroughly with clean water and get prompt medical attention.

7. Remove the battery from the battery box.

8. Remove the cover from the top of the battery.

CAUTION
Be careful not to spill battery electrolyte on painted or polished surfaces. The chemical is highly corrosive and will damage the finish. If it is spilled, neutralize it with a baking soda and water solution, then thoroughly rinse with clean water.

Battery Removal (Maintenance-free Battery)

1. Remove the seat (Chapter Fourteen).

2. Disconnect the negative (–) battery cable from the battery (A, **Figure 11**).

3. Unbolt and remove the battery holder (B, **Figure 11**).

4. Disconnect the positive (+) battery cable from the battery (C, **Figure 11**).

5. Remove the battery from the battery box.

Battery Cleaning and Inspection

1. Inspect the battery pads in the battery box for contamination or damage. Clean with a solution of baking soda and water. Replace damaged pads.

2. Check the entire battery case for cracks or other damage. If the battery case is warped, discolored or has a raised top, the battery has been suffering from overcharging or overheating. See **Figure 5** (standard battery) or **Figure 6** (maintenance-free battery).

4. Check the battery terminal bolts, spacers and nuts for corrosion, deterioration or damage. Clean parts thoroughly with a solution of baking soda and water. Replace severely corroded or damaged parts.

NOTE
When cleaning a standard battery, keep the cleaning solution out of the battery cells or the electrolyte level will be seriously weakened.

5. Clean the top of the battery with a stiff bristle brush using the baking soda and water solution. Rinse the battery with water.
6. Check the battery cables for corrosion and damage. Repair minor damage with a stiff wire brush. Replace severely corroded or damaged cables.
7. On standard batteries, check the vent hose. Make sure it is not kinked, plugged or damaged.

Adding Water (Standard Battery)

1. Place the battery on a level surface.
2. Check the electrolyte level on the side of the battery. The level must be within the upper and lower marks on the battery case (**Figure 12**). If the level is low in one or more cells, continue with Step 3.

NOTE
Do not overfill the battery cells. The electrolyte expands due to heat from charging and will overflow if the level is above the upper level line.

3. Remove the fill caps (**Figure 13**) and add distilled water to bring the level within the upper and lower level lines on the battery case (**Figure 12**). Install the caps and tighten securely.

Battery Installation (Standard Battery)

1. Install the battery cover on top of the battery.
2. Install the battery with its terminals facing out. The positive (+) battery terminal (A, **Figure 10**) should face toward the front of the vehicle. Slide the battery forward in its box until it stops.
3. Reconnect the battery vent hose (B, **Figure 10**) to the battery fitting. Make sure it is correctly connected.

NOTE
For further information on vent hose routing, refer to the Battery Vent Hose Routing decal mounted on the rear fender under the seat.

WARNING
After installing the battery, make sure the vent hose is not pinched. A pinched or kinked hose would allow pressure to accumulate in the battery and cause the electrolyte to overflow. If the vent hose is damaged, replace it.

4. Install and tighten the positive (+) battery cable (A, **Figure 10**).
5. Slide the battery holder (**Figure 9**) toward the front and insert its tabs into the receptacles in the battery box. Push the battery holder all the way forward until it stops, then align the bolt hole.
6. Install the bolt (**Figure 9**) securing the battery holder and tighten securely.
7. Install and tighten the negative (–) battery cable (**Figure 8**).

CAUTION
Be sure the battery cables are connected to their proper terminals. Connecting the battery backward will reverse the polarity and damage the rectifier and ignition system.

8. Coat the battery connections with dielectric compound or petroleum jelly to retard corrosion. Also apply the compound to the holder mounting bolt.
9. Install the left rear wheel (Chapter Twelve).
10. Install the rear fender (Chapter Fourteen).

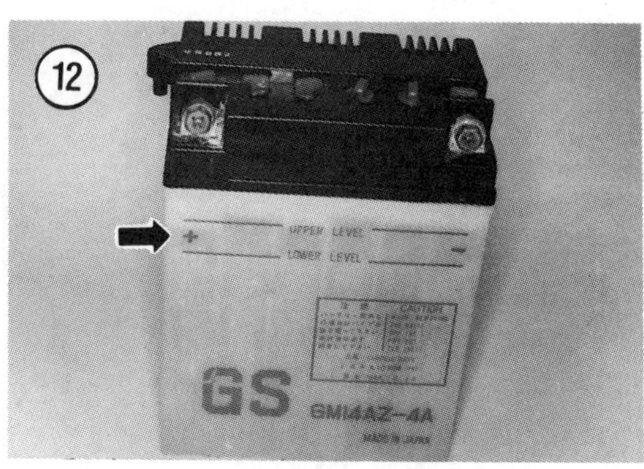

Battery Installation (Maintenance-free Battery)

1. Install the battery so that the battery terminals (A and C, **Figure 11**) face toward the front of the vehicle.

2. Connect the positive (+) battery cable to the battery (C, **Figure 11**).

3. Install and tighten the battery holder (B, **Figure 11**).

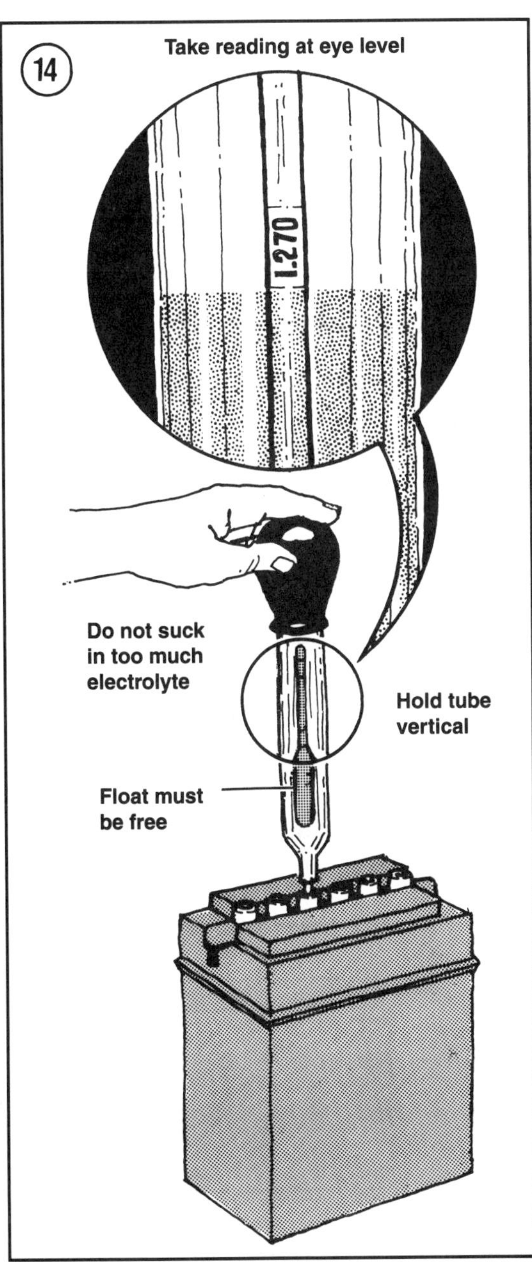

4. Connect the negative (–) battery cable to the battery (A, **Figure 11**).

5. Install the seat (Chapter Fourteen).

Hydrometer Battery Test (Standard Battery)

Hydrometer testing is the best way to check the battery's state of charge. Use a hydrometer with numbered graduations from 1.100 to 1.300 rather than one with just color-coded bands. To use the hydrometer, squeeze the rubber ball, insert the tip into the cell and release the ball (**Figure 14**).

NOTE

Do not attempt to test a battery with a hydrometer immediately after adding water to the cells. Charge the battery for 15-20 minutes at a rate high enough to cause vigorous gassing, then check the specific gravity.

Draw enough electrolyte to float the weighted float inside the hydrometer. If using a temperature-compensated hydrometer, release the electrolyte and repeat this process several times to make sure the thermometer has adjusted to the electrolyte temperature before taking the reading.

Hold the hydrometer vertically and note the number in line with the surface of the electrolyte (**Figure 14**). This is the specific gravity for this cell. Return the electrolyte to the cell from which it came. The specific gravity of a cell is the indicator of the cell's state of charge. A fully charged cell will read 1.260 or more at 80° F (26.7° C). A cell that is 75% charged will read from 1.220-1.230 while a cell with a 50% charge will read from 1.170-1.180. Any cell reading 1.120 or less should be considered discharged. See **Table 4**. All cells should be within 30 points specific gravity of each other. If over 30 points variation is noted, the battery's condition is questionable. Charge the battery and recheck the specific gravity. If 30 points or more variation remains between cells after charging, the battery has failed and must be replaced.

NOTE

If a temperature-compensated hydrometer is not used, add 0.004 to the specific gravity reading for every 10° above 80° F (25° C). For every 10° below 80° F (25° C), subtract 0.004.

Open-Circuit Battery Test (Maintenance-free Battery)

The open-circuit voltage test is used on maintenance-free batteries. To do the test, the battery must be disconnected from the wiring harness and allowed to set for at least 4 hours to allow the battery voltage to stabilize.

1. Remove the seat (Chapter Fourteen).
2. Disconnect the negative (–) battery cable from the battery (A, **Figure 11**).
3. Disconnect the positive (+) battery cable from the battery (C, **Figure 11**).
4. Wait 4 hours.
5. Measure the battery voltage with a digital voltmeter (**Figure 15**). Connect the positive (+) lead to the battery positive terminal; connect the negative (–) lead to the battery negative terminal. Note the voltmeter reading:
   a. The correct reading is 12.6 volts or higher.
   b. If the voltmeter reads 12.4 volts or less, the battery needs charging.
6. Disconnect the voltmeter leads.
7. Connect the positive (+) battery cable to the battery (C, **Figure 11**).
8. Connect the negative (–) battery cable to the battery (A, **Figure 11**).
9. Install the seat (Chapter Fourteen).

Charging

A good state of charge should be maintained in batteries used for starting. When charging the battery, note the following:

a. When charging a standard battery, the cells will show signs of gas bubbling. If one cell has no gas bubbles, or if its specific gravity is low, the cell is probably defective.
b. If a battery not in use loses its charge within a week after charging or if the specific gravity drops quickly, the battery is defective. A good battery should only self-discharge approximately 1% each day.

CAUTION
Always remove the battery from the vehicle before connecting the charging equipment.

WARNING
During charging, highly explosive hydrogen gas is released from the battery. Charge the battery in a well-ventilated area only, away from open flames (including pilot lights on some gas home appliances). Do not allow smoking in the area. Never check the charge of the battery by arcing across the terminals; the resulting spark can ignite the hydrogen gas resulting in a violent explosion.

1. Remove the battery from the vehicle as described in this chapter.
2. Connect the positive (+) charger lead to the positive (+) battery terminal and the negative (–) charger lead to the negative (–) battery terminal.
3. On standard batteries, remove all fill/vent caps (**Figure 13**) from the battery, set the charger at 12 volts and switch it ON. Normally, a battery should be charged at a slow charge rate of 1/10 its given capacity.

CAUTION
*Maintain the electrolyte level at the upper level (**Figure 12**) during the charging cycle.*

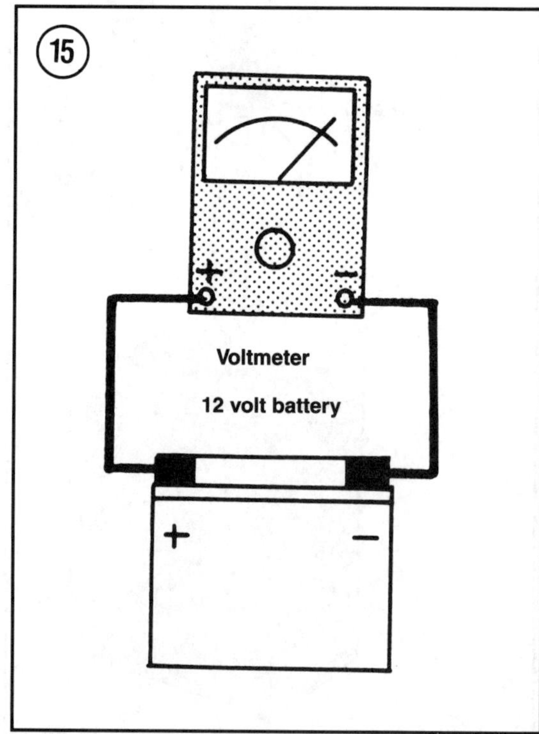

4. The charging time depends on the discharged condition of the battery.

5A. Standard battery: After the battery has charged for the predetermined time, turn the charger off, disconnect the leads and check the specific gravity as described under *Hydrometer Battery Test (Standard Battery)* in this chapter. It should be within the limits specified in **Table 4**. If it is, and remains stable for one hour, the battery is charged.

5B. Maintenance-free battery: After disconnecting the battery charger leads, wait 30 minutes for the battery voltage to stabilize, then check the battery voltage as described under *Open-Circuit Battery Test (Maintenance-free Battery)* in this chapter.

New Battery Installation

A new battery must be fully charged before installation in a vehicle. When electrolyte is added to a new battery, its charge or capacity at that time is approximately 80%. To bring the battery to full charge, it must receive an initial or booster charge. Using a new battery without an initial charge will cause permanent battery damage. That is, the battery will never be able to hold more than an 80% charge. Charging a new battery after it has been used will not bring its charge to 100%. When purchasing a new battery verify its charge status. If necessary, charge the battery prior to installation.

NOTE
Recycle your old battery. When you replace the battery, be sure to turn in the old battery at that time. The lead plates and the plastic case can be recycled. Most motorcycle dealers will accept your old battery in trade when you purchase a new one. Never place an old battery in your household trash since it is illegal, in most states, to place any acid or lead (heavy metal) contents in landfills. There is also the danger of the battery being crushed in the trash truck and spraying acid on the truck or landfill operator.

LUBRICANTS

Engine Oil

Oil is graded according to its viscosity, which is an indication of how thick it is. The Society of Automotive Engineers (SAE) distinguishes oil viscosity by numbers, called weights. Thick (heavy) oils have higher viscosity numbers than thin (light) oils. For example, a 5 weight (SAE 5) oil is a light oil while a 90 weight (SAE 90) oil is relatively heavy. The viscosity of the oil has nothing to do with its lubricating properties.

Grease

Unless otherwise specified, waterproof grease should be used when grease is needed. Water does not wash grease off parts as easily as it washes off oil. In addition, grease maintains its lubricating qualities better than oil over a longer period of time.

CLEANING SOLVENT

A number of solvents can be used to remove old dirt, grease and oil. See your Yamaha dealership or a motorcycle or auto parts store.

WARNING
Never use gasoline as a cleaning solvent. Gasoline is extremely volatile and contains tremendously destructive potential energy. The slightest spark could cause a fatal explosion if it occurs near gasoline vapor.

PERIODIC LUBRICATION

Engine Oil/Transfer Gearcase Oil

The transfer gearcase (A, **Figure 16**) is mounted at the rear of the engine. The components operating inside the gearcase are lubricated by engine oil. Beacuse the engine and transfer gearcase are equipped with separate oil fill and drain plugs, you can change the engine and transfer gearcase oil separately or at the same time. Although the engine oil level is checked using the dipstick (**Figure 17**), the oil level in the gearcase cannot be checked. It is therefore recommended to change the engine and transfer gearcase oil at the same time. Lubricant capacities are provided in **Table 6**.

Engine oil level check

The engine oil also lubricates the transfer gearcase components.

1. Park the vehicle on level ground and set the parking brake.
2. On the right side of the engine, unscrew the dipstick (**Figure 17**) and wipe it off with a clean lint-free cloth.
3. Insert the dipstick into the clutch cover opening and rest it on the cover—do not screw the dipstick into the threads in the cover. It must be sitting on the clutch cover.
4. Remove the dipstick. The oil level must be within the minimum and maximum dipstick marks (**Figure 18**).
5. If the oil level is low, add the recommended grade and vicosity oil listed in **Table 5** to correct the level.
6. Inspect the O-ring seal on the dipstick and replace if it is starting to deteriorate or harden.
7. Install the dipstick and tighten securely.
8. If the oil level is too high, draw out thc cxccss oil with a syringe or suitable pump.
9. Recheck the oil level and adjust if necessary.

Engine Oil and Filter Change

Regular oil changes will contribute more to engine longevity than any other maintenance performed. The factory recommended oil and filter change intervals are listed in **Table 1**. This assumes that the vehicle is operated in moderate climates. If it is operated under dusty conditions, the oil will get dirty more quickly and must be changed more frequently than recommended.

Use only a high quality detergent motor oil with an API classification of SE. The classification is stamped or printed on top of the can or label on plastic bottles (**Figure 19**). Try to use the same brand of oil at each oil change. Refer to **Figure 20** for the correct oil weight to use under anticipated ambient temperatures (not engine oil temperature).

To change the engine oil and filter you need the following:

a. Drain pan.
b. Funnel.
c. Wrench and sockets.
d. New oil (see **Table 6**).

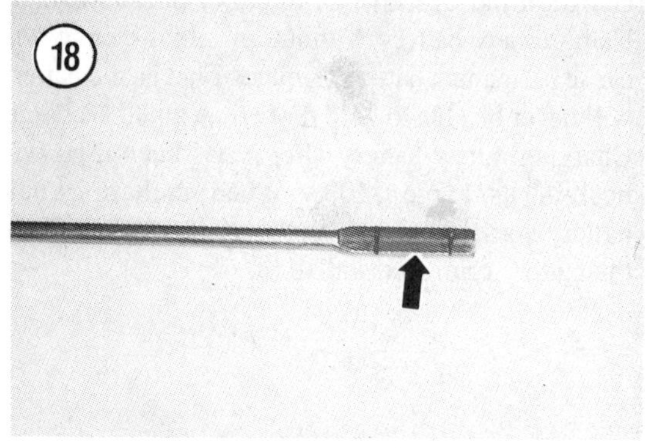

e. New oil filter.

NOTE
Never dispose of motor oil in the trash, on the ground, or down a storm drain. Many service stations accept used motor oil and waste haulers provide curbside used motor oil collection. Do not combine other fluids with motor oil to be recycled. To locate a recycler, contact the American Petroleum Institute (API) at ***www.recycleoil.org****.*

1. Ride the vehicle until normal operating temperature is reached, then park the vehicle on a level surface and set the parking brake. Turn the engine off.

NOTE
Warming the engine allows the oil to heat up and flow freely. Warm oil also carries more contamination and sludge out with it.

2. Place a drain pan under the engine drain plug (**Figure 21**).

NOTE
In ***Figure 21*** *the drain plug is not visible but is accessible through the large recess and access hole in the engine guard.*

3. Loosen the drain plug (**Figure 21**) mounted in the bottom of the engine. Then remove the drain plug, spring, oil strainer and O-ring (**Figure 22**).

4. Loosen the dipstick (**Figure 17**) to help speed up the flow of oil.

5. Place another drain pan under the transfer gearcase drain plug (**Figure 23**) and remove it and its washer. Allow the oil to drain out.

6. Replace the oil filter as described under *Oil Filter Replacement* in this section.

7. Check the drain plug O-ring (**Figure 22**) and replace if leaking or damaged.

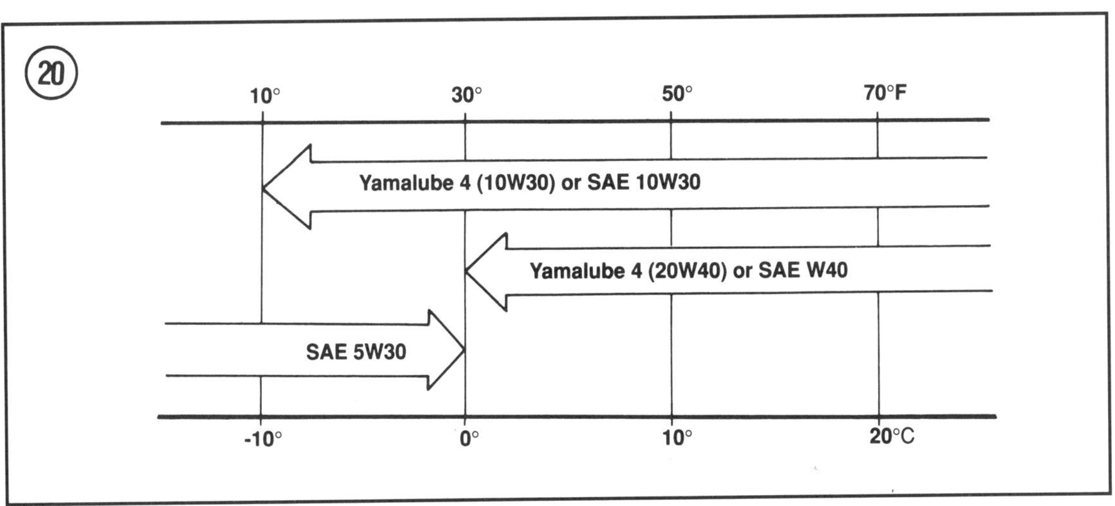

8. Clean and inspect the oil strainer (**Figure 22**). Replace if damaged.

9. Assemble the oil strainer, spring and engine drain bolt as shown in **Figure 22**. Then install the drain plug into the engine (**Figure 21**) and tighten as specified in **Table 7**.

10. Install the transfer gearcase drain plug and washer (**Figure 23**) and tighten as specified in **Table 7**.

11. Insert a funnel into the engine oil fill hole and fill the engine with the correct weight (**Figure 20**) and quantity of oil. Refer to **Table 6** for refill capacities.

12. Remove the funnel and screw in the dipstick securely.

13. Fill the transfer gearcase through the oil fill hole with the correct amount of engine oil specified in **Table 6**. Then install the transfer gearcase oil fill plug (B, **Figure 16**) and tighten as specified in **Table 7**.

14. Start the engine and allow to run at idle speed.

NOTE
*If you are just starting a rebuilt engine, check the engine oil pressure as described under **Engine Oil Pressure Check** in this chapter.*

15. Check the oil filter covers and both drain plugs for leaks.

16. Turn off the engine and allow the oil to settle. Then check the engine oil level as described in this chapter. Adjust the oil level if necessary.

WARNING
Prolonged contact with oil may cause skin cancer. It is advisable to wash your hands thoroughly with soap and water as soon as possible after handling or coming in contact with motor oil.

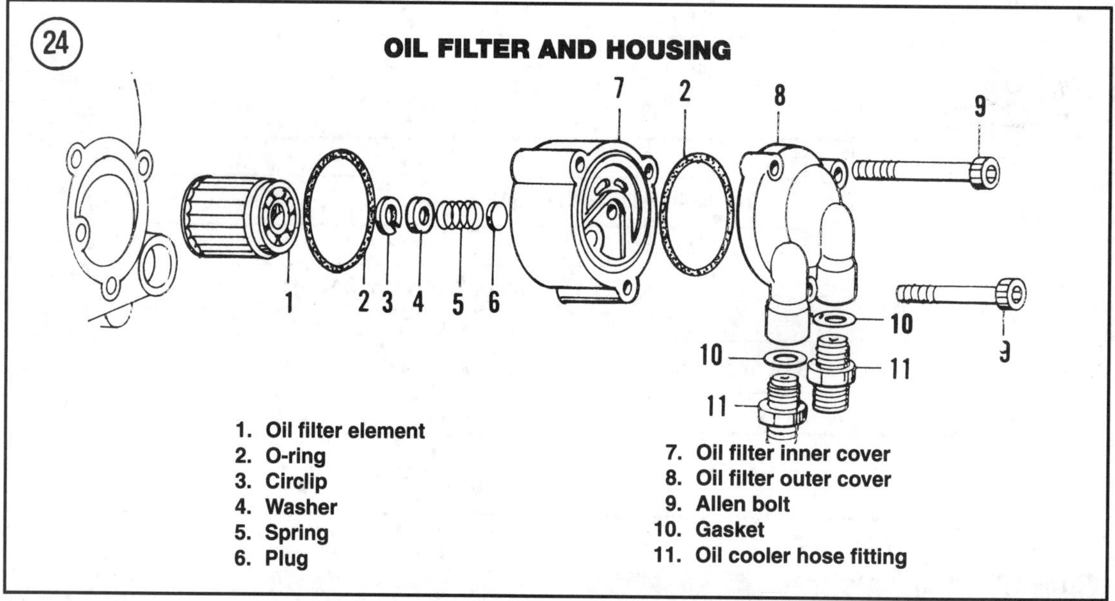

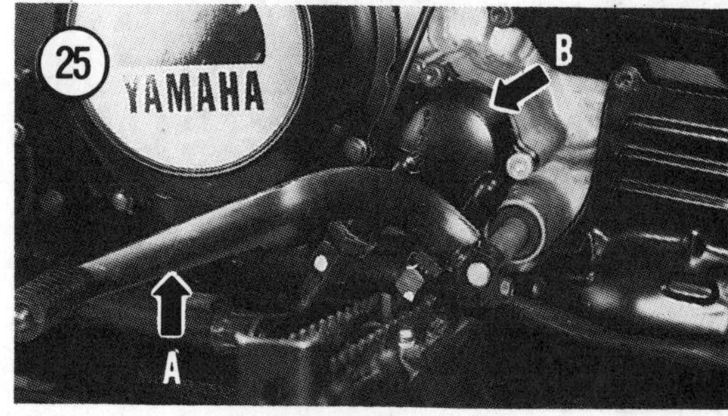

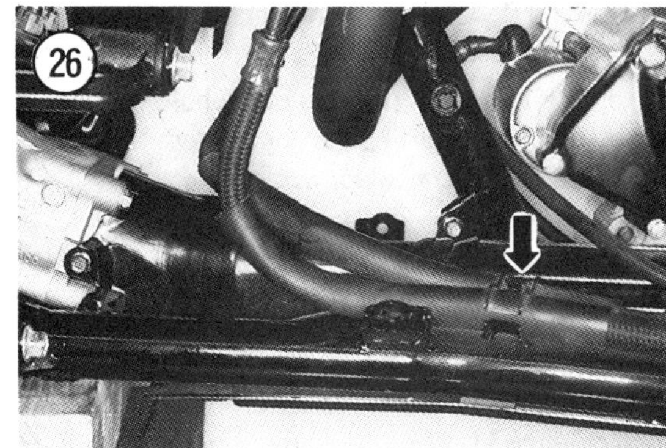

Oil Filter Replacement

Refer to **Figure 24** for this procedure.

1. Drain the engine oil as described in this section.
2. Unbolt and remove the shift lever (A, **Figure 25**).
3. Remove the bolt and clamp (**Figure 26**) securing the oil cooler hoses to the frame adjacent to the oil filter assembly.

NOTE
Do not disconnect the oil cooler hoses from the oil filter outer cover.

4. Remove the 3 Allen bolts securing the oil filter outer (B, **Figure 25**) and inner covers to the crankcase. Note that the upper bolt is different from the 2 lower bolts.
5. Remove the oil filter outer (8, **Figure 24**) and inner (7, **Figure 24**) covers and the 2 O-rings.
6. Remove the oil filter (A, **Figure 27**) from the filter cavity and discard it.
7. Inspect the O-ring in each side the of inner cover (**Figure 28** and **Figure 29**). Replace both O-rings if either is leaking or damaged.
8. Clean and dry the inner and outer covers.
9. The circlip shown in **Figure 30** secures the washer, spring and plug into the inner cover. If necessary, remove the circlip and the spring assembly and clean these parts thoroughly. Then reinstall and secure with a new circlip.
10. Thoroughly clean the crankcase cavity and O-ring mating surface (B, **Figure 27**).
11. Lubricate the 2 inner cover O-rings with a lithium soap base grease and install them in the inner cover grooves. Both O-rings are identical (same part number).
12. Install the oil filter so its sealing surface (**Figure 31**) goes into the crankcase first. The open or flow

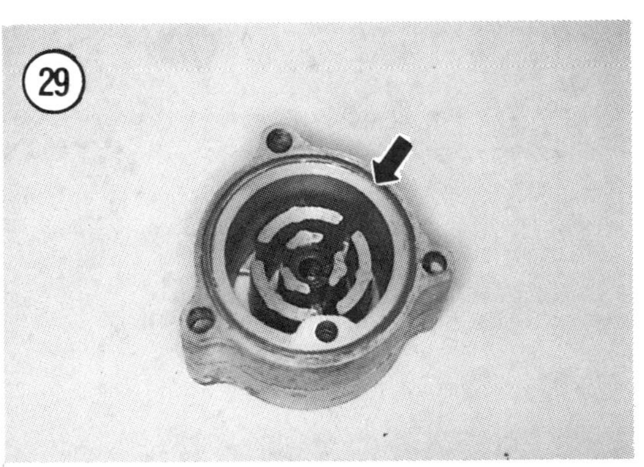

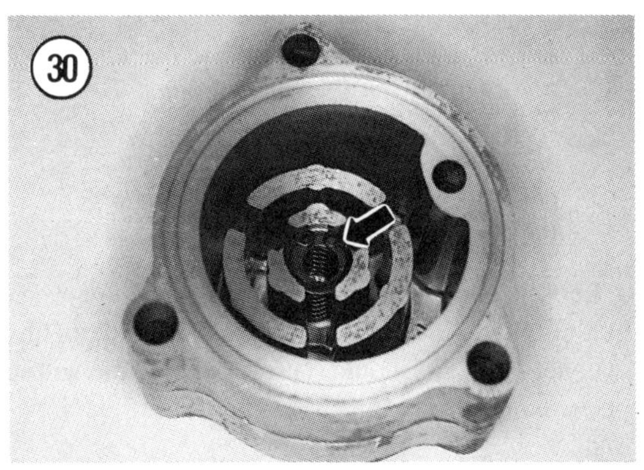

side of the filter must face out as shown in A, **Figure 27**.

13. Align the oil flow paths (**Figure 32**) of the inner and outer covers and install both covers over the oil filter.

14. Apply Gasgacinch gasket sealer (or equivalent) onto the threads of the 3 oil filter cover mounting bolts. Then install the bolts (9, **Figure 24**) and tighten as specified in **Table 7**. The upper Allen bolt is different from the lower 2 Allen bolts.

NOTE
Apply a light coat of gasket sealant (not a threadlocking compound) to the bolt threads prior to installation to help prevent an oil leak.

15. Install and tighten the oil filter cover mounting bolts as specified in **Table 7**.

16. Reposition the oil cooler hoses, then secure the hoses in place with the clamp (**Figure 26**) and mounting bolt.

17. Align the shift lever slot with the mark on the end of the shift shaft and install the shift lever (A, **Figure 25**). Install the pinch bolt and tighten securely.

Engine Oil Pressure Test

This test allows you to check engine oil flow. Always check the engine oil pressure after reassembling the engine, when troubleshooting the lubrication system or after installing one of the external oil pipes.

1. Park the vehicle on level ground and set the parking brake.
2. Check the engine oil level as described in this chapter.
3. Start the engine and allow to idle.

CAUTION
Oil passages deliver engine oil from the oil pump to engine components. Because the oil flowing through these passages is under pressure, do not increase engine speed above idle when checking the oil pressure.

4. Loosen, but do not remove, the oil pressure check bolt (**Figure 33**) mounted on the right side of the cylinder head. Oil should seep out of the hole within one minute after starting the engine. Note the following:

   a. If oil flows out of the bolt hole, the oil pressure is correct.
   b. If oil does not flow out of the hole within one minute of starting the engine, turn the engine off to prevent engine seizure.

5. Turn the engine off.
6. Tighten the oil pressure check bolt as specified in **Table 7**.
7. Wipe up the oil that seeped from the bolt hole.
8. If there was no oil visible at the oil pressure check bolt (**Figure 33**) when the engine was running, drain the engine oil and remove the oil filter as described in this chapter. Inspect the oil, oil filter and oil strainer and the filter for contamination, sludge and any other abnormal conditions. If the oil and filter are in good condition, remove and inspect the oil pipe, oil pump and oil cooler (Chapter Five).

WARNING
Prolonged contact with oil may cause skin cancer. It is advisable to wash your hands thoroughly with soap and water as soon as possible after handling or coming in contact with motor oil.

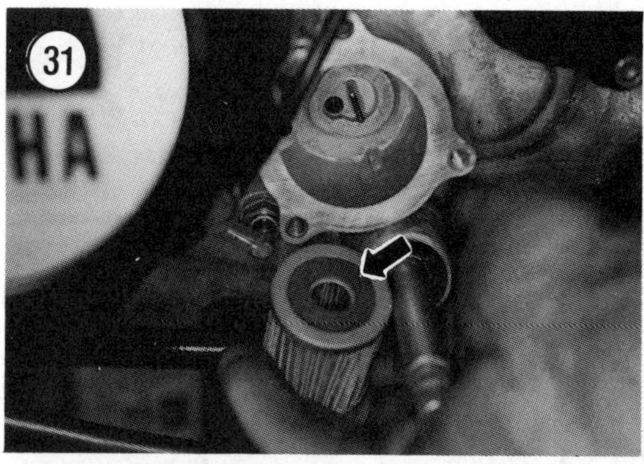

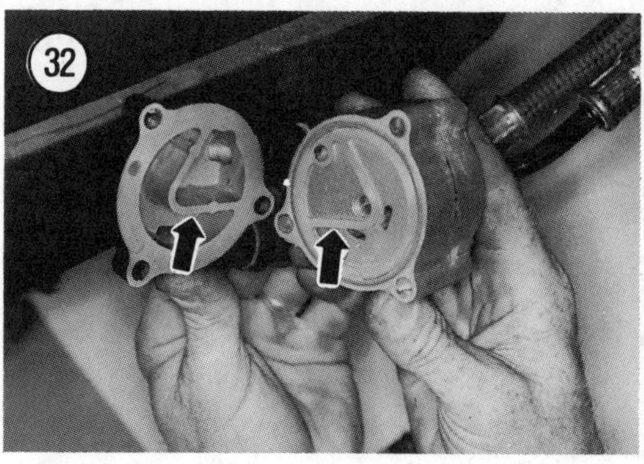

Transfer Gearcase Oil Change

1. Ride the vehicle until normal operating temperature is reached, then park the vehicle on a level surface and set the parking brake. Turn the engine off.
2. Place a drain pan under the transfer gearcase drain plug (**Figure 23**) and remove it and its washer.
3. Remove the transfer gearcase oil fill plug (B, **Figure 16**).
4. When the oil stops draining out of the drain hole, install the transfer gearcase drain bolt and washer (**Figure 23**) and tighten as specified **Table 7**.
5. Fill the transfer gearcase (A, **Figure 16**) with the correct amount of engine oil specified under transfer gear oil in **Table 6**.
6. Install the transfer gearcase oil fill plug(B, **Figure 16**) and tighten as specified in **Table 7**.

Front Differential Gearcase

Oil level check

1. Park the vehicle on a level surface and set the parking brake.

2. Wipe the area around the oil fill cap clean and unscrew the oil fill cap (**Figure 34**).
3. The oil level should be level with the bottom thread of the fill bolt hole. If the oil level is low, add hypoid gear oil (**Table 5**) until the level is correct.
4. Inspect the oil fill cap O-ring and replace if damaged.
5. Screw on the oil fill cap and tighten as specified in **Table 7**.

Oil change

The factory recommended oil change interval is listed in **Table 1**.

To drain the oil you need the following:

a. Drain pan.
b. Funnel.
c. Hypoid gear oil. See **Table 5** (oil type) and **Table 6** (oil quantity).

Discard old oil in the same manner as outlined under *Engine Oil Change* in this chapter.

NOTE
A short ride allows the front differential gearcase oil to heat up; thus it flows freely and carries contamination and sludge out with it.

1. Ride the vehicle until normal operating temperature is reached, then park the vehicle on a level surface and set the parking brake. Turn the engine off.
2. Place a drain pan underneath the 2 drain plugs (**Figure 35**). Both drain plugs can be removed with the skid plate installed on the vehicle.
3. Remove the oil fill cap (**Figure 34**).
4. Remove the front and rear drain plugs (**Figure 35**) and allow the oil to drain.
5. Inspect the sealing washer on each drain plug. Replace if leaking or damaged.
6. Install and tighten the front and rear drain plugs as specified in **Table 7**. Note that different torque specifications are used for the front and rear plugs.
7. Insert a funnel into the oil fill cap hole and add the recommended type (**Table 5**) and quantity (**Table 6**) of gear oil.
8. Remove the funnel and check the oil level. It should come up to the bottom thread of the fill cap hole. Add additional oil if necessary.
9. Inspect the oil fill bolt O-ring and replace if damaged.

10. Install the oil fill cap(**Figure 34**) and tighten as specified in **Table 7**.

11. Test ride the vehicle and check for leaks. After the test ride recheck the oil level and adjust if necessary.

Rear Final Drive Gearcase

Oil level check

1. Park the vehicle on a level surface and set the parking brake.

2. Wipe the area around the oil fill plug and remove it (**Figure 36**).

3. The oil level should be level with the bottom thread of the oil fill plug hole. If the oil level is low, add hypoid gear oil (**Table 5**) until the level is correct.

4. Inspect the oil fill plug O-ring and replace if damaged.

5. Screw on the oil fill plug and tighten as specified in **Table 7**.

Oil change

The factory recommended oil change interval is listed in **Table 1**.

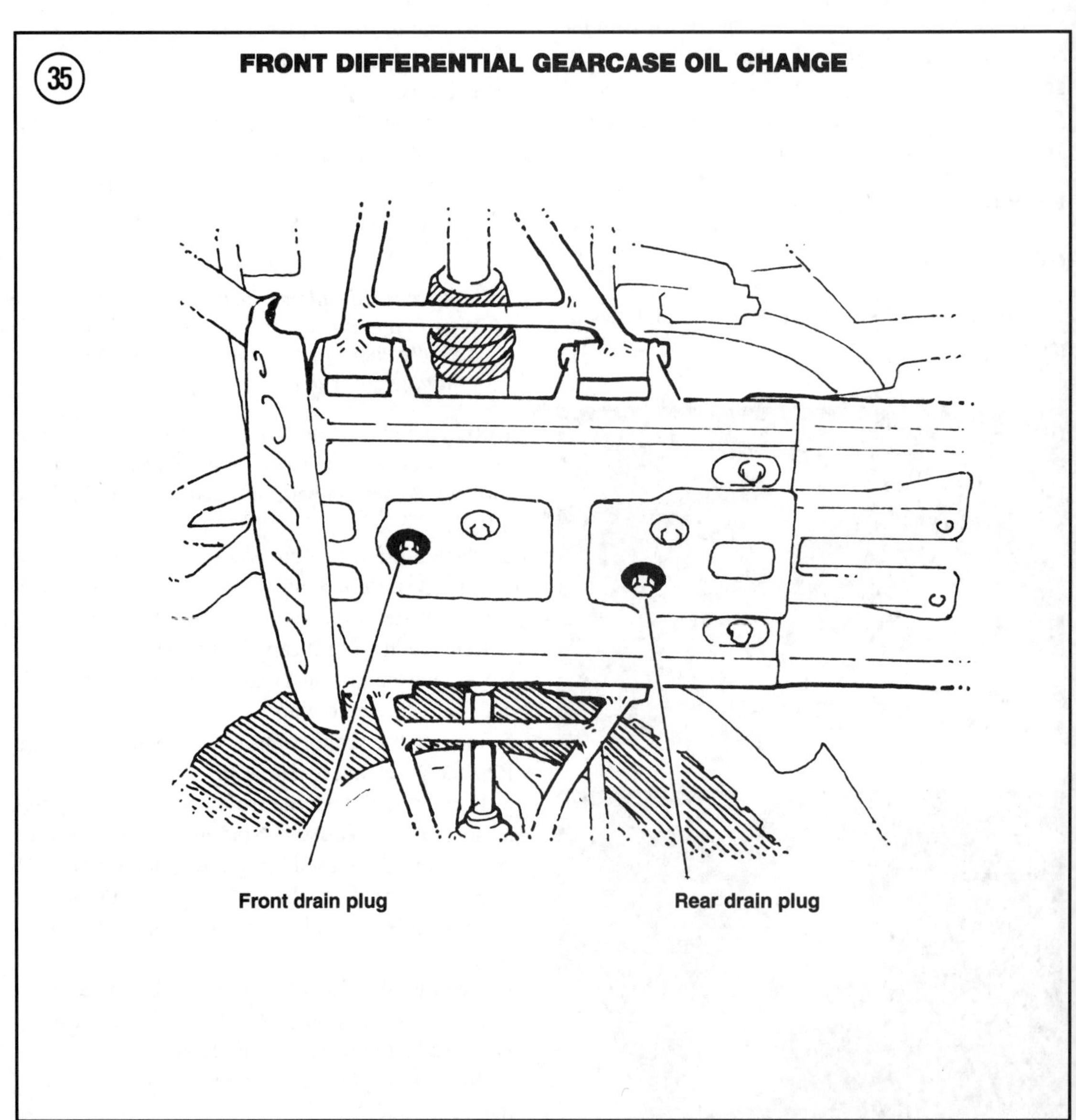

To drain the oil you need the following:

a. Drain pan.

b. Funnel.

c. Hypoid gear oil. See **Table 5** (oil type) and **Table 6** (oil quantity).

Discard old oil in the same manner as outlined under *Engine Oil Change* in this chapter.

NOTE

A short ride allows the rear final gearcase oil to heat up; thus it flows freely and carries contamination and sludge out with it.

1. Ride the vehicle until normal operating temperature is reached, then park the vehicle on a level surface and set the parking brake. Turn the engine off.

NOTE

***Figure 37** shows the drain bolt with the skid plate removed for clarity. It is not necessary to remove the skid plate to drain the oil.*

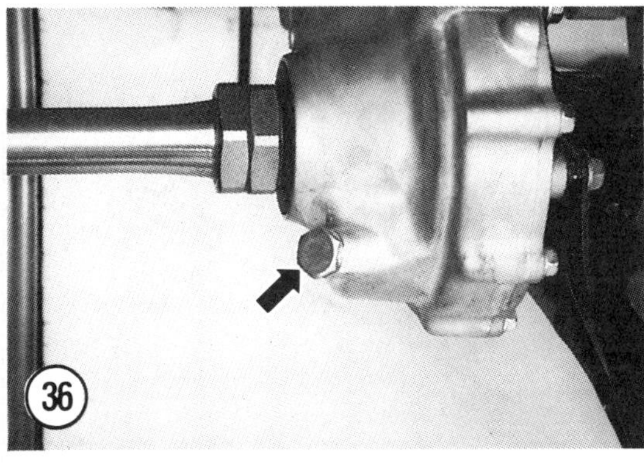

36

37

2. Place a drain pan underneath the drain plug (**Figure 37**) and remove it. Allow the oil to drain out.

3. Wipe the area around the oil fill bolt clean and unscrew the oil fill plug (**Figure 36**).

4. Inspect the drain plug washer and replace if leaking or damaged.

5. When the oil stops draining out, install the drain plug and gasket and tighten as specified in **Table 7**.

6. Insert a funnel into the oil fill hole and add the recommended type (**Table 5**) and quantity (**Table 6**) of gear oil.

7. Remove the funnel and check the oil level. It should come up to the bottom thread of the fill bolt hole. Add additional oil if necessary.

8. Inspect the oil fill plug O-ring and replace if damaged.

9. Screw on the oil fill plug and tighten as specified in **Table 7**.

10. Test ride the vehicle and check for leaks. After the test ride recheck the oil level and adjust if necessary.

General Lubrication

At the service intervals listed in **Table 1**, lubricate the following items with engine oil:

a. Brake pedal.

b. Brake levers.

Control Cable Lubrication

Clean and lubricate the throttle, rear brake and parking brake cables at the intervals indicated in **Table 1**. In addition, check the cables for kinks, excessive wear, damage or fraying that could cause the cables to fail or stick. Cables are expendable items and will not last forever under the best of conditions.

The most positive method of control cable lubrication involves the use of a cable lubricator and a can of cable lube or a general lubricant . Do not use chain lube as a cable lubricant.

1. Disconnect the cable to be lubricated.

2. Attach a cable lubricator to the end of the cable following its manufacturer's instructions (**Figure 38**).

3. Inject cable lubricant into the cable until it begins to flow out of the other end of the cable. If you cannot get the cable lube to flow through the cable at one

end, remove the lubricator and try at the opposite end of the cable.

NOTE
Place a shop cloth at the end of the cable to catch the oil as it runs out.

4. Disconnect the lubricator.
5. Apply a light coat of grease to the cable ends before reconnecting them. Reconnect the cable and adjust as described in this chapter.
6. After lubricating the throttle cable, operate the throttle lever at the handlebar. It should open and close smoothly with no binding.
7. After lubricating the brake cable(s), check brake operation.

UNSCHEDULED LUBRICATION

The services listed in this section are not included in **Table 1** (maintenance and lubrication schedule). However, lubricate these items throughout the service year. Lubrication and service intervals depend on vehicle use. Use a waterproof bearing grease when grease is called for in the following sections.

Steering Shaft Lubrication

Remove the steering shaft (Chapter Ten) and lubricate the upper bearing blocks and split dust seals with grease. At the same time, check the lower bearing and oil seals for damage.

Front Upper and Lower Arm Lubrication

Remove the upper and lower arm pivot bolts and lubricate the bolts and their bushings with grease. Refer to Chapter Ten for service.

Front Wheel Seals

Lubricate the front hub seals with grease. If the front wheel bearings are not sealed, lubricate them also. Refer to Chapter Ten for service.

Rear Shock Absorber Mounting Bolt Lubrication

Remove the front (Chapter Ten) and rear (Chapter Twelve) shock absorbers and lubricate the mounting bolts with grease.

PERIODIC MAINTENANCE

Periodic maintenance intervals are listed in **Table 1**.

Air Box Check Hose

Inspect the check hose (**Figure 39**) mounted on the bottom of the air box. When the hose is filled with water, dirt and other debris, clean and reoil the air filter. Then clean the air box and drain the check hose at the same time.

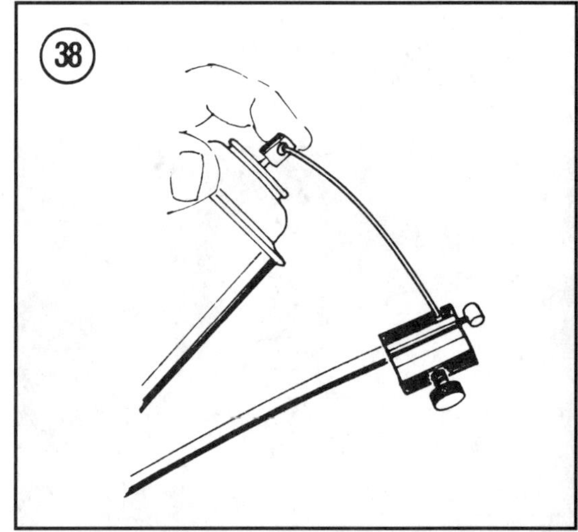
38

39

Air Filter

A clogged air filter will decrease the efficiency and life of the engine. Never run the engine without an air filter properly installed. Even minute particles of dust can cause severe internal engine wear and clogging of carburetor passages.

Removal and installation

1. Remove the seat (Chapter Fourteen).

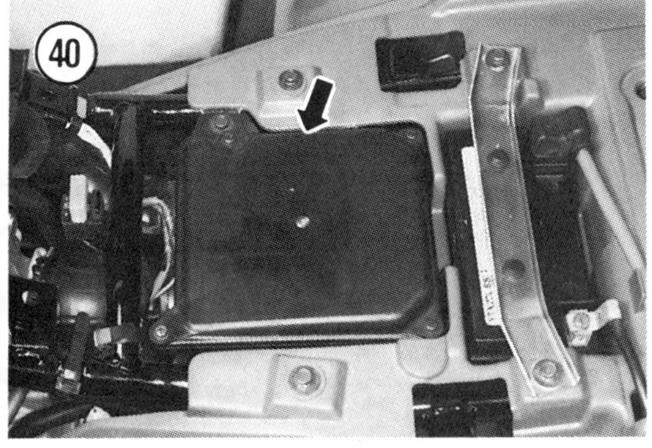
40

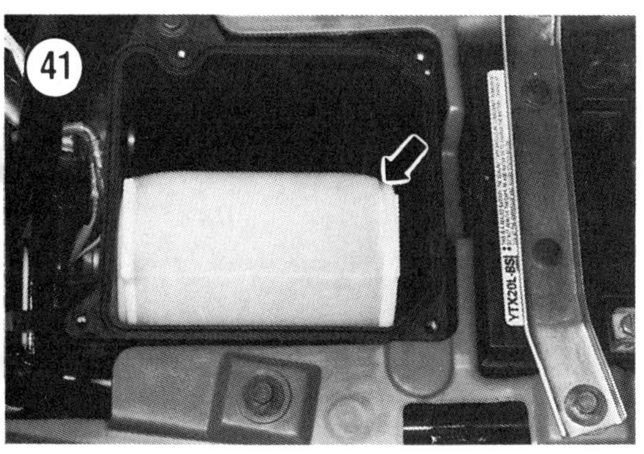
41

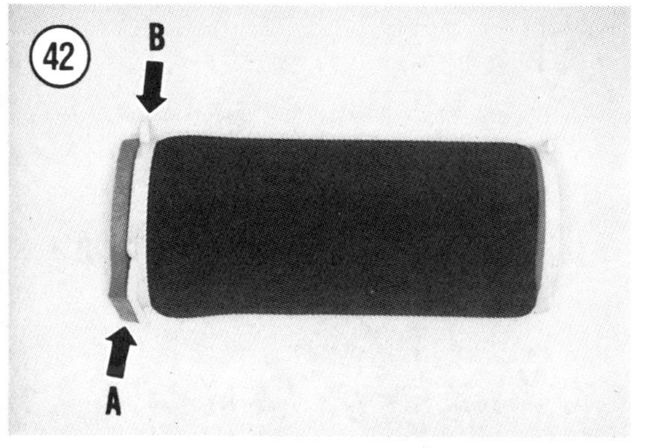

42

NOTE
This procedure is shown with the rear fender removed for clarity. It is not necessary to remove the rear fender for this procedure.

2. Unbolt and remove the air box cover (**Figure 40**).
3. Pull the air filter assembly (**Figure 41**) out of the air box.
4. Disassemble, clean and oil the air filter as described in the following procedure.
5. Check the air box and carburetor boot for dirt or other contamination.
6. Wipe the inside of the air box with a clean rag. If you cannot clean the air box with it bolted to the frame, remove and clean the air box (Chapter Eight).
7. Cover the air box opening with a clean shop rag.
8. Inspect all fittings, hoses and connections from the air box to the carburetor.
9. Assemble the air filter as described under *Air Filter Cleaning and Reoiling* in this chapter.
10. Coat the foam gasket (A, **Figure 42**) on the front of the air filter with wheel bearing grease.
11. Install the filter guide (B, **Figure 42**) into the receptacle in the air box and install the air filter (**Figure 41**) into the bottom of the air box.

NOTE
The rear portion of the air filter will rest on the molded tab in the bottom of the air box.

12. Make sure the air filter cover O-ring gasket is in place, then install the air filter cover (**Figure 40**). Tighten the screws securely.
13. Install the seat (Chapter Fourteen).

Air filter cleaning and reoiling

Service the air filter element in a well-ventilated area, away from all sparks and flames.

1. Turn the cap (A, **Figure 43**) 90° and remove it from the air filter element and filter holder.
2. Separate the air filter element (A, **Figure 44**) from the filter screen/holder (B, **Figure 44**) and remove the element.

WARNING
Do not clean the air filter element with gasoline.

3. Clean the filter element with filter solvent to remove oil and dirt. Allow the element to air dry.
4. Carefully inspect the element. Replace if it is torn or damaged in any area.
5. Fill a clean pan with liquid detergent and warm water.
6. Submerge the filter into the cleaning solution and gently work the cleaner into the filter pores. Soak and squeeze (gently) the filter to clean it.

CAUTION
Do not wring or twist the filter when cleaning it. This could damage the filter pores or tear the filter loose at a seam. This would allow unfiltered air to enter the engine and cause severe and rapid wear.

7. Rinse the filter under warm water while soaking and gently squeezing it.
8. Repeat Step 6 and Step 7 until there is no dirt being rinsed from the filter.
9. After cleaning the element, inspect it again carefully. If it is torn or broken in any area, replace it. Do not run the engine with a damaged element.
10. Set the filter aside and allow it to dry thoroughly.
11. Clean and dry the filter screen/holder. Check the screen for damage and replace if necessary.

CAUTION
Make sure the filter is completely dry before oiling it.

12. Properly oiling an air filter element is a messy job. Wear a pair of disposable rubber gloves when performing this procedure. Oil the filter as follows:
  a. Place the air filter into a storage bag (A, **Figure 45**).
  b. Pour foam air filter oil (B, **Figure 45**) onto the filter to soak it.
  c. Gently squeeze the filter to let the air out of the bag and close the bag.
  d. Gently squeeze and release the filter to soak filter oil into the filter's pores. Repeat until all of the filter's pores are saturated with oil.
  e. Remove the filter from the bag and check the pores for uneven oiling. This is indicated by light or dark areas. If necessary, soak the filter and squeeze it again.
  f. When the filter oiling is even, squeeze the filter a final time.
  g. Pour the leftover filter oil from the bag back into the bottle for reuse.
  h. Dispose of the plastic bag.
13. Apply wheel bearing grease to the front surface of the filter screen/holder (**Figure 46**) where it seats against the filter element.
14. Slide the filter element (A, **Figure 44**) over the filter screen/holder (B, **Figure 44**).
15. Install the cap and turn it 90° until the screen/holder raised tab (B, **Figure 43**) aligns with the arrows (C, **Figure 43**) on the cap.

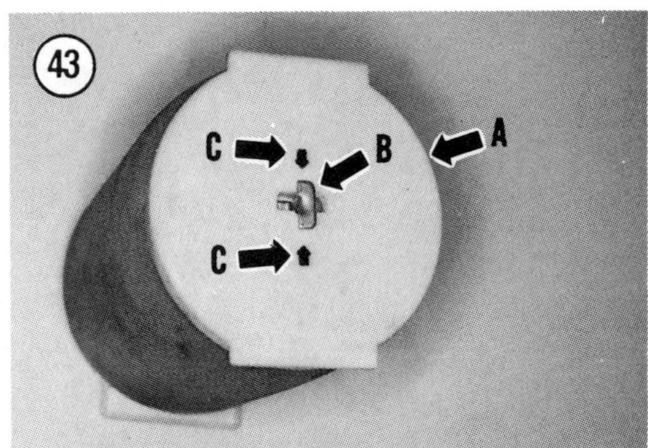

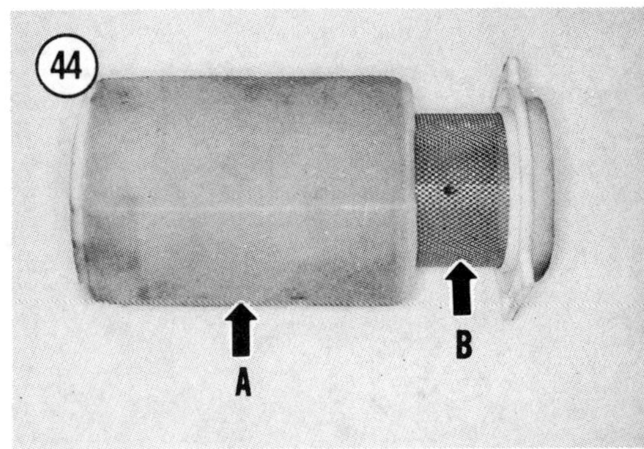

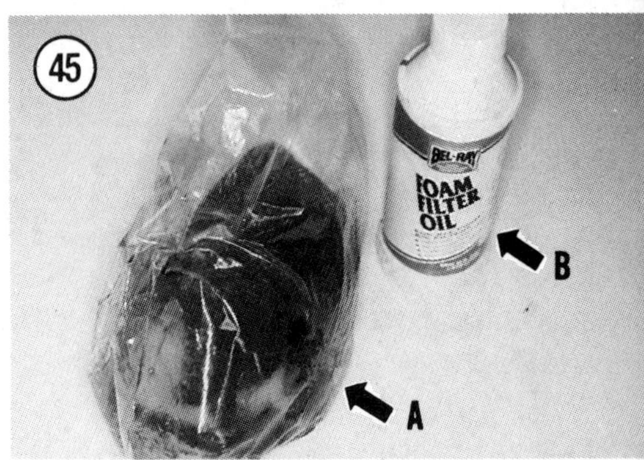

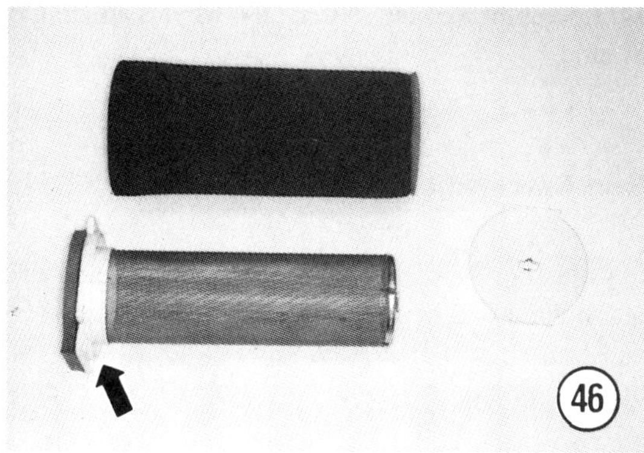
46

16. Install the air filter as described in this chapter.

Fuel Line Inspection

WARNING
Some fuel may spill when performing this procedure. Because gasoline is extremely flammable, perform the following procedure away from all open flames (including appliance pilot lights) and sparks. Do not smoke or allow someone who is smoking in the work area. Always work in a well-ventilated area. Wipe up any spills immediately.

47

Inspect the fuel line (**Figure 47**) and replace it if cracked, leaks or shows evidence of age deterioration or other damage. Make sure each end of the hose is secured with a hose clamp. Check the carburetor overflow and vent hose ends for contamination.

WARNING
A damaged or deteriorated fuel line presents a very dangerous fire hazard to both the rider and machine.

48

Fuel Tank Vent Hose

Check the fuel tank vent hose (**Figure 48**) for proper routing and make sure it is not kinked. Check the end of the hose for contamination.

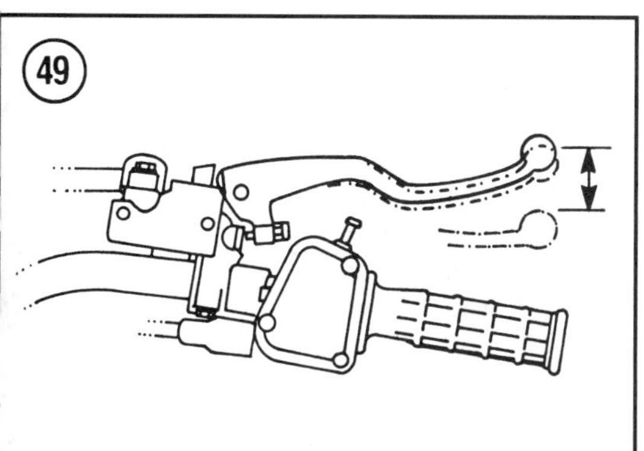
49

Front Brake Lever Free Play Adjustment

The free play on these models is measured at the tip of the brake lever.

1. Apply the front brake lever and measure the amount of free play travel until the adjuster touches the master cylinder piston (**Figure 49**). The correct lever free play measurement is 2-5 mm (0.08-0.020 in.).
2. To adjust the free play, loosen the adjuster locknut and turn the adjuster (**Figure 50**) until the correct amount of free play is achieved.
3. Tighten the locknut securely.
4. Support the vehicle with the front and rear wheels off the ground.
5. Have an assistant spin both front wheels by hand while you apply the front brake lever. Measure the amount of lever movement until just before the brake is actually applied (**Figure 51**). The correct lever free

play is 25-30 mm (1.0-1.2 in.). If the brake linings contact the brake drum too early or too late, adjust the front brakes as described in the following procedure.

NOTE
Contamination inside the brake drum can cause the brakes to apply too soon. If it sounds or feels like there is dirt and other debris inside the drum, remove the brake drum and inspect the drum surface and brake linings as described in Chapter Thirteen.

Front Drum Brake Adjustment

1. Support the vehicle with both the front and rear wheels off the ground.
2. Remove the front wheels (Chapter Ten).
3. Remove the rubber plug (**Figure 52**) from one of the brake drums.

NOTE
***Figure 53** shows the adjusters for the front (A) and rear (B) wheel cylinders with the brake drum removed for clarity.*

4. Rotate the brake drum until the hole is adjacent to the front wheel cylinder adjuster (A, **Figure 53**).
5. Insert a slotted screwdriver into the hole (**Figure 54**) and rotate the adjuster (A, **Figure 55**) away from the center of the hub until the drum is locked and can no longer rotate.
6. From this position, rotate the adjuster in the opposite direction 3 clicks. Apply the front brake lever several times.
7. Rotate the drum and make sure the brake is not dragging on the drum. If it is, turn the adjuster until the brake is no longer dragging.
8. Turn the brake drum until its adjustment hole is adjacent to the rear wheel cylinder adjuster (B, **Figure 53**).
9. Repeat Steps 5-7 for the rear wheel cylinder adjuster.
10. Install the rubber plug (**Figure 52**) into the brake drum.
11. Repeat Steps 3-10 for the opposite front wheel and brake.
12. Recheck brake lever free play, and readjust if necessary.
13. Install the front wheels (Chapter Ten).
14. Lower the vehicle so that all 4 wheels are on the ground.

Rear Brake Adjustment

Adjusting the rear brake consists of adjusting the rear brake pedal height and then the rear brake lever and brake pedal free play. Always adjust the rear brake in this order to maintain proper brake operation.

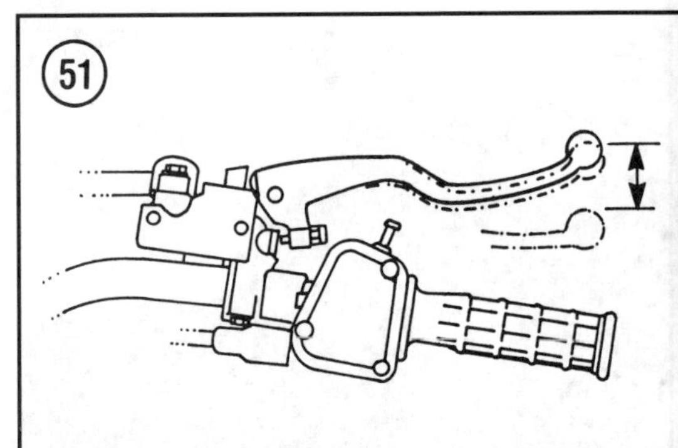

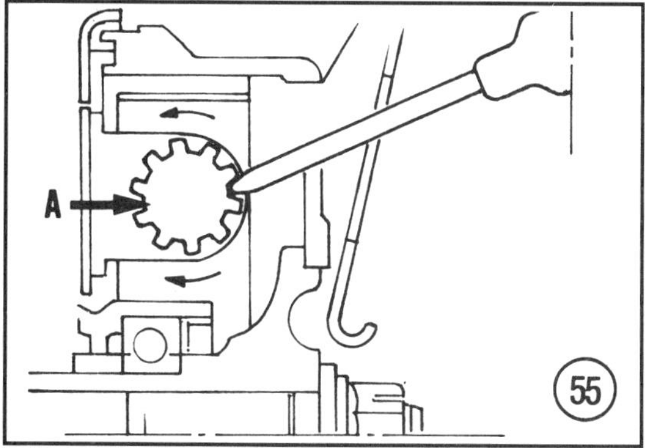

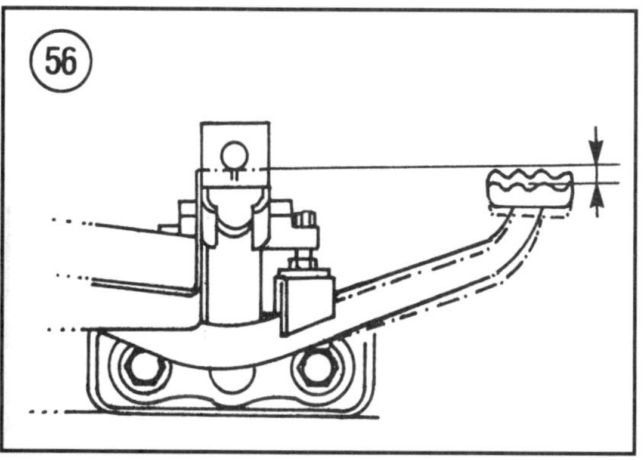

NOTE
Adjust the rear brake pedal height before adjusting the rear brake lever and brake pedal free play.

Rear brake pedal height adjustment

1. Measure the brake pedal height as shown in **Figure 56**. The correct brake pedal height is 5 mm (0.2 in.) below the top of the footpeg. If out of adjustment, loosen the locknut (A, **Figure 57**) and turn the adjuster (B, **Figure 57**) as necessary to achieve the correct brake pedal height. Tighten the locknut and recheck the pedal height.
2. Perform the *Rear Brake Lever and Brake Pedal Free Play Adjustment* in this section.

Rear brake lever and brake pedal free play adjustment

1. Check and adjust the rear brake pedal height as described under *Rear Brake Pedal Height Adjustment* in this section.
2. Check the brake lever and brake pedal free play as follows:
   a. Apply the rear brake lever (**Figure 58**) and measure the free play distance it travels until the rear brake is applied (A, **Figure 58**). The correct rear brake lever free play is 5-8 mm (0.20-0.31 in.).
   b. At the brake pedal, apply the rear brake and check the pedal free play. With the pedal in the at rest position, apply the brake pedal and check the distance it travels until the rear brake is applied (**Figure 59**). The correct brake pedal free play is 20-30 mm (0.8-1.2 in.).

c. If either adjustment is incorrect, continue with Step 3.

3. Apply the rear brake pedal 2-3 times to set the cable and linkage.

4. At the handlebar brake lever, loosen the cable adjuster locknut (B, **Figure 58**) and turn the adjuster (C, **Figure 58**) all the way in to obtain maximum cable slack.

5. At the rear drum brake assembly, perform the following:

a. Fully loosen the rear brake lever cable adjuster (A, **Figure 60**).

b. Turn the rear brake rod adjuster (B, **Figure 60**) until the brake pedal free play is 20-30 mm (0.8-1.2 in.).

c. Turn the brake cable adjuster (A, **Figure 60**) clockwise until the gap between the barrel and the end of the caliper lever (C, **Figure 60**) is 0-1 mm (0.00-0.04 in.).

6. Check the rear brake pedal free play. Push the rear brake pedal down and check the distance the pedal travels from the at-rest position until the rear brake is applied (**Figure 59**). The correct free play distance is 20-30 mm (0.8-1.2 in.). If out of specification, repeat this procedure.

7. At the handlebar brake lever, turn the adjuster (C, **Figure 58**) until the brake lever free play (A, **Figure 58**) is 5-8 mm (0.20-0.31 in.). Then tighten the locknut (B, **Figure 58**) securely.

8. Support the vehicle with both the front and rear wheels off the ground.

9. Rotate the rear wheels and make sure the drum brakc is not dragging. If the brake is dragging, repeat this procedure until there is no drag.

NOTE

Brake drag can also be caused by dirt and other contamination in the brake drum and on the brake linings. If necessary, remove the brake drum (Chapter Thirteen) and check the brake drum and linings.

10. Lower the vehicle so that all 4 wheels are on the ground

Brake Fluid Level Check

1. Turn the handlebar so that the master cylinder is level.

2. Check the brake fluid level through the master cylinder inspection window (A, **Figure 61**). The level should be above the LOWER level line. If necessary, add brake fluid as follows.

3. Clean any dirt from the cover and master cylinder.

4. Remove the 2 top cover screws, cover (B, **Figure 61**) and diaphragm.

5. Add new DOT 3 or DOT 4 brake fluid to raise the brake fluid level.

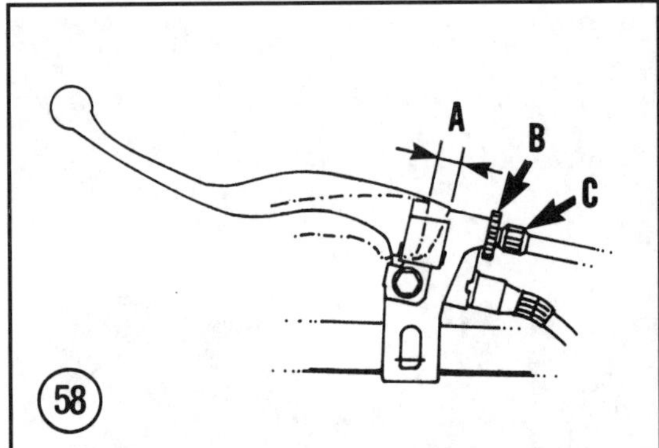

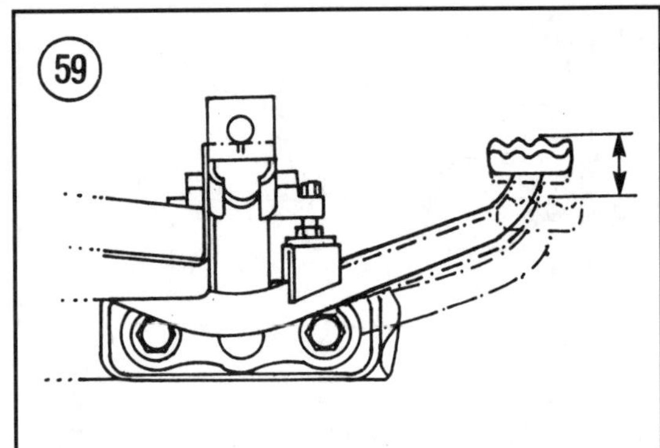

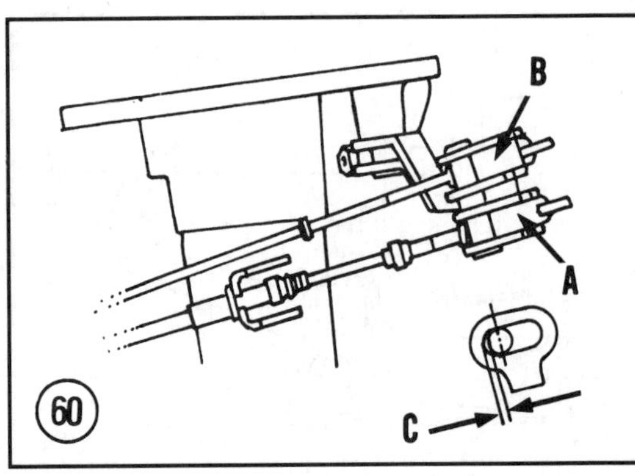

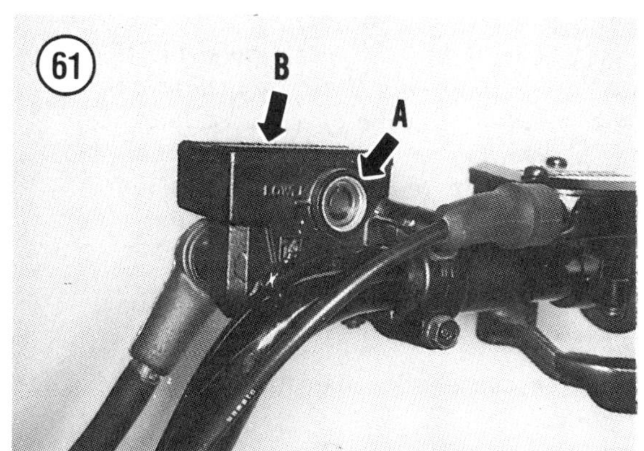

WARNING

Use brake fluid clearly marked DOT 3 or DOT 4. Others may cause brake failure. Do not intermix different brands or types of brake fluid as they may not be compatible. Do not intermix a silicone based (DOT 5) brake fluid as it can cause brake component damage leading to brake system failure.

CAUTION

Be careful when handling brake fluid. Do not spill it on painted or plastic

62

REAR BRAKE LINING INSPECTION

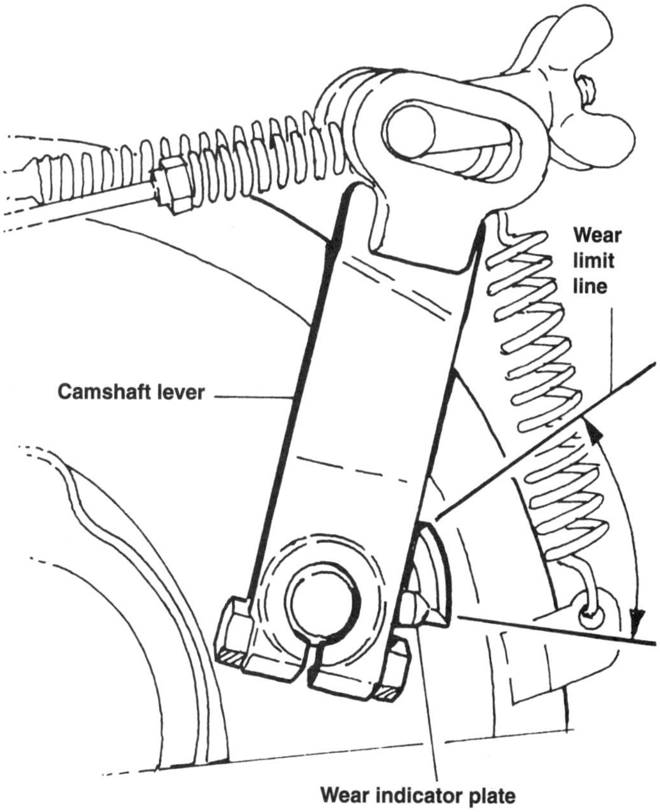

Wear limit line

Camshaft lever

Wear indicator plate

surfaces as it will destroy the surface. Wash the area immediately with soap and water and thoroughly rinse it off.

6. Reinstall the diaphragm and top cover. Install the screws and tighten securely.

Disc Brake Hoses

Inspect the brake hoses for cracks, cuts, bulges, deterioration and leaks. Check the metal brake lines for cracks and leaks. Replace the brake hoses at the intervals specified in **Table 1**. Refer to Chapter Thirteen for service procedures.

Front Brake Lining Wear

Inspect and measure the front brake linings as described under *Front Brake Shoe Replacement* in Chapter Thirteen.

Rear Brake Lining Wear

To check the condition of the rear brake linings, have an assistant depress the rear brake pedal while you watch the movement of the rear brake wear indicator (**Figure 62**). Replace the rear brake linings when the wear indicator pointer aligns with the wear limit line when the rear brakes are applied. Replace the rear brake linings as described in Chapter Thirteen.

Disc Brake Fluid Change

Every time the master cylinder top cover is removed, a small amount of dirt and moisture can enter the brake fluid. The same thing happens if a leak occurs or if any part of the hydraulic system is loosened or disconnected. Dirt can clog the system and cause unnecessary wear and brake failure. Water in the brake fluid will contaminate the hydraulic system, impairing the hydraulic action and reducing the brake's stopping ability.

To maintain peak performance, change the brake fluid every 2 years or whenever rebuilding or replacing the master cylinder or a wheel cylinder. To change brake fluid, follow the brake bleeding procedure in Chapter Thirteen.

WARNING
Use brake fluid clearly marked DOT 3 or DOT 4 only. Others may cause brake failure. Dispose of any used fluid according to local EPA regulations—never reuse brake fluid. Contaminated brake fluid can cause brake failure.

Clutch Adjustment

Adjust the clutch at the intervals specified in **Table 1**.

This adjustment pertains only to the manual clutch as the centrifugal clutch requires no adjustment. Since there is no clutch cable, the mechanism is the only component that requires adjustment. This adjustment takes up slack due to clutch component wear.

1. Loosen the clutch adjust screw locknut (A, **Figure 63**).
2. Turn the adjust screw (B, **Figure 63**) counterclockwise until resistance is felt, then stop.
3. From this point, turn the adjust screw (B, **Figure 63**) clockwise 1/8 of a turn, then stop.

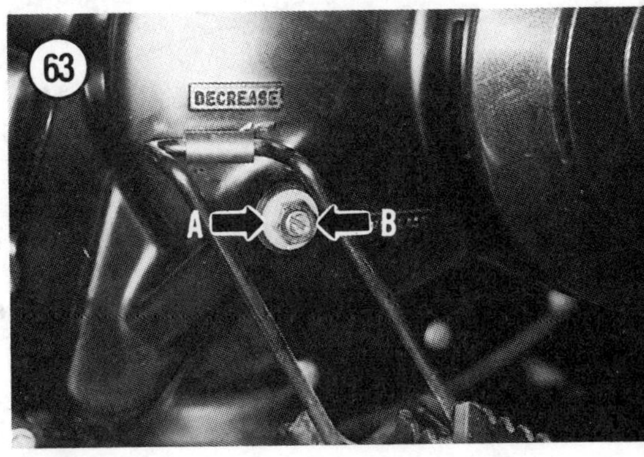

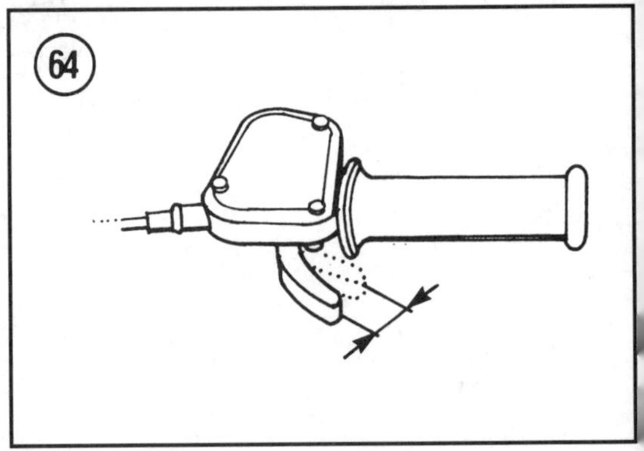

NOTE
Make sure the adjust screw does not move when tightening the locknut in Step 4.

4. Hold the adjust screw and tighten the locknut (A, **Figure 63**) as specified in **Table 7**.
5. Test ride the vehicle and make sure the clutch is operating correctly. Readjust if necessary.

NOTE
If the clutch adjustment is hard to make, the friction plates may be worn. Remove the clutch cover and inspect the friction plates as described in Chapter Six.

Throttle Cable Check and Adjustment

Check the throttle cable free play at the interval indicated in **Table 1** or whenever it seems too tight or too loose. The throttle cable should have 3-5 mm (0.12-0.20 in.) of free play measured at the tip of the throttle lever (**Figure 64**).

In time, the throttle cable free play will become excessive from cable stretch. This will delay throttle response and affect low speed operation. However, if there is no throttle cable free play, an excessively high idle can result.

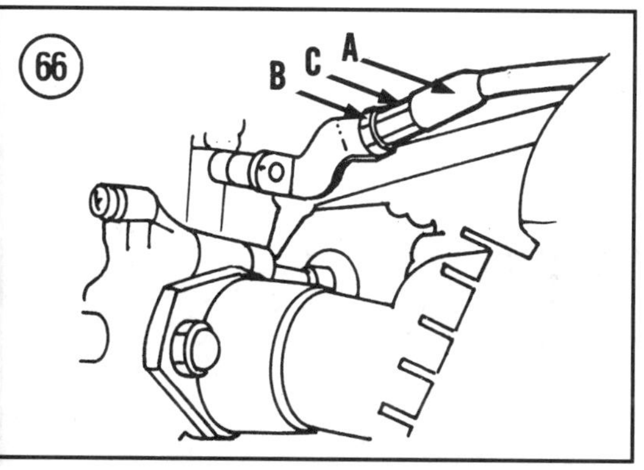

1. At the upper throttle cable adjuster (handlebar), pull the rubber boot (A, **Figure 65**) off the adjuster and check that the adjuster locknut (B, **Figure 65**) and adjuster (C, **Figure 65**) are tight. If the adjuster is loose, tighten it securely, then slide the rubber boot back over the adjuster and continue with Step 2.
2. At the carburetor, slide the rubber boot (A, **Figure 66**) off the adjuster. Then loosen the locknut (B, **Figure 66**) and turn the adjuster (C, **Figure 66**) as necessary to achieve the correct amount of free play. Hold onto the adjuster (C, **Figure 65**) and tighten the locknut (B, **Figure 65**) securely. Slide the rubber boot (A, **Figure 65**) back into position.
3. If the proper amount of free play cannot be achieved at the carburetor end of the cable, adjust the upper throttle cable end, starting with Step 4.
4. At the throttle housing, slide the rubber boot (A, **Figure 65**) off the adjuster. Loosen the locknut (B, **Figure 65**) and turn the adjuster (C, **Figure 65**) to achieve the correct amount of free play. Hold onto the adjuster (C, **Figure 65**) and tighten the locknut (B, **Figure 65**) securely. Slide the rubber boot back into place.
5. If the throttle cable cannot be adjusted properly, the cable is stretched excessively and must be replaced.
6. Make sure the throttle lever moves freely from its fully closed to fully open positions and has 3-5 mm (0.12-0.20 in.) of free play.
7. Apply the parking brake.
8. Start the engine and allow it to idle in NEUTRAL. Turn the handlebar from side to side. If the engine speed increases as the handlebar is being turned, the throttle cable is routed incorrectly or there is not enough cable free play. Readjust the throttle cable, or if necessary, replace the throttle cable as described in Chapter Eight.

NOTE
A damaged throttle cable will prevent the engine from idling properly.

Speed Limiter Screw Adjustment

The throttle housing is equipped with a speed limiter screw (**Figure 67**) that can be set to prevent the rider from opening the throttle all the way. The speed limiter screw can be set for beginning riders or to control engine speed when breaking in a new engine.

Set the speed limiter adjustment by varying the length of the speed limiter screw. The standard exposed length is 12 mm (0.47 in.). Loosen the locknut, then turn the screw out to increase engine speed or turn the screw in to decrease engine speed.

WARNING

Do not operate the vehicle with the speed limiter screw removed from the housing. If you are adjusting the speed limiter for a beginning rider, start and ride the vehicle yourself, making sure the vehicle's speed is not too fast.

Transmission Range Select Lever Cable Adjustment

The transmission range select lever shifts the transmission into one of the dual-range modes, either HIGH or LOW, or shifts the transmission into REVERSE. The select lever is mounted on the top of the left side crankcase cover.

CAUTION

Before moving the select lever in this procedure, make sure the vehicle is at a complete stop with the throttle lever in its closed position; otherwise, the transmission components may be damaged.

The 2 control cables (No. 1 and No. 2) must be adjusted in the sequence described in this procedure. Shift the transmission into NEUTRAL and turn off the engine. See A, **Figure 68** (No. 1 cable) and B, **Figure 68** (No. 2 cable).

1. Shift the select lever (B, **Figure 68**) into its LOW position. Make sure the lever is properly seated in the LOW position and the button has returned to the out position.

NOTE

The select lever must be in the LOW position at all times when adjusting the No. 1 and No. 2 controls cables in this procedure.

2. Check and adjust the No. 2 control cable (B, **Figure 68**) as follows:
   a. Check that the spring (A, **Figure 69**) is just tight enough to take the slack out of the No. 2 cable (B, **Figure 69**), but not so that tight that it pulls on the cable.
   b. If the spring tension is incorrect, loosen the locknuts (A, **Figure 70**) and turn them alternately until the spring tension is correct.
   c. Tighten both locknuts securely and recheck the spring tension.

3. Verify that the select lever cannot be shifted into REVERSE without first depressing the brake pedal. Then, when operating the brake pedal, check that the No. 2 control cable moves a minimum of 5 mm (0.2

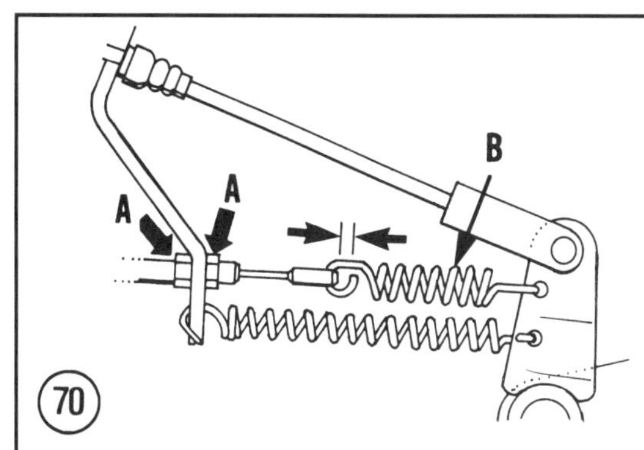

70

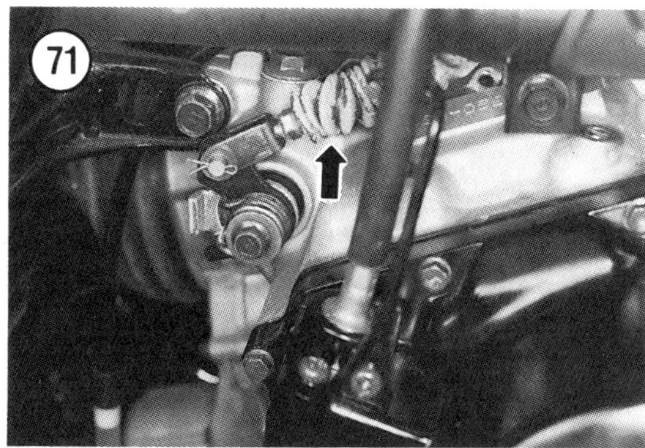
71

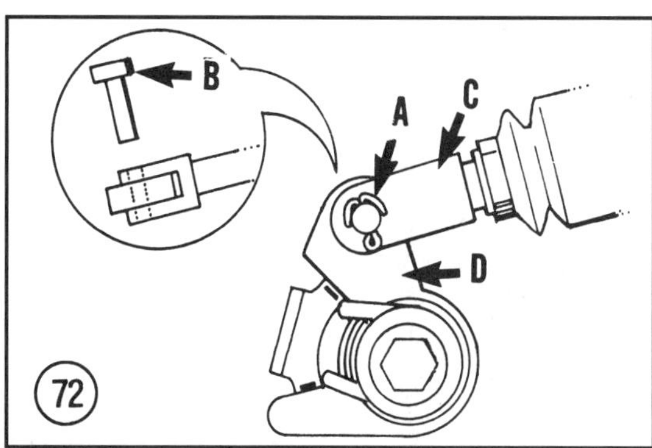

72

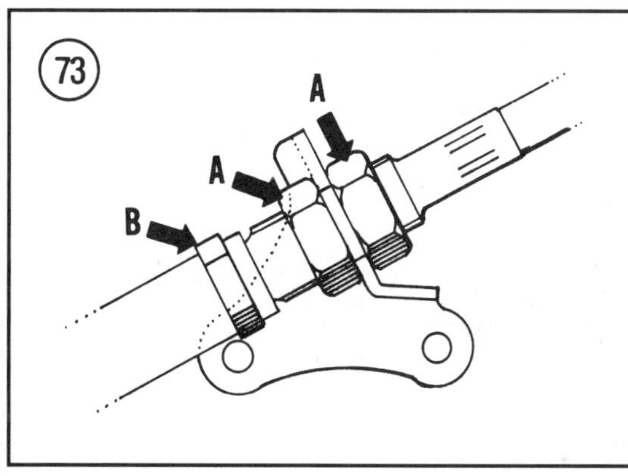

73

mm) at the point indicated in B, **Figure 70**. If the select lever can be moved into REVERSE without depressing the brake pedal, or the No. 2 control cable travel is less than the minimum, readjust the No. 2 control cable and recheck the rear brake pedal adjustment.

4. Adjust the No. 1 control cable (**Figure 71**) as follows:
   a. At the right-rear side of the engine, remove the cotter pin (A, **Figure 72**), washer and the clevis pin (B, **Figure 72**) from the cable fitting.
   b. Loosen both locknuts (A, **Figure 73**) and turn them alternately until the holes in the cable fitting (C, **Figure 72**) align with the hole in the arm (D, **Figure 72**). Insert the clevis pin through the holes to check alignment. The pin must slide in and out of its mounting hole easily and with no binding.
   c. Remove the clevis pin and tighten the No. 1 control cable locknuts as specified **Table 7**. Make sure the cable fitting does not move when tightening the locknuts.
   d. Recheck the clevis pin hole alignment and readjust if necessary.
   e. When the adjustment is correct, spray the clevis pin with a silicone lubricant. Then install the clevis pin (B, **Figure 72**) and washer and secure it with a new cotter pin. Bend the cotter pin ends over to lock it in place.

5. Lubricate the No. 1 control cable end with grease by moving the dust cover (**Figure 71**) forwards and then backwards to expose inner cable. Then center the dust cover so that it covers the part of the cable that was lubricated.

6. Check the select lever operation by verifying that the select lever cannot be shifted into REVERSE without first depressing the brake pedal.

Steering System and Front Suspension Inspection

Inspect the steering system and front suspension at the interval indicated in **Table 1**.

If any of the following mentioned front suspension and steering fasteners are loose, refer to Chapter Ten for the correct service procedures and tightening torque's.

1. Park the vehicle on level ground and set the parking brake.

3

2. Visually inspect all components of the steering system. Repair or replace damaged components as described in Chapter Ten.
3. Check the shock absorbers as described in this next section.
4. Carefully lift up and unhook the indicator light assembly from the handlebar.
5. Check the handlebar holder bolt tightness.
6. Make sure the front axle nuts are tight and that all cotter pins are in place.
7. Check that the cotter pins are in place on all steering components. If any cotter pin is missing, check the nut(s) for looseness. Torque the nut(s) and install new cotter pins.
8. Check steering shaft play as follows:
   a. To check steering shaft radial play, move the handlebar from side to side (without attempting to move the wheels). If radial play is excessive, the upper steering bearings are probably worn or the bearing holder (**Figure 74**) mounting bolts are loose. Replace the upper steering bearings or tighten the bearing holder bolts as necessary.
   b. To check steering shaft thrust play, lift up and then push down on the handlebar. If excessive thrust play is noted, check the lower steering shaft nut (**Figure 75**) for looseness. If the nut is tightened properly, check the lower steering shaft bearing for severe wear or damage.
   c. Service the steering shaft as described in Chapter Ten.
9. Check steering knuckle and tie rod ends as follows:
   a. Turn the handlebar quickly from side to side. If there is appreciable looseness between the handlebar and tires, check the tie rod ends for excessive wear or damage. See A, **Figure 76**, typical.
   b. Service the steering knuckle and tie rods as described in Chapter Ten.

NOTE
If any cotter pins were removed in this section, install new cotter pins during reassembly.

Shock Absorber Inspection

1. Check the front and rear shock absorbers for oil leaks, a bent damper rod or other damage.
2. Compare the 2 front shock absorbers for spring fatigue.
3. If necessary, replace the shock absorbers as described in Chapter Ten (front) or Chapter Twelve (rear).

Front Axle Joint Boot Inspection

At the interval specified in **Table 1**, inspect the front axle joint boots (B, **Figure 76**) for tearing or

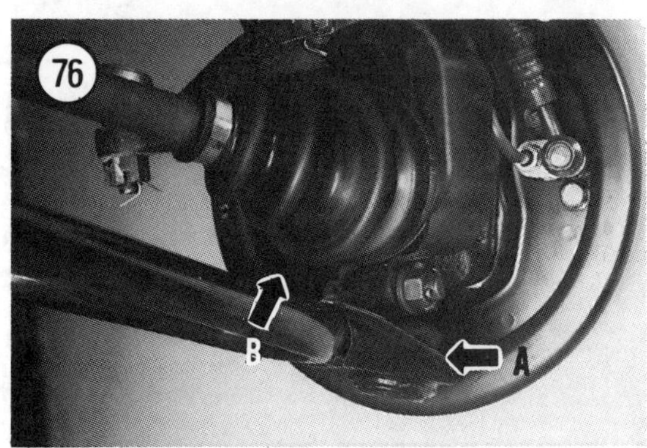

other damage. Replace damaged boots as described in Chapter Eleven.

Toe-In Adjustment

Toe-in is a condition where the front of the tires are closer together than the back (**Figure 77**). Check the toe-in adjustment at the interval specified in **Table 1**, after servicing the front suspension or when replacing the tie rods.

Toe-in is adjusted by changing the length of the tie rods.

1. Inflate all 4 tires to the recommended pressure specified in **Table 2**.
2. Park the vehicle on level ground and set the parking brake. Then raise and support the front of the vehicle so that both front tires just clear the ground.
3. Turn the handlebar so the wheels are facing the straight-ahead position.
4. Using a tape measure, carefully measure the distance between the center of both front tires as shown in A, **Figure 77**. Mark the tires with a piece of chalk at these points. Record the measurement.

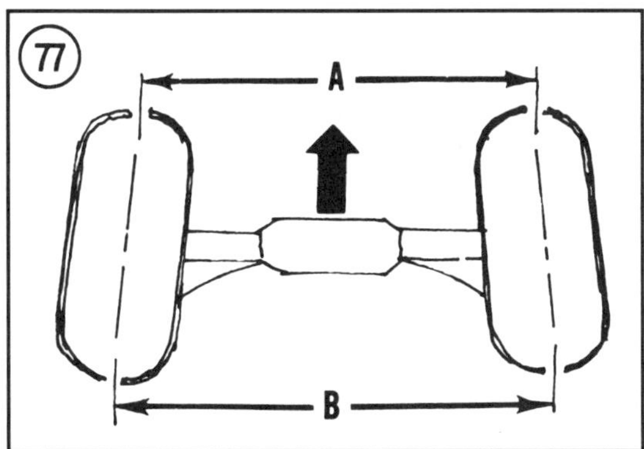

5. Turn each tire exactly 180° and measure the distance between the center of both front tires at B, **Figure 77**. Record the measurement.
6. Subtract the measurement in Step 4 from Step 5 as shown in **Figure 77**. Toe-in is correct if the difference is 0-10 mm (0-0.39 in.). If the toe-in measurement is incorrect, continue with Step 7. If the toe-in is correct, go to Step 10.
7. Loosen the locknut (A, **Figure 78**) at each end of both tie rods.
8. Use a wrench on the flat portion (B, **Figure 78**) of the tie rods and slowly turn both tie rods the same amount until the toe-in measurement is correct.

NOTE
Turn both tie rods the same number of turns. This ensures that the tie rod length will remain the same on each side. If you feel that the left- and right-side tie rod lengths are different, refer to ***Tie Rods*** *in Chapter Ten.*

NOTE
If the tie rods are not adjsuted equally, the handlebar will not be centered even though the front wheels are facing straight forward.

9. When the toe-in adjustment is correct, hold each tie rod in place and tighten the locknuts as specified in **Table 7**.
10. Lower the vehicle so that both front wheels are on the ground.
11. Start the engine and make a slow test ride on level ground. Ride in a straight-ahead position while checking that the handlebar does not turn toward the left- or right-side.

Nuts, Bolts, and Other Fasteners

Constant vibration can loosen many of the fasteners on the vehicle. Check the tightness of all fasteners, especially those on:

a. Engine mounting hardware.
b. Cylinder head bracket bolts.
c. Engine crankcase covers.
d. Handlebar.
e. Gearshift lever.
f. Brake pedal and lever.
g. Exhaust system.

3

UNSCHEDULED MAINTENANCE

Exhaust System

1. Inspect the exhaust pipe for cracks or dents which could alter performance.
2. Check all of the exhaust pipe fasteners and mounting points for loose or damaged parts.

Exhaust Pipe Muffler Baffle Cleaning

1. Remove the bolt and washer (A, **Figure 79**) securing the baffle to the muffler housing.
2. Pull the baffle (B, **Figure 79**) out of the muffler.
3. Use a stiff brush to remove all carbon residue from the baffle.
4. Reinstall the baffle and its mounting bolt. Tighten the bolt securely.

Fuel Tank Shutoff Valve Cleaning

Periodically remove and clean the fuel tank shutoff valve as described in Chapter Eight.

Carburetor Cleaning

Remove, disassemble and clean the carburetor as described in Chapter Eight.

Handlebar

Inspect the handlebar for cracks, bending and other damage. Replace a bent or damaged handlebar. The knurled section of the bar should be very rough. Clean the clamps with a wire brush. Any time that the bars slip in the clamps they should be removed and wire brushed clean to prevent small bits of aluminum from gathering in the clamps and reducing gripping ability.

Handlebar Grips

Inspect the handlebar grips for tearing, looseness or excessive wear. Install new grips when required. Follow their manufacturer's instructions when installing grips.

Frame Inspection

Routinely inspect the frame, brackets and all welded joints for cracks or other damage.

ENGINE TUNE-UP

The number of definitions of the term tune-up is probably equal to the number of people defining it. For the purposes of this book, a tune-up is general adjustment and maintenance to ensure peak engine performance.

The following paragraphs discuss each phase of a proper tune-up which should be performed in the order given. Unless otherwise specified, the engine should be thoroughly cool before starting any tune-up procedure.

Have the new parts on hand before you begin.

To perform a tune-up on your Yamaha, you will need the following tools and equipment:

a. 14 mm spark plug wrench.
b. Socket wrench and assorted sockets.
c. Phillips head screwdriver.

d. Spark plug feeler gauge and gap adjusting tool.

e. Feeler gauge set.

Camshaft Chain Adjustment

An automatic camshaft chain tensioner assembly is used. No adjustment is required.

81

82

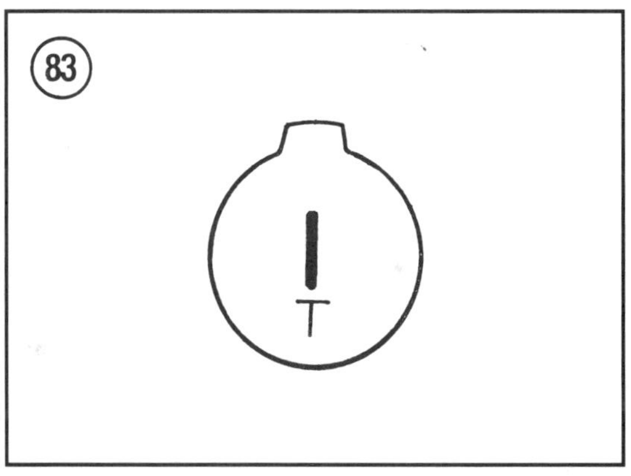

83

Valve Clearance Check and Adjustment

Check and adjust the valve clearance with the engine cold. The exhaust valve is located in the front of the engine and the intake valve is at the rear of the engine next to the carburetor.

1. Park the vehicle on level ground and set the parking brake.
2. Remove the seat and front fender (Chapter Fourteen).
3. Remove the fuel tank (Chapter Eight).
4. Remove the recoil starter assembly (Chapter Five).
5. Remove the ignition timing window plug and O-ring (**Figure 80**).
6. Remove the cylinder head side cover and O-ring (A, **Figure 81**).
7. Remove the exhaust and intake valve covers and O-ring seals.
8. Remove the spark plug. This will make it easier to turn the engine by hand.
9. The engine must be set at top dead center (TDC) on its compression stroke when checking and adjusting the valve clearance. Perform the following:
   a. Place a wrench on the crankshaft starter pulley (B, **Figure 81**), turn the crankshaft counterclockwise and align the camshaft sprocket index mark (A, **Figure 82**) with the cylinder head mark (B, **Figure 82**).
   b. Now check that the T mark on the rotor is aligned with the crankcase index mark. See **Figure 80** and **Figure 83**. If these marks are not aligned, turn the crankshaft one revolution counterclockwise and align the rotor T mark with the crankcase index mark (**Figure 83**).
   c. When the camshaft sprocket and rotor marks are properly aligned, both rocker arms will have a valve clearance, indicating that both the intake and exhaust valves are closed. Check by moving each rocker arm by hand. There should be some side movement.
10. Check the clearance of both the intake valve and exhaust valve by inserting a flat feeler gauge between the rocker arm pad and the valve stem as shown in **Figure 84**. See **Table 8** for the intake and exhaust valve clearances. When the clearance is correct, there will be a slight resistance on the feeler gauge when it is inserted and withdrawn.
11. To correct the valve clearance, perform the following:

a. Loosen the locknut and turn the adjuster (**Figure 85**) in or out until the clearance is correct. There should be a slight resistance felt when the feeler gauge is drawn from between the adjuster and valve tip.
b. Hold the adjuster to prevent it from turning further and tighten the locknut securely.
c. Then recheck the clearance to make sure the adjuster did not move when the locknut was tightened. If necessary, readjust the valve clearance.

12. Inspect the valve cover, cylinder head side cover and timing hole plug O-rings. Replace if leaking or damaged. Lubricate these O-rings with a lithium-soap base grease before installation.
13. Install the valve covers with their inner ridge (**Figure 86**) facing up. Install and tighten the valve cover mounting bolts as specified in **Table 7**.
14. Install the cylinder head side cover, O-ring and mounting bolts. Tighten as specified in table 7.
15. Install the ignition timing window plug and O-ring. Tighten the plug securely.
16. Install the spark plug and tighten as specified in **Table 7**. Reconnect the spark plug cap.
17. Install the recoil starter (Chapter Five).
18. Install the fuel tank (Chapter Eight).
19. Install the front fender and seat (Chapter Fourteen).

Cylinder Compression

A cylinder compression test is one of the quickest ways to check the condition of the rings, head gasket, piston and cylinder. It is a good idea to check compression at each tune-up, and compare it with the reading you get at the next tune-up. This will help you spot any developing problems.

1. Warm the engine to normal operating temperature.
2. Remove the spark plug. Then insert the plug into the plug cap and ground the plug against the cylinder head (**Figure 87**).
3. Thread or insert the tip of a compression gauge into the cylinder head spark plug hole (**Figure 88**). Make sure the gauge is seated properly against the hole.

NOTE
The battery must be fully charged when turning the engine over with the starter motor or a false compression reading may be obtained. If necessary, use the recoil starter to turn the engine over.

4. Hold the throttle wide open and crank the engine with the starter motor for several revolutions until the gauge stabilizes and gives its highest reading. Record the pressure reading and compare to the compression specifications listed in **Table 8**.

5. If the reading is higher than normal, there may be a buildup of carbon deposits in the combustion chamber or on the piston crown.

6. If a low reading is obtained, it indicates a leaking cylinder head gasket, valve(s) or piston ring trouble. To determine which, pour about a teaspoon of engine oil through the spark plug hole onto the top of the piston. Crank the engine once to clear some of the excess oil, then make another compression test and record the reading. If the compression increases significantly, the valves are good but the rings are worn or damaged. If compression does not increase, the valves require servicing. A valve could be hanging open or a piece of carbon could be on the valve seat.

84

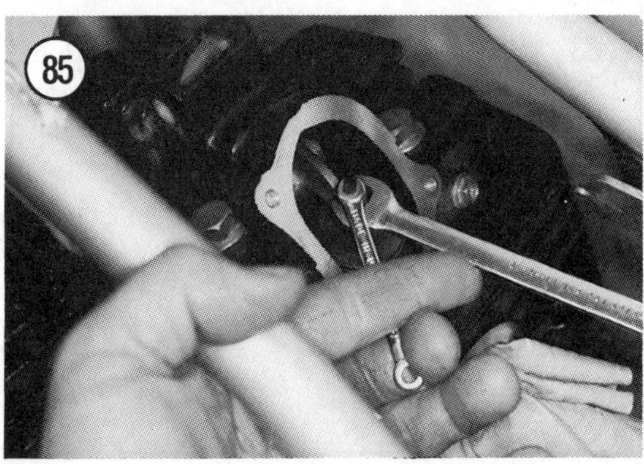
85

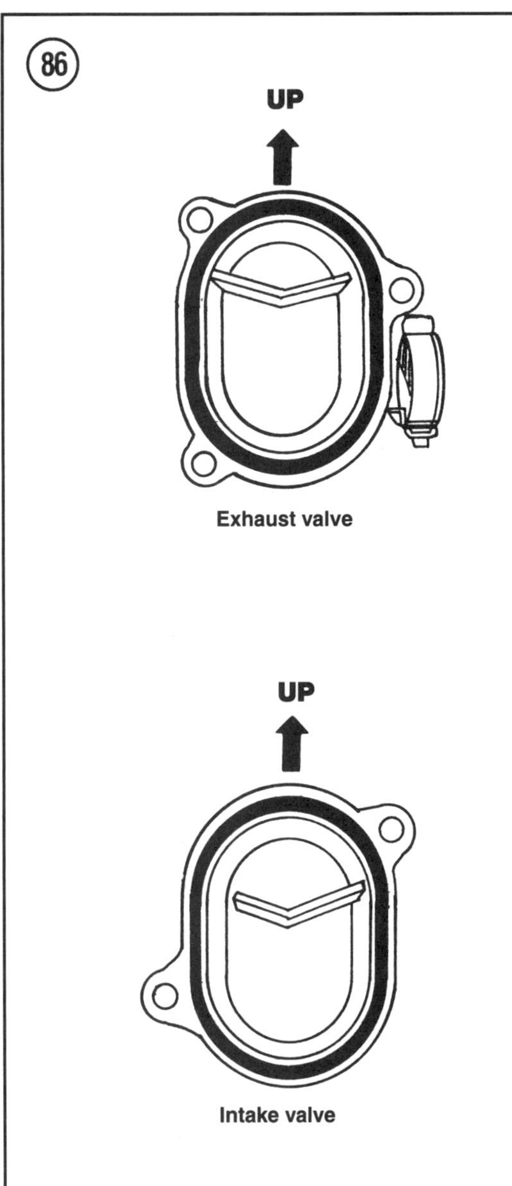

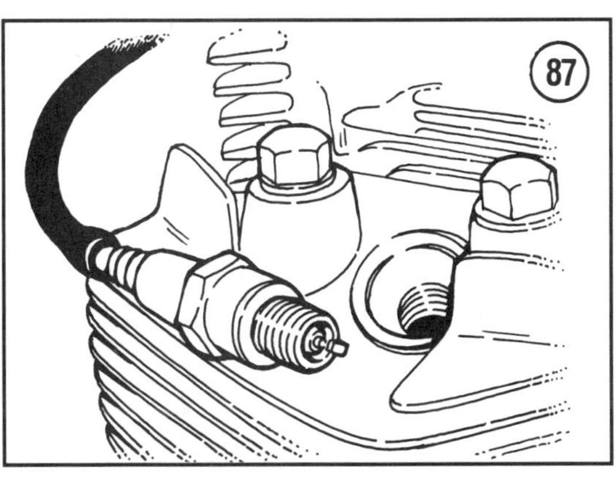

7. Remove the compression tester. Install the spark plug and reconnect the spark plug cap.

NOTE
If the compression is low, the engine cannot be tuned to maximum performance.

3

Correct Spark Plug Heat Range

Spark plugs are available in various heat ranges, hotter or colder than the plugs originally installed at the factory.

Select plugs of the heat range designed for the loads and conditions under which your Yamaha will operate. Use of the incorrect heat range can cause the plug to foul or overheating and piston damage.

In general, use a hot plug for low speeds and low temperatures. Use a cold plug for high speeds, high engine loads and high temperatures. The plug should operate hot enough to burn off unwanted deposits, but not so hot that it burns itself or causes preignition. A spark plug of the correct heat range will show a light tan color on the insulator after the plug has been in service.

The reach (length) of a plug is also important. A plug that is too short will cause excessive carbon buildup, hard starting and plug fouling. A plug that is too long will cause overheating or may contact the top of the piston. Both conditions will cause engine damage. See **Figure 89**.

Table 8 lists the standard heat range spark plug.

Spark Plug Removal

CAUTION
Whenever the spark plug is removed, dirt around it can fall into the plug hole. This can cause expensive engine damage.

1. Grasp the spark plug lead (**Figure 90**) as near the plug as possible and pull it off the plug. If it is stuck to the plug, twist it slightly to break it loose.
2. Blow away any dirt that has collected around the spark plug.
3. Remove the spark plug with a spark plug socket.

NOTE
If the plug is difficult to remove, apply penetrating oil, like WD-40 or Liquid Wrench, around the base of the plug and let it soak about 10-20 minutes.

4. Inspect the plug carefully. Look for a broken center porcelain, excessively eroded electrodes and excessive carbon or oil fouling.

Gapping and Installing the Plug

Carefully adjust the electrode gap on a new spark plug to ensure a reliable, consistent spark. Use a spark plug gapping tool and a wire feeler gauge.

1. If necessary, screw the small terminal end onto the end of the plug (**Figure 91**).
2. Insert a wire feeler gauge between the center and side electrode of the plug (**Figure 92**). The correct gap is listed in **Table 8**. If the gap is correct, you will fccl a slight drag as you pull the wire through. If there is no drag, or the gauge will not pass through, bend the side electrode with a gap adjusting tool (**Figure 93**) to set the proper gap.
3. Apply antiseize compound to the plug threads before installing the spark plug. Do not use engine oil on the plug threads.

NOTE
Antiseize compound can be purchased at most automotive parts stores.

4. Screw the spark plug in by hand until it seats. Very little effort should be required. If force is necessary, you may have the plug cross-threaded. Unscrew it and try again.
5. Use a spark plug wrench and tighten the spark plug as specified in **Table 7**. If you do not have a torque wrench, tighten the plug an additional 1/4 to 1/2 turn after the gasket has made contact with the head. If you are installing a used spark plug, only tighten an additional 1/4 turn.

NOTE
Do not overtighten. This will only crush the gasket and destroy its sealing ability.

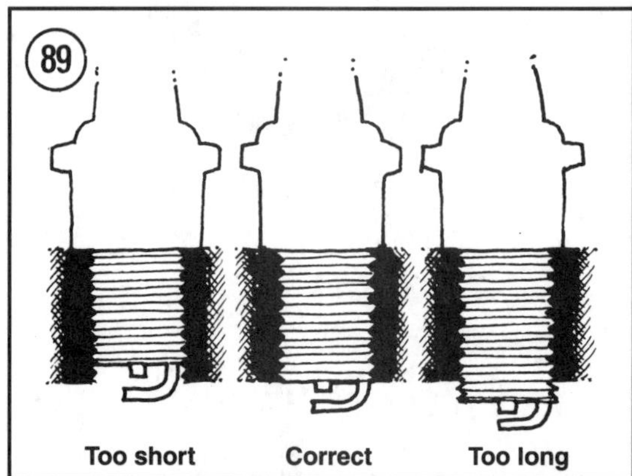

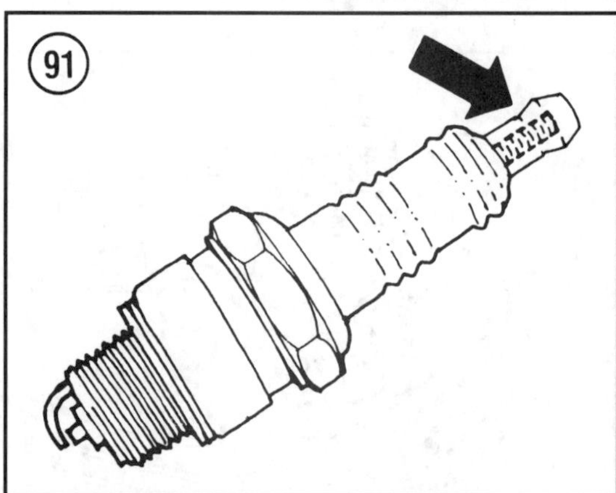

Reading Spark Plugs

Much information about engine and spark plug performance can be determined by careful examination of the spark plug. This information is only valid after performing the following steps.

1. Ride the vehicle a short distance at full throttle.

2. Push the engine stop switch to the OFF position before closing the throttle and simultaneously shift to neutral, then coast and brake to a stop.

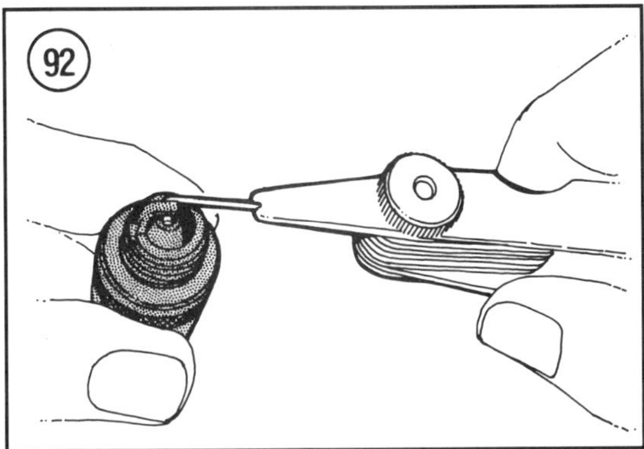

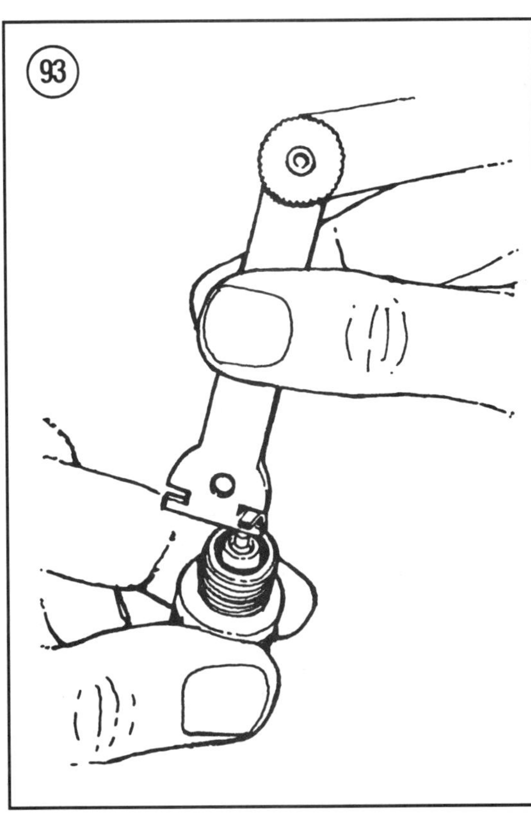

3. Remove the spark plug and examine it. Compare it to **Figure 94** and note the following:

Normal condition

If the plug has a light tan- or gray-colored deposit and no abnormal gap wear or erosion, good engine, carburetion and ignition condition are indicated. The plug in use is of the proper heat range and may be serviced and returned to use.

Carbon fouled

Soft, dry sooty deposits covering the entire firing end of the spark plug are evidence of incomplete combustion. Even though the firing end of the plug is dry, the plug's insulation decreases. The carbon on the plug can create an electrical path that bypasses the electrodes and causes a misfire.

a. Excessively rich air/fuel mixture.
b. Spark plug too cold.
c. Restricted air filter.
d. Retarded ignition timing.
e. Ignition failure.
f. Low compression.
g. Excessive operation at idle speed.

Oil fouled

If the tip of an oil fouled plug has a black insulator tip, a damp oily film over the firing end and a carbon layer over the entire nose. The electrodes are worn. Common causes for this condition are:

a. Incorrect carburetor jetting.
b. Low idle speed or prolonged idling.
c. Ignition component failure.
d. Spark plug heat range too cold.
e. Engine still being broken in.

Oil fouled spark plugs may be cleaned in an emergency, but it is better to replace them. It is important to correct the cause of fouling before the engine is returned to service.

Gap bridging

A plug with this condition will have its electrode gap shorted out by combustion deposits between the electrodes. If this condition is encountered, check for an improper oil type or excessive carbon in the

SPARK PLUG CONDITION

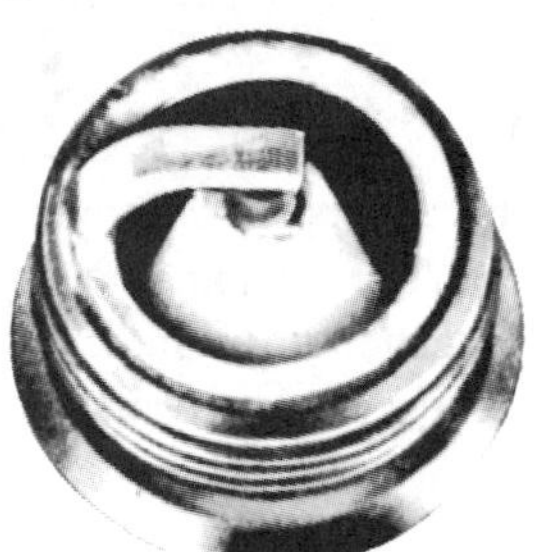

NORMAL

- Identified by light tan or gray deposits on the firing tip.
- Can be cleaned.

GAP BRIDGED

- Identified by deposit buildup closing gap between electrodes.
- Caused by oil or carbon fouling. If deposits are not excessive, the plug can be cleaned.

OIL FOULED

- Identified by wet black deposits on the insulator shell bore and electrodes.
- Caused by excessive oil entering combustion chamber through worn rings and pistons, excessive clearance between valve guides and stems or worn or loose bearings. Can be cleaned. If engine is not repaired, use a hotter plug.

CARBON FOULED

- Identified by black, dry fluffy carbon deposits on insulator tips, exposed shell surfaces and electrodes.
- Caused by too cold a plug, weak ignition, dirty air cleaner, too rich a fuel mixture or excessive idling. Can be cleaned.

LEAD FOULED

- Identified by dark gray, black, yellow or tan deposits or a fused glazed coating on the insulator tip.
- Caused by highly leaded gasoline. Can be cleaned.

WORN

- Identified by severely eroded or worn electrodes.
- Caused by normal wear. Should be replaced.

FUSED SPOT DEPOSIT

- Identified by melted or spotty deposits resembling bubbles or blisters.
- Caused by sudden acceleration. Can be cleaned.

OVERHEATING

- Identified by a white or light gray insulator with small black or gray brown spots and with bluish-burnt appearance of electrodes.
- Caused by engine overheating, wrong type of fuel, loose spark plugs, too hot a plug or incorrect ignition timing. Replace the plug.

PREIGNITION

- Identified by melted electrodes and possibly blistered insulator. Metallic deposits on insulator indicate engine damage.
- Caused by wrong type of fuel, incorrect ignition timing or advance, too hot a plug, burned valves or engine overheating. Replace the plug.

combustion chamber. Be sure to locate and correct the cause of this condition.

Overheating

Badly worn electrodes and premature gap wear, along with a gray or white blistered porcelain insulator surface are signs of overheating. The most common cause for this condition is using a spark plug of the wrong heat range (too hot). If you have not changed to a hotter spark plug but the plug is overheated, consider the following causes:

a. Lean fuel mixture.
b. Ignition timing too advanced.
c. Engine lubrication system malfunction.
d. Engine vacuum leak.
e. Improper spark plug installation (too tight).
f. No spark plug gasket.

Worn out

Corrosive gases formed by combustion and high voltage sparks have eroded the electrodes. Spark plugs in this condition require more voltage to fire under hard acceleration. Replace with a new spark plug.

Preignition

If the electrodes are melted, preignition is almost certainly the cause. Check for carburetor mounting or intake manifold leaks and over advanced ignition timing. It is also possible that a plug of the wrong heat range (too hot) is being used. Find the cause of the preignition before returning the engine into service.

Ignition Timing

All models are equipped with a capacitor discharge ignition system (CDI). This system uses no breaker points, but timing does have to be checked to make sure all components of the ignition system are functioning properly.

Incorrect ignition timing can cause a drastic loss of engine performance and efficiency. It may also cause overheating.

Before starting this procedure, check all electrical connections related to the ignition system. Make sure all connections are tight and free from corrosion and that all ground connections are clean and tight.

1. Start the engine and let it warm approximately 2-3 minutes.
2. Park the vehicle on level ground and apply the parking brake. Shut off the engine.
3. Remove the ignition timing window plug and O-ring (**Figure 95**).
4. Connect a portable tachometer following its manufacturer's instructions.
5. Connect a timing light following its manufacturer's instructions.
6. Restart the engine and let it run at the idle speed indicated in **Table 8**.
7. Adjust the idle speed if necessary as described in this chapter.
8. Aim the timing light at the timing window and pull the trigger. The F mark on the flywheel should line up with the fixed mark on the crankcase as shown in **Figure 96**. If the ignition timing is incorrect, troubleshoot the ignition system as described in Chapter Two.
9. Turn the ignition switch off and disconnect the timing light and portable tachometer.
10. Install the ignition timing window plug and O-ring and tighten securely.

Pilot Air Screw Adjustment

Carefully turn the pilot air screw (**Figure 97**) in until it lightly seats, then back it out the number of turns listed in **Table 8**.

NOTE

Figure 97 *shows the pilot air screw with the carburetor removed for clarity.*

Idle Speed Adjustment

1. Start the engine and let it warm to normal operating temperature.
2. Park the vehicle on level ground, apply the parking brake and shut off the engine.
3. Connect a portable tachometer to the engine following its manufacturer's instructions.
4. Restart the engine and turn the idle speed adjust screw (**Figure 98**) to set the idle speed. See **Table 8** for idle speed specifications.
5. Open and close the throttle a couple of times and check for variation in idle speed. Readjust if necessary.

WARNING

With the engine idling, move the handlebar from side to side. If idle speed increases during this movement, the throttle cable needs adjusting or may be incorrectly routed through the frame. Correct this problem immediately. Do not ride the vehicle in this unsafe condition.

6. Turn the engine off and disconnect the portable tachometer.

STORAGE

Several months of inactivity can cause serious problems and a general deterioration of your Yamaha. This is especially true in areas of weather extremes. This section describes procedures on how to prepare your Yamaha for long term storage. Long term storage is considered to be 60 days or more of non-operation.

Selecting a Storage Area

The most likely place to store your vehicle is in your home garage or workshop. If you do not have a home garage or suitable building, facilities suitable for long-term vehicle storage are readily available for rent or lease in most areas. When selecting a building, consider the following points.

1. The storage area must be dry. Heating is not necessary, but the building should be well insulated to minimize extreme temperature variation.
2. Buildings with large window areas should be avoided, or such windows should be masked (also a good security measure) if direct sunlight can fall on the vehicle.

Preparing Vehicle for Storage

Careful preparation will minimize deterioration and make it easier to restore the vehicle to service later. Use the following procedure.

1. Wash the vehicle completely. Make certain to remove all dirt in all the hard to reach areas. Completely dry all parts.

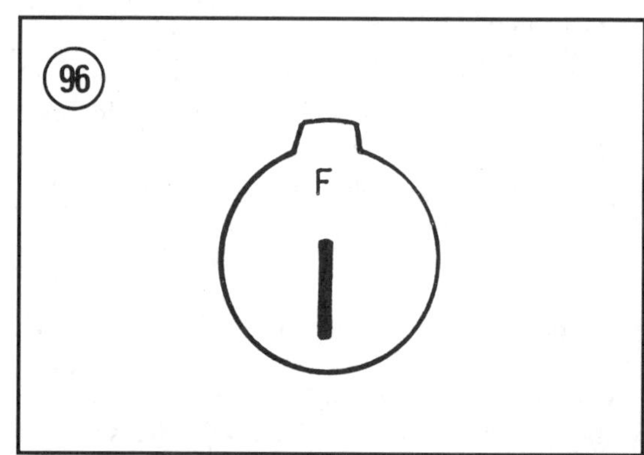

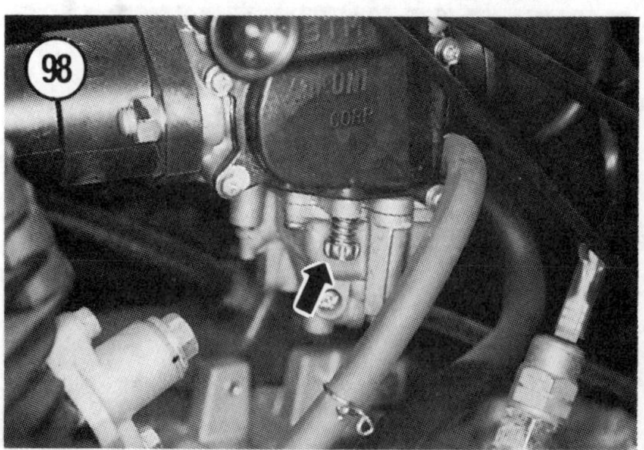

2. Run the engine long enough to warm the engine oil. Drain the oil, regardless of the time since the last oil change. Refill with the normal quantity and type of oil as described in this chapter.
3. Drain all gasoline from the fuel tank, fuel hose, and carburetor. Make sure the fuel tank filler cap is tightened securely and that the vent hose is connected properly.
4. Clean and lubricate the control cables as described in this chapter.
5. Remove the spark plug and add about one tablespoon of engine oil into the cylinder. Then turn the engine over the recoil starter to distribute the oil to the cylinder wall and piston. Reinstall the spark plug and connect the spark plug cap.
6. Tape or tie a plastic bag over the end of the muffler to prevent the entry of moisture.
7. Inflate the tires to the correct pressure and move the vehicle to the storage area. Support the vehicle with all 4 wheels off the ground.
8. Remove the battery and charge it as described in this chapter. Then store the battery in a safe area away from freezing or excessively warm temperatures. Inspect and charge the battery once a month.
9. Clean the battery terminals of all corrosion, then lubricate them with dielectric grease.
10. If the vehicle is being stored in a humid or salt-air area, spray all exposed metal surfaces with a light film of oil. Do not spray the seat, tires or any rubber part.
11. Cover the vehicle with a tarp, blanket or heavy plastic drop cloth. Place this cover over the vehicle mainly as a dust cover—do not wrap it tightly, especially any plastic material, as it may trap moisture, and resulting in rust. Leave room for air to circulate around the vehicle.

Restoring Vehicle to Service

A vehicle that has been properly prepared and stored in a suitable area requires only light maintenance to restore to service.
1. Before removing the vehicle from the storage area, inflate the tires to the correct pressure. Air loss during storage may have nearly flattened the tires.
2. Remove the plug from the end of the muffler.
3. When the vehicle is brought to the work area, refill the fuel tank with fresh gasoline.
4. Install a fresh spark plug and start the engine.
5. Perform the standard tune-up as described earlier in this chapter.
6. Check the operation of the engine stop switch. Oxidation of the switch contacts during storage may make it inoperative.
7. Check the brakes and throttle controls before riding the vehicle.

Table 1 MAINTENANCE AND LUBRICATION SCHEDULE

Every 20-40 hours of engine operation
Clean air filter element.
Initial 1st month
Check and adjust valve clearance.
Check spark plug condition.
Change engine and transfer gear oil.
Clean oil strainer (mounted on engine drain bolt).
Change front differential gear oil.
Change final gear oil.
Check front brake operation and brake fluid level.
Check rear brake operation and adjustment.
Check/adjust clutch operation.
Check wheel condition and runout.
Check wheel bearings for damage.
Check steering operation.
Check/adjust toe-in adjustment.
(continued)

Table 1 MAINTENANCE AND LUBRICATION SCHEDULE (continued)

Check front axle rubber boots for damage.
Check battery condition. Check breather hose (1993-1995) routing.
Check for loose and missing fasteners.

Initial 3 months:
- Check spark plug condition.
- Check/adjust carburetor idle speed and choke operation.
- Check front brake operation and brake fluid level.
- Check rear brake operation and adjustment; adjust if necessary.
- Check steering operation.
- Check/adjust toe-in adjustment.
- Check battery condition. Check breather hose (1993-1995) routing.
- Check for loose and missing fasteners.

Initial 6 months:
- Check and adjust valve clearance.
- Check fuel line for cracks and damage.
- Check/adjust carburetor idle speed and choke operation.
- Check spark plug condition.
- Change engine and transfer gear oil.
- Clean oil strainer (mounted on engine drain bolt).
- Check front brake operation and brake fluid level.
- Check/adjust rear brake operation and adjustment.
- Check clutch operation; adjust if necessary.
- Check/adjust drive select lever adjustment.
- Check wheel condition and runout.
- Check wheel bearings for damage.
- Check steering operation.
- Check/adjust toe-in adjustment.
- Check battery condition. Check breather hose (1993-1995) routing.

Every 6 months after initial 6 month operation:
- Check and adjust valve clearance
- Check fuel line for cracks and damage.
- Check/adjust carburetor idle speed and choke operation.
- Check spark plug condition.
- Check front brake operation and brake fluid level.
- Check/adjust rear brake operation and adjustment.
- Check clutch operation; adjust if necessary.
- Check drive select lever adjustment; adjust if necessary.
- Check wheel condition and runout.
- Check wheel bearings for damage.
- Check steering operation.
- Check/adjust toe-in adjustment.
- Check battery condition. Check breather hose (1993-1995) routing.

Once a year
- Perform the procedures listed under every 6 months after initial 6 month operation, plus the following.
- Change engine and transfer gear oil.

Once a year (continued)
- Clean oil strainer (mounted on engine drain bolt).
- Change front differential gear oil.
- Change final gear oil.
- Inspect front axle rubber boots for damage.

Table 2 TIRE INFLATION PRESSURE

Year	Front psi (kPa)	Rear psi (kPa)
1993-1995	2.4-3.3 (17-23)	3.2-3.9 (22-27)
1996-on	3.2-3.9 (22-27)	3.2-3.9 (22-27)

Table 3 BATTERY CAPACITY

Year	Capacity
1993-1995	12 volt, 14 amp hour
1996-on	12 volt, 18 amp hour

Table 4 BATTERY STATE OF CHARGE

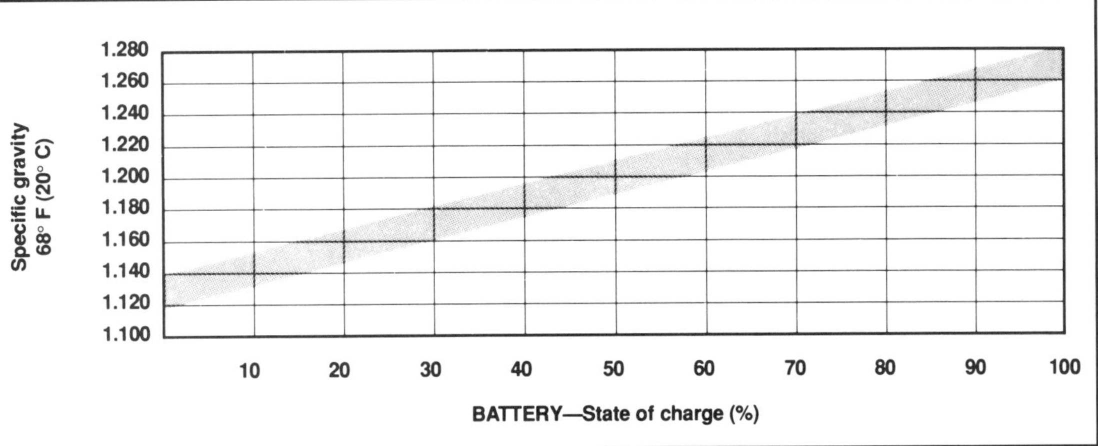

Table 5 RECOMMENDED LUBRICANTS AND FLUIDS

Engine oil	
Grade	API SE
Viscosity	SAE 10W-30, 10W-40, 20W-40
Final gear oil	SAE 80 API GL-4 hypoid gear oil
Front differential gear oil (4-wheel drive)	SAE 80 API GL-4 hypoid gear oil
Battery refill	Distilled water
Brake fluid	DOT 4

Table 6 REFILL CAPACITIES

	ml	U.S. qts.	Imp. qts.
Engine oil and transfer oil			
Without oil filter replacement			
Engine oil only	2400	2.5	2.1
Transfer gear oil only	300	0.32	0.26
Total engine oil and transfer gear oil	2700	2.9	2.4
With oil filter replacement			
Total engine oil and transfer gear oil	2800	3.0	2.5
Engine overhaul total change	3700	3.9	3.3
Final gear case oil			
Oil change	190	0.20	0.17
Overhaul capacity	240	0.26	0.22
Differential gear case			
Oil change	470	0.50	0.41
Overhaul capacity	500	0.53	0.44

Table 7 MAINTENANCE TORQUE SPECIFICATIONS

	N•m	in.-lb.	ft.-lb.
Cam chain tensioner			
Body bolt	10	88	—
Tensioner cap plug	23	—	17
Clutch adjuster locknut	15	—	11
Cylinder head cover screws	10	88	—
Engine oil drain bolt	32	—	23
Front differential gearcase			
Oil fill cap	23	—	17
Drain plugs			
Front	23	—	17
Rear	16	—	11
No. 1 control cable locknuts	25	—	18
Oil filter cover mounting bolts	10	88	—
Oil pressure check bolt	7	62	—
Rear (final) differential gearcase			
Oil fill cap	20	—	14
Drain plug	23	—	17
Spark plug	18	—	13
Tie rod locknuts			
1993-1995	30	—	22
1996-on	35	—	25
Transfer gear case			
Oil fill plug	23	—	17
Drain plug	20	—	14
Valve adjusting nut	20	—	14
Valve cover bolts	10	88	—
Wheel lug nuts			
Front and rear	55	—	40

Table 8 TUNE-UP SPECIFICATIONS

Item	Specification
Carburetor adjustment	
Idle speed	1350-1450 rpm
Pilot air screw (turns out)	2.0
Engine compression	
Standard	920 kPa (131 psi)
Minimum	740 kPa (105 psi)
Maximum	1,020 kPa (145 psi)
Ignition timing	Non-adjustable, see text for procedure
Spark plug	
Type	
Canada and Europe	NGK DR8EA
U.S. and all other	NGK D8EA
Gap	0.6-0.7 mm (0.024-0.028 in.)
Valve clearance (engine cold)	
Intake	0.06-0.10 mm (0.002-0.004 in.)
Exhaust	0.16-0.20 mm (0.006-0.008 in.)

CHAPTER FOUR

ENGINE TOP END

4

The engine is an air-cooled, single camshaft, 2-valve single. Valves are operated by a single chain-driven camshaft.

This chapter provides complete service and overhaul procedures, including information for disassembly, removal, inspection, service and reassembly of the engine top end components. These include the camshaft, valves, cylinder head, piston, piston rings and cylinder block. The components located in the lower end of the engine are covered in Chapter Five.

Before starting any work, refer to Chapter One and read the service hints and the detailed information relating to the use of the measuring equipment that must be used in this chapter. You will do a better job with this information fresh in your mind.

Table 1 lists general engine specifications and **Table 2** lists engine top end service specifications. **Tables 1-4** are at the end of the chapter.

ENGINE PRINCIPLES

Figure 1 explains basic 4-stroke engine operation. This information is helpful when troubleshooting and repairing the engine.

CYLINDER HEAD

The cylinder head can be removed with the engine mounted in the frame or after the entire engine assembly is removed. Refer to **Figure 2** when servicing the cylinder head assembly.

Removal

1. Remove the following components as described in Chapter Fourteen:
   a. Seat.
   b. Front carrier rack.
   c. Front fender.
2. Disconnect the negative battery cable as described in Chapter Three.
3. Remove the following components as described in Chapter Eight:
   a. Fuel tank.
   b. Carburetor.
   c. Exhaust pipe assembly.

NOTE

In Step 4, the mounting bracket must be removed from the cylinder head and the frame to gain enough room for cylinder head removal with the engine in the frame.

4. Remove the bolt and nut (A, **Figure 3**) securing the front engine mounting bracket to the cylinder head. Remove the bolts (B, **Figure 3**) securing the mounting bracket to the frame and remove the bracket.

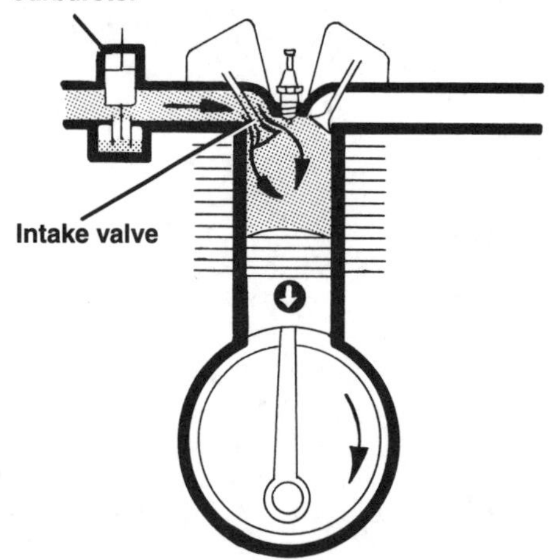

As the piston travels downward, the exhaust valve is closed and the intake valve opens, allowing the new air/fuel mixture from the carburetor to be drawn into the cylinder. When the piston reaches the bottom of its travel (BDC) the intake valve closes and remains closed for the next 1 1/2 revolutions of the crankshaft.

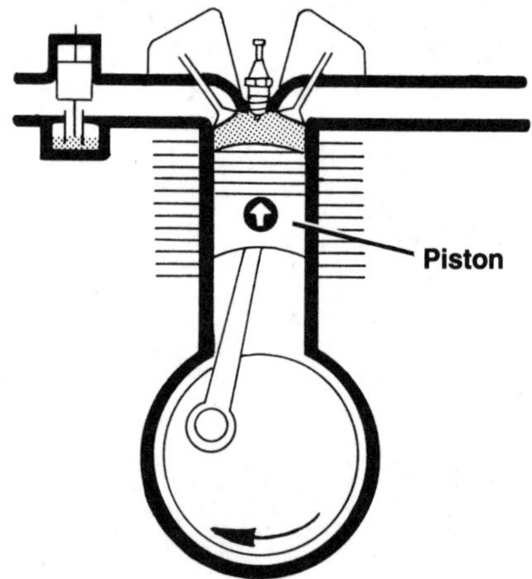

While the crankshaft continues to rotate, the piston moves upward, compressing the air-fuel mixture.

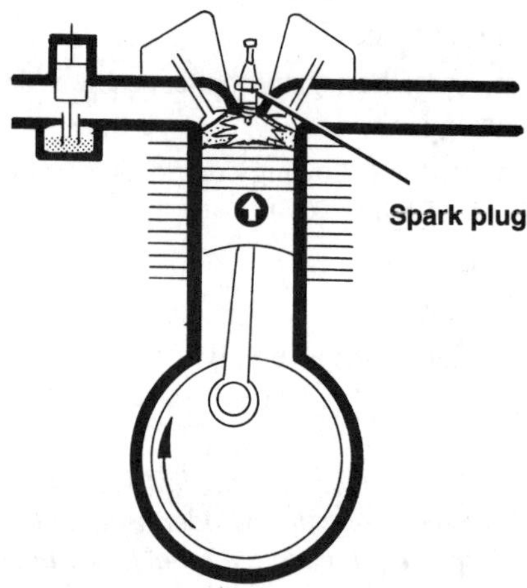

As the piston almost reaches the top of its travel, the spark plug fires, igniting the compressed air/fuel mixture. The piston continues to top dead center (TDC) and is pushed downward by the expanding gases.

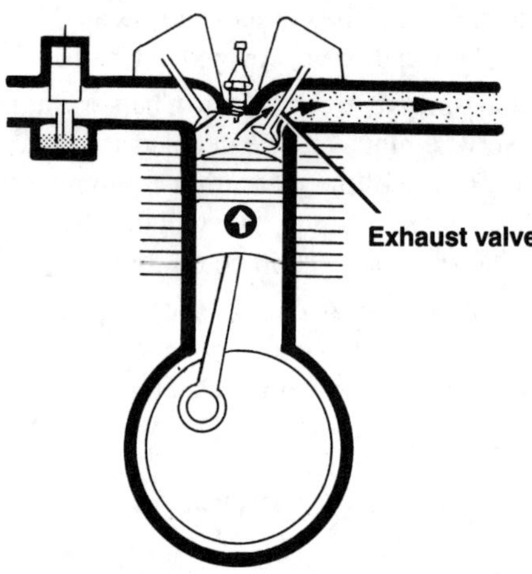

When the piston almost reaches BDC, the exhaust valve opens and remains open until the piston is near TDC. The upward travel of the piston forces the exhaust gses out of the cylinder. After the piston has reached TDC, the exhaust valve closes and the cycle starts all over again.

(2)

CYLINDER HEAD

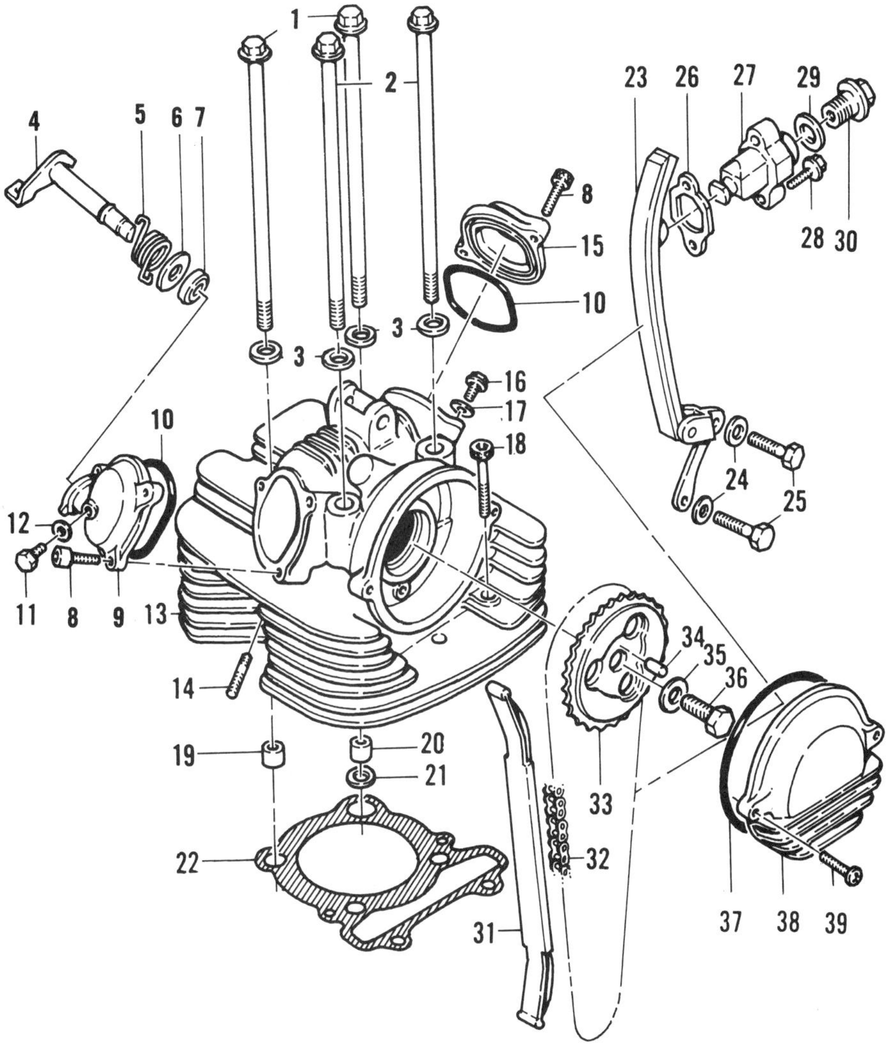

1. Bolt
2. Bolt
3. Washer
4. Decompression lever
5. Spring
6. Washer
7. Seal
8. Allen bolt
9. Valve cover (exhaust)
10. O-ring
11. Pin bolt
12. Washer
13. Cylinder head
14. Studs
15. Valve cover (intake)
16. Bolt
17. Washer
18. Allen bolt
19. Dowel pin
20. Dowel pin
21. Seal
22. Head gasket
23. Rear chain guide
24. Washer
25. Bolt
26. Gasket
27. Chain tensioner
28. Bolt
29. Washer
30. Tensioner plug
31. Front chain guide
32. Cam chain
33. Sprocket
34. Pin
35. Washer
36. Bolt
37. O-ring
38. Cover
39. Bolt

4

5. Remove the recoil starter assembly as described in Chapter Five.
6. Remove the transmission range selector lever cover mounting screws (A, **Figure 4**) and cover (B, **Figure 4**).
7. Remove the ignition timing window plug and O-ring (**Figure 5**).
8. Remove the cylinder head side cover and O-rings (A, **Figure 6**).
9. Remove the exhaust (**Figure 7**) and intake valve covers and O-rings.
10. Remove the spark plug. This will make it easier to turn the engine by hand.
11. The engine must be set at top dead center (TDC) on its compression stroke before removing the upper camshaft sprocket bolt and sprocket in the following procedure. Perform the following:
   a. Turn the crankshaft (B, **Figure 6**) counterclockwise and align the camshaft sprocket index mark (A, **Figure 8**) with the cylinder head mark (B, **Figure 8**).
   b. Now look through the window plug opening (**Figure 5**) and check that the T mark on the rotor is aligned with the crankcase index mark (**Figure 9**). If these marks are not aligned, turn the crankshaft one revolution counterclockwise and align the rotor T mark with the crankcase index mark (**Figure 9**).
   c. When the camshaft sprocket and rotor marks are properly aligned, both rocker arms can be moved sideways by hand. This indicates that the intake and exhaust valves are closed.
12. Remove the transmission range select lever as described in Chapter Seven.
13. To remove the camshaft chain tensioner:
   a. Loosen, but do not remove, the camshaft chain tensioner plug (A, **Figure 10**).

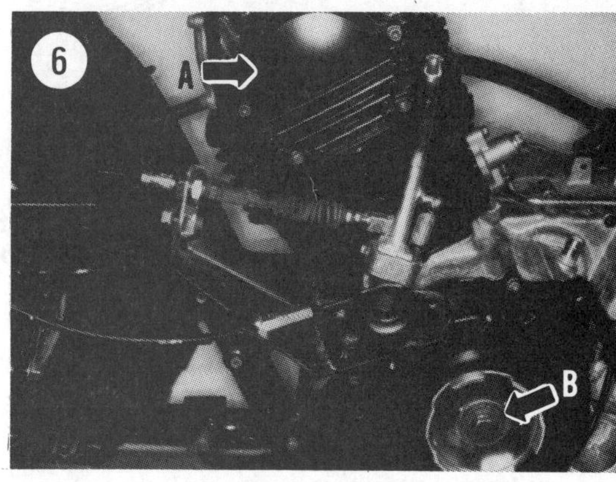

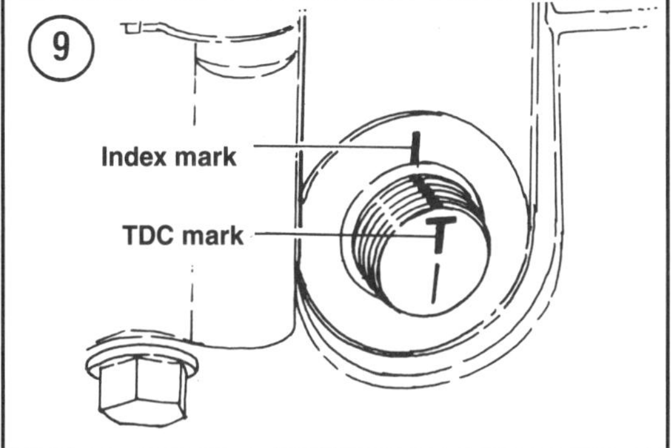

b. Remove the camshaft chain tensioner mounting bolts (B, **Figure 10**) and remove the tensioner body from the cylinder block.

14. Secure the camshaft chain with safety wire. This will prevent the chain from falling down into the cylinder chain tunnel.

15. Hold the crankshaft starter pulley with a wrench and loosen the camshaft sprocket bolt (C, **Figure 8**).

16. Remove the camshaft sprocket bolt and washer. Then slide the camshaft sprocket (A, **Figure 11**) off of the camshaft. Disengage the chain (B, **Figure 11**) from the sprocket and remove the sprocket. Do not drop the locating pin (C, **Figure 11**) installed in the end of the camshaft into the engine.

17. Tie the camshaft chain to the frame with a piece of wire to keep the chain from falling down into the crankcase.

18. Place a clean shop cloth into the cylinder head cavity and remove the locating pin (C, **Figure 11**) from the end of the camshaft.

NOTE

*The camshaft and both rocker arms can be removed with the cylinder head mounted in the frame. To do so, refer to **Camshaft and Rocker Arm Removal** in this chapter.*

19. Following the pattern shown in **Figure 12**, loosen the cylinder head mounting bolts in equal amounts until all of the bolts are loose.

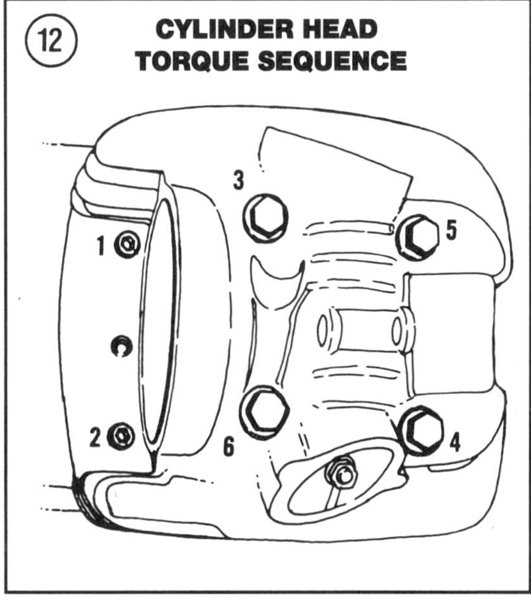

4

20. Remove the 2 cylinder head Allen bolts (D, **Figure 8**).
21. Remove the 4 cylinder head mounting bolts and washers.

CAUTION
The cooling fins are fragile and may be damaged if tapped or pried on too hard. Never use a metal hammer when loosening the cylinder head in Step 22.

22. Tap the cylinder head with a rubber mallet to break it free from the head gasket.
23. Lift the cylinder head slightly then pivot the rear of the head (intake side) up and toward the right-hand side and remove the cylinder head. Guide the camshaft chain through the cavity in the cylinder head.
24. Tie the camshaft chain (A, **Figure 13**) to the frame.
25. Remove the cylinder head gasket.
26. Remove the exhaust side camshaft chain guide (B, **Figure 13**).
27. Remove the dowel pins and O-ring (C, **Figure 13**) from the top of the cylinder block. Discard the O-ring seal as a new one must be used during installation.
28. Cover the cylinder block with a clean shop rag or paper towels.
29. If necessary, remove the camshaft and rocker arms as described in this chapter.

Cylinder Head Inspection

1. Perform the *Solvent Test* listed under *Valves and Valve Components* in this chapter. If there is fluid leakage during this test, follow the instructions listed in the procedure to find the cause of the leak.
2. Remove all traces of gasket residue from the cylinder head (**Figure 14**) and cylinder block mating surfaces. Do not scratch the gasket surface.
3. Without removing the valves, remove all carbon deposits from the combustion chamber (**Figure 14**). Use a fine wire brush dipped in solvent or make a scraper from hardwood. Take care not to damage the head, valves or spark plug threads.

CAUTION
If the combustion chamber is cleaned while the valves are removed, you may damage the valve seat surfaces. A damaged or even slightly scratched valve seat will cause poor valve seating.

4. Examine the spark plug threads in the cylinder head for damage. If damage is minor or if the threads are dirty or clogged with carbon, clean the threads with a spark plug thread tap. If necessary, repair the threads using a steel thread insert. Thread insert kits can be purchased at automotive supply stores or you can have the inserts installed at a Yamaha dealership or machine shop.

NOTE
When using a tap to clean spark plug threads, coat the tap with an aluminum tap cutting fluid or kerosene.

NOTE
Aluminum spark plug threads are commonly damaged due to galling, cross-threading and overtightening. To prevent galling, apply an antiseize compound on the plug threads before installation and do not overtighten.

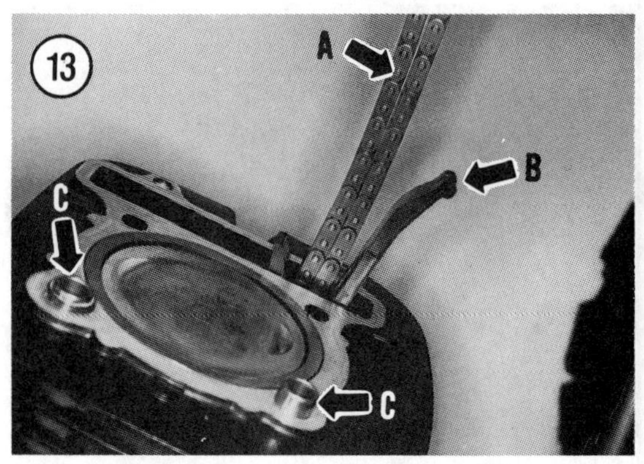

5. After removing carbon from the combustion chamber and valve ports and cleaning the spark plug hole, clean the entire head in solvent.

NOTE
If the cylinder head is bead-blasted, clean the head thoroughly with solvent and then with hot soapy water. Residue grit seats in small crevices and other areas and can be hard to get out. Also chase each exposed thread with a tap to remove grit between the threads. Residue grit left in the engine will contaminate the oil and cause premature piston, ring and bearing wear.

6. Examine the piston crown. The crown should show no signs of wear or damage. If the piston crown appears pecked or spongy-looking, also check the spark plug, valves and combustion chamber for aluminum deposits. If these deposits are found, the cylinder is suffering from excessive heat caused by a lean fuel mixture or preignition.

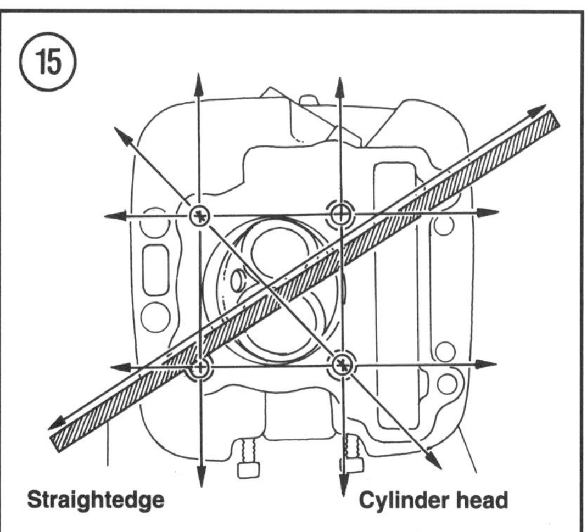

7. Inspect the intake manifold for cracks or other damage that would allow unfiltered air to enter the engine.
8. Check the combustion chamber (**Figure 14**) and both ports for cracks. A cracked head must be replaced if it cannot be repaired by welding.
9. Inspect the exhaust pipe studs for damage. If necessary, clean the threads with the correct size metric die. If necessary, securely tighten the studs.
10. Measure cylinder head warpage by placing a straightedge across the gasket surface at several points (**Figure 15**). Insert a feeler gauge between the straightedge (**Figure 15**) and cylinder head at each location. **Table 2** lists the maximum allowable warpage limit. Warpage or nicks in the cylinder head surface could cause an air leak and result in overheating. If warpage exceeds this limit, the cylinder head must be resurfaced or replaced. Consult a Yamaha dealership or machine shop experienced in this type of work.
11. Examine the camshaft bearing and bearing surface during *Camshaft Inspection* in this chapter.
12. Check the cylinder head for cracked or missing cooling fins.
13. Check the mounting boss in the top of the cylinder head for cracks or other damage.
14. Remove the cylinder head oil flow check plug and washer (**Figure 16**). Apply compressed air to the oil gallery hole in the cylinder head, make sure the gallery is clear. Clean the passage if contaminated.
15. Check the cylinder head bolts for thread damage, cracks and twisting. Check the washers for cracks and other damage.
16. Check the machined surface on the cylinder head where the cylinder head bolts and washers ride. This surface must be smooth to provide a good seat for the washer and bolt so the bolts can be properly tightened to the correct torque value.

Camshaft Chain Tensioner Inspection

Inspect the automatic camshaft chain tensioner for damaged parts prior to reassembly.

1. Remove the plug and washer and withdraw the spring (**Figure 17**).
2. Remove all gasket residue from the camshaft chain tensioner and cylinder block gasket surfaces.
3. Clean all parts in solvent and dry thoroughly.
4. Inspect the entire body and mounting flanges (**Figure 17**) for wear or damage.

5. Check the plug for cracks or damaged threads.
6. Check the spring for bending, unequally spaced coils or other damage.
7. Check the tensioner rack teeth for damage (**Figure 18**).
8. Replace any component as required.

Installation

1. Clean all gasket material from the cylinder head and cylinder mating surfaces.
2. If removed, install the following components as described in this chapter:
   a. Valves.
   b. Camshaft.
   c. Rocker arms and shafts.
3. Install the 2 cylinder head dowel pins (C, **Figure 13**) into the cylinder block. Install a *new* O-ring around the rear dowel pin (C, **Figure 13**).
4. Install a new cylinder head gasket over the dowel pins and cylinder block.
5. If the crankshaft was rotated away from TDC, perform the following:
   a. Lift the camshaft chain and engage it with the lower crankshaft chain sprocket. Hold the chain in this position when turning the crankshaft.

CAUTION
The camshaft chain must be kept tight against its sprocket when turning the crankshaft. Otherwise, the chain can roll off the sprocket and bind in the lower end, causing chain damage.

   b. Turn the crankshaft counterclockwise and align the T mark on the rotor with the crankcase index mark (**Figure 9**).
6. Install the exhaust side camshaft chain guide into the cylinder head chain guide slot (B, **Figure 13**). Make sure the chain guide's sliding surface faces toward the camshaft chain.
7. Position the cylinder head between the frame and cylinder block and run the camshaft chain and its safety wire through the cylinder head chain tunnel. Tie the safety wire to the frame.
8. Move the cylinder head into position, then check that the dowel pins, O-ring and head gasket are still in place (**Figure 19**).
9. Install the cylinder head into position and push it down until it is completely seated over the dowel pins and head gasket.
10. Retie the camshaft chain to the frame.
11. Lubricate the cylinder head bolt threads, bolt head lower surfaces and the washers with engine oil. This will ensure the bolts will be tightened to the correct torque specification.
12. Install the 4 cylinder head hex head bolts and washers (**Figure 20**).

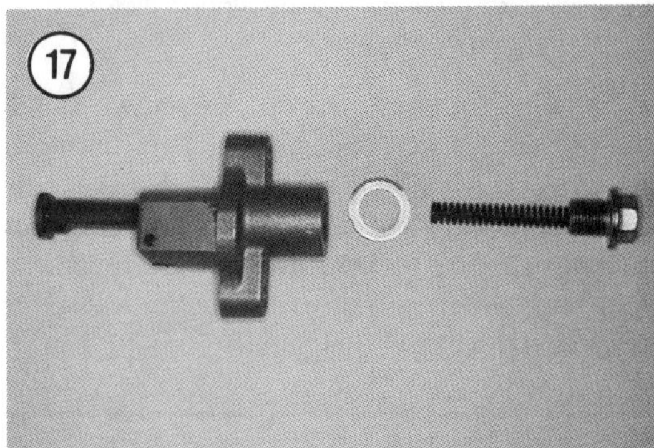

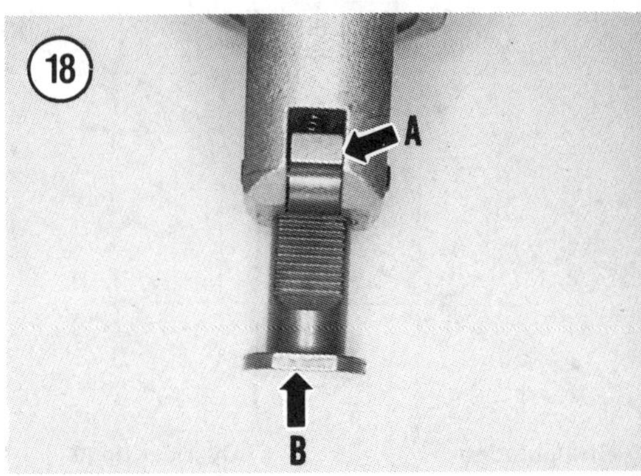

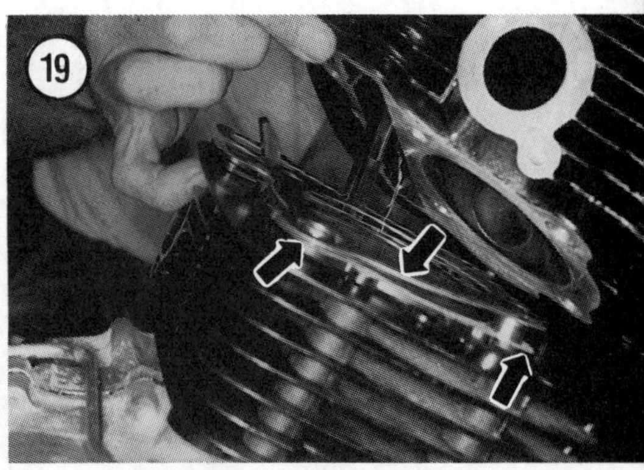

13. Install the 2 Allen bolts (no washers) as shown in D, **Figure 8**.

14. Tighten the 4 cylinder head mounting bolts finger-tight, then the 2 Allen bolts finger-tight.

15. Tighten the 4 hex head bolts (10 mm) and 2 Allen bolts (8 mm) in 2-3 stages in the pattern shown in **Figure 21**. Tighten to the final torque specification listed in **Table 3**.

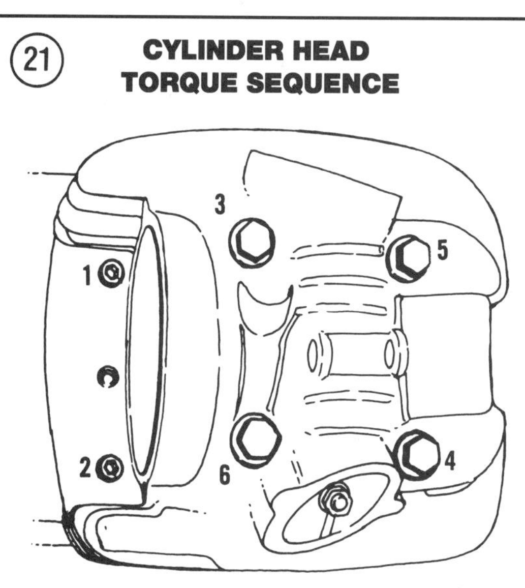

CYLINDER HEAD TORQUE SEQUENCE

16. Confirm that the flywheel T mark is aligned with the crankcase timing mark as shown in **Figure 9**. If not, repeat Step 5.

17. Place a clean shop cloth in the cylinder head cavity to prevent the locating pin from falling down into the crankcase when installing it in Step 18.

NOTE

Spray aerosol electrical contact cleaner into the locating hole in the camshaft. This will remove any residual cleaning solvent or oil from the hole. If solvent or oil remains in the hole, the locating pin will not stay in place and will tend to pop back out when it is pushed into place due to trapped air.

18. Install the locating pin (**Figure 22**) into the hole in the camshaft. Push the pin until it bottoms out. Make sure it stays in place and does not start to pop out.

NOTE

Because of chain slack, the camshaft chain can easily slip off of the crankshaft sprocket. Pull up on the chain and make sure it is properly engaged with the crankshaft sprocket when installing the camshaft sprocket in the following steps.

19. Untie and remove the wire from the camshaft chain .

20. Turn the camshaft so its locating pin (A, **Figure 23**) aligns with the cylinder head index mark (B, **Figure 23**).

21. Mesh the camshaft sprocket with the drive chain so that its timing mark (C, **Figure 23**) faces out and aligns with the cylinder head index mark (B, **Figure 23**).

22. Slide the camshaft sprocket onto the camshaft, engaging the notch in the sprocket with the camshaft locating pin (**Figure 23**).
23. Make sure the camshaft sprocket timing mark (C, **Figure 23**) is aligned with the cylinder head index mark (B, **Figure 23**). If not, remove the sprocket and reposition it in the drive chain, then reinstall it.
24. When the timing marks are correct, install the camshaft sprocket mounting bolt and washer and tighten finger-tight (**Figure 24**).

CAUTION
Do not rotate the crankshaft more than 1/2 turn (180°) or piston and valve damage may occur.

25. Turn the crankshaft clockwise and then counterclockwise (less than 1/4 turn both ways) and then realign the timing marks. This step removes slack from the camshaft chain.
26. Insert your finger through the camshaft chain tensioner hole in the cylinder block and push hard against the camshaft chain. Make sure the camshaft sprocket timing mark aligns with the cylinder head timing mark. If not, remove the camshaft sprocket and reinstall it so the timing marks are aligned.
27. Hold the starter pulley with a wrench and torque the camshaft sprocket bolt (**Figure 24**) as specified in **Table 3**.
28. Install the camshaft chain tensioner as follows:
   a. Remove the camshaft chain tensioner end cap, washer and spring, if you have not previously done so.
   b. Release the camshaft chain tensioner one-way latch (A, **Figure 25**) with your finger and push the tensioner rod (B, **Figure 25**) into the tensioner body until it stops and locks in place. See **Figure 26**.
   c. Install a new gasket onto the camshaft chain tensioner.
   d. Insert the camshaft chain tensioner into the cylinder with the one-way latch facing down.
   e. Install the tensioner body 6 mm mounting bolts (**Figure 27**) and tighten as specified in **Table 3**.
   f. Install the spring, washer and end cap bolt (**Figure 28**). Push the end cap bolt into position and thread it into the tensioner body. Tighten the tensioner end cap bolt as specified in **Table 3**.

29. Check valve adjustment as described in Chapter Three.

30. Install the spark plug and reconnect the spark plug cap.

31. Inspect the valve cover and side cover O-rings and replace if damaged. Apply a lithium-soap base grease to the O-rings and install them into their cover grooves.

32. Install the valve covers with their inner ridge facing up as shown in **Figure 29**. Install and tighten

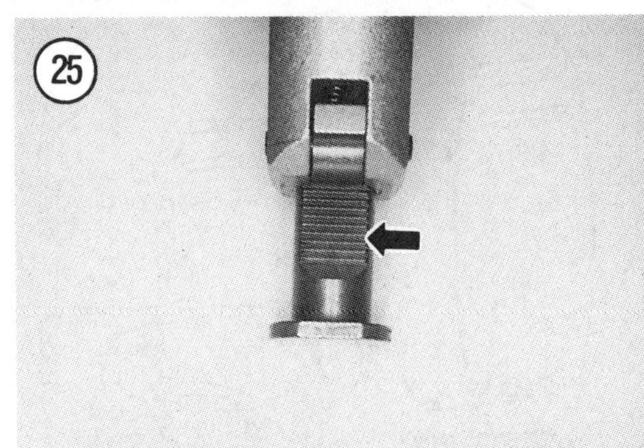

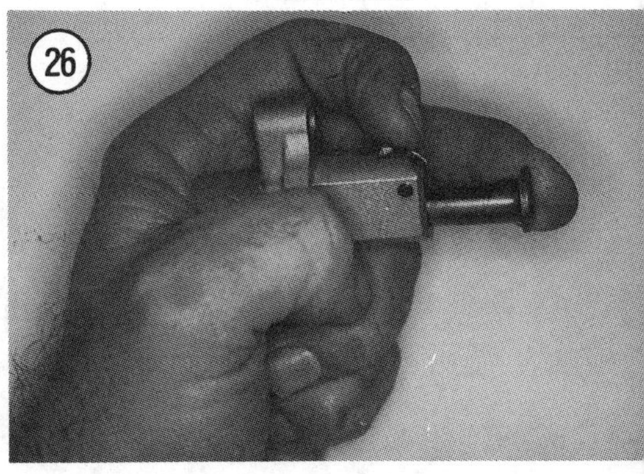

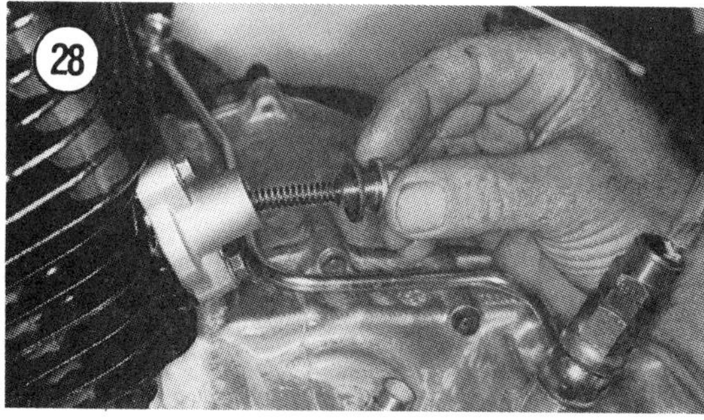

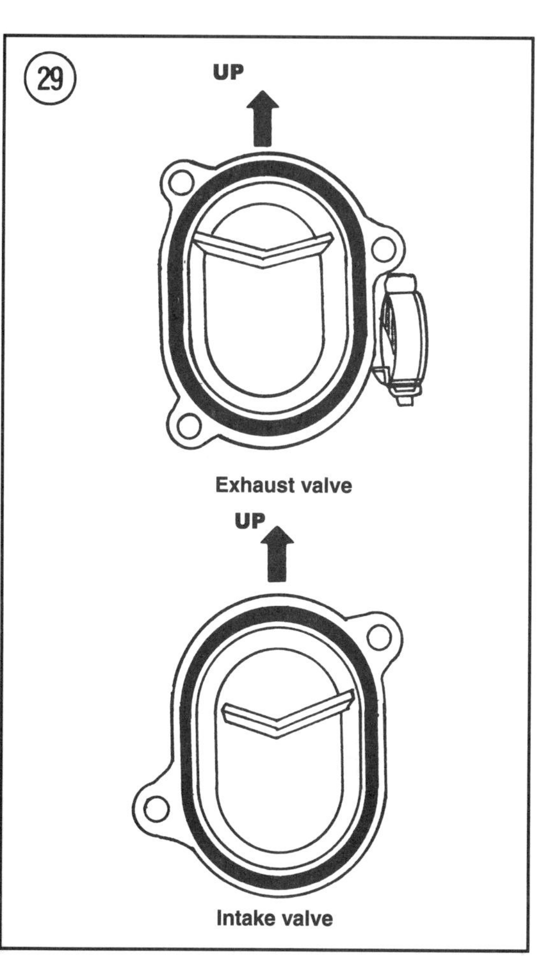

the valve cover mounting bolts as specified in **Table 3**.

33. Install the cylinder head side cover and O-ring (A, **Figure 6**). Tighten the side cover mounting bolts as specified in **Table 3**.

34. Install the ignition timing window plug and O-ring and tighten securely.

35. Install the recoil starter assembly as described in Chapter Five.

36. Install the transmission range select lever as described in Chapter Seven.

37. Install the upper front engine mounting bracket to the frame and install the mounting bolts (B, **Figure 3**). Install the bolt and nut (A, **Figure 3**) securing the front engine mounting bracket to the cylinder head. Tighten the bolts and nut as specified in **Table 3**.

38. Install the following components as described in Chapter Eight:

   a. Exhaust pipe.
   b. Carburetor.
   c. Fuel tank.

39. Reconnect the negative battery cable at the battery as described in Chapter Three.

40. Install the following components as described in Chapter Fourteen:

   a. Front fender.
   b. Front carrier rack.
   c. Seat.

41. Start the engine and check for fuel, exhaust and compression leaks.

CAMSHAFT AND ROCKER ARMS

A single camshaft is mounted in the cylinder head. The camshaft is held in place with a ball bearing and needle bearing. The camshaft is driven by a chain from the timing sprocket on the crankshaft. The camshaft and both rocker arms can be removed with the engine in the frame.

Refer to **Figure 30** when performing this procedure.

Special Tools

The Yamaha slide hammer set (part No. YU-01083) or equivalent is required to remove the rocker arms shafts from the cylinder head. If you are going to fabricate or assemble a slide hammer assembly, the threaded shaft requires M6 × 1.00 mm threads.

NOTE
This procedure is shown with the cylinder head removed from the engine. As previously mentioned the camshaft can be removed with the engine either in or out of the frame.

Removal

1. Park the vehicle on level ground and set the parking brake.

2. Remove the camshaft sprocket as described under *Cylinder Head Removal* in this chapter.

NOTE
If the engine is mounted in the frame, it is unnecessary to remove the upper engine mount bracket, carburetor and exhaust pipe when removing the camshaft and rocker arms.

3. Pry back the lockwasher tabs and remove the 2 camshaft retainer bolts (A, **Figure 31**).

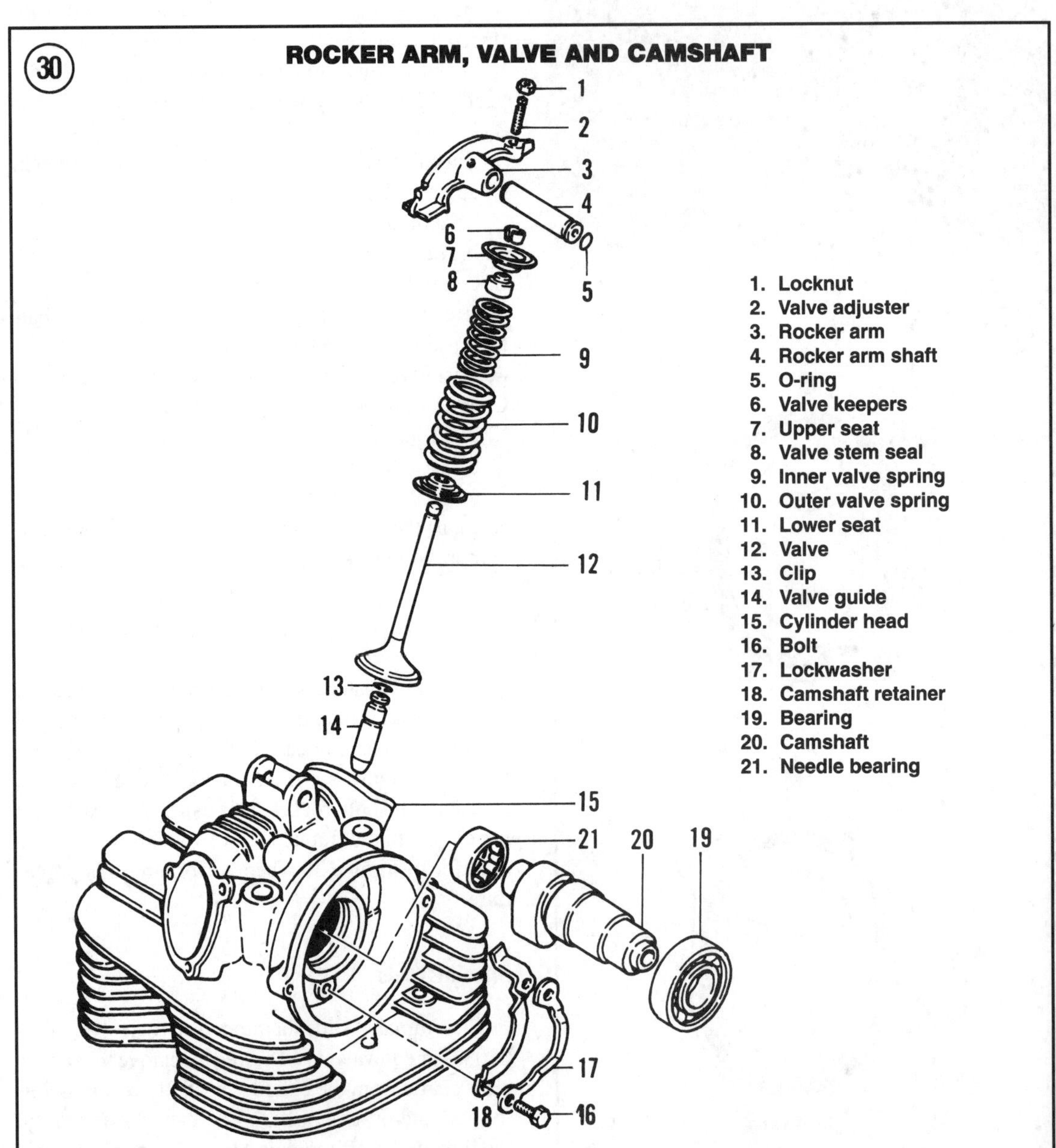

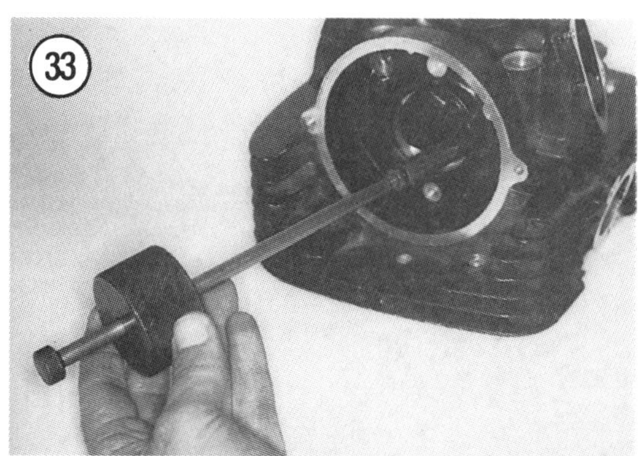

4. Remove the lockwasher (B, **Figure 31**) and camshaft retainer (C, **Figure 31**).

5. Thread the camshaft sprocket mounting bolt into the camshaft and carefully pull the camshaft out of the cylinder head. See **Figure 32**.

NOTE
Both rocker arms and shafts are identical (same part numbers). However, because these parts have developed a wear pattern, label the rocker arms and shafts to avoid mixing the parts. When removing the rocker arm assemblies in the following steps, mark them in sets: E (exhaust) or I (intake).

6. Thread a slide hammer (Yamaha part No. YU-01083) or equivalent into one of the rocker arm shafts. Operate the slide hammer and remove the rocker arm shaft and O-ring (**Figure 33**). Then remove the rocker arm (**Figure 34**).

7. Repeat Step 6 for the opposite rocker arm assembly.

Camshaft Inspection

When measuring the camshaft components, compare the measurements to the specifications in **Table 2**. Replace parts that are out of specification or show damage as described in this section.

1. Check the camshaft lobes (A, **Figure 35**) for wear. The lobes should not be scored and the edges should be square.

2. Measure the camshaft lobe height (**Figure 36**) and the base circle diameter (**Figure 37**) with a micrometer.

3. Check the camshaft bearing journal (B, **Figure 35**) for wear and scoring.

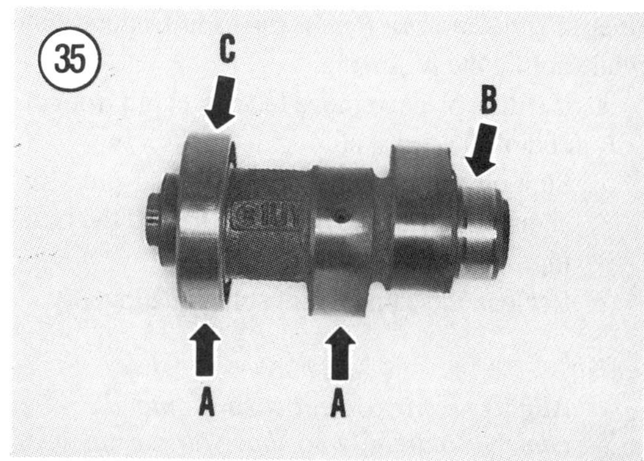

4

4. The left-hand camshaft bearing (C, **Figure 35**) is a press-fit. Do not remove the bearing unless you are going to replace it or the camshaft. Refer to *Camshaft Bearings* in this section.
5. Place the camshaft between centers and measure its runout with a dial indicator—position the dial indicator stem against the camshaft bearing journal.
6. Clean the camshaft oil holes and passages with compressed air.

Camshaft Bearings Inspection/Replacement

The camshaft bearing assembly consists of the following:

a. The left-hand bearing is a single row ball bearing, rubber shielded on one side (C, **Figure 35**). This bearing is a press-fit on the camshaft.
b. A caged needle bearing, which supports the right-hand camshaft journal, is pressed into a recess in the cylinder head (**Figure 38**).

NOTE
Do not remove the bearings unless they require replacement.

1. Clean the camshaft/bearing assembly in solvent. Blow dry with compressed air.
2. Hold the camshaft and rotate the outer bearing race (C, **Figure 35**) with your hand. The bearing should turn smoothly with no roughness, binding or excessive play. The bearing should show no signs of overheating. Bearing shield should not be dented or otherwise damaged. If the bearing does not show visual damage but turns roughly, reclean the bearing and recheck. If the condition still persists, replace the bearing as described in Step 3.
3. To replace the left-hand bearing (C, **Figure 35**), refer to *Ball-Bearing Replacement* in Chapter One while noting the following:

a. If still in place, remove the dowel pin from the end of the camshaft.
b. Support the bearing in a press and press the camshaft off of the bearing. Discard the bearing.
c. Reclean the camshaft in solvent. Blow dry.

CAUTION
Align and press the bearing onto the camshaft carefully so that you do not damage the bearing outer shield. A damaged shield will leak oil.

d. Align the new bearing with the camshaft (shielded side facing out) and press the bearing onto the camshaft shoulder until it bottoms out on the camshaft shoulder.
e. Lubricate the bearing with new engine oil.

NOTE
If the camshaft is not going to be immediately installed in the engine, store the

36

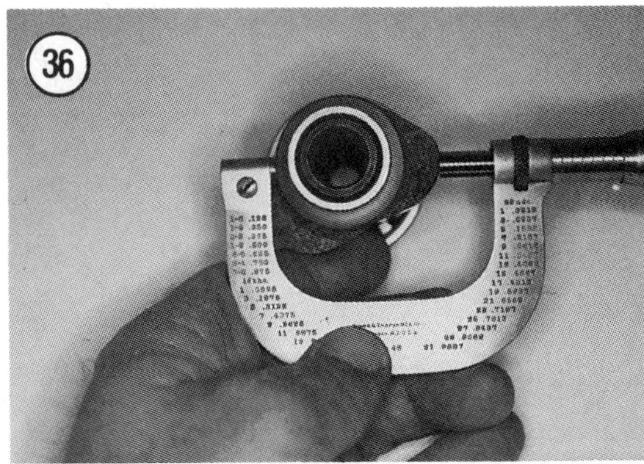

37

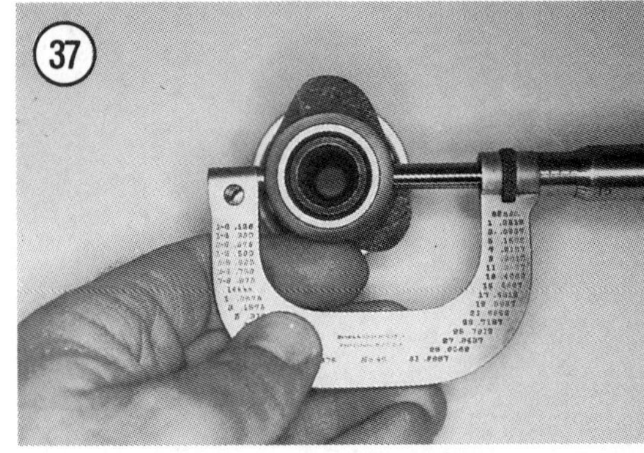

38

camshaft/bearing assembly in a plastic bag to prevent bearing contamination.

4. Inspect the needle bearing (**Figure 38**) for visual damage. Then turn the bearing rollers with a finger, checking for roughness or damaged rollers. If the bearing is damaged, replace the bearing as described in Step 5.

5. To replace the needle bearing (**Figure 38**):
   a. Support the cylinder head and remove the needle bearing with a universal internal (blind)bearing remover.
   b. Clean the cylinder head in solvent. Blow dry with compressed air.
   c. Support the cylinder head and press the new bearing into the cylinder recess until it bottoms out. Install the bearing with its manufacturer's numbers facing out.

39

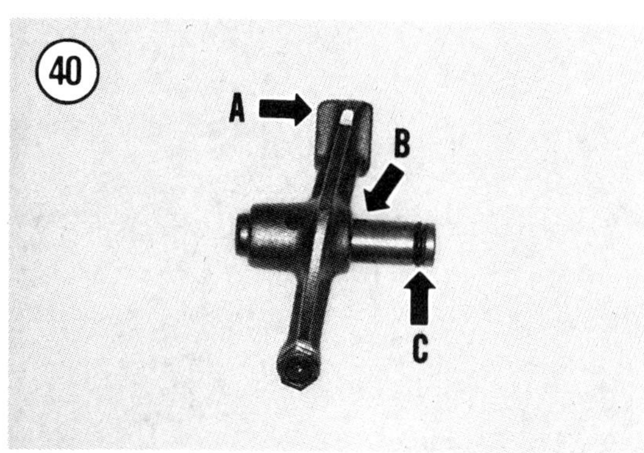

40

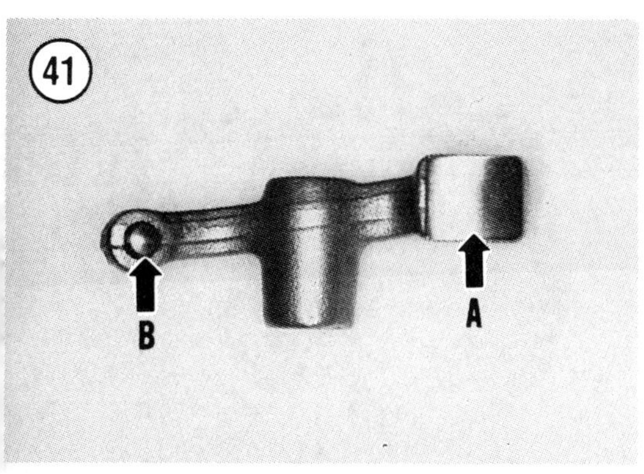

41

Camshaft Sprocket Inspection

Inspect the upper camshaft sprocket (**Figure 39**) for worn, broken or chipped teeth. If the upper sprocket is damaged or worn, inspect the chain guides, cam chain and the lower sprocket (mounted on the crankshaft) for damage.

Rocker Arms and Shafts Inspection

When measuring the rocker arms (A, **Figure 40**) and shafts (B, **Figure 40**) in this section, compare the measurements to the specifications in **Table 2.** Replace parts that are out of specification or show damage as described in this section.

1. Clean and dry all parts.
2. Inspect the rocker arm pad (A, **Figure 41**) where it rides on the camshaft lobe and where the adjuster rides on the valve stem (B, **Figure 41**). Check for scratches, flat spots, uneven wear and scoring.
3. Replace the valve adjuster (B, **Figure 41**) if it has stretched or damaged in anyway.
4. Inspect the rocker arms (A, **Figure 40**) for excessive wear or damage.
5. Inspect the rocker arm shaft (B, **Figure 40**) for signs of wear or scoring.
6. Install a new O-ring (C, **Figure 40**) onto the rocker arm shaft prior to installing the rocker arm.
7. Insert the rocker arm shaft into the rocker arm (**Figure 40**). Rotate it slowly while checking for any binding or roughness.
8. Calculate the rocker arm-to-shaft clearance as follows:
   a. Measure the rocker arm (A, **Figure 40**) bore diameter with a small hole gauge, then measure the small hole gauge with a micrometer and record the measurement.
   b. Measure the rocker arm shaft (B, **Figure 40**) outer diameter and record the measurement.
   c. Subtract the measurement in substep b from the measurement in substep a to determine

rocker arm-to-shaft clearance. Compare the actual clearance to the specification in **Table 2**.

9. Repeat for the other rocker arm assembly.

Installation

1. Install a new O-ring (C, **Figure 40**) in each rocker arm shaft groove.
2. Coat the rocker arm shaft, O-ring and rocker arm bore with assembly oil.

NOTE
Install the rocker arms and shafts in their original positions in the cylinder head. Refer to your marks made during the removal procedure.

3. Install the exhaust rocker arm in the cylinder head with the valve adjuster facing out (**Figure 42**).
4. Position the rocker arm shaft with the O-ring end going in last (**Figure 43**) and install it part way into the cylinder head and part way through the rocker arm.
5. Install a M6 × 1.00 mm bolt into the end of the rocker arm.

NOTE
*The exhaust rocker arm shaft is held in place by one of the cylinder head mounting bolts. Make sure the end of the shaft is clear of the mounting bolt hole (**Figure 44**); otherwise, the mounting bolt cannot be installed during cylinder head installation.*

6. Hold onto the rocker arm to make sure alignment is correct and carefully tap the rocker arm shaft into the cylinder head with a soft faced mallet (**Figure 45**). Continue to drive the rocker arm shaft through the cylinder head until it aligns and enters the rocker arm and bottoms in the cylinder head (**Figure 46**). Remove the bolt installed in Step 5.

NOTE
*After installing the rocker arm shaft, check the end of the rocker arm shaft (**Figure 46**) for bits of rubber, indicating that the O-ring was torn during installation. If any damaged material is noted, remove the rocker arm shaft, replace the O-ring and reinstall the shaft.*

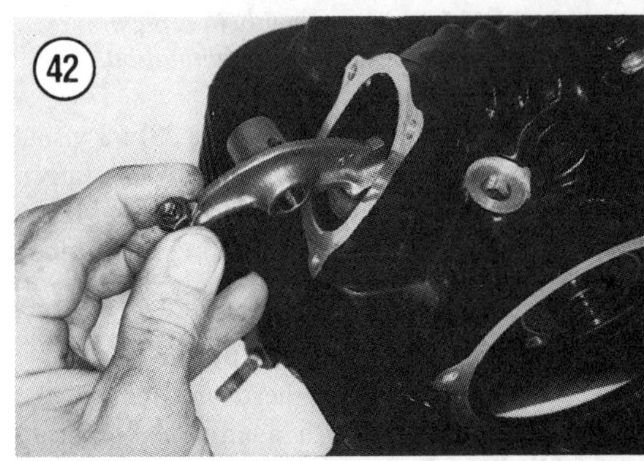
42

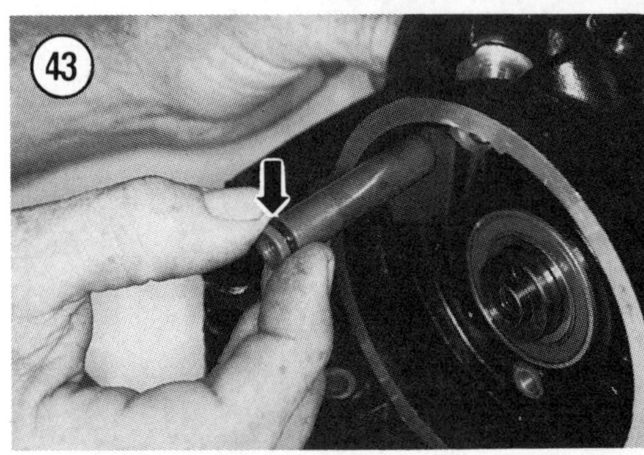
43

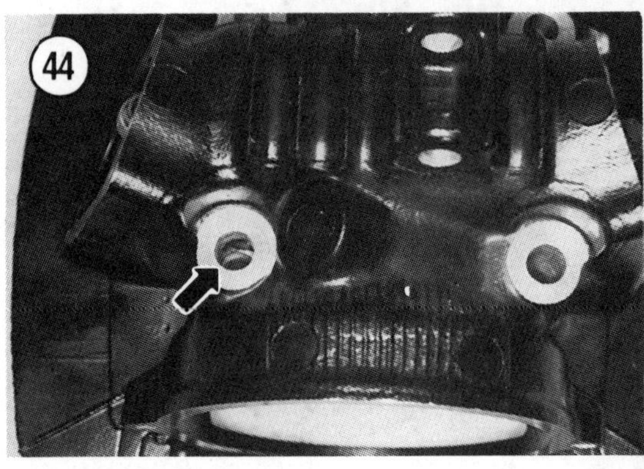
44

45

7. Repeat Steps 3-6 to install the intake rocker arm and shaft.

8. Coat the camshaft journal, lobes and bearing rollers with engine oil.

9. Hold the rocker arms up with your finger and thumb, then insert the camshaft through the cylinder head opening and seat it into the needle bearing. Push the camshaft in until it bottoms out. Position the camshaft so that its locating pin hole (**Figure 47**) faces up.

10. Install the camshaft retainer (**Figure 48**). The long arm on the retainer goes into the intake rocker arm shaft receptacle.

11. Install the lockwasher (A, **Figure 49**) and the 2 camshaft retainer bolts (B, **Figure 49**). Tighten the camshaft retainer bolts as specified in **Table 3**. Bend the lockwasher tabs over the bolt heads.

12. Install the cylinder head and camshaft sprocket as described in this chapter.

4

CAMSHAFT CHAIN

A continuous camshaft chain is used on all models. Do not cut the chain, as replacement link components are not available.

Removal/Installation

1. Remove the camshaft sprocket as described under *Cylinder Head Removal* in this chapter.

2. Remove the magneto rotor as described in Chapter Five.

3. Slip the camshaft chain (A, **Figure 50**) off of the lower sprocket and remove it.

4. Install by reversing these steps.

Inspection

NOTE
Service specifications for the camshaft chain are not available. If the chain is noisy and the tensioner is working properly, the chain is probably excessively worn.

1. Clean the camshaft chain in solvent. Blow dry with compressed air.
2. Check the camshaft chain for:
   a. Worn or damaged pins and rollers.
   b. Cracked or damaged side plates.
3. Replace the camshaft chain if damaged. If the chain is severely worn, replace the upper sprocket (**Figure 39**) at the same time. The lower sprocket on the crankshaft cannot be replaced separately. If worn or damaged, the crankshaft assembly must be rebuilt or replaced.

CAUTION
Do not attempt to repair the camshaft chain as this could lead to expensive engine damage if the chain should break during engine operation.

CHAIN GUIDES

A front guide and rear chain guide/damper are used along with the chain tensioner to maintain the correct amount of tension on the camshaft chain.

Removal/Installation

1. Remove the front chain guide as described under *Cylinder Head Removal* in this chapter.
2. To remove the rear chain guide/damper, perform the following:
   a. Remove the cylinder as described in this chapter.
   b. Remove the magneto rotor as described in Chapter Five.
   c. Remove the rear chain guide/damper mounting bolts and washers, then remove the rear chain guide/damper (B, **Figure 50**).
3. Install by reversing these steps. Tighten the rear chain guide/damper mounting bolts as specified in **Table 3**.

Inspection

1. Check the chain guide surfaces for excessive wear, cracks or other damage. Replace if necessary.
2. Inspect the rear chain guide/damper and the mounting bracket and pivot shaft for severe wear or damage.

VALVES AND VALVE COMPONENTS

A complete valve job, consisting of reconditioning the valve, valve seats and replacing the valve guides, requires a number of specialized tools and the experience to use them. This section describes on checking the valve components for wear and how to determine what type of service is required. Refer all valve service work requiring grinding and guide replacement to a motorcycle dealership.

Special Tools

A valve spring compressor is required to remove and install the valves. This tool compresses the valve springs so the valve keepers can be released from the valve stem. Do not attempt to remove or install the valves without a valve spring compressor. Because of the limited working area found in the typical ATV and motorcycle cylinder heads, most automotive type valve spring compressors will not work. Instead, rent or purchase a valve spring compressor designed for ATV and motorcycle applications.

Solvent Test

For proper engine operation, the valves must seat tightly against their seats. Any condition that

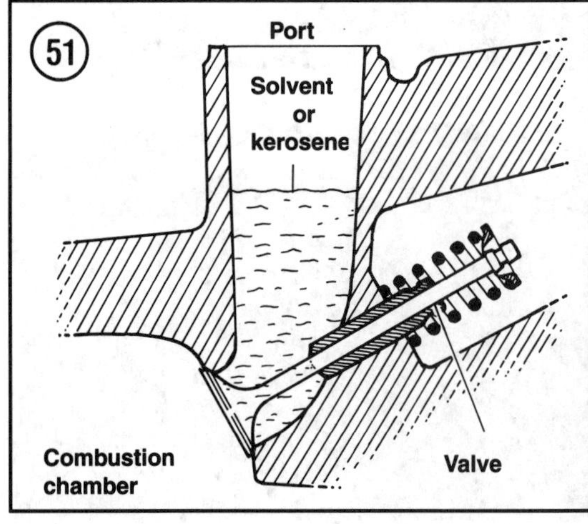

prevents the valves from seating properly can cause valve burning and reduced engine performance.

Before removing the valves from the cylinder head, perform the following solvent test to check valve seating.

1. Remove the cylinder head as described in this chapter.
2. Support the cylinder so that the exhaust port faces up (**Figure 51**). Then pour solvent or kerosene into the port as shown in **Figure 51**. Wait a few seconds then check the combustion chamber for fluid leaking past the exhaust valve seat.

3. Repeat Step 2 for the intake port and intake valve and seat.

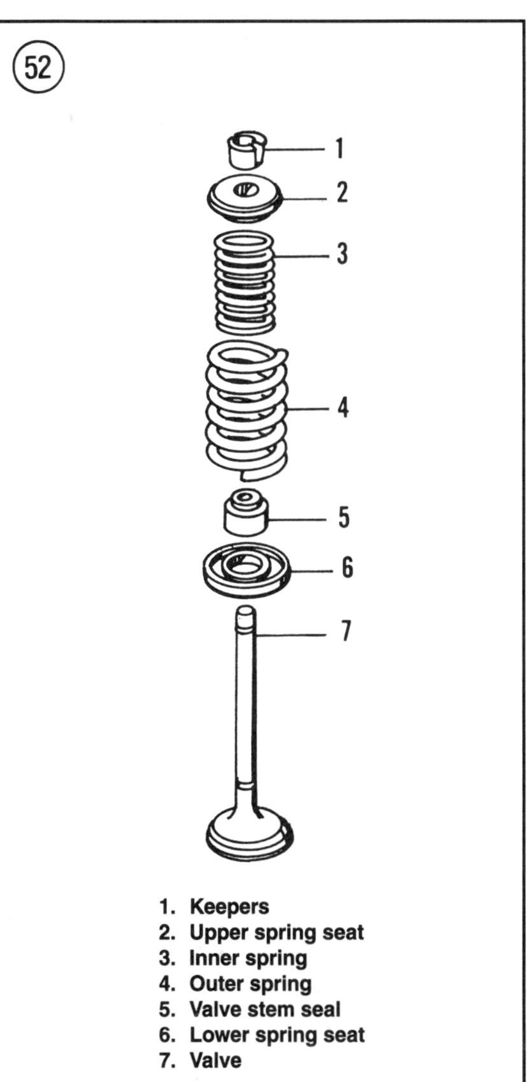

1. Keepers
2. Upper spring seat
3. Inner spring
4. Outer spring
5. Valve stem seal
6. Lower spring seat
7. Valve

4. If there is fluid leaking around one or both valve seats, the valve(s) is not seating properly on its seat. The following condition will cause poor valve seating:

a. A vent valve stem.
b. A worn or damaged valve seat (in cylinder head).
c. A worn or damaged valve face.
d. A crack in the combustion chamber.

4

Removal

A valve spring compressor is required to remove and install the valves.

Refer to **Figure 52** for this procedure.

1. Remove the cylinder head as described in this chapter.
2. Install a valve spring compressor squarely over the valve spring seat with the other end of tool placed against valve head (**Figure 53**). Position the compressor head so you can reach and remove the valve keepers in Step 3.

NOTE
When compressing the valve springs in Step 3, do not compress them any more than necessary to remove the valve keepers.

3. Tighten the valve spring compressor to remove all tension from the upper spring seat and valve keepers. Then lift valve keepers out through the valve spring compressor with needlenose pliers (**Figure 54**) or a magnet.
4. Slowly loosen the valve spring compressor and remove it from the head.
5. Remove the upper spring seat (**Figure 55**) and both valve springs.

CAUTION
*Remove any burrs from the valve stem grooves (**Figure 56**) before removing the valves; otherwise, the valve guides will be damaged as the valve stems pass through them.*

6. Remove the valve from the cylinder head.
7. Pull the seal (**Figure 57**) off of the valve guide and discard it.
8. Remove the lower spring seat.

CAUTION
All component parts of each valve assembly must be kept together. Do not intermix components from the different valves or excessive wear may result.

9. Repeat Steps 2-8 and remove the remaining valve.

54

55

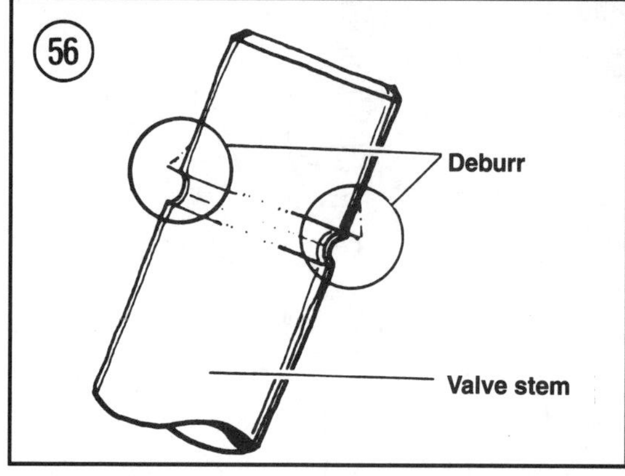

56

57

Inspection

When measuring the valve components (**Figure 52**) in this section, compare the actual measurements to the new and service limit specifications in **Table 2**. Replace parts that are out of specification or show damage as described in this section. Always replace the valve guide(s) when replacing the valve(s).

Refer to the troubleshooting chart in **Figure 58** when performing valve inspection procedures in this section.

1. Clean the valves in solvent. Do not gouge or damage the valve seating surface.
2. Inspect the contact surface (**Figure 59**) of each valve for burning. Minor roughness and pitting can be removed by lapping the valve as described in this chapter. Excessive unevenness to the contact surface is an indication that the valve is not serviceable.
3. Inspect the valve stems for wear and roughness. Then measure the valve stem diameter for wear (**Figure 60**).
4. Remove all carbon and varnish from the valve guides with a stiff spiral wire brush before measuring wear.

NOTE
If you do not have the required measuring tools, proceed to Step 7.

5. Measure each valve guide at the top, center and bottom inside diameter with a small hole gauge.

58

VALVE TROUBLESHOOTING

Symptom	Check
Valve deposits	Check: • Worn valve guide • Carbon buildup from incorrect engine tuning • Carbon buildup from incorrect carburetor adjustment • Dirty or gummed fuel
Valve sticking	Check: • Worn valve guide • Bent valve stem • Deposits collected on valve stem • Valve burning or overheating
Valve burning	Check: • Valve sticking • Cylinder head warped • Valve seat distorted • Valve clearance incorrect • Incorrect valve spring • Valve spring worn • Worn valve seat • Carbon buildup in engine • Engine ignition and/or carburetor adjustments incorrect
Valve seat/face wear	Check: • Valve burning • Incorrect valve clearance • Abrasive material on valve face and seat
Valve damage	Check: • Valve burning • Incorrectly installed or serviced valve guides • Incorrect valve clearance • Incorrect valve, spring seat and retainer assembly • Detonation caused by incorrect ignition and/or carburetor adjustments

Then measure the small hole gauge with a micrometer to determine the valve guide inside diameter.

6. Subtract the measurement made in Step 3 from the measurement made in Step 5. The difference is the valve stem-to-guide clearance. Replace any guide or valve that is not within tolerance. Refer valve guide replacement to a dealership.

7. If a small hole gauge is not available, insert each valve in its guide. Hold the valve just slightly off its seat and rock it sideways. If the valve rocks more than slightly, the guide is probably worn. However, as a final check, take the cylinder head to a dealer or machine shop and have the valve guides measured.

8. Check the inner and outer valve springs as follows:

   a. Check each valve spring for visual damage.
   b. Use a square and check each spring for distortion or tilt (**Figure 61**).
   c. Measure the valve spring free length with a vernier caliper (**Figure 62**).
   d. Replace worn or damaged springs as a set.

9. Check the valve spring seats and valve keepers for cracks or other damage.

10. Inspect the valve seats (**Figure 63**) for burning, pitting, cracks, excessive wear or other damage. If worn or burned, they may be reconditioned as described in this chapter. Seats and valves in near-perfect condition can be reconditioned by lapping with fine carborundum paste. Check as follows:

   a. Clean the valve seat and valve mating areas with contact cleaner.
   b. Coat the valve seat with machinist's blue marking compound.
   c. Install the valve into its guide and rotate it against its seat with a valve lapping tool. See *Valve Lapping* in this chapter.
   d. Lift the valve out of the guide and measure the seat width (**Figure 64**) with vernier calipers.
   e. The seat width for intake and exhaust valves should measure within the specifications listed in **Table 2** all the way around the seat. If the seat width exceeds the service limit, have the seats reconditioned at a Yamaha dealership.
   f. Remove all machinist's blue residue from the seats and valves.

11. Measure valve stem runout with a V-block and dial indicator as shown in **Figure 65**.

12. Measure the head diameter of each valve using a vernier caliper or micrometer (**Figure 66**).

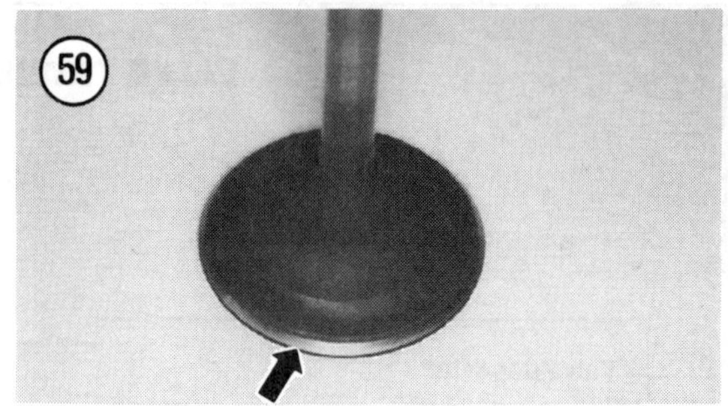

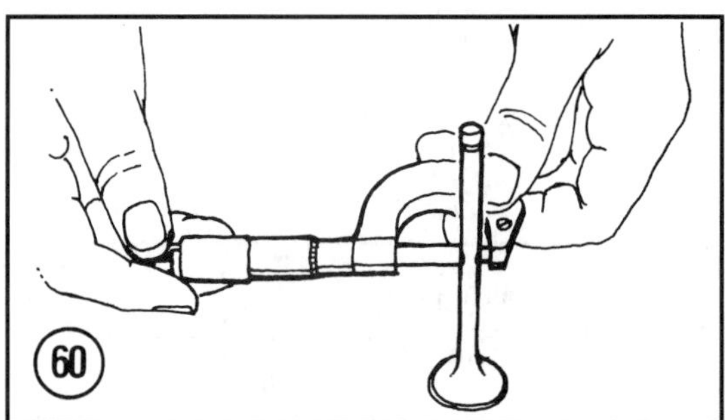

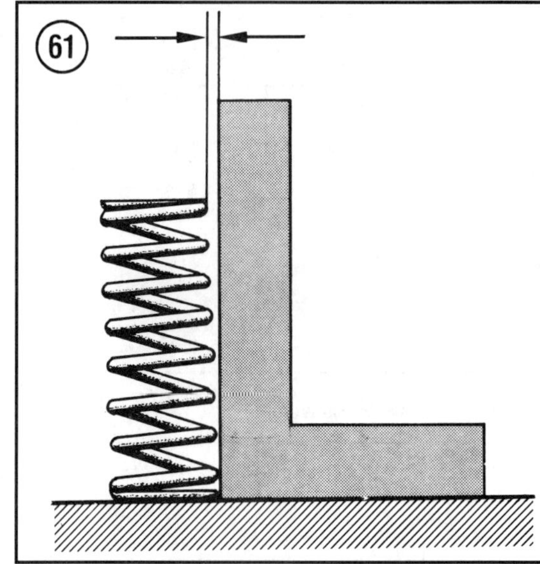

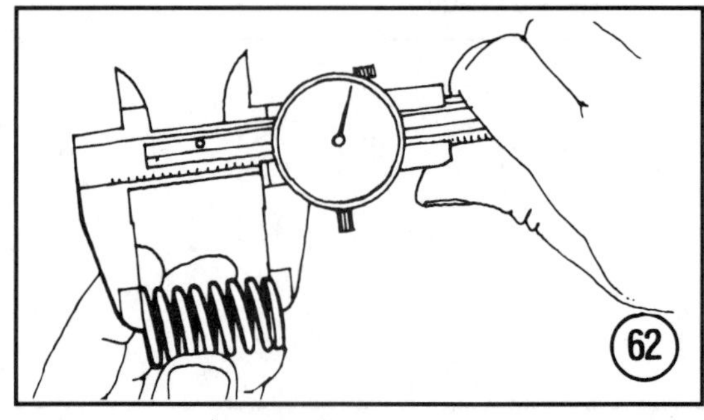

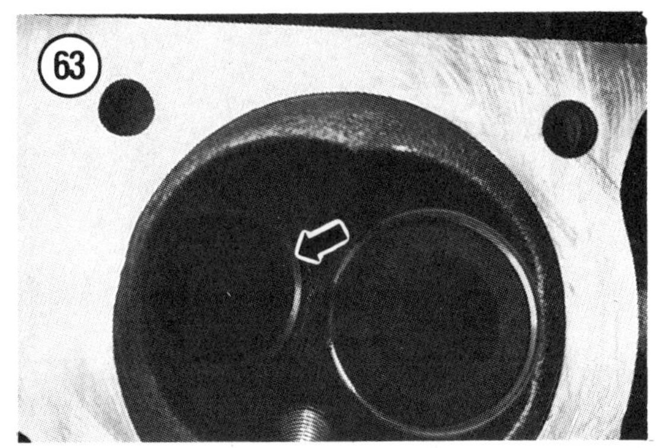

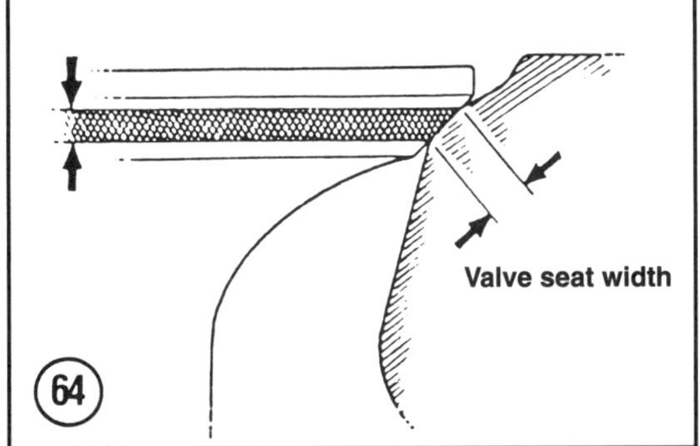

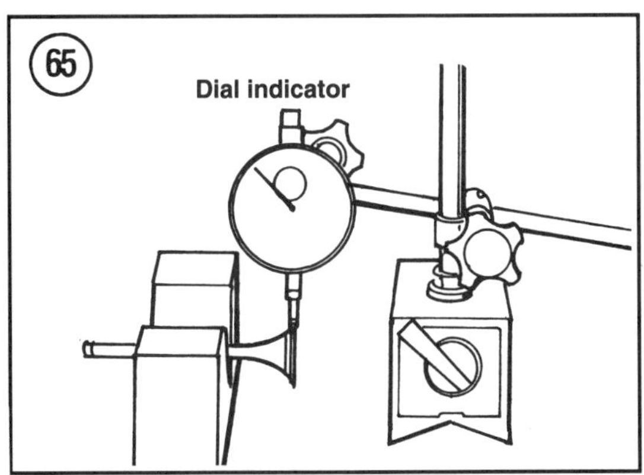

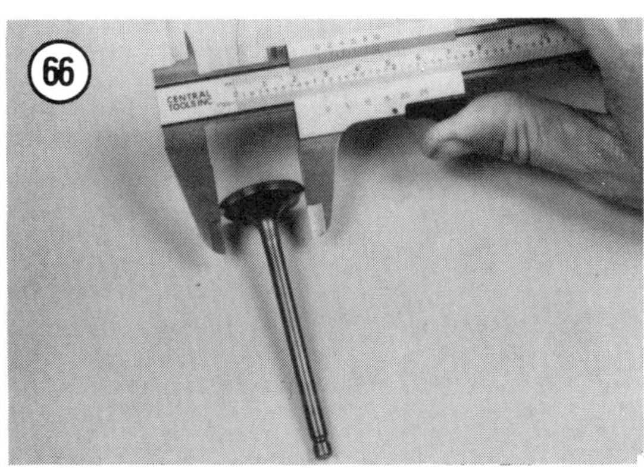

Valve Guide Replacement

Refer valve guide replacement to a Yamaha dealership. If you are going to do the work yourself, a 7 mm (0.275 in.) valve guide reamer is required.

Valve Seat Reconditioning

The valve seats are an integral part of the cylinder head and cannot be replaced separately. Minor valve seat wear and damage can be repaired by grinding or cutting. Refer this service to a Yamaha dealership. If you are equipped and have the experience to do the work yourself, refer to **Figure 67** for the valve seat cutter angles required. Refer to **Table 2** for the valve seat specifications.

4

Valve Lapping

Valve lapping is a simple operation which can restore the valve seal without machining—if the amount of wear or distortion is not too great.

This procedure should only be performed after determining that the valve seat width and outside diameter are within specifications. See the *Inspection* procedure in this section.

1. Smear a light coating of fine-grade valve lapping compound on seating surface of valve.
2. Insert the valve into the head.
3. Wet the suction cup of the lapping stick and stick it onto the head of the valve. Lap the valve to the seat by spinning the lapping stick in both directions. Every 5 to 10 seconds, rotate the valve 180° in the valve seat. Continue this action until the mating surfaces on the valve and seat are smooth and equal in size.

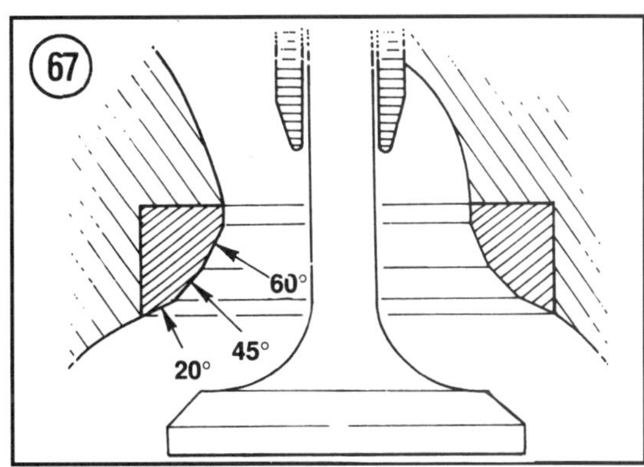

4. Closely examine valve seat in cylinder head. It should be smooth and even with a smooth, polished seating ring.
5. Thoroughly clean the valves and cylinder head in solvent and then with hot soapy water to remove all lapping compound. Any compound left on the valves or the cylinder head will end up in the engine and cause excessive wear and damage. After drying the cylinder head, lubricate the valve guides with engine oil to prevent rust.
6. After installing the valves into the cylinder, test the valve seat seal as described under *Solvent Test* in this section. If fluid leaks past any of the seats, remove that valve assembly and repeat the lapping procedure until there is no leakage. When there is no leakage, remove both valve sets and reclean the cylinder head assembly as described in Step 5.

Valve Installation

1. Clean and dry all parts. If the valve seats were reground or lapped, or the valve guides replaced, thoroughly clean the valves and cylinder head in solvent and then with hot soapy water to remove all lapping and grinding compound. Any abrasive residue left on the valves or in the cylinder head will contaminate the engine and cause excessive wear and damage. After drying the cylinder head, lubricate the valve guides with engine oil to prevent rust.
2. Install the lower spring seat (**Figure 68**) with its shoulder side facing up.
3. Install *new* oil seals as follows:

NOTE
New valve stem seals must be installed whenever the valves are removed.

a. Lubricate the inside of each new seal with molybdenum disulfide paste.
b. Install the new seal over the valve guide and seat it into place (**Figure 69**).
c. Repeat for the other oil seal.

4. Coat a valve stem with molybdenum disulfide paste and install into its correct guide.

NOTE
*Install valve springs with the narrow pitch end (end with coils closest together) facing the cylinder head (**Figure 70**).*

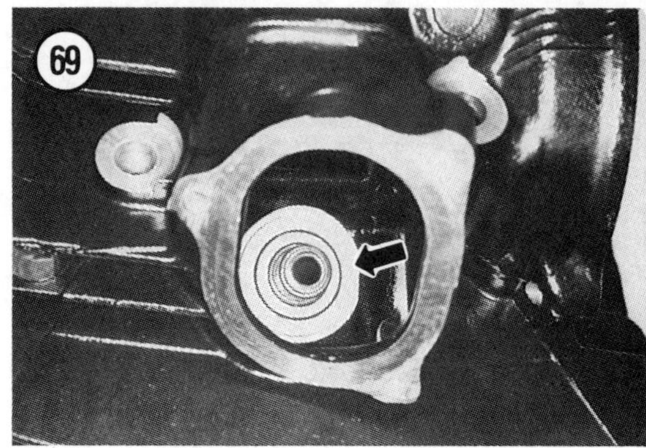

5. Install the inner and outer valve springs (**Figure 71**).
6. Install the upper spring seat (**Figure 72**).
7. Install the valve spring compressor. Push down on the upper valve seat and compress the springs, then install the valve keepers. Release tension from the compressor, checking that the keepers are seated around the end of the valve. Then tap the end of the valve stem with a soft-faced hammer. This will ensure that the keepers are properly seated. See **Figure 73**.
8. Repeat Steps 2-7 for the opposite valve.
9. After installing the cylinder head onto the engine, check and adjust valve clearance as described in Chapter Three.

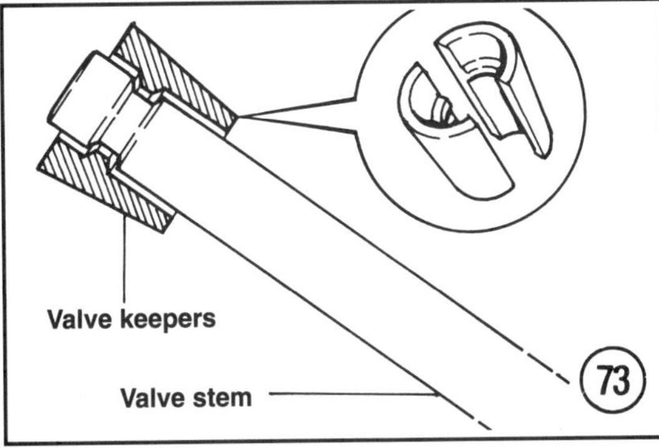

CYLINDER BLOCK

The alloy cylinder block has a pressed-in cast iron cylinder liner which can be bored to 0.50 mm (0.020 in.) oversize and again to 1.0 mm (0.040 in.) oversize. These oversize piston and ring sizes are available through Yamaha dealerships and aftermarket piston suppliers.

The cylinder block can be removed with the engine mounted in the frame. Refer to **Figure 74** when servicing the cylinder block in the following section.

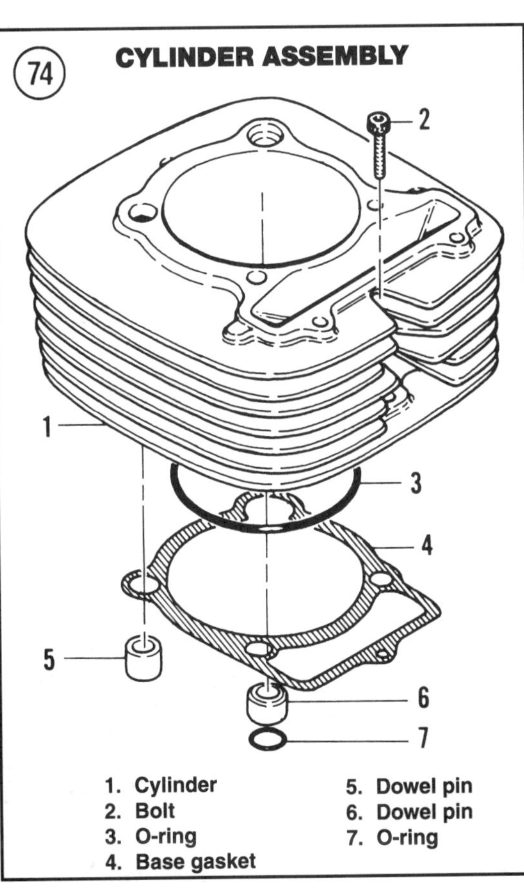

Removal

1. Remove the cylinder head as described under *Cylinder Head Removal/Installation* in this chapter.
2. Remove the Allen bolt (**Figure 75**) securing the cylinder block to the crankcase .

CAUTION

The cooling fins are fragile and may be damaged if tapped or pried on too hard. Never use a metal hammer when loos-

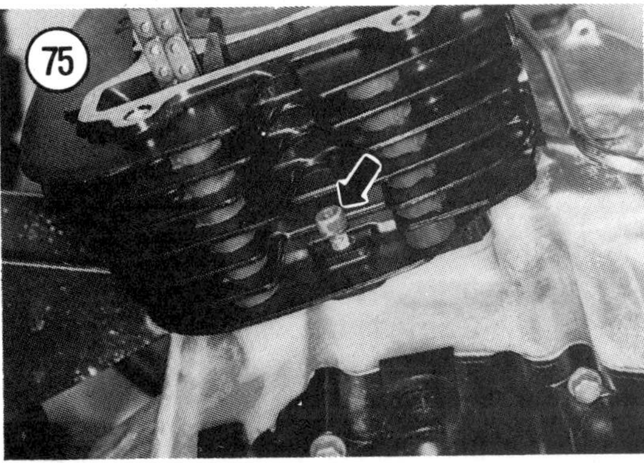

ening the cylinder block in the following step.

3. Loosen the cylinder block by tapping around its perimeter with a rubber or plastic mallet.
4. Untie the camshaft chain wire from the frame and allow the chain to fall into the crankcase.
5. Pull the cylinder block straight up and off the crankcase. Hold onto the piston as it becomes free from the cylinder bore and rest it onto the crankcase.
6. Remove the base gasket.
7. Remove the 2 dowel pins (A, **Figure 76**) and O-ring (B, **Figure 76**).
8. If necessary, remove the piston as described under *Piston Removal/Installation* in this chapter.
9. Cover the crankcase opening with a clean shop cloth to prevent objects and abrasive dust from falling into the crankcase.

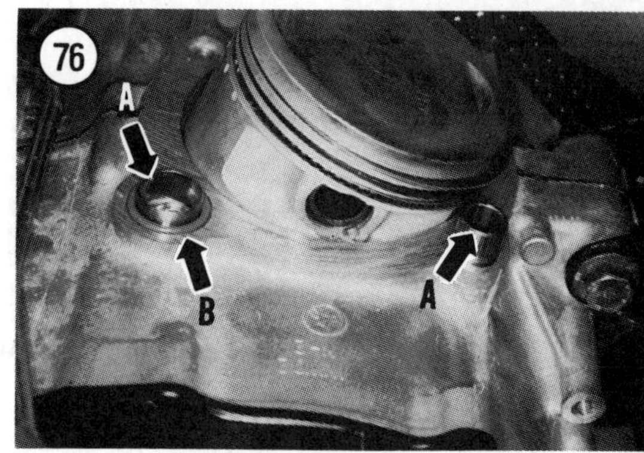

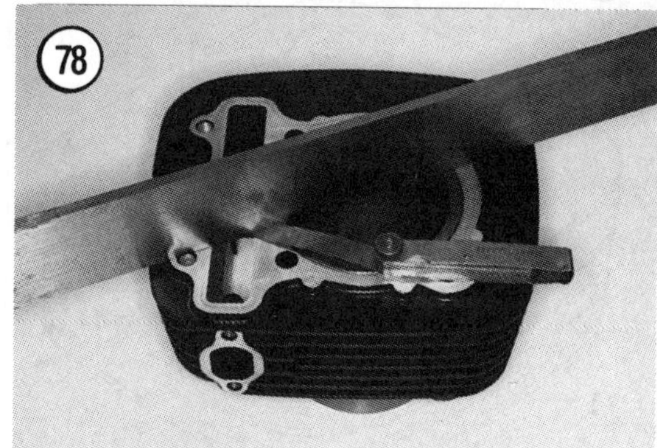

Inspection

When measuring the cylinder block in this section, compare the actual measurements to the service specifications in **Table 2**. Service the cylinder bore if damaged or out of specification.

1. Remove the cylinder block O-ring (**Figure 77**) before washing the cylinder block in solvent. If the O-ring is not damaged it can be reused.
2. Remove all gasket residue from the top and bottom cylinder block gasket surfaces.
3. Wash the cylinder block in solvent and dry with compressed air.
4. After cleaning the cylinder block, place a straightedge across the top gasket surface at several points and check for warpage with a feeler gauge (**Figure 78**). Warpage or nicks in the cylinder block surface could cause an oil leak. If the warpage exceeds the service limit in **Table 2**, resurface or replace the cylinder block. Refer this service to a Yamaha dealership.
5. Check the dowel pin holes for cracks or other damage.
6. Check cylinder block for cracked, damaged or missing fins.
7. Measure the cylinder bore with a bore gauge or inside micrometer. Measure the cylinder bore 40 mm (1.57 in.) from the top of the cylinder as shown in **Figure 79**. Measure in line with the piston pin and 90° to the pin. This measurement determines cylinder bore out-of-round. Now measure in 3 axes (**Figure 80**)—aligned with the piston pin and at 90° to

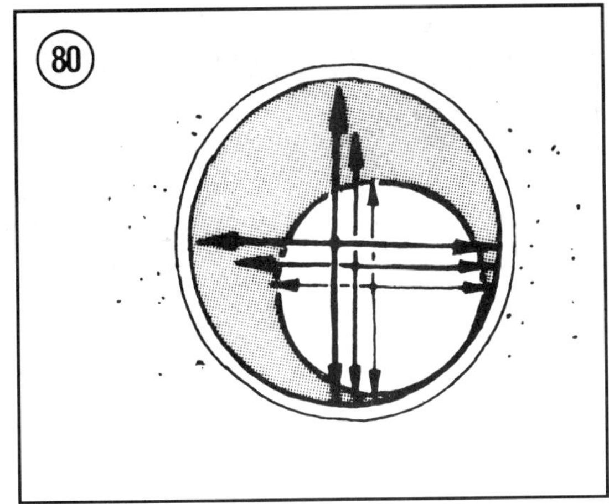

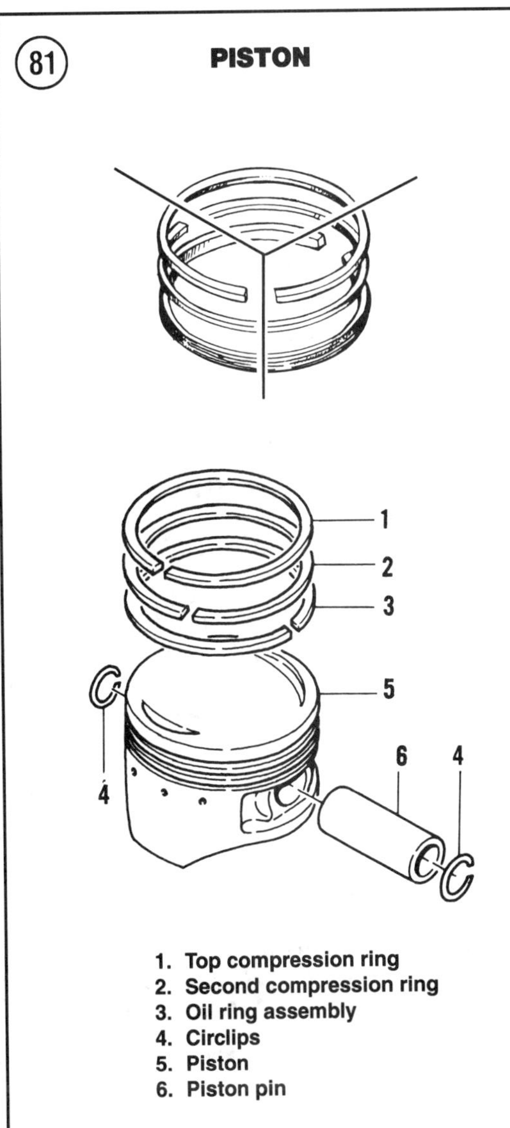

1. Top compression ring
2. Second compression ring
3. Oil ring assembly
4. Circlips
5. Piston
6. Piston pin

the pin. If the cylinder taper or out-of-round is excessive, rebore the cylinder to the next oversize and install a new piston and rings.

NOTE
*Purchase the new piston before the cylinder is bored so the piston can be measured. The cylinder must be bored to match the piston. Piston-to-cylinder clearance is listed in **Table 2**.*

8. Check the bore surface for scratches or gouges. The bore still may require boring and reconditioning.
9. After the cylinder has been serviced, wash the bore in hot soapy water. This is the only way to clean the cylinder wall of the fine grit material left from the bore or honing job. After washing the cylinder wall, run a clean white cloth through it. The cylinder wall should show no traces of grit or other debris. If the rag is dirty, the cylinder wall is not clean and must be rewashed. After the cylinder is clean, lubricate the cylinder wall with engine oil to prevent the cylinder liner from rusting.

CAUTION
A combination of soap and water is the only solution that will completely clean the cylinder wall. Solvent and kerosene cannot wash fine grit out of cylinder crevices. Grit left in the cylinder will cause premature wear to the new rings.

Installation

1. Check that the top and bottom cylinder surfaces are clean of all gasket residue.
2. If removed, install the piston as described in this chapter.

CAUTION
Make sure the piston pin circlips are installed and seated correctly.

3. Install the cylinder O-ring by pushing it into the groove in the bottom of the cylinder block (**Figure 77**).
4. Install the 2 dowel pins (A, **Figure 76**) into the crankcase receptacles. Install a *new* O-ring (B, **Figure 76**) around the rear dowel pin.
5. Install a new base gasket. Make sure all holes align.

6. Stagger the piston rings around the piston as shown in **Figure 81**.
7. Lubricate the cylinder bore, piston and rings liberally with engine oil.
8. Carefully align the cylinder block with the piston and start installing the cylinder over the piston. Compress each ring (**Figure 82**) with your fingers before it enters the cylinder.
9. When all of the rings are in the cylinder, hold onto the piston and carefully push the cylinder block down and seat it over the dowel pins and O-ring, and against the base gasket.
10. Run the chain and wire up through the cylinder block and retie it to the frame.
11. Install the Allen bolt (**Figure 75**) and tighten as specified in **Table 3**.
12. Install the cylinder head as described in this chapter.

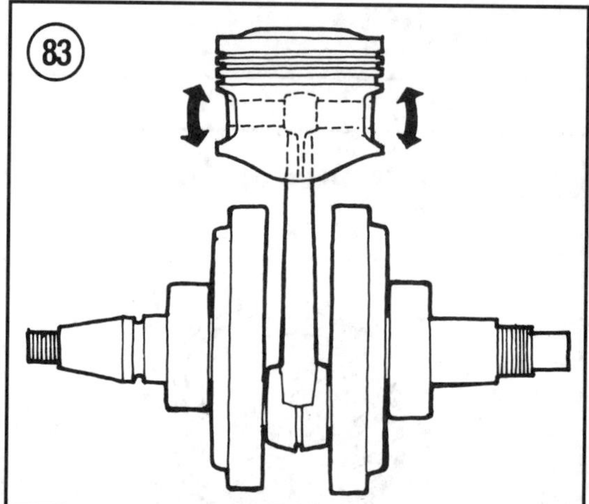

PISTON AND PISTON RINGS

The piston is made of aluminum alloy. The piston pin is made of steel and is a precision fit in the piston. The piston pin is held in place by a clip at each end.

Refer to **Figure 81** when servicing the piston and rings in the following section.

Piston Removal/Installation

1. Remove the cylinder block as described in this chapter.
2. Seal the crankcase below the piston with clean shop cloth or paper towels to prevent the piston pin circlips from falling into the crankcase.
3. Before removing the piston, hold the rod tightly and rock the piston (**Figure 83**). Any rocking motion (do not confuse with the normal sliding motion) indicates wear on the piston pin, pin bore, or more likely, a combination of all three.
4. Remove the circlips from the piston pin bore (**Figure 84**).

NOTE
Discard the piston circlips. New circlips must be installed during reassembly.

5. Push the piston pin out of the piston by hand and remove the piston. If the pin is tight, use a homemade tool (**Figure 85**) to remove it. Do not drive the piston pin out as this may damage the piston pin, connecting rod and/or piston.

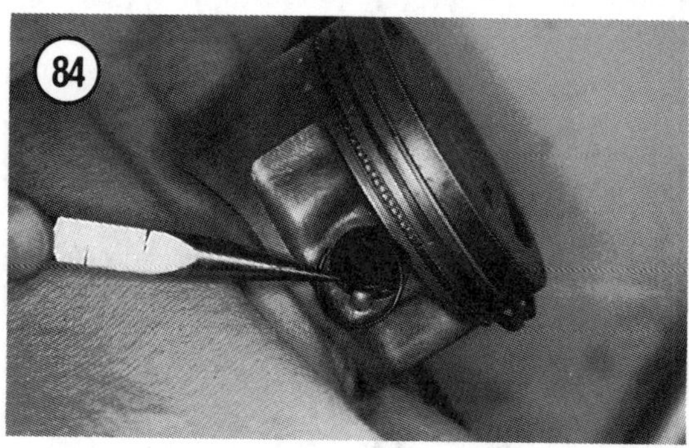

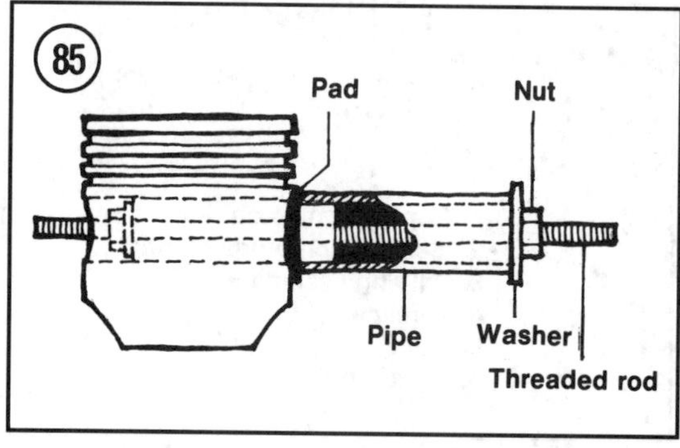

6. Inspect the piston and rings as described in this chapter.

Piston Inspection

1. Remove the piston rings as described in this chapter.
2. Carefully clean the carbon from the piston crown (**Figure 86**) with a soft scraper or wire wheel mounted in a drill. Large carbon accumulations reduce piston cooling and results in detonation and piston damage. Do not remove or damage the carbon ridge around the circumference of the piston above the top ring. If the piston, rings and cylinder are found to be dimensionally correct and can be reused, removal of the carbon ring from the top of the piston or the carbon ridges from the cylinder bore will promote excessive oil consumption.

CAUTION
Do not wire brush the piston skirt.

3. After cleaning the piston, examine its crown. The crown must not be worn or damaged. If the crown appears pecked or spongy, also check the spark plug, valves and combustion chamber for aluminum deposits. If these deposits are found, the engine has been overheating.

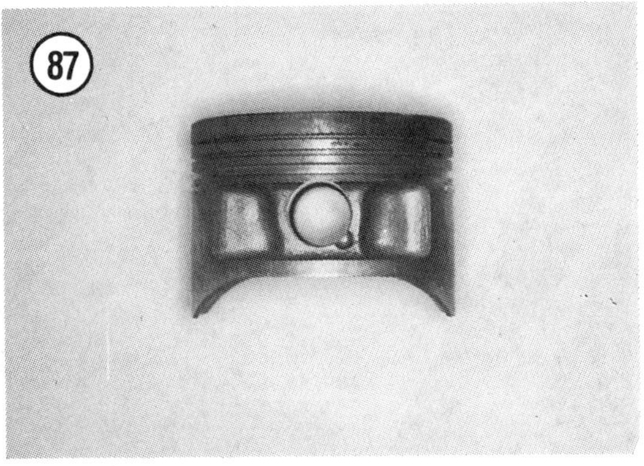

4. Examine each ring and groove (**Figure 87**) for burrs, dented edges or other damage. Pay particular attention to the top compression ring groove as it usually wears more than the others. Because the oil rings are constantly bathed in oiled, these rings and grooves wear little compared to compression rings and their grooves. If there is evidence of oil ring groove wear or if the oil ring assembly is tight and difficult to remove, the piston skirt may have collapsed due to excessive heat and is permanently deformed. If so, replace the piston.
5. Check the oil control holes in the piston for carbon or oil sludge buildup. Clean the holes with wire and compressed air.
6. Check the piston skirt (**Figure 87**) for cracks or other damage. If the piston shows signs of partial seizure (bits of aluminum on the piston skirt), the piston should be replaced and the cylinder bored (if necessary) to reduce the possibility of engine noise and further piston seizure.

NOTE
If the piston skirt is worn or scuffed unevenly from side to side, the connecting rod may be bent or twisted.

7. Check the piston circlip grooves (**Figure 87**) for wear, cracks or other damage. Check the circlip fit by installing a new circlip into each groove and then attempt to move the circlip from side to side. If the circlip has any side play, the groove is worn and the piston must be replaced.
8. Measure piston-to-cylinder clearance as described under *Piston Clearance* in this chapter.
9. If necessary, select a new piston as described under *Piston Clearance* in this chapter.

Piston Pin Inspection

When measuring the piston pin components, compare the actual measurements to the specifications in **Table 2**. Replace parts that are out of specification or show damage as described in this section.

1. Clean and dry the piston pin.
2. Inspect the piston pin (A, **Figure 88**) for chrome flaking or cracks. Replace if necessary.

4

3. Oil the piston pin and install it in the connecting rod. Slowly rotate the piston pin and check for radial play (**Figure 89**). If any play exists, the piston pin and/or connecting must be replaced. Confirm piston pin clearance by performing the following steps.
4. Oil the piston pin and install it in the piston. Slowly rotate the piston pin and check for radial play (**Figure 90**). If any play exists, the piston pin and/or piston must be replaced. Determine wear by performing the following steps.
5. Measure the piston pin (A, **Figure 88**) outer diameter using a micrometer and compare to **Table 2**.
6. Measure the piston pin bore (B, **Figure 88**) using a small hole gauge. Then measure the small hole gauge with a micrometer and compare to **Table 2**.
7. Subtract the measurement made in Step 5 from the measurement made in Step 6. The difference is piston pin-to-piston clearance. If out of specification, replace the piston and pin.

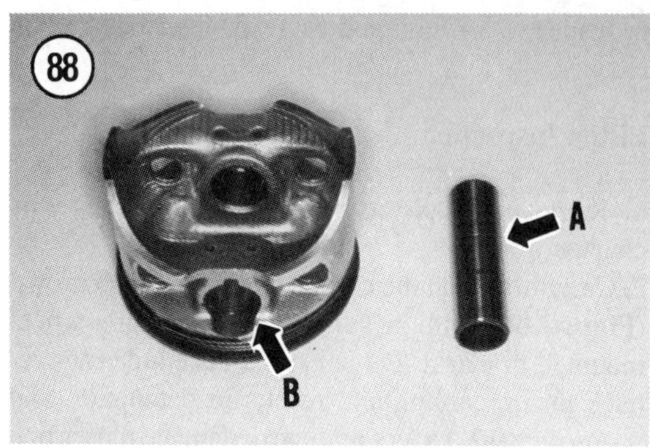

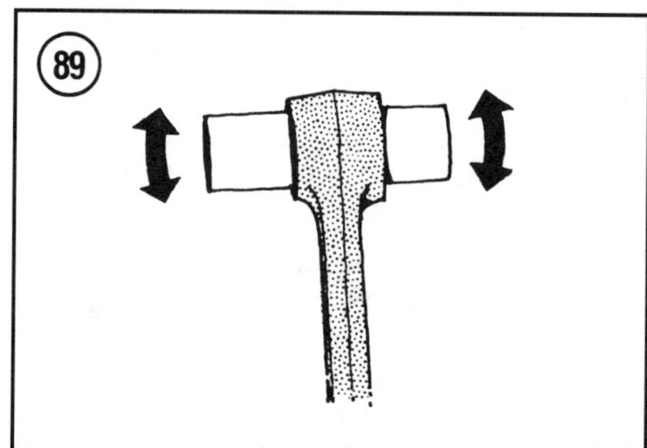

Piston Clearance

1. Make sure the piston and cylinder walls are clean and dry.
2. Measure the cylinder bore with a bore gauge or inside micrometer. Measure the cylinder bore 40 mm (1.57 in.) from the top of the cylinder as shown in **Figure 91**. Measure aligned with the piston pin and 90° to the pin. Write down the bore diameter measurement.
3. Measure the piston diameter with a micrometer at a right angle to the piston pin bore (**Figure 92**). Measure 5.5 mm (0.22 in.) up from the bottom edge of the piston skirt.
4. Subtract the piston diameter from the largest bore diameter to determine piston-to-cylinder clearance. If the clearance exceeds the service limit in **Table 2**, bore the cylinder to the next oversize and install an oversize piston and rings. To determine the oversize cylinder diameter, measure the new (oversize) piston and add the preferred piston-to-cylinder clearance specification to the piston diameter.

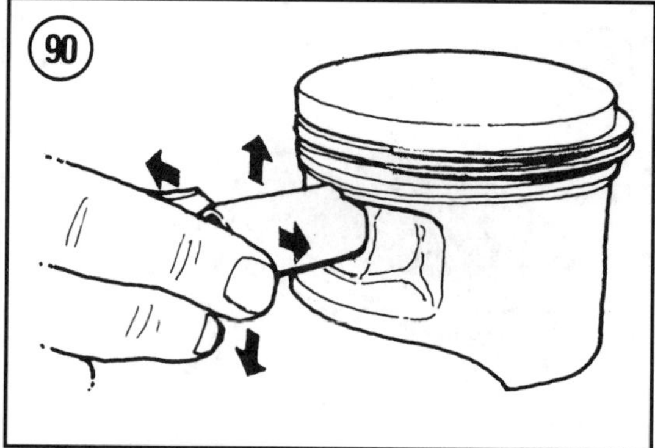

NOTE

If the piston-to-cylinder clearance is excessive, but the cylinder bore diameter is still within specification, installing a new piston may bring the clearance to within operating clearance. The new piston will take up some of the excessive

piston-to-cylinder clearance. Check carefully before deciding to rebore or to just install a new piston.

Piston Installation

1. Make sure all parts are clean before starting assembly.
2. Install the piston rings onto the piston as described in this chapter.

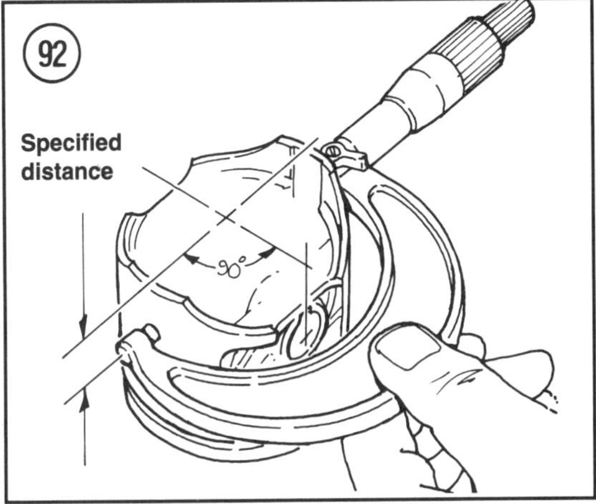

3. Coat the connecting rod bore, piston pin and piston with engine oil.
4. Slide the piston pin into the piston until its end is flush with the piston pin boss.
5. Place the piston over the connecting rod so that the arrow on the piston crown (**Figure 93**) faces forward.
6. Align the piston pin with the hole in the connecting rod. Push the piston pin through the connecting rod and into the other side of the piston until it is centered in the piston.
7. Install new piston pin clips (**Figure 94**) in both piston grooves. Make sure they are seated in the piston grooves completely.

CAUTION

*Do not align the piston pin circlip end gap with the cutout in the piston (**Figure 95**).*

Piston Ring Inspection and Removal

A 3-ring type piston and ring assembly is used (**Figure 81**). The top and second rings are compression rings. The bottom ring is an oil control ring assembly (consisting of 2 ring rails and an expander spacer). **Table 4** identifies the piston rings.

When measuring the piston rings in this section, compare the actual measurements to the new and service limit specifications in **Table 2**. Replace parts

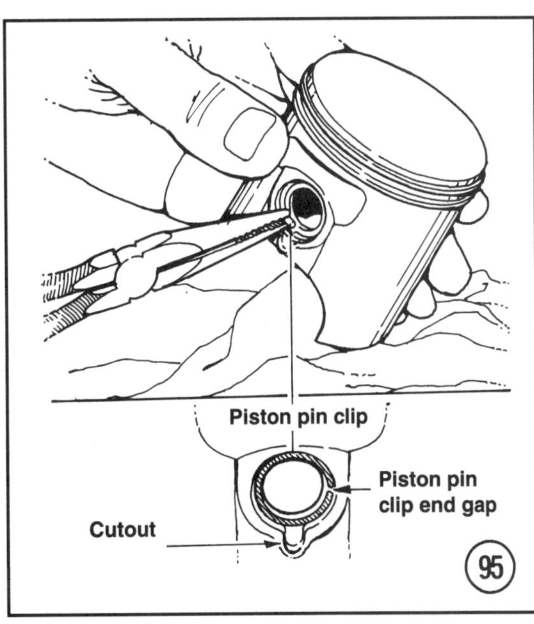

that are out of specification or damaged as described in this section.

NOTE
If necessary, clean the carbon and oil residue from the piston ring grooves and rings before checking the side clearance in Step 1. Remove the rings as described later in this procedure.

1. Measure the side clearance of each ring in its groove with a flat feeler gauge (**Figure 96**) and compare with the specifications in **Table 2**. Replace the rings if the clearance is greater than specified. Replace the piston if the clearance is still excessive with new rings.

WARNING
The edges of all piston rings are very sharp. Be careful when handling them to avoid cut fingers.

NOTE
Store the rings in order of removal.

2. Remove the compression rings with a ring expander tool (**Figure 97**) or by spreading the ring ends with your thumbs and lifting the rings up evenly (**Figure 98**).
3. Remove the oil ring assembly (**Figure 99**) by first removing the upper (A, **Figure 100**) and lower (B, **Figure 100**) ring rails. Then remove the expander spacer (C, **Figure 100**).
4. Using a broken piston ring, carefully remove carbon and oil residue from the piston ring grooves (**Figure 101**). Do not remove aluminum material from the ring grooves as this will increase ring side clearance.
5. Inspect the ring grooves for burrs, nicks or broken or cracked lands. Then roll each compression ring around its piston groove as shown in **Figure 102** and check for binding. Minor binding may be cleaned up with a fine-cut file. Replace the piston if the binding cannot be cleaned up or repaired.
6. Measure the end gap of each ring. To check, insert the ring into the bottom of the cylinder bore (**Figure 103**) approximately 20 mm (3/4 in.) and square it with the cylinder wall by tapping it with the piston (**Figure 103**). Measure the end gap with a feeler gauge (**Figure 103**). Replace rings as a set if the end gap for any one ring is too large. If the end gap on a new ring is smaller than specified, hold a small file

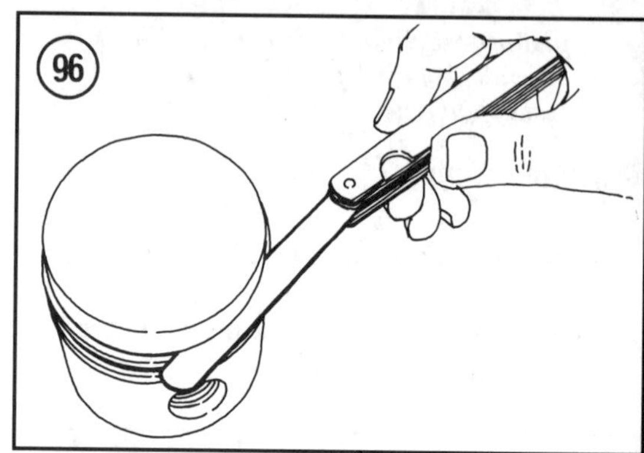
96

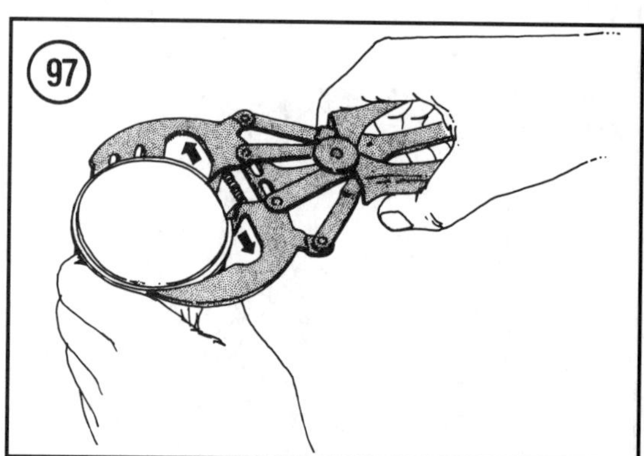
97

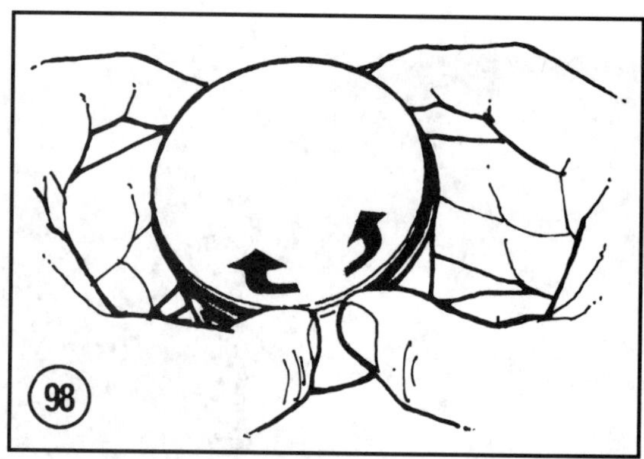
98

99

in a vise, grip the ends of the ring with your fingers and enlarge the gap.

NOTE
*When measuring oil control ring end gap, measure end gap of the upper and lower ring rails only. Do not measure the expander spacer (C, **Figure 100**).*

Piston Ring Installation

1. Deglaze or hone the cylinder when installing new piston rings. This procedure will help the new rings to seat properly. If necessary, refer honing service to a Yamaha dealership or motorcycle repair shop. After honing, measure the end gap of each ring and compare to the specifications in **Table 2**.

NOTE
*If the cylinder block was deglazed or honed, clean the cylinder block as described under **Cylinder Block Inspection** in this chapter.*

2. Clean the piston and rings in solvent. Dry with compressed air.

NOTE
*The top and second compression rings are different. Refer to **Table 4** to identify the rings.*

3. Install the piston rings as follows:

NOTE
Install the piston rings—first the bottom, then the middle, then the top ring—by carefully spreading the ends with your thumbs and slipping the rings over the top of the piston. Install the piston rings with their marks facing up toward the top of the piston.

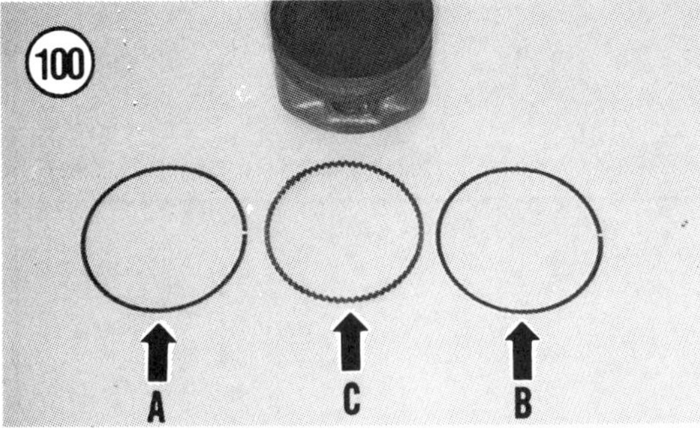

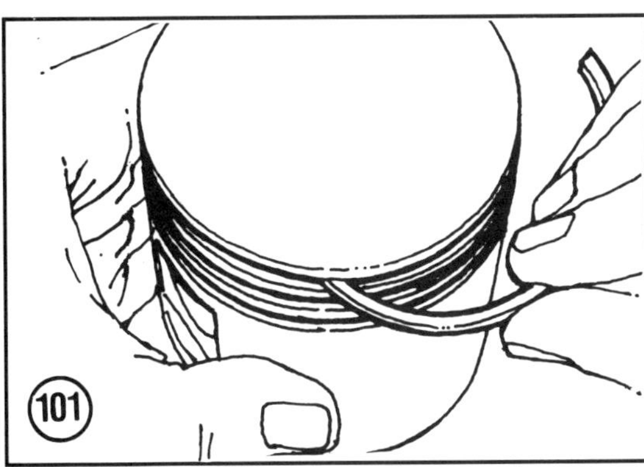

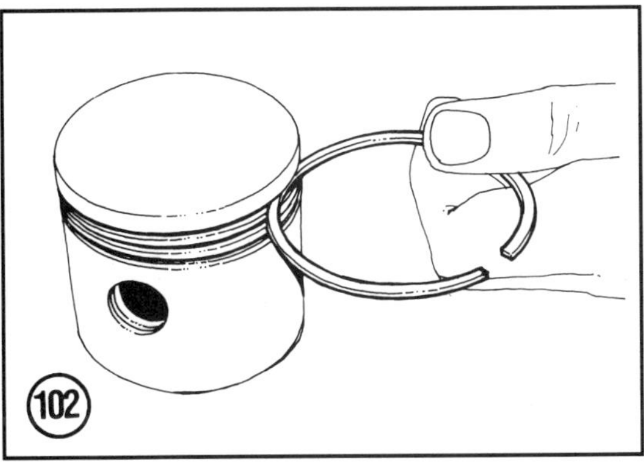

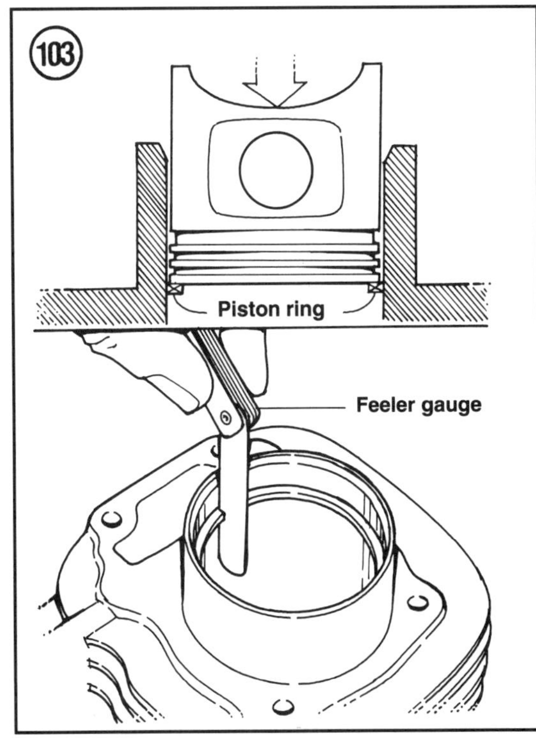

4

a. Install the oil ring assembly into the bottom ring groove. First install the expander spacer (C, **Figure 100**). Position the expander spacer so that its ends butt together as shown in **Figure 104**. Do not overlap the ends. Then install the bottom (B, **Figure 100**) and top (A, **Figure 100**) ring rails.

NOTE
*The 2 ring rails (A and B, **Figure 100**) are identical.*

b. Install the 2nd or middle compression ring with its mark facing up.
c. Install the top compression ring with its mark facing up.

4. Make sure the rings are seated completely in their grooves all the way around the piston and that the end gaps are distributed around the piston as shown in **Figure 81**. It is important that the ring gaps are not aligned with each other when installed to prevent compression pressure from escaping past them.
5. When installing oversize compression rings, check the number to make sure the correct rings are being installed. The ring numbers should be the same as the piston oversize number.
6. If new parts are installed, the engine should be broken-in just as though it were new. Refer to *Engine Break-In* in Chapter Five.

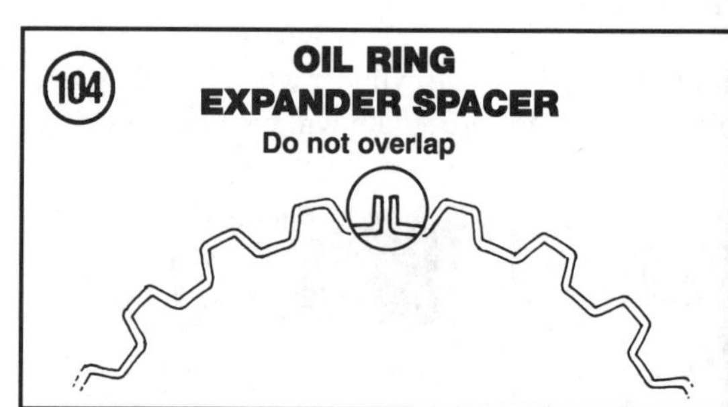

Table 1 GENERAL ENGINE SPECIFICATIONS

Engine	4-stroke, SOHC
Cooling system	Air cooled
Bore × stroke	83.0 × 71.5 mm (27 × 2.81 in.)
Displacement	386 cc (23.6 cu. in.)
Compression ratio	8.6:1
Compression pressure (standard)	920 kPa (133 psi)

4

Table 2 ENGINE SERVICE SPECIFICATIONS

Item	New mm (in.)	Service limit mm (in.)
Cylinder head warpage limit	—	0.03 (0.0012)
Camshaft		
Lobe height		
Intake	40.29-40.39 (1.586-1.590)	40.26 (1.585)
Exhaust	40.28-40.38 (1.586-1.590)	40.25 (1.585)
Base circle diameter	32.14-32.24 (1.265-1.269)	32.11 (1.264)
Runout	—	0.03 (0.0012)
Cylinder block		
Bore diameter	82.97-83.02 (3.2665-3.2685)	83.15 (3.2746)
Measuring point from top cylinder surface	40 (1.57)	—
Out-of-round limit	— —	0.01 (0.0004)
Taper limit	—	0.01 (0.0004)
Top surface warp limit	—	0.03 (0.0012)
Piston diameter		
Standard size	82.92-82.97 (3.265-3.267)	—
Oversize	Measure new piston	
Piston-to-cylinder clearance	0.04-0.06 (0.0016-0.0024)	0.1 (0.0039)
Piston pin bore diameter	19.004-19.015 (0.7482-0.7486)	—
Piston pin diameter	18.990-18.995 (0.7476-0.7487)	—
Piston pin-to-piston clearance	0.009-0.025 (0.0004-0.0010)	0.07 (0.003)
Piston rings		
End gap		
Top and second ring	0.2-0.4 (0.008-0.0016)	0.5 (0.020)
Oil ring	0.3-0.9 (0.012-0.035)	—
Side clearance		
Top	0.04-0.08 . (0.0016-0.0031)	0.12 (0.0047)
Second	0.03-0.07 (0.0012-0.0028)	0.12 (0.0047)

(continued)

Table 2 ENGINE SERVICE SPECIFICATIONS (continued)

Item	New mm (in.)	Service limit mm (in.)
Valves		
Head diameter		
Intake	39.9-40.1 (1.571-1.579)	—
Exhaust	33.9-34.1 (1.335-1.343)	—
Face width	2.26 (0.089)	—
Seat width	1.2-1.4 (0.047-0.055)	1.6 (0.06)
Margin thickness		
Intake	1.0-1.4 (0.0394-0.0551)	—
Exhaust	0.8-1.2 (0.0315-0.0472)	—
Stem diameter		
Intake	6.975-6.990 (0.2746-0.2752)	6.95 (0.274)
Exhaust	6.955-6.970 (0.2738-0.2744)	6.915 (0.272)
Valve guide inside diameter	7.000-7.012 (0.2756-0.2761)	7.03 (0.277)
Valve stem-to-guide clearance		
Intake	0.010-0.037 (0.0004-0.0015)	0.08 (0.0031)
Exhaust	0.030-0.057 (0.0012-0.0022)	0.1 (0.004)
Valve stem runout	—	0.02 (0.0008)
Valve springs		
Free length		
Inner	39.9 (1.57)	37.9 (1.49)
Outer	43.27 (1.70)	36.6 (1.4)
Installed length		
Inner	33.6 (1.3)	—
Outer	36.6 (1.4)	—
Tilt limit		
Inner and outer springs	—	1.6 (0.063)
Rocker arm bore diameter	12.000-12.018 (0.4724-0.4731)	12.078 (0.4755)
Rocker arm shaft diameter	11.981-11.991 (0.4717-0.4721)	11.951 (0.4705)
Rocker arm-to-shaft clearance	0.009-0.037 (0.0004-0.0015)	0.08 (0.0031)

Table 3 ENGINE TOP END TIGHTENING TORQUES

	N.m	in.-lb.	ft.-lb.
Cam chain guide bolt	10	88	—
Cam chain tensioner			

(continued)

Table 3 ENGINE TOP END TIGHTENING TORQUES (continued)

	N•m	in.-lb.	ft.-lb.
Tensioner body	10	88	—
Tensioner plug	23	—	17
Camshaft sprocket bolt	60	—	44
Camshaft retainer bolts	8	71	—
Cylinder head bolts			
8 mm	20	—	14
10 mm	40	—	29
Cylinder head cover			
Camshaft cover	10	88	—
Valve covers	10	88	—
Cylinder head-to-frame mounting bolts and nuts			
Upper mounting bolts	42	—	30
Lower mounting bolt and nut	33	—	24
Cylinder block Allen bolt	10	88	—
Oil check bolt	7	7	—
Rear chain guide/damper mounting bolts	10	88	—
Spark plug	18	—	13
Valve adjust nut	20	—	14

4

Table 4 PISTON RING SECTIONAL DIMENSIONS

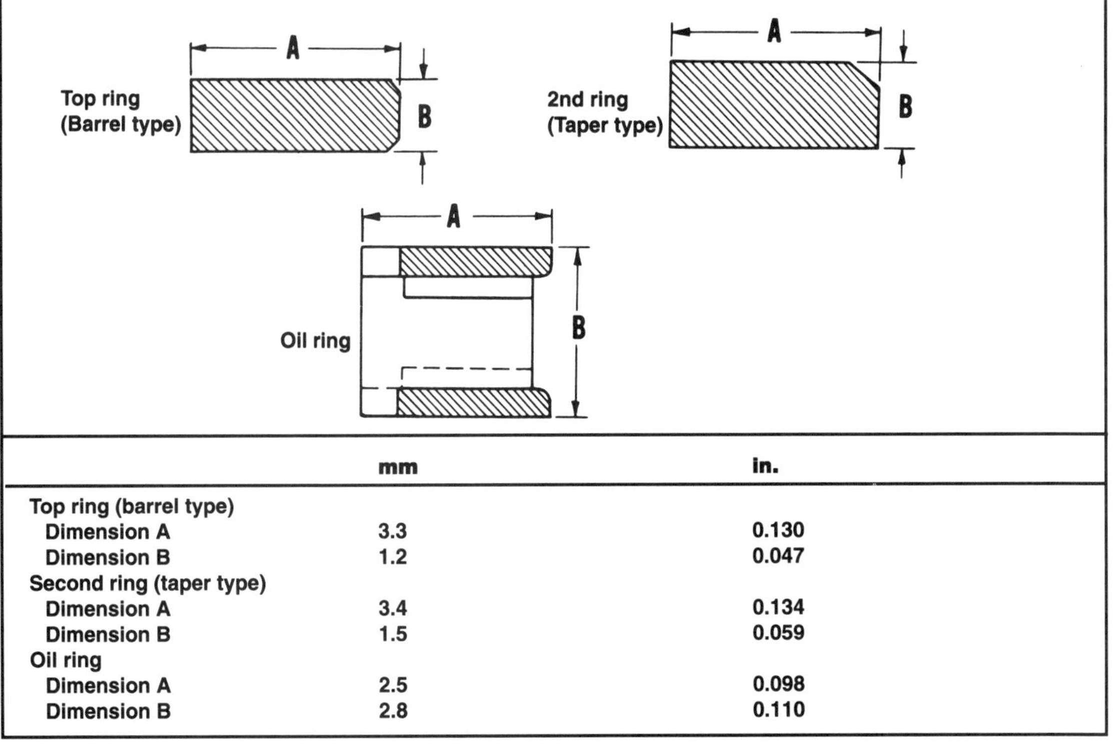

	mm	in.
Top ring (barrel type)		
Dimension A	3.3	0.130
Dimension B	1.2	0.047
Second ring (taper type)		
Dimension A	3.4	0.134
Dimension B	1.5	0.059
Oil ring		
Dimension A	2.5	0.098
Dimension B	2.8	0.110

CHAPTER FIVE

ENGINE LOWER END

This chapter describes service procedures for the following lower end components:

a. Crankcase.
b. Crankshaft and connecting rod.
c. Balancer assembly.
d. Transmission shafts and shift assembly (removal and installation).
e. Middle drive and reverse shaft and shift assembly (removal and installation).
f. Middle driven gear assembly.
g. CDI magneto assembly and starter gears.
h. Internal shift mechanism (removal and installation).
i. Recoil starter (models so equipped).

Prior to removing and disassembling the crankcase, clean the entire engine and frame with a good grade commercial degreaser, like Gunk or Bel-Ray engine degreaser or equivalent. It is easier to work on a clean engine and you will do a better job.

Before starting any work, refer to Chapter One and read the service hints and the detailed information relating to the use of the measuring equipment that must be used in this chapter. You will do a better job with this information fresh in your mind.

Engine specifications are listed in **Table 1**. **Table 1** and **Table 2** are at the end of the chapter.

SERVICING ENGINE IN FRAME

The following components can be serviced while the engine is mounted in the frame (the vehicle's frame is a great holding fixture—especially for breaking loose stubborn bolts and nuts):

a. Cylinder head (Chapter Four).
b. Cylinder block and piston (Chapter Four).
c. External gearshift mechanism.
d. Clutch assemblies.
e. Recoil starter.
f. Oil pump
g. CDI magneto assembly and starter gears.
h. Starter motor
i. Carburetor.
j. Transfer gear assembly.

Engine Removal

This procedure describes engine removal. If service work requires only the removal of a top end component, the engine can be left in the frame and the top end disassembled only as far as required to remove the desired subassembly. If the engine requires crankcase disassembly, it is easier to remove all of the subassemblies from the engine before removing the engine from the frame. By following this method, the frame can be used as a holding

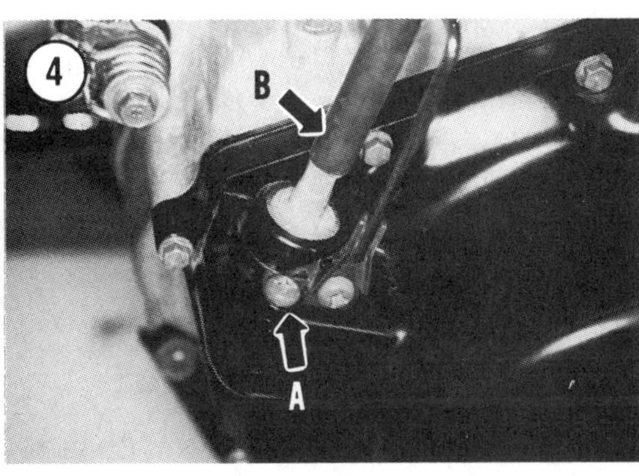

fixture as the engine is disassembled. Disassembling the complete engine while it is placed on a workbench is more time consuming and also requires an assistant to help hold the engine when loosening many of the larger nuts and bolts.

NOTE
This procedure is shown with all of the subassemblies removed from the crankcase.

1. Support the vehicle on a level surface. Set the parking brake and block the rear wheel so the vehicle will not roll in either direction.
2. Remove the battery (Chapter Three).
3. Remove the front carrier rack, the front fender, the rear carrier rack and rear fender as described in Chapter Fourteen.
4. Remove the fuel tank (Chapter Eight).
5. Drain the engine oil and remove the oil filter assembly (Chapter Three). Move the oil cooler hoses out of the way.
6. Remove the exhaust pipe and muffler (Chapter Eight)
7. Remove the air filter box and carburetor (Chapter Eight).
8. Remove the transmission range select lever assembly from the left side of the vehicle (Chapter Seven).
9. Remove the cotter pin and clevis pin (**Figure 1**) and disconnect the No. 1 control cable from the select lever on the crankcase.
10. Remove the No. 1 control cable bracket mounting bolts (**Figure 2**). Tie the cable and bracket away from the engine.
11. Disconnect the brake cables (A, **Figure 3**) from the camshaft lever at the right rear wheel.
12. Disconnect the breather hose (B, **Figure 3**) from the rear brake housing.
13. Remove the left footpeg assembly.
14. Remove the shift pedal pinch bolt and shift pedal.
15. Remove the screw (A, **Figure 4**) and disconnect the speedometer cable (B, **Figure 4**) from the clutch cover.
16. Remove the rear brake pedal assembly (Chapter Thirteen).
17. Disconnect the crankcase ventilation hose (A, **Figure 5**).
18. Disconnect the following electrical connectors:
   a. Spark plug lead from the spark plug.
   b. Thermoswitch connector (B, **Figure 5**).

c. Engine ground cable (C, **Figure 5**).
d. Reverse switch connector (D, **Figure 5**).
e. CDI magneto and neutral switch leads (E, **Figure 5**).

19. Remove the starter motor (Chapter Nine).
20. Remove the rear drive unit and swing arm (Chapter Twelve).
21. Remove the transfer gear assembly as described in this chapter.
22. Remove the front drive shaft (Chapter Eleven).
23. If the engine requires disassembly, remove the following subassemblies:
   a. Cylinder Head (Chapter Four).
   b. Cylinder block and piston (Chapter Four).
   c. CDI magneto/starter clutch (this chapter).
   d. Both clutch assemblies (Chapter Six).
   e. Oil pump (this chapter).
24. If the engine is being removed with the top end installed, perform the following:
   a. Remove the bolt and nut (A, **Figure 6**) securing the front engine mounting bracket to the cylinder head.
   b. Remove the bolts (B, **Figure 6**) securing the mounting bracket to the frame and remove the bracket.
25. Remove the engine assembly as follows:
   a. Place a jack underneath the engine. Raise the jack so the pad just rests against the bottom of the engine. If necessary, place a block of wood on the jack pad to protect the engine case.
   b. Loosen the front mounting bracket (A, **Figure 7**) bolts and nuts.
   c. Loosen the upper rear mounting bolt and nut (B, **Figure 7**).
   d. Loosen the lower rear mounting bolt and nut (C, **Figure 7**).
   e. Move all cables, wires and harnesses out of the way so they will not interfere with engine removal.
   f. Remove the front mounting bracket bolts, nut and the brackets (A, **Figure 7**). Reinstall the bolts and nuts onto the mounting brackets to avoid misplacing them
   g. Remove the lower mounting bolt and nut (C, **Figure 7**) and the upper mounting bolt and nut (B, **Figure 7**).

NOTE
A minimum of 2 people are required to safely remove an assembled engine from the frame.

NOTE
If the engine is disassembled down to the crankcase, there will still be approximately 0.5 qt. (0.47 l) of oil in the bottom of the crankcase. If the engine is tipped to the left side during removal, this remaining oil will drain out of the oil filter element receptacle.

   g. Remove the engine from the left side of the frame.

26. While the engine is removed, check the engine frame mounts for cracks or other damage.

Engine Installation

1. Clean all engine mount bolts and nuts in solvent. Dry with compressed. Remove corrosion from bolts with a wire brush or wheel.
2. Prior to installation, spray the engine mount bolts with a commercial type of rust inhibitor.

NOTE
A minimum of 2 people are required to safely install an assembled engine into the frame.

3. Place a jack in the area directly under the frame where the engine sits. Adjust the height so the engine will sit correctly on it when installed into the frame.

4. Install the engine into the frame from the left side.

5. Install all of the engine mounting bolts (**Figure 7**) from the vehicle's right side. Tighten the engine mounting nuts and bolts as specified in **Table 2**.

6. If the cylinder head is mounted on the engine, tighten the cylinder head-to-frame mounting bolts as specified in **Table 2**. The mounting bolts are identified as follows:

   a. Upper mounting bolts (B, **Figure 6**).
   b. Lower mounting bolt (A, **Figure 6**) and nut.

7. In the following steps, lubricate all of the drive shaft splines with molybdenum disulfide grease.

8. Install the front drive shaft into the front drive unit (Chapter Eleven).

9. Install the front transfer gear assembly as described under *Transfer Gear Assembly* in this chapter, plus the following:
   a. Finger-tighten the mounting bolts (A, **Figure 8**) on the crankcase side of the transfer gear assembly. Do not tighten the bolts at this time.

NOTE
*The 2 bolts marked B in **Figure 8** were not loosened during disassembly. These bolts secure the rear case half to the front case half.*

   b. Tighten the middle gearcase mounting bolts (A, **Figure 9**), except the 2 lower mounting bolts, as specified in **Table 2**. Do not tighten these 2 bolts at this time.

10. Check the front drive shaft operation as follows:

WARNING
Support the vehicle securely to prevent it from falling over.

   a. Support the vehicle so that the front wheels are off the ground.
   b. While an assistant secures the vehicle, turn the front wheels back and forth. At the same time, check the front drive shaft operation. The front drive shaft should turn smoothly.

11. If the transfer gear assembly was overhauled, have the middle gear lash adjusted at a Yamaha dealership.

12. Tighten the transfer gear assembly mounting bolts (A, **Figure 8**) as specified in **Table 2**.

13. Install the front drive shaft protector halves (front and rear) as described in Chapter Eleven.

14. Install the rear swing arm and drive unit as described in Chapter Twelve.

15. If the engine is partially assembled, install the following subassemblies:
   a. Oil pump (this chapter).
   b. Clutch assemblies (Chapter Six).
   c. CDI magneto/starter clutch (this chapter).
   d. Piston and cylinder block(Chapter Four).
   e. Cylinder head (Chapter Four).

16. Install the starter motor (Chapter Nine).

17. Clean the electrical connectors with contact cleaner.
18. Reconnect the following electrical connectors:
   a. Spark plug lead to spark plug.
   b. Thermo unit connector (B, **Figure 5**).
   c. Engine ground cable (C, **Figure 5**).
   d. Reverse switch connector (D, **Figure 5**).
   e. CDI magneto and neutral switch leads (E, **Figure 5**).
19. Reconnect the crankcase ventilation hose (A, **Figure 5**).
20. Install the brake pedal assembly (Chapter Thirteen).
21. Connect the speedometer cable (B, **Figure 4**) into the clutch cover. Secure the cable with its screw (B, **Figure 4**).
22. Install the shift pedal and secure it with its pinch bolt.
23. Install the left footpeg assembly.
24. Reconnect the breather hose (B, **Figure 3**) onto the rear brake housing.
25. Reconnect the brake cables (A, **Figure 3**) onto the camshaft lever at the right rear wheel.
26. Adjust the rear brake and parking brake as described in Chapter Three.
27. Install the No. 1 control cable bracket and secure it with its mounting bolts (**Figure 2**). Tighten the bolts securely.
28. Reconnect the No. 1 control cable at the select lever on the crankcase. Install the clevis pin and secure it with a new cotter pin (**Figure 1**).
29. Install the transmission range select lever assembly as described in Chapter Seven.
30. Install the carburetor and air filter box (Chapter Eight).
31. Install the exhaust pipe and muffler (Chapter Eight).
32. Install the oil filter and refill the engine with new oil as described in Chapter Three.
33. Install the fuel tank (Chapter Eight).
34. Install the rear fender, rear carrier rack, front fender and front carrier rack (Chapter Fourteen).
35. Install the battery (Chapter Three).
36. Adjust the No. 1 and No. 2 select lever control cables as described in Chapter Three.
37. Start the engine and check for oil leaks.
38. Check the following indicator lights for proper operation:
   a. Neutral.
   b. Reverse.
   c. Oil temperature.
39. Check the headlight for proper operation.
40. Check engine idle speed and adjust as described in Chapter Three.

TRANSFER GEAR ASSEMBLY

Removal

The transfer gear assembly can be removed with the engine mounted in the frame.

1. Support the vehicle on a level surface. Set the parking brake and block the rear wheels.
2. Remove the battery (Chapter Three).
3. Remove the front carrier rack, the front fender, the rear carrier rack and rear fender as described in Chapter Fourteen.
4. Remove the fuel tank (Chapter Eight).
5. Drain the transfer gear oil (Chapter Three).
6. Remove the exhaust pipe and muffler (Chapter Eight).
7. Remove the rear axle and swing arm assembly as described in Chapter Twelve.
8. Remove the engine rear guard (B, **Figure 9**).
9. Loosen the 2 inner bolts (A, **Figure 8**) securing the transfer gear assembly to the rear of the crankcase. Do not loosen the 2 outer bolts (B, **Figure 8**).
10. Remove the bolts securing the transfer gear assembly (A, **Figure 9**) to the side of the crankcase. Note the location of the cable clamp and the washers under these bolts. The washers and cable clamp must be reinstalled in the same location.

CAUTION
The transfer gear assembly is heavy. In Step 6, be sure to hold onto it while removing the 2 remaining bolts to avoid dropping it.

11. Hold onto the transfer gear assembly and remove the 2 inner bolts (A, **Figure 8**). Remove the transfer gear assembly. Do not lose the locating dowels.
12. Inspect the transfer gear assembly as described in this chapter.

Inspection

Because of the number special tools required to work on the transfer gear and middle driven gear assembly, refer all service to a Yamaha dealership

Figure 10 is an exploded view of the transfer gearcase assembly.

1. Clean off all gasket residue from the middle driven gear cover and the mating surface on the crankcase.

2. Clean the assembly in solvent and dry with compressed air.

3. Inspect the middle driven gear (A, **Figure 11**) for chipped or missing teeth. If the gear is worn or damaged, inspect the middle drive gear (**Figure 12**) in the crankcase. It may also be damaged.

4. Check the ball bearing (B, **Figure 11**) for wear or damage. It must rotate freely with no binding or excess play.

5. Check the O-ring (A, **Figure 13**) for wear, hardness or deterioration. If necessary, replace the O-ring as follows:

   a. Remove the 2 bolts (**Figure 14**) securing the middle driven gear cover to the transfer case and remove the cover (B, **Figure 13**).

   b. When the cover is removed, the 2 split shims (C, **Figure 13**) may come off with the cover

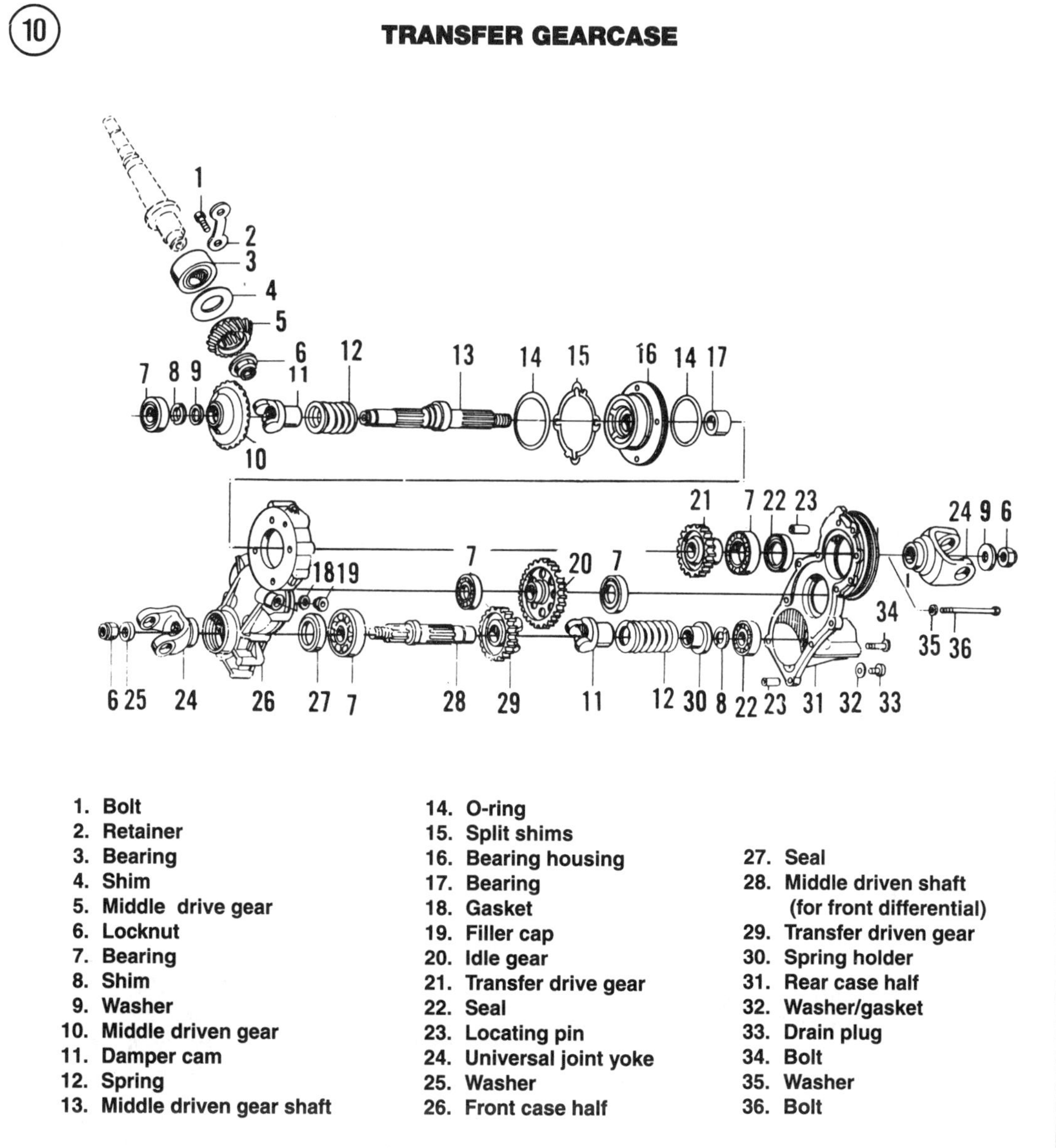

(10) **TRANSFER GEARCASE**

1. Bolt
2. Retainer
3. Bearing
4. Shim
5. Middle drive gear
6. Locknut
7. Bearing
8. Shim
9. Washer
10. Middle driven gear
11. Damper cam
12. Spring
13. Middle driven gear shaft
14. O-ring
15. Split shims
16. Bearing housing
17. Bearing
18. Gasket
19. Filler cap
20. Idle gear
21. Transfer drive gear
22. Seal
23. Locating pin
24. Universal joint yoke
25. Washer
26. Front case half
27. Seal
28. Middle driven shaft (for front differential)
29. Transfer driven gear
30. Spring holder
31. Rear case half
32. Washer/gasket
33. Drain plug
34. Bolt
35. Washer
36. Bolt

or stay with the transfer case. Do not lose the shims.

c. Remove the O-ring (A, **Figure 13**) and install a new one.

d. Make sure the split shims are still in place and then install the cover and 2 bolts (**Figure 14**). Tighten the transfer gear rear case mounting bolts as specified in **Table 2**.

6. Check both universal joints (**Figure 15**) for wear or excess play.

7. Remove the short drive shaft from the final drive unit on the swing arm.

8. Check both universal joint inner splines (**Figure 16**) for wear or damage.

9. Check the short drive shaft outer splines and the front drive shaft outer splines for wear or damage. See **Figure 17**, typical.

10. Insert the short drive shaft into the universal joint (**Figure 18**). It must fit snug with no rotational play. Repeat for the front drive shaft. Replace any component with damaged splines.

11. Inspect the split shims (15, **Figure 10**) for wear or damage. If damaged, replace with the same thickness shim(s).

Installation

1. Apply a light coat of gasket sealant to the sealing surface of the cover.

2. Make sure the locating dowels (C, **Figure 11**) are in place in the crankcase.

3. Apply a light coat of engine oil to the O-ring (A, **Figure 13**).

4. Engage the transfer gear assembly with the front drive shaft, then install it onto the crankcase and install the 2 mounting bolts (A, **Figure 8**) to hold the assembly in place. Tighten the bolts finger-tight only.

5. Install the middle gearcase (A, **Figure 9**) and its mounting bolts. Install the cable clamp and the washers under the correct bolts. At this time, tighten the middle gearcase mounting bolts as specified in **Table 2**.

6. Tighten the 2 transfer gearcase-to-crankcase mounting bolts (A, **Figure 8**) as specified in **Table 2**.

7. Install the engine rear guard (B, **Figure 9**).

8. Install the rear axle and swing arm assembly (Chapter Twelve).

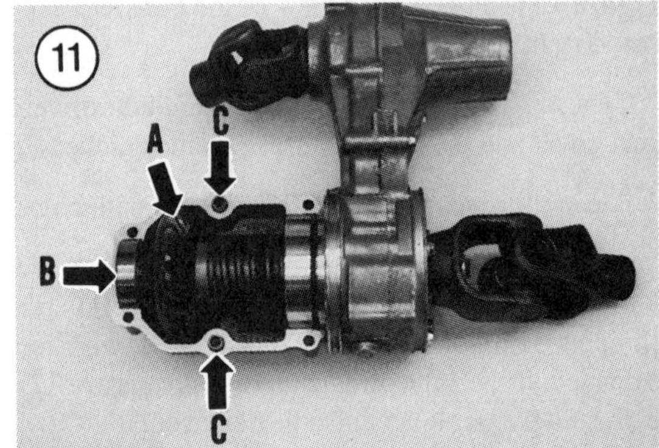

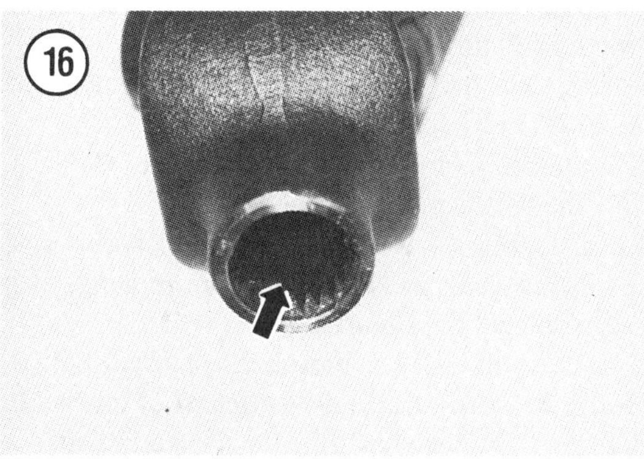

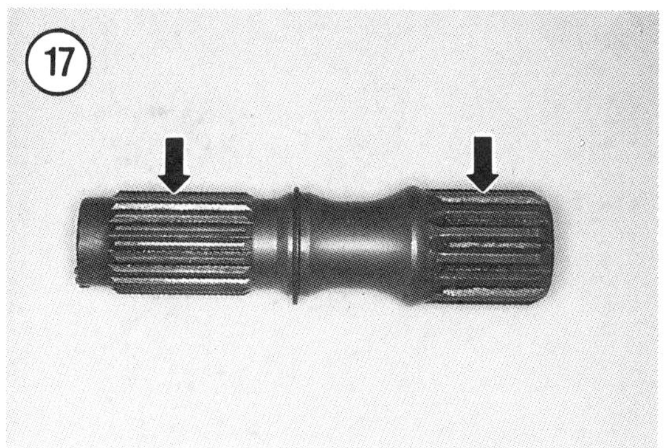

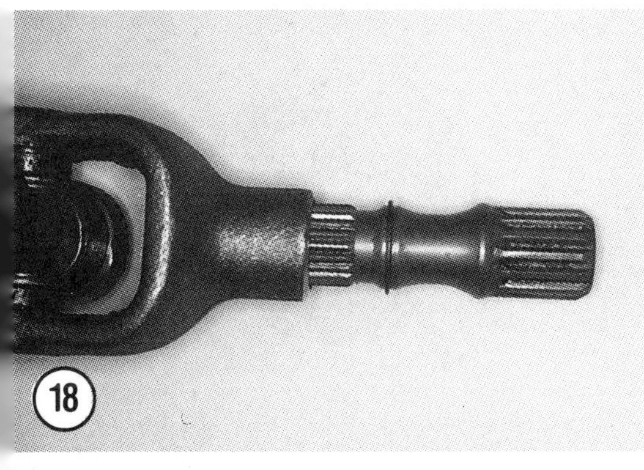

9. Install the exhaust pipe and muffler (Chapter Eight).

10. Refill the transfer gear oil as described in Chapter Three.

11. Install the fuel tank (Chapter Eight).

12. Install the rear fender and rear carrier and the front fender and front carrier rack (Chapter Fourteen).

13. Install the battery (Chapter Three).

MIDDLE DRIVE GEAR

The middle drive gear (5, **Figure 10**) is mounted on the middle drive shaft and positioned outside the left crankcase.

Removal

1. Remove all engine subassemblies from the engine, then remove the engine from the frame as described in this chapter.

2. If still installed, remove both clutch assemblies as described in Chapter Six.

3. Shift the transmission into first gear.

4. Reinstall the manual clutch boss onto the transmission shaft. Install the lockwasher and nut and tighten the nut hand tight.

CAUTION
Do not damage the grooves in the clutch boss when installing the clutch holding tool in Step 5.

5. Carefully install a clutch holding tool (**Figure 19**) onto the clutch boss splines.

6. Use a small chisel or drift and bend the locking portion of the nut away from the flat on the middle drive gear shaft (**Figure 20**).
7. Hold the clutch boss with the holding tool and loosen the middle drive gear nut. Remove the nut (**Figure 20**) and discard the nut. A new nut must be installed during assembly.
8. Remove the clutch holding tool.
9. Slide the middle drive gear (**Figure 20**) off the middle drive shaft, then remove the shim (4, **Figure 10**) located between the gear and crankcase.
10. Remove the nut, lockwasher and manual clutch boss from the transmission shaft (**Figure 19**).

Inspection

1. Check the gear for chipped or missing teeth (**Figure 21**). If the gear is worn or damaged, inspect the middle driven gear on the middle driven gear assembly.
2. Check the inner splines (**Figure 21**) for wear or damage. If the splines are worn or damaged, inspect the splines on the middle drive shaft.

Installation

1. Reinstall the manual clutch boss only onto the transmission shaft (**Figure 19**). Install the lockwasher and nut and tighten the nut hand tight.

CAUTION
Do not damage the grooves in the clutch boss when installing the clutch holding tool in Step 2.

2. Carefully install a clutch holding tool (**Figure 19**) onto the clutch boss splines.
3. Install the shim and the middle drive gear (**Figure 20**) onto middle drive shaft. Push them on until they bottom out.
4. Install a *new* nut onto the shaft (**Figure 20**).
5. Shift the transmission into first gear.
6. Hold the clutch boss and tighten the middle drive gear nut (**Figure 20**) as specified in **Table 2**.
7. Remove the clutch holding tool.
8. Use a drift and bend the locking portion of the nut down onto the flat on the middle drive gear shaft (**Figure 20**).
9. Remove the nut, lockwasher and clutch boss from the transmission shaft (**Figure 19**).
10. Install the engine in the frame, then install all engine subassemblies onto the engine.

BALANCER GEAR AND OIL PUMP DRIVE GEAR ASSEMBLY

The balancer shaft and oil pump gears (**Figure 22**) are mounted on the right side of the engine.

Removal

1. Remove all engine subassemblies from the engine, then remove the engine from the frame as described in this chapter.
2. If still installed, remove both clutch assemblies as described in Chapter Six.
3. Bend the lockwasher tab (B, **Figure 23**) away from the balancer driven gear nut.
4. Place a brass washer between the balancer drive and driven gears to keep them from rotating, then loosen the nut (A, **Figure 23**).
5. Remove the nut (A, **Figure 23**), lockwasher (B, **Figure 23**) and balancer driven gear (C, **Figure 23**). Remove the square key from the balancer shaft.

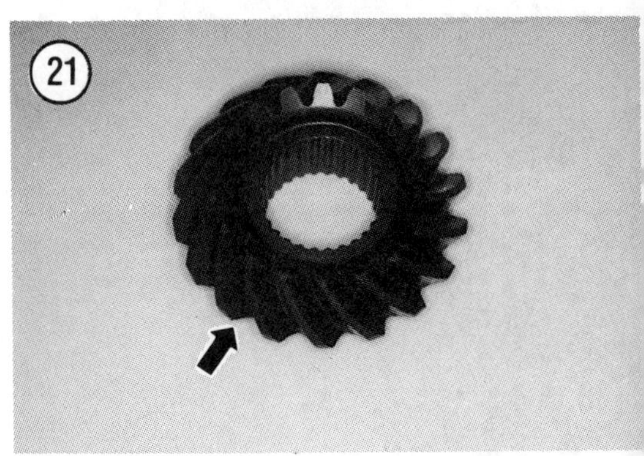

6. Slide the collar off the balancer shaft.

7. Remove the circlip (A, **Figure 24**), then slide the holding plate (B, **Figure 24**) off the crankshaft.

NOTE
There are 6 small springs and 3 small pins located in the balancer drive gear. They will usually stay with the gear when it is removed, but be prepared to catch the springs if they come free during gear removal.

8. Carefully slide the balancer drive gear assembly (**Figure 25**) straight off the buffer boss.

9. To prevent the loss of the springs and pins, secure each set to the gear with small tie wraps as shown in **Figure 26**. Every other spring has one of the pins located within it.

NOTE
The buffer boss is pressed onto the end of the crankshaft and must be removed with a puller.

CAUTION
*In Step 10, the puller jaws **must** be placed behind the steel washer (A, **Figure 27**). The washer is strong enough to*

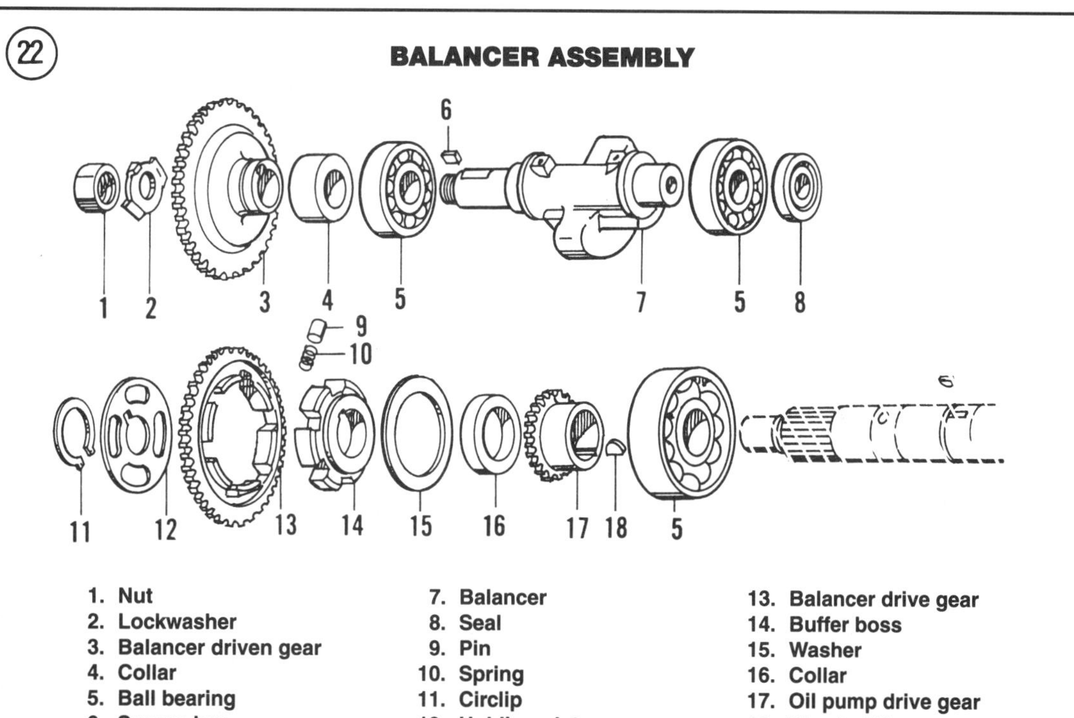

withstand the pressure of the puller. Do ***not*** *place the puller jaws behind the oil pump drive gear (B,* ***Figure 27****) as the gear will be damaged during removal.*

10. Install a jaw puller behind the steel washer and the buffer boss (C, **Figure 27**). Make sure the center post of the puller is centered on the end of the crankshaft, then slowly tighten the puller. The buffer boss is *extremely tight* on the crankshaft and a considerable amount of pressure is required to remove it from the crankshaft.

NOTE

The buffer boss must be replaced every time it is removed from the crankshaft. A new boss must be pressed on to maintain the required tight fit of the boss to the crankshaft.

11. Remove the puller, buffer boss and washer from the crankshaft. Discard the buffer boss.
12. Remove the buffer boss Woodruff key (**Figure 28**) from the crankshaft.
13. Slide off the collar (A, **Figure 29**) and the oil pump drive gear (B, **Figure 29**).
14. Remove the oil pump drive gear Woodruff key (**Figure 30**) from the crankshaft.

Inspection

1. Clean and dry all parts (**Figure 31**).
2. Check the balancer drive gear and oil pump drive gear gears for broken or chipped teeth, heat discoloration and excessive wear.
3. Check the Woodruff keyway in the oil pump drive gear for wear or damage.

25

26

27

28

29

30

31

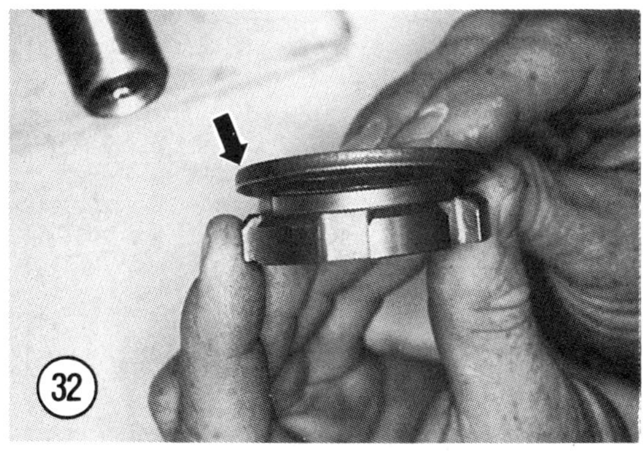
32

33

4. Check the balancer drive gear springs for sagging or wear. Replace all springs as a set if any are weak or damaged.
5. Check both Woodruff keys and the crankshaft keyways for wear or damage.

Installation

1. Install the oil pump drive gear Woodruff key (**Figure 30**) into the crankshaft keyway.
2. Slide the oil pump drive gear (B, **Figure 29**) onto the crankshaft. Align the gear keyway with the Woodruff key and push the gear on until it stops.
3. Install the collar (A, **Figure 29**) and seat it against the oil pump drive gear.
4. Install the buffer boss Woodruff key (**Figure 28**) into the crankshaft keyway.
5. Install the washer onto the backside of a *new* buffer boss (**Figure 32**).

NOTE
*In Step 6, install the buffer boss with its index mark (**Figure 33**) facing out.*

6. Align the buffer boss keyway with the crankshaft Woodruff key, then install the buffer boss onto the crankshaft until it stops.
7. Support the crankcase with wooden blocks.
8. Place a suitable size pipe against the buffer boss (**Figure 34**) and start driving the boss onto the crankshaft with a hammer. Stop frequently to check its position on the shaft and its alignment with the Woodruff key. Continue to drive the boss on until it moves past the circlip groove in the crankshaft (**Figure 35**), then stop.
9. Once the complete circlip groove is visible, install the holding plate (A, **Figure 36**) over the Woodruff key and seat it against the buffer boss. Make sure the

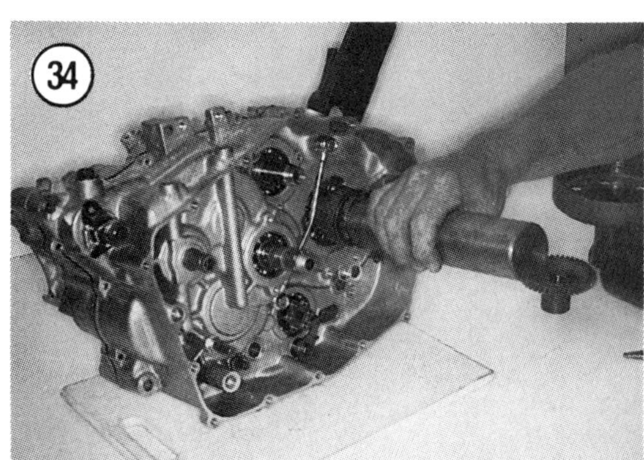
34

5

circlip groove is still visible (B, **Figure 36**) with sufficient room to install the circlip.

10. Remove the holding plate.

11. Remove the small tie wraps from the balancer drive gear. Make sure the springs are still in place with the pins located in every other spring.

NOTE
In Step 12, install the balancer drive gear with its index mark facing out.

12. Align the index mark on the balancer drive gear with the buffer boss (**Figure 37**), then install the gear onto the buffer boss. See **Figure 25**.

13. Install the holding plate (B, **Figure 24**) and use it to push the drive gear completely onto the buffer boss. Then remove the holding plate, making sure the springs (**Figure 37**) are properly seated in both parts.

14. Recheck the index marks (**Figure 38**) on both parts for proper alignment.

15. Install the holding plate by aligning its keyway with the end of the Woodruff key (**Figure 39**).

16. Install the circlip (A, **Figure 24**) into the crankshaft groove. Make sure it seats in the groove completely.

17. Hold onto the end of the connecting rod and turn the crankshaft several times. Make sure it moves smoothly and with no roughness or binding.

18. Slide the collar (B, **Figure 29**) onto the balancer shaft.

19. Align the index mark on the balancer driven gear with the index mark on the balancer drive gear (**Figure 40**), then install the driven gear (C, **Figure 23**).

20. Rotate the crankshaft and align the balancer driven gear and balancer shaft keyways. Hold the

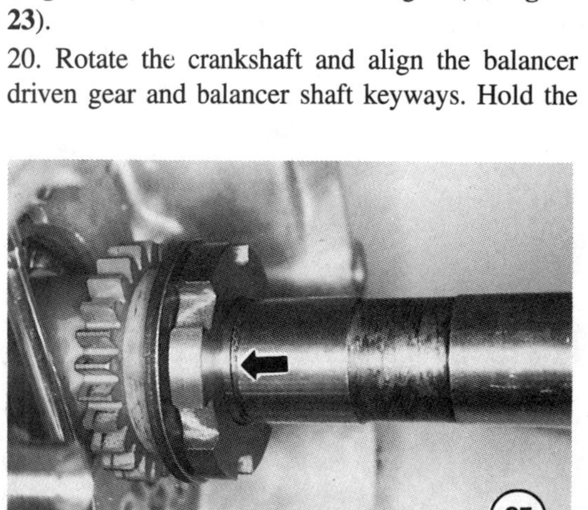

driven gear in this position and install the square key (A, **Figure 41**) into the gear and balancer shaft.

21. Install a new lockwasher (A, **Figure 42**). Insert the lockwasher tang (B, **Figure 41**) into the driven gear keyway (B, **Figure 42**).

22. Install the balancer driven gear nut (A, **Figure 43**) and tighten finger-tight.

23. Place a copper or brass washer between the drive and driven gears (B, **Figure 43**). Doing so will prevent the driven gear from turning when tightening the nut.

24. Tighten the balancer driven gear nut (A, **Figure 43**) as specified in **Table 2**. Then remove the copper or brass washer.

25. Bend the lockwasher tab against one flat on the balancer driven gear nut.

26. Install the engine in the frame and install all engine subassemblies onto the engine as described in this chapter.

5

OIL PUMP

The oil pump is mounted behind the clutch on the right side of the engine. The oil pump can be removed with the engine mounted in the frame. This procedure is shown with the engine removed from the frame.

Removal

1. Remove both clutch assemblies as described in Chapter Six.

2. If the oil pump is going to be disassembled, loosen the oil pump assembly cover screw (**Figure 44**).

CAUTION
An impact driver with a No. 3 Phillips bit must be used to loosen the oil pump mounting screws in Step 3. Attempting to loosen the screws with a Phillips screwdriver will ruin the screw heads.

3. Loosen and remove the oil pump assembly mounting screws (A, **Figure 45**).
4. Remove the oil pump and driven gear assembly (B, **Figure 45**) from the crankcase.

Oil Pump Disassembly/Inspection

When measuring the oil pump operating clearances in this section, compare the actual measurements to the specifications in **Table 1**. Replace the oil pump if parts are out of specification or are damaged as described in this section. Always replace the oil pump as an assembly.

Refer to **Figure 46** for this procedure.

1. Remove and discard the gasket.
2. Remove the Phillips head screw (**Figure 44**) securing the pump cover to the pump body and disassemble the oil pump assembly. Do not lose the small locating pins.
3. Remove all gasket residue from the oil pump body and crankcase mating surfaces.

NOTE
Before cleaning the oil pump driven gear in Step 4, make sure the solvent is compatible with the plastic gear.

4. Clean and dry all parts.
5. Inspect the oil pump body and cover for cracks.

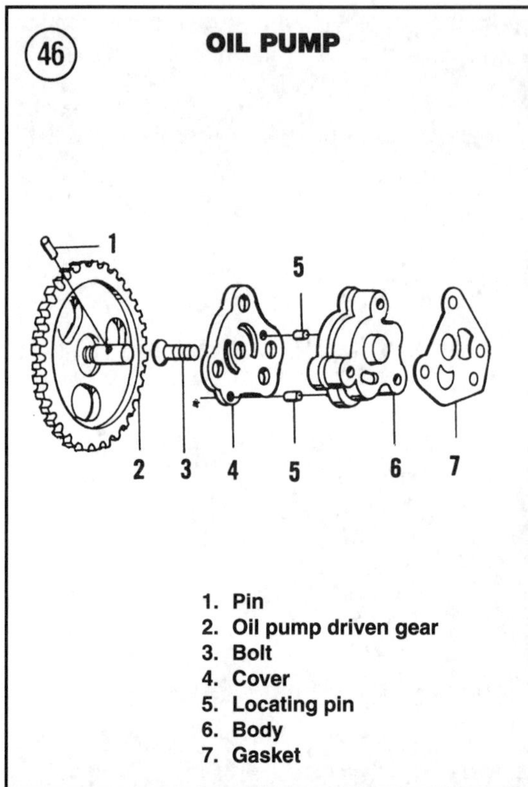

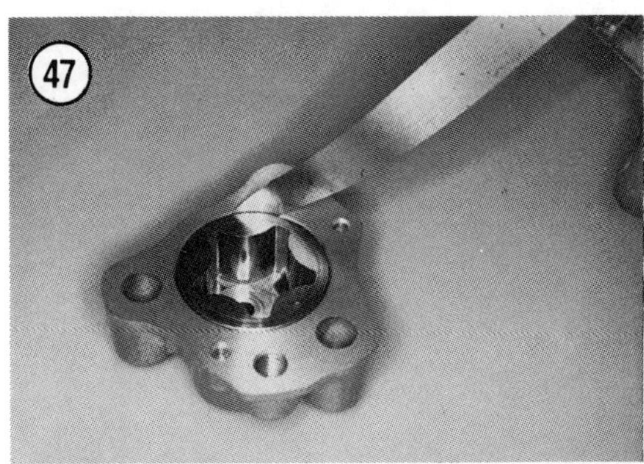

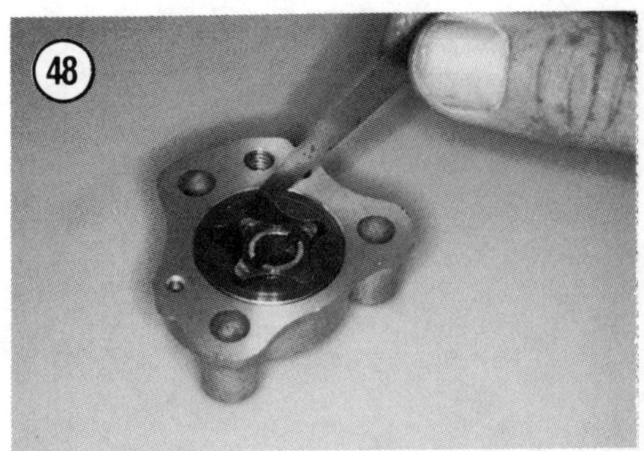

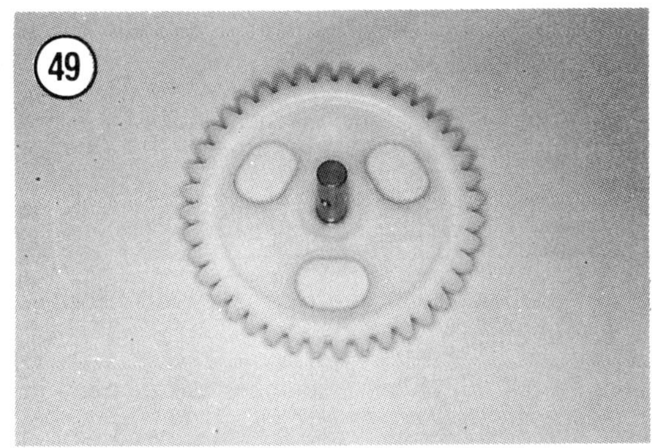

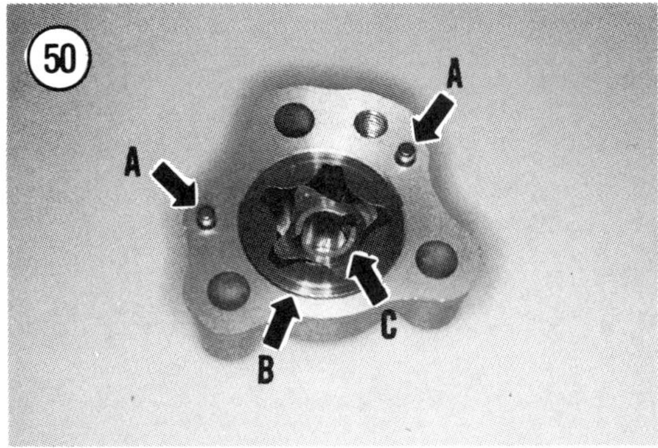

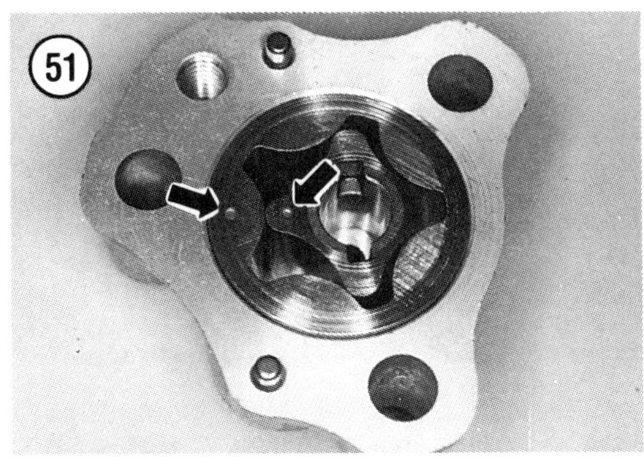

6. Inspect the inner and outer rotors for cracks, scoring or other damage.
7. Install the outer rotor into the oil pump body. Then measure the outer rotor- to-oil pump body side clearance with a flat feeler gauge (**Figure 47**).
8. Install the inner rotor into the oil pump body. Then measure the inner rotor-to-outer rotor tip clearance with a flat feeler gauge (**Figure 48**).
9. Inspect the oil pump driven gear (**Figure 49**) for:
   a. Broken or chipped teeth.
   b. Surface degradation.
   c. Shaft or keyway wear or damage.

5

Oil Pump Assembly

1. Coat all parts with clean engine oil prior to assembly.
2. Install the small locating pins (A, **Figure 50**) into the oil pump body
3. Position the outer rotor (B, **Figure 50)** with its punch mark facing up and install it in the body.
4. Position the inner rotor (C, **Figure 50**) with its punch mark facing up and install it in the body and outer rotor.
5. Make sure both rotor punch marks are facing up (**Figure 51**).
6. Install the outer cover over the oil pump shaft (**Figure 52**).
7. Install the pin (**Figure 53**) through the oil pump shaft hole.
8. Align the slot in the inner rotor (A, **Figure 54**) parallel to the small locating pins (B, **Figure 54**).
9. Align the 2 locating pins (**Figure 55**) parallel with the small locating pin holes in the cover.
10. Turn the cover and driven gear over and align the cover locating pin holes with the oil pump body locating pins and install the cover.

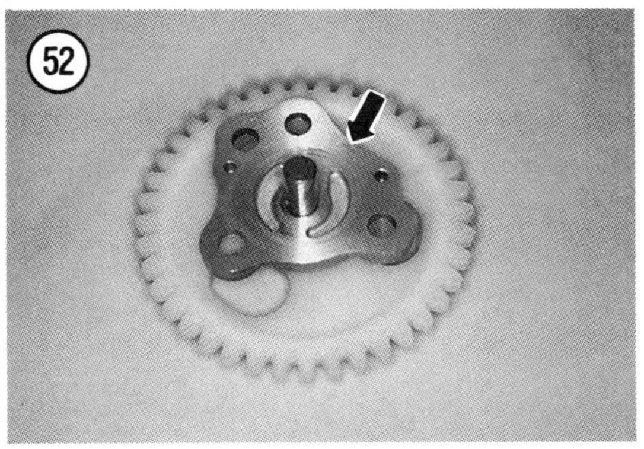

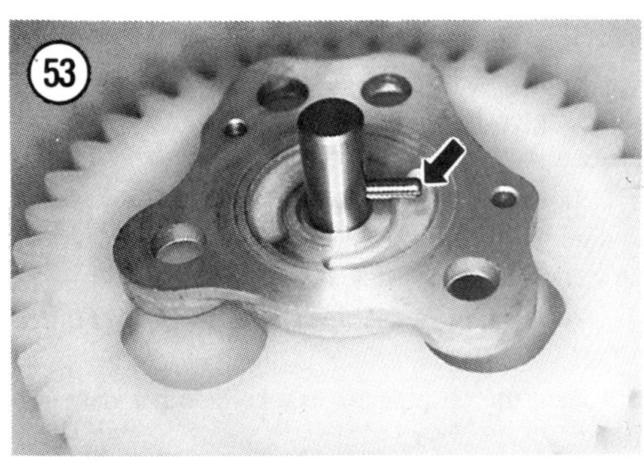

11. Push the cover onto the body. Make sure they come completely together with no gap. Do not try to force the 2 parts together with the mounting screw as the oil pump will be damaged.
12. Install the Phillips screw (**Figure 44**) securing the cover to the body and tighten as specified in **Table 2**.

NOTE
If the body screw is difficult to tighten, tighten it finger-tight now. Then tighten to its final torque specification after installing the oil pump onto the crankcase.

13. After tightening the screw, turn the driven gear to make sure the oil pump rotates smoothly with no binding. If there is any binding, disassemble the pump and correct the problem.

Oil Pump Installation

1. Install a new oil pump gasket onto the body.
2. Move the oil pump up into position and mesh the driven gear (B, **Figure 45**) with the oil pump drive gear.
3. Align the mounting holes and install the oil pump mounting screws (A, **Figure 45**). Tighten the screws finger-tight.
4. If necessary, tighten the oil pump body screw (**Figure 44**) as specified in **Table 2**.
5. Tighten the oil pump mounting screws (A, **Figure 45**) as specified in **Table 2**.
6. Install both clutch assemblies as described in this chapter.

INTERNAL OIL PIPE

Removal/Installation

1. Remove both clutch assemblies as described in Chapter Six.
2. Remove the balancer *driven gear* as described in this chapter. It is not necessary to remove the balancer drive gear and buffer boss.
3. Remove the 2 banjo bolts (A, **Figure 56**), washers and oil pipe (B, **Figure 56**). Discard the washers as new ones must be installed.
4. Clean and dry the oil pipe and banjo bolts (**Figure 57**).
5. Check the oil pipe for cracks or other damage. Replace if necessary.
6. Install the oil pipe by reversing these steps, while noting the following:
   a. Install a new washer on each side of the banjo fittings as shown in **Figure 57**.
   b. Tighten the internal oil pipe banjo bolts as specified in **Table 2**.
   c. Install the balancer driven gear as described in this chapter.
   d. Install the clutch assemblies as described in this chapter.

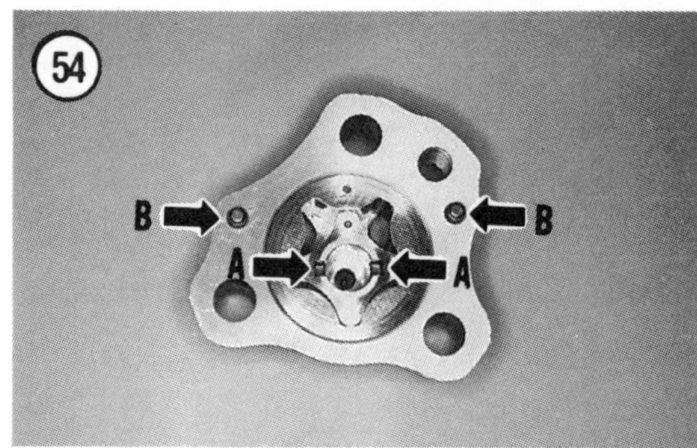

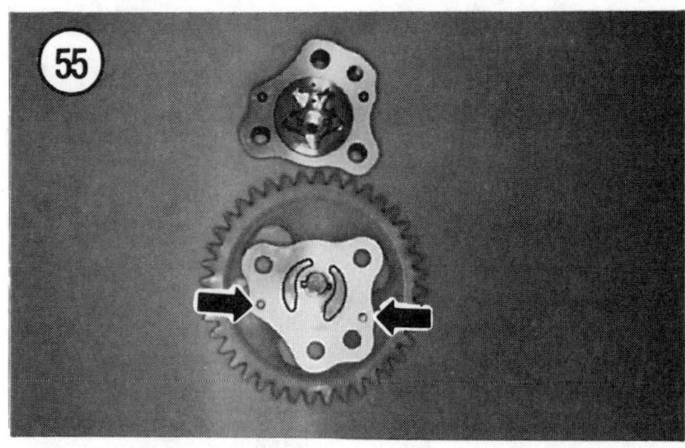

EXTERNAL OIL PIPE

Removal/Installation

NOTE
This procedure is shown with additional components removed for clarity. Remove only the components listed in this procedure.

1. Remove the carburetor as described in Chapter Eight.

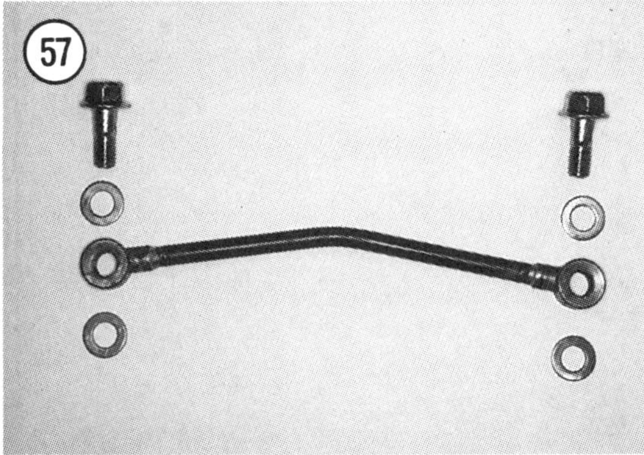
57

58

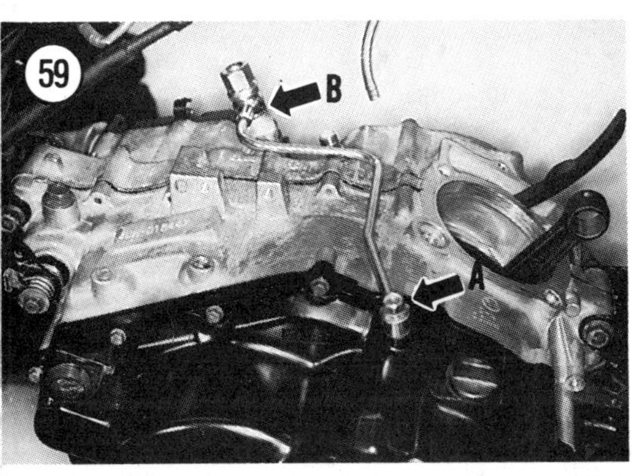

59

2. Disconnect the thermo unit electrical connector (**Figure 58**).
3. Loosen and remove the thermo unit (**Figure 58**) and washer.
4. Loosen and remove the right banjo bolt (A, **Figure 59**) and washers. Discard the washers.
5. Loosen and remove the left banjo bolt (B, **Figure 59**) and washers. Discard the washers.
6. Remove the external oil pipe.
7. Clean and dry the oil pipe and banjo bolts.
8. Check the oil pipe for cracks or other damage. Replace if necessary.
9. Install the external oil pipe by reversing these steps, while noting the following.
10. Tighten the external oil pipe banjo bolts as follows:
   a. Install a new washer on each side of the banjo fittings.
   b. Tighten the left banjo bolt (B, **Figure 59**) as specified in **Table 2**.
   c. Tighten the right banjo bolt (A, **Figure 59**) as specified in **Table 2**.
11. Install the thermo unit and a new washer. Tighten the thermo unit as specified in **Table 2**.
12. Install the carburetor as described in this Chapter Eight.

5

OIL COOLER AND HOSES

Two hoses connect the oil cooler to the oil filter cover at the engine. The oil hoses and oil cooler can be removed separately or the oil cooler and hoses can be removed at the same time.

Refer to **Figure 60** for this procedure.

1. Remove the front carrier rack and front fender as described in Chapter Fourteen.
2. Drain the engine oil as described in Chapter Three.
3. Remove the bolt and clamp securing the oil cooler hoses to the frame.
4. Remove the shift lever pinch bolt and remove the shift lever.
5. To remove only the oil cooler hoses, perform the following:
   a. Loosen one of the oil hose fittings at the oil filter outer cover (**Figure 61**). Disconnect the fitting and remove the gasket.
   b. Repeat for the other oil hose.
   c. Loosen one of the oil hose fittings (A, **Figure 62**) at the oil cooler. Disconnect the fitting and remove the O-ring and dowel pin.

d. Repeat for the other oil hose.

e. Plug the oil hose ends to prevent oil leakage and hose contamination.

NOTE
The 2 oil hoses are different. Identify the hoses before removing them.

f. Carefully remove the oil cooler hoses from the frame.

CAUTION
The oil cooler fins are fragile. Handle the oil cooler carefully during the following steps.

6. To remove the oil cooler only, perform the following:

a. Loosen one of the oil hose fittings (A, **Figure 62**) at the oil cooler. Disconnect the fitting and remove the O-ring and dowel pin. Plug the oil hose opening to prevent oil leakage and hose contamination.

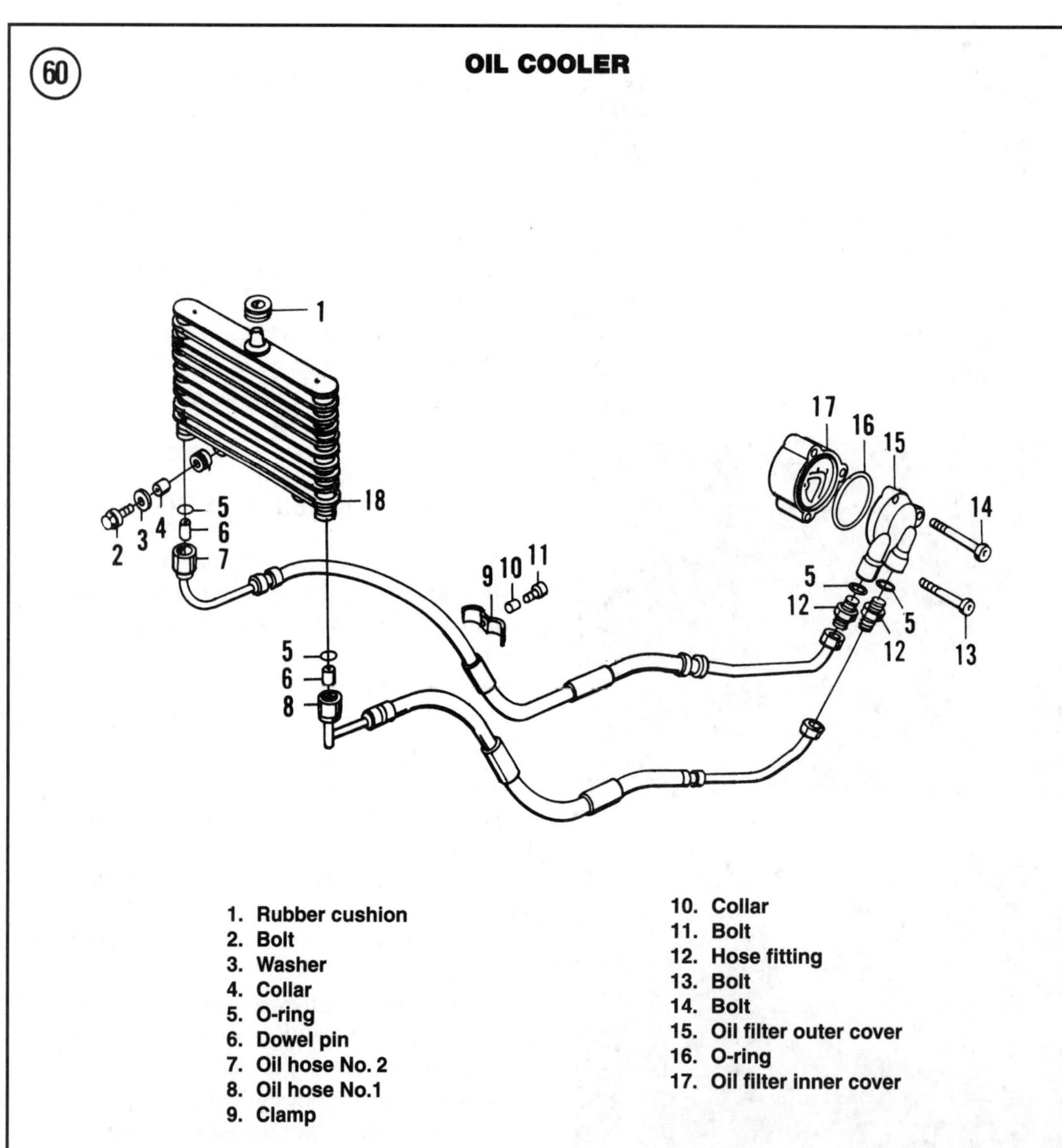

b. Repeat for the opposite hose.

c. Remove the oil cooler mounting bolts and washers (B, **Figure 62**).

d. Pull the oil cooler down and release the top locating pin from the mounting tab on the frame.

e. Carefully remove the oil cooler (C, **Figure 62**) from the frame. Don't lose the metal collars located inside the rubber grommet mounting tabs.

7. To remove the oil cooler and both lines as an assembly, perform the following:

a. Loosen one of the oil hose fittings at the oil filter outer cover (**Figure 61**). Disconnect the fitting and remove the gasket. Plug the oil hose to prevent oil leakage and hose contamination.

b. Repeat for the other oil hose.

c. Remove the oil cooler mounting bolts and washers (B, **Figure 62**).

d. Pull the oil cooler down and release the top locating pin from the mounting tab on the frame.

61

62

e. Carefully remove the oil cooler (C, **Figure 62**) from the frame. Do notlose the metal collars located inside the rubber grommet mounting tabs.

8. Replace the O-rings (5, **Figure 60**) if leaking or damaged.

9. Replace the gaskets if leaking or damaged.

10. Install by reversing these removal steps, while noting the following:

a. Lubricate the O-rings (5, **Figure 60**) with engine oil.

b. Tighten the oil cooler mounting bolts as specified in **Table 2**.

c. Tighten the oil hose fittings as specified in **Table 2**.

d. Refill the engine with oil as described in Chapter Three.

e. Start the engine and check for any oil leaks before installing the front fender assembly. Tighten any fittings as necessary.

ELECTRIC FAN

The electric fan is mounted behind the oil cooler. It can be removed after removing the oil cooler from the frame. When removing the oil cooler, you do not need to disconnect the oil hoses.

Refer to **Figure 63** (1993-1995) or **Figure 64** (1996-on) when servicing the electric fan.

Fan Testing

Refer to Chapter Nine.

Removal/Installation

1. Remove the front carrier rack and front fender as described in Chapter Fourteen.

2. To remove the oil cooler without disconnecting the oil hoses, perform the following:

a. Remove the oil cooler mounting bolts and washers (B, **Figure 62**).

b. Pull the oil cooler down and release the top locating pin from the mounting tab on the frame.

c. Carefully move the oil cooler (C, **Figure 62**) away from the fan. Do not lose the metal collars located inside the rubber grommets.

3. Disconnect the fan electrical connector.

4. Remove the bolts (**Figure 65**) securing the fan to the frame.

5. Disconnect the vent hose (**Figure 66**) from the fan and remove the fan.

6. Replace any missing or damaged fan grommets or collars.

7. Install the fan by reversing these removal steps, noting the following.

8. Tighten the fan mounting bolts securely.

Fan Blade Removal/Installation

1. On 1993-1995 models, remove the cover.

2. Remove the nut and the fan blade. See **Figure 63** or **Figure 64**.

3. Install the fan blade with its correct side facing out.

4. Install and tighten the nut.

5. On 1993-1995 models, install the cover.

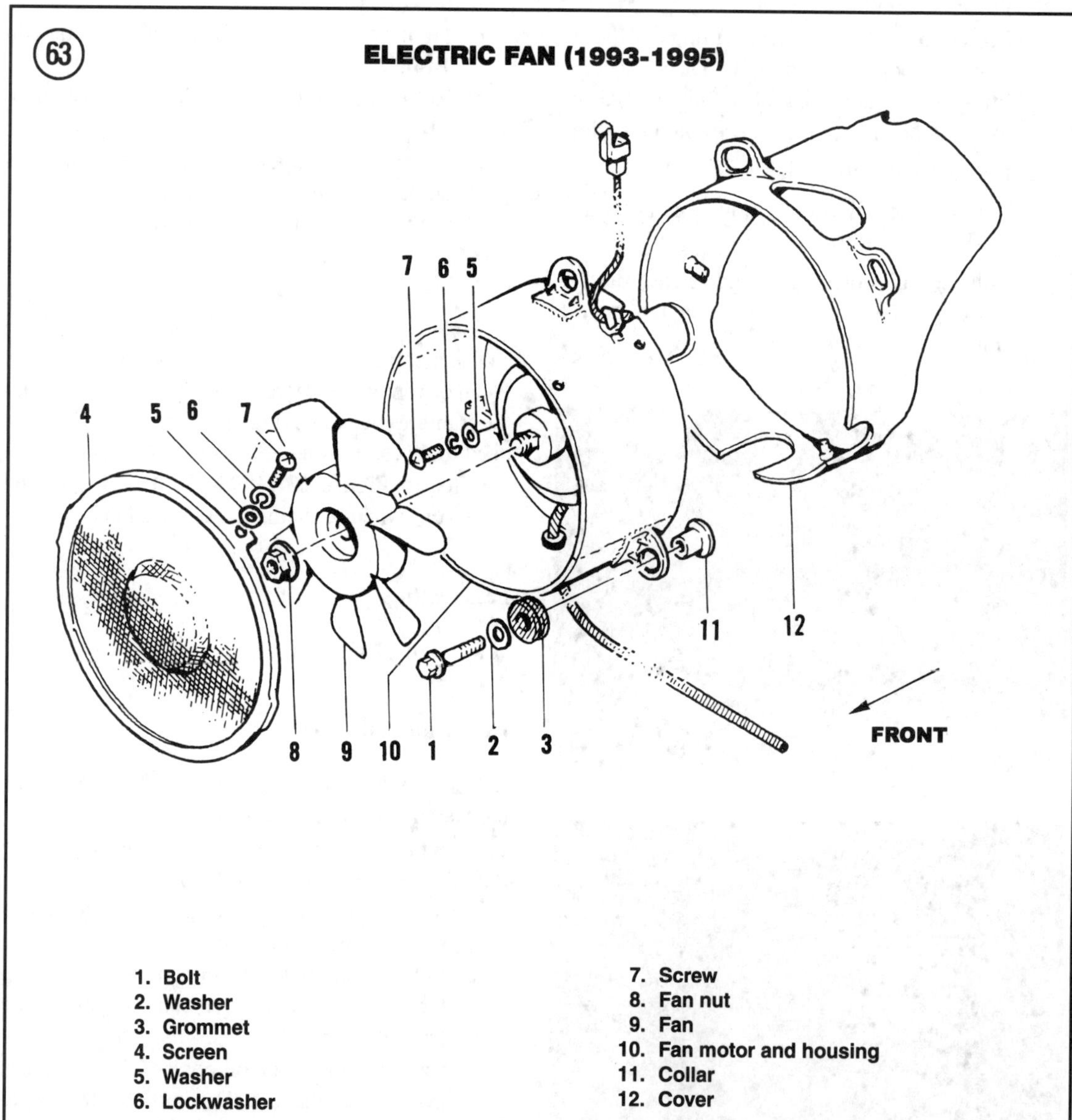

MAGNETO STATOR AND STATOR HOUSING

The stator coil is mounted inside the stator housing on the left side of the engine. The stator housing is also referred to as the left crankcase cover.

Refer to **Figure 67**.

Stator Housing Removal

1. Drain the engine oil as described in Chapter Three.
2. Remove the shift lever and the left side footpeg assembly.
3. Remove the transmission range select lever assembly as described in Chapter Seven.
4. Remove the recoil starter assembly and the starter drum as described in this chapter.
5. Disconnect the stator coil electrical connectors from the wiring harness.

5

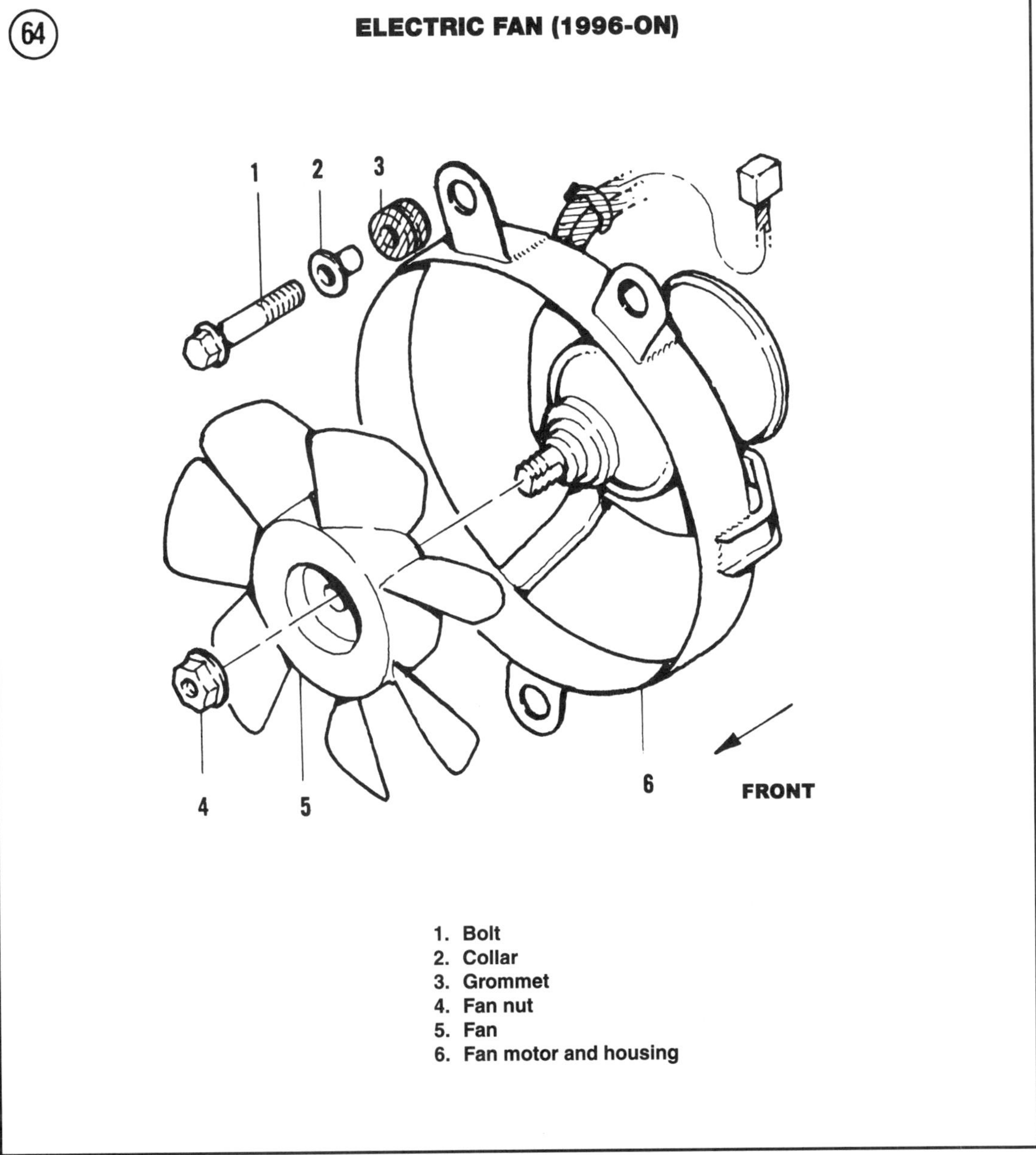

NOTE
When removing the stator housing mounting bolts, note the location of the sealing washer and wiring harness clamp.

6. Remove the stator housing (**Figure 68**) mounting bolts. Remove the sealing washer from the bolt.
7. Remove the stator housing.
8. Remove the gasket and 2 dowel pins.
9. If necessary, remove the stator as described in this chapter.
10. If further disassembly or testing is not required, store the stator housing assembly in a plastic bag until reassembly.

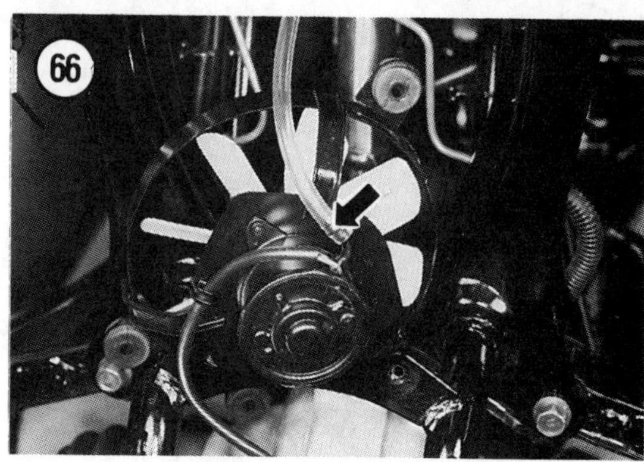

Stator Coil Testing

Refer to *Charge Coil Testing* and *Source Coil and Pickup Coil Testing* in Chapter Nine.

Stator Coil Removal/Installation

The stator coil consists of the charge, pickup and source coil assemblies. The pickup coil is a separate unit from the main stator coil assembly. Do not cut any of the stator coil wires. If either the pickup coil or one of the internal stator coils (charge or source coil) is faulty, the stator coil must be replaced as an assembly.

1. Remove the stator housing as described in this section.
2. Remove the pickup coil mounting screws (A, **Figure 69**).
3. Remove the source coil wire guide screws and remove the guide (B, **Figure 69**).
4. Remove the stator coil mounting screws (C, **Figure 69**), lockwashers and flat washers.
5. Remove the stator coil assembly from the housing.
6. If you are going to replace the stator housing oil seal and/or bearing, do so now as described in the following procedure.
7. Remove all threadlocking residue from the pickup and stator coil screws and threaded holes.
8. Apply a medium strength threadlocking compound to all of the mounting screws before installing them in the following steps.
9. Install the stator coil into the housing by aligning the stator coil and stator housing holes. Install the

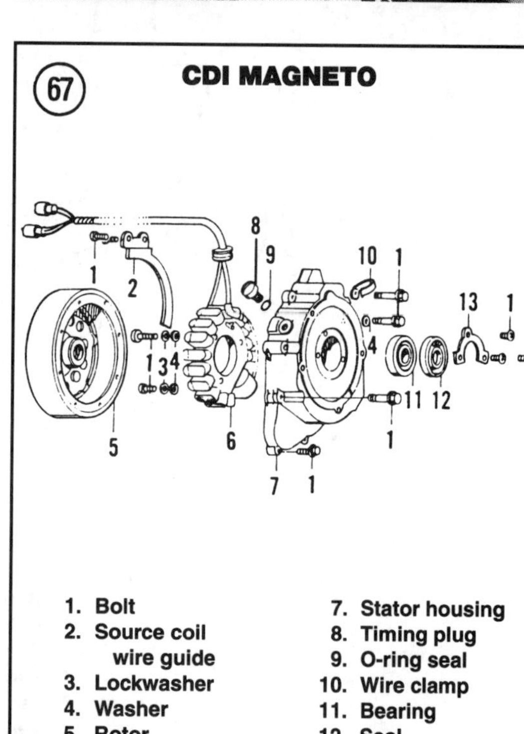

67 CDI MAGNETO

1. Bolt
2. Source coil wire guide
3. Lockwasher
4. Washer
5. Rotor
6. Stator assembly
7. Stator housing
8. Timing plug
9. O-ring seal
10. Wire clamp
11. Bearing
12. Seal
13. Seal plate

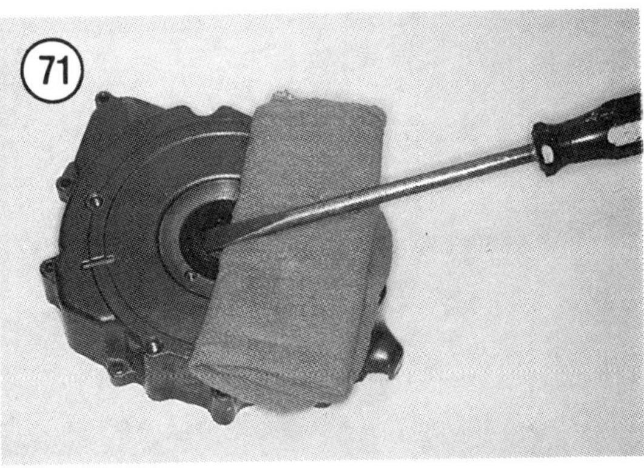

mounting screws (C, **Figure 69**), lockwashers and flat washers. Tighten the stator coil mounting screws as specified in **Table 2**.

10. Align the pickup coil with the stator housing screw holes (A, **Figure 69**), then install and tighten the pickup coil mounting screws as specified in **Table 2**.

11. Route the stator coil wiring harness in the housing. Then push the rubber grommet into the housing notch.

12. Install the stator coil wire guide and guide screws (B, **Figure 69**) and tighten securely.

Stator Housing Seal and Bearing Replacement

1. If the bearing is going to be replaced, remove the stator coil from the housing as described in the previous procedure.
2. To remove the seal (A, **Figure 70**) perform the following:
   a. Remove the seal plate T-25 Torx screws and remove the seal plate (B, **Figure 70**).

   WARNING
   The seal is usually a tight fit in the housing. Wear safety glasses during seal removal.

   b. Pry the oil seal out of the housing with a large slotted screwdriver (**Figure 71**) or seal remover. Support the screwdriver with a rag to avoid damaging the housing. Pry at different points around the seal so it does not bind in its bore.
3. To remove the bearing:
   a. Support the housing in a press so its inner housing faces up as shown in **Figure 72**.
   b. Press the bearing out of the housing.
   c. Discard the bearing.
4. To install the new bearing:
   a. Support the housing in a press so that the outside of the housing faces up.
   b. Align the bearing with the housing so that the manufacturer's name and size code on the bearing is facing up.
   c. Press the bearing into the housing until it bottoms out.
5. To install the oil seal:
   a. Pack the seal lips with a waterproof bearing grease.

b. Align the seal with the housing so its manufacturer's name and size code on the seal faces out.

c. Press in the seal until its outer surface is flush with or slightly below the seal bore inside surface (A, **Figure 70**).

6. Install the seal plate (B, **Figure 70**) onto the stator housing. If the seal plate does not sit flush on the housing, the oil seal is not pressed in far enough.

7. Apply a medium strength threadlocking compound onto the seal plate Torx screws. Then install the Torx screws and tighten securely.

8. If removed, install the stator coil as described in the previous section.

Stator Housing Installation

Refer to **Figure 67** for this procedure.

1. Install the 2 dowel pins and a new gasket (**Figure 73**).

2. Apply RTV sealant onto the rubber plug (**Figure 74**) installed in the stator housing.

3. Install the stator housing (**Figure 68**) onto the crankcase.

4. Install the stator housing mounting bolts, sealing washer and wiring harness clamp. Install the sealing washer and wiring harness clamp in their original positions. See **Figure 67**.

5. Tighten the stator housing mounting bolts as specified in **Table 2**.

6. Connect the magneto stator electrical cable connectors to the wiring harness.

7. Install the recoil starter assembly and the starter drum as described in this chapter.

8. Install the transmission range select lever as described in Chapter Seven.

9. Install the shift lever and the left side footpeg assembly.

10. Refill the engine with oil as described in Chapter Three.

ROTOR AND STARTER CLUTCH

The starter clutch assembly is mounted on the backside of the rotor.

Refer to **Figure 75** for this procedure.

Removal

1. Park the vehicle on level ground and set the parking brake.

2. Remove the stator housing as described in this chapter.

NOTE

*The Yamaha flywheel puller (part No. YM-01404) or equivalent is required to remove the rotor. See **Figure 76**.*

72

73

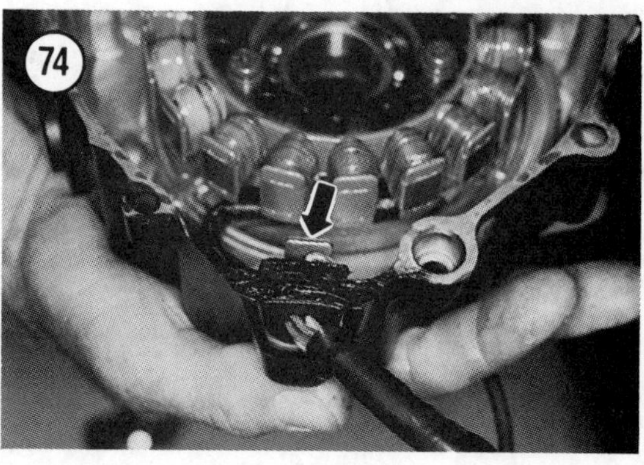
74

3. Screw the flywheel puller body (C, **Figure 77**) onto the rotor until it stops. Then wipe the end of the pressure bolt with grease (**Figure 77**) and screw the bolt into the body until it stops.

CAUTION

Do not try to remove the rotor without a puller; any attempt to do so will ultimately lead to some form of damage to the engine and/or the rotor. If you cannot buy or borrow one, have the rotor removed at a dealership.

4. Hold the puller body with a wrench and gradually tighten the pressure bolt (**Figure 78**) until the rotor pops loose from the crankshaft taper. Remove the puller from the rotor.

CAUTION

If normal rotor removal attempts fail, do not force the puller as the threads may be stripped off of the rotor causing expensive damage. Take the vehicle to a dealership and have the rotor removed.

5. Remove the Woodruff key (A, **Figure 79**) from the crankshaft groove.

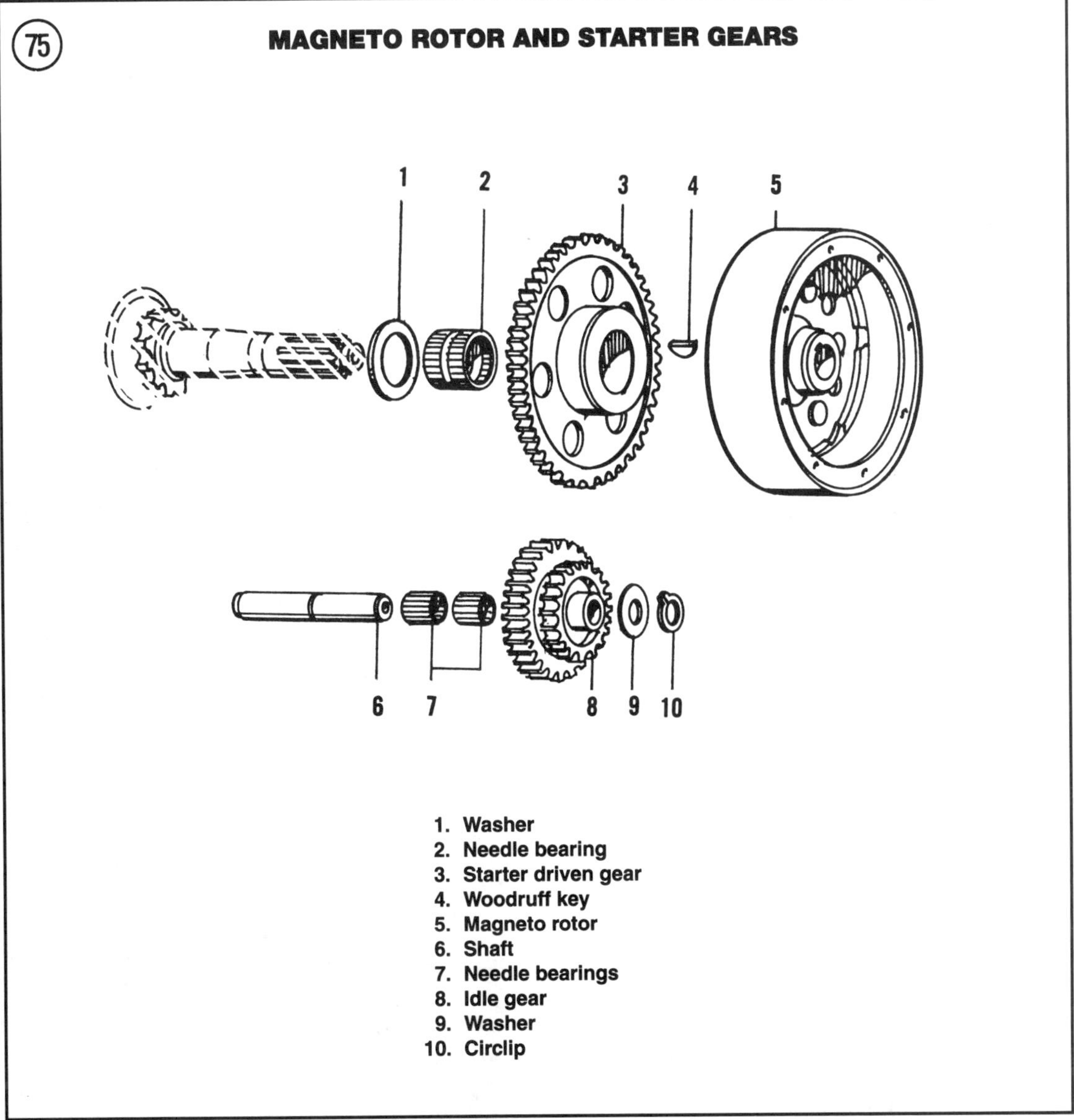

1. Washer
2. Needle bearing
3. Starter driven gear
4. Woodruff key
5. Magneto rotor
6. Shaft
7. Needle bearings
8. Idle gear
9. Washer
10. Circlip

6. Remove the starter driven gear (B, **Figure 79**)
7. Slide the needle bearing (A, **Figure 80**) and washer (B, **Figure 80**) off the crankshaft.
8. Remove the starter idle gear assembly (**Figure 81**).

Starter Clutch Inspection

1. Wash all parts in solvent. Blow dry with compressed air.
2. Disassemble the idle gear assembly (**Figure 75**):
   a. Check for broken or chipped gear teeth.
   b. Check for a worn or scored shaft surface.
   c. Check each needle bearing for wear or damage.
   d. Install the needle bearings onto the shaft and rotate them. Check for smooth operation.
   e. Reassemble the idle gear assembly (**Figure 75**).
3. Remove the starter driven gear from the rotor:
   a. Check for broken or chipped gear teeth.
   b. Check the needle bearing (2, **Figure 75**) for wear or damage.
   c. Check the inner surface of the driven gear (3, **Figure 75**) where the needle bearing rides for wear or damage.
   d. Check driven gear outer surface where it rides in the rotor. Check for wear or damage.
4. To check starter clutch (**Figure 82**) operation, perform the following:
   a. Install the starter driven gear (**Figure 83**) into the starter clutch.
   b. Turn the starter wheel gear *counterclockwise*. The gear (**Figure 83**) should turn freely.
   c. Now try to turn the starter wheel gear *clockwise*. The gear (**Figure 83**) should engage with the starter clutch and should not turn.
   d. If the starter clutch fails to operate as described in substep b or c, replace it as described in the following step.
5. To replace the starter clutch, perform the following:

CAUTION
The Allen bolts are staked on the backside and are difficult to loosen. An impact driver with a Allen wrench bit must be used to loosen the starter clutch housing mounting bolts. Attempting to loosen the bolts with an Allen wrench may strip the bolt heads.

80

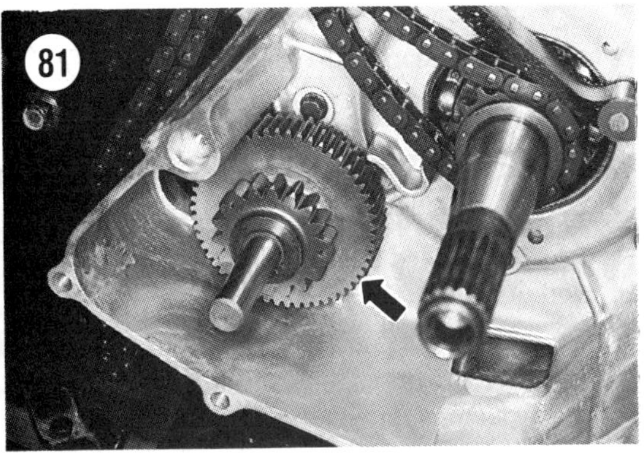
81

a. Using an impact driver and socket bit, remove the Allen bolts (**Figure 84**) securing the starter clutch housing to the rotor.

b. Remove the starter clutch.

c. Remove all sealer residue from the starter clutch bolts and the bolt threads in the rotor.

d. Position the new starter clutch with the arrow (A, **Figure 85**) facing out, away from the backside of the rotor. Install the new starter clutch onto the rotor.

e. Apply a medium strength threadlocking compound onto the starter clutch mounting bolt threads. Then install the bolts (**Figure 84**) and tighten as specified in **Table 2**.

f. Stake the starter clutch mounting bolt ends with a punch (B, **Figure 85**).

Rotor Inspection

1. Clean and dry the rotor.
2. Check the rotor (**Figure 84**) for cracks or breaks.

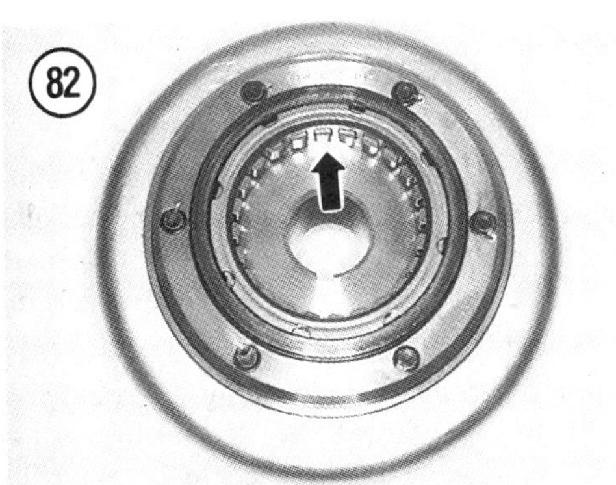
82

83

84

85

WARNING
A cracked or chipped rotor must be replaced. A damaged rotor may fly apart at high speed, throwing metal fragments into the engine. Do not attempt to repair a damaged rotor.

3. Check the rotor tapered bore and keyway for damage.
4. Check the rotor threads for damage.
5. Replace the rotor if damaged.

Installation

1. Assemble the idle gear assembly as shown in **Figure 75**. Make sure the circlip is fully seated in the shaft groove.
2. Install the idle gear assembly into the crankcase (**Figure 81**). Engage the idle gear with the starter motor drive gear.
3. Install the washer (B, **Figure 80**) and needle bearing (A, **Figure 80**) onto the crankshaft.
4. Install the Woodruff key into the crankshaft keyway.
5. Install the starter driven gear into the rotor (**Figure 83**).

CAUTION
*Carefully inspect the inside of the rotor (**Figure 84**) for small bolts, washers or other metal debris that may have been picked up by the magnets. These small metal parts can cause severe damage to the stator coil assembly.*

6. Align the keyway in the rotor with the Woodruff key and install the rotor (**Figure 86**) onto the crankshaft. If necessary, rotate the idle gear until the gears mesh. Then push the rotor on until it bottoms out.
7. Install the stator housing as described in this chapter.

CRANKCASE AND CRANKSHAFT

Disassembly of the crankcase—splitting the cases—and removal of the crankshaft assembly requires engine removal from the frame. However, the cylinder head, cylinder and all other attached subassemblies should be removed with the engine in the frame.

The crankcase is made in 2 halves of precision die cast aluminum alloy and is of the thin-walled type. To avoid damage to them, do not hammer or pry on any of the interior or exterior projected walls. These areas are easily damaged if stressed beyond what they are designed for. They are assembled without a gasket; only gasket sealer is used while dowel pins align the crankcase halves when they are bolted together. The crankcase halves are sold as a matched set only. If one crankcase half is severely damaged, both must be replaced.

The crankshaft assembly is made up of 2 full-circle flywheels pressed together on a crankpin. The connecting rod big end bearing on the crankpin is a caged needle bearing assembly (**Figure 87**). The crankshaft assembly is supported by 2 ball bearings in the crankcase.

The procedure which follows is presented as a complete, step by step major lower end overhaul that should be followed if the engine is to be completely reconditioned.

Remember that the right and left sides of the engine relates to the engine as it sits in the frame, not as it may sit on your workbench.

Special Tools

When splitting the crankcase assembly, a few Yamaha special tools are required. These tools allow easy disassembly and reassembly of the engine without prying or hammer use. Remember, the crankcase halves can be easily damaged by improper disassembly or reassembly techniques.

a. Yamaha crankcase separating tool (part No. YU-01135 [**Figure 88**]). This tool threads into the crankcase and is used to separate the

crankcase halves and to press the crankshaft out of the crankcase.

b. Yamaha crankshaft installing set (part No. YU-90050 [A, **Figure 89**]), Yamaha adapter (part No. YU-1383 [B, **Figure 89**]) and the Yamaha adapter (part No. YM-91044 [C, **Figure 89**]). These tools are used together to pull the crankshaft back into the crankcase assembly.

Crankcase Disassembly

This procedure describes disassembly of the crankcase halves and removal of the crankshaft, transmission shaft assemblies, middle drive shaft, reverse shaft assembly and internal shift mechanism. Disassembly and reassembly of the transmission, reverse assembly and internal shift mechanism assembly is described in Chapter Seven.

(87)

CRANKSHAFT ASSEMBLY

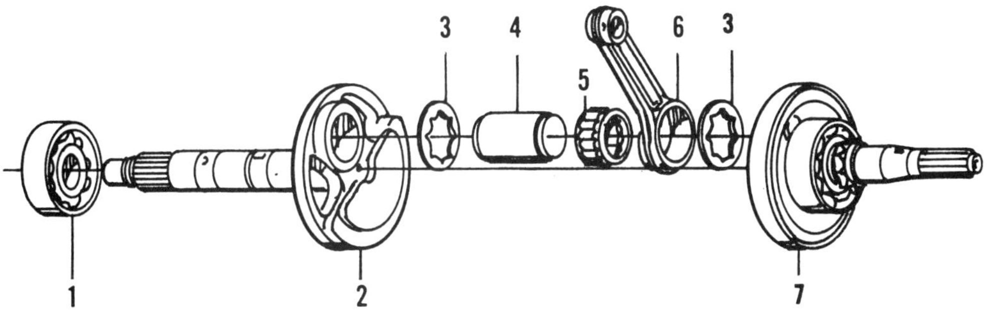

1. Ball bearing
2. Right-hand crank half
3. Thrust washer
4. Crankpin
5. Needle bearing
6. Connecting rod
7. Left-hand crank half

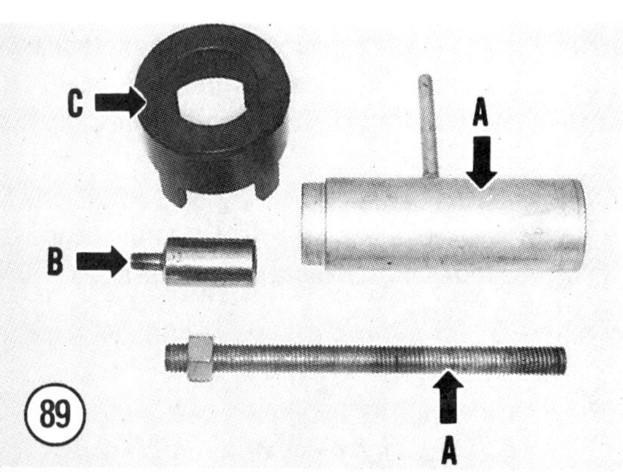

1. Remove all exterior engine subassemblies as described in this chapter and other related chapters:
   a. Cylinder head (Chapter Four).
   b. Cylinder block and piston (Chapter Four).
   c. External gearshift mechanism.
   d. Clutch assemblies.
   e. Recoil starter.
   f. Oil pump
   g. CDI magneto assembly and starter gears.
   h. Starter motor (Chapter Nine).
   i. Carburetor (Chapter Eight).
   j. External oil pipe.
2. Remove the bolt and washer (A, **Figure 90**) securing the shift drum No. 2 select lever assembly. Remove the assembly (B, **Figure 90**).
3. Remove the shift drum No. 2 detent bolt and washer (**Figure 91**), spring and ball (**Figure 92**).
4. Place the engine assembly on 2 wooden blocks with the left side facing up (**Figure 93**).
5. Following a crisscross pattern, loosen all screws one-quarter turn at a time.

NOTE

To prevent loss and to ensure proper screw location during assembly, draw the crankcase outline on cardboard, then punch holes to correspond with screw locations. Insert the screws in their appropriate locations.

6. Remove all screws loosened in Step 5 and install them in the cardboard. Be sure to remove all of them.
7. Turn the crankcase over so the right side faces up.

CAUTION

Do not pry between the crankcase mating surfaces when separating the crankcase halves. Doing so will result in oil leaks, requiring replacement of both case halves.

8. Use a soft-faced mallet and tap on the balancer shaft (A, **Figure 94**), transmission main shaft (B) and middle gear drive shaft (C) while lifting the right side crankcase half (D) off of the engine.
9. Immediately check the bearings in the right crankcase for washers that may be stuck to the bearings. If any are found, install them on their respective axle shaft. See **Figure 95**.

NOTE

This engine is equipped with a large number of shaft assemblies, shift drums

90

91

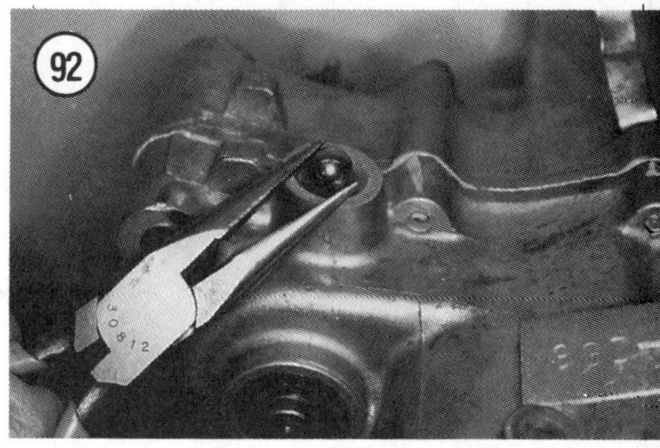
92

93

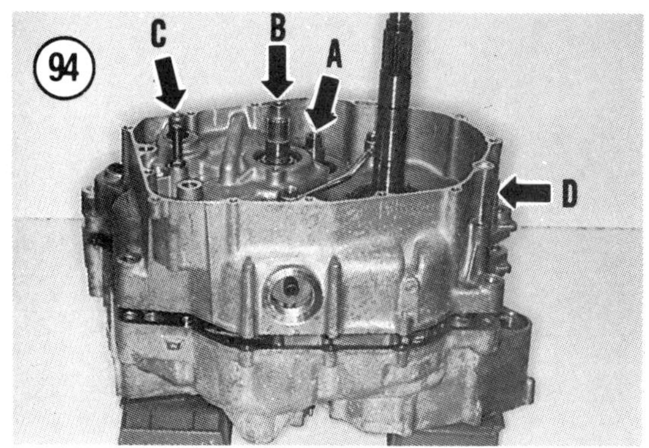

and shift forks. To avoid mixing up the parts, place each assembly in a separate plastic bag or box.

10. Remove the reverse shaft assembly (**Figure 96**). Do not lose the outer washer on the top gear.

11. Remove the high/low combination gear shaft (**Figure 97**). Do not lose the washers on the upper and lower end of the shaft.

12. Remove the shift drum No. 2 (A, **Figure 98**), the shift fork shaft and shift forks (B, **Figure 98**).

13. Remove the middle drive gear shaft assembly (A, **Figure 99**), the shift fork shaft and shift forks (B, **Figure 99**).

14. Remove the mainshaft shift fork shaft, shift forks and transmission mainshaft assembly (**Figure 100**).

15. Remove the balancer shaft (**Figure 101**).

16. Remove the countershaft shift fork shaft, shift forks and transmission countershaft assembly (**Figure 102**). Do not lose the outer washer on the countershaft.

17. Remove the shift drum No. 1 (A, **Figure 103**).

18. Remove the crankshaft (B, **Figure 103**) as follows:

5

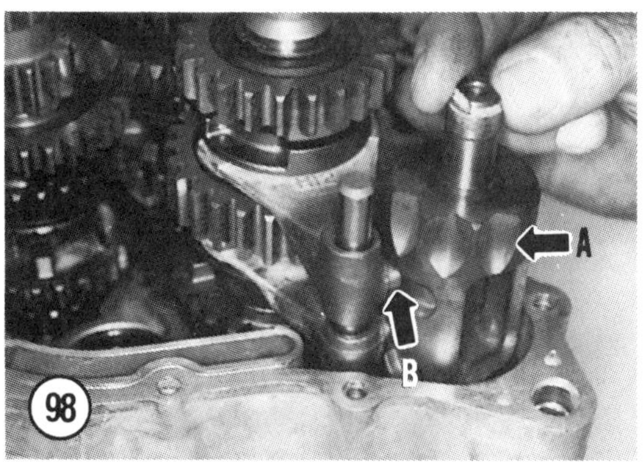

a. Install the Yamaha tool attachment (part No. YM-1382) onto the left side of the crankshaft.
b. Install the crankcase separating tool (**Figure 104**) into the threaded holes on the left crankcase half. Center the pressure bolt against the end of the crankshaft.
c. Tighten the tool's mounting bolts into the crankcase, making sure the tool body is parallel with the crankcase. If necessary, back out one of the bolts.
d. Hold onto the tool and tighten the puller *clockwise* to push the crankshaft out of the crankcase.

Crankcase Inspection

1. Remove all of the external crankcase seals as described under *External Seal Replacement* in this chapter.
2. Remove all sealer and gasket residue from all gasket surfaces.

CAUTION

When drying the crankcase bearings in Step 3, do not allow the inner bearing race to spin. The bearing will be without lubrication and damage will result. When drying the bearings, hold the inner race with your finger. In addition, when drying bearings with compressed air, never allow the air jet to rotate the bearing. The jet is capable of rotating the bearing at speeds far in excess of those for which they were designed. The likelihood of a bearing disintegrating and causing serious injury and damage is very great.

3. Clean both crankcase halves inside and out and all crankcase bearings with cleaning solvent. Refer to **Figure 105** and **Figure 106**. Dry with compressed air.
4. Unscrew the neutral indicator switch and washer (**Figure 107**) from the left-hand crankcase.
5. Clean all crankcase oil passages with compressed air.
6. If still installed, check the tightness of the internal oil line banjo bolts (**Figure 108**). If necessary, tighten as specified in **Table 2**.
7. Lightly oil the crankcase bearings with engine oil before checking them in Step 8.

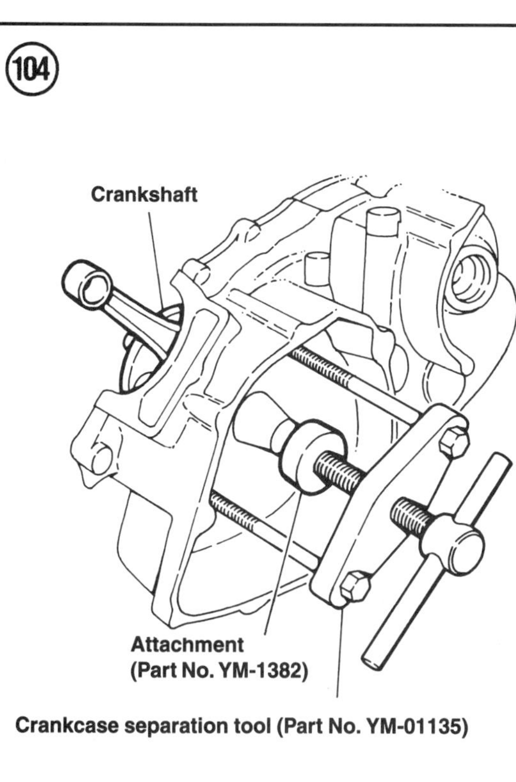

8. Check the crankcase bearings (**Figure 105** and **Figure 106**) for roughness, pitting, galling and excessive play by rotating them slowly by hand. If any roughness or play can be felt, replace the bearing.

NOTE
Always replace the opposite bearing at the same time.

9. Replace any worn or damaged bearings as described in this chapter.
10. Carefully inspect the cases for cracks and fractures, especially in the lower areas where they are vulnerable to rock damage.
11. Check the areas around the stiffening ribs, around bearing bosses and threaded holes for damage. If necessary have the crankcase repaired at a shop specializing in crankcase repair.
12. Check the threaded holes in both crankcase halves for thread damage, dirt or oil buildup. If necessary, clean or repair the threads with a suitable size metric tap. Coat the tap threads with kerosene or an aluminum tap fluid before use.
13. Check the shift shaft pin bolt for damage and replace it as necessary. During replacement, install

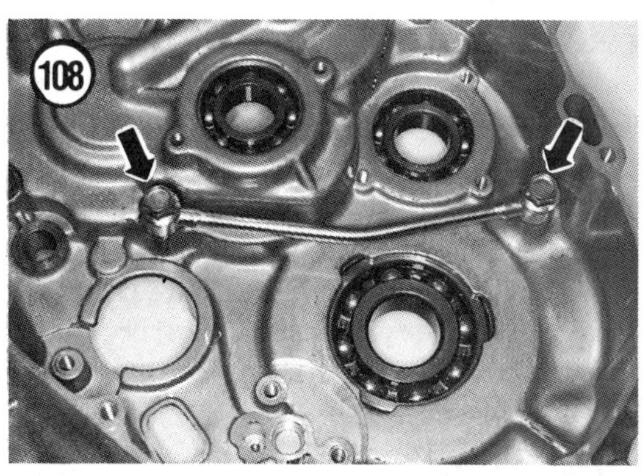

5

a new lockwasher and bend the lockwasher tab over one flat on the pin bolt to lock it.

External Seal Replacement

Replace the shift shaft and the shift drum No. 2 external seals whenever the engine is disassembled or if they are leaking or damaged.

1. Pry out the seal (**Figure 109**, typical) with a screwdriver. Place a rag underneath the screwdriver to avoid damaging the crankcase.
2. Clean the seal mounting bore.
3. Pack the seal lip with a waterproof bearing grease.
4. Install the seal with its manufacturer's name and size code facing out.
5. Press or drive in the seal in until its outer surface is flush with or slightly below the seal bore inside surface.

Internal Seal and Bearing Replacement

Internal seals are those installed on the inside of the crankcase, located between the bearing and crankcase wall. When replacing bearings and seals in the following steps, note the following:

1. A pilot bearing remover (**Figure 110**), or equivalent, is required to remove the bearings described in this section.
2. Because bearing removal usually damages the internal oil seal, if applicable, install new oil seals during the procedure.
3. Because of the number of bearings used in the left- and right-hand crankcase, make sure to identify the bearings before removing them. The size code found on the bearings and oil seals can be used for identification. See **Figure 111**, typical.
4. Refer to *Ball Bearing Replacement* in Chapter One for general information on bearing removal and installation.
5. Prior to removing the seal(s), note and record the direction in which the lip of the seal(s) faces for proper reinstallation. See **Figure 112**, typical.
6. The left-hand main bearing (A, **Figure 113**) is part of the left-hand crankshaft half and must be replaced with the left-hand crankshaft half. The bearing and left-hand crankshaft half cannot be replaced separately.

Crankshaft Inspection

When measuring the crankshaft components (**Figure 87**), compare the actual measurements to the specifications in **Table 1**. Rebuild or replace the crankshaft if out of specification as described in this section. See *Crankshaft Overhaul* in this chapter.

1. Clean the crankshaft (**Figure 113**) thoroughly with solvent. Clean the crankshaft oil passageway with compressed air. Dry the crankshaft with com-

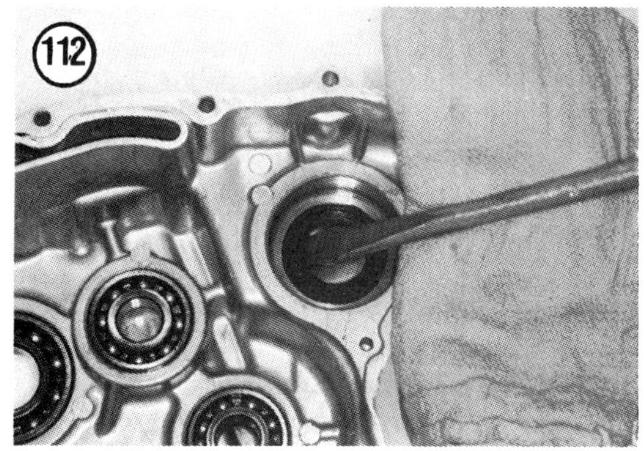

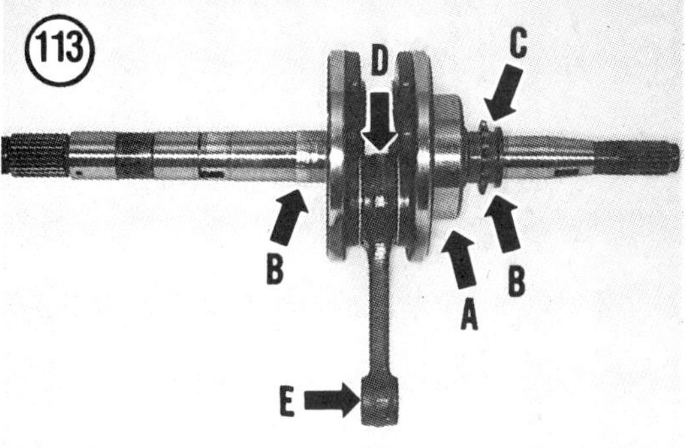

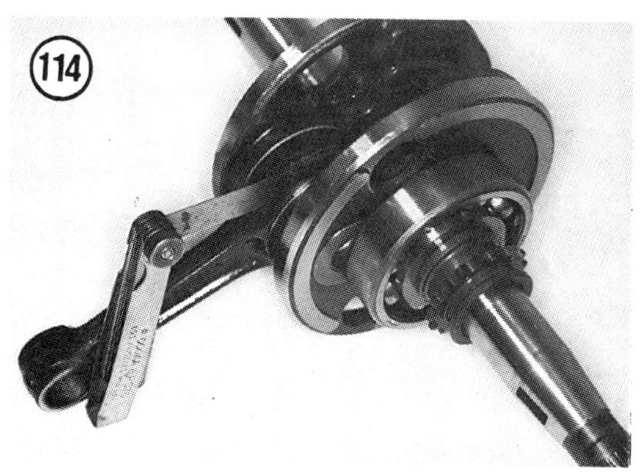

pressed air. Then lubricate all bearing surfaces with a light coat of engine oil.

2. Check the crankshaft journals (B, **Figure 113**) for scratches, heat discoloration or other damage.

3. Check crankshaft bearing surfaces for chatter marks and excessive or uneven wear. Repair minor damage with 320 grit carborundum cloth. If 320 cloth is used, clean crankshaft in solvent and check surfaces. If they did not clean up properly, disassemble the crankshaft and replace the damaged part.

4. Check rotor taper and keyway for damage.

5. Inspect the crankshaft splines for severe wear or damage.

6. Inspect the camshaft chain timing sprocket (C, **Figure 113**) for wear or damage. Because the camshaft chain timing sprocket is part of the left-hand crank half, it cannot be replaced separately.

7. Check the connecting rod big end (D, **Figure 113**) for evidence of seizure, bearing or thrust washer damage or connecting rod damage.

8. Check the connecting rod small end (E, **Figure 113**) for evidence of excessive heat (blue discoloration) or other damage.

9. Slide the connecting rod to one side and check the connecting rod side clearance with a flat feeler gauge (**Figure 114**).

10. Measure the crankshaft width with micrometer or vernier caliper (**Figure 115**) and compare to the specifications listed in **Table 1**. Measure around the crankshaft wheel circumference on the outer machined edge—do not measure on cast surfaces.

11. Check crankshaft runout at points A and B with a dial indicator and V-blocks as shown in **Figure 116**. Compare the runout to the specifications listed in **Table 1**.

12. If necessary, overhaul the crankshaft as described in this chapter.

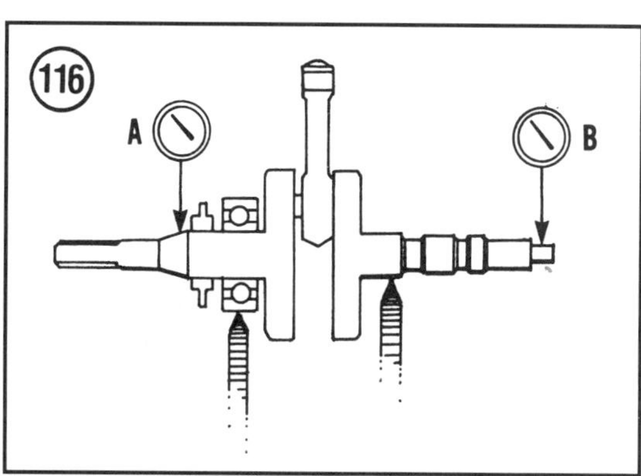

Crankshaft Overhaul

Crankshaft overhaul requires a 20 ton hydraulic press (minimum capacity), holding jigs, crankshaft alignment jig, dial indicators and a micrometer or vernier caliper. For this reason, refer crankshaft overhaul to a Yamaha dealership or motorcycle repair shop. If having the crankshaft rebuilt, instruct the dealership or shop to align the crankshaft and crank pin oil passages as shown in **Figure 117**.

Balancer Shaft and Driven Gear Inspection

1. Check the balancer shaft bearing journals (**Figure 118**) for deep scoring, excessive wear, heat discoloration or cracks.

2. Check the balancer shaft keyway for cracks or excessive wear. Check the square key for wear, cracks or other damage.

3. Check the balancer driven gear for chipped or missing teeth or a damaged keyway.

4. Replace excessively worn or damaged parts as required.

Transmission, Reverse and Middle Driven Shaft Assemblies Inspection

Refer to Chapter Seven for all disassembly, inspection and reassembly procedures.

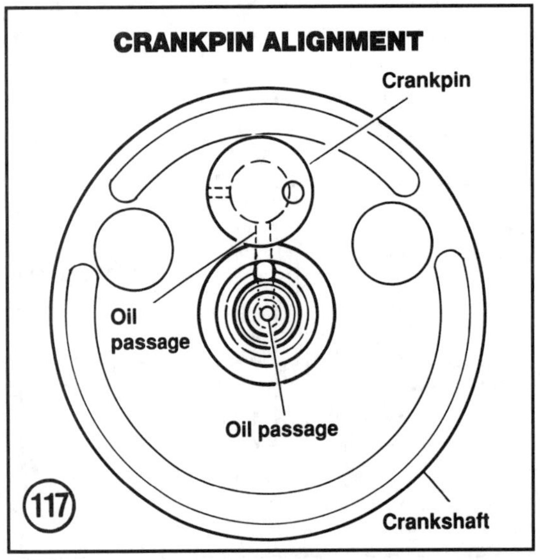

Crankcase Assembly

1. Pack all of the crankcase seals with a high-temperature grease.

2. Lubricate the crankshaft bottom end bearing with engine oil.

3. If removed, install the neutral switch (**Figure 107**) and its washer and tighten as specified in **Table 2.**
4. Use the Yamaha tools (**Figure 119**) and install the crankshaft into the left-hand crankcase as follows:

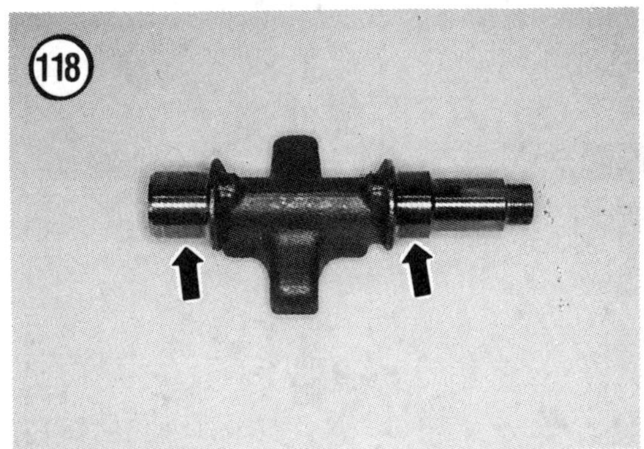

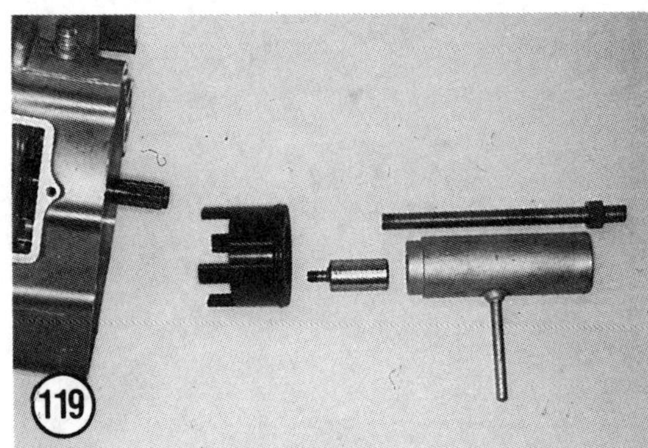

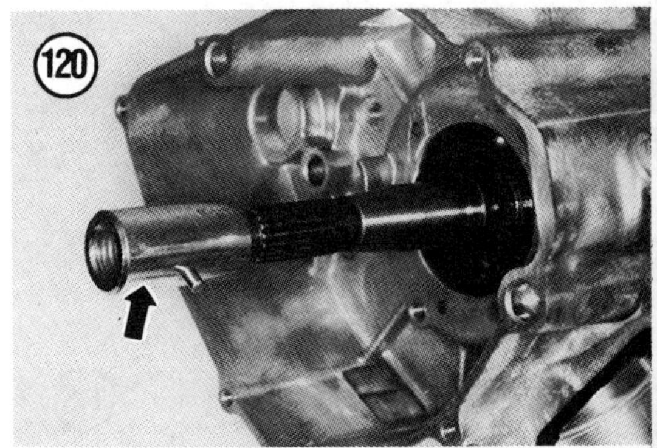

CAUTION
If you do not have the necessary crankshaft installation tools, have the crankshaft installed at a Yamaha dealership or machine shop. Do not drive the crankshaft and bearing into the crankcase with a hammer as the crankshaft will become distorted resulting in severe engine damage.

a. Apply a light coat of engine oil to the left-hand crankshaft bearing journal.

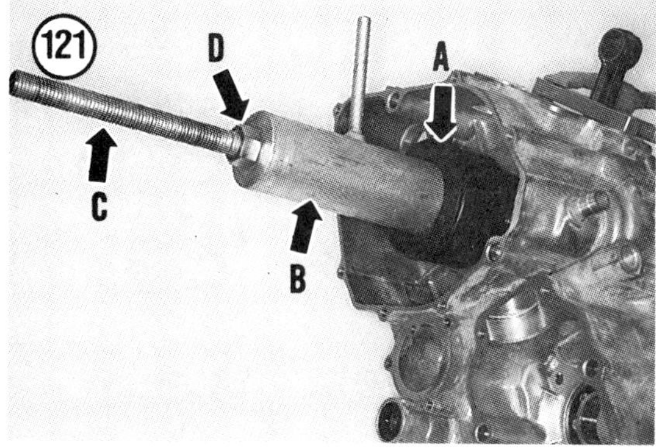

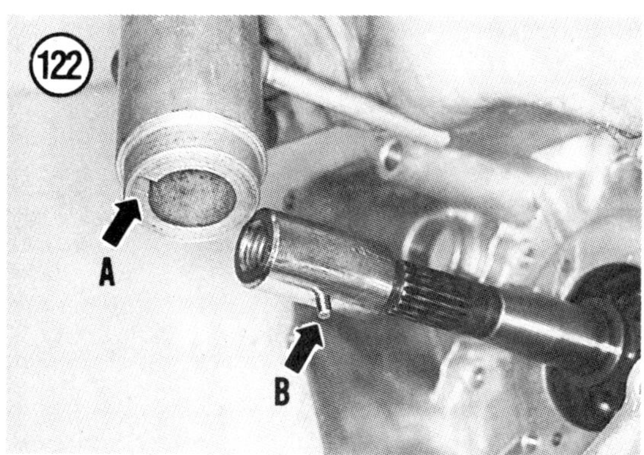

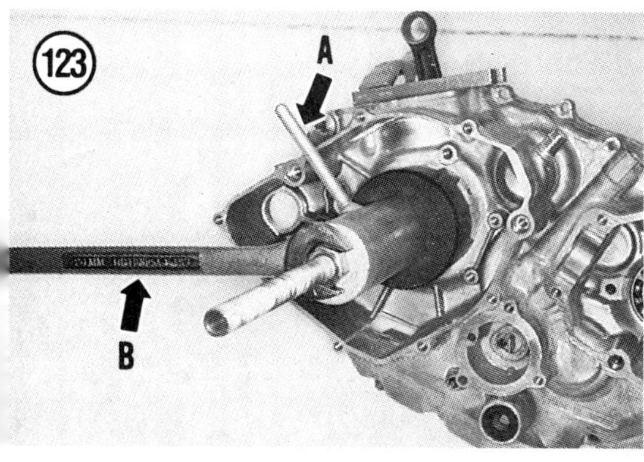

b. Insert the short end of the crankshaft (end with bearing) into the left-hand crankcase until the left-hand main bearing is square with its crankcase mounting bore. Using hand pressure only, push the crankshaft into the crankcase until the bearings stops in its bore. Rotate the crankshaft until the connecting rod is at the bottom of it stroke (BDC).

CAUTION
When installing the crankshaft, make sure to center the connecting rod within the top opening in the crankcase. If the connecting rod moves out of this opening it could catch onto the side of the crankcase and cause connecting rod, crankshaft and crankcase damage as the crankshaft is pressed into position.

c. Thread the crankshaft small adapter (**Figure 120**) into the end of the crankshaft. Tighten it securely.
d. Install the crankshaft large adapter (A, **Figure 121**) over the crankshaft and place it against the crankcase.
e. Align the groove in the crankcase installer (A, **Figure 122**) with the small adapter pin (B, **Figure 122**) and attach the installer (B, **Figure 121**).
f. Install the threaded rod (C, **Figure 121**) through the installer and screw it into the end of the crankshaft adapter (**Figure 120**) until it bottoms out.
g. Thread the nut (D, **Figure 121**) all the way down until it bottoms out against the top of the installer.
h. Hold the crankcase installer bar (A, **Figure 123**) and slowly tighten the nut with a wrench (B, **Figure 123**) to press the crankshaft into the crankcase. Check the crankshaft often to make sure it is being pulled straight in with no side load and that the connecting rod is positioned at TDC or BDC (**Figure 124**). Press the crankshaft in until its bearing bottoms out in its mounting bore.
i. After installing the crankshaft, remove the crankshaft installer set.
j. Turn the crankshaft slowly by hand. It should turn freely with no roughness or binding.

5

5. Place the left-hand crankcase assembly onto wooden blocks with the right crankshaft end facing up.

6. Lubricate all of the left crankcase bearings with engine oil.

7. Install the shift drum No. 1 (**Figure 125**).

8. Install the transmission mainshaft and shift fork assembly into the crankcase as follows:

NOTE
The 2 top gears are removed from the shaft to more clearly show the shift fork installation procedure. It is not necessary to remove these gears.

a. Properly mesh the shift forks and shaft into the transmission mainshaft (**Figure 126**) and install the assembly into the crankcase.
b. Push the transmission shaft into the crankcase bearing until it is completely seated (A, **Figure 127**).
c. Slightly lift the shift forks and their respective gears (B, **Figure 127**) and engage the shift fork pins with the shift drum No. 1 grooves.
d. Insert the shift fork shaft (C, **Figure 127**) into its receptacle in the crankcase and push it down until it is completely seated (**Figure 128**).
e. Make sure the shift fork pins are correctly seated in the shift drum No. 1 grooves and that the shift fork shaft is pushed all the way down (**Figure 128**).

9. Install the balancer shaft (**Figure 129**).

10. Install the transmission countershaft and shift fork assembly into the crankcase as follows:.

a. Properly mesh the shift fork and shaft into the transmission countershaft. Lubricate the shift

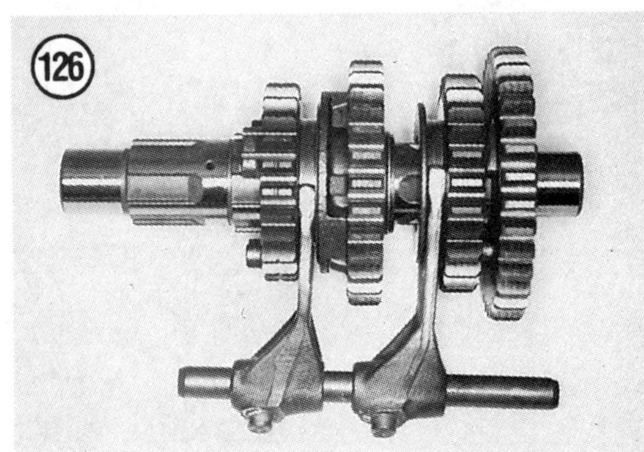

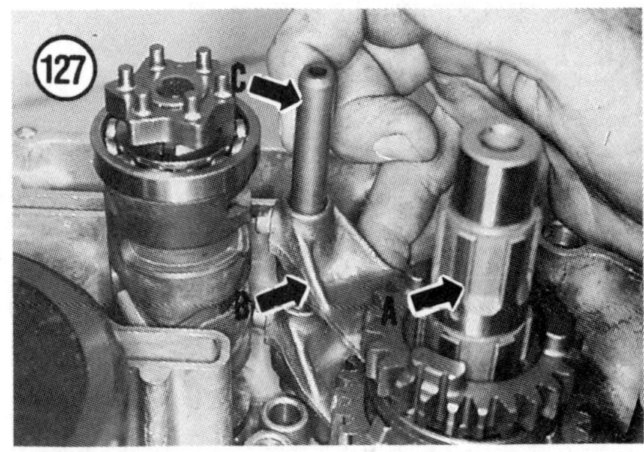

fork shaft O-rings (**Figure 130**) with engine oil.

b. Install the assembly (A, **Figure 131**) into the crankcase while holding up the gears on the mainshaft (B, **Figure 131**) to allow the gears of both shafts to mesh properly .

c. Push the transmission shaft into the crankcase bearing until it is completely seated.

d. Slightly lift up on the shift fork and its respective gear and engage the shift fork pin with the shift drum No. 1(A, **Figure 132**) groove.

e. Insert the shift fork shaft (B, **Figure 132**) into its receptacle in the crankcase and push it down until it is completely seated.

f. Make sure the shift fork pin is correctly seated in the shift drum No. 1 groove and that the shift fork shaft is pushed all the way down.

11. Install the middle drive shaft and shift fork assembly into the crankcase as follows:.

a. Mesh the shift forks, shaft spring and cup into the transmission countershaft (**Figure 133**).

b. Install the assembly into the crankcase, making sure the spring and cup (**Figure 134**) are still in place on the end of the shift fork shaft.

Do not insert the shift fork shaft into its receptacle at this time. First, move it back (**Figure 135**) to allow room to install the shift drum No. 2.

c. Push the middle drive shaft into the crankcase bearing until it is completely seated (**Figure 136**).
d. Partially install shift drum No. 2 (A, **Figure 137**), then move the shift forks and shaft over and mesh the shift fork pins (B, **Figure 137**) into the No. 2 drum grooves.
e. Push the shift drum No. 2 and shift fork shaft down until both are correctly seated. Make sure the shift fork shaft cup is correctly seated into its receptacle in the crankcase.
f. Make sure the shift fork pins are correctly seated in the shift drum No. 2 grooves and that the shift fork shaft is pushed all the way down (**Figure 138**).

12. Install the high/low combination gear as follows:
    a. Position the high/low combination gear with the smaller diameter gear going in first.
    b. Install the lower washer (**Figure 139**) onto the lower end of the high/low combination gear and shaft.
    c. Align the flat (A, **Figure 140**) on the end of the shaft with the flat (B, **Figure 140**) within the shaft receptacle in the crankcase.
    d. Install the high/low combination gear into the crankcase receptacle while slightly moving the shaft back and forth to ensure proper indexing of the shaft flat with the receptacle flat. This alignment is necessary so the shaft can seat correctly within the crankcase and to keep the shaft from rotating during engine operation.
    e. Push the shaft down until it is completely seated.
13. Install the reverse gear shaft (**Figure 141**) and push it down until it is completely seated.
14. Install the reverse gear and washer (**Figure 142**).
15. Make sure the washer is in place on top of the high/low combination gear, countershaft and reverse gear assemblies (**Figure 143**).

NOTE

Step 16 is best done with the aid of a helper as the assemblies are loose and do not spin easily. Have the helper spin the transmission shaft while you turn the shift drum through all the gears.

135

136

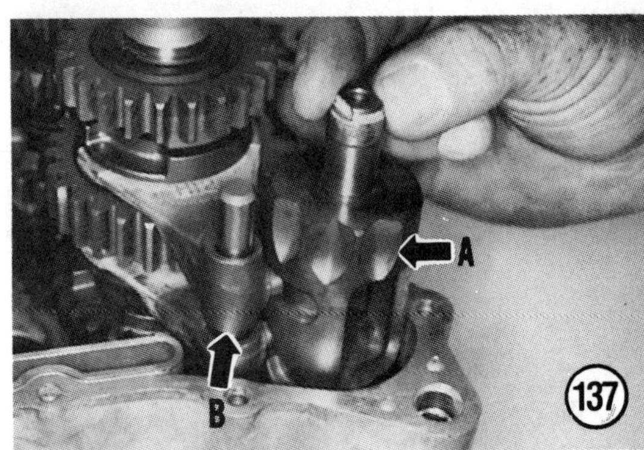

137

138

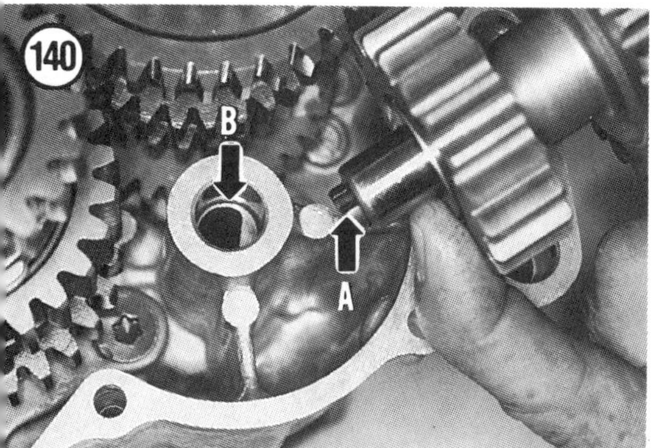

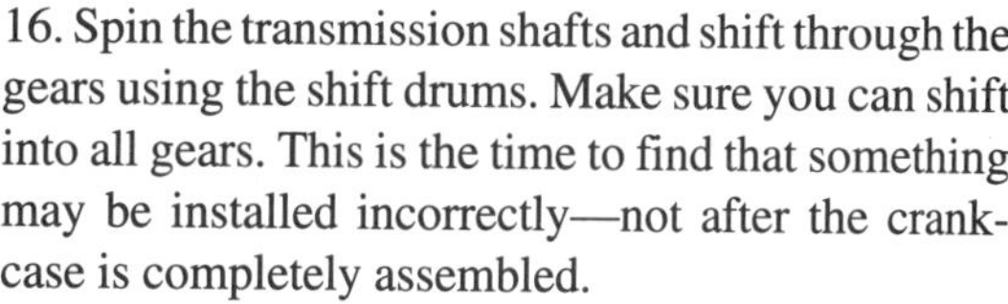
16. Spin the transmission shafts and shift through the gears using the shift drums. Make sure you can shift into all gears. This is the time to find that something may be installed incorrectly—not after the crankcase is completely assembled.

17. After making sure the transmission shifts into all of the gears correctly, shift the main transmission assembly into NEUTRAL.

18. Install the 2 locating dowels. **Figure 144** shows one of the locating dowels.

NOTE
Make sure the left- and right-hand crankcase surfaces are clean and free of all old gasket material. This is to make sure you get a leak free seal.

19. Apply a light coat of *non-hardening liquid gasket* sealer, such as Yamabond No. 4 or ThreeBond 1104, onto the mating surfaces of both crankcase halves.

20. Align the right-hand crankcase half with the axle shafts and crankshaft install it. Push it down squarely into place until it engages the dowel pins (**Figure 145**) and seats completely against the lower case half.

5

CAUTION

If everything is aligned properly, the right-hand crankcase half should be easy to install. Force is not be required. If the crankcase halves do not fit together completely, do not attempt to pull them together with the crankcase screws. Separate the crankcase halves and investigate the cause of the interference. If any of the transmission and/or other gear shaft assemblies were disassembled, make sure that a gear is not installed backward. Crankcase halves are a matched set and are very expensive. Do not risk damage by trying to force them together.

21. Turn all of the exposed axle shafts, crankshaft and shift drums. There should be no tightness. If everything turns okay, continue with Step 22.
22. Install several of the crankcase screws to hold the crankcase halves together prior to turning the assembly over. Be sure to install the copper washer under the one bolt as shown in **Figure 146**.
23. Turn the engine over so that the left-hand crankcase faces up. Install all of the crankcase mounting bolts finger-tight.
24. Tighten the crankcase mounting bolts in 2-3 stages in a crisscross pattern to the final torque specified in **Table 2**.
25. Rotate the axle shafts, crankshaft and shift drums to make sure there is no binding. If there is any binding, remove the crankcase mounting bolts and the right-hand crankcase half and correct the problem.
26. Install the shift drum No. 2 detent assembly as follows:
    a. Position the shift drum No. 2 onto the LOW position (flats on the end of the shaft in a horizontal position).
    b. Install the steel ball (**Figure 147**).
    c. Install the spring, washer and bolt (**Figure 148**). Make sure the bolt fits over the spring and that the spring goes up into the hollow bolt.
    d. Tighten the shift drum No. 2 detent bolt as specified in **Table 2**.
27. Install the shift drum No. 2 select lever as follows:
    a. Install the spring onto the shift drum No. 2 select lever (**Figure 149**).

b. Align the flat on the lever with the flats on the shift drum No. 2 (**Figure 150**).
c. Install and tighten the shift drum No. 2 select lever bolt as specified in **Table 2**.

28. Install all exterior engine subassemblies as described in this chapter and other related chapters:
a. External oil pipe.
b. Carburetor (Chapter Eight).
c. Starter motor (Chapter Nine).
d. Rotor assembly and starter gears.
e. Oil pump.

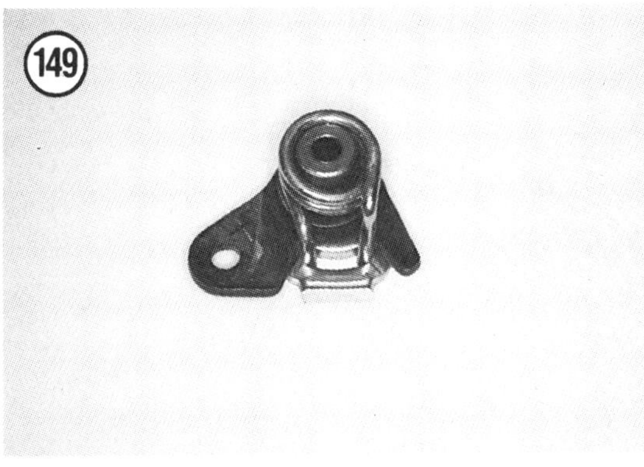

f. Recoil starter (models so equipped).
g. Clutch assemblies.
h. External gearshift mechanism.
i. Piston, rings and cylinder (Chapter Four).
j. Cylinder head (Chapter Four).

RECOIL STARTER

The recoil starter assembly is mounted on the stator housing. Pulling the rope handle causes the pulley shaft to rotate against spring tension, moving the drive pawl into engagement with the starter pulley on the crankshaft, thereby cranking the engine. When the rope handle is released, the spring inside the assembly reverses direction of the shaft and winds the rope around the sheave.

Recoil starters are relatively trouble-free. A broken or frayed rope is the most common problem.

Recoil Starter Housing Removal/Installation

1. Park the vehicle on level ground. Set the parking brake and block the rear wheels so the vehicle will not roll in either direction.
2. Remove the bolts securing the recoil starter housing (**Figure 151**) to the stator housing. Then remove the starter housing and gasket.
3. Install by reversing these steps while noting the following:.
a. Install a new gasket.
b. Tighten the recoil starter housing mounting bolts as specified in **Table 2**.
c. Pull the starter rope and make sure starter drum and housing assembly engage properly.

Starter Drum Removal/Inspection/Installation

The starter drum (**Figure 152**) is bolted to the end of the crankshaft.

1. Remove the starter housing as described in the previous section.
2. Hold the starter drum using the Yamaha rotor holding tool (part No. YU-01235) or a square bar. See **Figure 153**.
3. Hold the starter drum and loosen the rotor mounting bolt (**Figure 153**).

5

152

RECOIL STARTER

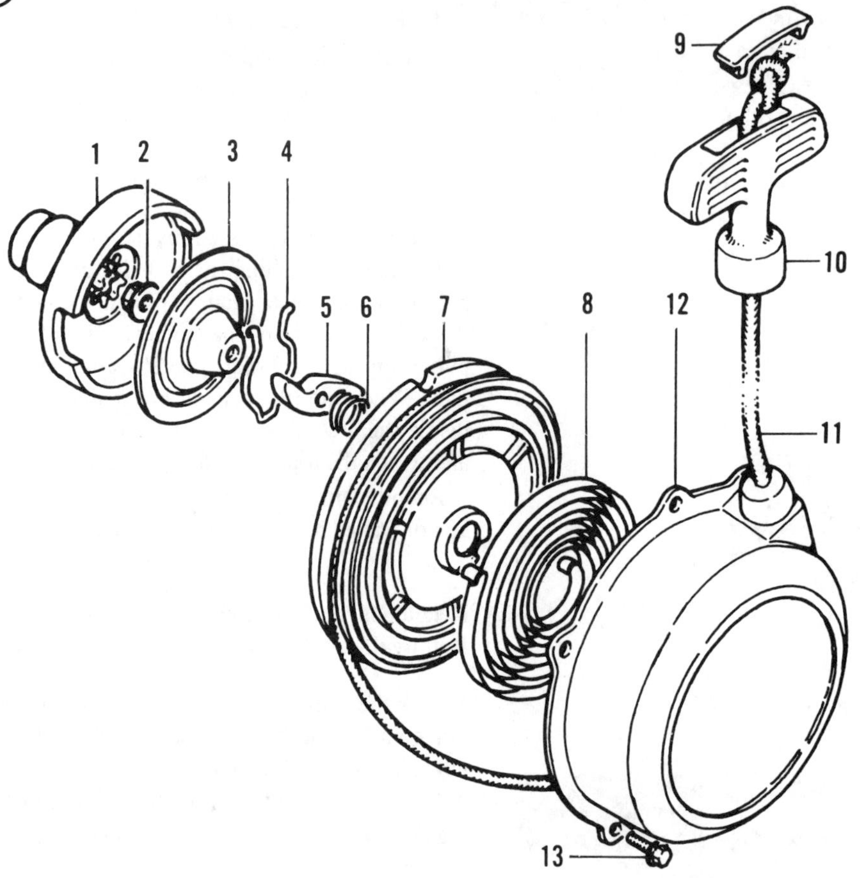

1. Starter drum
2. Nut
3. Friction plate
4. Pawl spring
5. Drive pawl
6. Drive pawl spring
7. Pulley
8. Starter rewind spring
9. Cap
10. Starter handle
11. Rope
12. Starter housing
13. Bolt

153

154

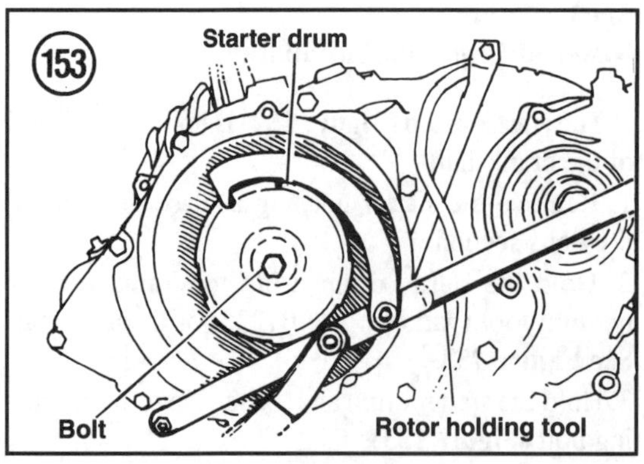

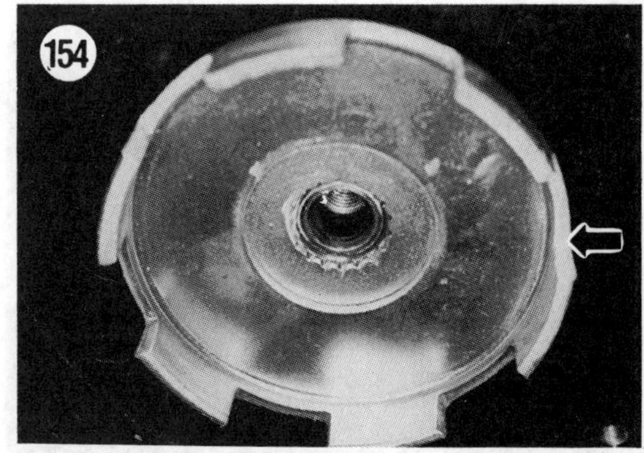

4. Remove the bolt, lockwasher, flat washer and starter drum (**Figure 154**).

5. Inspect the O-ring (A, **Figure 155**) inside the starter drum. Replace if it is hard or starting to deteriorate. Lubricate the O-ring with engine oil.

6. Inspect the starter drum arms (B, **Figure 155**) for severe wear, cracks or other damage.

7. Lubricate stator housing seal with engine oil.

8. Install the starter drum onto the crankshaft, taking care not to damage the seal within the stator housing and the O-ring seal in the drum.

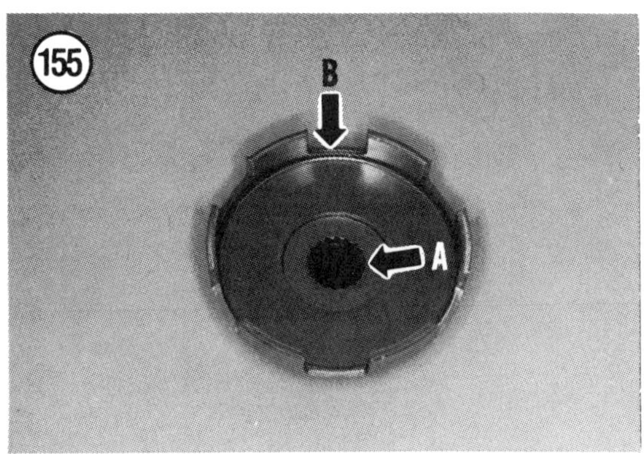

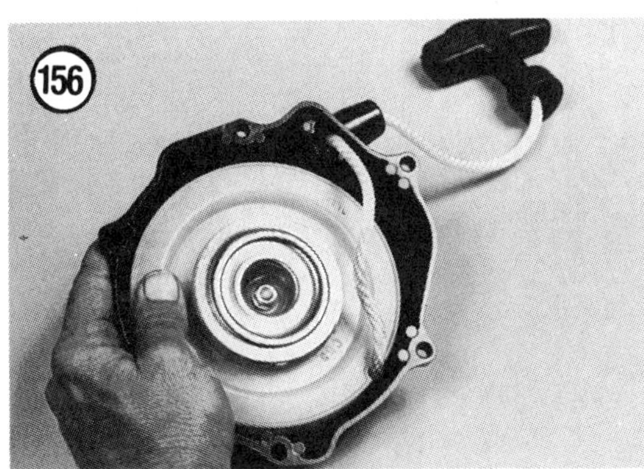

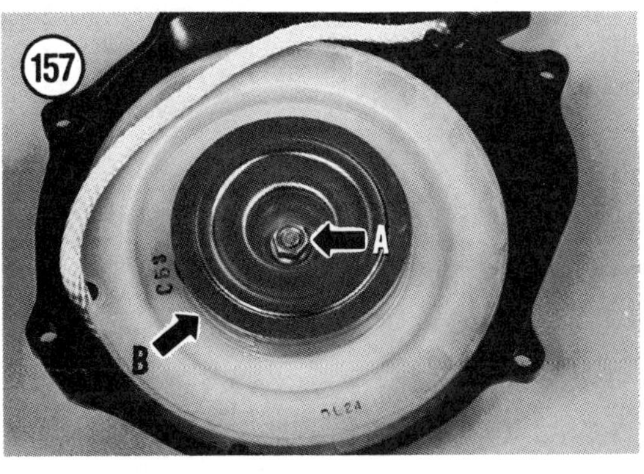

9. Push the drum on until it bottoms, then install the bolt, lockwasher and flat washer.

10. Use the same tool set up to prevent the starter drum from turning and tighten the rotor mounting bolt as specified in **Table 2**.

11. Install the starter housing as described in the previous section.

Starter Housing Disassembly

Refer to **Figure 152** for this procedure.

WARNING
Wear safety glasses when disassembling the recoil starter. The starter rewind spring is under pressure and may jump out when disassembling the starter housing. While the spring is not very strong, it can cause eye injury and is often sharp enough to cut fingers and hands.

1. Remove the starter housing as described in this chapter.

2. Pull the starter handle and rope partway out and hold the rope pulley with your thumb (**Figure 156**) to prevent the sheave drum from unwinding.

3. Pull the rope partway out from between the starter housing and the rope pulley. Pull the rope through the pulley notch as shown in **Figure 156**.

4. Remove your thumb and allow the pulley to unwind *slowly*.

5. Remove the starter handle as follows:
   a. Pry the cap from the end of the handle.
   b. Slide the rope trough the handle and untie the knot.
   c. Remove the starter handle from the rope.

6. Remove the starter shaft nut (A, **Figure 157**). Then remove the following parts in order:
   a. Friction plate (B, **Figure 157**).
   b. Drive pawl (**Figure 158**).
   c. Drive pawl spring (A, **Figure 159**).

WARNING
The starter rewind spring may remain wound in the starter housing or it may fly out when removing the sheave drum in Step 7. Protect yourself accordingly.

7. Slowly lift the rope pulley (B, **Figure 159**) and starter rope from the starter housing.

5

8. If necessary, remove the rewind spring (**Figure 160**) as follows:
   a. Place the starter housing on the floor with the spring side facing down.
   b. Tap the housing while holding it tightly against the floor. The spring will fall and unwind from the starter housing.

Inspection

Replace damaged or worn parts as described in this chapter.

1. Clean all parts, except the starter rope, in solvent and dry thoroughly.
2. Check the starter shaft for cracks and excessive wear. Check the shaft threads for damage.
3. Check the guide where the rope passes through the starter housing for wear or roughness that would damage the rope.
4. Inspect the rope pulley for damage at the center hub where the rewind spring attaches and where the pawl attaches. Check the top and bottom surfaces of the pulley for cracks or other damage.
5. Inspect the drive pawl (**Figure 161**) for damage, especially near the operating ends.
6. Inspect the friction plate for warpage, cracks or other damage.
7. Replace the rope if frayed or broken. Carefully measure the diameter and length of the old rope to make sure that the replacement rope is identical.
8. Check the starter spring (**Figure 162**). Make sure that neither end is broken off, cracked, or otherwise damaged. Clean the entire length of the spring and check for cracks, bends or other damage.

Attaching Rope to Rope Pulley

1. Heat the starter rope ends (**Figure 163**) to prevent fraying and to keep the knots from untying.
2. Remove and disassemble the starter assembly as described in this chapter.
3. Insert one end of the rope through the hole in the pulley.
4. Tie a knot in the rope end (**Figure 164**).

NOTE
*Make sure the knot is both tight and small enough to fit into the pulley pocket (**Figure 165**).*

5. Wind the rope 4 1/2 turns clockwise into the sheave drum and through the notch as shown in **Figure 165**. Cut the rope about 45 cm (18 in.) beyond the notch.

6. Heat the cut end of the rope to prevent fraying and to make it easier to thread the end through the starter housing and handle.

7. Assemble the starter assembly as described in this chapter.

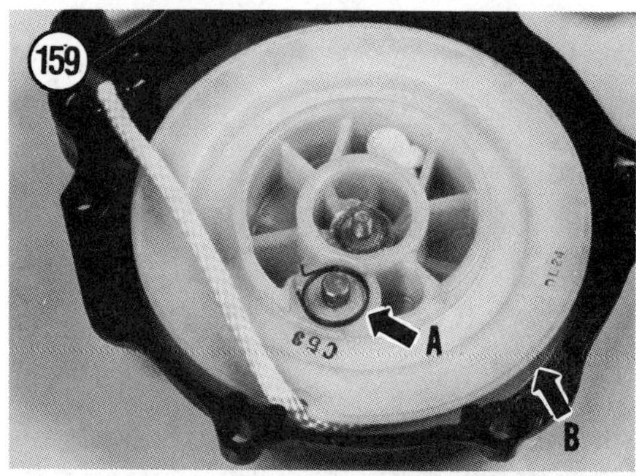

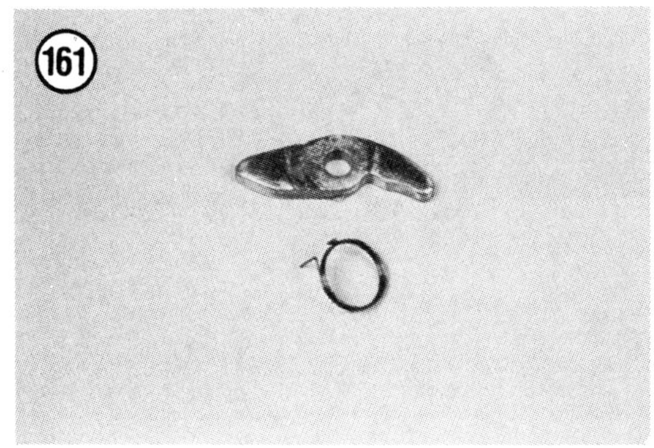

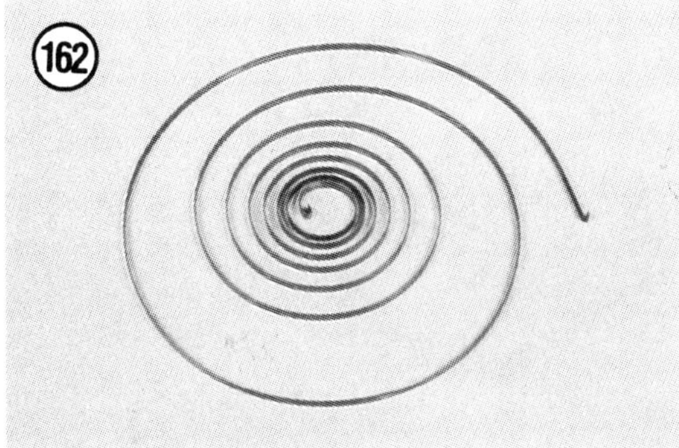

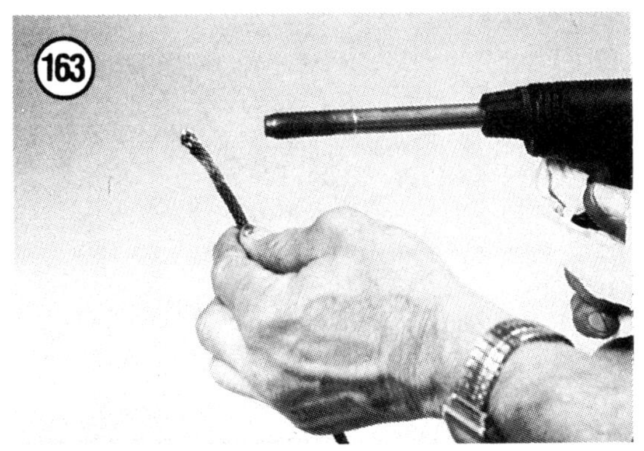

Rewind Spring Installation

WARNING
Wear safety glasses when installing the starter spring and assembling the starter housing.

1. Remove and disassemble the starter assembly as described in this chapter.
2. Install the rewind spring in the starter housing as follows:
   a. Lubricate the entire length of the spring and the inside of the cavity in the start housing with water proof grease.
   b. Attach the hooked end of the rewind spring onto the slot in the starter housing.
   c. Wind the spring clockwise into the housing as shown in B, **Figure 160**.

NOTE
*The spring should lay flat in the housing as shown in **Figure 160**.*

Starter Housing Assembly

WARNING
Wear safety glasses when assembling the starter housing in the following steps.

1. Install the rewind spring and starter rope as described in this chapter.
2. Install the rope pulley over the shaft in the starter housing (**Figure 166**). Keep the rope coiled into the pulley groove and exiting through the pulley notch.
3. Engage the inner end of the spring with the notch in the pulley center hub. Make sure that the pulley is

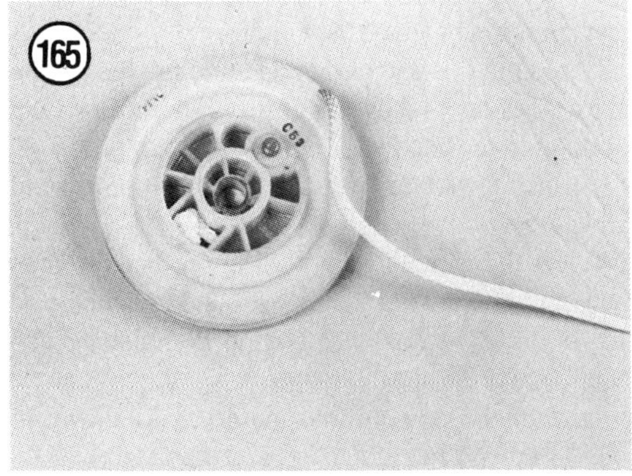

5

fully seated in the starter housing and that the spring is attached to the hub.

4. Turn the pulley clockwise while holding the rope in the notch to check for spring pressure. After checking, carefully release spring pressure while keeping the rope in the pulley notch. The rope should be coiled 4 1/2 turns around the pulley (**Figure 167**).

5. Install the pawl spring and drive spring as follows:

   a. Install the long end of the pawl spring into the pulley hole. See A, **Figure 159** and **Figure 168**.
   b. Install the drive pawl into the spring so that the short end of the pawl spring fits into the drive pawl notch (**Figure 158**).
   c. Preload the drive pawl spring by turning it one turn counterclockwise, then push the drive pawl into the cutout in the pulley.

6. Make sure that the pawl spring is correctly installed in the friction plate (**Figure 169**).

7. Install the pawl spring and friction plate assembly as shown in **Figure 170**.

8. Install the retaining nut (A, **Figure 157**) and tighten securely.

NOTE
There should be 4 1/2 turns of the starter rope wrapped into the pulley. When preloading the rewind spring in the following step, do not unwind the rope from the pulley groove.

9. Grasp the starter rope where it exits the notch in the pulley and preload the rewind spring by rotating the pulley 3 turns clockwise.

10. Hold the pulley in this position to keep it from turning and feed bout 30 cm (1 foot) of rope through the rope guide in the starter housing.

11. Tie a loose knot in the rope to prevent the rope from rewinding into the housing. Be sure to leave enough room to attach the handle.

12. Feed the free end of the rope through the handle and tie the knot as shown in **Figure 164**. Pull the knot down onto the handle.

13. Untie the loose knot and let the rope rewind around the pulley.

14. Test the assembly by pulling the handle, then releasing it to rewind the rope around the pulley.

15. If the rope does not rewind completely, add additional preload as follows:

   a. Pull the rope up into the notch as shown in **Figure 156**.

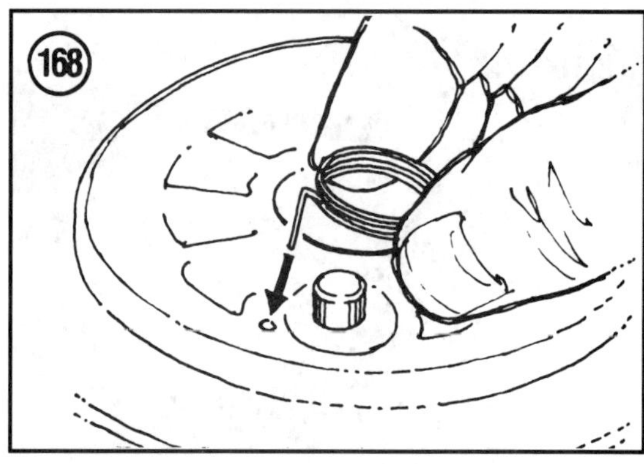

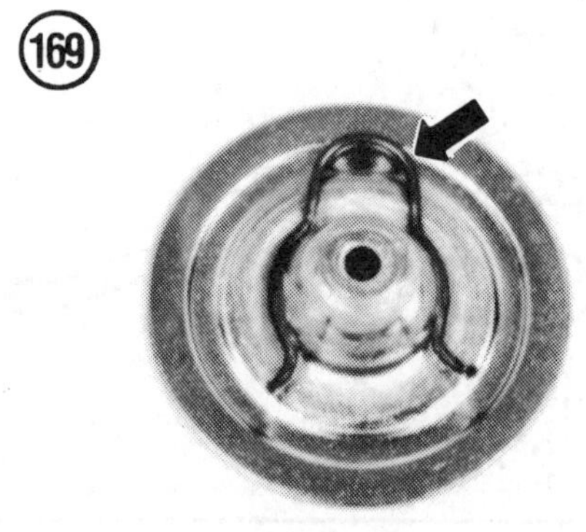

b. Hold the rope in the notch and turn the pulley clockwise one additional turn.
c. Recheck starter operation.

16. Operate the starter and check that the pawl extends properly. If the pawl does not extend, the friction plate and/or pawl spring may be damaged or installed incorrectly. Correct the problem at this time.

ENGINE BREAK-IN

The performance and durability of your Kodiak ATV engine will depend on a sensible and accurate engine break-in procedure. If the rings were replaced, a new piston installed, the cylinder replaced, the crankshaft rebuilt or replaced, or new engine bearings installed, the engine must be broken in just as if it were new. If a proper engine break-in procedure is not followed, accelerated engine wear and overheating will result, reducing engine life.

Before starting the break-in procedure, note the following:

a. Make sure the crankcase is filled with the correct type and quantity engine oil. See Chapter Three.
b. Make sure the air filter is clean, oiled, and properly installed.
c. Make sure the correct heat range spark is installed in the engine.
d. Check clutch operation to make sure there is no clutch slipping or dragging.
e. Perform the break-in procedure on flat ground. To prevent engine overheating, avoid riding in sand, mud or up hills.
f. Do not run the engine with the throttle in the same position for more than a few seconds.
g. Short bursts of full throttle operation (no more than 2-3 seconds at a time) are acceptable. However, rest the engine after each full throttle operation by cruising at a low engine speed for a few minutes. This will allow the engine to rid itself of any excessive heat buildup.
h. Check the spark plug frequently during the break-in procedure. The electrode should be dry and clean and the color of the insulation should be light to medium tan. Refer to Chapter Three for further information on spark plug reading.
i. To control throttle operation at 1/2 and 3/4 throttle positions during break-in, adjust the speed limiter (**Figure 171**) mounted on the throttle housing.
j. Keep accurate time records of the break-in procedure.

1. For the first 10 hours, keep the engine speed below 1/2 throttle. Stop and turn the engine off after every hour of continuous riding and allow the engine to cool down for 5 to 10 minutes before continuing. During this time period, shift the transmission frequently to avoid lugging the engine while at the same time avoiding high engine rpm. Do not operate the vehicle for any length of time in any one throttle position.
2. For the next 10 hours, do not ride the vehicle above 3/4 throttle. During this period, shift the transmission frequently to avoid lugging the engine while avoiding high engine rpm.
3. After the first 20 hours of engine operation, the engine break-in is complete.

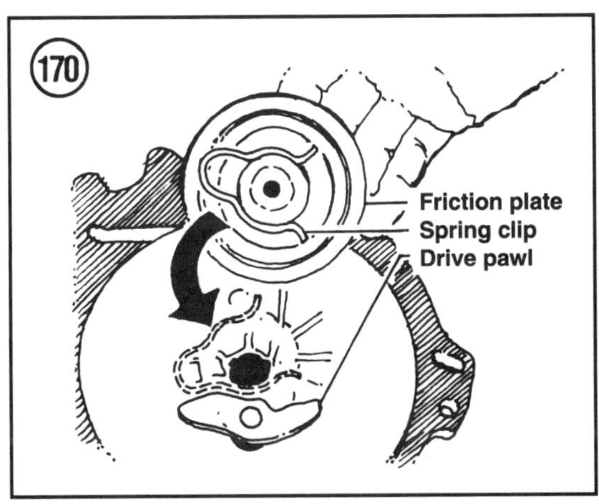

5

Table 1 ENGINE BOTTOM END SERVICE SPECIFICATIONS

Item	New mm (in.)	Service limit mm (in.)
Connecting rod big end side clearance	0.35-0.85 (0.014-0.033)	0.7 (0.028)
Crankshaft		
Runout limit		
Point A	—	0.02 (0.0008)
Point B	—	0.06 (0.0024)
Wheel width	58.95-59.00 (2.321-2.323)	—
Big end radial clearance	0.010-0.025 (0.0004-0.0010)	—
Small end free play	0.8-1.0 (0.0315-0.0394)	2.0 (0.0787)
Oil pump		
Outer rotor-to-oil pump body side clearance	0.04-0.09 (0.0016-0.0035)	—
Inner rotor-to-outer rotor tip clearance	—	0.15 (0.006)

Table 2 ENGINE BOTTOM END TIGHTENING TORQUES

	N•m	in.-lb.	ft.-lb.
Balancer driven gear nut	60	—	44
Bearing retainer (middle drive axle)	25	—	18
Crankcase mounting bolts	10	88	—
Crankcase covers	10	88	—
Cylinder head-to-frame mounting bolts and nuts			
Upper mounting bolts	42	—	30
Lower mounting bolt and nut	33	—	24
Engine mounting nuts and bolts			
8 mm	33	—	24
10 mm	42	—	30
Exhaust system			
Muffler and frame bolts	27	—	19
Muffler and exhaust pipe bolt	20	—	14
Exhaust pipe and cylinder head nuts	12	106	—
Exhaust pipe and protector bolts	11	97	—
Flywheel bolt	50	—	36
Middle drive gear nut	120	—	88
Middle driven axle and U-joint nut	90	—	66
Middle gear case mounting bolts	10	88	—
Neutral switch	20	—	14
Oil cooler hoses			
Oil hose and oil cooler nuts	35	—	25
Oil hose and crankcase nuts	35	—	25
Hose clamps	7	62	—
Oil cooler mounting bolts	7	62	—
Oil drain plug	10	88	—
Oil filter cover	10	88	—
Oil pipe banjo bolts			
External oil pipe			
Left banjo bolt	35	—	35
Right banjo bolt	16	—	11
Internal oil pipe banjo bolts*	16	—	11

(continued)

Table 2 ENGINE BOTTOM END TIGHTENING TORQUES (continued)

	N•m	in.-lb.	ft.-lb.
Oil pump			
Body screw	7	62	—
Mounting screws	7	62	—
Recoil starter housing mounting bolts	10	88	—
Rotor mounting bolt	50	—	36
Shift drum No. 2 detent bolt	10	88	—
Shift drum No. 2 select lever bolt	14	—	10
Shift drum segment	12	106	—
Shift pedal pinch bolt	10	88	—
Starter clutch mounting bolts	30	—	22
Starter motor mounting bolts	10	88	—
Stator coil assembly			
Pickup coil mounting screws	5	44	—
Stator coil mounting screws	8	70	—
Stator housing mounting bolts	10	88	—
Thermosensor	20	—	14
Transfer gear assembly			
Crankcase mounting bolts	25	—	18
Rear case mounting bolts	25	—	18

* The internal oil pipe is installed behind the clutch and inside the crankcase.

CHAPTER SIX

CLUTCH AND EXTERNAL SHIFT MECHANISM

This chapter describes service procedures for the following subassemblies:

a. Clutch cover.
b. Clutch release mechanism.
c. Clutch assemblies (primary and secondary).
d. External shift mechanism.

These subassemblies can be removed with the engine in the frame. Clutch service specifications are listed in **Table 1** and **Table 2**. **Tables 1-3** are located at the end of the chapter.

CLUTCH COVER

The clutch release mechanism is mounted in the clutch cover.

Removal

1. Park the vehicle on a level ground and set the parking brake.
2. Remove the right-hand footpeg assembly as described in Chapter Fourteen.
3. Drain the engine oil as described in Chapter Three.
4. Remove the exhaust pipe guard plate (A, **Figure 1**).
5. If necessary, remove the protector cover screws and protector cover (B, **Figure 1**).
6. Remove the oil pipe banjo bolt and washers (C, **Figure 1**).
7. Remove the screw and disconnect the speedometer cable (A, **Figure 2**) from the clutch cover.
8. Remove the oil filler cap/dipstick. This must be removed prior to removing the cover due to an interference between the lower end of the dipstick and a clutch component.

CAUTION
*If the external oil pipe is not going to be removed, **carefully** lift the right-hand end up and off the clutch cover. Do not pull up too high as the oil line may become kinked resulting in reduced oil flow or an oil leak.*

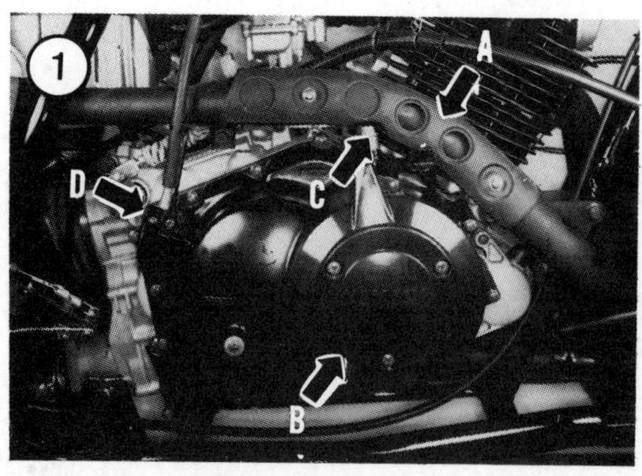

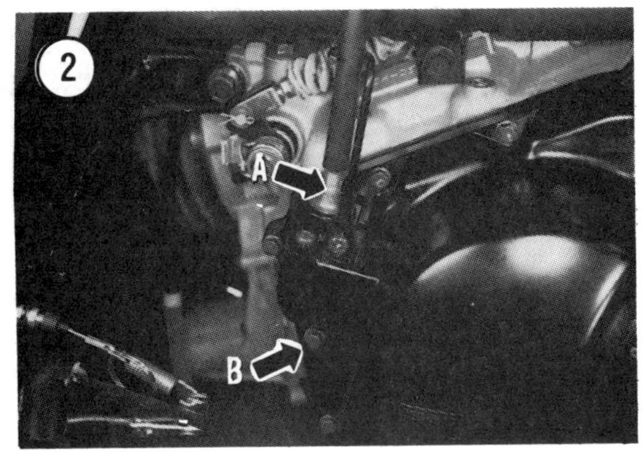

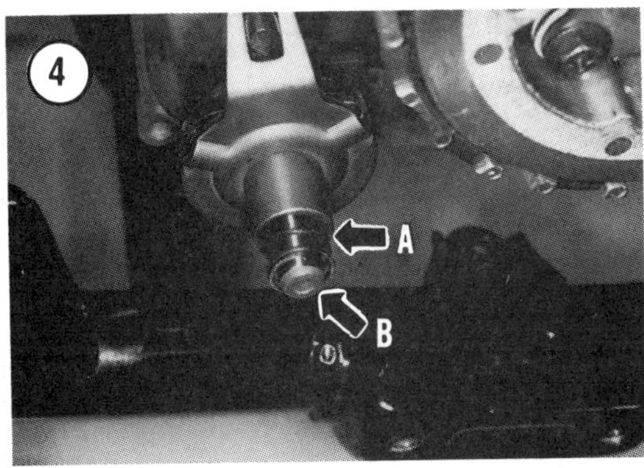

9. Remove the clutch cover mounting bolts. Note the sealing washer used on the bolt shown in B, **Figure 2**.

10. Tap the clutch cover lightly to break its gasket seal, then remove the cover and its 2 dowel pins.

11. Remove and discard the gasket.

12. Note the position of the speedometer drive gear (**Figure 3**). It may still be on the middle drive gear shaft or came off inside the clutch cover.

13. Do not lose the small coil spring (A, **Figure 4**) on the end of the shift guide.

14. Remove all gasket residue from the cover and crankcase gasket surfaces.

15. If necessary, service the clutch release mechanism as described under *Clutch Release Mechanism* in this chapter.

Clutch Cover Bearing, Washer and Seal Inspection and Replacement

The bearing, washer and seal installed in the clutch cover are an integral part of the engine's lubrication system. Oil passages in the clutch cover and crankshaft allow circulation of oil to the crankshaft big end bearing. The end of the crankshaft operates in the bearing. The oil seal, installed behind the bearing, seals the crankshaft and clutch cover oil passages so that oil does not leak out.

Replace the seal whenever the bearing is removed from the clutch cover or when rebuilding an engine that was damaged from overheating or suffered a crankshaft failure.

When removing the bearing and oil seal from the clutch cover, note and record the direction in which the bearing (manufacturer's marks) and oil seal (closed side) faces for proper reinstallation.

1. Turn the clutch cover bearing (A, **Figure 5**) by hand. The bearing should turn smoothly without catching, binding or excessive noise. If the bearing is damaged or if the seal requires replacement, continue with Step 2.

2. Support the clutch cover and remove the bearing retainer screws and remove the retainer (B, **Figure 5**).

3. Support the clutch cover and remove the bearing (A, **Figure 5**) with a blind bearing remover.

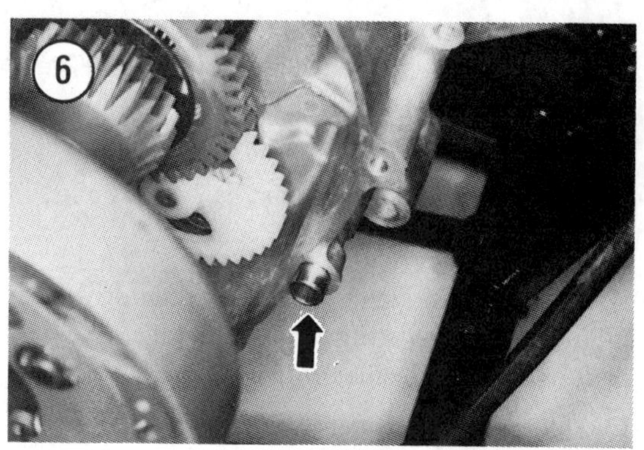

CLUTCH RELEASE MECHANISM/SHIFT SHAFT

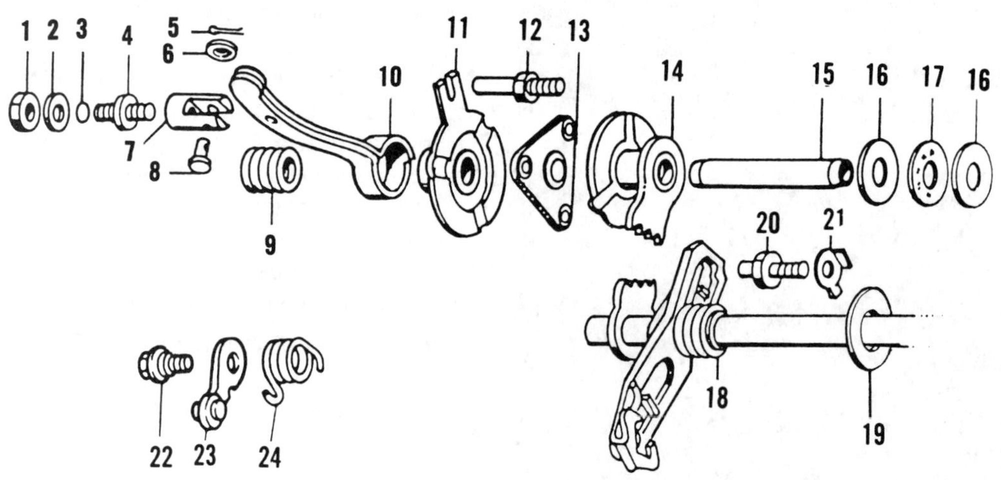

1. Locknut
2. Washer
3. O-ring
4. Adjust screw
5. Cotter pin
6. E-clip
7. Holder
8. Clevis pin
9. Spring
10. Release lever
11. Release cam No. 2
12. Stopper bolt
13. Release bearing
14. Release cam No. 1
15. Shaft
16. Bearing washers
17. Radial bearing
18. Shift shaft
19. Washer
20. Stopper bolt
21. Lockwasher
22. Bolt
23. Stopper lever
24. Spring

NOTE
Note the direction of the oil seal so the new seal will be reinstalled in the right direction.

4. Carefully pry the seal out of the bore with a slotted screwdriver or oil seal removal tool. Pad the tool so that it does not damage the bearing bore.
5. Clean the clutch cover in solvent and dry thoroughly.
6. Clean the clutch cover oil passage with compressed air.
7. Support the clutch cover and install the new seal. Install the seal so that its closed side faces in the direction recorded during disassembly.
8. Press the new bearing into the clutch cover bearing bore.
9. Apply a medium strength threadlocking compound to the bearing retainer screws. Then install the bearing retainer and screws and tighten securely.

Installation

1. Clean the clutch cover oil passage with compressed air.
2. Install the speedometer drive gear (**Figure 3**) on the end of the middle drive gear shaft.
3. Make sure the small coil spring (A, **Figure 4**) is installed on the end of the shift guide.
4. Install the clutch cover dowel pins. **Figure 6** shows one of the dowel pins.
5. Install a new clutch cover gasket.
6. Move the clutch cover into place and make sure of the following:
   a. The release lever (A, **Figure 7**) properly engages the shift guide (B, **Figure 4**).

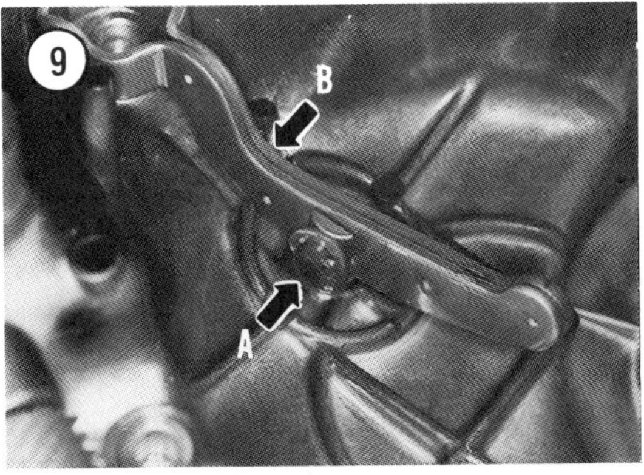

   b. The crankshaft end enters the bearing (B, **Figure 7**) in the cover.
7. Install the clutch cover and its mounting bolts. Be sure to install a new sealing washer under the bolt shown in B, **Figure 2**. Tighten the bolts securely in a crisscross pattern.
8. Install the oil filler cap/dipstick and tighten it securely.
9. Install the oil pipe banjo bolt and washers (C, **Figure 1**). Install a new washer on each side of the banjo fitting. Tighten the external oil pipe banjo bolt as specified in **Table 3**.
10. Install protector cover (B, **Figure 1**) and tighten the screws securely.
11. Install the exhaust pipe guard plate (A, **Figure 1**).
12. Adjust the clutch as described in Chapter Three.
13. Refill the engine with oil as described in Chapter Three.
14. Install the right-hand footpeg (Chapter Fourteen).

CLUTCH RELEASE LEVER MECHANISM

Refer to **Figure 8** when servicing the clutch release mechanism.

Removal

1. Remove the clutch cover as described in this chapter.
2. Remove the cotter pin and E-clip (A, **Figure 9**) securing the clevis pin and holder to the clutch release lever.
3. Remove the locknut, washer, O-ring and clutch adjust screw (**Figure 8**).
4. Remove the clutch release lever and spring (B, **Figure 9**) from the clutch cover.

NOTE
*While the clutch release cams and release bearing are part of the clutch release mechanism, these items are covered under **External Shift Mechanism** in this chapter.*

Inspection

1. Clean and dry all parts.
2. Replace the clutch adjust screw O-ring if leaking or damaged.

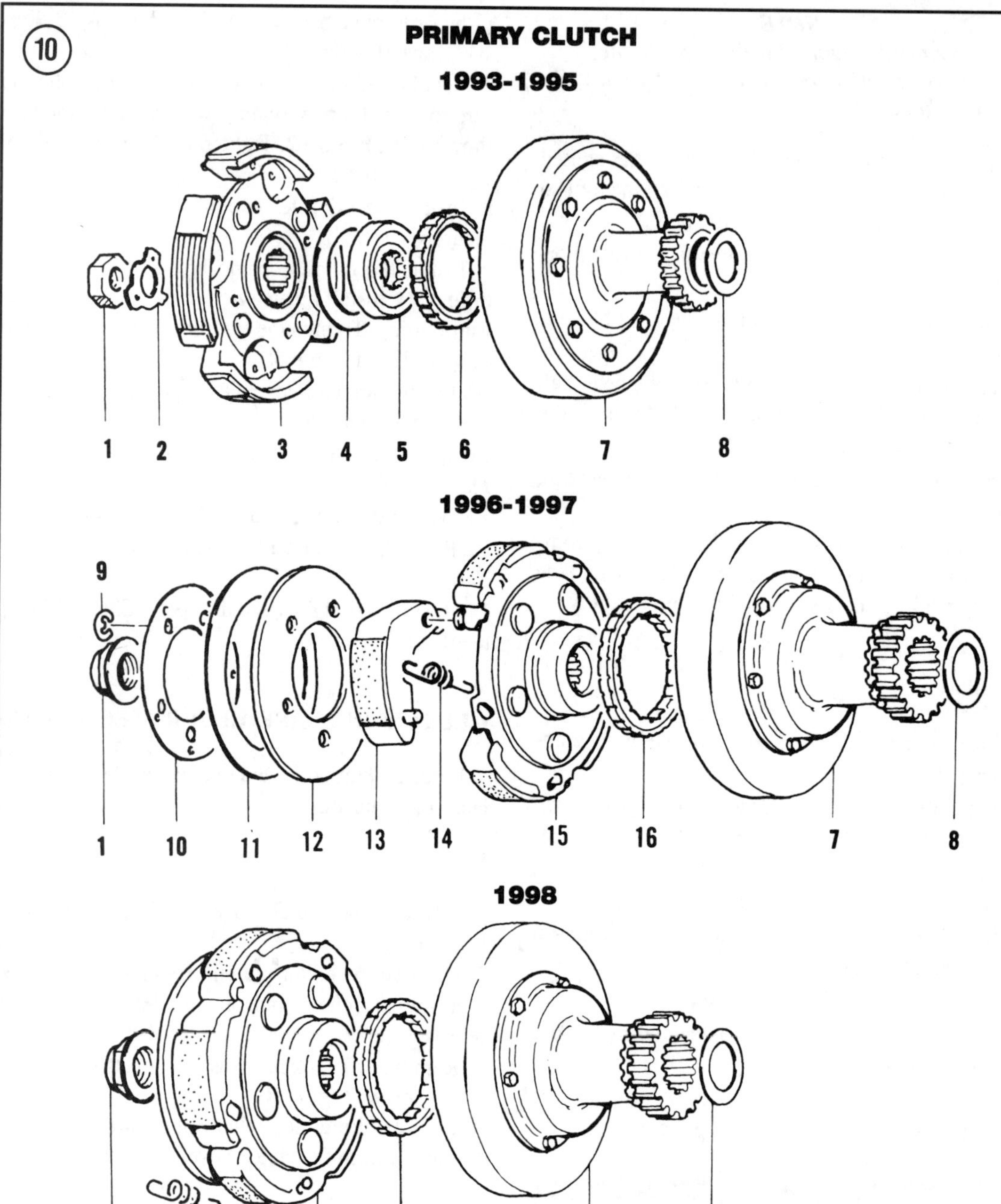

1. Nut
2. Lockwasher
3. Clutch carrier
4. Washer
5. Inner race and bearing
6. One-way clutch
7. Primary clutch housing and drive gear
8. Washer
9. E-clip
10. Thrust weight plate
11. Spring washer
12. Friction ring
13. Clutch shoe
14. Spring
15. Clutch carrier
16. One-way clutch
17. Clutch carrier

3. Check the clutch release lever for excessive wear or damage.
4. Check the large spring for weakness or other damage.
5. Replace all worn or damaged parts.

Installation

1. Install the clutch release lever and spring (B, **Figure 9**) onto the clutch cover.
2. Install the clutch adjust screw, O-ring and locknut onto the clutch cover (**Figure 8**). Install the clevis pin through the release lever and holder.
3. Install the E-clip and a new cotter pin (A, **Figure 9**). Bend the ends over completely.
4. Install the clutch cover as described in this chapter.
5. Adjust the clutch as described in Chapter Three.

CLUTCH ASSEMBLIES

Refer to **Figure 10** and **Figure 11** for this procedure.

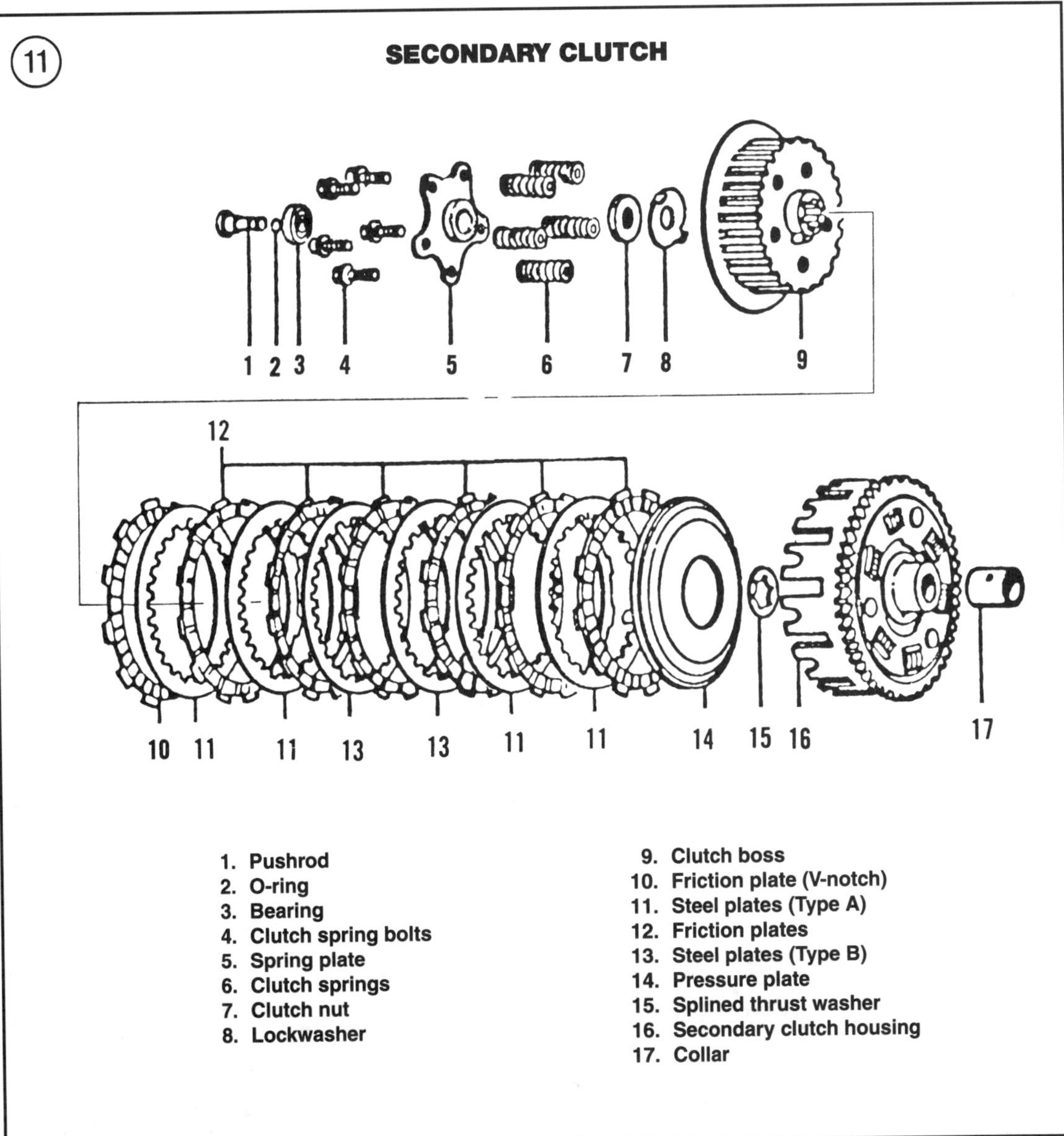

1. Pushrod
2. O-ring
3. Bearing
4. Clutch spring bolts
5. Spring plate
6. Clutch springs
7. Clutch nut
8. Lockwasher
9. Clutch boss
10. Friction plate (V-notch)
11. Steel plates (Type A)
12. Friction plates
13. Steel plates (Type B)
14. Pressure plate
15. Splined thrust washer
16. Secondary clutch housing
17. Collar

6

Removal

1. Remove the clutch cover as described in this chapter.
2. Perform the *One-Way Clutch Check* described in this chapter.
3. Remove the clutch release cams and release bearing as described under *External Shift Mechanism* in this chapter.
4. Remove the speedometer drive gear (**Figure 3**).

NOTE
*Steps 5-11 describe removal of the primary clutch assembly (**Figure 10**).*

5. Flatten the primary clutch locknut (**Figure 12**) with a punch or similar tool.
6. Remove the recoil starter housing as described in Chapter Five.
7. Have an assistant secure the starter pulley using a rotor holding tool (**Figure 13**) or metal bar. Do not hold the rotor mounting bolt.
8. Loosen and remove the primary clutch locknut (**Figure 12**).
9. Rotate the secondary clutch housing until the curved recess (**Figure 14**) is aligned with the gear portion of the primary clutch housing. This alignment is necessary to slide the primary clutch housing past the secondary clutch housing.
10. Remove the primary clutch assembly using a 2-jaw puller (**Figure 15**).
11. Remove the washer (**Figure 16**).

NOTE
*Steps 12-20 describe removal of the secondary clutch assembly (**Figure 11**).*

12. Loosen the clutch spring bolts (A, **Figure 17**) in a crisscross pattern. Then remove the bolts.

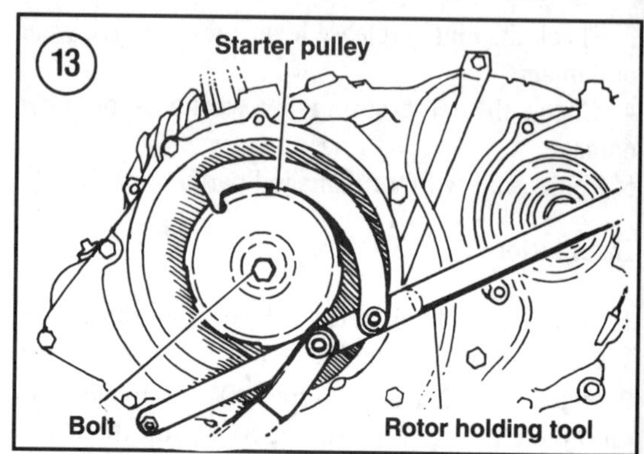

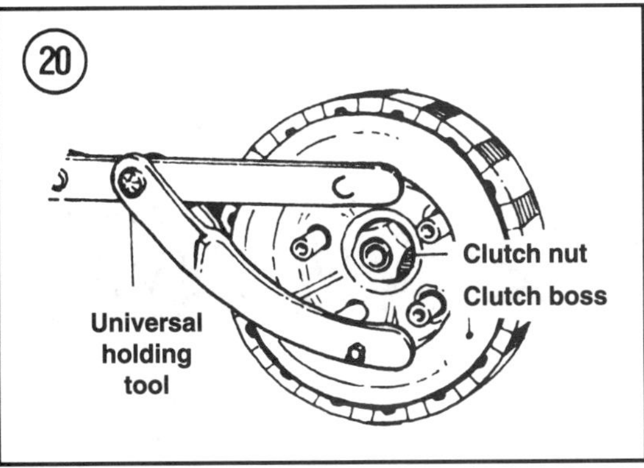

13. Remove the spring plate (B, **Figure 17**), bearing, pushrod and 3 clutch springs (**Figure 18**).

14. Reinstall 2 of the clutch bolts (A, **Figure 19**) over the 2 rings and tighten securely. This will hold the clutch assembly together for easier removal.

15. Straighten the locking tab (B, **Figure 19**) on the lockwasher.

NOTE

The Yamaha rotor holder (part No. YU-01235) shown in Step 16 has 2 pins that fit into the 2 clutch boss holes identified in C, ***Figure 19****. This tool is used to hold the clutch boss when loosening and tightening the secondary clutch nut.*

16. Hold the clutch boss with the Yamaha rotor holder (**Figure 20**) or equivalent and loosen the secondary clutch nut.

17. Remove the secondary clutch nut (B, **Figure 19**) and lockwasher.

18. Slide the clutch boss (C, **Figure 19**), clutch plates and pressure plate off the transmission shaft.

19. Remove the splined thrust washer (**Figure 21**).

20. Remove the secondary clutch housing (**Figure 22**) and collar (**Figure 23**).

21. Inspect all clutch components as described in this chapter.

Primary Clutch Shoe Inspection

When measuring the primary clutch components, compare the actual measurements to the specifications listed in **Table 1**. Replace parts that are damaged or out of specification as described in this section. Refer to **Figure 10** when performing this procedure.

1. Remove the clutch shoe assembly. On 1993-1995 models, remove the large flat washer.
2. Check the primary clutch shoe linings (**Figure 24**) for cracks, missing friction material, uneven wear or discoloration. If any of the shoe linings are damaged, replace the primary shoe lining assembly.
3. Check for weak or damaged springs.
4. Measure the groove depth of each primary clutch shoe (**Figure 25**). If one or more shoes are out of specification, note the following:
   a. On 1993-1995 and 1998 models, the primary clutch shoes are not available separately. Replace the primary clutch shoe assembly.
   b. On 1996-1997 models, the primary clutch shoes are available separately. Replace the shoes as a set (**Figure 11**). After replacing the shoes, make sure the E-clips seat in the shaft grooves completely.
5. Inspect the clutch shoe springs for fatigue, stretched coils or other damage. If the clutch shoes are worn unevenly, remove the springs from the clutch carrier assembly and measure the free length of each spring with a vernier caliper. If out of specification, replace the springs as a set.

22

23

Primary Clutch Housing and One-Way Clutch Inspection

The primary clutch housing is a subassembly consisting of the primary clutch housing, one-way clutch and primary drive gear. **Figure 10** shows the differences between the 1993-1995, 1996-1997 and 1998 primary clutch assemblies.

Replace worn or damaged parts as described in this section.

1. Clean and dry the primary clutch housing assembly.

2A. On 1993-1995 models, turn the inner race (**Figure 26**) and check the one-way clutch assembly for excessive wear, binding or roughness. Then remove the inner race from the housing.

2B. On 1996-on models, turn the clutch shoe assembly and check the one-way clutch for excessive wear, binding or roughness. Then remove the clutch shoe assembly from the housing.

3. To remove the one-way clutch, insert a slotted screwdriver underneath the one-way clutch (**Figure 27**) and carefully pry it out of the hub bore.

4. On 1993-1995 models, inspect the inner race (A, **Figure 28**) for cracks, scoring or heat damage.

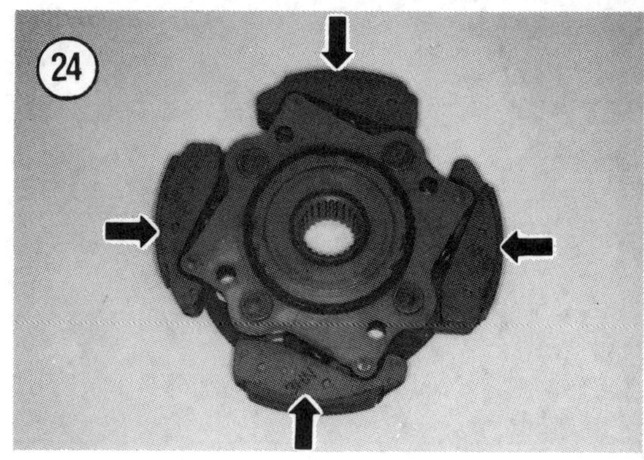

24

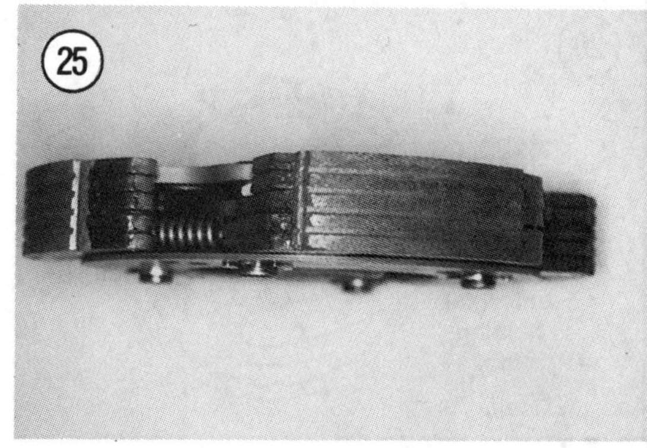

25

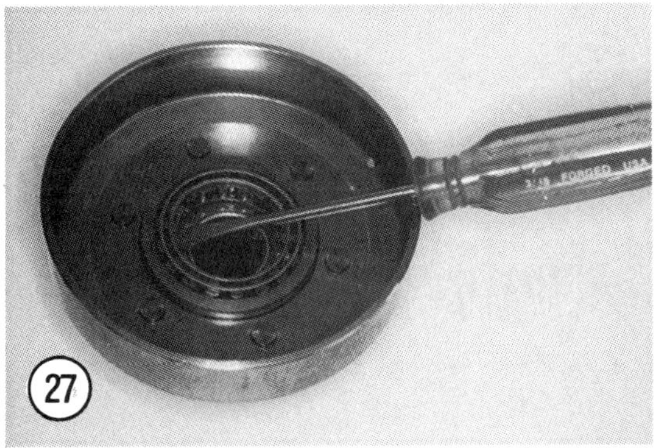

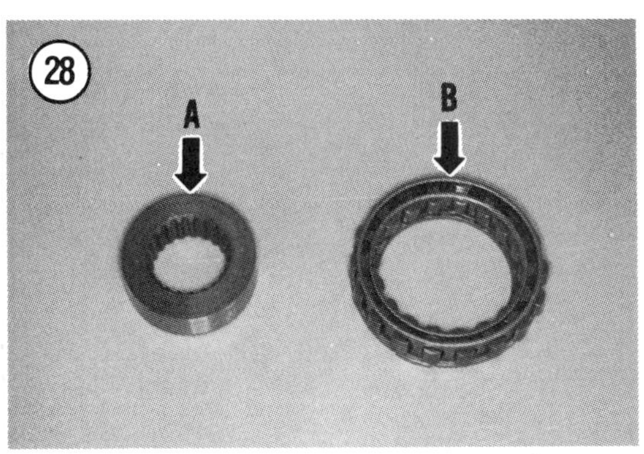

Check the splines for cracks or other damage. On 1996-on models, check the clutch carrier shoulder for the same conditions.

5. Check the one-way clutch bearing (B, **Figure 28**). Check the bearing cage for cracks. Check the bearing rollers for flat spots, binding or other damage.

6. Inspect the one-way clutch outer race (**Figure 29**) for excessvie wear, grooves or other damage.

7. Inspect the primary clutch housing (**Figure 10**) inner and outer bushings for excessive wear or damage.The bushings cannot be replaced separately. If damaged, replace the primary clutch housing.

8. Inspect the primary clutch housing-to-clutch shoe contact area (**Figure 30**) for excessive wear, grooves or other damage.

9. Inspect the primary drive gear (**Figure 10**) for worn or chipped gear teeth.

10. Check the primary clutch housing (**Figure 11**) for wear, fractures or damage.

11. Inspect the inner splines of the primary clutch shoe assembly for wear or damage. Replace if necessary.

12. Assemble the one-way clutch assembly as follows:

   a. The one-way clutch has a shoulder on one end (A, **Figure 31**).
   b. Install the one-way clutch so that its shoulder (B, **Figure 31**) seats into the groove in the bottom of the outer race (B, **Figure 31**).

Secondary Clutch Inspection

When measuring the secondary clutch components (**Figure 11**), compare the actual measurements to the new and service limit specifications in **Table 2**. Replace worn or damaged parts as described in this section. When replacing the clutch plates, al-

6

ways replace the steel plates and/or the friction plates as a set. Never replace 1 or 2 plates at a time.

1. Remove the 2 clutch spring bolts and springs (**Figure 32**) securing the friction plates, clutch plates, clutch boss and pressure plate together. Separate all components in the order shown in **Figure 11**.
2. Clean and dry all parts.
3. Measure the free length of each clutch spring (**Figure 33**) with a vernier caliper. Replace the springs as a set if any one spring is too short.
4. **Table 1** lists the number of friction plates used in the stock clutch. Inspect the friction plates for cracks or other obvious defects.
5. Measure the thickness of each friction plate at several places around the plate (**Figure 34**) with a vernier caliper or micrometer.
6. The friction plate tabs slide in the clutch housing grooves. Inspect each friction plate tab for cracks or galling that can cause the plate to grab or cause clutch housing groove wear. The tabs and clutch housing grooves must be smooth for chatter-free clutch operation. Repair light damage with a smooth or second cut file. Excessive friction plate tab and clutch housing groove wear can cause clutch drag.
7. **Table 2** lists the number of steel plates and their respective thickness used in the stock clutch. Inspect the steel plates for heat discoloration and damage.

NOTE
The secondary clutch uses 2 different steel plate thicknesses.

8. Place each steel plate on a surface plate or a thick piece of glass and check for warpage with a feeler gauge (**Figure 35**).
9. The steel plates inner teeth mesh with the clutch boss (**Figure 36**) splines. Check the splines for notches, cracks or galling. They must be smooth for

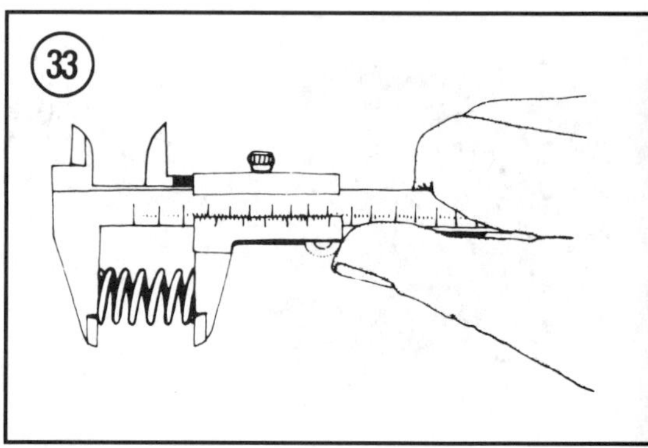

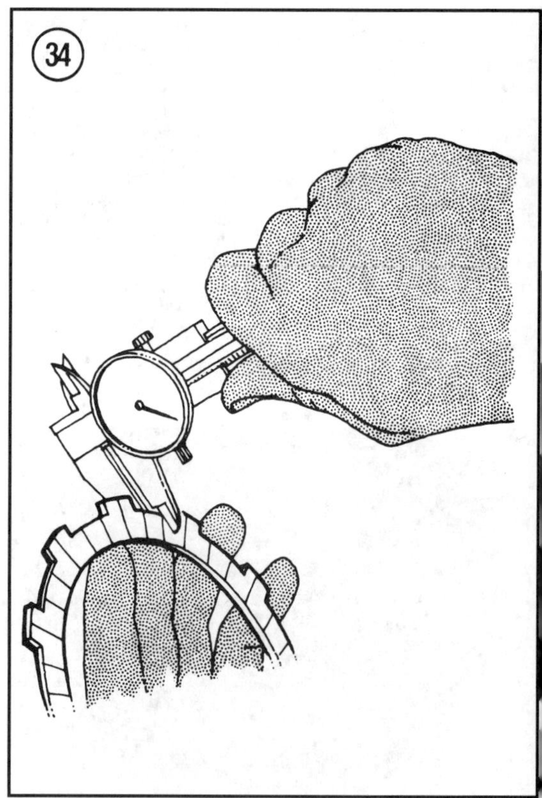

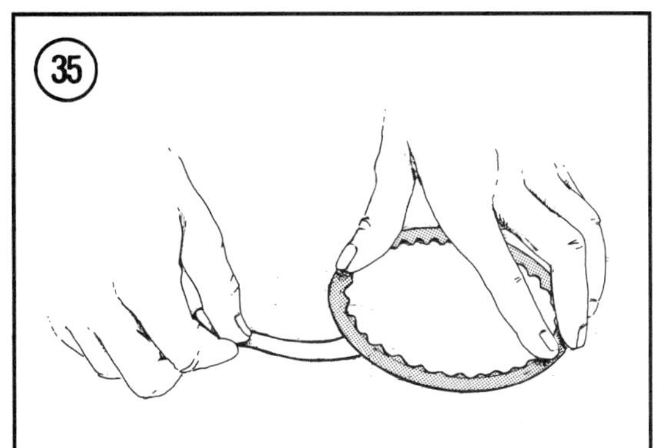
35

36

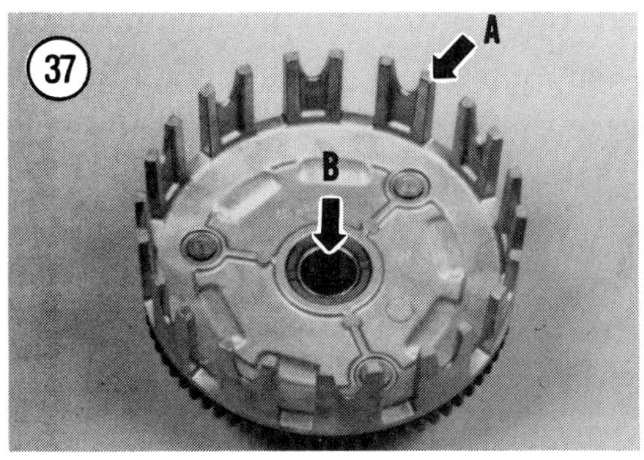

37

38

chatter-free clutch operation. Repair light damage with a smooth or second cut file. If the clutch boss splines are worn, check the steel plate teeth for wear or damage.

10. Inspect the clutch boss shaft splines (**Figure 36**) and the friction plate mating surface for scoring or other damage.

11. Inspect the secondary clutch housing tabs (A, **Figure 37**) for notches, cracks or galling. Minor damage can be repaired with a smooth or second cut file.

12. Check the secondary clutch housing gear for severely worn or damaged gear teeth. Then check the gear for loose mounting rivets.

13. Inspect the secondary clutch housing bushing (B, **Figure 37**) and spacer for wear or other damage.

14. Apply a light coat of clean engine oil to the spacer and insert the spacer into the clutch housing bushing. Rotate the bushing and check for excessive wear or binding.

15. Inspect the pressure plate (A, **Figure 38**) for damaged splines or for cracked or broken spring towers. Inspect the threaded studs for thread damage. Repair if necessary.

16. Inspect the spring plate (B, **Figure 38**) bolt holes for elongation or cracks. Replace if necessary.

17. Inspect the clutch release bearing (C, **Figure 38**) for damage. Hold the outer bearing race and turn the inner race by hand. The bearing should turn smoothly with no roughness or excessive noise.

18. Check the pushrod (D, **Figure 38**) for flattened ends, heat discoloration or other damage. Inspect the O-ring for cracks or severe wear.

Installation

NOTE

*Steps 1-15 describe installation of the secondary clutch assembly (***Figure 11***).*

1. Before installing the clutch plate assembly, note the following:

   a. The stock clutch uses 7 friction plates, of which there are 2 different types. The friction plate installed against the clutch boss has a V-notch cut into one plate tab (A, **Figure 39**). The remaining 6 friction plates (B, **Figure 39**) do not have the V-notch.

   b. The stock clutch uses 6 steel plates, of which there are 2 different types: Type A and Type B.

6

The 4 Type A steel plates have a smaller inside diameter than the 2 Type B plates.

2. Assemble the friction and clutch plates onto the clutch boss (**Figure 36**) as follows:
   a. Lubricate the friction and steel clutch plates with engine oil.
   b. Install the friction plate with the V-notch onto the clutch boss (**Figure 40**).
   c. Install a Type A steel plate (**Figure 41**).
   d. Install the remaining clutch plates in the order shown in **Figure 42**. The last plate installed is a friction plate.
3. Align the V-notch on the first friction plate tab with the arrow mark on the clutch boss (**Figure 43**). Then align all of the friction plate tabs.
4. Align the pressure plate index mark (A, **Figure 44**) with the clutch boss index mark (B, **Figure 44**) and install the pressure plate. See **Figure 45**.

NOTE
Make sure the pressure plate sits flush against the outer friction plate. If not, check the index marks and realign the pressure plate.

5. Temporarily install 2 clutch springs and bolts (**Figure 46**) to hold the assembly together. Tighten the bolts finger-tight.
6. Install the collar (**Figure 47**) onto the transmission shaft.
7. Install the secondary clutch housing (A, **Figure 48**) and splined thrust washer (B, **Figure 48**).
8. Install the clutch boss assembly into the secondary clutch housing. When doing so, center the clutch boss index mark (A, **Figure 49**) with the 2 clutch housing index marks (B, **Figure 49**).
9. Install a new lockwasher (A, **Figure 50**) by inserting its tab into the clutch boss notch.
10. Install the clutch nut (B, **Figure 50**) and tighten finger-tight.
11. Secure the clutch with the same tool used during disassembly (**Figure 51**) and tighten the secondary clutch nut as specified in **Table 3**.
12. Bend one of the lockwasher tabs against one side of the clutch nut.
13. Remove the 2 bolts and clutch springs (C, **Figure 50**).
14. Install the clutch springs onto the pressure plate posts.
15. Install the spring plate, bearing, pushrod and clutch spring mounting bolts (**Figure 52**). Tighten the clutch spring bolts in a crisscross pattern in 2-4 steps to the torque specification in **Table 3**.

NOTE
*Steps 16-21 describe installation of the primary clutch assembly (**Figure 10**).*

16. Install the flat washer (**Figure 53**) onto the crankshaft.
17. Install the primary clutch housing as follows:
   a. Rotate the secondary clutch housing until its curved recess (**Figure 54**) aligns with the gear

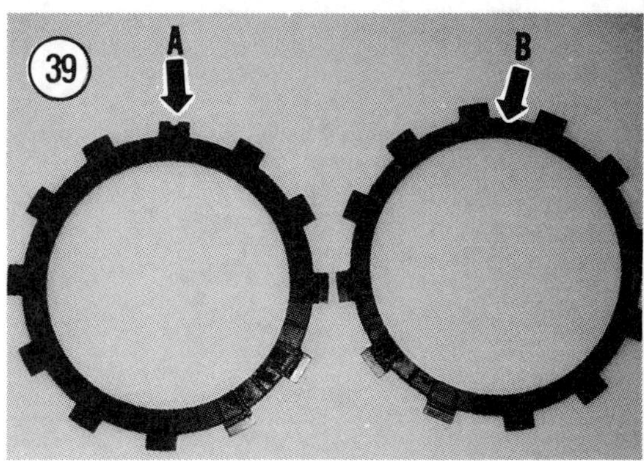

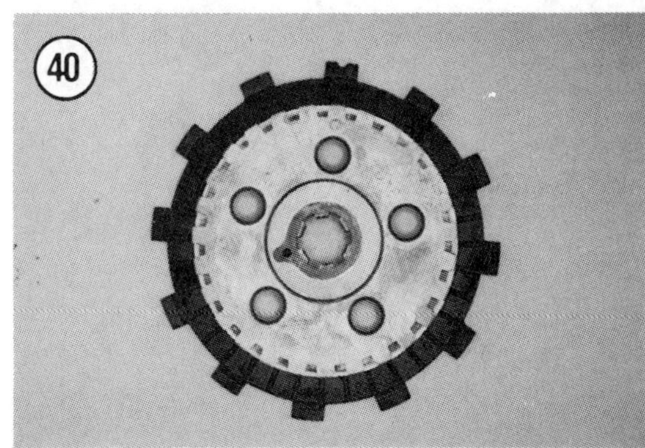

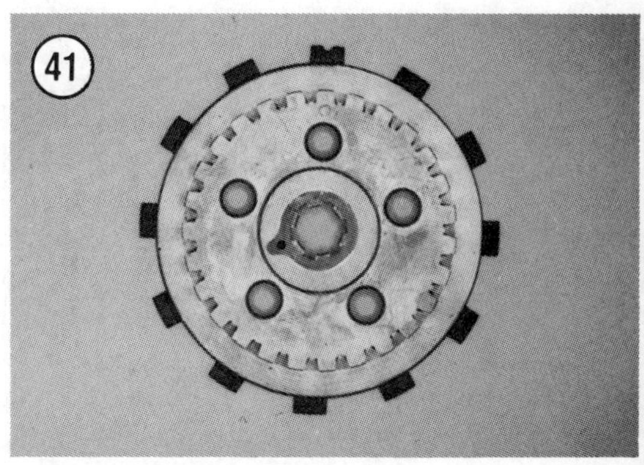

42

SECONDARY CLUTCH PLATES

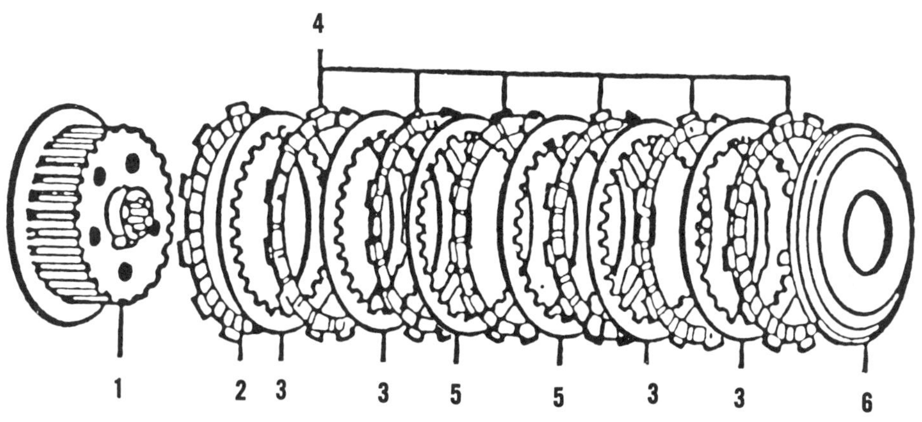

1. Clutch boss
2. Friction plate (V-notch)
3. Steel plates (Type A)
4. Friction plates
5. Steel plates (Type B)
6. Pressure plate

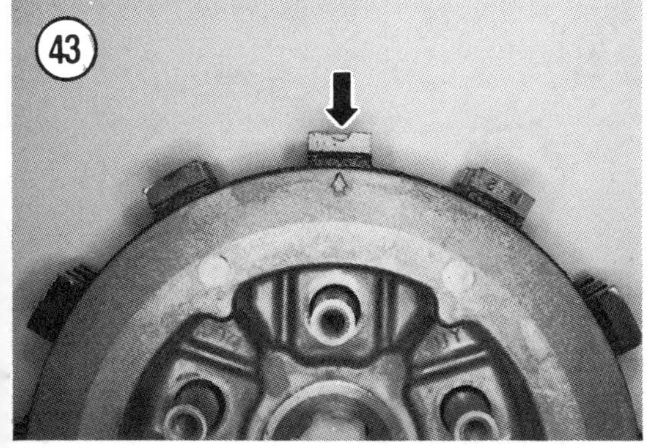

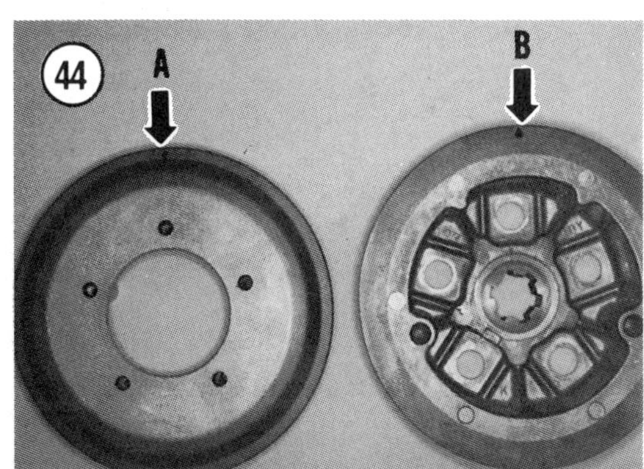

6

mounted on the primary clutch housing. This alignment is necessary to slide the primary clutch housing past the secondary clutch housing.

b. Slide the primary clutch housing onto the crankshaft (**Figure 54**). Mesh the gear with the secondary clutch housing.

18A. On 1993-1995 models, install the clutch shoe assembly (**Figure 10**) as follows:

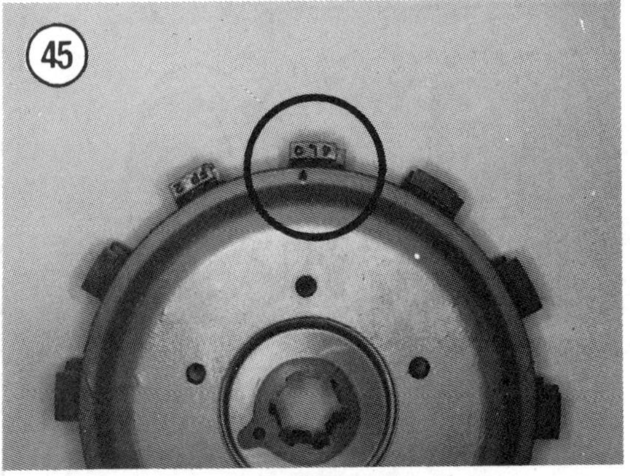

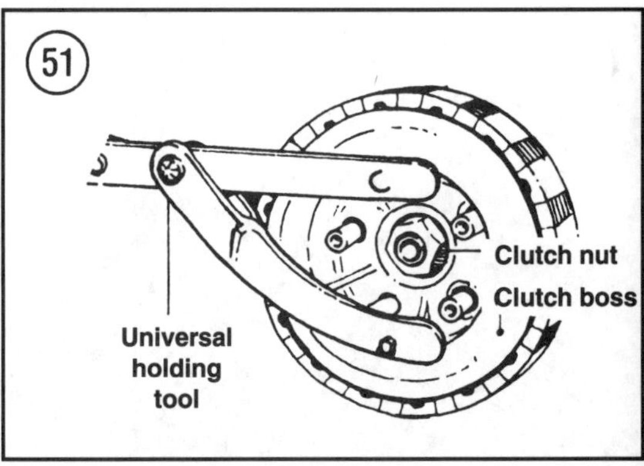

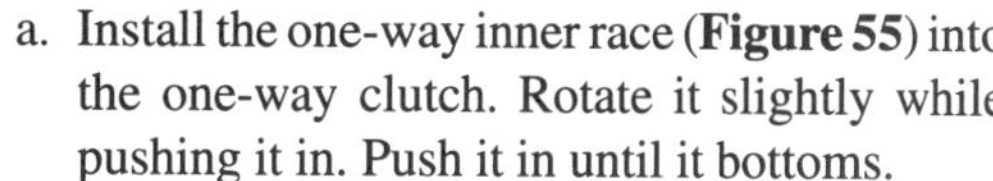

a. Install the one-way inner race (**Figure 55**) into the one-way clutch. Rotate it slightly while pushing it in. Push it in until it bottoms.

b. Install the washer (**Figure 56**) onto the inner race. Make sure it is seated properly.

c. Align the splines and slide the primary clutch shoe assembly (**Figure 57**) into the primary clutch housing.

18B. On 1996-on models, install the clutch shoe assembly (**Figure 10**) as follows:

a. Lubricate the primary clutch shoe assembly shoulder with engine oil.

b. Align the splines and slide the primary clutch shoe assembly (A, **Figure 58**) into the primary clutch housing.

19. Install a *new* primary clutch nut (B, **Figure 58**) and tighten finger-tight.

20. Have an assistant secure the starter drum with a rotor holding tool (**Figure 59**) or metal bar. Do not hold the rotor mounting bolt. Then tighten the primary clutch nut (B, **Figure 58**) as specified in **Table 3**.

21. Using a punch, drive part of the clutch nut shoulder against the flat surface machined into the crankshaft threads (**Figure 60**).
22. Install the speedometer drive gear (**Figure 61**).
23. Install the clutch release cams and release bearing as described in this chapter.
24. Install the clutch cover as described in this chapter.
25. Adjust the clutch as described in Chapter Three.
26. Start the engine and allow to warm up to normal operating temperature. The shift the transmission into first gear and check clutch operation.

ONE-WAY CLUTCH CHECK

This procedure checks the one-way clutch assembly installed in the primary clutch housing.
1. Remove the clutch cover as described in this chapter.
2. Stand on the right side of the vehicle and turn the primary clutch housing (**Figure 62**) by hand. The primary housing should turn counterclockwise freely but should not turn clockwise.
3. If the one-way clutch does not operate as described in Step 2, remove the primary clutch housing and one-way clutch as described under *Clutch Removal* in this chapter. Inspect the one-way clutch components as described under *Primary Clutch Housing and One-Way Clutch Inspection* in this chapter. Replace worn or damaged parts.
4. Reassemble the one-way clutch and install the primary clutch housing as described under *Clutch Installation* in this chapter.
5. Install the clutch cover as described in this chapter.

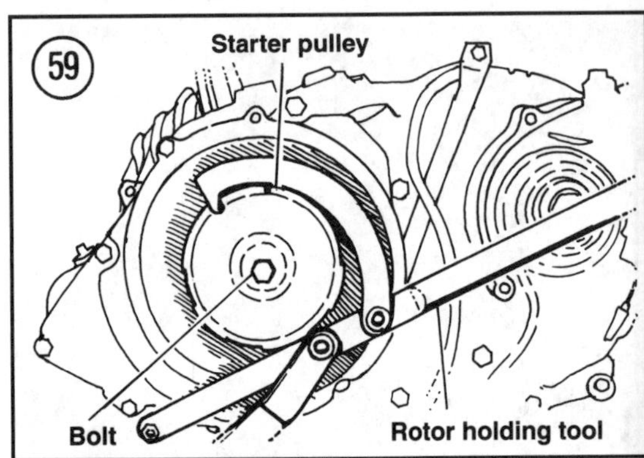

EXTERNAL SHIFT MECHANISM

The external shift mechanism is located on the same side of the crankcase as the clutch and can be removed with the engine in the frame. To remove the shift drums and shift forks, remove and disassemble the engine as described in Chapter Five.

Removal

Refer to **Figure 63** for this procedure.
1. Remove the clutch cover as described in this chapter.
2. Remove the shift pedal from the left side of the vehicle.

3. Remove the spring, the outer release cam and the release bearing assembly (**Figure 64**) from the shift shaft.

4. Remove both clutch assemblies as described in this chapter.

5. Disengage the shift pawl (**Figure 65**) from the shift drum and remove the shift shaft assembly. Do not lose the inner washer on the shaft.

6. Remove the mounting bolt (**Figure 66**) and remove the shift drum No. 1 stopper arm and spring.

(63)

CLUTCH RELEASE MECHANISM/SHIFT SHAFT

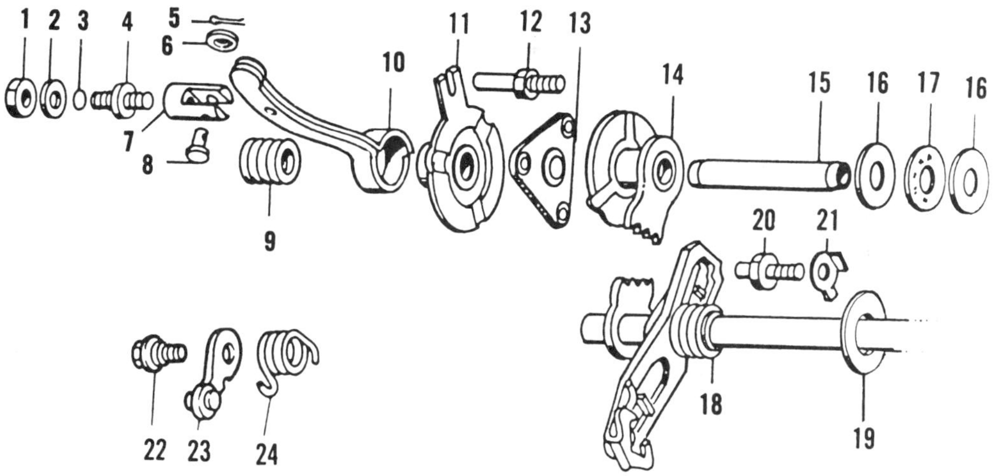

1. Locknut
2. Washer
3. O-ring
4. Adjust screw
5. Cotter pin
6. E-clip
7. Holder
8. Clevis pin
9. Spring
10. Release lever
11. Release cam No. 2
12. Stopper bolt
13. Release bearing
14. Release cam No. 1
15. Shaft
16. Bearing washers
17. Radial bearing
18. Shift shaft
19. Washer
20. Stopper bolt
21. Lockwasher
22. Bolt
23. Stopper lever
24. Spring

Disassembly/Inspection

Replace parts that show damage as described in this section.

Refer to **Figure 63** for this procedure.

1. Disassemble the release cam and bearing assembly.

2. Clean and dry all parts.

3. Check the shift shaft (A, **Figure 67**) for cracks or bending. Check the shaft splines (B, **Figure 67**) for damage.

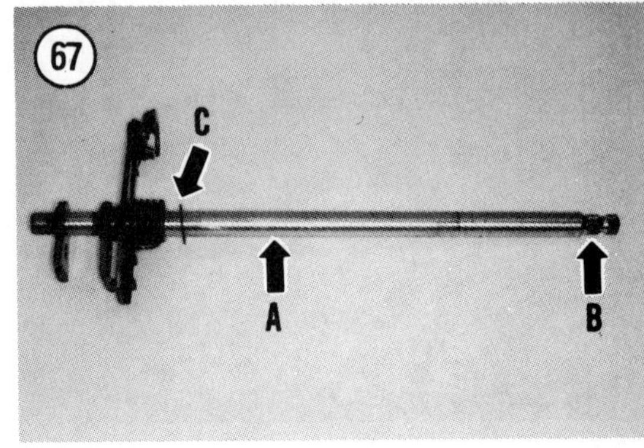

4. Check the shift shaft springs for weakness or damage.
5. Inspect the sector gear and release cam No. 1 gear teeth for wear or damage.
6. Inspect the 2 release cams for scoring or other damage.
7. Inspect the release bearing (**Figure 68**) for scoring, flat spots or other damage.
8. Inspect the radial bearing for scoring, flat spots or other damage.
9. Check the release cam and bearing shaft for wear or damage.
10. Reassemble the release cam and bearing assembly. Refer to **Figure 63** and **Figure 69**.

Installation

1. Install the bolt and spring onto the shift drum No. 1 stopper arm (**Figure 70**).
2. Install the stopper arm assembly (**Figure 66**) and tighten the bolt securely. Engage the stopper arm roller with the shift drum cam as shown in **Figure 66**.
3. Install the washer (C, **Figure 67**) onto the shift shaft.
4. Lubricate the shift shaft with engine oil and install the shaft (**Figure 65**) into the crankcase. Engage the shift pawl arms with the shift drum pins (**Figure 65**). Then check that the return spring is centered around the return post (**Figure 65**).
5. Install both clutch assemblies as described in this chapter.
6. Hold the release bearing assembly (**Figure 69**) together and install the assembly and shaft part way into the receptacle in the crankcase.
7. Guide the release cam No. 2 fork onto the crankcase post (**Figure 71**) while aligning the punch marks (**Figure 72**) on the sector gears. Push the assembly on until it bottoms.
8. Install the shift pedal and its pinch bolt. Tighten the bolt securely.
9. Install the clutch cover as described in this chapter.

71

72

Table 1 PRIMARY CLUTCH SERVICE SPECIFICATIONS

Item	New mm (in.)	Service limit mm (in.)
Clutch shoe thickness	2.0 (0.08)	1.5 (0.06)
Clutch shoe spring free length	42.5 (1.67)	—
Clutch engagement speed		
1993-1995	1850-2150 rpm	
1996-on	1750-2050 rpm	
Clutch stall speed		
1993-1995	3050-3450 rpm	
1996-on	3000-3400 rpm	

Table 2 SECONDARY CLUTCH SERVICE SPECIFICATIONS

Item	New mm (in.)	Service limit mm (in.)
Friction plate thickness	2.94-3.06 (0.116-0.120)	2.8 (0.11)
Steel plate thickness		
Type A	1.5-1.7 (0.059-0.067)	—
Type B	1.9-2.1 (0.075-0.083)	—
Clutch plate warp limit	—	0.2 (0.008)
Clutch spring free length	44.0 (1.73)	42.8 (1.69)
Number of clutch plates		
Friction plates	7	
Steel plates		
Type A	4	
Type B	2	

Table 3 CLUTCH TIGHTENING TORQUES

	N•m	in.-lb.	ft.-lb.
Primary clutch nut	140	—	103
Secondary clutch			
Clutch nut	80	—	59
Clutch spring bolts	8	70	—
External oil pump banjo bolt	16	—	11

CHAPTER SEVEN

TRANSMISSION, SELECT LEVER AND INTERNAL SHIFT MECHANISMS

The transmission is a 5-speed dual-range unit with reverse for a total of 11 possible gear combinations. To gain access to the transmission and internal shift mechanism it is necessary to remove the engine and split the crankcase (Chapter Five). Once the crankcase has been split, the removal of the transmission shafts, middle drive gear shaft, reverse gears, No. 1 and No. 2 shift drums and forks can then be accomplished.

Transmission gear ratios are listed in **Table 1** located at the end of the chapter.

TRANSMISSION/REVERSE SYSTEM IDENTIFICATION

With the forward and reverse systems, there are 9 different assemblies in the transmission system covered in this chapter. The different assemblies are identified in **Figure 1** and listed as follows:

a. Shift drum No. 1 (A).
b. Shift drum No. 1 shift forks and shaft (B).
c. Mainshaft (C).
d. Reverse shaft (D).
e. Countershaft (E).
f. Middle drive shaft (F).
g. Shift drum No.2 (G).
h. Shift drum No.2 shift forks and shaft (H).
i. High/low combination gear shaft (I).

TRANSMISSION TROUBLESHOOTING

Refer to Chapter Two.

TRANSMISSION OVERHAUL

Removal/Installation

Remove and install the transmission shafts and internal shift assemblies as described under *Crankcase Disassembly and Crankcase Assembly* in Chapter Five.

Transmission Preliminary Inspection

After the transmission shaft assemblies are removed from the crankcase, clean and inspect the assemblies prior to disassembling them. Place the assembled shaft into a large can or plastic bucket and thoroughly clean with solvent and a stiff brush. Dry with compressed air or let it sit on rags to drip dry. Repeat for all other shaft assemblies.

1. After cleaning, visually inspect the components for excessive wear. Any burrs, pitting or roughness on the teeth of a gear will cause wear on the mating gear.

NOTE

Defective gears should be replaced. It is a good idea to replace the mating gear on the other shaft even though it may not show as much wear or damage.

2. Inspect all engagement dogs. If any are chipped, worn, rounded or missing, replace the affected gear.
3. Rotate the transmission bearings in the crankcase halves by hand. Check for roughness, noise and radial play. Replace any questionable bearing.
4. If the transmission shafts are satisfactory and are not going to be disassembled, apply clean engine oil to all components and reinstall them in the crankcase as described in Chapter Five.

Transmission Service Notes

1. Use a divided container to help maintain correct alignment and position of the parts as they are removed from the transmission and reverse shaft assemblies. Due to the number of shaft assemblies and gears, service only one shaft at a time.
2. The circlips are a tight fit on the transmission shafts. All circlips removed during disassembly must be discarded and new circlips installed.
3. Circlips will turn and fold over, making removal and installation difficult. To ease replacement, open the circlip with a pair of circlip pliers while at the same time holding the back of the circlip with a pair of pliers.
4. When installing the *new circlips* during transmission assembly, align the open ends of the circlip with the transmission shaft spline groove as shown in **Figure 2**. Never expand a circlip more than necessary to slide it over the shaft.
5. When installing the circlips next to a washer or gear, install the circlip so its sharp-edge corner faces away from the washer or gear as shown in **Figure 3**.

Mainshaft Disassembly/Assembly

A hydraulic press and a bearing splitter is required to disassemble and reassemble the mainshaft as the second gear is pressed onto the shaft. If you do not have access to a press, refer mainshaft overhaul to a Yamaha dealership.

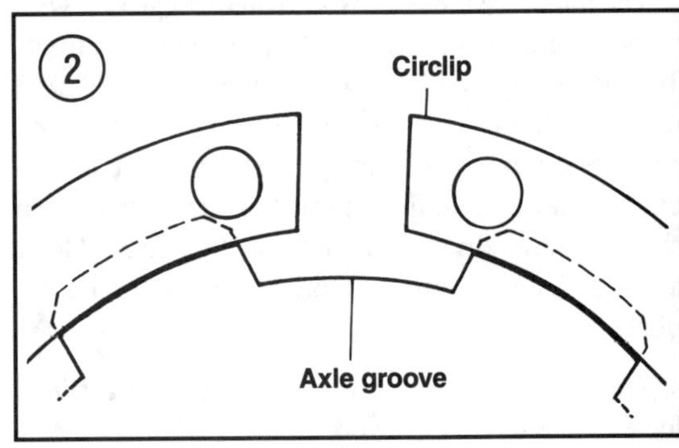

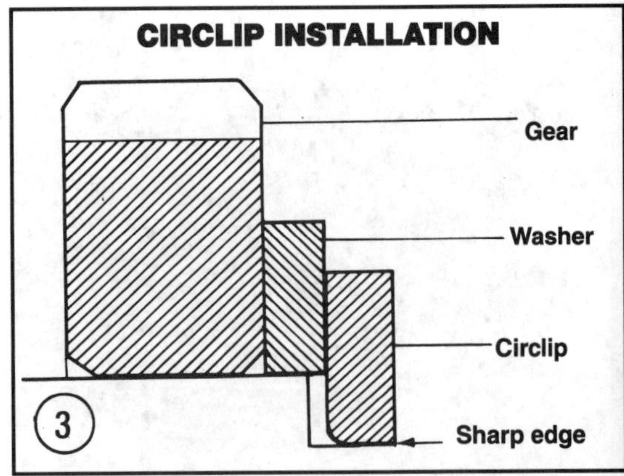

CAUTION

Second gear can only be removed and installed on the mainshaft 2 times before the shaft suffers excessive wear. Because the mainshaft is made of softer material than second gear, repeated removal and installation will result in the shaft becoming so worn that it will be impossible to secure the gear to the shaft properly. Therefore, replace the mainshaft (not second gear) if it becomes necessary to remove second gear from the shaft for the third time.

Refer to **Figure 4** for this procedure.

1. Press off mainshaft second gear as follows:
   a. Measure the overall width of the installed gears (**Figure 5**) on the mainshaft with a vernier caliper and record measurement. Then measure the clearance between mainshaft second and fourth gears with a flat feeler gauge and record the measurement. These measurements will be used during mainshaft reassembly.
   b. Install a bearing splitter below second gear and tighten it. Then install the mainshaft in a press. Make sure the remainder of the gears are clear of the press bed and supports.
   c. Hold the mainshaft and press off second gear. Do not allow the shaft assembly to fall onto the shop floor.
   d. Remove second gear and the mainshaft assembly from the press.
2. Slide off fourth gear.
3. Slide off third gear.

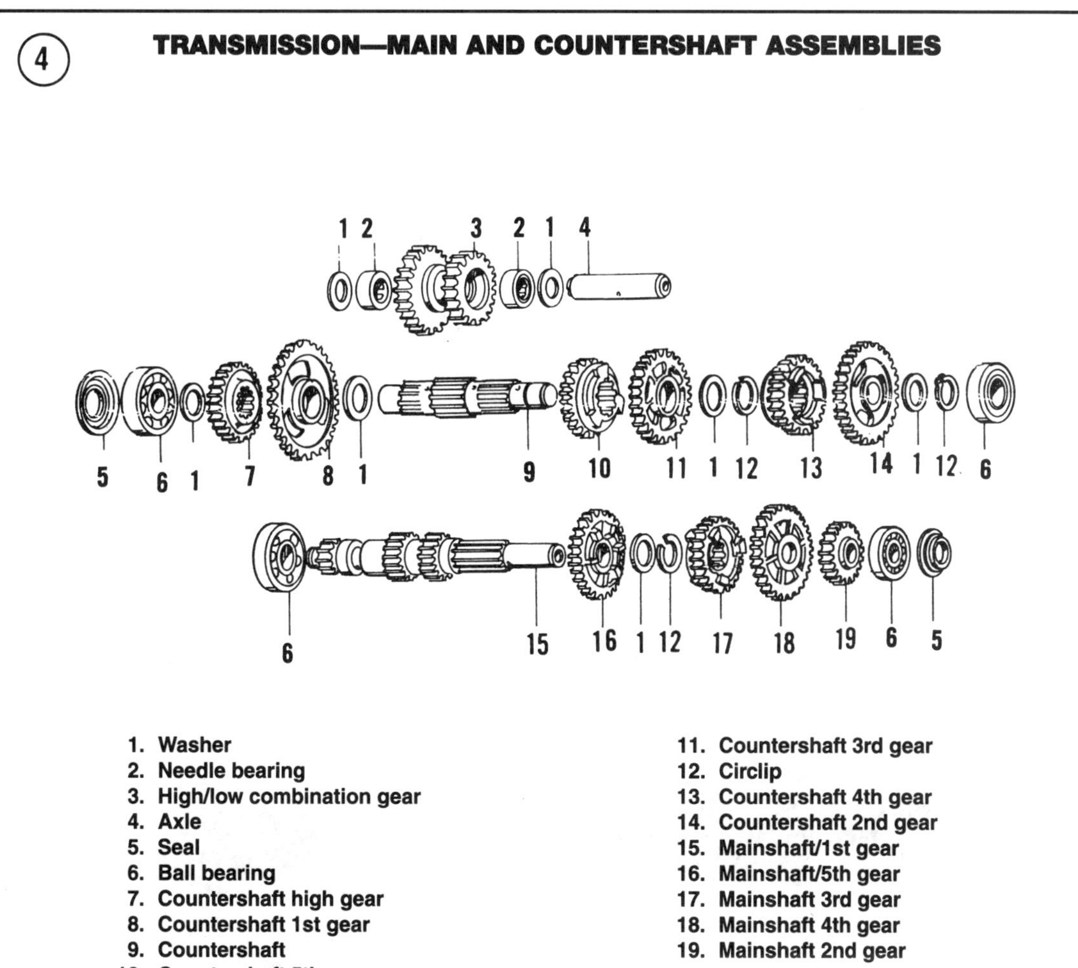

(4) **TRANSMISSION—MAIN AND COUNTERSHAFT ASSEMBLIES**

1. Washer
2. Needle bearing
3. High/low combination gear
4. Axle
5. Seal
6. Ball bearing
7. Countershaft high gear
8. Countershaft 1st gear
9. Countershaft
10. Countershaft 5th gear
11. Countershaft 3rd gear
12. Circlip
13. Countershaft 4th gear
14. Countershaft 2nd gear
15. Mainshaft/1st gear
16. Mainshaft/5th gear
17. Mainshaft 3rd gear
18. Mainshaft 4th gear
19. Mainshaft 2nd gear

4. Remove the circlip and washer and slide off fifth gear.

NOTE
Mainshaft first gear is an integral part of the mainshaft.

5. Inspect all parts as described under *Transmission Inspection* in this chapter.
6. Install fifth gear (**Figure 6**) with its gear dogs facing away from first gear.
7. Install the washer (A, **Figure 7**) and circlip (B, **Figure 7**). Seat the circlip in the groove next to fifth gear.
8. Install third gear with its shift fork groove (**Figure 8**) facing toward fifth gear.
9. Install fourth gear (**Figure 9**) with its gear dogs facing toward third gear.
10. Press second gear onto the mainshaft as follows:
   a. Lubricate the second gear bore and the mainshaft with assembly oil.
   b. Install second gear over the mainshaft with its shoulder side (**Figure 10**) facing toward fourth gear. Slide on second gear until it stops.
   c. Place the mainshaft in a press with second gear (A, **Figure 11**) facing up.
   d. Install a hollow driver (B, **Figure 11**)over mainshaft and center it onto second gear.

CAUTION
The inside diameter of the driver must be large enough and deep enough so it will not contact the mainshaft when second gear is pressed on; otherwise, the mainshaft will be damaged.

   e. Carefully press second gear onto the mainshaft. Periodically, stop and check the assembled gear length with a vernier caliper. Check

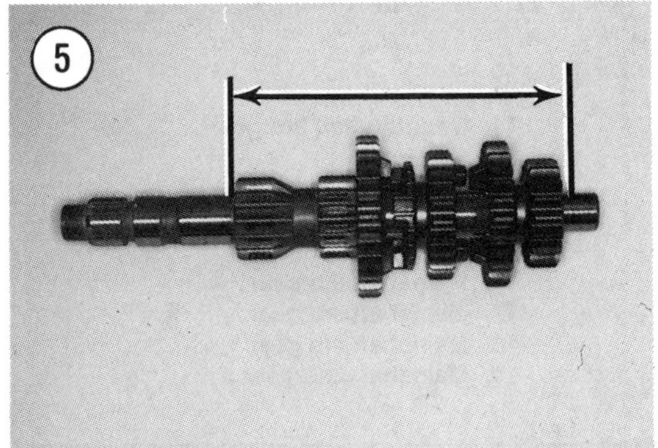

10

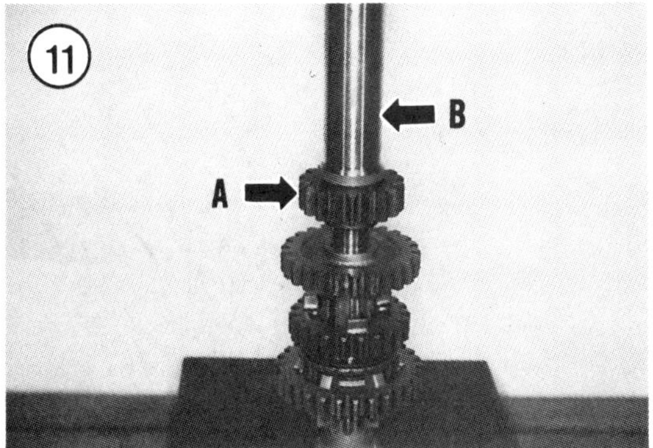

11

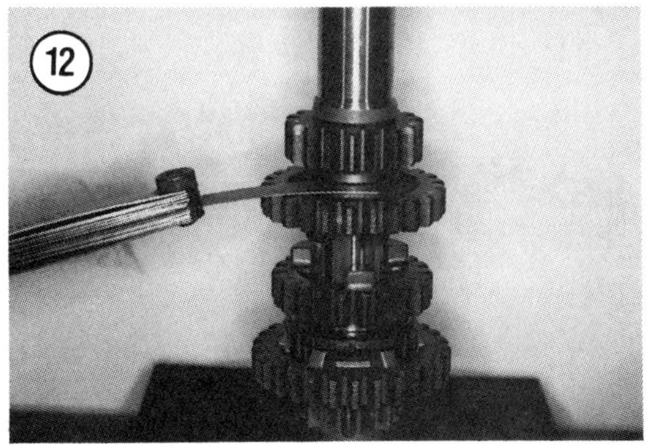
12

final positioning with a feeler gauge (**Figure 12**). Refer to the measurements taken prior to disassembly.

NOTE
A rule of thumb clearance between second and fourth gears is 0.014-0.080 mm (0.0006-0.0031 in.). If the clearance falls within this span, the second gear location is satisfactory.

f. Assembly is complete when the assembled gear length is the same as that recorded during disassembly and the second and fourth gear clearance is correct.

11. Refer to **Figure 13** for the correct placement of the mainshaft gears.

Countershaft Disassembly/Assembly

Refer to **Figure 4** for this procedure.

NOTE
All of the washers installed on the countershaft are different.

1. Remove the washer, high gear, first gear and washer.
2. Slide off fifth gear.
3. From the other end of the shaft, remove the circlip and washer.
4. Slide off second gear and fourth gear.
5. Remove the circlip and washer and slide off third gear.
6. Inspect the countershaft assembly as described under *Transmission Inspection* in this chapter.
7. Install third gear with its gear dogs facing toward the inside of the countershaft as shown in **Figure 14**.

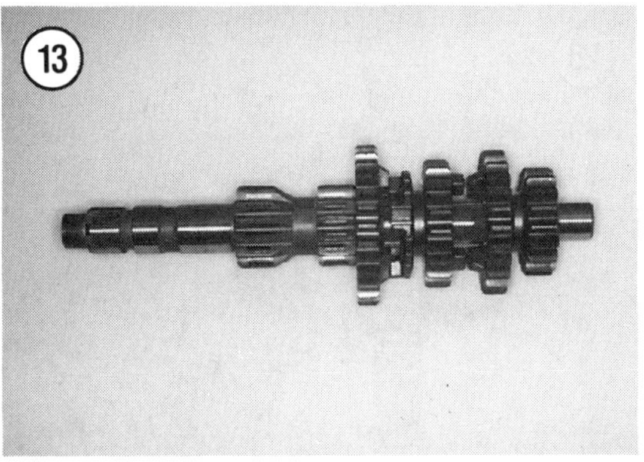
13

14

7

8. Install the washer (A, **Figure 15**) and circlip (B, **Figure 15**). Seat the circlip in the groove next to third gear.

9. Install fourth gear with its shift fork groove (**Figure 16**) facing toward third gear.

10. Install second gear with its shoulder side (**Figure 17**) facing away from fourth gear.

11. Install the washer and circlip (**Figure 18**). Seat the circlip in the groove next to second gear.

12. Working from the opposite end of the shaft, install fifth gear with its shift fork groove (**Figure 19**) facing toward third gear.

13. Install the washer (A, **Figure 20**).

14. Install first gear with its beveled side (B, **Figure 20**) facing toward fifth gear.

15. Install high gear with its shoulder (**Figure 21**) facing toward first gear.

16. Install the washer (**Figure 22**) and seat it against high gear.

17. Refer to **Figure 23** for the correct placement of all gears. Make sure all circlips are seated correctly in the shaft grooves.

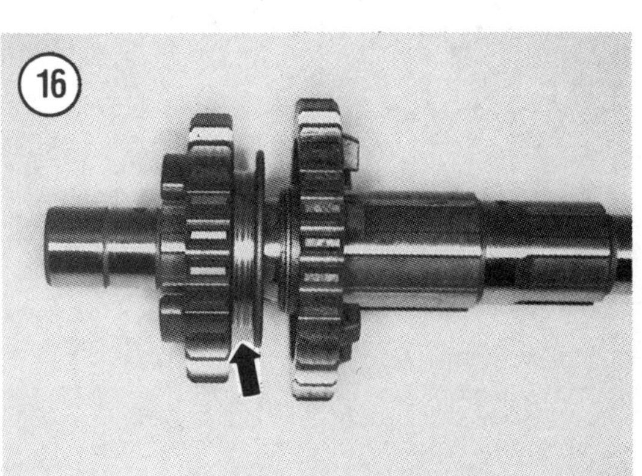

21

22

23

24

Transmission Inspection

This section describes inspection procedures for the mainshaft and countershaft assemblies. Replace damaged or worn parts as described in this section. When replacing a gear, replace the mating gear at the same time to ensure proper gear operation and to reduce premature wear to the new gear.

1. Clean and dry all parts.
2. Clean the oil holes in each shaft with compressed air.
3. Check each shaft for:
   a. Worn or damaged splines.
   b. Damaged circlip groove.
   c. Excessively worn or damaged bearing surfaces.
   d. Excessively worn or damaged bearing ball operating surfaces.
4. Check the transmission gears for:
   a. Missing, broken or chipped teeth.
   b. Worn, damaged or rounded-off gear dogs (**Figure 24**) and holes.
   c. Worn shift fork groove.
   d. Excessively worn or damaged gear dogs.
5. Place each shaft on a set of V-blocks or truing stand and measure runout with a dial indicator. Replace any shaft it its runout exceeds 0.08 mm (0.0031 in.).
6. Replace all circlips during reassembly. In addition, check the washers for burn marks, scoring or cracks. Replace if necessary.

MIDDLE DRIVE SHAFT

Removal/Installation

Remove and install the middle drive shaft and internal shift assemblies as described under *Crankcase Disassembly and Crankcase Assembly* in Chapter Five.

Refer to *Transmission Service Notes* and *Transmission Preliminary Inspection* in the previous section. The service notes and inspection procedures for the transmission shafts also apply to the middle drive shaft covered in this section.

Disassembly/Assembly

Refer to **Figure 25** for this procedure.

1. Remove the following parts in order:

7

TRANSMISSION—MIDDLE DRIVEN SHAFT AND REVERSE SHAFT ASSEMBLIES

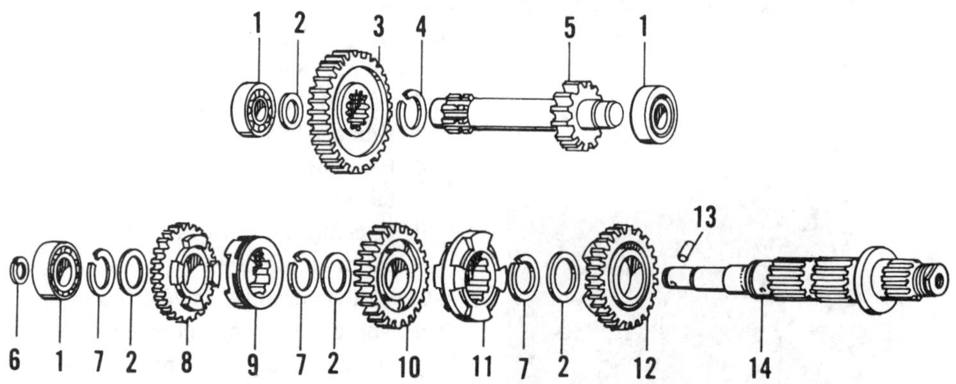

1. Ball bearing
2. Washer
3. No. 1 reverse gear
4. Circlip
5. Reverse shaft
6. Circlip
7. Circlip
8. Middle driven gear
9. Shifter
10. Middle drive gear
11. Dog clutch
12. No. 2 reverse gear
13. Pin
14. Middle driven shaft

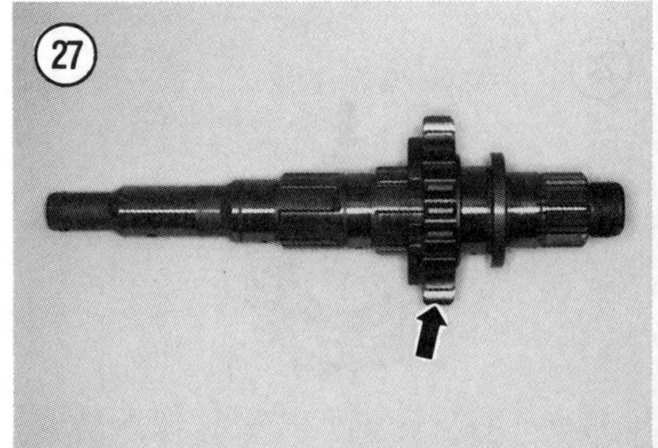

28

29

30

a. Circlip.
b. Washer.
c. Driven gear.
d. Shifter.
e. Circlip and washer.
f. Middle drive gear.
g. Dog clutch.
h. Circlip.
i. Washer.
j. No. 2 reverse gear.

2. Inspect all parts as described in this section. Discard the circlips.

3. Install the No. 2 reverse gear with its gear dogs (**Figure 26**) facing away from the middle drive shaft shoulder.

4. Install the washer (A, **Figure 27**) and circlip (B, **Figure 27**). Seat the circlip in the groove next to the No. 2 reverse gear.

5. Install the dog clutch with its larger diameter side (**Figure 28**) facing toward the No. 2 reverse gear.

6. Install the middle drive gear with its shift dog slots (**Figure 29**) facing toward the dog clutch.

7. Install the washer (A, **Figure 30**) and circlip (B, **Figure 30**). Seat the circlip in the groove next to the middle drive gear.

8. Install the shifter with its shift fork groove (**Figure 31**) facing toward the drive gear.

9. Install the middle driven gear (**Figure 32**) with its gear dogs facing toward the shifter.

10. Install the washer (A, **Figure 33**) and circlip (B, **Figure 33**). Seat the circlip in the groove next to the middle driven gear

11. Refer to **Figure 34** for the correct placement of all gears and components.

31

32

Middle Drive Shaft Inspection

Replace parts that show damage as described in this section. When replacing a gear, replace the mating gear at the same time to ensure proper gear operation and to reduce premature wear to the new gear.

1. Clean and dry all parts.
2. Clean the oil holes in the middle drive shaft with compressed air.
3. Check the middle drive shaft for:
   a. Worn or damaged splines.
   b. Damaged circlip groove.
   c. Severely worn or damaged bearing surfaces.
   d. Severely worn or damaged bearing ball operating surfaces.
4. Place the shaft on a set of V-blocks or truing stand and measure runout with a dial indicator. Replace any shaft it its runout exceeds 0.08 mm (0.0031 in.).
5. Check the speedometer drive gear tab (**Figure 35**) for wear or damage,
6. Inspect the shifter and dog clutch for:
   a. Excessively worn or damaged splines.
   b. Excessively worn or damaged shift fork groove.
   c. Excessively worn or damaged shift dogs.
7. Check each gear for:
   a. Missing, broken or chipped teeth.
   b. Worn, damaged or rounded-off gear dogs (**Figure 24**) and holes.
   c. Worn shift fork groove.
   d. Excessively worn or damaged gear dogs.
8. Replace all circlips during reassembly. In addition, check the washers for burn marks, scoring or cracks. Replace if necessary.

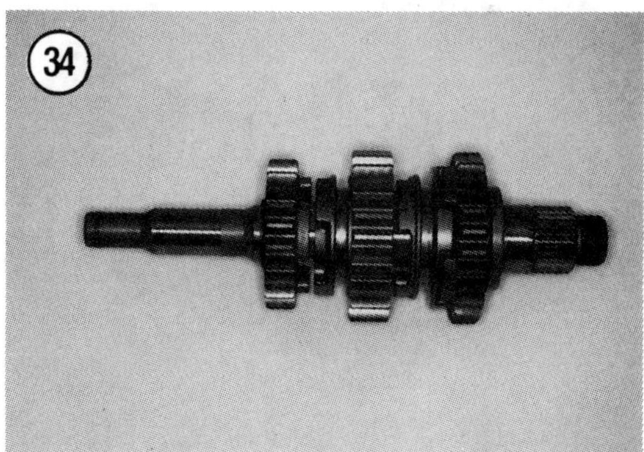

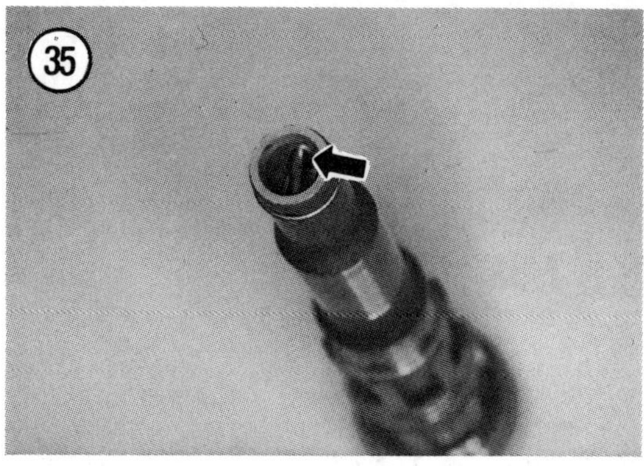

REVERSE GEAR AND SHAFT

Removal/Installation

Remove and install the reverse gear and shaft as described under *Crankcase Disassembly and Crankcase Assembly* in Chapter Five.

Refer to *Transmission Service Notes* and *Transmission Preliminary Inspection* in the previous section. The service notes and inspection procedures for the transmission shafts also apply to the reverse gear and shaft covered in this section.

Disassembly/Assembly

Refer to **Figure 25** for this procedure.

1. Remove the following parts from the reverse shaft:
   a. Washer.
   b. No. 1 reverse gear.
   c. Circlip.
2. Inspect all parts as described in this section.

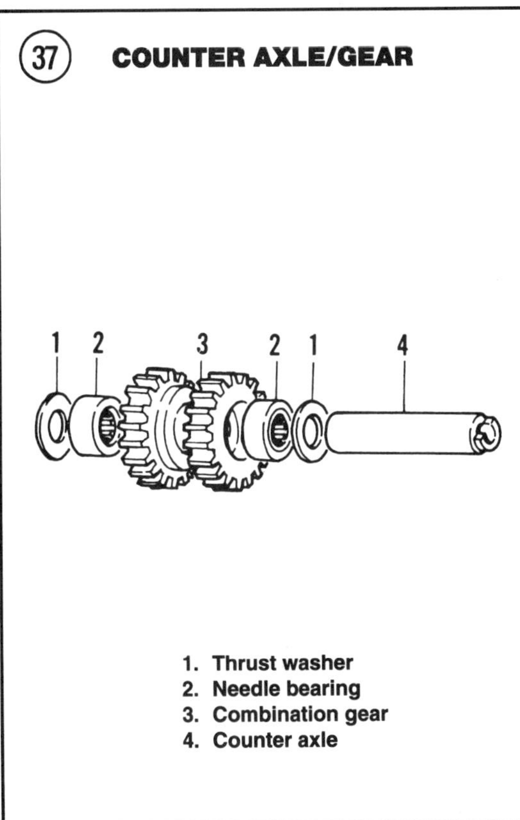

3. Install the circlip (A, **Figure 36**) into the reverse shaft groove.
4. Install the No.1 reverse gear (B, **Figure 36**).
5. Install the washer (C, **Figure 36**).

Inspection

Replace parts that show damage as described in this section. When replacing a gear, replace the mating gear at the same time to ensure proper gear operation and to reduce premature wear to the new gear.

1. Inspect the gears (**Figure 36**) for:
   a. Missing, broken or chipped teeth.
   b. Excessively worn or damaged gear bore.
2. Inspect the reverse shaft for:
   a. Damaged circlip groove.
   b. Excessively worn or damaged gear operating surface.
   c. Excessively worn or damaged splines.
3. Replace the circlip during reassembly.

7

HIGH/LOW COMBINATION GEAR ASSEMBLY

The high/low combination gear assembly consists of the combination gear, 2 needle bearings, 2 washers and shaft (**Figure 37**).

Removal/Installation

Remove and install the high/low combination gear assembly as described under *Crankcase Disassembly and Crankcase Assembly* in Chapter Five.

High/Low Gear Assembly Inspection

1. Clean and dry all parts.
2. Check the combination gear for broken or chipped teeth.
3. Check the shaft for burrs, excessive wear or damage.
4. Check the flat on the end of the shaft for wear or damage.
5. Check washers for galling or other damage.
6. Check the needle bearings (**Figure 38**) for loose or damaged needles. Check the bearing cage for

cracks or other damage. If necessary, replace both bearings as described in following procedure.

High/Low Gear Needle Bearing Replacement

1. Mount a blind bearing puller onto one of the bearings as shown in **Figure 39**. Either bearing can be removed first.

NOTE

Each bearing is installed against a shoulder inside the gear. Thus, both bearings must be removed from their end of the gear. Because of the gear shoulders, it is difficult to grasp the bottom of the bearings with a puller. Instead, install the bearing puller so that its arms wedge themselves into the middle of the bearing and tighten the puller arms securely.

2. Mount the combination gear into a bearing splitter. Install the bearing splitter (A, **Figure 40**) into the press so that the top of the bearing puller is positioned at the bottom (hanging upside down).
3. Insert a rod through top of the gear so that it is centered on the bearing remover arms as shown in B, **Figure 40**. Now press out the bottom bearing.
4. Repeat to remove the opposite bearing.
5. Discard both bearings.
6. Clean and dry the gear.
7. Inspect the gear bore for damage. Replace the gear if necessary.

NOTE

Install new bearings with their manufacturer's marks facing outward.

8. Place the combination gear in press and center a new bearing in gear's bore. Center a hollow pipe over bearing and press the bearing into gear until it bottoms out.
9. Turn the gear over and repeat to install opposite bearing.
10. Check the condition of both bearings.

INTERNAL SHIFT MECHANISM

The crankcase is equipped with two different sets of shift forks and shift drums. The No.1 shift drum and its 3 forks control the shifting of the transmission mainshaft and countershaft. The No.2 shift drum and its 2 shift forks control the high/low speeds and the reverse shifting of the middle drive gear assembly.

Refer to **Figure 41** for this procedure.

Removal/Installation

Remove and install the shift drums and shift forks along with the transmission and middle drive gear shaft assemblies as described under *Crankcase Disassembly and Crankcase Assembly* in Chapter Five.

Inspection

Replace parts that show excessive wear or damage as described in this section.

1. Inspect each shift fork for wear or damage. Examine the shift forks at the points where they contact the slider gear (**Figure 42**). This surface should be smooth with no wear or damage.
2. Check for any arc-shaped wear or burn marks on the shift forks. This indicates that the shift fork has contact with the gear. The shift fork fingers are excessively worn and the shift fork must be replaced.

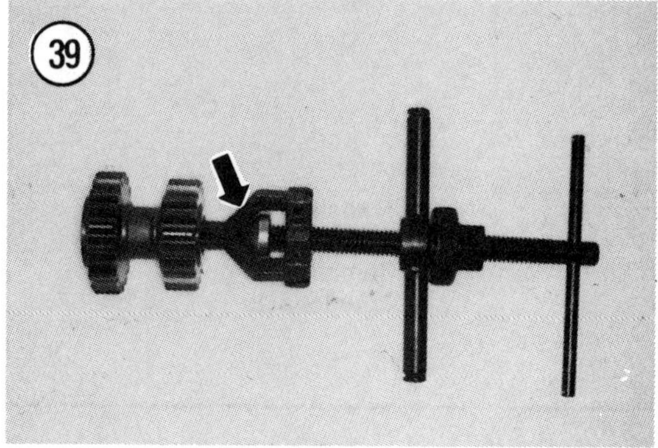

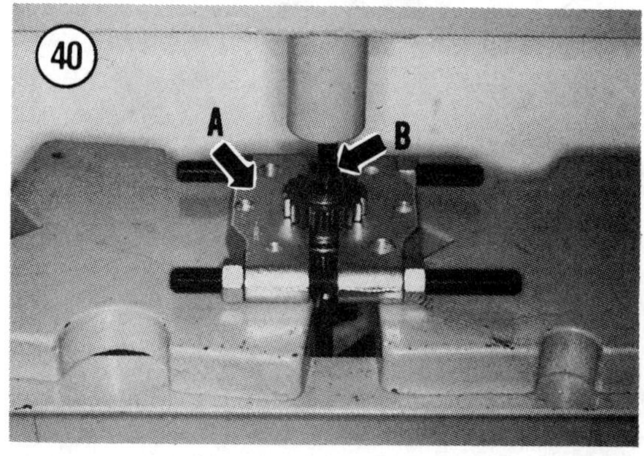

(41) **SHIFT MECHANISM (INTERNAL AND EXTERNAL)**

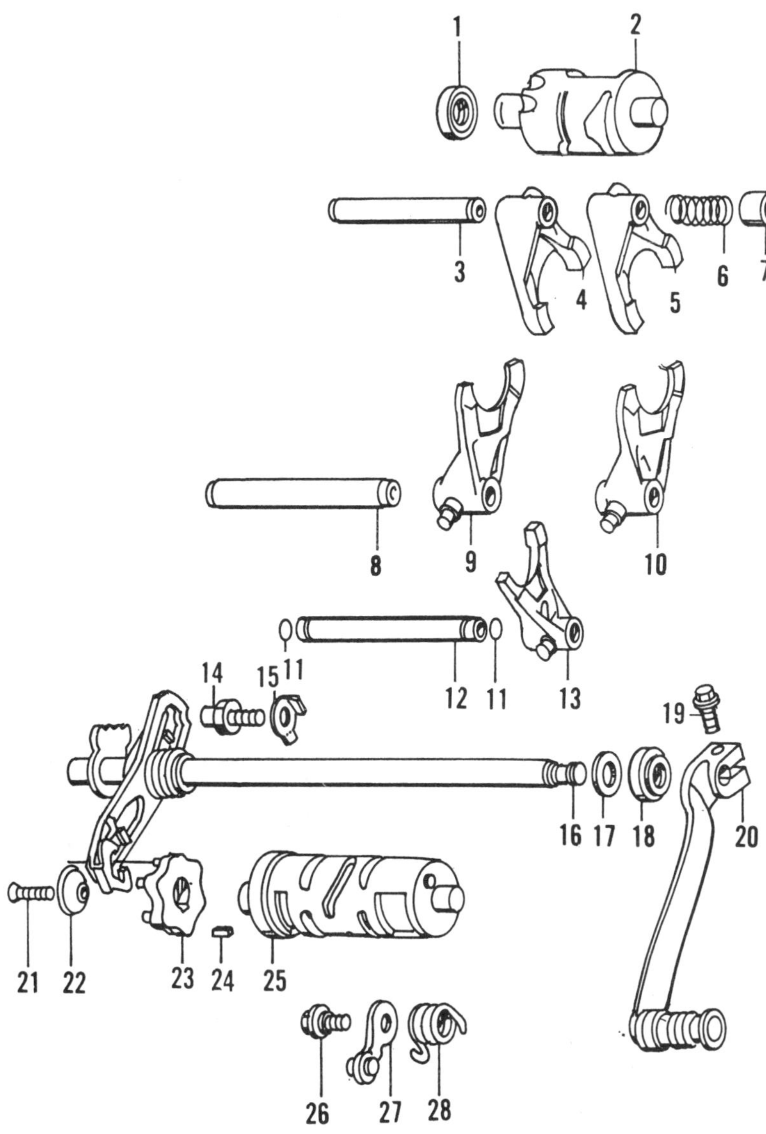

1. Seal
2. No. 2 shift drum
3. Shift fork shaft
4. Middle drive gear shift fork
5. Middle drive gear shift fork
6. Spring
7. Cup
8. Shift fork shaft (long)
9. Shift fork
10. Shift fork
11. O-ring
12. Shift fork shaft (short)
13. Shift fork
14. Stopper bolt
15. Lockwasher
16. Shift shaft
17. Washer
18. Shift shaft seal
19. Clamping bolt
20. Shift pedal
21. Bolt
22. Washer
23. Shift drum segment
24. Straight key
25. No. 1 shift drum
26. Bolt
27. Stopper lever
28. Spring

3. Place the shift fork shaft on a flat surface (a piece of plate glass) and roll the shaft. Any clicking or wobbling indicates a bent shaft that must be replaced.
4. Check each shift fork guide pin for severe wear or roughness.
5. Inspect each shift fork bore and both shift fork shafts (**Figure 42**) for excessive wear or roughness.
6. On models so equipped, inspect the shift fork shaft O-rings for hardness or deterioration. Replace if necessary.
7. Slide each shift fork onto its operating shaft. Each shift fork should slide freely without excessive play.
8. When inspecting the No. 2 shift drum and forks, inspect the spring (6, **Figure 41**) and cup (7) for excessive wear or damage.
9. Check the shift drum grooves (**Figure 43** and **Figure 44**) for wear or roughness.
10. Check the No. 1 shift drum (**Figure 43**) for:
   a. Severely worn or damaged bearing.
   b. Damaged pins.
   c. Damaged ramps.
11. Check the No. 2 shift drum (**Figure 44**) for seized or damaged shaft ends.

TRANSMISSION RANGE SELECT LEVER

The transmission range select lever shifts the transmission gears into one of the dual-range modes, either HIGH or LOW, or shifts the transmission into REVERSE. The select lever is mounted on top of the left crankcase cover.

Removal/Installation

Refer to **Figure 45** for this procedure.
1. Remove the plastic rivet (9, **Figure 45**) securing the shift knob and remove the knob.
2. Unscrew the No. 2 control cable (**Figure 46**) from the link shift bracket.
3. Remove the screws securing the cover and remove the cover (18, **Figure 45**) and the shifter control gate (17, **Figure 45**) as an assembly.
4. If both control cables are going to be removed, screw the No. 2 control cable (**Figure 46**) back into shifter bracket to keep both cables together during removal.
5. Remove the shifter bracket mounting bolts (**Figure 47**) and remove the shifter bracket from the top of the left crankcase cover.
6. Remove the cotter pin and clevis pin (**Figure 48**) and disconnect the No. 1 control cable from the select lever on the crankcase.
7. Remove the No. 1 control cable bracket mounting bolts (**Figure 49**).
8. Note the routing of the No. 1 control cable through the frame and remove the No. 1 control cable (**Figure 49**) from the frame.

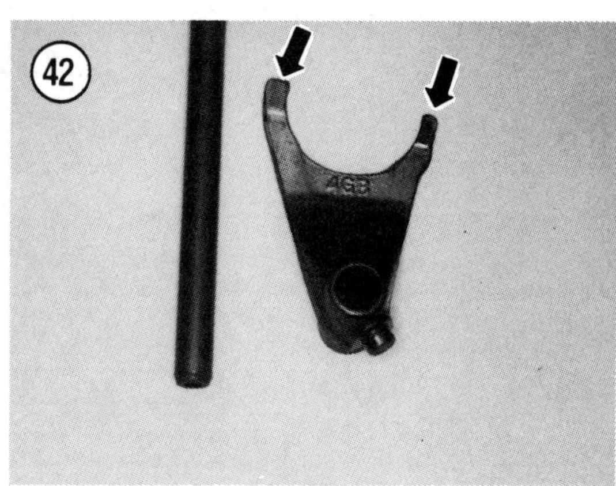
42

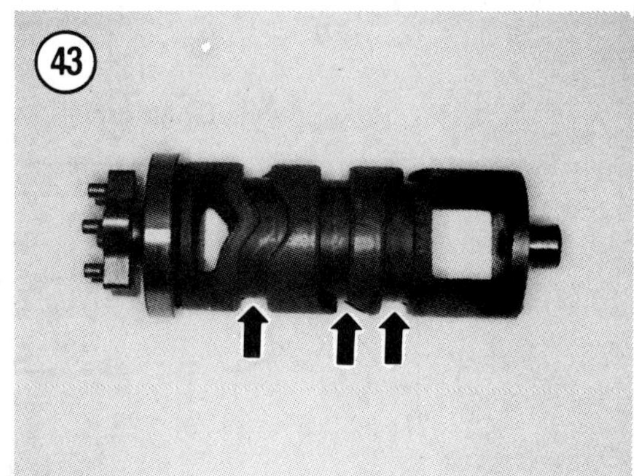
43

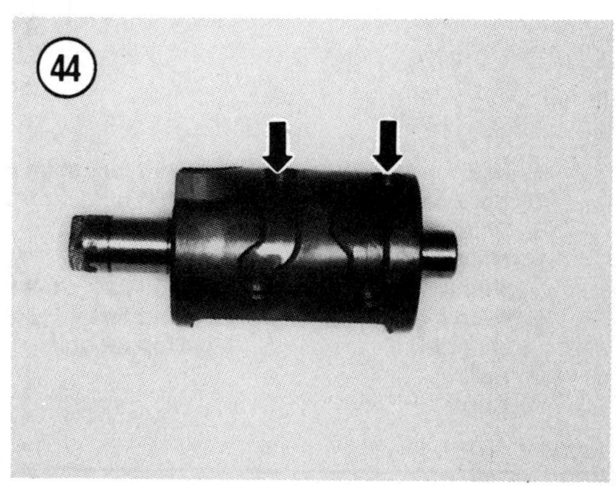
44

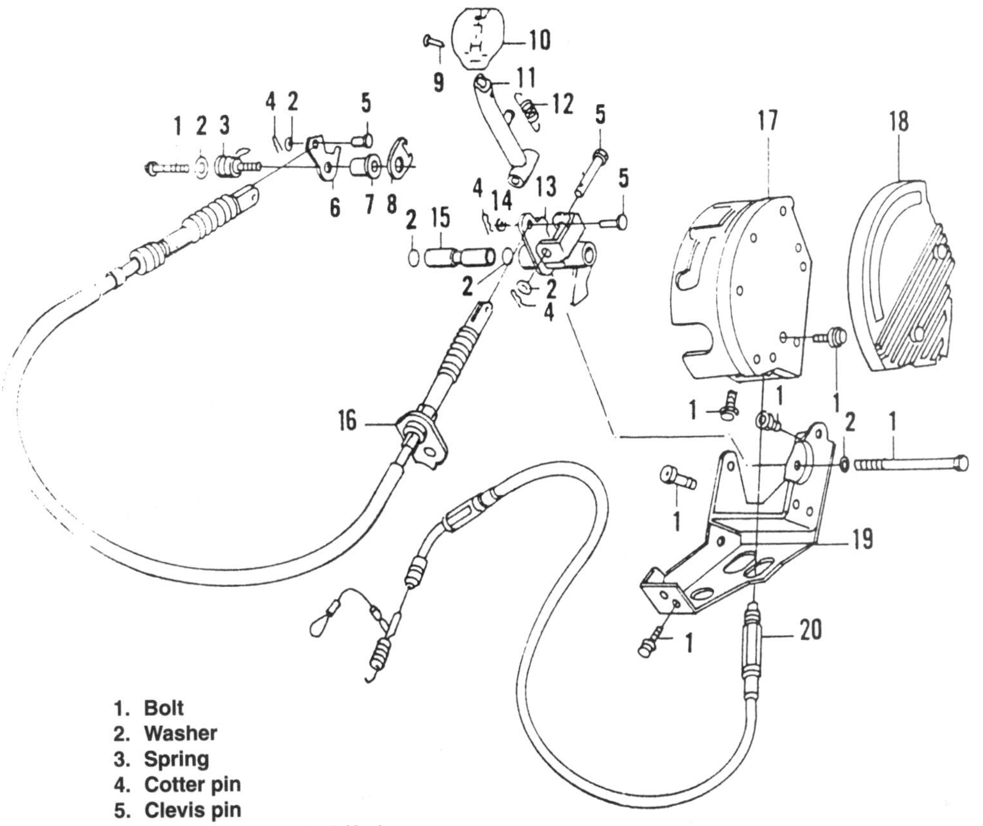

(45)

TRANSMISSION RANGE SELECT LEVER (CRANKCASE COVER MOUNTED)

1. Bolt
2. Washer
3. Spring
4. Cotter pin
5. Clevis pin
6. Select lever-No. 2 shift drum
7. Collar
8. Lever
9. Rivet
10. Shift knob
11. Shift lever
12. Spring
13. Shift lever linkage
14. Washer
15. Pivot collar
16. No.2 control cable
17. Shift control gate
18. Cover
19. Shift bracket
20. No. 1 control cable

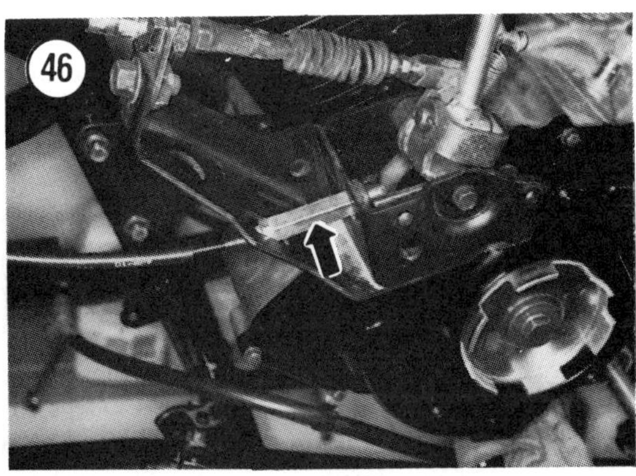

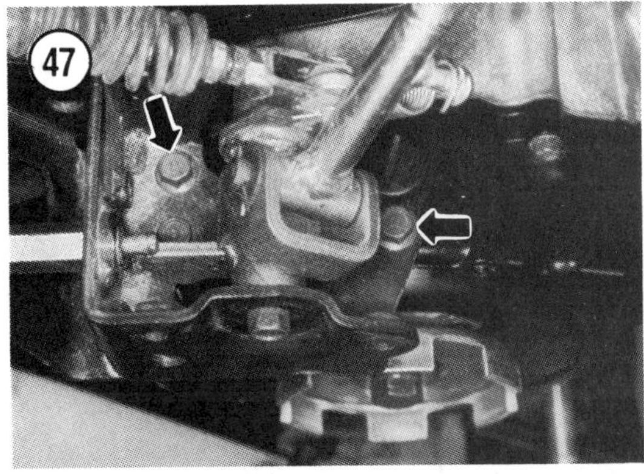

9. Unhook No. 2 control cable from the rear brake pedal bracket (**Figure 50**).

10. Disconnect No. 2 control cable from the frame bracket (A, **Figure 51**).

11. Note the routing of No.2 control cable through the frame and remove the control cable (B, **Figure 51**) from the frame.

12. Inspect the shift lever assembly as follows:

   a. Check that the spring (12, **Figure 45**) is sagged or broken, and replace if necessary.
   b. Make sure the cotter pin and washer (4 and 14, **Figure 45**) are securely in place.
   c. Make sure the adjust nuts (**Figure 52**) are tight.
   d. Inspect the rubber boot at the end of the No. 2 control cable for tears or damage. The boot cannot be replaced separately.
   e. Move the shift lever back and forth and from side-to-side and check for smooth operation. Apply clean engine oil to the pivot points if necessary.

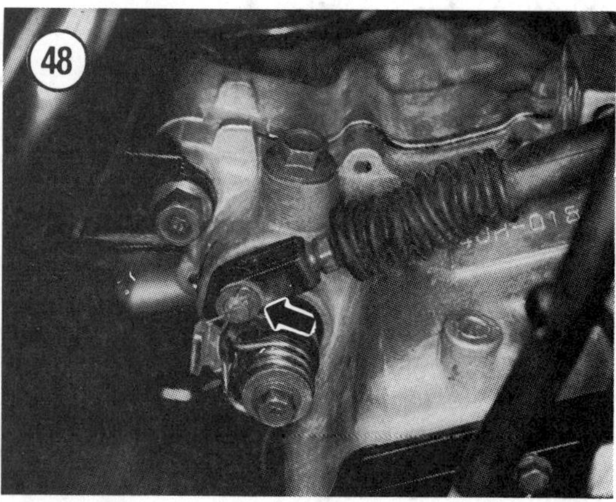

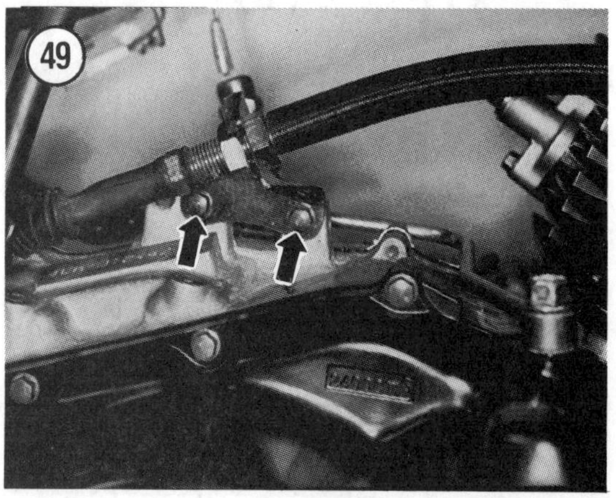

13. Install by reversing these removal steps, while noting the following:

   a. Route the control cables through the frame as noted during removal. Make sure the cables do not touch any moving parts.
   b. Tighten all mounting bolts securely
   c. Install the plastic rivet (9, **Figure 45**) securing the shift knob. To keep the rivet in place, install a small tie-wrap around the shift knob and over the rivet.
   d. Adjust the cables as described in Chapter Three.

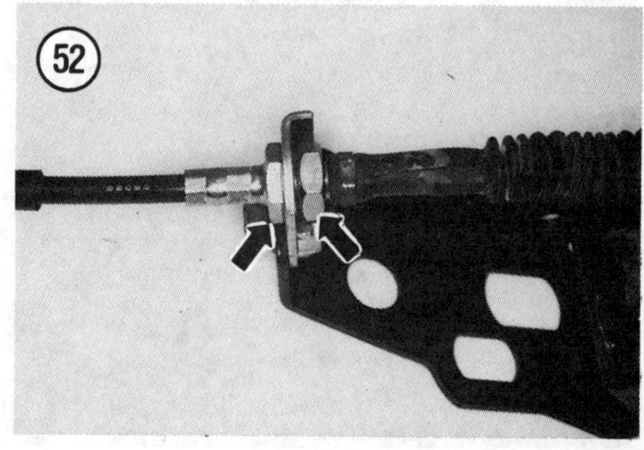

Table 1 TRANSMISSION SPECIFICATIONS

Primary reduction ratio	76/24 (3.167)
Secondary reduction ratio	24/18 × 33/09 (4.889)
Transmission	
Type	5-speed forward, 1-speed reverse dual-range, constant mesh
Gear ratio (high range)	
1st	38/13 × 24/23 × 23/24 (2.923)
2nd	34/18 × 24/23 × 23/24 (1.889)
3rd	30/22 × 24/23 × 23/24 (1.364)
4th	26/25 × 24/23 × 23/24 (1.040)
5th	24/29 × 24/23 × 23/24 (0.828)
Gear ratio (low range)	
1st	38/13 × 24/23 × 27/19 (4.335)
2nd	34/18 × 24/23 × 27/19 (2.801)
3rd	20/22 × 24/23 × 27/19 (2.022)
4th	26/25 × 24/23 × 27/19 (1.542)
5th	24/29 × 24/23 × 27/19 (1.227)
Reverse gear ratio	36/13 × 27/26 (4.673)

CHAPTER EIGHT

FUEL AND EXHAUST SYSTEMS

The fuel system consists of the fuel tank, fuel shutoff valve, a single carburetor and an air filter/air box assembly.

The exhaust system consists of an exhaust pipe and muffler assembly.

This chapter includes service procedures for all parts of the fuel system and exhaust system. Air filter service is covered in Chapter Three.

Carburetor specifications are listed in **Table 1**. **Tables 1** and **2** are located at the end of this chapter.

CARBURETOR OPERATION

An understanding of the function of each of the carburetor components and their relation to one another is a valuable aid for pinpointing a source of carburetor trouble.

The carburetor's purpose is to supply and atomize fuel and mix it in correct proportions with air that is drawn in through the air intake. At the primary throttle opening (idle), a small amount of fuel is siphoned through the pilot jet by the incoming air. As the throttle is opened further, the air stream begins to siphon fuel through the main jet and needle jet. The tapered needle increases the effective flow capacity of the needle jet as it is lifted, in that it occupies progressively less of the area of the jet.

At full throttle the carburetor venturi is fully open and the needle is lifted far enough to permit the main jet to flow at full capacity.

The choke circuit is a bystarter system in which the choke lever opens a valve rather than closing a butterfly valve in the venturi area as on many carburetors. In the open position, the slow jet discharges a stream of fuel into the carburetor venturi, to enrich the mixture when the engine is cold.

CARBURETOR

Removal/Installation

1. Park the vehicle on level ground and set the parking brake.
2. Remove the seat (Chapter Fourteen).
3. Remove the fuel tank as described in this chapter.
4. Loosen the hose clamp securing the intake hose (**Figure 1**) to the air box, then remove the intake hose.
5. Loosen the rear carburetor hose clamp (A, **Figure 2**) and slide the hose clamp down the hose and away from the carburetor.
6. Remove the 2 nuts (B, **Figure 2**) securing the carburetor to the intake manifold.
7. Push the carburetor back to remove it from the intake manifold, then remove it from its rear hose and lift it past the 2 upper frame rails.
8. Remove the carburetor side cover screws and remove the side cover (A, **Figure 3**).
9. Disconnect the air vent hose (A, **Figure 4**) from the carburetor.

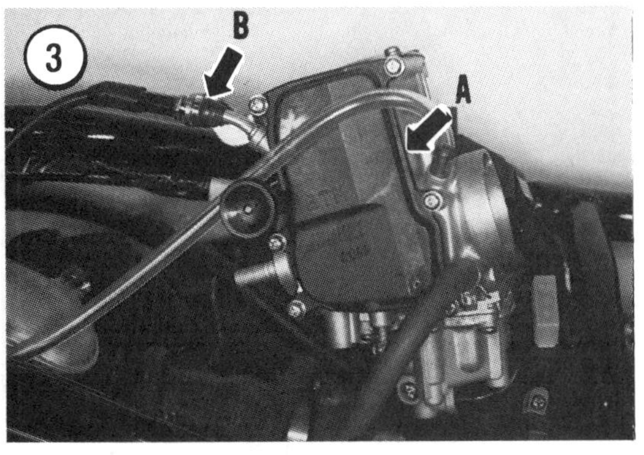

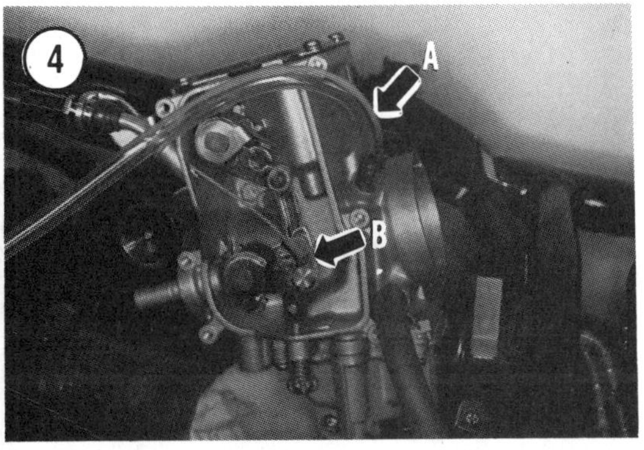

10. Disconnect the throttle cable (B, **Figure 4**) from the carburetor. Do not lose the connecting ball.

11. Remove the screw securing the throttle cable holder (B, **Figure 3**) to the carburetor body. Then remove the throttle cable from the carburetor.

12. Remove the carburetor from the frame.

13. Place a clean shop cloth into the intake manifold and air box boot openings to prevent the entry of foreign matter.

14. If necessary, service the carburetor as described in this chapter.

15. Install the carburetor by reversing these removal steps, noting the following.

16. If removed, install the front carburetor O-ring.

17. To reconnect the throttle cable to the throttle lever:

   a. Install the throttle cable through the carburetor and secure its mounting bracket (B, **Figure 3**) to the carburetor body with its mounting screw. Tighten the mounting screw securely.
   b. Connect the cable onto the ball (**Figure 5**).
   c. Lift the throttle lever and connect the throttle cable and ball (B, **Figure 4**) into the throttle lever.
   d. Operate the throttle lever at the handlebar a few times, making sure the throttle lever at the carburetor moves up and down smoothly and that the cable end does not pop out.

18. Install the side cover (A, **Figure 3**) and its O-ring. Tighten the side cover screws securely.

19. Tighten the carburetor mounting nuts (B, **Figure 2**) as specified in **Table 2**.

20. Install the intake hose (**Figure 1**) onto the air box by inserting the index tab on the intake hose between the 2 raised tabs on the air box (**Figure 6**). Tighten the hose clamp securely.

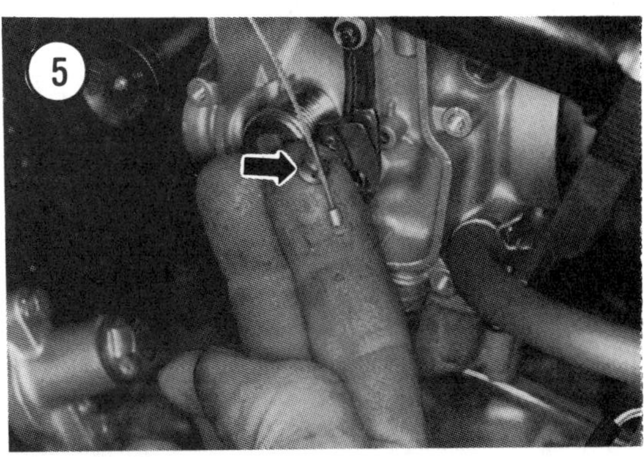

21. After assembly and installation are complete, adjust the carburetor as described in Chapter Three.

Piston Valve Removal

Refer to **Figure 7** for this procedure.

1. Remove the screws securing the cover (**Figure 8**). Remove the cover and gasket.
2. Remove the E-clip (A, **Figure 9**) and separate the arm (B, **Figure 9**) from the throttle lever (C, **Figure 9**).

PISTON VALVE/JET NEEDLE ASSEMBLY (DUAL THROTTLE CABLE MODELS)

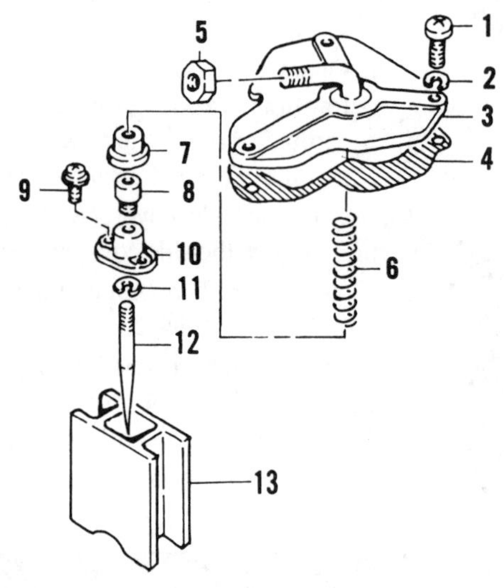

1. Screw
2. Lockwasher
3. Cover
4. Gasket
5. Nut
6. Spring
7. Spring seat
8. Guide
9. Screw
10. Jet needle holder
11. E-clip
12. Jet needle
13. Piston valve

3. Remove the screw (A, **Figure 10**) securing the throttle lever (B, **Figure 10**) to the shaft.

4. Slowly pull the arm (**Figure 11**) from the body. Remove the seal (A, **Figure 12**) and throttle lever (B, **Figure 12**) from the body.

5. Carefully remove the throttle lever and piston valve assembly (**Figure 13**).

6. Compress the small spring (A, **Figure 14**) and disconnect the throttle lever (B, **Figure 14**) from the piston valve assembly.

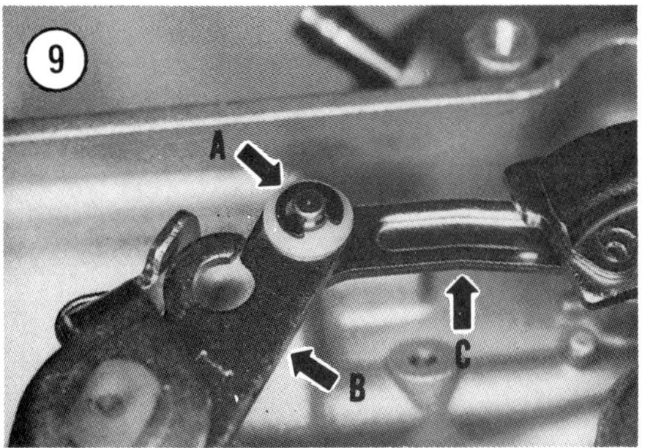

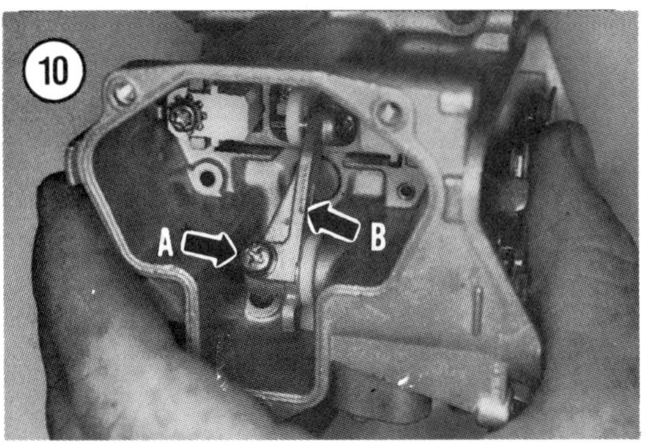

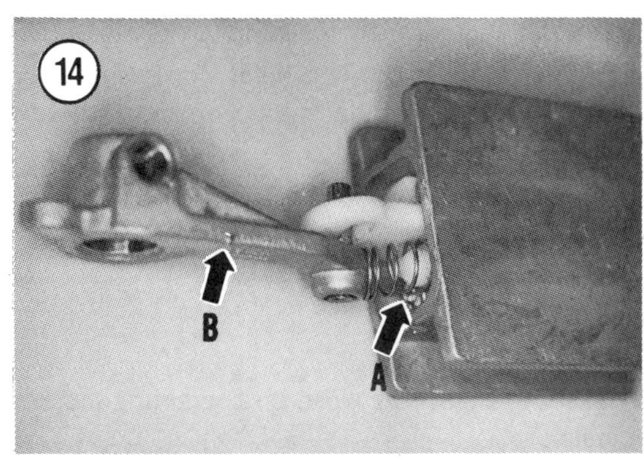

7. Remove the 2 jet needle holder screws (**Figure 15**) and remove the jet needle holder.
8. Remove the jet needle from the piston valve.
9. Clean and dry all parts.
10. Inspect the parts (**Figure 16**) for excessive wear or damage.

Installation

1. Make sure the E-clip is secured in the jet needle clip groove.

NOTE
*See **Table 1** for the stock jet needle clip position.*

2. Install the jet needle into the piston valve.
3. Install the jet needle holder and 2 screws (**Figure 15**). Tighten the screws securely.
4. Compress the small spring (A, **Figure 17**) and connect the throttle lever (B, **Figure 17**) onto the piston valve assembly.
5. Carefully install the throttle lever and piston valve assembly (**Figure 13**) into the body while guiding the jet needle into the needle jet.
6. Slowly slide the arm (A, **Figure 18**) into the body and install the seal (B, **Figure 18**) between the arm and body housing. See A, **Figure 12**.
7. Hold the throttle lever in position and push the arm and shaft (**Figure 19**) all the way into the body until it bottoms. Make sure the seal (A, **Figure 12**) is still positioned correctly and centered over the shaft.
8. Move the arm (B, **Figure 11**) into position until the screw holes align, then install the screw and washer (**Figure 11**) and tighten securely.
9. Slightly lift up on the arm (A, **Figure 20**) and install the end onto the raised post on the throttle lever (B, **Figure 20**).
10. Install the E-clip (A, **Figure 9**) onto the post and make sure it is correctly seated in the post groove.
11. After the E-clip is attached, slowly move the throttle arm and throttle lever back and forth and check for smooth operation.
12. Install the cover (**Figure 8**) and its gasket. Tighten the cover screws securely.

Disassembly

Refer to **Figure 21** when disassembling the carburetor.

1. Remove the carburetor as described in this chapter.

2. Remove the piston valve from the carburetor as described in this chapter.

3. Remove the coasting enrichener system as follows:

   a. Remove the cover screws and cover (**Figure 22**).

   b. Remove the spring and diaphragm (**Figure 23**).

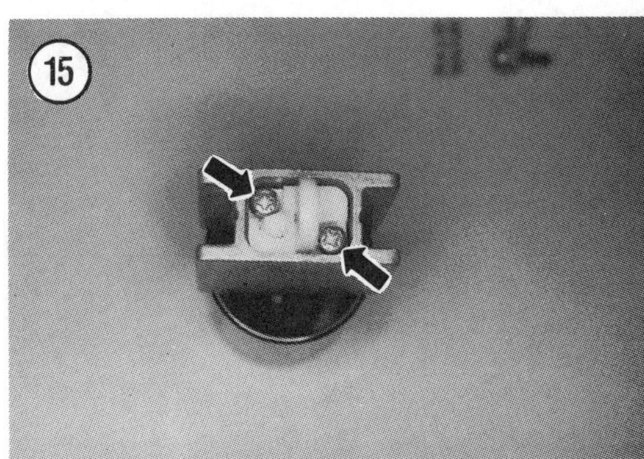

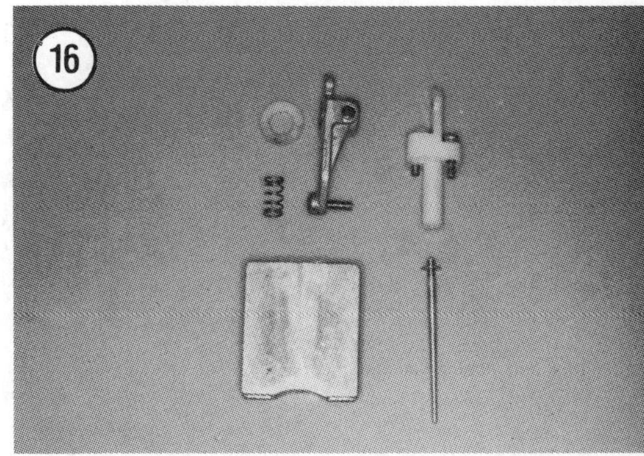

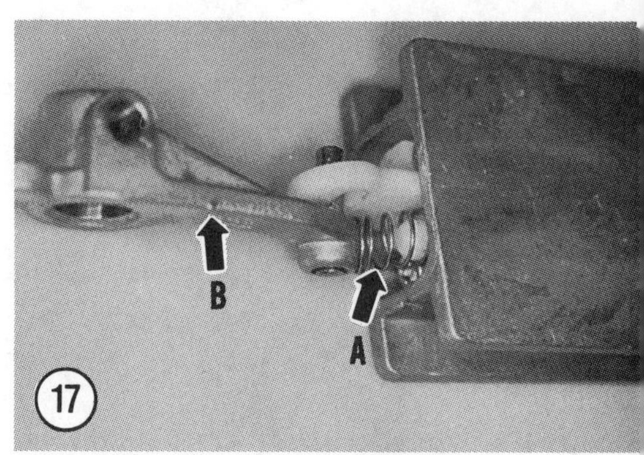

4. Loosen the bystarter valve nut (**Figure 24**) and remove the bystarter valve assembly.

5. Lightly seat the pilot air screw (**Figure 25**), counting the number of turns required for reassembly reference, then back screw out and remove it from the carburetor along with the spring.

6. Remove the float bowl screws (**Figure 26**) and lift off the float bowl.

7. Remove the main jet washer (A, **Figure 27**).

8. Remove the pilot jet (B, **Figure 27**).

9 Remove the float pin (A, **Figure 28**).

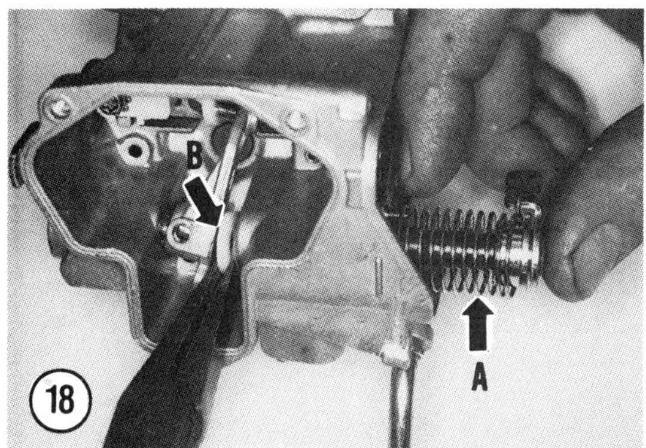

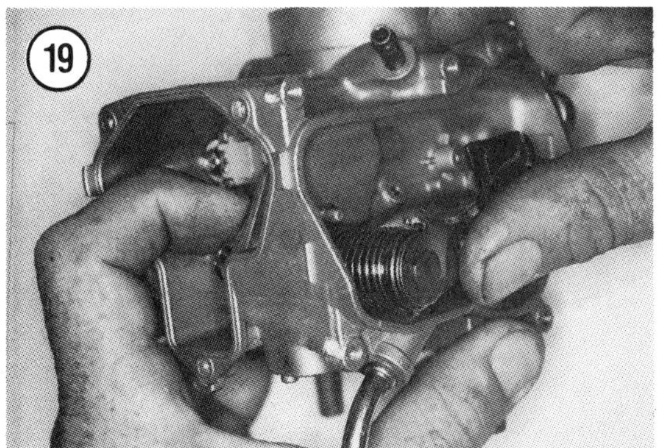

10. Lift the float (B, **Figure 28**) and needle valve (**Figure 29**) out of the main body.

11. Remove the screw and washer (A, **Figure 30**) securing the needle valve seat.

12. Remove the needle valve seat and O-ring (B, **Figure 30**).

13. Remove the main jet and washer (C, **Figure 30**).

14. Push the needle jet (**Figure 31**) out through the top of the carburetor.

15. Remove the starter jet (**Figure 32**) from the float bowl.

16. Remove the throttle adjust screw (A, **Figure 33**), washer and O-ring.

17. Remove the large O-ring (B, **Figure 33**).

NOTE
Further disassembly is neither necessary nor recommended. Do not remove the throttle shaft or valve (C, ***Figure 33****) as these parts are not available separately.*

18. Clean and inspect all parts as described in this chapter.

8

Cleaning and Inspection

1. Initially clean all parts in a petroleum based solvent. Then clean in hot soap and water and rinse with cold water. Blow dry with compressed air.

CAUTION
Do not submerse the carburetor body or any of the O-rings in a carburetor cleaner or other solution that will damage the rubber parts and seals.

CAUTION
If compressed air is not available, allow the parts to air dry before reassembly.

CAUTION
Do ***not*** *use wire or drill bits to clean jets as minor gouges in the jet can alter the flow rate and change the fuel/air mixture.*

2. Make sure the float bowl overflow tube is clear.

3. Inspect the float bowl O-ring gasket for damage or deterioration and replace if necessary. O-ring gaskets tend to become hardened after prolonged use and heat and therefore lose their ability to seal properly.

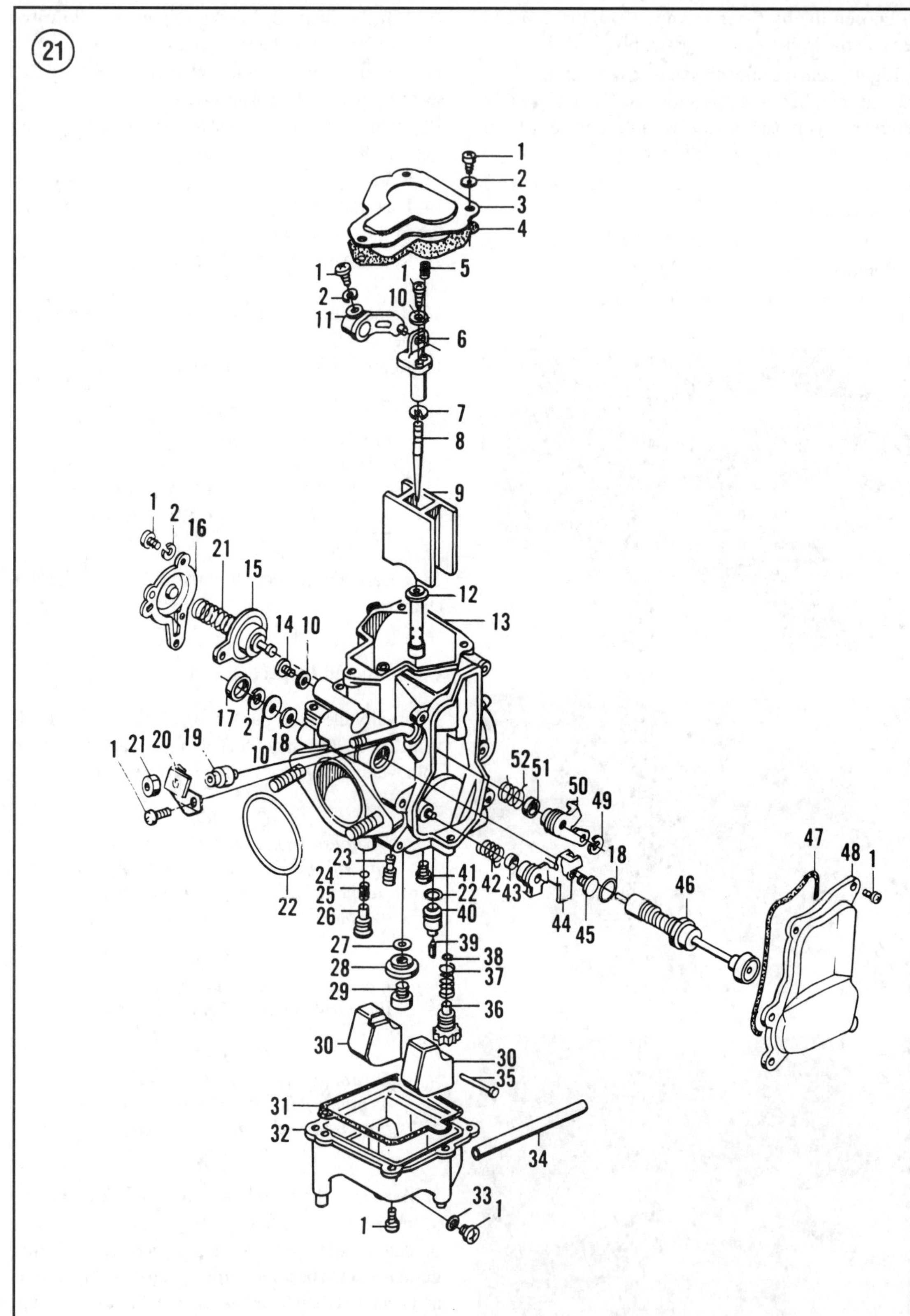
21
1
2
3
4
5
6
7
8
9
10
11
12
13
14
15
16
17
18
19
20
21
22
23
24
25
26
27
28
29
30
31
32
33
34
35
36
37
38
39
40
41
42
43
44
45
46
47
48
49
50
51
52

CARBURETOR (SINGLE CABLE)

1. Screw
2. Washer
3. Top cover
4. Gasket
5. Spring
6. Jet needle holder
7. E-clip
8. Jet needle
9. Piston valve
10. Washer
11. Throttle lever
12. Needle jet
13. Body
14. Screw
15. Coasting enrichener diaphragm
16. Cover
17. Cap
18. Seal
19. Cover
20. Plate
21. Nut
22. O-ring
23. Pilot jet
24. O-ring
25. Spring
26. Pilot air screw
27. Washer
28. Main jet washer
29. Main jet
30. Float
31. O-ring gasket
32. Float bowl
33. Washer
34. Hose
35. Float pivot pin
36. Idle speed adjust screw
37. Spring
38. O-ring
39. Needle valve
40. Needle valve seat
41. Screw
42. Spring
43. Seal
44. Arm
45. Throttle cable ball
46. Bystarter valve (choke)
47. Gasket
48. Cover
49. E-clip
50. Arm
51. Seal
52. Spring

22
MIKUNI

26

23
MIKUNI
CORP.

27
A
B

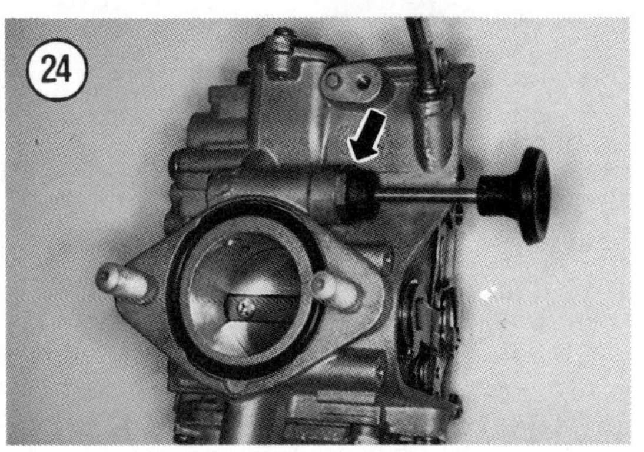
24

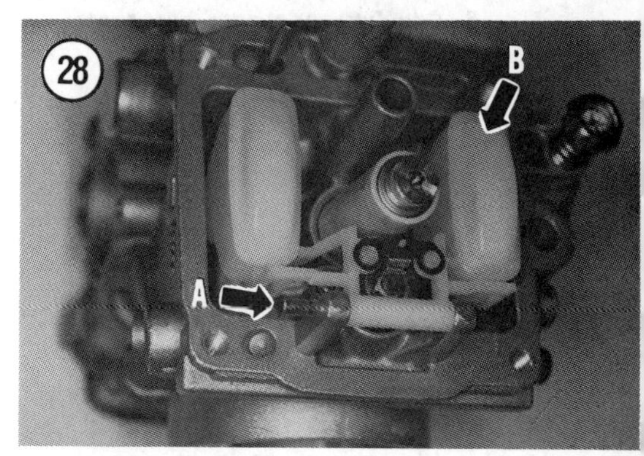
28
B
A

25

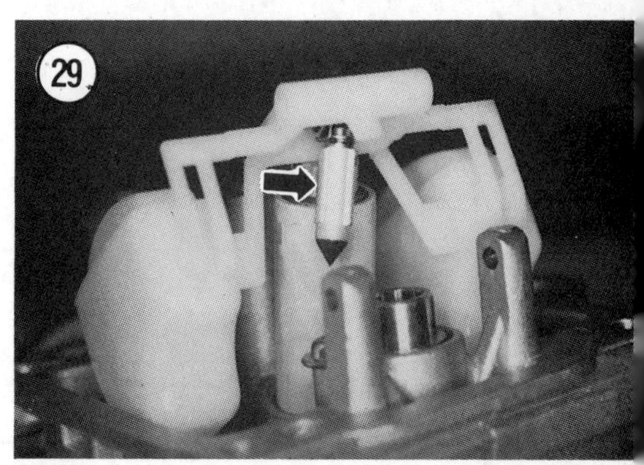
29

4. Inspect the coasting enrichener diaphragm (**Figure 34**) for cracks or other deterioration and replace if necessary. Check the spring (**Figure 34**) for weakness or damage.

5. Inspect the needle valve assembly as follows:

   a. Check the O-ring (A, **Figure 35**) for wear, hardness, cracks or other damage.

   b. Inspect the end of the inlet valve needle (**Figure 36**) for wear or damage.

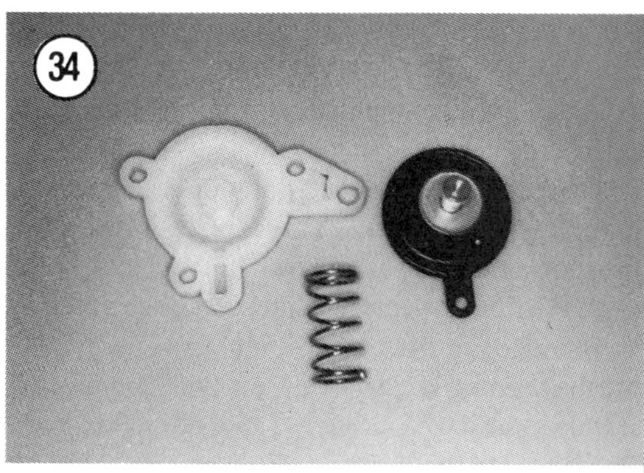

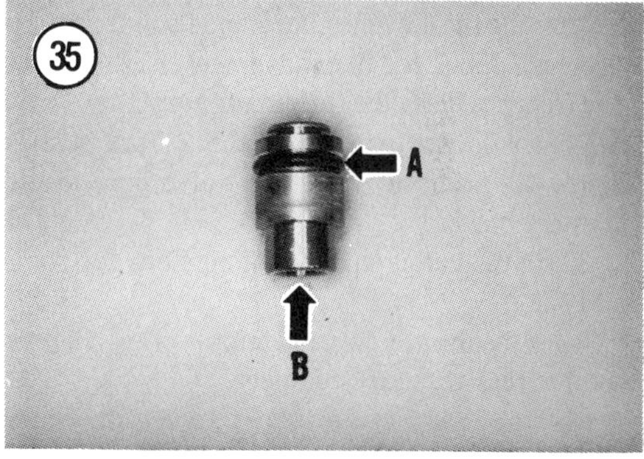

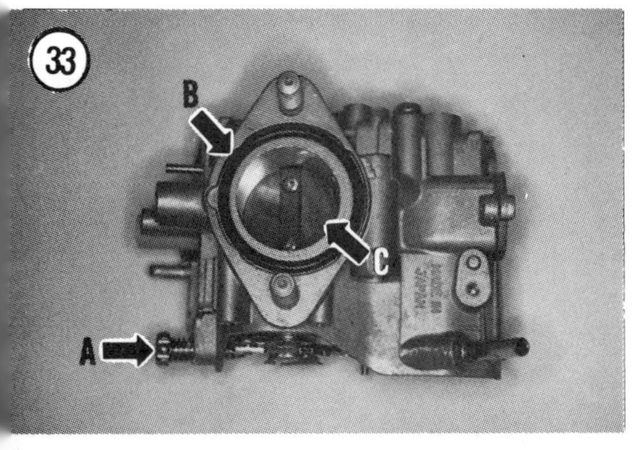

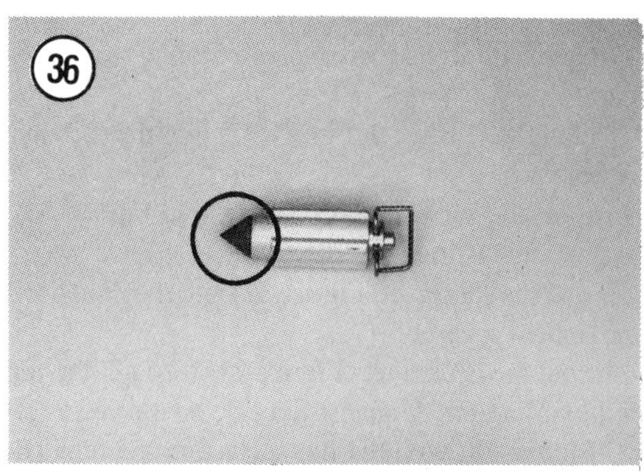

8

c. Check the inside of the inlet valve seat (B, **Figure 35**) for steps, uneven wear or other damage.
d. If the needle valve and/or seat are damaged, replace the needle valve assembly as a set.

6. Check the main jet and both washers for wear or damage.
7. Inspect the pilot air screw (**Figure 37**), O-ring and spring for damage. Replace the screw if the tip or threads are damaged.
8. Inspect the idle speed screw O-ring (**Figure 38**) for wear, hardness, cracks or other damage. Replace if necessary.
9. Inspect the bystarter valve assembly (**Figure 39**) for wear, damage or deterioration.
10. Make sure all of the small openings in the needle jet are clear.
11. Inspect the float for deterioration or damage. If the float is suspected of leakage, place it in a water filled container and push it down. If the float absorbs water, the float is damaged and must be replaced.
12. Remove the float bowl drain screw and make sure the opening is clear. Blow out with compressed air if necessary.
13. Make sure the throttle valve screws (C, **Figure 33**) are tight.
14. Move the throttle lever back and forth from stop to stop and check for free movement. If it does not move freely, replace the carburetor body.
15. Do not loosen or remove the 2 Torx screws (**Figure 40**) securing the piston valve bore to the carburetor body.
16. Check the carburetor mounting studs for damage.
17. Check the throttle arm and return spring (**Figure 41**) for excessive wear or damage.

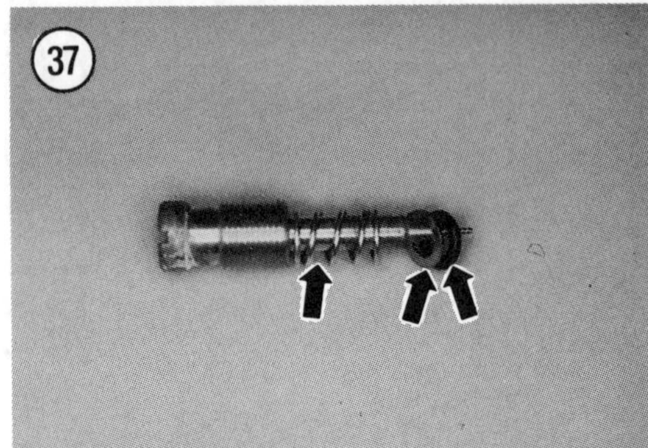

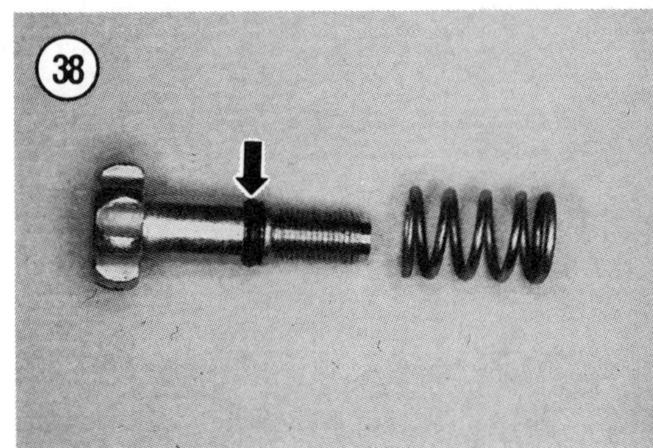

Assembly

Refer to **Figure 21** when reassembling the carburetor.

1. Install the O-ring (B, **Figure 33**) into the carburetor body.
2. Install the throttle adjust screw (A, **Figure 33**), washer and O-ring.
3. Install the starter jet (**Figure 32**) into the float bowl and tighten securely.
4. Install the needle jet (**Figure 31**) through the top of the carburetor. Align the flat side on the needle jet (A, **Figure 42**) with the flat surface in the tube (B,

Figure 42). Push the needle jet in place until it bottoms.

5. Install the main jet and washer (C, **Figure 30**).

6. Install the needle valve seat and O-ring (B, **Figure 30**) and push it down until it seats completely.

7. Install the screw and washer (A, **Figure 30**) securing the needle valve seat and tighten securely.
8. Install the needle valve onto the float tang (**Figure 29**) and carefully install the float assembly (B, **Figure 28**) into position.

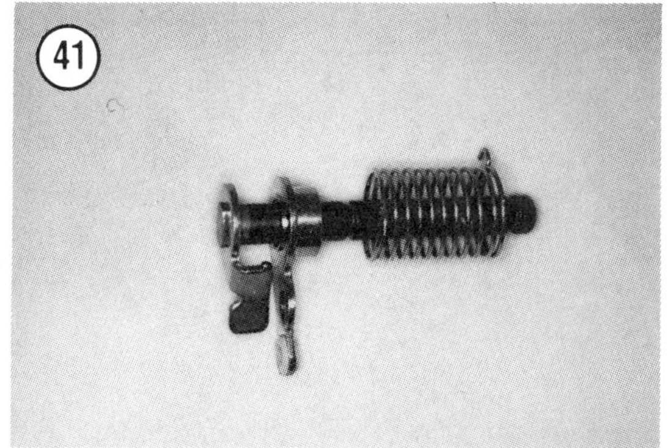

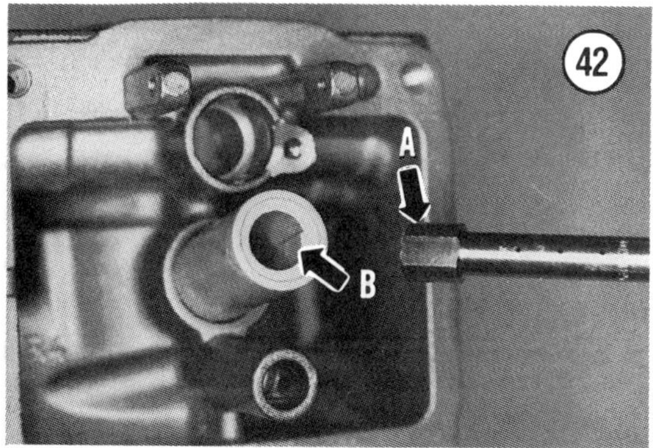

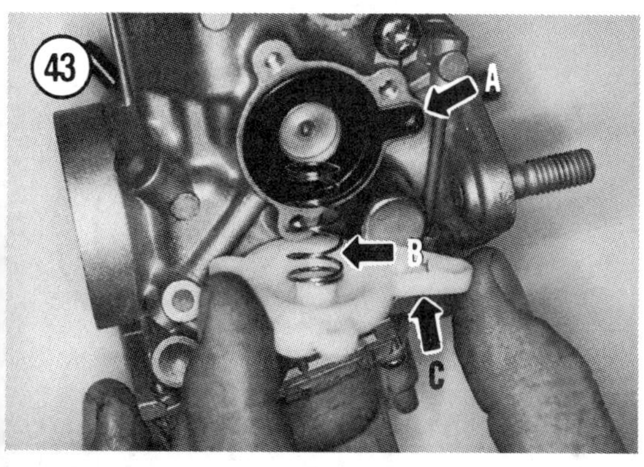

9. Install the float pin and push it in until it is completely seated (A, **Figure 28**).
10. Check the float height as described in this chapter.
11. Install the pilot jet (B, **Figure 27**).
12. Install the large main jet washer (A, **Figure 27**). Push it on until it is correctly seated.
12. If removed, install O-ring gasket into float bowl groove. Then install the float bowl (**Figure 26**) and its mounting screws. Tighten the screws securely.
14. Make sure the spring, washer and O-ring (**Figure 37**) are in place on the pilot screw. Install the pilot screw assembly (**Figure 25**) and lightly seat it. Then back it the out number of turns recorded during removal or to the setting listed in **Table 1**.
15. Install the coasting enrichener system as follows:
   a. Install the diaphragm (A, **Figure 43**) making sure the tab with the hole is aligned properly with the opening in the carburetor body.
   b. Install the spring (B, **Figure 43**) and hold it in place.
   c. Install the cover (C, **Figure 43**) and cover screws. Tighten the screws securely.

16. Install the bystarter valve and tighten the nut (**Figure 24**) securely.
17. Install the piston valve into the carburetor as previously described in this chapter.
18. Install the carburetor as described in this chapter.

8

CARBURETOR ADJUSTMENTS

Idle speed and pilot screw adjustment are covered in Chapter Three.

Float Adjustment

The fuel valve and float maintain a constant fuel level in the carburetor float bowl. Because the float level affects the fuel mixture throughout the engine's operating range, the level must be maintained within factory specification.

The carburetor assembly must be removed and partially disassembled for this adjustment.
1. Remove the carburetor as described in this chapter.
2. Remove the screws (**Figure 26**) securing the float bowl and remove the float bowl.
3. Hold the carburetor so the float arm is just touching the fuel valve—not pushing it down. Use a float level gauge, small ruler or vernier caliper (**Figure

44) and measure the distance from the carburetor body gasket surface to the float. The correct height is listed in **Table 1**.

4. If the float height is incorrect, adjust as follows:
   a. Pull the float pin out (A, **Figure 28**) and remove the float and needle valve (B, **Figure 28**). Remove the needle valve from the float arm.
   b. Carefully bend the float arm (**Figure 45**) with a small screwdriver to adjust the float level.
   c. Install the fuel valve onto the float arm and install the float and float pin.
   d. Recheck the float level as described in Step 3. Repeat until the float level adjustment is correct.
5. Make sure the float bowl O-ring is in place and reinstall the float bowl. Tighten the screws securely.
6. Install the carburetor as described in this chapter.

Fuel Level Adjustment

NOTE
Check and adjust the float level prior to adjusting the fuel level.

1. Park the vehicle on level ground and set the parking brake. Block the rear wheels so the vehicle will not roll in either direction.
2. Raise the front of the vehicle until the carburetor body is vertical. The fuel level in the float bowl must be horizontal to achieve an accurate fuel level measurement.
3. Attach a Fuel Level Gauge (Yamaha pat No. 01312-A) to the float bowl overflow hose tube (**Figure 46**).
4. Loosen the drain screw on the float bowl (**Figure 46**) and start the engine.
5. Place the tube next to the center of the mating line of the carburetor body and the float bowl as shown in **Figure 46**.
6. Measure the fuel level with the gauge. The correct fuel level is listed in **Table 1**.
7. Turn off the engine and close the drain screw.
8. Remove the special gauge and dispose of the fuel in the gauge properly.
9. Remove the jack from under the vehicle.
10. If the fuel level is incorrect, remove the carburetor and adjust the float tang as described under *Float Adjustment* in this chapter.
11. Repeat this procedure until the fuel level is correct.

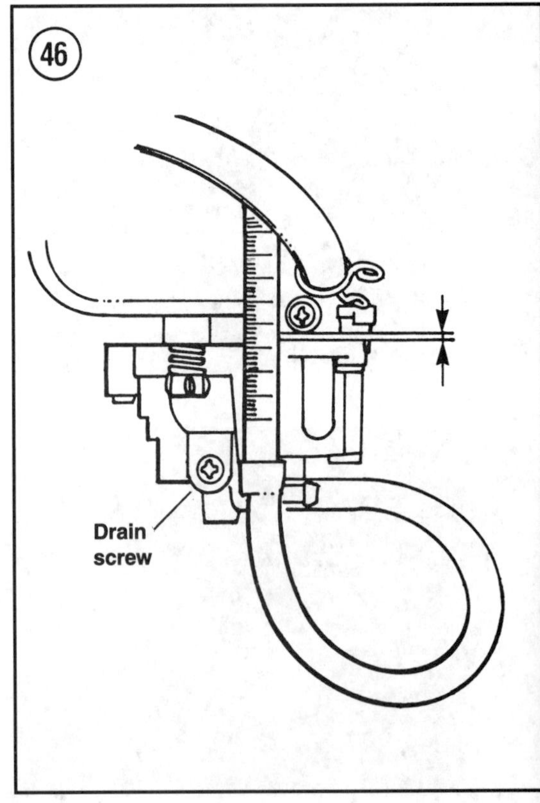

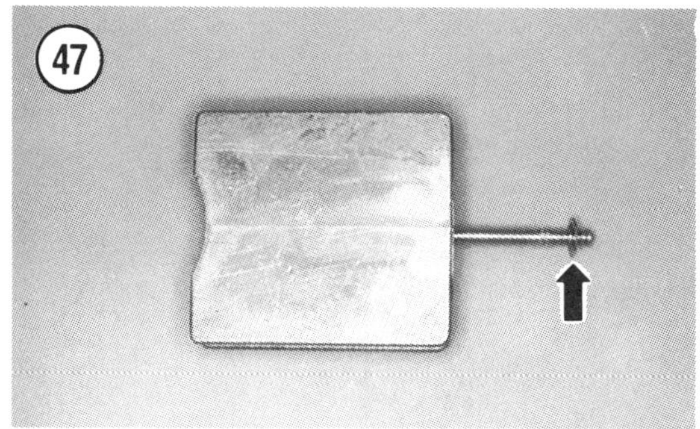

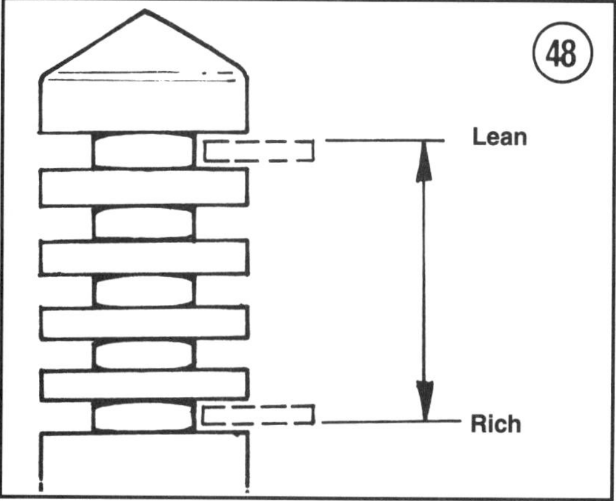

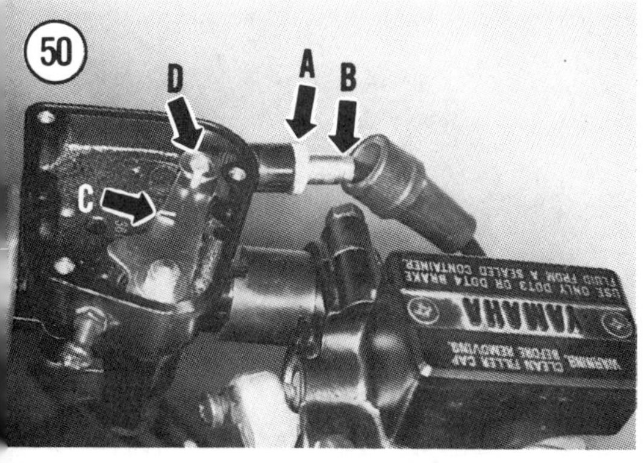

Jet Needle Adjustment

The position of the needle jet can be adjusted to affect the fuel/air mixture for medium throttle openings.

1. Remove the piston valve and jet needle (**Figure 47**) as described in this chapter.

NOTE
Record the clip position before removing it.

2. Raising the needle (lowering the clip) will enrichen the mixture during mid-throttle opening, while lowering the needle (raising the clip) will lean the mixture. Refer to **Figure 48**.
3. Refer to **Table 1** for the standard jet needle clip position.
4. Install the jet needle and piston valve as described in this chapter.

THROTTLE CABLE REPLACEMENT

1. Park the vehicle on level ground and set the parking brake.
2. Remove the seat.
3. Remove the front carrier/rack and fender as described in Chapter Fourteen.
4. Remove the fuel tank as described in this chapter.
5. Disconnect the throttle cable from the carburetor as described under *Carburetor Removal/Installation* in this chapter.
6. Disconnect the throttle cable from the throttle lever as follows:
   a. Slide the rubber boot (A, **Figure 49**) off of the cable adjuster.
   b. Remove the throttle lever housing cover screws and remove the cover (B, **Figure 49**) and gasket.
   c. Loosen the throttle cable adjuster locknut (A, **Figure 50**) and loosen the adjuster (B, **Figure 50**) to provide as much cable slack as possible.
   d. Pull the throttle arm (C, **Figure 50**) back and disconnect the throttle cable (D, **Figure 50**) from the throttle arm. If you cannot disconnect the cable end, remove the throttle arm nut, washer, lever and spring and disconnect the cable.
   e. Withdraw the throttle cable from the throttle lever housing.
7. Disconnect the throttle cable from any frame clips.

8. Make a note of the cable routing path through the frame, then remove it.
9. Lubricate the new cables described in Chapter Three.
10. Reverse Steps 1-8 to install the new cable assembly, while noting the following.
11. Reconnect throttle cable to the carburetor as described under *Carburetor Removal/Installation* in this chapter.
12. Apply grease to the cable end in the throttle lever housing.
13. Operate the throttle lever and make sure the carburetor throttle linkage is operating correctly without binding. If operation is incorrect or there is binding, make sure the cable is attached correctly and there are no tight bends in the cable.
14. Install the cover (B, **Figure 49**), gasket and mounting screws. Tighten the screws securely.
15. Adjust the throttle cable as described in Chapter Three.
16. Test ride the vehicle and make sure the throttle is operating correctly.

THROTTLE LEVER HOUSING

Removal/Installation

1. Remove the throttle cable from the throttle lever housing as described in the preceding procedure.
2. Remove the clamp screws and remove the clamp and the throttle lever housing (**Figure 51**) from the handlebar.
3. If necessary, disassemble and clean the housing as described in the following procedure.
4. Move the locating spacer (**Figure 52**) up against the master cylinder and index it with the post on the master cylinder as shown in A, **Figure 53**.
5. Install the throttle lever housing and index it with the spacer as shown in B, **Figure 53**.
6. Install the clamp and screws and tighten the screws securely.
7. Install the throttle cable onto the throttle lever assembly as described in the preceding procedure.

Disassembly/Assembly

1. Remove the throttle lever assembly as previously described.
2. Remove the nut and washer (A, **Figure 54**) securing the throttle arm.

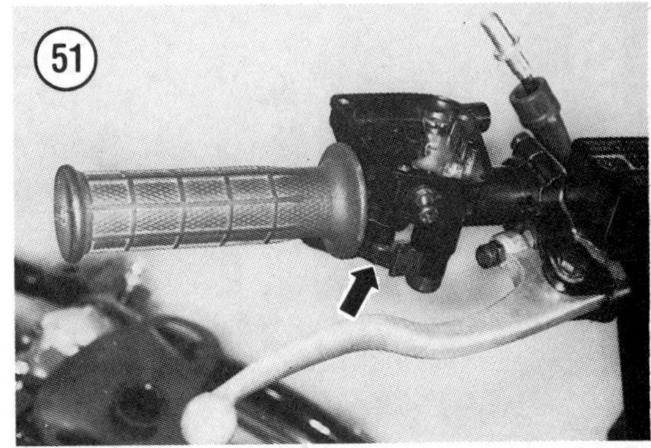

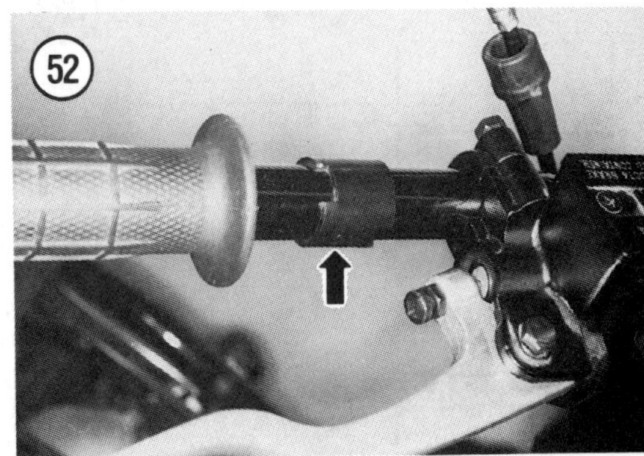

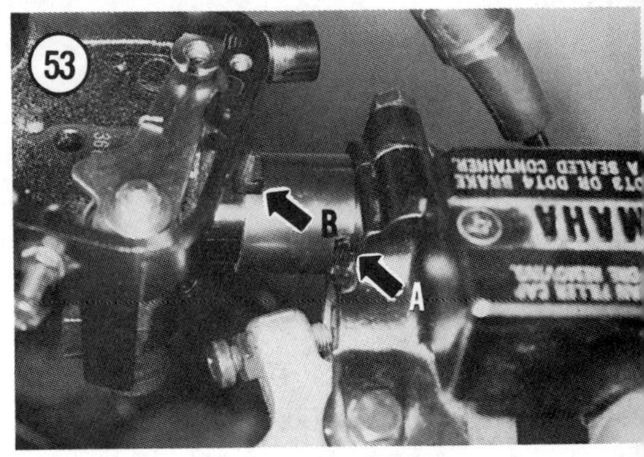

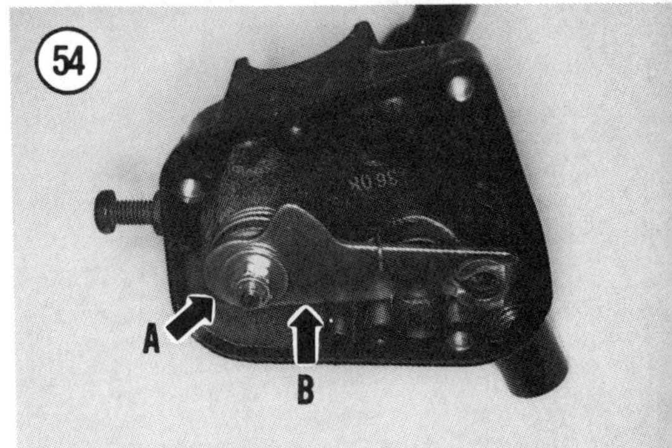

3. Remove the throttle arm and return spring (B, **Figure 54**).
4. Withdraw the throttle lever and washer from the housing.
5. Inspect all parts as described in the following procedure.
6. Apply a light coat of grease to the throttle arm shaft.
7. Install the washer (A, **Figure 55**) onto the throttle arm shaft and install the shaft (B, **Figure 55**) onto the housing.

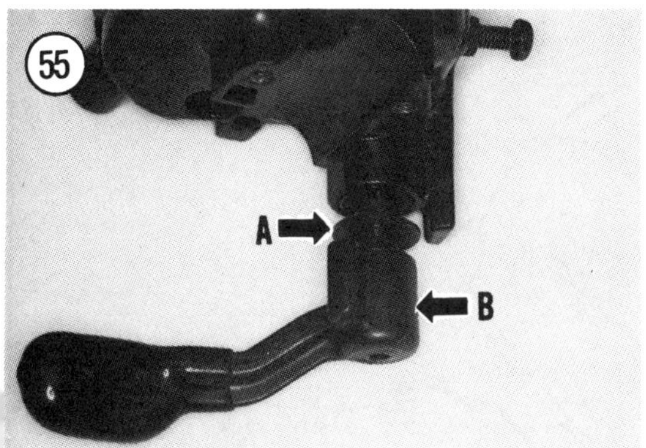

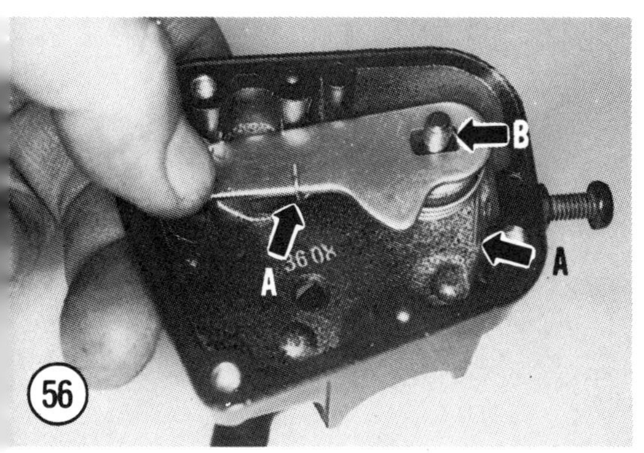

8. Hook the return spring onto the throttle arm against the housing as shown in A, **Figure 56**. Then install the throttle arm onto the end of the throttle arm shaft. Index the arm onto the flat shoulder on the end of shaft as shown in B, **Figure 56**.
9. Hold the throttle arm in this position (A, **Figure 56**) and install the washer and nut (A, **Figure 54**). Tighten the nut securely.
10. Hold the case and move the throttle lever back and forth several times to make sure it moves easily and that it returns to the at-rest position when released.

Inspection

Replace worn or damged parts as described in this section.

1. Clean and dry all parts.
2. Inspect the seal mounted in the base of the throttle housing for hardness or deterioration.
3. Inspect the bushing (**Figure 57**) in the top of the throttle housing for excessive wear or damage. Neither the bushing or throttle housing can be replaced separately. If any damage is noted, the throttle lever housing must be replaced as an assembly.
4. Check the throttle lever shaft for excessive wear or damage.
5. Check the throttle arm and return spring for excessive wear or damage.
6. Replace the cover gasket if damaged.

FUEL TANK

Removal/Installation

Refer to **Figure 58** (1993-1995) or **Figure 59** (1996-on) when servicing the fuel tank in this section.

WARNING
Fuel vapors will be present when removing the fuel tank. Because gasoline is extremely flammable, perform this procedure away from all open flames (including pilot lights) and sparks. Do not smoke or allow someone who is smoking in the work area as an explosion and fire may occur. Always work in a well-ventilated area. Wipe up any spills immediately.

8

(58)

FUEL TANK (1993-1995)

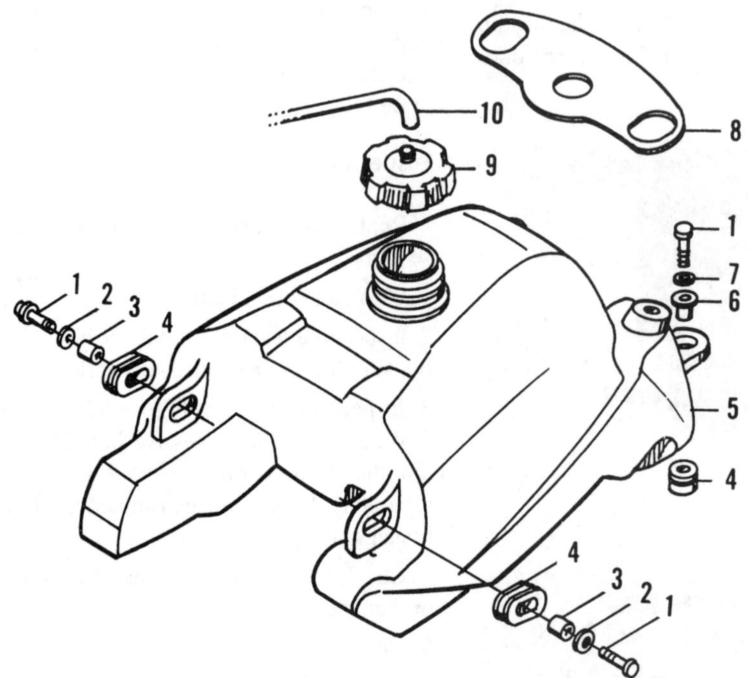

1. Bolt
2. Washer
3. Collar
4. Grommet
5. Fuel tank
6. Collar
7. Washer
8. Damper
9. Fill cap
10. Vent hose

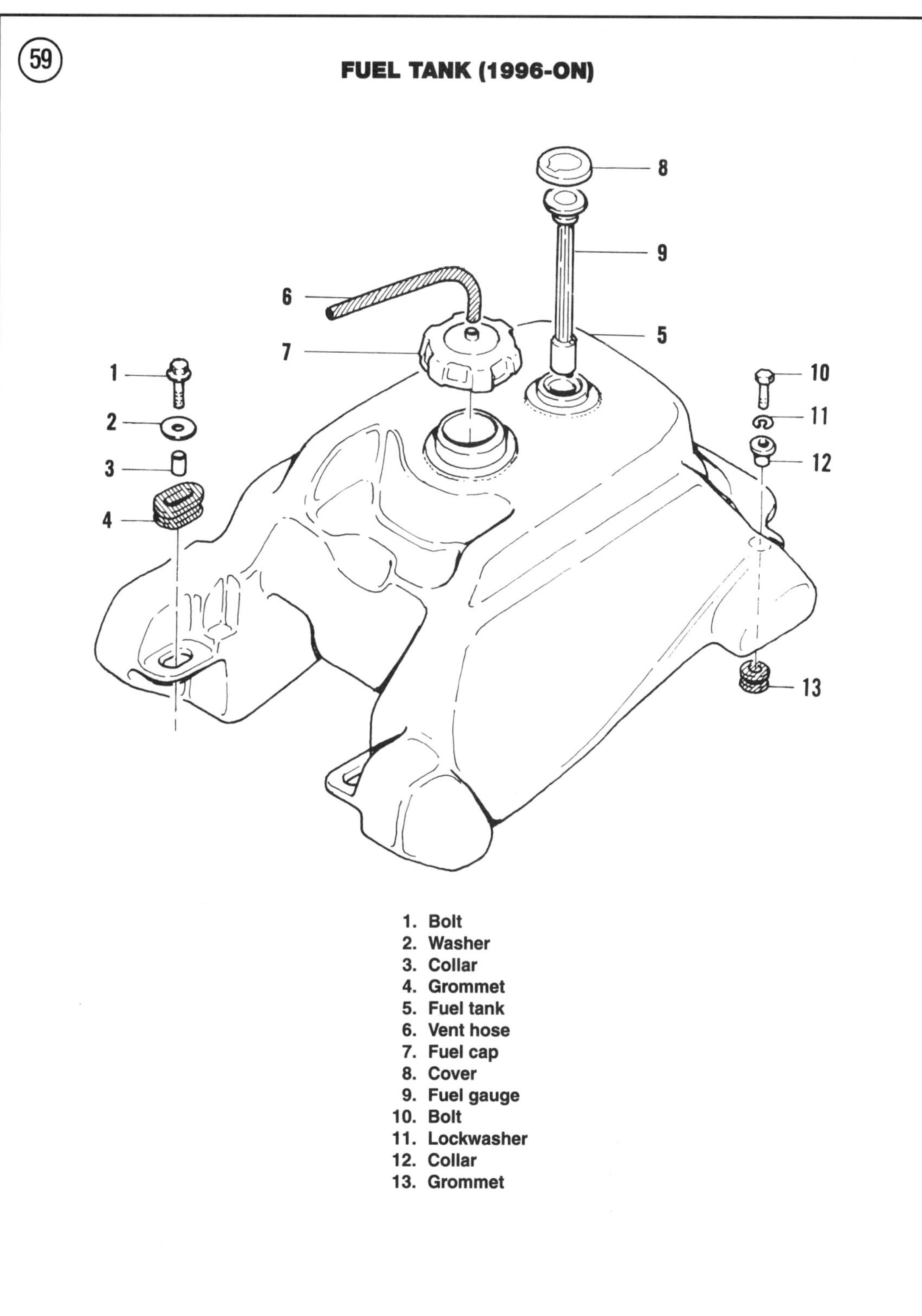

1. Bolt
2. Washer
3. Collar
4. Grommet
5. Fuel tank
6. Vent hose
7. Fuel cap
8. Cover
9. Fuel gauge
10. Bolt
11. Lockwasher
12. Collar
13. Grommet

1. Park the vehicle on level ground, set the parking brake and block the wheels so that vehicle will not roll in either direction.
2. Remove the seat (Chapter Fourteen).
3. Disconnect the battery negative lead (Chapter Three).
4A. On 1993-1995 models, remove the fuel tank cover (Chapter Fourteen).
4B. On 1996-on models, remove the front fender assembly (Chapter Fourteen).
5. Turn the fuel shutoff valve (A, **Figure 60**) to the OFF position and disconnect the fuel line (B, **Figure 60**) from the valve. Plug the open end of the fuel line to prevent contamination.
6. Remove the front and rear (A, **Figure 61**) fuel tank mounting bolts. Then remove the damper (B, **Figure 61**) assembly.
7. Pull the fuel tank to the rear and remove it.
8. Inspect the rubber cushion on each side of the fuel tank where the tank is held in place. Replace as a set if either are damaged or starting to deteriorate.
9. Inspect the fuel filler cap seal (**Figure 62**) for hardness or deterioration. If damaged, replace the cap as an assembly—the seal cannot be replaced separately.
10. Install by reversing these removal steps. Check for fuel leakage after installation is complete.

FUEL SHUTOFF VALVE

Removal/Installation

WARNING
Fuel vapor is present when removing the fuel tank and servicing the fuel shutoff valve. Because gasoline is extremely flammable, perform this procedure away from all open flames (including pilot lights) and sparks. Do not smoke or allow someone who is smoking in the work area as an explosion and fire may occur. Always work in a well-ventilated area. Wipe up any spills immediately.

Refer to **Figure 63** for this procedure.

1. Remove the fuel tank as described in this chapter.
2. Drain the fuel tank of all gasoline. Store the fuel in a can approved for gasoline storage.
3. Remove the screws (**Figure 64**) securing the fuel shutoff valve to the fuel tank and remove the valve and gasket.
4. To replace the fuel valve O-ring (6, **Figure 63**):
   a. Remove the 2 cover screws and disassemble the valve in the order shown in **Figure 63**.
   b. Replace the O-ring and reassemble the valve.
5. Install by reversing these steps, while noting the following:
   a. Install a new fuel shutoff valve O-ring (1, **Figure 63**). Tighten the screws securely.

FUEL VALVE

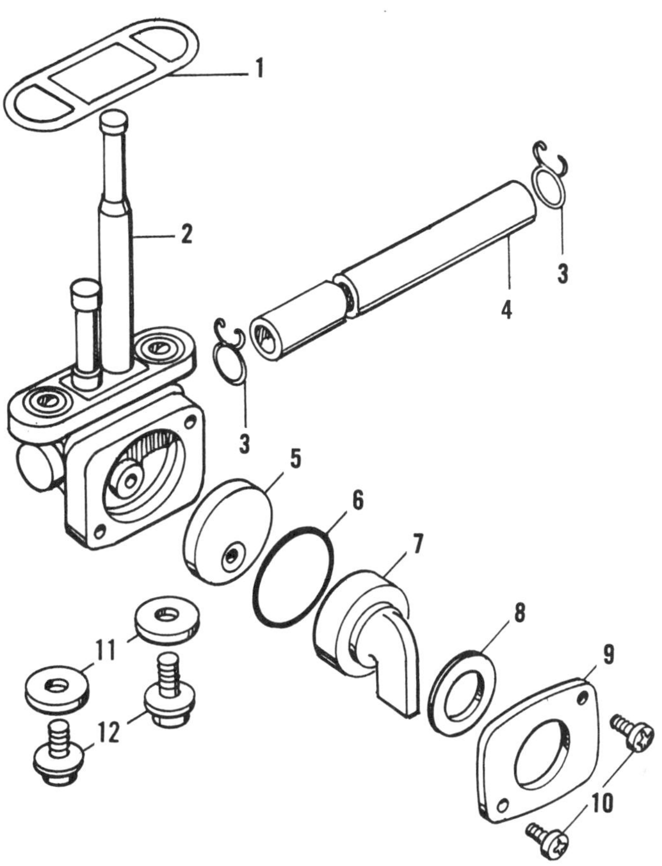

1. O-ring seal
2. Fuel valve body
3. Clamp
4. Fuel hose
5. Valve
6. O-ring
7. Lever
8. Wave washer
9. Plate
10. Screw
11. Washer
12. Screw

b. After reinstalling the fuel tank, pour a small amount of fuel into the tank and check the fuel valve for leaks.

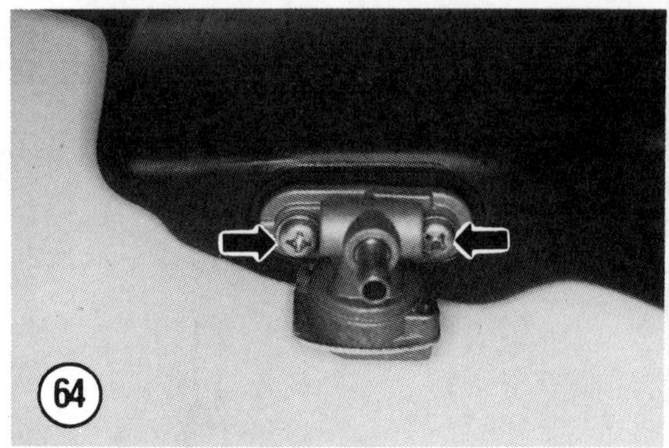
64

AIR FILTER AIR BOX

Removal/Installation

Refer to **Figure 65** (1993-1995) or **Figure 66** (1996-on) when servicing the air box. On 1996-on models, install the intake hose onto the air box by

65

AIR FILTER AIR BOX (1993-1995)

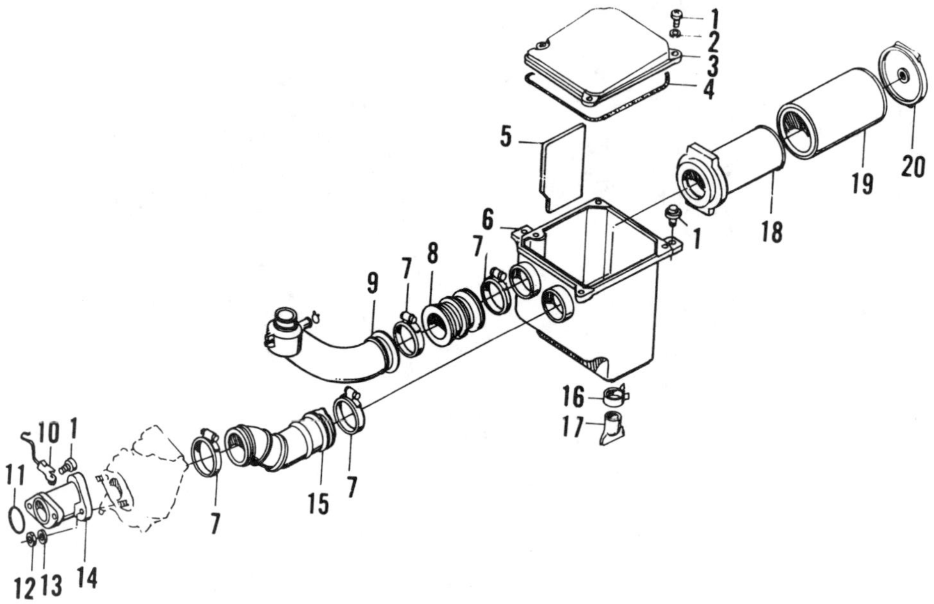

1. Screw
2. Washer
3. Cover
4. Gasket
5. Protector
6. Air box
7. Hose clamp
8. Rubber boot
9. Intake nozzle
10. Hose guide
11. O-ring
12. Nut
13. Washer
14. Intake manifold
15. Air box-to-carburetor air duct
16. Clamp
17. Drain valve
18. Filter screen holder
19. Air filter element
20. End cap

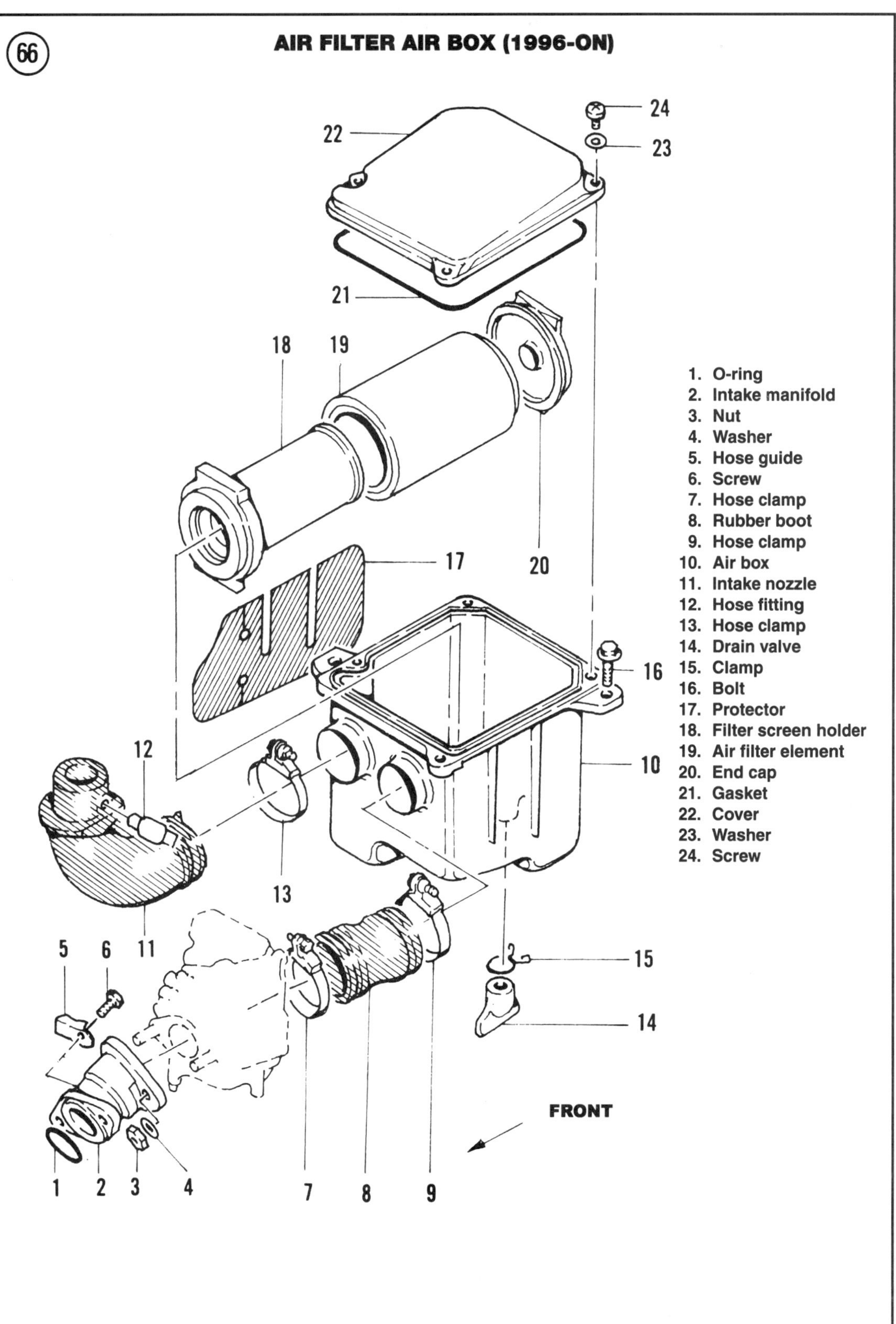
66
AIR FILTER AIR BOX (1996-ON)
1. O-ring
2. Intake manifold
3. Nut
4. Washer
5. Hose guide
6. Screw
7. Hose clamp
8. Rubber boot
9. Hose clamp
10. Air box
11. Intake nozzle
12. Hose fitting
13. Hose clamp
14. Drain valve
15. Clamp
16. Bolt
17. Protector
18. Filter screen holder
19. Air filter element
20. End cap
21. Gasket
22. Cover
23. Washer
24. Screw
FRONT

inserting the index tab on the intake hose between the 2 raised tabs on the air box (**Figure 67**). On all models, tighten the hose clamps securely.

EXHAUST SYSTEM

Check the exhaust system for deep dents and fractures and repair them or replace parts immediately. Check the muffler frame mounting flanges for fractures and loose fasteners. Check the cylinder head mounting flange for tightness. A loose exhaust

(68)

EXHAUST SYSTEM (1993-1995)

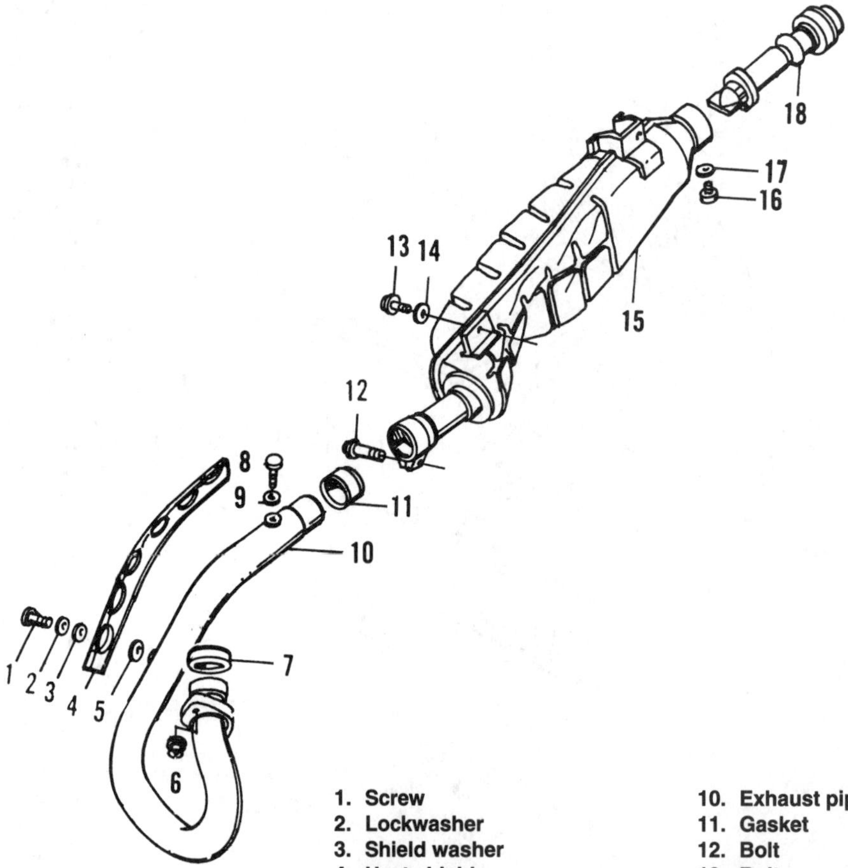

1. Screw
2. Lockwasher
3. Shield washer
4. Heat shield
5. Shield washer
6. Nut
7. Gasket
8. Screw (1993-1994)
9. Washer (1993-1994)
10. Exhaust pipe
11. Gasket
12. Bolt
13. Bolt
14. Washer
15. Muffler
16. Bolt
17. Washer
18. Baffle

pipe connection will cause excessive exhaust noise and decreased engine power.

The stock exhaust system consists of the exhaust pipe, muffler, gaskets and mounting fasteners. See **Figure 68** (1993-1995) or **Figure 69** (1996-on).

Removal/Installation

1. Park the vehicle on level ground and set the parking brake. Block the rear wheels so the vehicle will not roll in either direction.
2. Remove the seat as described (Chapter Fourteen).

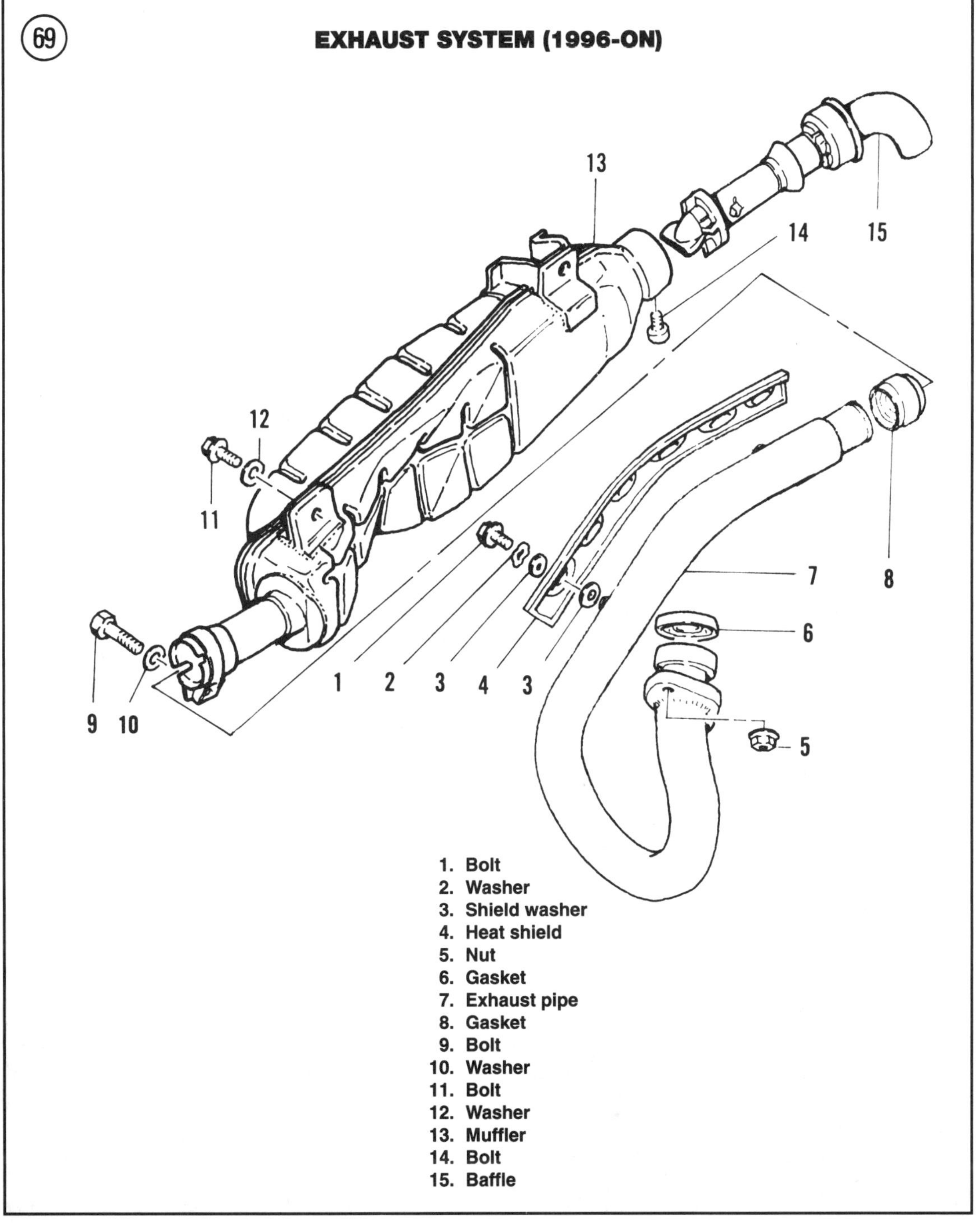

3. Loosen the exhaust pipe-to-muffler clamp bolt (**Figure 70**).

4. Remove the muffler mounting bolts and washers (**Figure 71**) and remove the muffler.

5. Remove the nuts (**Figure 72**) securing the exhaust pipe to the cylinder head.

6. Pull the exhaust pipe forward to clear the cylinder head studs and remove the exhaust pipe (**Figure 73**). Discard the exhaust port gasket.

7. Check the exhaust pipe mounting flange and the muffler mounting flanges for cracks or damage. Make sure the heat shield is secure. Tighten the screws if necessary.

8. Remove the baffle mounting bolt and lockwasher (A, **Figure 74**) and remove the baffle (B, **Figure 74**). Clean out the baffle and reinstall. Tighten the bolt securely.

9. Install by reversing these removal steps, while noting the following.

10. Install a new exhaust pipe gasket (**Figure 75**).

11. Replace the exhaust pipe-to-muffler gasket if leaking or damaged.

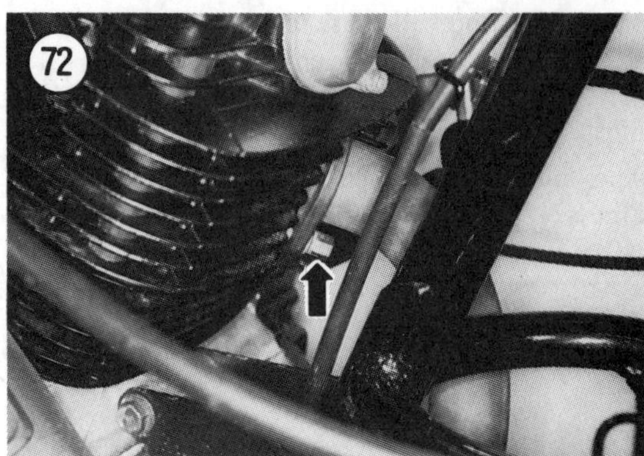

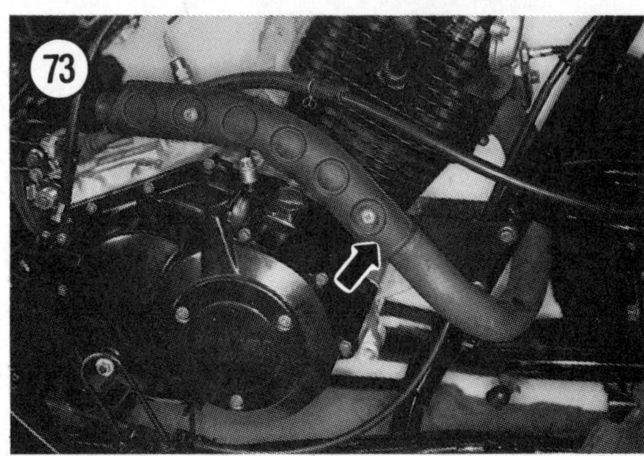

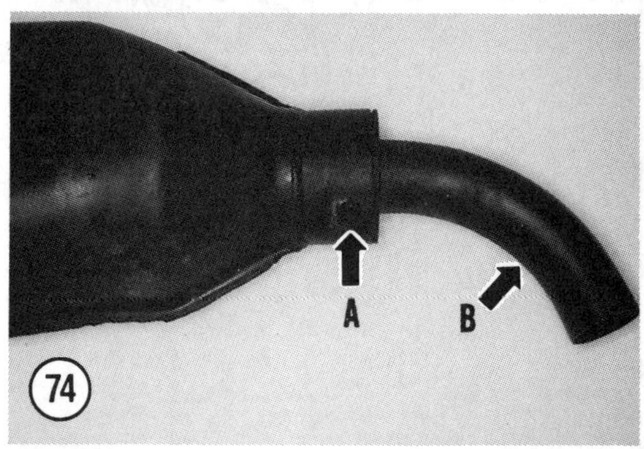

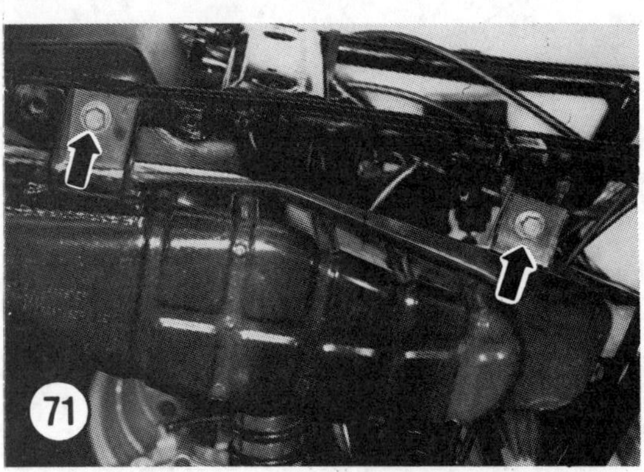

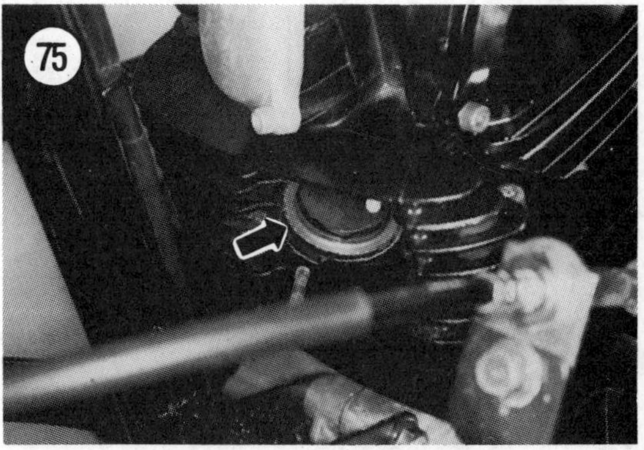

12. To minimize the chances of an exhaust leak at the cylinder head, first tighten the exhaust pipe-to-cylinder head nuts, then the muffler mounting bolts and last the exhaust pipe-to-muffler clamp bolt. Tighten the mounting bolts and nuts as specified in **Table 2**.

13. After installation is complete, start the engine and check for exhaust leaks.

Table 1 CARBURETOR SPECIFICATIONS

	1991-1995	1996-on
Carburetor	Mikuni	Mikuni
Model number	4GB 00	4SH 00
Main jet	122.5	105
Pilot jet	45	45
Main air jet	0.7	0.7
Jet needle	5H26	
Clip position	3rd	3rd
Needle jet	N-8	N-8
Pilot air jet		
No. 1	1.0	1.0
No. 2	0.9	0.9
Pilot outlet	0.75	0.75
Initial pilot air screw setting (turns out)	2.0	3 1/4
Starter jet	60	60
Float height	11.4-13.4 mm (0.45-0.53 in.)	11.4-13.4 mm 0.45-0.53 in.)
Fuel level	1.0-2.0 mm (0.04-0.08 in.)	1.0-2.0 mm 0.04-0.08 in.)

Table 2 FUEL AND EXHAUST SYSTEM TIGHTENING TORQUES

	N•m	in.-lb.	ft.-lb.
Carburetor mounting nuts	16	—	11
Exhaust system			
Muffler to frame mounting bolts	27	—	19
Muffler to exhaust pipe clamp bolt	20	—	14
Exhaust pipe to cylinder head nuts	12	106	—
Exhaust pipe and heat shield bolts	11	97	—

CHAPTER NINE

ELECTRICAL SYSTEM

This chapter contains service and test procedures for all electrical and ignition components. Since this type of vehicle may be subjected to moisture and water while operating under severe conditions, keep all electrical connections free of corrosion and completely coupled to each other. Apply dielectric compound (available from automotive parts stores) to all electrical connectors whenever they are disconnected. This will help seal out moisture and help to prevent corrosion of the electrical connector terminals.

Service procedures relating to the battery and spark plugs are covered in Chapter Three.

The electrical system includes the following systems:

a. Charging system.

b. Ignition system.

c. Starting system

d. Lighting system.

e. Electrical components.

Before starting any work, refer to Chapter One and read the service hints and the detailed information relating to the use of the electrical testing equipment that must be used in this chapter. You will do a better job with this information fresh in your mind.

NOTE

When using an analog ohmmeter, always touch the test leads, then zero the needle to ensure correct readings.

NOTE

Most ATV and motorcycle dealerships and parts suppliers will not accept the return of any electrical part. If you are unable to determine the cause of any electrical system malfunction, have a Yamaha dealership retest that specific system to verify your test results. If you purchase a new electrical component(s), install it, then find that the system still does not work properly, you will, in most cases, be unable to return the unit for a refund.

Tables 1-6 are located at the end of this chapter.

CHARGING SYSTEM

The charging system consists of the battery, CDI magneto, fuse and a voltage regulator/rectifier.

Alternating current generated by the CDI magneto is rectified to direct current. The voltage regulator maintains the voltage to the battery and additional electrical loads such as the lights and ignition system at a constant voltage regardless of variations in engine speed and load.

Charging System Output Test

If a charging system problem is suspected, make sure the battery is fully charged and in good condition before going any further. Clean and test the battery as described under *Battery Testing* in Chapter Three.

Also make sure all electrical connectors within the charging system are tight and free of corrosion prior to making this test.

1. Remove the seat (Chapter Fourteen).

2. Check the main fuse. Locate the fuse holder (**Figure 1**), open it and pull the fuse out and visually inspect it. If the fuse is blown, refer to *Fuse* in this chapter. If the main fuse is good, reinstall it, then proceed to the next step.

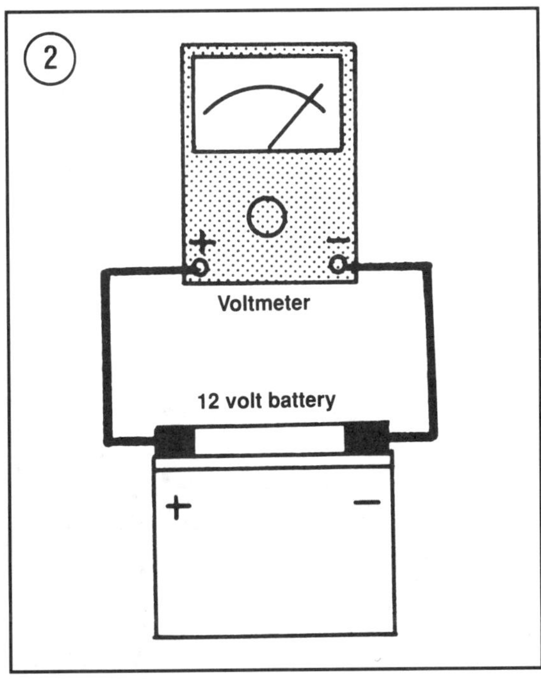

NOTE
Make sure the fuse is secure in its holder.

3. Test the specific gravity of each battery cell. See *Battery* in Chapter Three. Clean and charge the battery as required. if the battery is damaged or if it will not maintain its charge, replace it.

4. Connect a 0-20 DC voltmeter to the battery terminals as shown in **Figure 2**. Connect an inductive tachometer to the spark plug wire following the manufacturer's instructions.

5. Start the engine and increase engine speed to 5,000 rpm. Read the voltage indicated on the voltmeter. It should be between 14-15 volts. Note the following:

   a. Charging voltage correct: The charging system is operating properly.

   b. Charging voltage incorrect: Test the stator charge coil resistance as described under *Charge Coil Testing* in this chapter. If out of specification, replace the stator coil assembly as described in Chapter Five. If the resistance reading is correct, perform Step 6.

6. Check the charging system wiring harness and connectors for dirty or loose-fitting terminals; clean and repair as required. If the wiring harness and connectors are good, and you have not found the problem after performing the previous tests, the regulator/rectifier is probably faulty. Install a regulator/rectifier unit that is known to be in working order and retest.

7. After the test is completed, disconnect the voltmeter and tachometer.

8. Install the seat as described in Chapter Fourteen.

CHARGE COIL TESTING

It is not necessary to remove the stator coil assembly to perform the following tests. To get accurate resistance measurements, the stator coil must be at approximately 20° C (68° F).

1. Remove the seat and the rear carrier rack and rear fender as described in Chapter Fourteen.

2. Disconnect the 3-pin stator coil connector (**Figure 3**). The connector contains 3 white wires.

3. Use an ohmmeter set at R × 1 and measure the resistance between each white wire (**Figure 4**) on the stator coil side of the connector.

4. The specified resistance is listed in **Table 2**. If resistance is not as specified the stator coil assembly must be replaced as described in Chapter Five.
5. Make sure the electrical connectors are free of corrosion.
6. Apply dielectric compound (available from an automotive parts store) to the electrical connector prior to reconnecting it. This will help seal out moisture.
7. Make sure the electrical connector is completely coupled.

VOLTAGE REGULATOR/RECTIFIER

Testing

Service specifications for the voltage regulator/rectifier are not available. Replace the voltage regulator/rectifier when no other problem can be found in the charging system. See *Charging System* in Chapter Two.

Removal/Installation

1. Remove the rear fender (Chapter Fourteen).
2. Disconnect the voltage regulator/rectifier electrical connectors.
3. Unbolt and remove the voltage regulator/rectifier (**Figure 5**) from its mounting position on top of the tool box.
4. Install by reversing these removal steps, noting the following.
5. Make sure the electrical connector is free of corrosion. Clean off if necessary.
6. Apply dielectric compound (available from an automotive parts store) to the electrical connector prior to reconnecting it tohelp seal out moisture.

CAPACITOR DISCHARGE IGNITION

All vehicle models are equipped with a capacitor discharge ignition system.

CDI Precautions

Certain measures must be taken to protect the capacitor discharge system.
1. Never disconnect any electrical connectors while the engine is running.
2. Apply dielectric compound to all electrical connectors prior to reconnecting them to help seal out moisture.

3. Make sure all electrical connectors are free of corrosion and are completely coupled to each other.

4. The CDI unit is mounted within a rubber vibration isolator. Always make sure the isolator is in place when installing the unit.

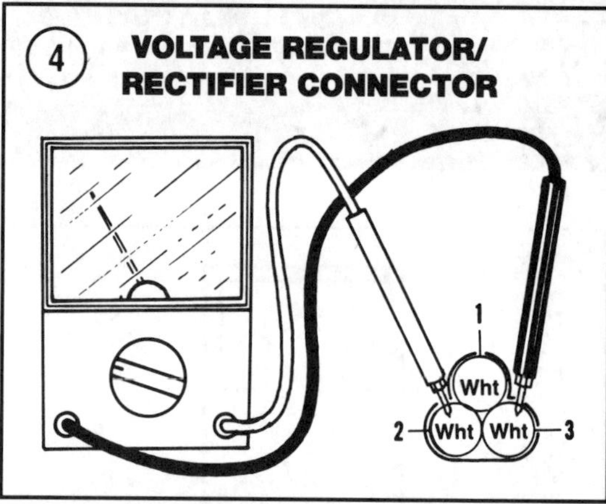

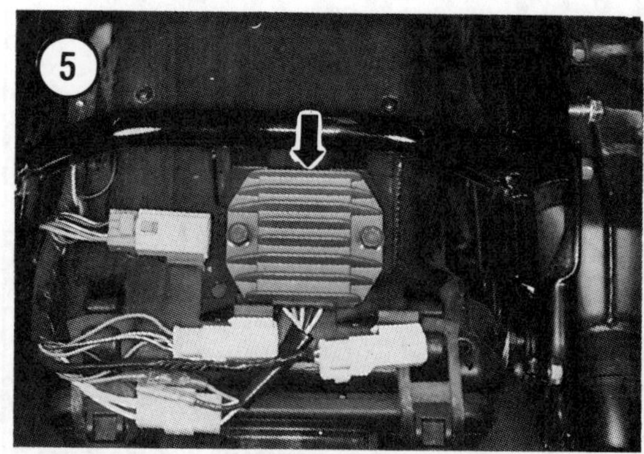

CDI Troubleshooting

Refer to Chapter Two.

CDI Unit Testing

Service specifications for the CDI unit are not available. Replace the CDI unit if no other problem can be found in the ignition system. See *Ignition System* in Chapter Two.

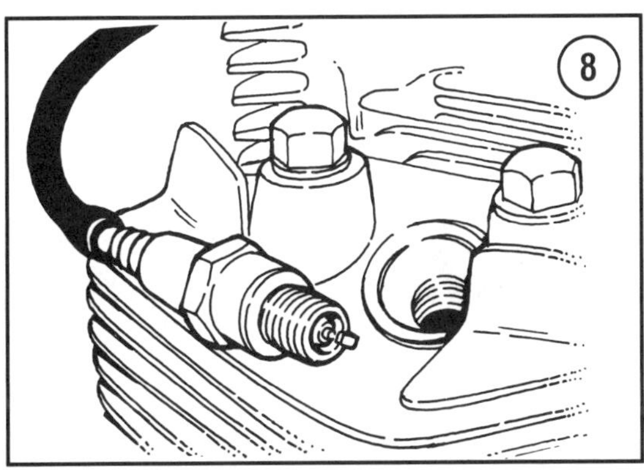

CDI Unit Replacement

1. Disconnect the CDI electrical connectors.
2. Unbolt and remove the CDI unit. See **Figure 6** (1993-1995) or **Figure 7** (1996-on).
3. Install by reversing these removal steps, noting the following.
4. Make sure the electrical connector is free of corrosion.
5. Apply dielectric compound (available from an automotive parts store) to the electrical connector prior to reconnecting it to help seal out moisture.
6. Make sure the electrical connector is completely coupled together.

IGNITION COIL

Testing

The ignition coil is a form of transformer that develops the high voltage required to jump the spark plug gap. The only maintenance required is that of keeping the electrical connections clean and tight and occasionally checking to see that the coil is mounted securely.

If the condition of the coil is doubtful, there are several checks which may be made.

First, disconnect the high voltage lead from the spark plug. Remove the spark plug from the cylinder head. Connect a new or known-good spark plug or spark tester to the high voltage lead and place the spark plug or spark tester base on a good ground like the engine cylinder head (**Figure 8**). Position the spark plug or spark tester so you can see the electrode or tester leads.

WARNING

If it is necessary to hold the high voltage lead, do so with insulated pliers. The high voltage generated by the CDI could produce serious or fatal shocks.

Crank the engine with the electric starter or recoil starter. If a crisp blue spark occurs, the coil is in good condition; if not proceed as follows.

Reinstall the spark plug in the cylinder head.

NOTE

To get an accurate resistance measurement, the ignition coil temperature must be approximately 20° C (68° F.)

1. Remove the front carrier rack and front fender as described in Chapter Fourteen.
2. Disconnect the spark plug cap (secondary lead) from the spark plug (A, **Figure 9**).
3. Disconnect the primary electrical connector (orange wire) from the ignition coil (B, **Figure 9**).
4. Test the spark plug cap as follows:
   a. Carefully remove the spark plug cap from the spark plug lead.
   b. Measure the spark plug cap resistance using an ohmmeter set at R × 1,000. Measure between each end of the cap as shown in **Figure 10**. The correct resistance is listed in **Table 3**.
   c. Replace the spark plug cap if the resistance is out of specification.
   d. Reinstall the spark plug cap.
5. Measure the ignition coil primary resistance using an ohmmeter set at R × 1. Measure resistance between the ignition primary terminal and the ignition coil body (**Figure 11**). See **Table 3** for test specifications.
6. With the spark plug cap installed on the spark plug lead, measure the secondary resistance using an ohmmeter set at R × 1,000. Measure the resistance between the spark plug lead and the ignition coil body (**Figure 11**). See **Table 3** for test specifications.
7. If the ignition coil resistance is out of specification in Step 5 or Step 6, replace the ignition coil.
8. Reconnect the ignition coil leads.

Removal/Installation

1. Remove the fuel tank (Chapter Eight).
2. Disconnect the spark plug cap from the spark plug (A, **Figure 9**).
4. Disconnect the primary lead (A, **Figure 12**) from the ignition coil.

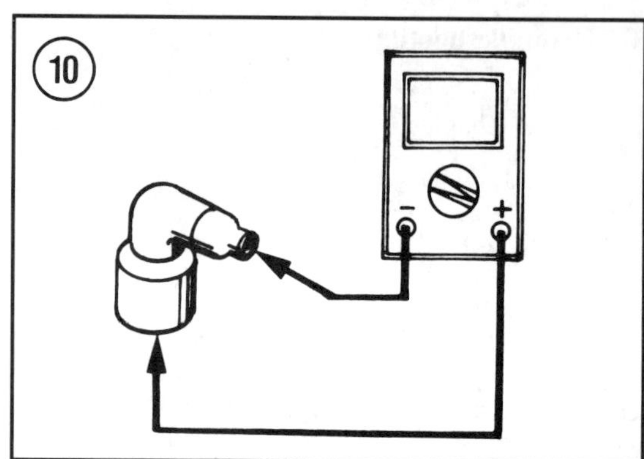

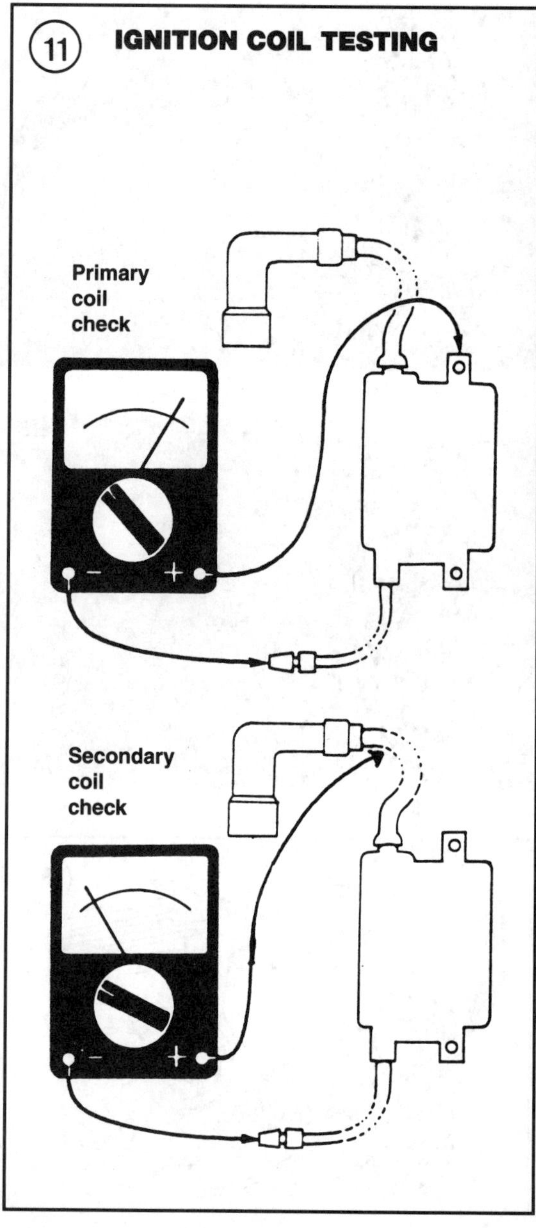

5. Remove the mounting screws and ground wire and remove the ignition coil (B, **Figure 12**).
6. Install by reversing these removal steps, making sure all electrical connections are tight and free of corrosion.

SOURCE COIL AND PICKUP COIL TESTING

The source and pickup coils can be tested while the stator coil is mounted on the engine. To get accurate resistance measurements, the stator assembly must be at approximately 20° C (68° F).

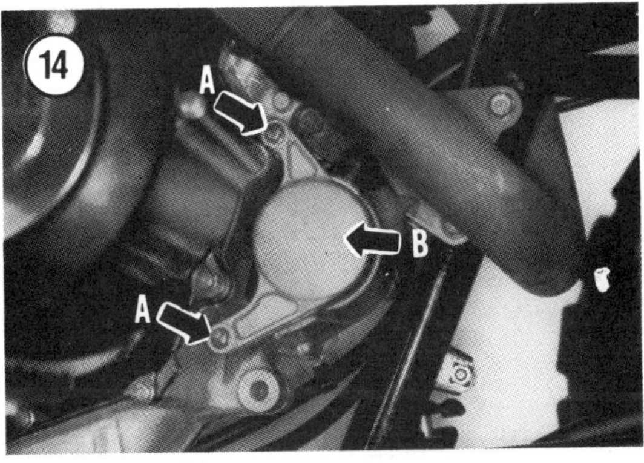

1. Disconnect the source coil 2-pin (brown and green wires) electrical connector (**Figure 3**).
2. Disconnect the pickup coil 2-pin (red and white wires) electrical connector (**Figure 3**).
3. Set an ohmmeter on the R × 100 scale.
4. Refer to **Table 3** for test connections and test values for the source and pickup coils. Compare the meter reading to the values in **Table 3**. If any of the readings differ from the stated values, replace the stator coil assembly as described in Chapter Five. Individual stator coils cannot be replaced.
5. Make sure the electrical connectors are free of corrosion.
6. Apply dielectric compound (available from an automotive parts store) to the electrical connectors prior to reconnecting them.

STARTING SYSTEM

The starting system consists of the starter motor, starter gears, starter relay, starter cutoff relay, neutral relay and the starter button. When the starter button is pressed, it engages the starter solenoid switch that completes the circuit allowing electricity to flow from the battery to the starter motor.

CAUTION
Do not operate the starter for more than 5 seconds at a time. Let it rest approximately 10 seconds, then use it again.

The starter gears are covered in Chapter Five.

Troubleshooting

Refer to Chapter Two.

Starter Motor Removal/Installation

1. Park the vehicle on level ground and set the parking brake.
2. Disconnect the battery negative lead (Chapter Three).
3. Pull back the rubber boot (**Figure 13**) and disconnect the black electric starter cable from the starter.
4. Remove the bolts (A, **Figure 14**) securing the starter to the crankcase.

5. Pull the starter (B, **Figure 14**) toward the right-hand side and remove it from the engine.

6. Install by reversing these removal steps. Make sure the electrical connector is free of corrosion and is tight.

Disassembly

Refer to **Figure 15** for this procedure.

1. Scribe an alignment mark across both end covers and the armature housing for reference during reassembly.

(15) **STARTER MOTOR**

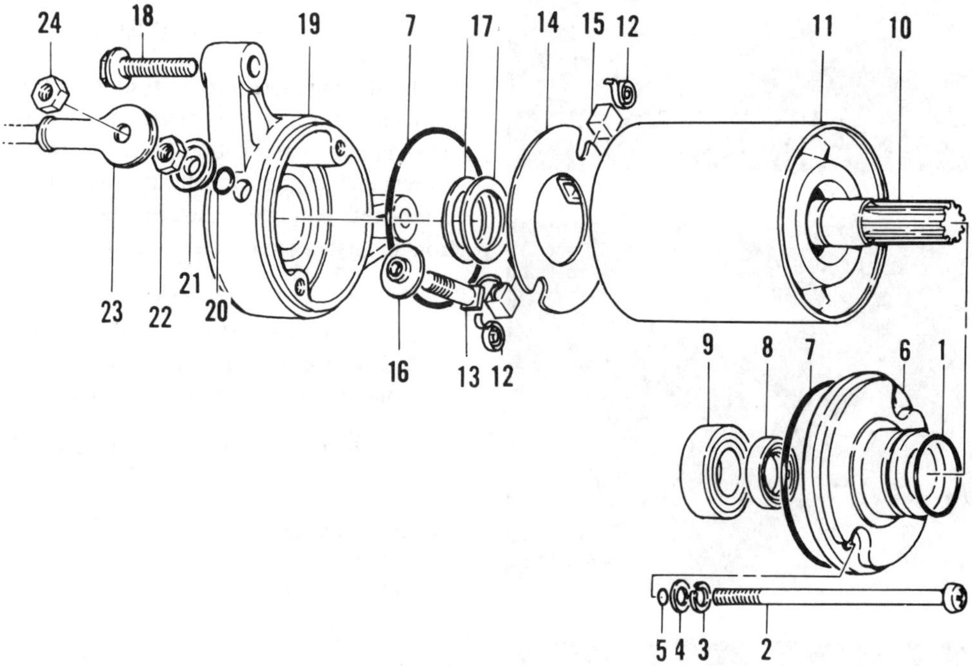

1. O-ring
2. Throughbolt
3. Lockwasher
4. Flat washer
5. O-ring
6. Rear cover
7. O-ring
8. Seal
9. Bearing
10. Armature
11. Housing
12. Spring
13. Brush
14. Brush plate
15. Brush
16. Insulator
17. Shims
18. Bolt
19. Front cover
20. O-ring
21. Insulator
22. Nut
23. Starter cable
24. Nut

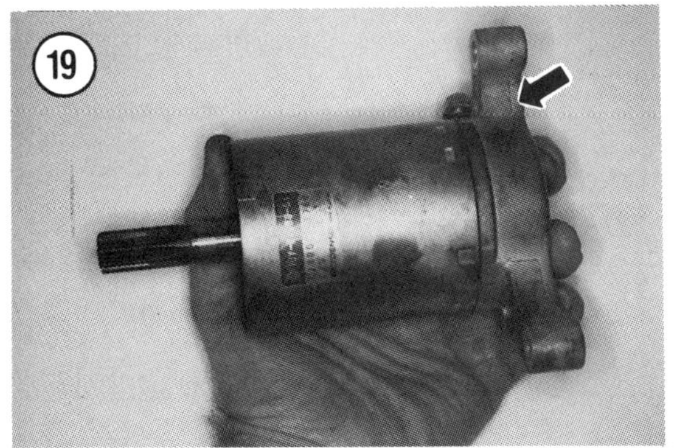

2. Remove the 2 throughbolts, washers, lockwashers and O-rings (**Figure 16**).

NOTE

Record the thickness and number of shims used on the shaft next to the front and rear covers when removing them in the following steps. Be sure to install these shims in their same position when reassembling the starter. The number of shims used in each starter motor varies. The starter motor you are working on may use a different number of shims from that shown in the following photographs.

3. Remove the rear cover (**Figure 17**) and shim(s) (**Figure 18**).
4. Slide the front cover (**Figure 19**) off of the armature. Remove the shim(s).
5. Slide the brush plate (**Figure 20**) off the armature shaft and remove the front cover and the brush plate.
6. Slide the armature (**Figure 21**) out of the housing and remove it.

CAUTION

Do not immerse the wire windings in the case or the armature coil in solvent as the insulation may be damaged. Wipe the windings with a cloth lightly moistened with solvent and dry thoroughly.

7. Clean all grease, dirt and carbon from the armature, case and end covers.

Inspection

When measuring the starter components in this section, compare the measurements to the specifica-

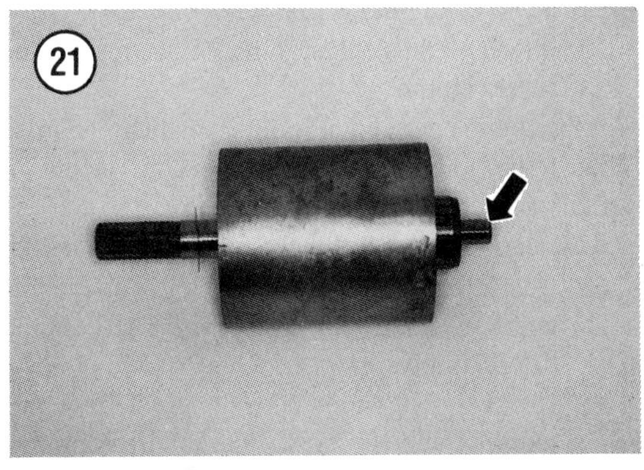

tions in **Table 4**. Replace parts that are damaged or out of specification as described in this section. Major components for the starter motor assembly, except for the brush assemblies, O-rings, washers and mounting bolts, are not available separately. If a major starter motor component is excessivlely worn or damaged, the starter motor must be replaced as an assembly. See your Yamaha dealership for part availability.

1. Pull the spring away from each brush and pull the brushes (A, **Figure 22**) out of their guides.
2. Measure the length of each brush with a vernier caliper (**Figure 23**). If necessary, replace the brushes as described under *Starter Brush Replacement* in this chapter.
3. Inspect the brush springs (B, **Figure 22**) for damage or weakness. If necessary, replace brush springs as follows:
   a. Make a drawing of the brush springs as they are installed on the brush holder, noting the direction in which the spring coils turn.
   b. Remove and replace both brush springs as a set.
4. Inspect the commutator (**Figure 24**). The mica in a good commutator is below the surface of the copper bars. On a worn commutator the mica and copper bars may be worn to the same level (**Figure 25**). If necessary, have the commutator serviced by a Yamaha dealership or electrical repair shop.
5. Inspect the commutator copper bars for discoloration. If a pair of bars are discolored, grounded armature coils are indicated.
6. Use an ohmmeter and make the following tests:
   a. Check for continuity between the commutator bars (**Figure 26**). There should be continuity between pairs of bars.
   b. Check for continuity between the commutator bars and the shaft (**Figure 27**). There should be no continuity (infinite resistance).
   c. If the unit fails either of these tests, replace the starter motor.
7. Measure the commutator outer diameter (**Figure 28**). If the commutator outer diameter is out of specification, replace the starter motor.
8. Use an ohmmeter and make the following tests:
   a. Check for continuity between the starter cable terminal and the end case cover. There should be continuity.
   b. Check for continuity between the starter cable terminal and the brush black wire terminal.

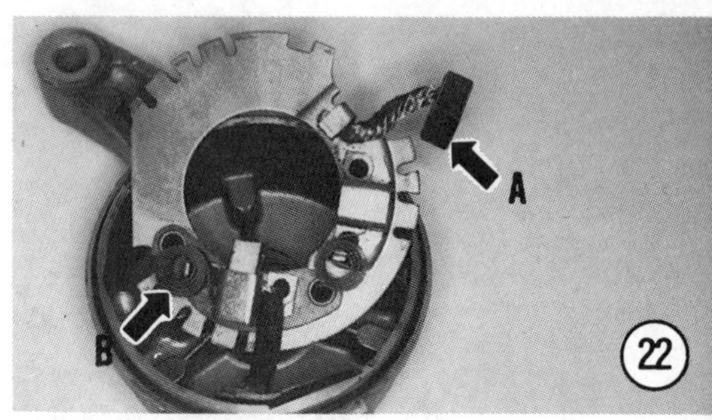

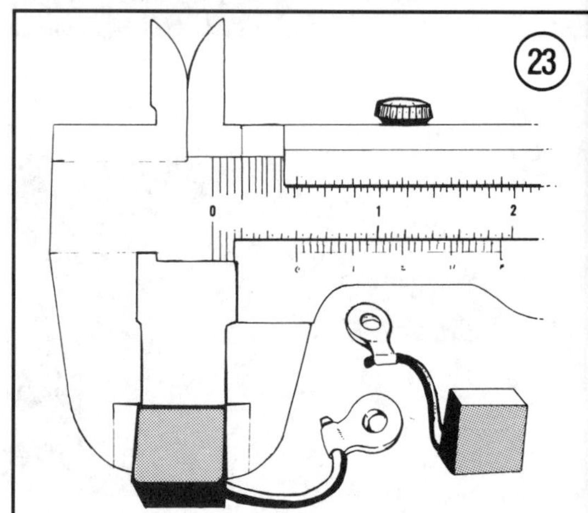

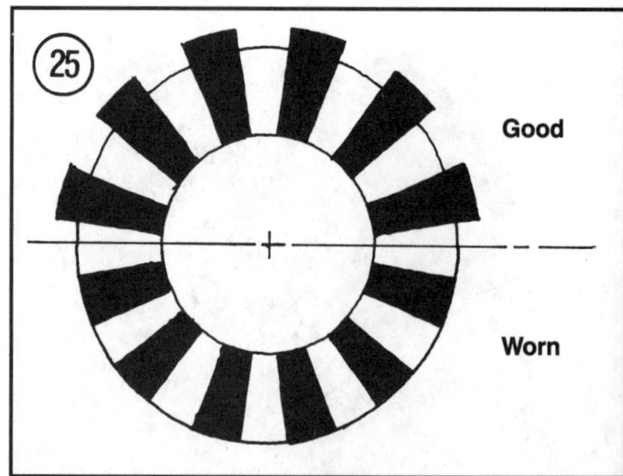

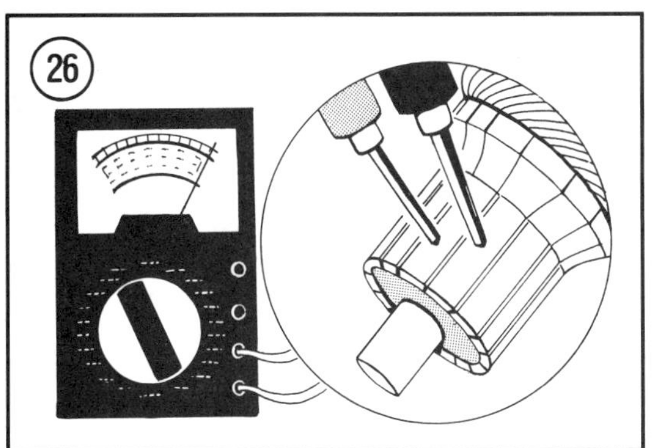
26

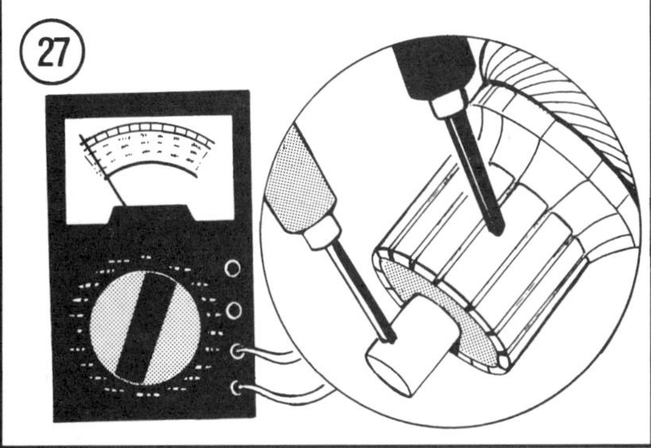
27

28

There should be no continuity (infinite resistance).

c. If the unit fails either of these tests, replace the starter motor.

9. Inspect the oil seal and needle bearing in the rear cover for wear or damage. If either is damaged, replace the starter motor.

10. Inspect the bushing in the front cover for wear or damage. If it is damaged, replace the starter motor.

11. Inspect the starter housing for cracks or other damage. Then inspect for loose, chipped or damaged magnets.

12. Inspect all of the starter O-rings for deterioration, flat spots or other damage. Replace as required.

Starter Brush Replacement

Replace both brushes as a set.

1. Remove the terminal nut (**Figure 29**) and slide off the insulator and O-ring (**Figure 30**).

2. Push the terminal (**Figure 30**) through the starter housing and remove the brush plate assembly. See **Figure 31**.

3. The terminal bolt and brush (A, **Figure 31**) are replaced as an assembly. Remove the terminal bolt and brush and replace it.

4. The other brush (B, **Figure 31**) is soldered to the brush plate. Replace the brush and plate at the same time.

5. Reverse Steps 1 and 2 to install the brush plate assembly. Tighten the terminal nut (**Figure 29**) securely.

29

30

Assembly

1. If removed, install the brushes into their holders and secure the brushes with the springs.
2. Insert the armature into the housing as shown in **Figure 21**.

> NOTE
> ***Figure 32** shows the correct installation position of the front and rear covers.*

3. Mount the armature in a vise (with soft jaws) so that the commutator end faces up.
4. Install the shim(s) over the armature shaft (**Figure 33**).
5. Compress the brushes and slide the brush plate over the commutator (**Figure 34**). Release the brushes.
6. Align the notch in the brush plate with the tab on the housing as shown in **Figure 35**. Then remove the starter from the vise and install the front cover over the armature as shown in **Figure 19**. Align the alignment marks on the front cover and housing made prior to disassembly. Then hold the front cover in place.
7. Install the shim(s) onto the armature shaft (**Figure 18**).
8. Install the rear cover (**Figure 17**) onto the housing, aligning the index marks made prior to disassembly.
9. Make sure the O-rings are installed on the starter mounting bolts (**Figure 15**) and install the bolts through the rear cover and thread into the front cover (**Figure 16**). If the bolts will not pass through the starter motor, the end covers and/or brush plate are installed incorrectly. Tighten the bolts securely.

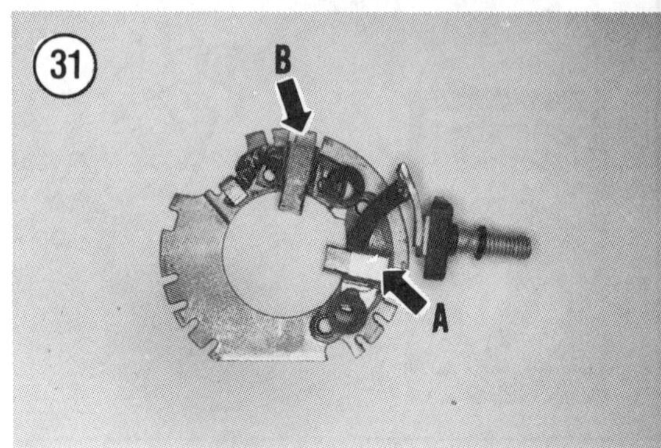

STARTER RELAY

The starter relay (**Figure 36**) is mounted on the left side of the vehicle.

System Test

Starter relay testing instructions are found under *Electric Starting System* in Chapter Two.

Starter Relay Resistance Test

Test the starter relay with an ohmmeter as follows.

1. Turn the ignition switch OFF.

2. Pull the boots off of the starter relay electrical connectors and disconnect the 2 cables (**Figure 37**).

3. Disconnect the starter relay 2-pin connector from the relay.

4. Switch an ohmmeter to R × 1 and measure the resistance across the blue/white and red/white starter relay connector pins (on the starter relay side).The specified resistance is listed in **Table 4**. Replace the starter relay if the resistance reading is incorrect.

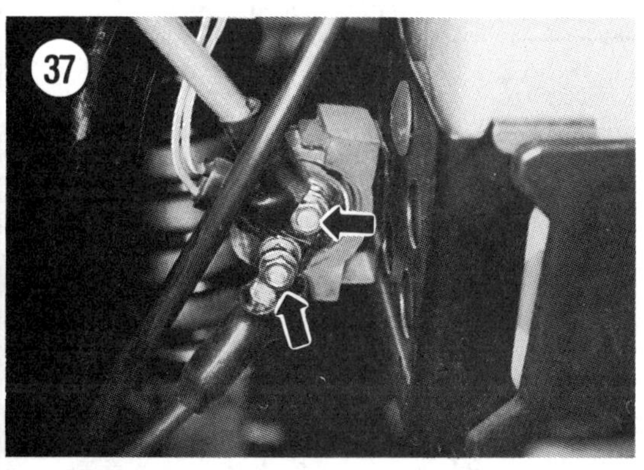

5. Reconnect the starter relay electrical connector and the 2 cables at the starter relay. Pull the boots over the 2 cable ends.

Removal/Installation

1. Disconnect the battery negative lead at the battery (Chapter Three).

2. Pull the boots off of the starter relay electrical connectors and disconnect the 2 cables (**Figure 37**).

3. Disconnect the starter relay 2-pin connector from the relay.

4. Remove the relay from the rubber mount on the frame.

5. Install the starter relay by reversing these removal steps.

LIGHTING SYSTEM

The lighting system consists of a headlight, taillight and indicator lights. **Table 6** lists replacement bulbs for these components.

Always use the correct wattage bulb as indicated in this section. The use of a larger wattage bulb will give a dim light and a smaller wattage bulb will burn out prematurely.

9

Troubleshooting

If the headlight and/or taillight do not work, refer to *Lighting System* in Chapter Two.

Headlight Bulb Replacement

Refer to **Figure 38** (1993-1995) or **Figure 39** (1996-on) for this procedure.

CAUTION
All models are equipped with quartz-halogen bulbs. Do not touch the bulb glass with your fingers. Traces of oil left on the bulb from your fingers can drastically reduce the life of the bulb. Clean any traces of oil or other chemicals from the bulb with a cloth moistened in alcohol or lacquer thinner.

38

HEADLIGHT (1993-1995)

1. Vertical adjust screw
2. Washer
3. Spring
4. Lens
5. Rubber damper
6. Plate
7. Screw
8. Bulb
9. Bulb holder

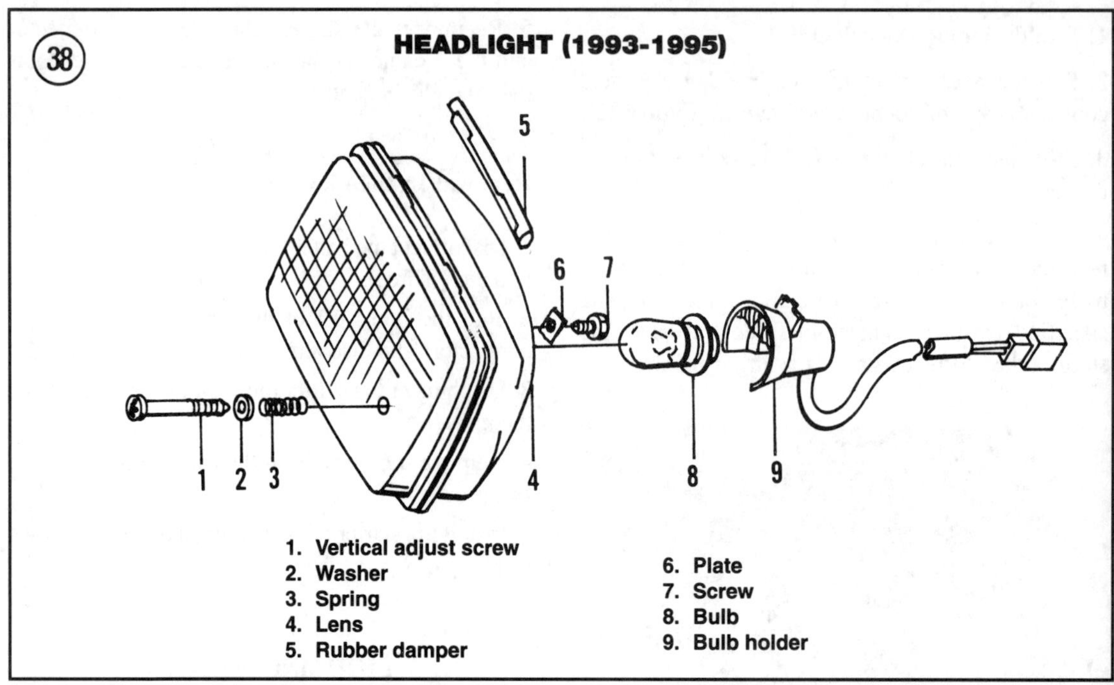

39

HEADLIGHT (1996-ON)

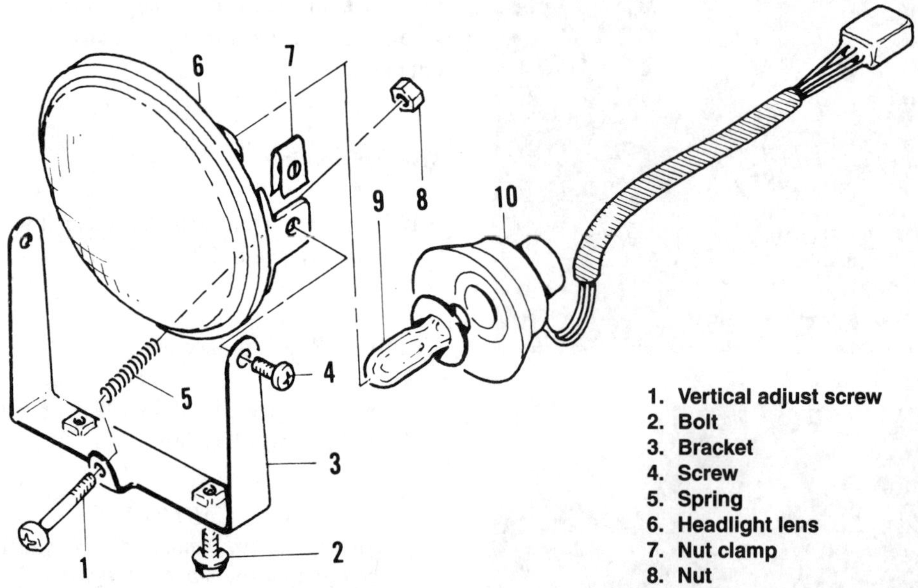

1. Vertical adjust screw
2. Bolt
3. Bracket
4. Screw
5. Spring
6. Headlight lens
7. Nut clamp
8. Nut
9. Bulb
10. Bulb holder

1993-1995 models

1. Remove the screws (**Figure 40**) securing the headlight assembly to the front fender.

2. Partially pull the headlight assembly out of the front fender. Do not pull out too far as the electrical harness wires are not very long.

3. Carefully pull the rubber cover off the socket assembly.

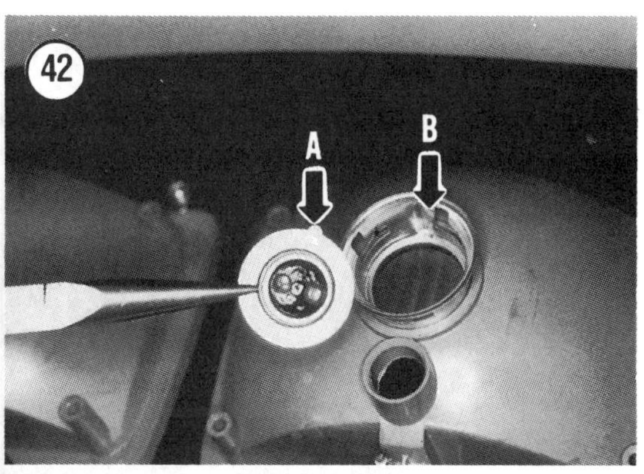

4. Push down and turn the socket (**Figure 41**) *counterclockwise* and remove it from the lens assembly.

5. Remove the bulb from the lens assembly.

6. Replace the bulb by inserting its locating tab (A, **Figure 42**) into the indexed groove in the socket (B, **Figure 42**).

7. Install by reversing these steps. Start the engine and check the headlight operation.

1996-on

1. Carefully pull the rubber cover off the socket assembly.

2. Push down and turn the socket (**Figure 43**) *counterclockwise* and remove it from the lens assembly.

3. Remove the bulb from the lens assembly.

4. Replace the bulb by inserting its locating tab (A, **Figure 42**) into the indexed groove in the socket (B, **Figure 42**).

5. Install by reversing these steps. Start the engine and check the headlight operation.

Headlight Adjustment

The headlight is equipped with a vertical adjust screw located at the base of the headlight. See **Figure 44** (1993-1995) or **Figure 45** (1996-on). There is no horizontal adjustment screw.

Turn the adjust screw *clockwise* to move the light up and *counterclockwise* to move the light down. Repeat for the opposite headlight.

Taillight Bulb and Lens Replacement

Refer to **Figure 46** for this procedure.

1. Remove the 2 screws (**Figure 47**) securing the taillight lens and remove the lens and gasket.

2. Carefully press in on the bulb (A, **Figure 48**) and turn it *counterclockwise* to remove it.

3. Replace the bulb.

4. Install by reversing these steps. Make sure the lens rubber gasket (B, **Figure 48**) is seated all the way around the base plate.

Taillight Assembly Replacement

Refer to **Figure 46** for this procedure.

(43) **HEADLIGHT BULB REPLACEMENT SET (1996-ON)**

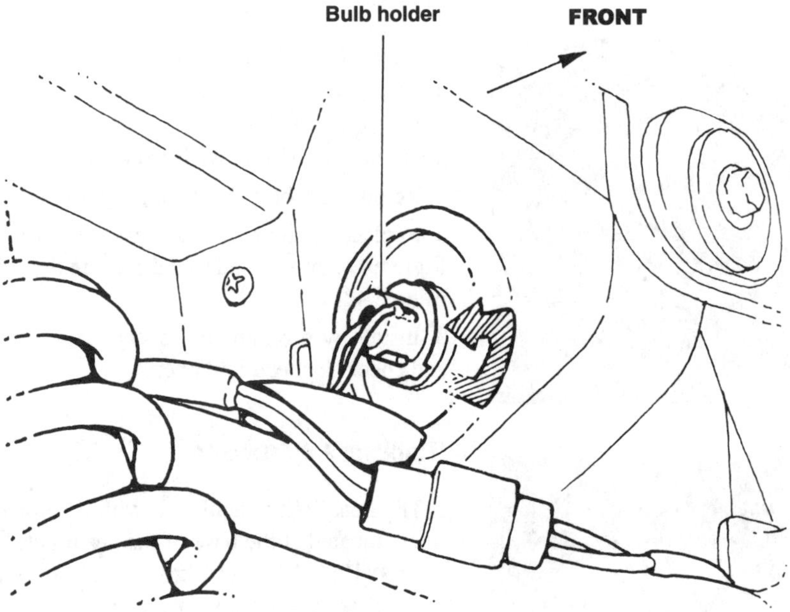

Bulb holder

FRONT

1. Remove the lens and bulb as previously described.

2. Unhook the rubber hooks (C, **Figure 48**) and open the tool box cover.

3. Remove the cap nuts, spring washers, washers, collars, rubber grommets and washers securing the base plate to the tool box cover.

4. Carefully pull the base plate away from the cover and disconnect the electrical connectors from the wiring harness.

5. Install by reversing these removal steps. Make sure the electrical connectors are free of corrosion and are tight.

INDICATOR LIGHTS

Troubleshooting

Refer to *Indicator Light System* in Chapter Two.

46 TAILLIGHT

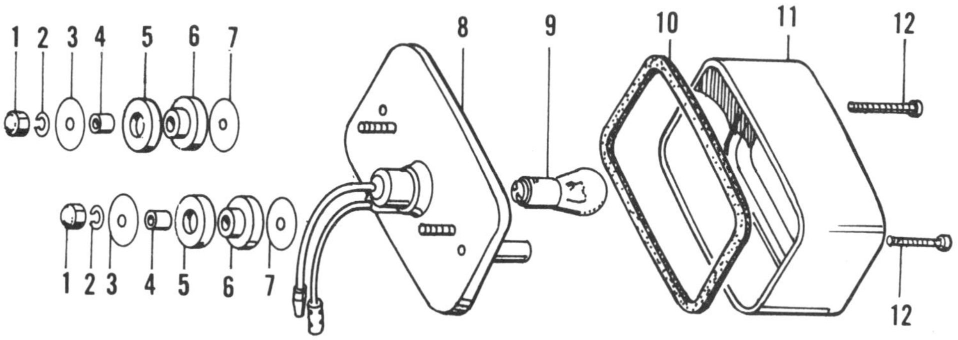

1. Cap nut
2. Spring washer
3. Washer
4. Collar
5. Special washer
6. Rubber cushion
7. Washer
8. Base plate
9. Bulb
10. Gasket
11. Lens
12. Screw

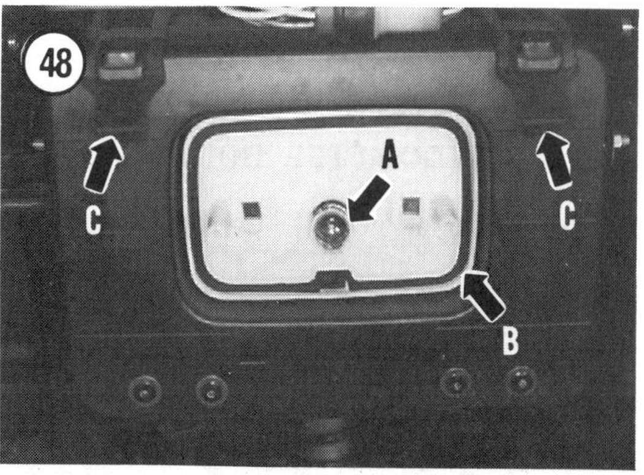

Oil Temperature Light Replacement

The oil temperature light (A, **Figure 49**) is mounted inside the handlebar cover.

1. Carefully pull the handlebar cover (B, **Figure 49**) off of the handlebar.
2. Remove the bulb holder from the handlebar cover and replace the bulb (**Figure 50**). See **Table 6** for bulb specifications.
3. Install by reversing these steps, plus the following.
4. Check the indicator light wire routing when installing the handlebar cover. Do not pinch the wires between the handlebar and cover.

Neutral, Reverse and Speedometer Housing Lights Replacement

The neutral, reverse and speedometer housing lights are located within the speedometer assembly (**Figure 51**) mounted on the handlebar. The neutral and reverse bulbs are indicator lights. The speedometer housing bulb illuminates the speedometer housing for night riding.

1. Carefully pull the handlebar cover (B, **Figure 49**) off of the handlebar and set aside.
2. Remove the clips and washers (A, **Figure 52**) securing the speedometer housing to its mounting bracket.
3. Pull the speedometer housing (B, **Figure 52**) up and off its mounting bracket. Do not disconnect the speedometer cable unless necessary.
4. Withdraw the bulb holder and remove the defective bulb(s). See **Figure 53**. See **Table 6** for bulb specifications.
5. Install the new bulb and install the bulb holder into the speedometer housing.
6. Reverse Steps 1-3 to install the speedometer housing.

SPEEDOMETER HOUSING

Removal/Installation

Refer to **Figure 51** for this procedure

1. Carefully pull the handlebar cover (B, **Figure 49**) off of the handlebar and set aside.
2. Disconnect the speedometer cable (C, **Figure 52**) from the speedometer housing.
3. Remove the clips, washers and dampers (A, **Figure 52**) securing the speedometer housing to its mounting bracket.
4. Pull the speedometer housing (B, **Figure 52**) up and off its mounting bracket.
5. Withdraw the 3 bulb holders (**Figure 53**) and set them aside.
6. Remove the speedometer housing.
7. Install the speedometer housing by reversing these removal steps, plus the following.
8. Seat the speedometer housing onto its damper. Check that there are no gaps or damage that would allow water to leak into the housing.

Speedometer Housing Mounting Bracket Replacement

1. Remove the speedometer (A, **Figure 54**) as described in this chapter.
2. Remove the handlebar (Chapter Ten).
3. Unbolt and remove the speedometer housing mounting bracket (B, **Figure 54**) from the steering stem bracket.
4. Install by reversing these removal steps.

(51)

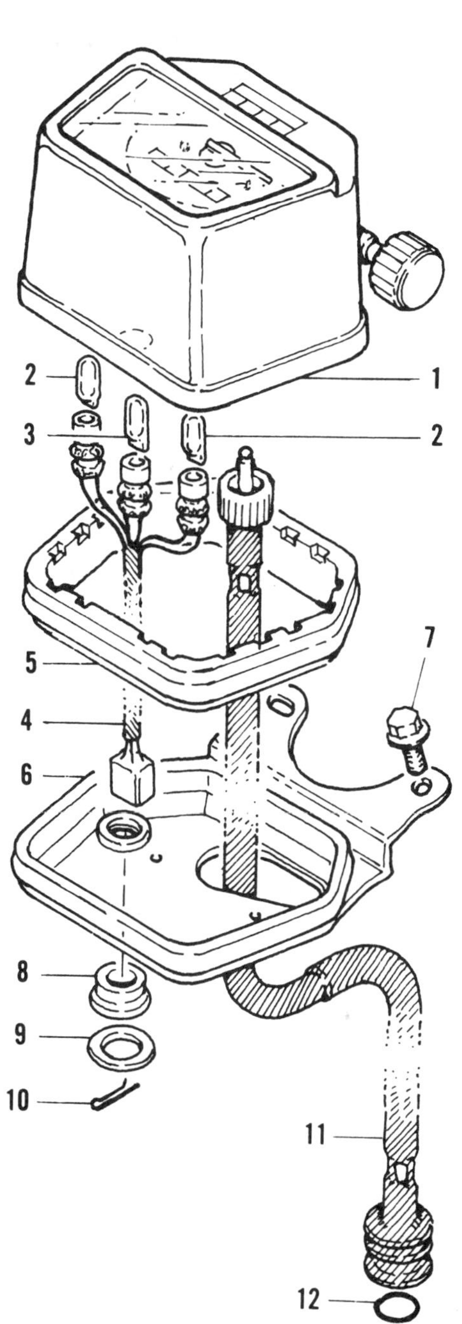

1. Speedometer
2. Bulb
3. Bulb
4. Bulb holder
5. Damper
6. Speedometer housing mounting bracket
7. Bolt
8. Damper
9. Washer
10. Clip
11. Speedometer cable
12. O-ring

SWITCHES

Testing

Switches can be tested for continuity with an ohmmeter (see Chapter One) or a self-powered test lamp at the switch connector plug by operating the switch in each of its operating positions and comparing results with its switch operating diagram. For example, **Figure 55** shows a continuity diagram for the main switch. It shows which terminals should have continuity when the switch is in a given position.

When the main switch is in the ON position, there should be continuity between the brown and red terminals. This is indicated by the line on the continuity diagram. An ohmmeter connected between these 2 terminals should indicate little or no resistance or a test light should light. When the main switch is OFF, there should be no continuity between the same terminals.

When testing switches, note the following:

a. First check the fuse as described under *Fuse* in this chapter.
b. Check the battery as described under *Battery* in Chapter Three. Charge the battery to the correct state of charge, if required.
c. Disconnect the battery negative lead from the battery if the switch connectors are not disconnected from the circuit.

CAUTION
Do not attempt to start the engine with the battery negative lead disconnected.

d. When separating 2 connectors, pull on the connector housings and not the wires.
e. After locating a defective circuit, check the connectors to make sure they are clean and properly connected. Check all wires going into a connector housing to make sure each wire is properly positioned and that the wire end is not loose.
f. Reconnect the connectors by pushing them together until they click or snap into place.

Replace the switch if it does not perform properly. Refer to the following figures when testing the switch:

a. Main (ignition) switch: **Figure 55**.
b. Start switch: **Figure 56**.
c. Engine stop switch: **Figure 57**.

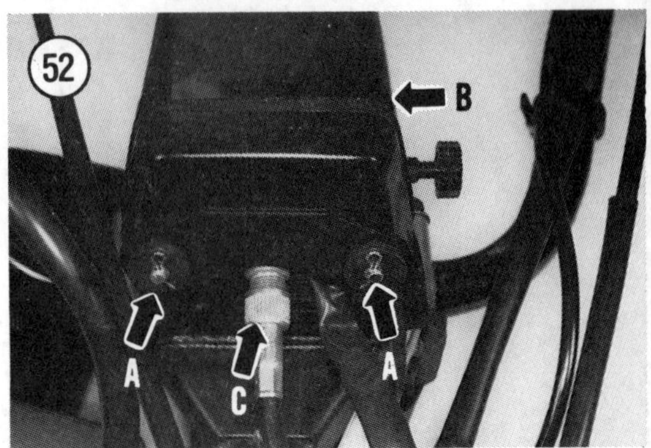

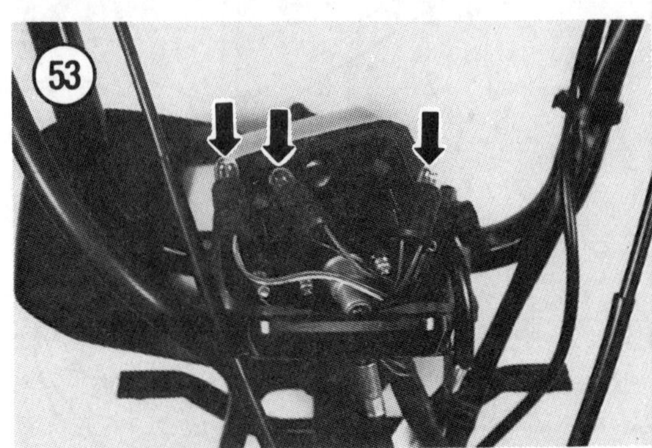

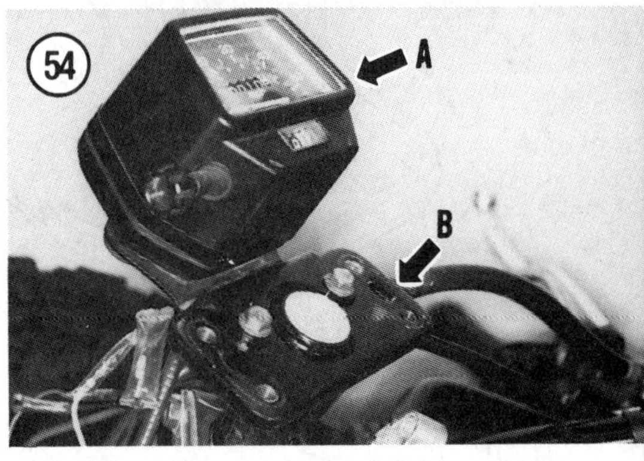

MAIN (IGNITION) SWITCH

	B/W	B	R	Br
OFF	●—	—●		
ON			●—	—●

55

START SWITCH

	B	R/W
OFF		
PUSH	●	●

ENGINE STOP SWITCH

	B/W	B
OFF	●	●
ON		
OFF	●	●

BRAKE SWTCH

	G/Y	B
FREE	●	●
PULL		

HEADLIGHT—TAILLIGHT DIMMER SWITCH

	Br	L	G	Y
OFF				
LO	●	●	●	
HI	●	●		●

d. Brake switch: **Figure 58**.
e. Headlight dimmer switch: **Figure 59**.
f. Reverse switch: **Figure 60**.
g. Neutral switch: **Figure 61**.

Left-hand Handlebar Switch Housing Replacement

The left-hand handlebar switch housing assembly is equipped with the following switches:

a. Light switch (A, **Figure 62**).
b. Engine stop switch (B, **Figure 62**).
c. Starter switch (C, **Figure 62**).

NOTE
The switches mounted in the left-hand handlebar switch housing assembly are not available separately. If one switch is damaged, the complete switch housing must be replaced as an assembly.

1. Remove the front carrier rack and front fender (Chapter Fourteen).
2. Remove or cut any clamps securing the switch wiring harness to the handlebar.

REVERSE SWITCH

	G/Y	B
Forward	●	●
Reverse		

NEUTRAL SWITCH

	Sb	B
In gear		
Neutral	●	●

3. Disconnect the left-hand switch electrical connector.
4. Remove the screws securing the switch to the handlebar.
5. Pivot the switch to the open position (**Figure 63**) and remove the switch assembly from the handlebar.
6. Install by reversing these steps.
7. Start the engine and check each switch function.

Brake Switch

The brake light switch (**Figure 64**) is mounted in the left-hand brake lever assembly.
1. Remove the front carrier rack and front fender (Chapter Fourteen).
2. Remove or cut any clamps securing the switch wiring harness to the handlebar.
3. Disconnect the left-hand switch electrical connector.
4. Depress the switch locking tab and remove the switch (**Figure 64**) from the brake lever assembly.
5. Install by reversing these steps.
6. Start the engine and check the brake light switch operation.

Main Switch Replacement

The main switch (A, **Figure 65**) is mounted in handlebar cover.
1. Loosen the main switch plastic nut (A, **Figure 65**).
2. Carefully pull the handlebar cover (B, **Figure 65**) off of the handlebar.
3. Disconnect the main switch electrical connector.
4. Remove the plastic nut and remove the main switch (**Figure 66**).
5. Install a new main switch by reversing these removal steps, plus the following.
6. Align the square tab on the main switch with the square hole in the handlebar cover when installing the main switch.

Neutral Switch Testing/Replacement

The neutral switch is mounted on the left crankcase half, just in front of the shift lever shaft (**Figure 67**).
1. Disconnect the neutral switch electrical connector at the switch (**Figure 67**). Connect an ohmmeter (set

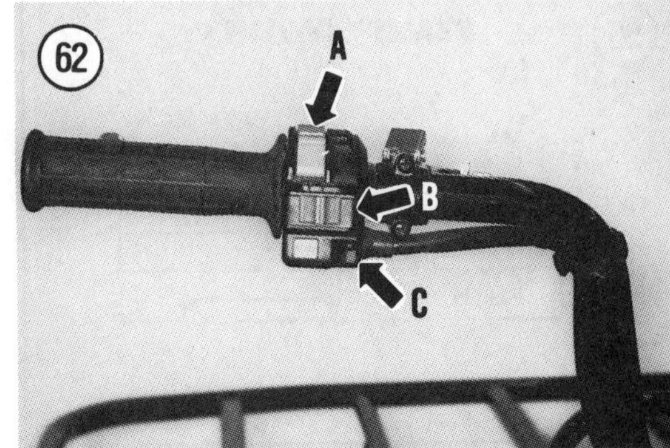

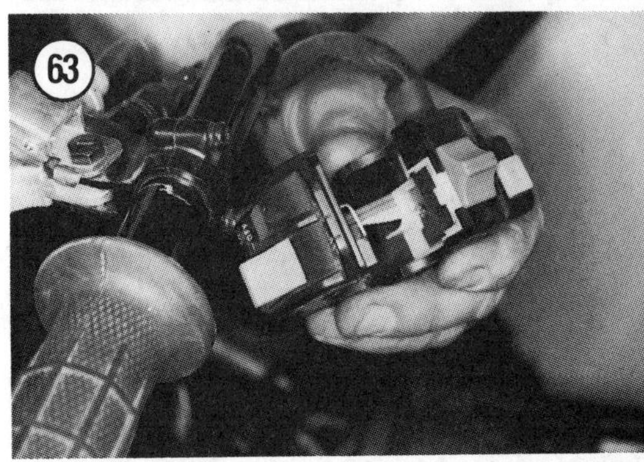

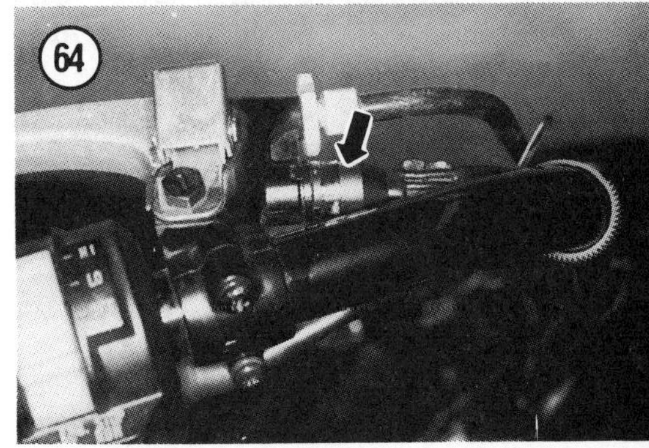

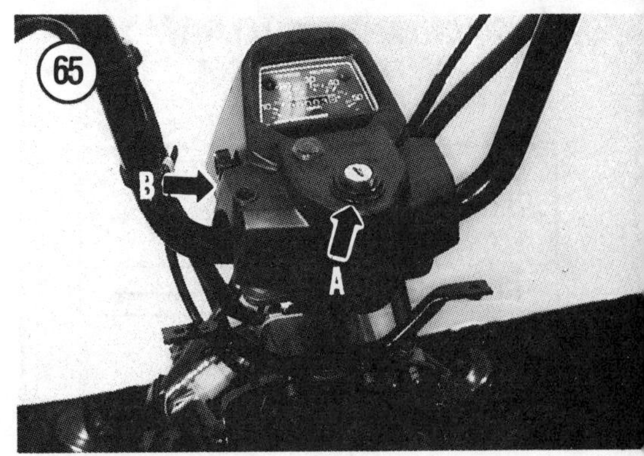

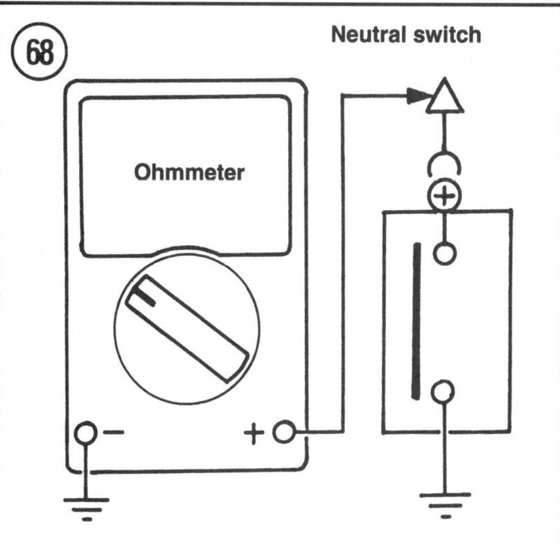

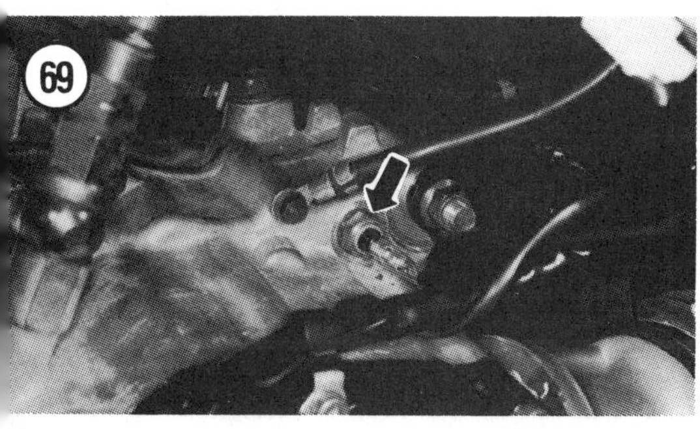

on R × 1) between the neutral switch lead (on the switch) and ground as shown in **Figure 68**. With the transmission in NEUTRAL, the ohmmeter should show continuity (0 ohms). With the transmission in gear, the ohmmeter should read infinity. If the meter reading is incorrect for one or both tests, neutral switch is faulty and should be replaced.

2. To replace neutral switch:
   a. Drain the engine oil and remove the oil filter as described in Chapter Three.
   b. Loosen and remove the neutral switch (**Figure 67**).
   c. Install the neutral switch and tighten securely.
3. Make sure the electrical connector is free of corrosion, then reconnect the neutral switch wire at the switch.
4. Refill the engine oil as described in Chapter Three.

Reverse Switch Testing/Replacement

The reverse switch is mounted at the rear left-hand crankcase just behind the engine ground strap (**Figure 69**).

1. Disconnect the reverse switch green/yellow wire (**Figure 69**) from the wiring harness. Connect an ohmmeter (set on R × 1) between the switch lead and ground as shown in **Figure 70**. With the range select lever (**Figure 71**) in the HI or the LO forward position, the ohmmeter should show continuity (0 ohms). With the select lever in the REVERSE position, the ohmmeter should show infinity. If the meter reading is incorrect for one or both tests, the reverse switch is faulty and should be replaced.

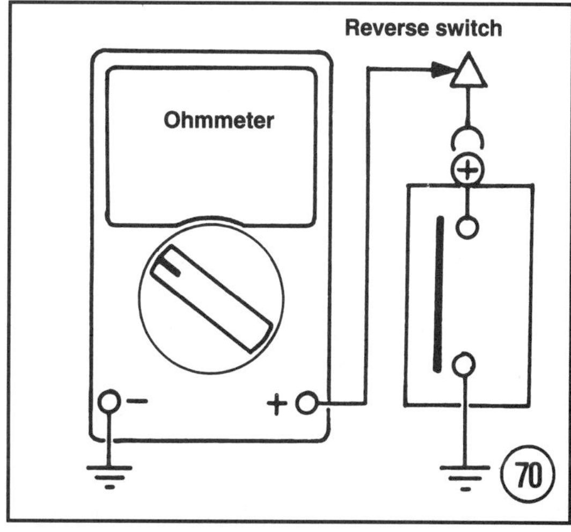

2. To replace reverse switch:

   a. Disconnect the wire connector from the reverse switch.

   b. Loosen, then remove the reverse switch (**Figure 69**).

   c. Install the reverse switch and tighten securely.

3. Make sure the electrical connector is free of corrosion, then reconnect the reverse switch wire at the switch.

RELAYS

Reverse Relay Testing/Replacement

The reverse relay (A, **Figure 72**) is mounted on top of the tool box.

1. Remove the rear carrier rack and rear fender (Chapter Fourteen).

2. Disconnect the electrical connector from the reverse relay (A, **Figure 72**) and remove the relay from the frame.

3. Switch an ohmmeter to the R × 1 scale and connect it to the reverse relay contacts as shown in **Figure 73**. See **Table 5** for the correct resistance reading. Disconnect the ohmmeter leads and note the following:

   a. If the reading is correct, perform Step 4.

   b. If the reading is incorrect, replace the reverse relay.

WARNING
Sparks may be produced when connecting and disconnecting the battery leads in Step 4. Perform this step away from all flammable materials to prevent an explosion and fire.

4. Connect an ohmmeter and 12-volt battery to the reverse relay contacts as shown in **Figure 74**. The ohmmeter should read infinity with the battery connected and zero ohms with the battery leads disconnected. Disconnect the ohmmeter leads. If either reading does not meet specifications, replace the reverse relay.

5. Reverse these steps to install the reverse relay.

Starter Circuit Cutoff Relay Testing/Replacement

The starter circuit cutoff relay (B, **Figure 72**) is mounted on top of the tool box.

1. Remove the rear carrier rack and rear fender (Chapter Fourteen).

2. Disconnect the electrical connector from the starter circuit cutoff relay (B, **Figure 72**) and remove the relay from the frame.

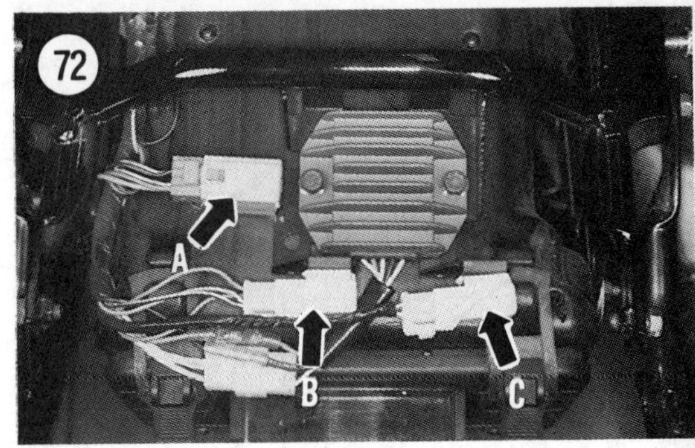

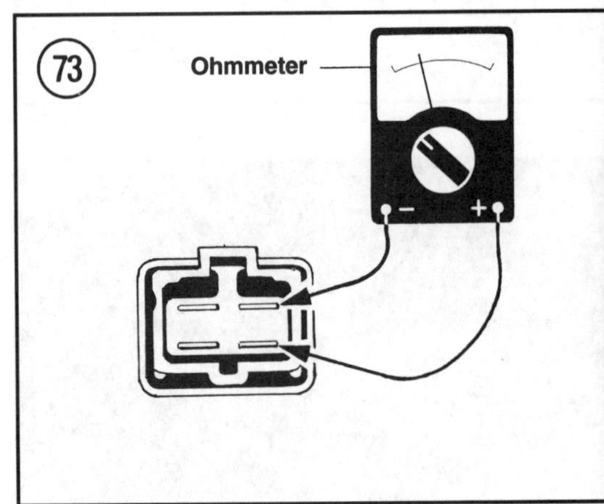

3. Switch an ohmmeter to the R × 1 scale and connect it to the starter circuit cutoff relay contacts as shown in **Figure 73**. See **Table 5** for the correct resistance reading. Disconnect the ohmmeter leads and note the following:

  a. If the reading is correct, perform Step 4.
  b. If the reading is incorrect, replace the starter circuit cutoff relay.

WARNING
Sparks may be produced when connecting and disconnecting the battery leads in Step 4. Perform this step away from all flammable materials to prevent an explosion and fire.

4. Connect an ohmmeter and 12-volt battery to the starter circuit cutoff relay contacts as shown in **Figure 74**. The ohmmeter should read infinity with the battery connected and zero ohms with the battery leads disconnected. Disconnect the ohmmeter leads. If either reading does not meet specifications, replace the starter circuit cutoff relay.
5. Reverse these steps to install the starter circuit cutoff relay.

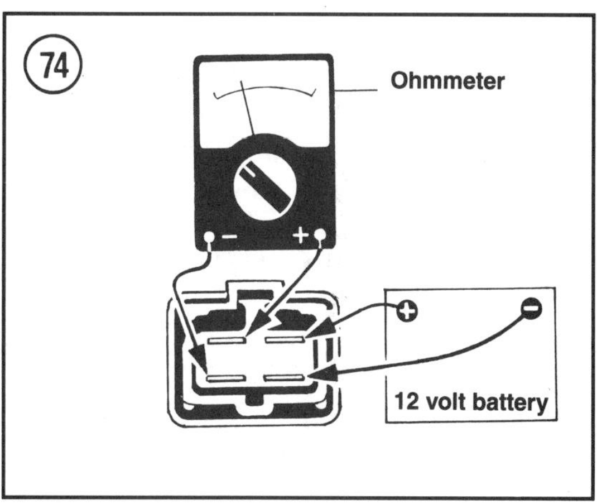

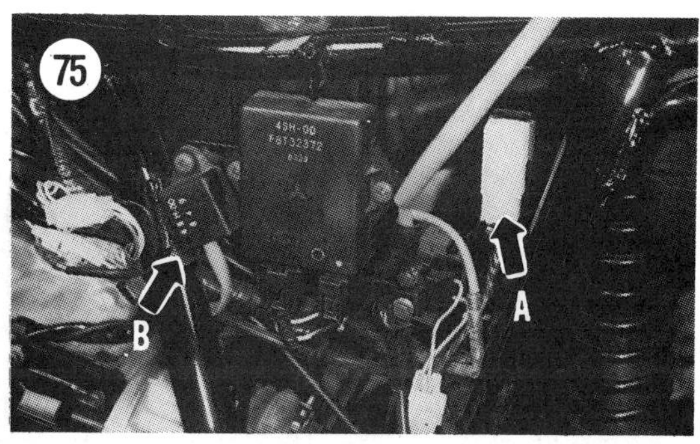

Neutral Relay

The neutral relay (C, **Figure 72**) is mounted on top of the tool box.

1. Remove the rear carrier rack and rear fender (Chapter Fourteen).
2. Disconnect the electrical connector from the neutral relay (C, **Figure 72**) and remove the relay from the frame.
3. Switch an ohmmeter to the R × 1 scale and connect it to the neutral relay contacts as shown in **Figure 73**. See **Table 5** for the correct resistance reading. Disconnect the ohmmeter leads and note the following:

  a. If the reading is correct, perform Step 4.
  b. If the reading is incorrect, replace the neutral relay.

WARNING
Sparks may be produced when connecting and disconnecting the battery leads in Step 4. Perform this step away from all flammable materials to prevent an explosion and fire.

4. Connect an ohmmeter and 12-volt battery to the neutral relay contacts as shown in **Figure 74**. The ohmmeter should read infinity with the battery connected and zero ohms with the battery leads disconnected. Disconnect the ohmmeter leads. If either reading does not meet specifications, replace the neutral relay.
5. Reverse these steps to install the neutral relay.

Fan Motor Relay

The fan motor relay is mounted on the left side of the vehicle. A, **Figure 75** shows the fan motor relay mounting position for 1996 and later models. On 1993-1995 models, the fan motor relay is mounted on the left side of the CDI unit.

1. Remove the rear carrier rack and rear fender (Chapter Fourteen).
2. Disconnect the electrical connector from the fan motor relay (A, **Figure 75**) and remove the relay from the frame.
3. Switch an ohmmeter to the R × 1 scale and connect it to the fan motor relay contacts as shown in **Figure 73**. See **Table 5** for the correct resistance reading. Disconnect the ohmmeter leads and note the following:

  a. If the reading is correct, perform Step 4.

9

b. If the reading is incorrect, replace the fan motor relay.

WARNING
Sparks may be produced when connecting and disconnecting the battery leads in Step 4. Perform this step away from all flammable materials to prevent an explosion and fire.

4. Connect an ohmmeter and 12-volt battery to the fan motor relay contacts as shown in **Figure 74**. The ohmmeter should read infinity with the battery connected and zero ohms with the battery leads disconnected. Disconnect the ohmmeter leads. If either reading does not meet specifications, replace the fan motor relay.
5. Reverse these steps to install the fan motor relay.

FAN MOTOR CONTROL UNIT

Testing/Replacement

The fan motor control unit (B, **Figure 75**) is mounted on the left side of the vehicle.

1. Remove the rear carrier rack and rear fender (Chapter Fourteen).
2. Connect a jumper wire between the fan motor control unit white/green wire and ground (**Figure 76**). Then turn the main switch on and note the following:
   a. If the fan motor turns, the fan motor control unit is good.
   b. If the fan motor does not turn, the fan motor control unit is faulty and must be replaced as described in Step 3.
   c. Turn the main switch off and disconnect the jumper wire.
3. Disconnect and remove the fan motor control unit (B, **Figure 75**).
4. Reverse these steps to install a new fan motor control unit.

THERMO UNIT

Removal/Installation

The thermo unit (**Figure 77**) is mounted in the top of the left crankcase.

1. Disconnect the electrical connector from the thermo unit.
2. Loosen and remove the thermo unit (**Figure 77**).
3. Install by reversing these steps. Tighten the thermo unit securely.

Testing

A specific procedure for testing the thermo unit is not available. If the fan motor does not run, perform the *Cooling System Testing* procedure in Chapter Two. During this procedure, all of the cooling system components parts are tested individually. If all of the parts are eliminated as the source of the

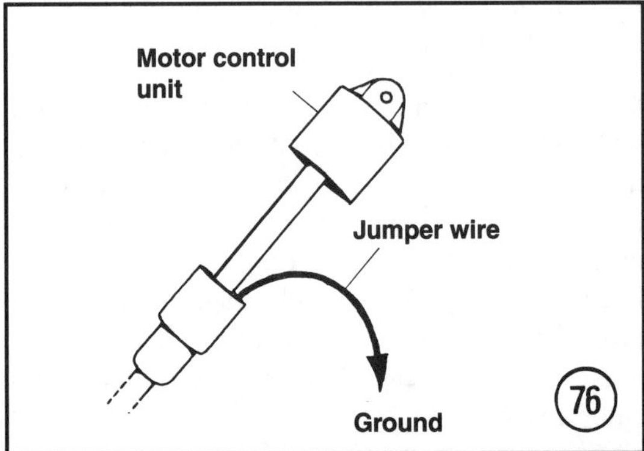

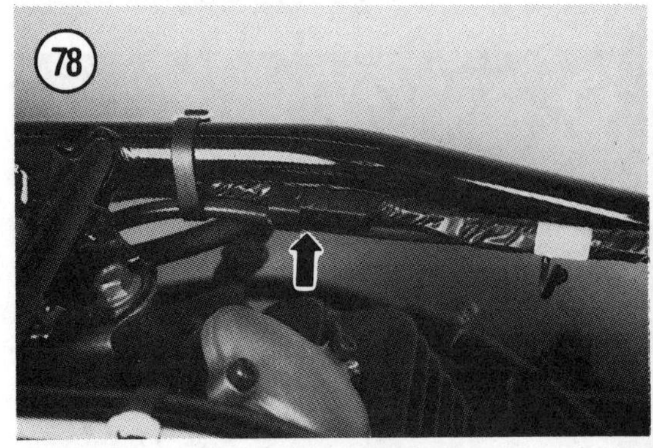

problem, the thermo unit can be considered defective by a process of elimination.

DIODE

The diode (**Figure 78**) is plugged into the part of the wiring harness that is routed along the upper right frame rail.

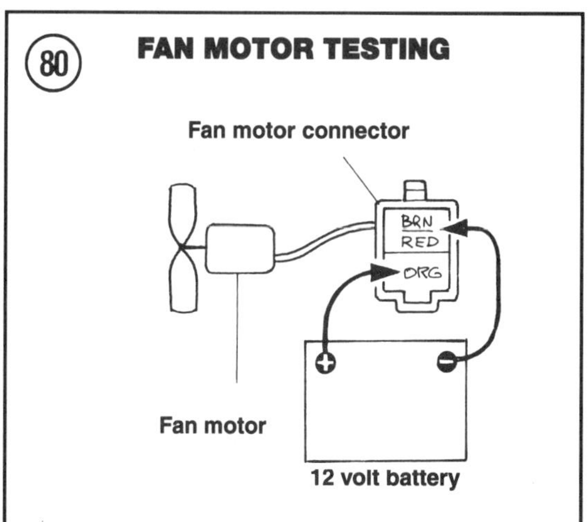

ELECTRIC FAN TESTING

The electric fan is mounted at the front of the vehicle, directly behind the oil cooler. **Figure 79** shows the electric fan with the oil cooler removed for clarity.

1. Remove the front fender (Chapter Fourteen).
2. Disconnect the fan motor electrical connector.

WARNING
Sparks may be produced when connecting and disconnecting the battery leads in Step 3. Perform this step away from all flammable materials to prevent an explosion and fire.

3. Momentarily connect a 12-volt battery to the fan motor electrical connector as shown in **Figure 80**. The fan motor should start. If the fan motor did not run, replace the fan motor as described under *Electric Fan* in Chapter Five.
4. Reverse Steps 1 and 2.

FUSES

A single main fuse is installed in the wiring system to prevent excessive current from destroying the wiring system and possibly causing the vehicle to catch fire.

Whenever a fuse blows, find out the reason for the failure before replacing the fuse. Usually, the trouble is a short circuit in the wiring. This may be caused by worn-through insulation or a disconnected wire shorted to ground. **Table 1** lists the fuse ratings for all models.

When replacing a blown fuse, purchase an additional spare fuse and carry it on the vehicle.

If the new fuse blows immediately after installing it, there is a short circuit in the wiring system.

CAUTION
Always turn the main switch off before replacing a fuse.

Main Fuse (1993-1995)

These models use a 30 amp glass type fuse.

1. The main fuse is mounted on the right side of the vehicle. If necessary, remove the rear fender assembly.
2. Open the fuse holder (**Figure 81**) and remove the fuse.

9

3. Install the new fuse and close the fuse holder.

Main Fuse (1996-on)

These models use a 30 amp blade-type fuse.

1. Remove the seat.
2. Open the fuse holder and remove the fuse (**Figure 82**).
3. Install the new fuse and close the fuse holder.

CIRCUIT BREAKER

A circuit breaker is installed in the fan circuit. If the fan motor does not turn, remove and test the circuit breaker as follows.

Replacement/Testing

1. Remove the front fender (Chapter Fourteen).
2. The circuit breaker is installed in the wiring system at the front of the vehicle. Remove the tape holding the circuit breaker (**Figure 83**) to the wiring harness, then disconnect and remove it.
3. Inspect the circuit breaker (**Figure 84**) for burns or other damage.
4. Switch an ohmmeter to the R × 1 scale. With the circuit breaker removed from the wiring harness, connect the ohmmeter between the circuit breaker leads as shown in **Figure 85**. The reading should be zero ohms. Replace the circuit breaker if its resistance is not as specified.
5. Reverse Steps 1 and 2 to install the circuit breaker.

WIRING DIAGRAMS

Wiring diagrams for all models are located at the end of this book.

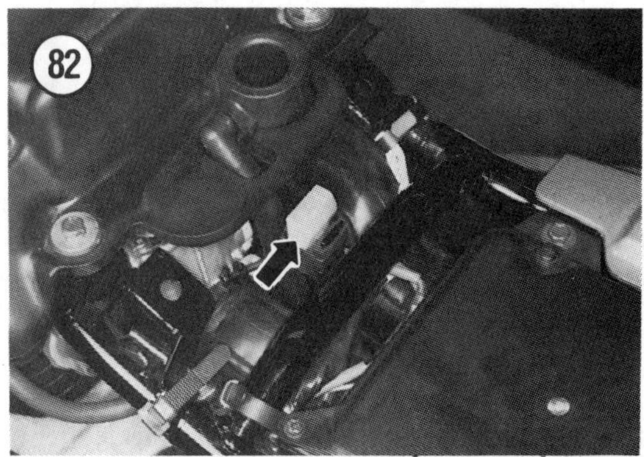

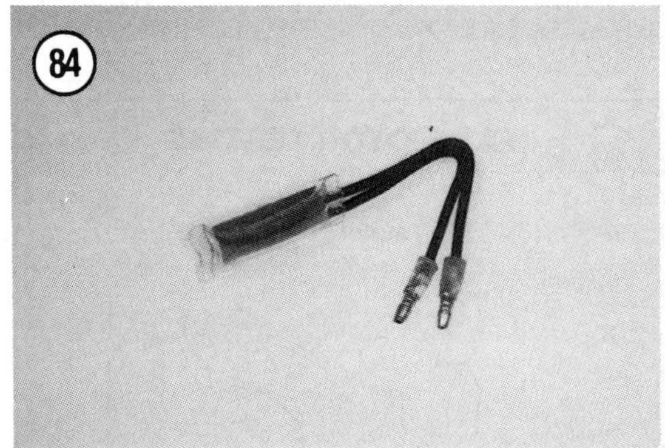

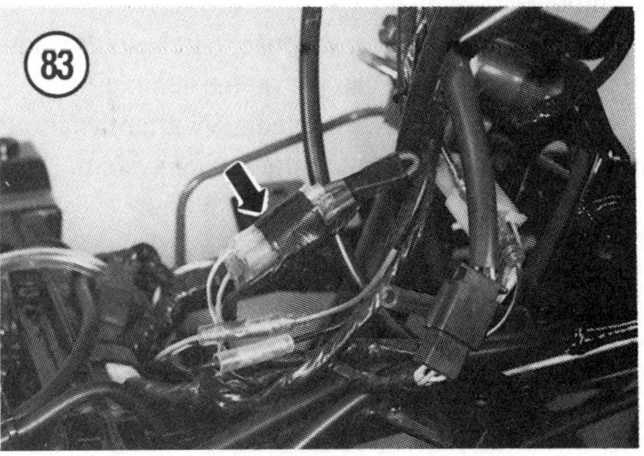

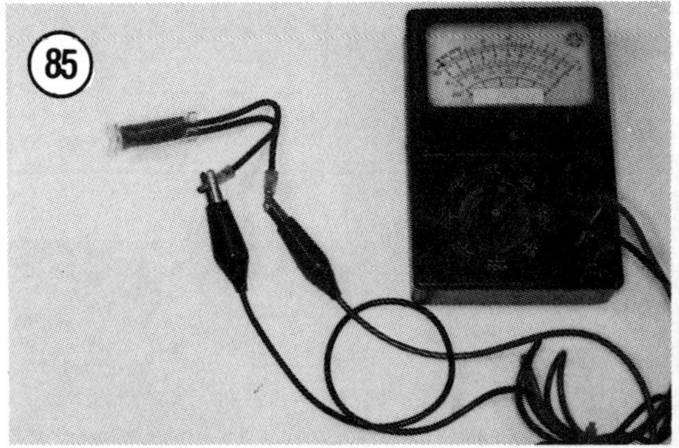

Table 1 ELECTRICAL SYSTEM GENERAL SPECIFICATIONS

Item	Specification
Battery capacity	
1993-1995	12 volt, 14 amp hour
1996-on	12 volt, 18 amp hour
Battery type	
1993-1995	GM14AZ-4A
1996-on	YTX20L-BS
CDI magneto	
Type	CDI magneto generator
Fuse size	
Main	30 amp
Fan motor	20 amp

Table 2 CHARGING SYSTEM TEST SPECIFICATIONS

Item	Specification
Type	AC magneto generator
Nominal output	12 volts, 17 amps @ 3,000 rpm
Stator coil	
Resistance	0.70-0.86 ohms*
Wire colors	white to white
Rectifier	
Capacity	
1993-1995	15 amps
1996-on	20 amps
Withstand voltage	200 volts

* For accurate resistance readings, perform tests at 20° C (68° F).

Table 3 IGNITION SYSTEM TEST SPECIFICATIONS

Item	Specification*
Ignition coil	
Minimum spark gap	6 mm (0.24 in.)
Primary resistance	0.36-0.48 ohms
Secondary resistance	5440-7360 ohms
Spark plug cap resistance	10,000 ohms
Pickup coil resistance/wire color	
1993-1995	171-209 ohms (red to white)
1996-on	459-561 ohms (red to white)
Source coil resistance/wire color	270-330 ohms (brown to green)

* For accurate resistance readings, perform tests at 20° C (68° F).

Table 4 STARTER SYSTEM TEST SPECIFICATIONS

Item	Specification
Starter motor	
Output	0.7 killowatts
Armature coil resistance*	0.011-0.013 ohms
Brush length	
New	12 mm (0.47 in.)
Service limit	8.5 mm (0.33 in.)
Spring force	650-950 g (22.9-33.5 oz.)

(continued)

9

Table 4 STARTER SYSTEM TEST SPECIFICATIONS (continued)

Item	Specification
Commutator	
Outer diameter	
New	28 mm (1.10 in.)
Minimum	27 mm (1.06 in.)
Mica undercut	0.6 mm (0.02 in.)
Starter relay	
Amperage rating	
1993-1995	150 amps
1996-on	100 amps
Coil winding resistance/wire colors*	
1993-1995	3.06-3.74 ohms (blue/white to red/white)
1996-on	4.18-4.62 ohms (blue/white to red/white)

* For accurate resistance, all components must be tested at 20° C (68° F).

Table 5 RELAY TEST SPECIFICATIONS

Item	Specification*
Fan motor relay resistance	72-88
Neutral relay resistance	72-88
Reverse relay resistance	72-88
Starter circuit cutoff relay resistance	72-88

* For accurate resistance, all components must be tested at 20° C (68° F).

Table 6 REPLACEMENT BULBS

Item	Specification
Headlight	
1993-1995	12 volt, 25/25 watt
1996-on	12 volt, 30/30 watt
Taillight	12 volt, 7.5 watt
Meter light	12 volt, 3.4 watt
Indicator lights	
Neutral	
1993-1995	12 volt, 3.4 watt
1996-on	12 volt, 1.7 watt
Oil temperature	12 volt, 3.4 watt
Reverse	
1993-1995	12 volt, 3.4 watt
1996-on	12 volt, 1.7 watt

CHAPTER TEN

FRONT SUSPENSION AND STEERING

This chapter describes repair and maintenance of the front wheels, hubs, front control arms and steering components.

Refer to **Table 1** for general front suspension and steering specifications. **Tables 2-4** list service specifications and torque specifications. **Tables 1-4** are located at the end of this chapter.

FRONT WHEEL

Removal/Installation

1. Park the vehicle on level ground and set the parking brake. Block the rear wheels so the vehicle cannot roll in either direction.

2. Mark the front tires with an L (left side) or R (right side) so they can be installed onto the same side of the vehicle from which they were removed.
3. Loosen the lug nuts (**Figure 1**) securing the wheel to the hub/brake drum.
4. Raise the front of the vehicle so the front wheel(s) is off the ground. Support the vehicle with safety stands or wooden blocks. Make sure they are properly placed before beginning work.
5. Remove the lug nuts and remove the front wheel.
6. Clean the wheel lug nuts in solvent and dry thoroughly.
7. Inspect the wheel for cracks, bending or other damage. If necessary, replace the wheel as described under *Tires and Wheels* in this chapter.
8. Install the wheel onto the studs. The rotation arrow (**Figure 2**) on each tire must face forward.
9. Install the lug nuts with their tapered end (**Figure 3**) facing toward the wheel. Tighten the nuts finger-tight to center the wheel squarely against the brake drum.
10. Tighten the front wheel lug nuts (**Figure 1**) as specified in **Table 4**.
11. Rotate the wheel, then apply the front brake several times to make sure that the wheel rotates freely and that the brake is operating correctly.

12. Measure wheel runout using a dial indicator as described in this chapter.
13. Raise the front of the vehicle and remove the safety stands or wooden blocks.
14. Lower the vehicle so both front wheels are on the ground and remove the jack.

FRONT BRAKE DRUM INSPECTION

Inspection (Hub Installed)

Inspect the wheel hub and follows:

CAUTION
Do not remove the wheel bearings for inspection purposes as they can be damaged during the removal process. Remove the wheel bearings only if they must replaced.

1. Check that wheel nuts (**Figure 1**) are tightened as specified in **Table 4**.
2. Park the vehicle on level ground and set the parking brake. Block the rear wheels so the vehicle cannot roll in either direction.
3. Raise the front of the vehicle so the front wheels are off the ground. Support the vehicle with safety stands or wooden blocks. Make sure they are properly placed before beginning work.

NOTE
Operating a dial indicator against a dented rim will not provide an accurate runout indication for the front bearings in Step 4. If the rim is not smooth, remove the front wheel and inspect the bearings by turning the front hub/brake drum by hand.

4. Mount a dial indicator against the rim as shown in **Figure 4**. Turn the tire slowly by hand and measure the wheel's radial (up-and-down) and lateral (side-to-side) runout. See **Table 2** for specifications.
   a. If runout limit is excessive, first check for a bent or damaged wheel.
   b. Next, remove the wheel and turn the brake drum by hand. The brake drum should turn smoothly without excessive play or other abnormal conditions. If the brake drum does not turn smoothly, remove the front hub/brake drum assembly and check the bearings located in the steering knuckle. Refer to *Steering Knuckle* in this chapter.

FRONT HUB/BRAKE DRUM

Removal/Installation

The front hub is an integral part of the brake drum. Refer to Chapter Thirteen for the front hub/brake drum removal and installation procedure.

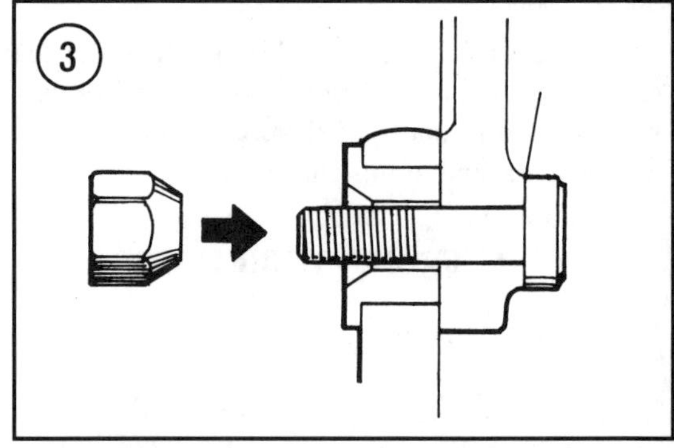

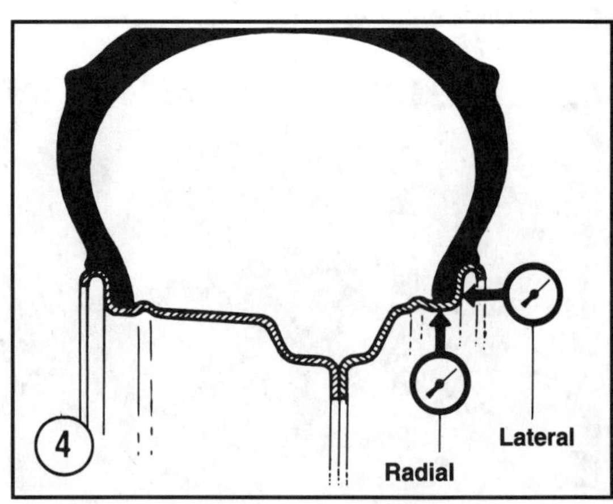

Front Wheel Bearings

The front wheel bearings are mounted inside the steering knuckle assembly. Refer to *Steering Knuckle* in this chapter for all service procedures.

SHOCK ABSORBER

Spring Preload Adjustment

A cam mounted at the bottom of each shock spring allows the springs to be adjusted to 5 preload positions (**Figure 5**). The No. 1 position is soft and the No. 5 position is hard. Turn the cam to adjust the spring preload position. Set both front shock absorbers to the same preload position.

Removal/Installation

1. Remove the front wheel(s) as described in this chapter.
2. Remove the upper and lower shock absorber mounting nuts and bolts and remove the shock absorber. See **Figure 6**.

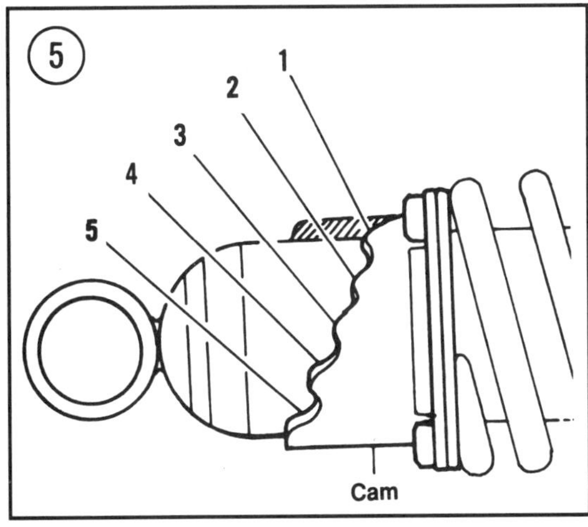

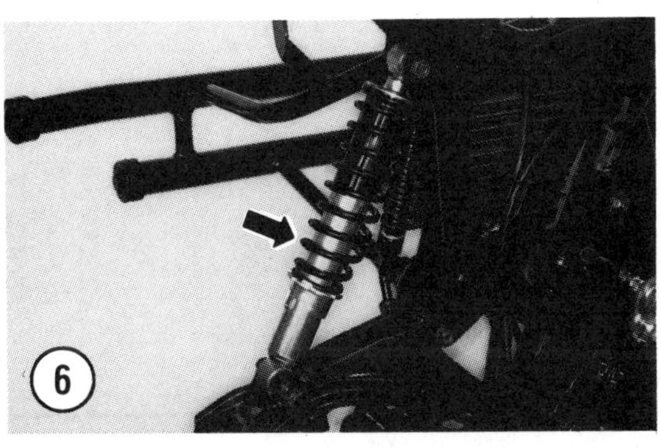

3. Inspect the shock absorber as described in this section.
4. Clean and dry the shock mounting nuts and bolts.
5. Lubricate the shock bolts with grease.
6. Install the shock mounting bolts from the front side.
7. Tighten the upper and lower shock mounting nuts as specified in **Table 4**.
8. Repeat for the other side as required.

Inspection

The stock shock absorbers cannot be disassembled. If any part of the shock is damaged or if the damper is leaking, replace it.

1. Check the damper unit for dents, fluid leakage or other damage.

WARNING
The stock shock absorbers are permanently sealed and should not be disassembled. Doing so can release gas that is under pressure and cause possible eye injury.

2. Check the shock absorber bushings for deterioration,excessive wear or other damage. If either bushing is worn or damaged, replace the shock absorber.

STEERING KNUCKLE

Refer to **Figure 7** when servicing the steering knuckle.

Removal

1. Remove the front wheel as described in this chapter.
2. Remove the brake drum and backing plate (A, **Figure 8**) as described in Chapter Thirteen.
3. Remove the shock absorber as described in this chapter.
4. Remove the metal boot protector, if used.
5. Unbolt the front brake hydraulic and vent hose bracket and move it out of the way.

CAUTION
Do not drive the ball joints out of the steering knuckle with a hammer. Doing so will damage the ball joint stud and threads.

6. Disconnect the tie rod ball joint from the steering knuckle as follows:

   a. Remove the cotter pin from the tie rod ball joint stud (**Figure 9**). Discard the cotter pin.

   b. Loosen the tie rod mounting nut and then turn it an additional 5-6 turns so it is positioned away from the steering knuckle. Do not remove the nut completely.

NOTE

By leaving the tie rod nut installed on the stud, it can chase the tie rod threads if minor thread damage occurs when using the puller. Also, the nut prevents the tie rod from flying out of the steering knuckle when it breaks loose. This helps to prevent damage to the ball joint stud threads and rubber boot.

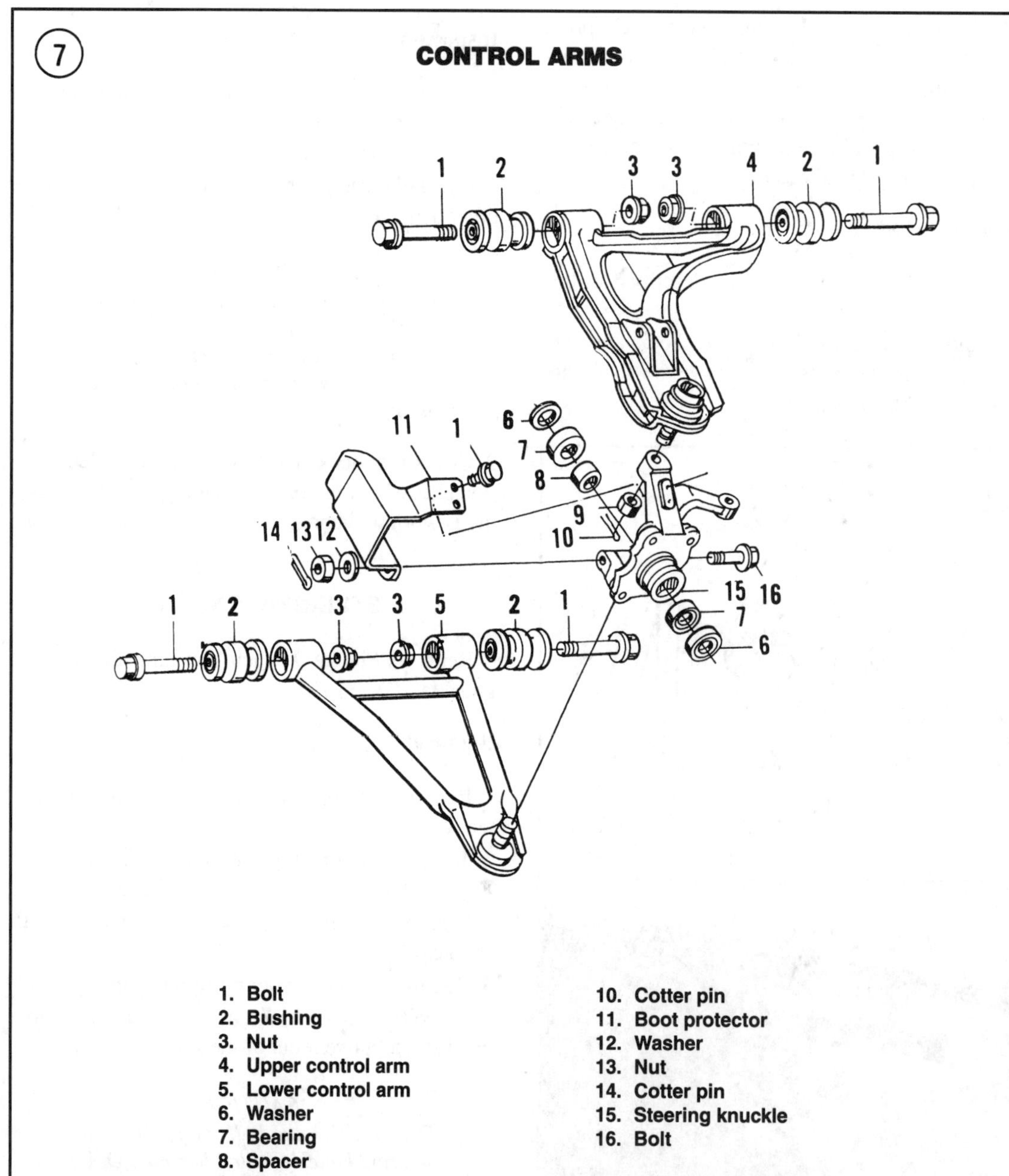

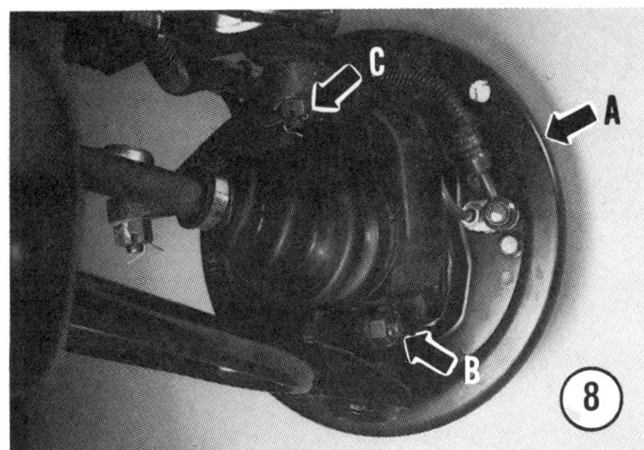

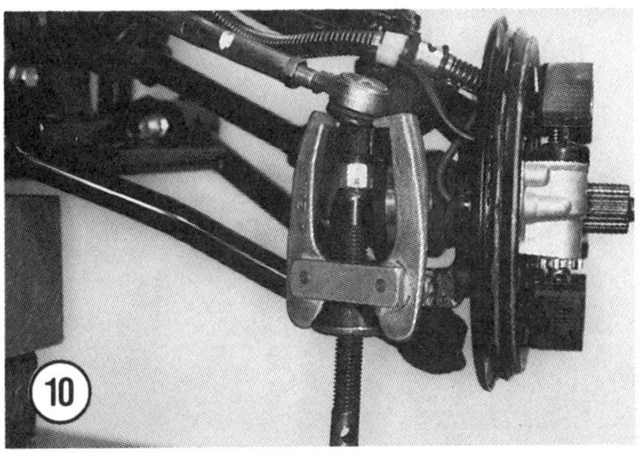

c. Install a 2-jaw puller onto the steering knuckle and center the puller's pressure bolt against the ball joint stud (**Figure 10**). Position the puller arms so that it does not pinch the ball joint rubber seal (**Figure 11**).

d. Operate the puller and apply pressure against the ball joint stud. When the ball joint stud is under pressure, strike the top of the puller with a hammer to free the ball joint from the steering knuckle.

7. Disconnect the lower control arm ball joint from the steering knuckle as follows:

a. Remove the cotter pin, nut, washer and bolt (B, **Figure 8**) from the lower control arm pinch bolt.

b. Separate the lower arm ball joint from the steering knuckle.

8. Disconnect the upper control arm ball joint from the steering knuckle as follows:

a. Remove the cotter pin from the upper control arm ball joint stud (C, **Figure 8**). Discard the cotter pin.

b. Loosen the upper control arm ball joint mounting nut and then turn it an additional 5-6 turns so that it positioned away from the steering knuckle. Do not remove the nut completely.

c. Use a puller as described in Step 5 to separate the upper arm ball joint from the steering knuckle. If there is not enough room to mount a puller onto the steering knuckle, continue with substep d.

d. Remove the upper control arm from the frame as described in this chapter.

e. Carefully pull the steering knuckle and upper arm (**Figure 12**) out and off of the front axle. Rest the front axle on the lower control arm.

f. Use a 2-jaw puller as described in Step 5 to separate the upper arm ball joint from the steering knuckle.

9. Remove the steering knuckle.

Inspection

1. Inspect the steering knuckle (**Figure 13**) for bending, thread damage, cracks or other damage.

2. Inspect the steering knuckle seals (**Figure 14** and **Figure 15**). Replace if they are deteriorated or starting to harden.

3. Turn each bearing inner race (**Figure 16**). Each bearing should turn smoothly without excessive play or noise.
4. If necessary, replace the seals and bearings as described under *Seal and Bearing Replacement* in this section.
5. Check the ball joint tapered holes for cracks, excessive wear or other damage.
6. Check the backing plate threaded holes for thread damage or other damage.

Seal andBearing Replacement

The front wheel bearings are installed in the steering knuckle. Always replace both bearings at the same time.

Refer to **Figure 17** for this procedure.

1. Remove the steering knuckle as described in this chapter.
2. Remove both seals (**Figure 14** and **Figure 15**) from the steering knuckle.

NOTE
If the bearings are not going to be replaced, install the new seals starting with Step 13.

3. Mount the steering knuckle in a vise with soft jaws.
4. Insert a steel or brass drift into one side of the knuckle and push the spacer over to one side, then place the drift on the inner race of the inner bearing. Tap the bearing out of the hub using a hammer working around the perimeter of the inner race.
5. Remove the spacer.
6. Insert a bearing driver through the steering knuckle and drive out the opposite bearing.
7. Clean and dry the steering knuckle and spacer.

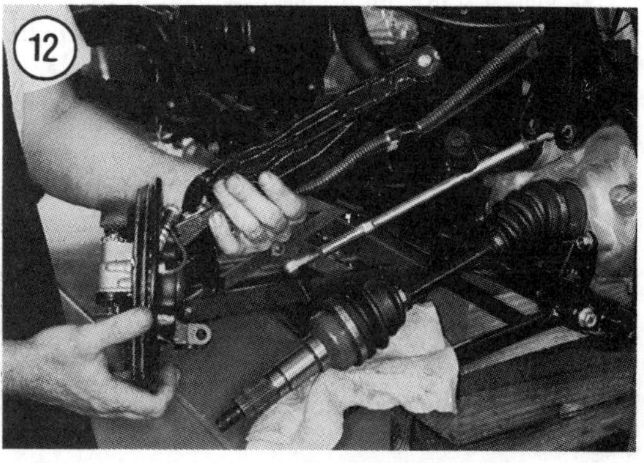

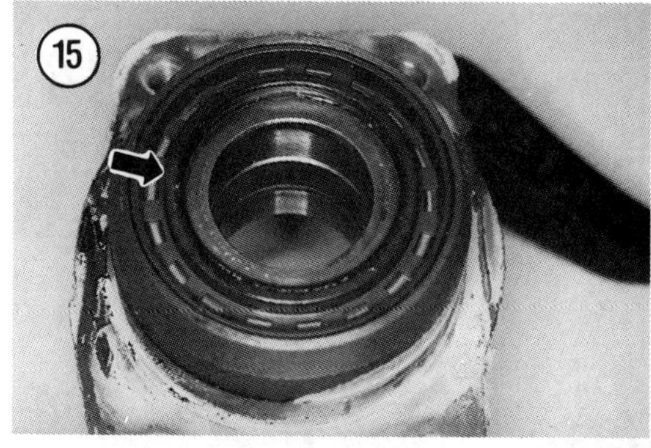

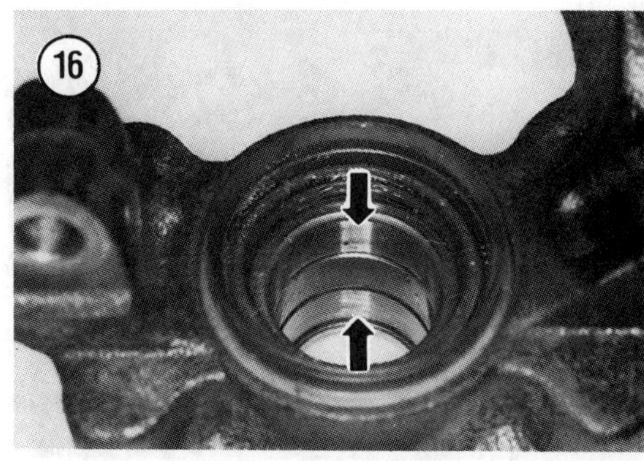

8. Check the bearing bore for cracks or other damage.

9. Pack unsealed bearings with a good quality lithium base grease. Work the grease in between the balls thoroughly. Turn the bearing by hand a couple of times to make sure the grease is distributed evenly inside the bearing.

10. Apply a light coat of lithium base grease to the interior surface of the knuckle, hub and to the spacer.

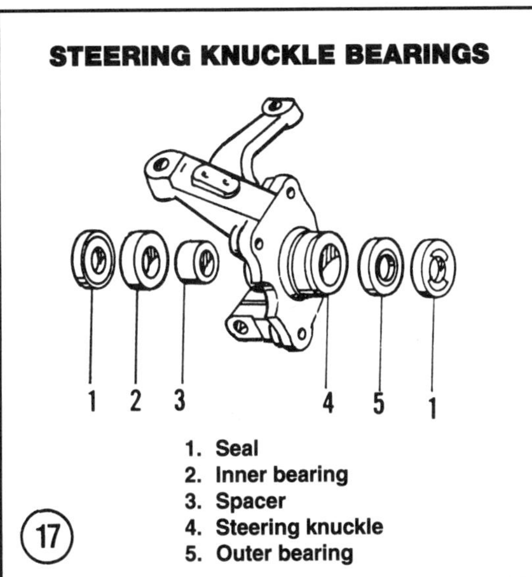

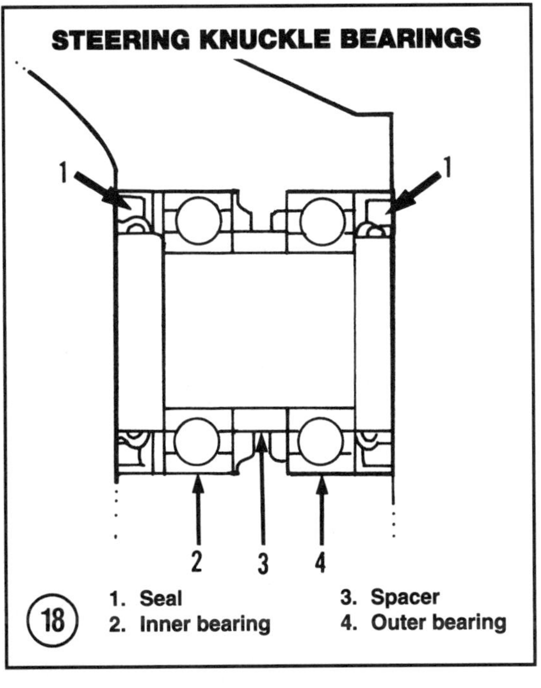

CAUTION

Install the bearings with their sealed side facing out. During installation, tap the bearings squarely into place and tap on the outer race only. Use a driver that matches the outer race diameter. Do not tap on the inner race or the bearing may be damaged. Be sure that the bearings are completely seated.

11. Install the outer bearing (**Figure 18**) first.

12. Install the spacer, then the inner bearing.

13. Apply a light coat of lithium base grease to both seals.

14. Position the seals with their sealed side facing toward the outside and install both seals. Refer to **Figure 14** and **Figure 15**.

Installation

1. If removed, install the upper control arm (**Figure 12**) as described in this chapter.

2. If removed, install the front axle as described in Chapter Eleven.

3. Carefully install the front axle through the steering knuckle (**Figure 19**).

4. Install the upper control arm ball joint (C, **Figure 8**) through the steering knuckle. Install the nut finger-tight.

5. Install the lower control arm ball joint (B, **Figure 8**) through the steering knuckle. Align the ball joint groove with the steering knuckle bolt hole, then install the bolt, washer and nut and tighten finger-tight.

6. Install the tie rod ball joint through the steering knuckle and install the nut finger-tight.

7. Make sure all of the parts are installed correctly onto the steering knuckle.

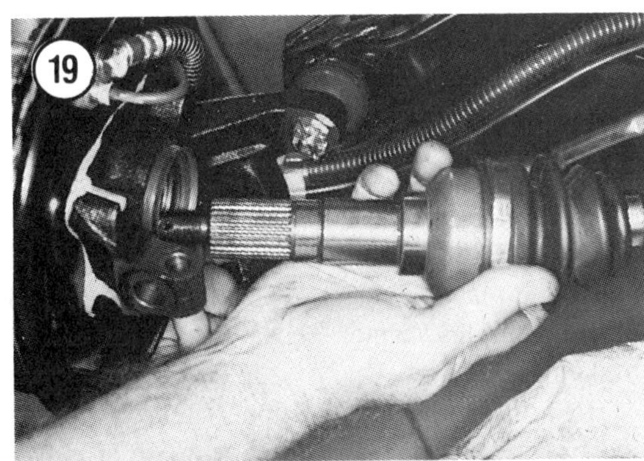

10

8. Tighten the steering knuckle and upper arm nut (C, **Figure 8**) as specified in **Table 4**. Secure the nut with a new cotter pin.
9. Tighten the steering knuckle and lower arm bolt and nut (B, **Figure 8**) as specified in **Table 4**. Secure the nut with a new cotter pin.
10. Tighten the steering knuckle and tie rod end nut (**Figure 9**) as specified in **Table 4**. Secure the nut with a new cotter pin.

WARNING
Always use new cotter pins.

11. Install and tighten the front brake hose hydraulic and vent hose bracket and mounting bolt.
12. Install the shock absorber as described in this chapter.
13. Turn handlebar from side to side and check that the steering knuckle and front axle moves smoothly.
14. Install the metal boot protector, if used.
15. Install the backing plate (A, **Figure 8**) and brake drum as described in Chapter Thirteen.
16. Install the front wheel as described in this chapter.

CONTROL ARMS

Refer to **Figure 7** when servicing the upper and lower control arms.

Removal/Preliminary Inspection

1. Unbolt and remove the front guard.
2. Disconnect the control arm(s) from the steering knuckle as described under *Steering Knuckle* in this chapter.

NOTE
If the upper arm must be removed to disconnect it from the steering knuckle, reinstall it back onto the frame to check bushing wear described in Steps 3 and 4.

3. Hold onto the end of the upper control arm and move it from side to side and check for side play. If noticeable play is evident, replace the bushings as described in this chapter. Repeat for the lower control arm.
4. Hold onto the end of the upper control arm and move it up and down and check for ease of movement. If movement is tight, or rough, replace the bushings as described in this chapter. Repeat for the lower control arm.
5. Unbolt and remove the upper control arm (**Figure 20**) from the frame.
6. Unbolt and remove the lower control arm (**Figure 21**) from the frame.

Control Arm Cleaning and Inspection

NOTE
When cleaning the control arms, do not wash the ball joints in solvent. Handle the ball joints carefully to avoid contaminating the grease or damaging the rubber boot.

1. Clean and dry the control arm, bolts and nuts.
2. Inspect both control arms for cracks, fractures and dents. Replace if necessary.
3. Inspect each bushing (**Figure 22**) for excessive wear or damage.
4. Inspect pivot bolts for bending or other damage. Replace damaged bolts.

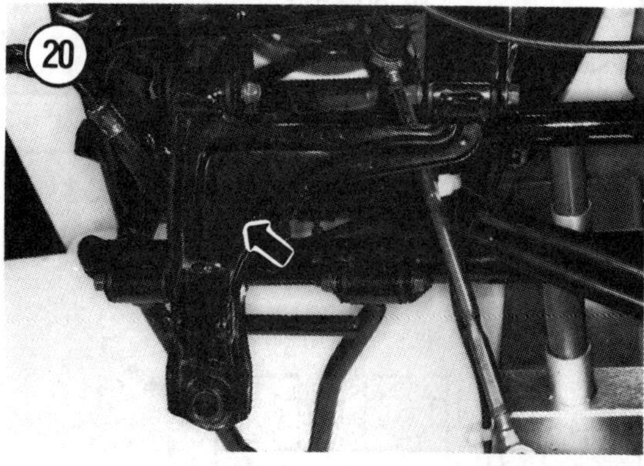

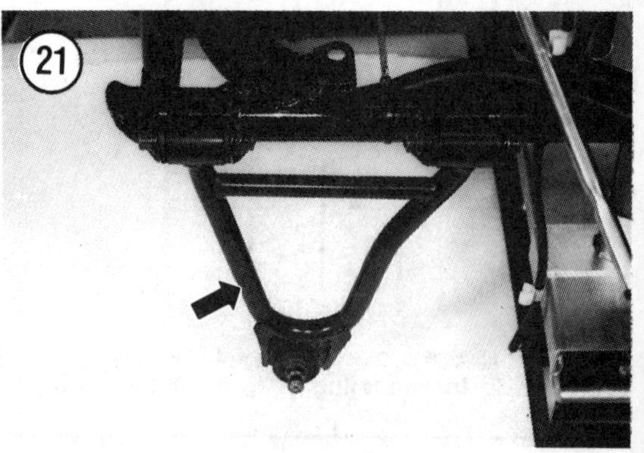

5. Inspect the shock absorber mounting bracket on the upper control arm for cracks or bolt hole elongation.

6. To replace the control arm bushings:

   a. Support control arm and drive or press out the bushing. Repeat for each bushing.

   b. Clean and dry the bushing mounting bores. Remove all rust and dirt residue.

   c. Check the mounting bores for cracks or other damage.

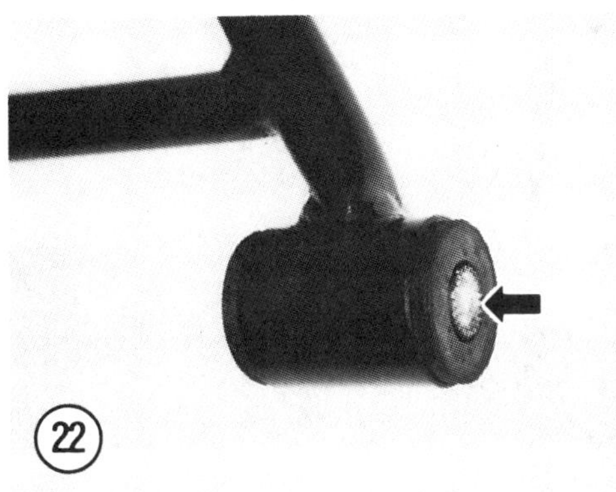

22

23

24

   d. Support control arm and press bushing into bore until bushing shoulder bottoms out.

7. Inspect the ball joints as described under *Ball Joint Inspection and Replacement* in this chapter.

8. Inspect the control arm mounting brackets on the frame for cracks or bolt hole elongation.

Ball Joint Inspection and Replacement

A single ball joint (**Figure 23**) is mounted on each control arm. The ball joints are an integral part of the control arm and cannot be replaced separately. Inspect the ball joint rubber boot. The swivel joint is packed with grease. If the rubber boot or ball joint is severely worn or damaged, replace the control arm assembly.

Installation

1. Lubricate the pivot bolts and inner bushing surfaces with a lithium-base grease.
2. Install the lower control arm as follows:
   a. Install the lower control arm between its mounting brackets (**Figure 21**). The ball joint should be facing up.
   b. Install the pivot bolts from the outer surfaces of the control arm (**Figure 24**). When properly installed, the nuts will face each other.
   c. Install the nuts (**Figure 24**) and tighten finger-tight.
3. Install the upper control as follows:
   a. Install the upper control arm between its mounting brackets (**Figure 20**). The ball joint should be facing down.
   b. Install the pivot bolts from the outer surfaces of the control arm (**Figure 24**). When properly installed, the nuts will face each other.
   c. Install the nuts (**Figure 24**) and tighten finger-tight.
4. Connect the control arm ball joints to steering knuckle as described under *Steering Knuckle* in this chapter.
5. Tighten the upper and lower control arm pivot bolt nuts as specified in **Table 4**.
6. Install the front shock absorber as described in this chapter.
7. Install the front guard and tighten the bolts securely.

HANDLEBAR

Removal

1. Cover the fuel tank and front fender with a heavy cloth or plastic tarp to protect them from accidentally spilling brake fluid.

NOTE
Wash any spilled brake fluid off any painted or plastic surface immediately as it will destroy the finish. Use soapy water and rinse thoroughly.

2. Carefully pull the handlebar cover (**Figure 25**) off of the handlebar.
3. Remove the front master cylinder as described in Chapter Thirteen. Do not disconnect the hydraulic hose.

CAUTION
Do not allow the weight of the master cylinder to hang by its hose. This could damage the hose.

4. Remove the throttle lever housing as described in Chapter Eight.
5. Remove the bands securing the left switch housing wiring harness to the handlebar.
6. Remove the screws securing the left switch assembly (A, **Figure 26**). Then separate the switch housing and remove from the handlebar.
7. Remove the screws and clamp (B, **Figure 26**) securing the parking brake assembly to the handlebar and remove the assembly. Position the assembly so the cables do not get crimped or damaged.
8. Remove the bolts securing the handlebar upper holders and remove the holders (A, **Figure 27**).
9. Remove the handlebar (B, **Figure 27**).
10. Reverse these steps to install the handlebar, plus the following:
11. Clean the knurled section of the handlebar and the handlebar holders with a wire brush.

NOTE
*The upper handlebar holders are directional; each holder is machined with one side offset from the other (A, **Figure 28**). The front side is marked with a punch mark (B, **Figure 28**). To ensure correct handlebar installation, install the upper holders as described in Step 12.*

12. Install the upper handlebar holders (**Figure 27**) with their punch mark (B, **Figure 28**) facing toward the front of the vehicle.
13. Install the handlebar holder bolts (**Figure 27**). Tighten the front bolts to the torque specification in **Table 4**. Then tighten the rear bolts to the same torque specification. After tightening the holder bolts, make sure there is a gap at the rear side of each holder as shown in **Figure 29**.

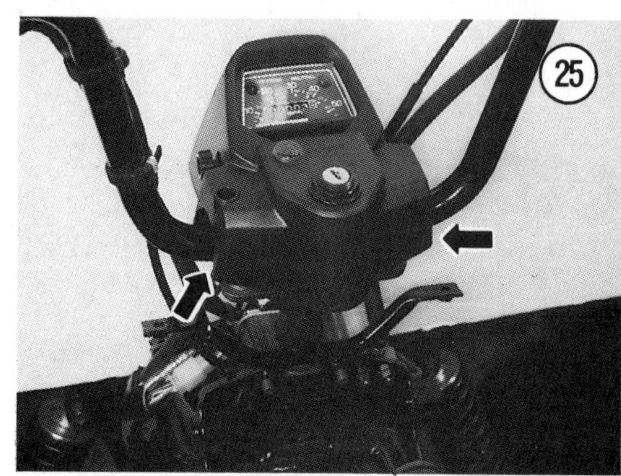

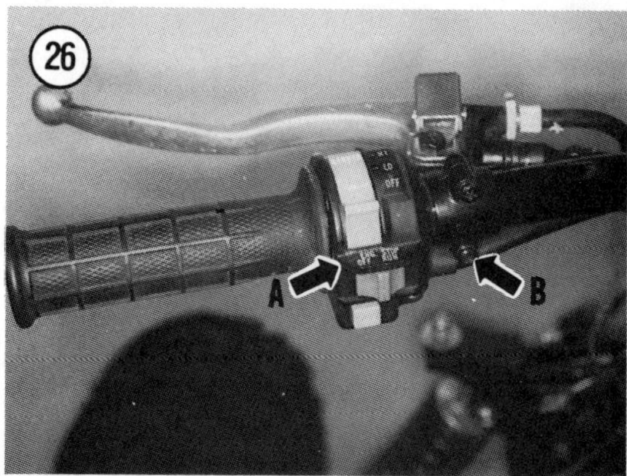

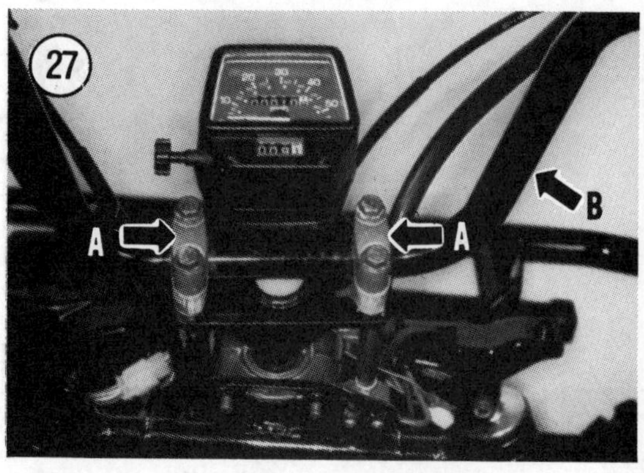

14. When installing new handlebar grips, follow their manufacturer's directions for installing and sealing the grips to handlebar.

15. After assembly, test each switch and control cable for proper operation. Correct any problem at this time.

TIE RODS

Figure 30 shows an exploded view of the steering shaft and tie rod assembly. The tie rods consists of a shaft with a ball joint at each end. The individual parts that make up the tie rod assembly can be replaced separately.

Removal

The *outer* tie rod end (20, **Figure 30**) can be replaced without having to disconnect the tie rod from the steering shaft. When replacing the inner tie rod end (13, **Figure 30**), remove the tie rod from the vehicle so that the inner tie rod can be properly adjusted.

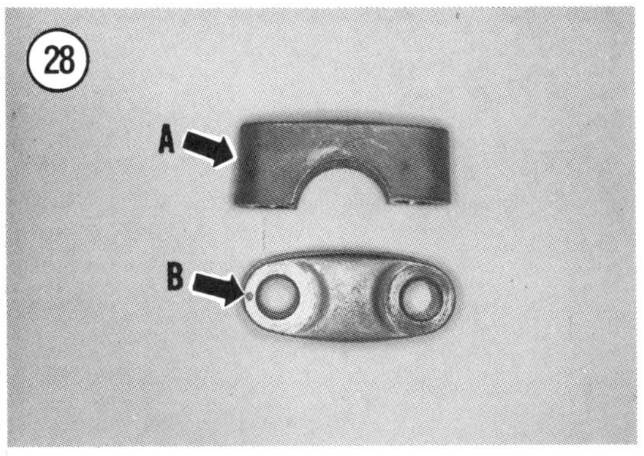

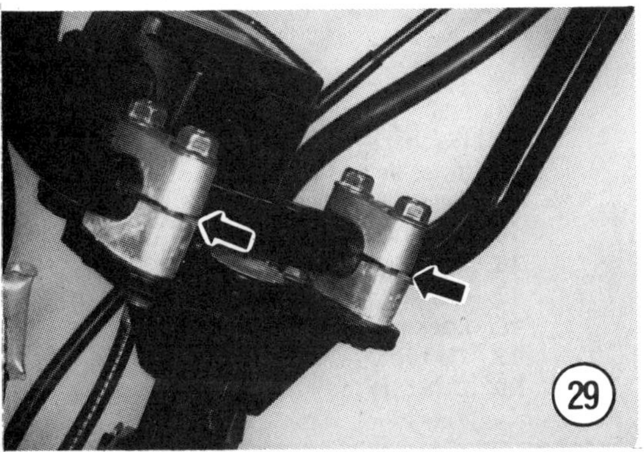

1. Support the vehicle and remove the front wheel(s) as described in this chapter.
2. Mark the tie rods with an R (right side) or L (left side). The tie rods must be reinstalled on the same side of the vehicle from which they were removed.

CAUTION
Do not drive the ball joint out of the steering knuckle with a hammer. Doing so will damage the ball joint stud and threads.

3. Disconnect the tie rod ball joint from the steering knuckle as follows:
   a. Remove the cotter pin from the tie rod ball joint stud (**Figure 31**). Discard the cotter pin.
   b. Loosen the tie rod mounting nut and then turn it an additional 5-6 turns so it is positioned away from the steering knuckle. Do not remove the nut completely.

NOTE
By leaving the tie rod nut installed on the stud, it can chase the tie rod threads if minor thread damage occurs when using the puller. Also, the nut prevents the tie rod from flying out of the steering knuckle when it breaks loose. This helps to prevent damage to the ball joint stud threads and rubber boot.

   c. Install a 2-jaw puller onto the steering knuckle and center the puller's pressure bolt against the ball joint stud (**Figure 32**). Position the puller arms so that they do not pinch the ball joint rubber seal (**Figure 33**).
   d. Operate the puller to apply pressure against the ball joint stud. When the ball joint stud is under pressure, strike the top of the puller with a hammer to free the ball joint from the steering knuckle.
4. Repeat Step 3 to remove the tie rod ball joint from the steering shaft (**Figure 34**).
5. Remove the tie rod.
6. Repeat for the other tie rod if necessary.

Inspection

NOTE
If you are going to clean the tie rod in solvent, work carefully to prevent the

(30)

STEERING KNUCKLE

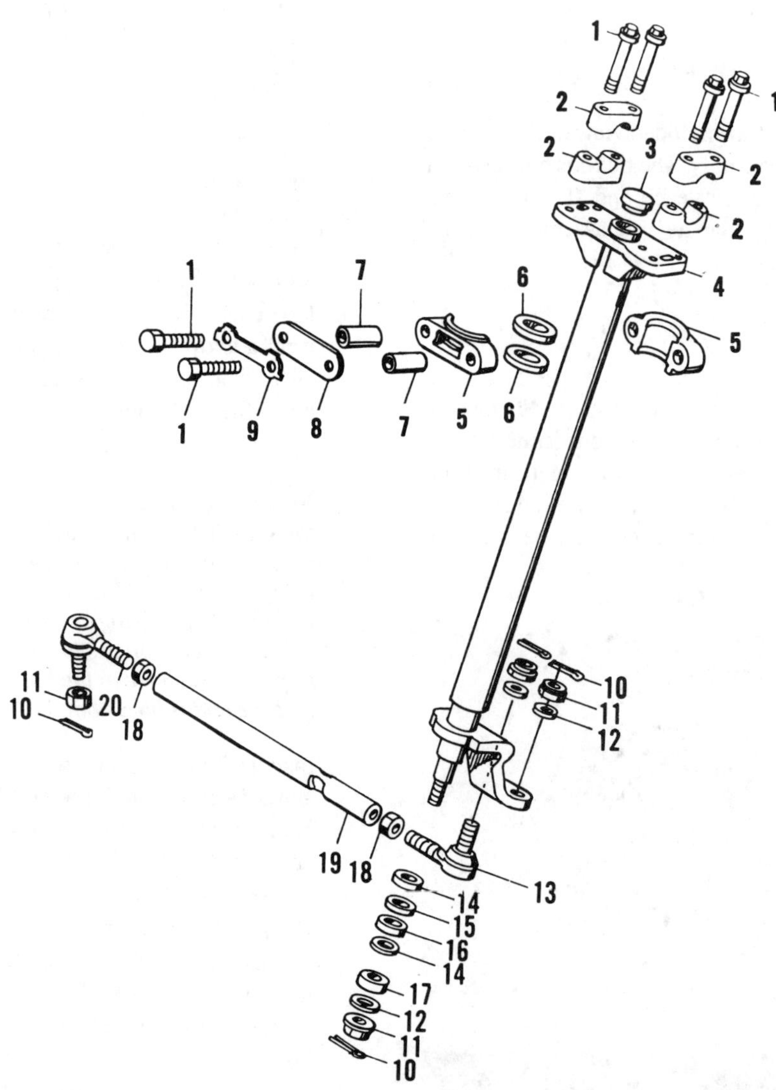

1. Bolt
2. Handlebar holders
3. Cap
4. Steering shaft
5. Upper bearing blocks
6. Dust seal
7. Collar
8. Plate
9. Lockwasher
10. Cotter pin
11. Nut
12. Washer
13. Inner tie rod end
14. Seal
15. Bearing holder
16. Bearing
17. Collar
18. Locknut
19. Tie rod
20. Outer tie rod end

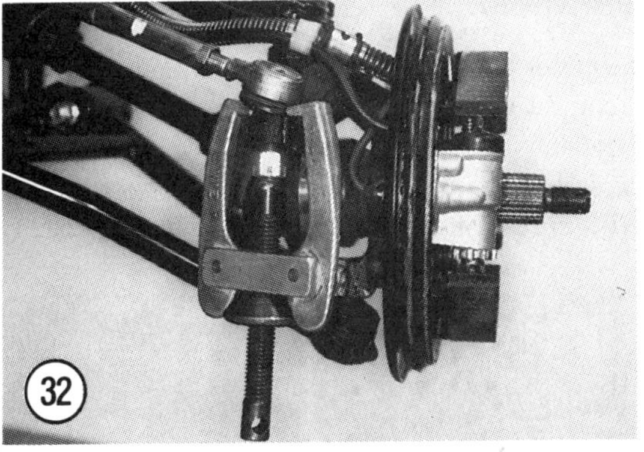

solvent from contaminating the grease in the rubber boot.

1. Inspect the tie rod shaft (A, **Figure 35**) for damage. There should be no creases or bends along the shaft. Check with a straightedge placed against the tie rod shaft.

2. Inspect the rubber boot (**Figure 36**) at each tie rod end. The tie rod ends are permanently packed with grease. If the rubber boot is damaged, dirt and moisture can enter the joint and destroy it. If the boot is damaged, disassemble the tie rod and replace the tie rod end. Refer to *Tie Rod Disassembly/Assembly* in the following procedure.

3. Pivot the tie rod end back and forth by hand. If the tie rod end moves roughly or has excessive play, replace it as described in the following procedure.

Tie Rod Disassembly/Assembly

Refer to **Figure 37** for this procedure.

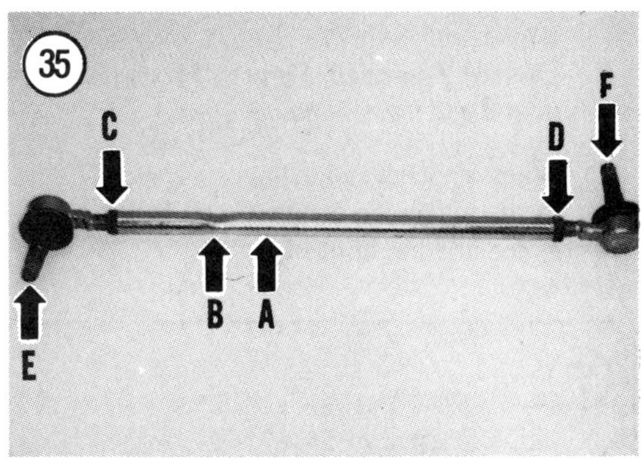

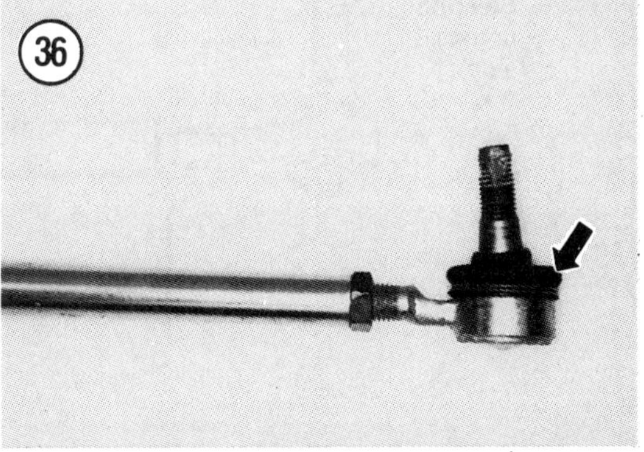

1. Hold the tie rod with a wrench across the shaft flat (B, **Figure 35**) and loosen the locknut for the tie rod end being replaced.

NOTE
*The locknut securing the outside tie rod end (C, **Figure 35**) has left-hand threads. The inside tie rod end locknut (D, **Figure 35**) has right-hand threads.*

2. Unscrew and remove the damaged tie rod end(s).
3. Clean the shaft and tie rod end threads with contact cleaner.
4. Identify the new tie rod end with the drawing in **Figure 37**. The outside and inside tie rod ends are different. Likewise, the left- and right-side tie rod shafts (A, **Figure 35**) are different.
5. Thread the tie rod (with the locknut) into the tie rod shaft.
6. Adjust the tie rod length and tighten the tie rod ends as follows:
   a. Adjust the tie rod ball joints to obtain a length of 344.5 mm (13.6 in.) as shown at A, **Figure 37**.

NOTE
*When adjusting the tie rod ends, the exposed threads (B, **Figure 37**) on each tie rod end must be equal.*

   b. When the length adjustment is correct, tighten the tie rod and locknuts (C and D, **Figure 35**) as specified in **Table 4**.

NOTE
*The locknut securing the outside tie rod end (D, **Figure 35**) has left-hand threads. The inside tie rod end locknut (C, **Figure 35**) has right-hand threads.*

Installation

NOTE
The left- and right-hand tie rod assemblies are different. While the right-hand tie rod assembly was originally marked with a white paint mark on its shaft, this mark may no longer be visible on some vehicles.

1. Refer to your identification marks made during removal and install the left and right side tie rod assemblies onto the vehicle.
2. Attach the tie rod assembly to the steering shaft (**Figure 34**) and to the steering knuckle (**Figure 31**).

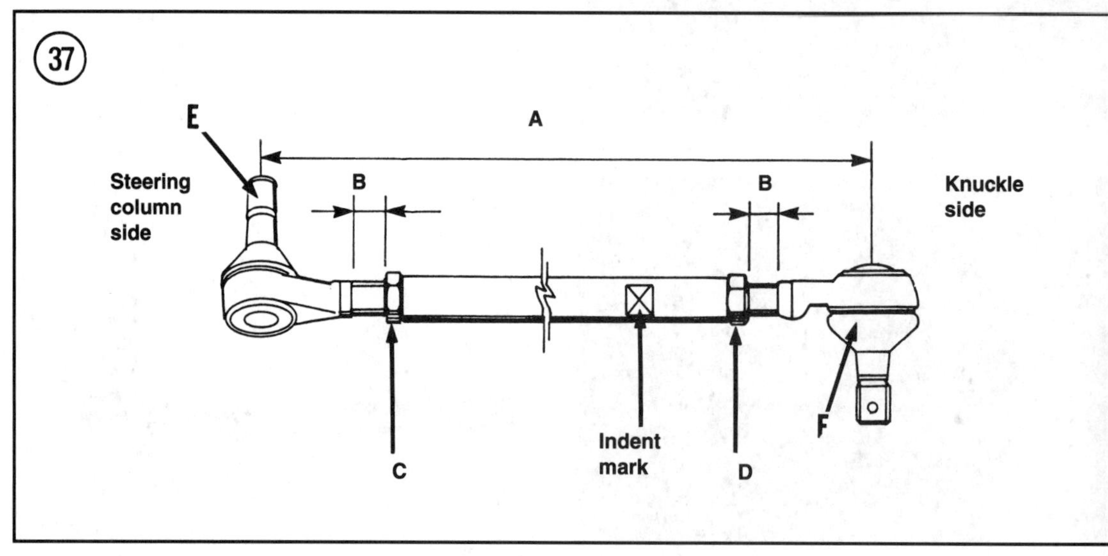

3. Thread the nut onto each ball joint stud and tighten as specified in **Table 4**.

4. Install new cotter pins through all ball joint studs. Open and bend the cotter pin arms to lock them in place.

WARNING
Always use new cotter pins.

5. Install the front wheels as described in this chapter.

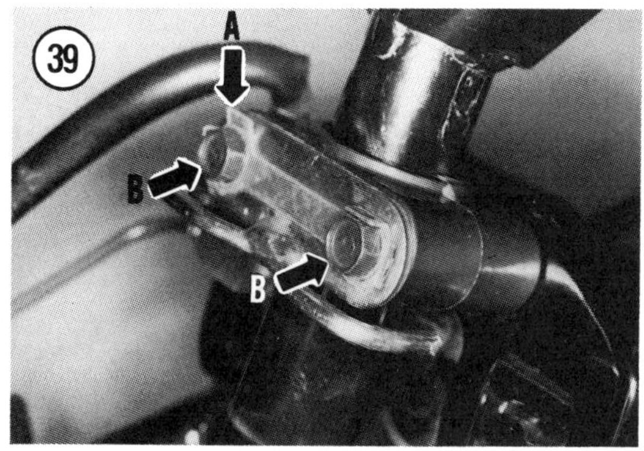

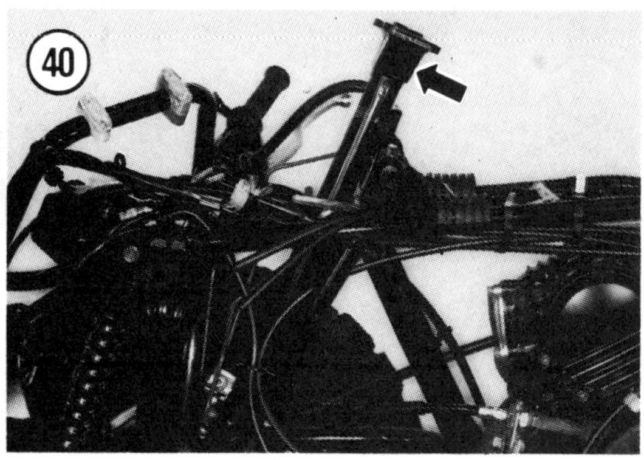

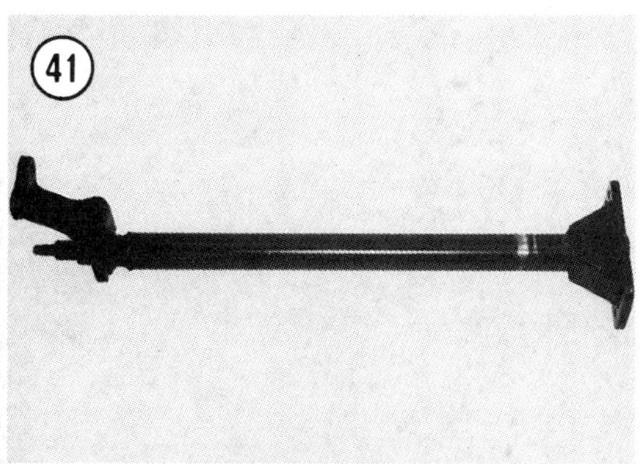

6. Check the toe-in adjustment, and adjust if necessary, as described in Chapter Three.

STEERING SHAFT

Figure 30 is an exploded views of the steering shaft and the components that are connected to it. The steering shaft pivots on split bearing halves at the upper end and a ball bearing at the lower end.

Removal

1. Remove the fuel tank (Chapter Eight).
2. Remove the front fender (Chapter Fourteen).
3. Remove both front wheels as described in this chapter.
4. Remove the handlebar assembly as described in this chapter.
5. Remove the speedometer (Chapter Nine).
6 Disconnect both tie rods from the steering shaft (**Figure 34**) as described under *Tie Rods* in this chapter.
7. Remove the cotter pin, nut and washer (**Figure 38**) from the bottom of the steering shaft.
8. Make a diagram of the cables and wiring harnesses as they pass around the steering shaft for reassembly reference.
9. Pry the lockwasher tabs (A, **Figure 39**) away from the upper bearing block mounting bolts.
10. Loosen and remove the upper bearing block mounting bolts (B, **Figure 39**). Then remove the outer block, collars, split dust seals and inner block assembly.
11. Remove the steering shaft (**Figure 40**) from the lower frame mount and remove it.

10

Inspection

1. Wash and dry all parts.
2. Check for a bent or damaged steering shaft (**Figure 41**). Check the shaft straightness with set of V-blocks and dial indicator (**Figure 42**).

NOTE
Running a damaged or bent shaft will cause rapid and excessive wear to the bearings as well as place undue stress on other components in the frame and steering system. ***Figure 43*** *shows the type of damage that can occur to a bent*

*steering shaft. The area were the upper bearing block rides (see arrow in **Figure 43**) is excessively worn.*

3. Inspect the tie rod attachment holes in the lower section of the steering shaft. Check the holes for elongation, cracks or wear. Replace the steering shaft if necessary.
4. Inspect the handlebar holder plate and the attachment holes in the upper section of the steering shaft. Check for hole elongation, cracks or wear. Replace the steering shaft if necessary.
5. Check the tie rod mounting bracket for wear, cracks or damage.
6. Inspect the upper bearing assembly (**Figure 44**) for:
   a. Worn or damaged dust seals.
   b. Worn or damaged bearing block halves.
   c. Bent or damaged bolts and collars. Make sure the collars and bearing block halves fit together without binding.
7. Inspect the lower steering shaft seal and bearing surfaces (**Figure 45**). Replace the steering shaft if the machined surfaces show severe wear or damage.
8. Inspect the steering bearing seals (**Figure 46**). Replace damaged seals as described in this chapter.
9. Turn the steering bearing inner race (**Figure 47**) and check for any roughness or excessive play. If damaged, replace the bearing as described in this chapter.

Steering Shaft Seal and Bearing Replacement

A 30 mm hex driver is required to remove and install the bearing retainer in the following steps. Use the Yamaha fork damper rod holder (part No. YM-01327 [**Figure 48**]) along with a ratchet and

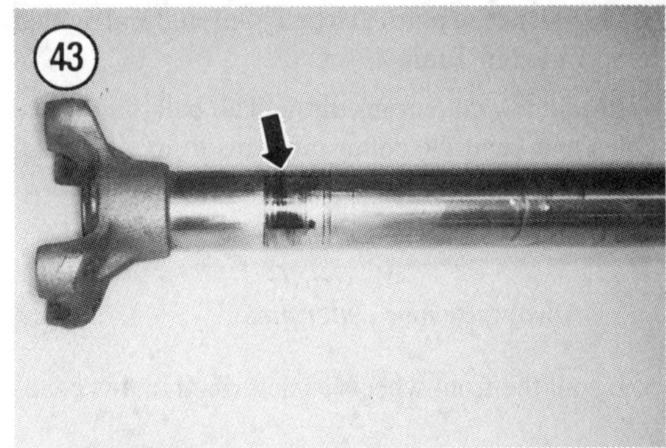
43

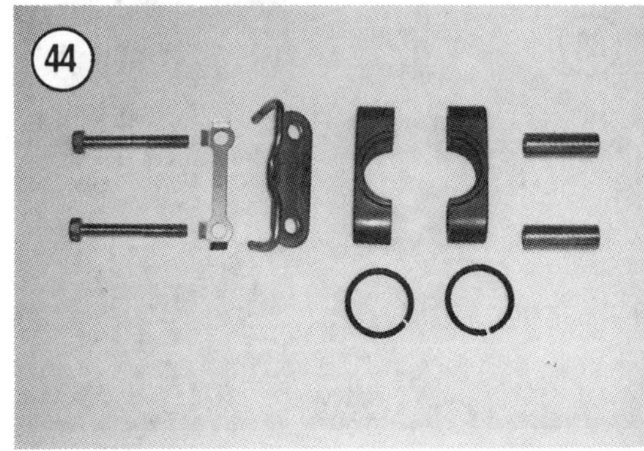
44

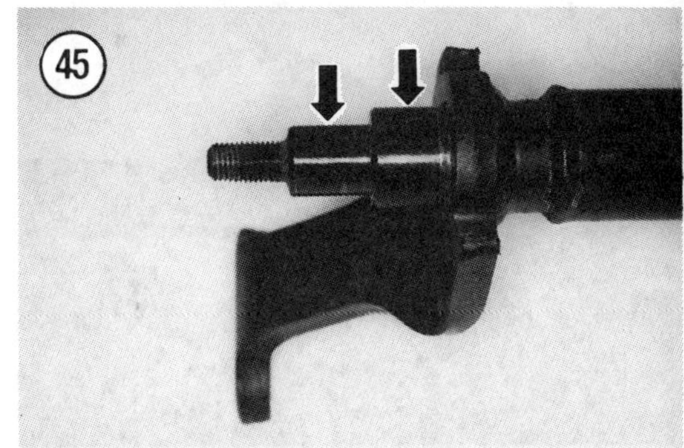
45

42

46

YAMAHA FORK DAMPER ROD HOLDER—30 mm (PART NO. YM-01327)

48

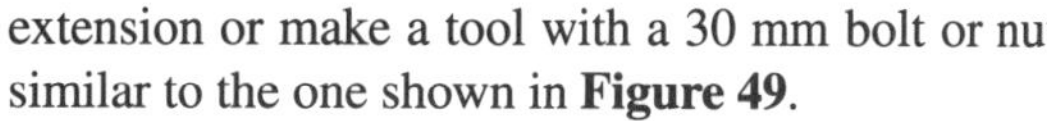

extension or make a tool with a 30 mm bolt or nut similar to the one shown in **Figure 49**.

1. Remove the collar from the lower seal (**Figure 50**).
2. Pry the upper and lower seals out of the frame tube with a slotted screwdriver (**Figure 51**). Pad the screwdriver to avoid damaging the frame. Discard both seals.
3. Use the 30 mm hex driver and remove the bearing retainer from the top of the bearing mounting bore in the frame. Then remove the tool and bearing retainer and lift out the bearing (**Figure 52**).
4. Clean and dry the bearing retainer and collar.
5. Clean the bearing retainer threads in the frame.
6. Install the new bearing in the frame with its manufacturer's name and size code facing up. Make sure the bearing seats squarely in its mounting bore.
7. Thread the bearing retainer—shoulder side facing down (**Figure 53**)—into the frame. Hand tighten the bearing retainer against bearing. Then tighten the bearing retainer as specified in **Table 4**.
8. Install the upper and lower seals as follows:
   a. The upper seal (A, **Figure 54**) is larger than the lower seal (B, **Figure 54**).

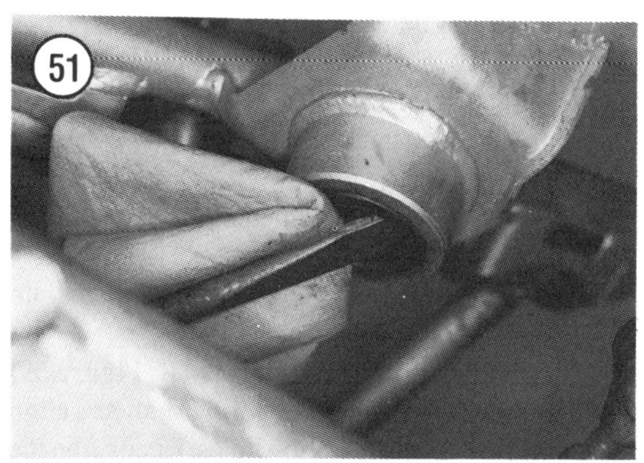

b. Install both seals with their closed side facing out (away from bearing).
c. Pack the lip of each seal with a waterproof grease.
d. Drive in the lower seal until its outer surface if flush with or slightly below the oil seal bore inside surface (**Figure 55**).
e. Install the upper seal with a piece of threaded rod, 2 large washers and 2 nuts (**Figure 56**). Assemble these pieces as shown in **Figure 57** and press in the seal until its outer surface is flush with the mounting bore inside surface. Hold the lower nut and turn upper nut to install the seal.

9. Insert the collar (**Figure 50**) into the lower seal.

Installation

1. Coat the steering bearing seals (**Figure 55**) with grease.
2. Apply a coat of grease to the steering shaft where it operates in the bearing.
3. Install the steering shaft into the frame (**Figure 40**)—with the tie rod mounting bracket toward the back—and carefully install it into the lower bearing assembly until it bottoms out.
4. Install the washer and the nut (**Figure 58**) and tighten finger-tight.
5. Assemble and install the upper bearing assembly as follows:
   a. Grease the inner diameter of both bearing block halves.
   b. Grease the dust seals and install them into steering shaft (A, **Figure 59**).
   c. Install the inner bearing block (B, **Figure 59**) between the frame and steering shaft and align with the frame mounting holes. Reposition the

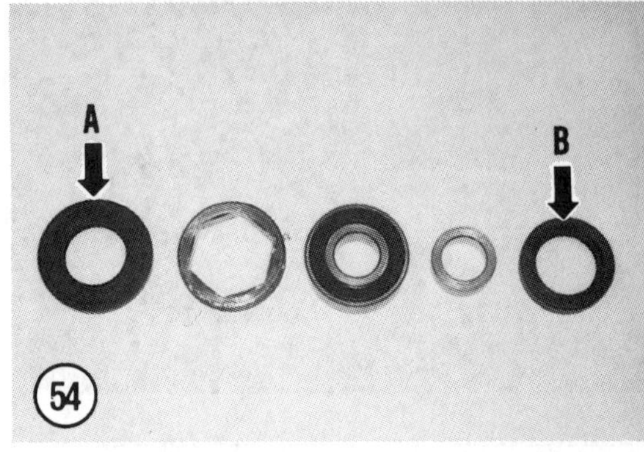

54

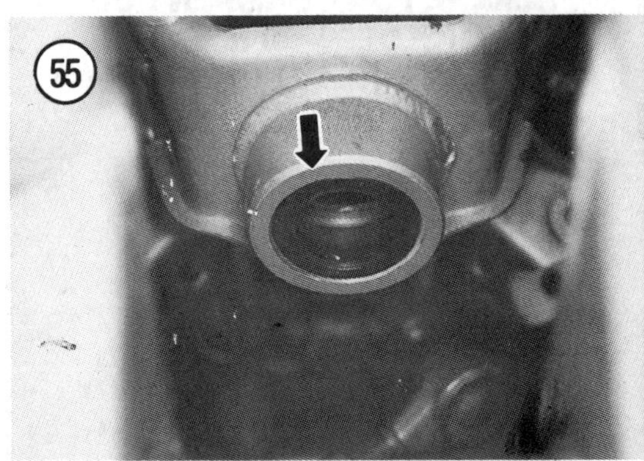
55

56

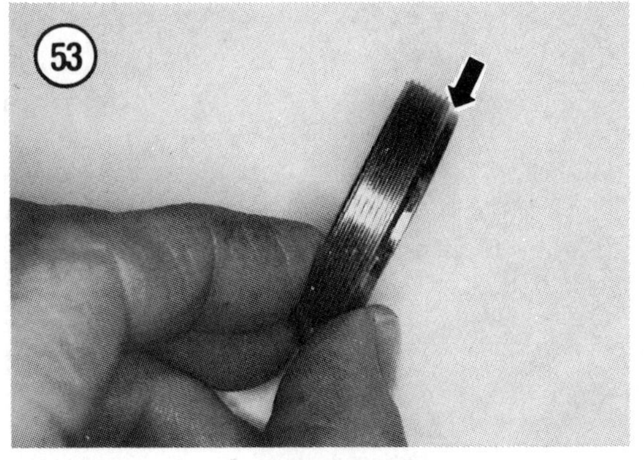
53

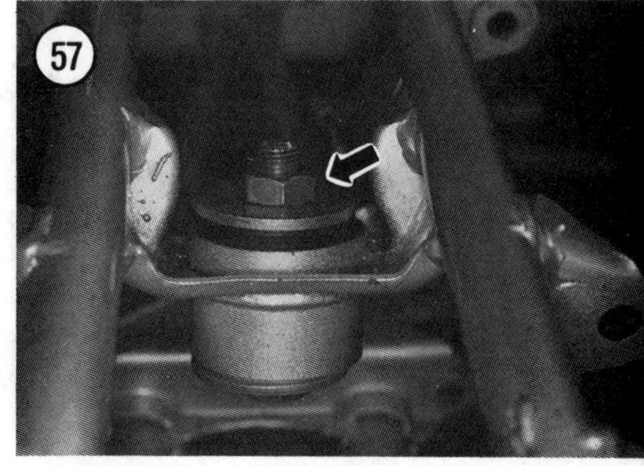
57

dust seals if necessary so they sit flush in the bearing block grooves.

NOTE
The inner and outer bearing block halves are identical.

d. Install the 2 collars (**Figure 60**) into the inner bearing block. Push them in until they bottom.
e. Install the outer bearing block (**Figure 61**), engaging the block grooves with the dust seals. Push it on until it seats flush against the inner block.
f. Install the bearing block mounting bolts (**Figure 62**) and lockwasher and tighten finger-tight.
g. Tighten the steering shaft nut (**Figure 58**) as specified in **Table 4**. Install a new cotter pin through the steering shaft hole. Bend the cotter pin arms around the steering shaft.
h. Tighten the 2 steering shaft bearing block bolts (**Figure 62**) as specified in **Table 4**.

6. Turn the steering shaft from side to side. The steering shaft should turn smoothly without excessive play.
7. Bend the lockwasher tabs (**Figure 62**) that secure the bearing block bolts onto the bolt heads.
8. Reconnect both tie rods to the steering shaft as described under *Tie Rods* in this chapter.
9. Install the speedometer (Chapter Nine).
10. Install the handlebar assembly as described in this chapter.
11. Install the front wheels as described in this chapter.
12. Install the front fender (Chapter Fourteen).
13. Install the fuel tank (Chapter Eight).
14. Check toe-in as described in Chapter Three.

TIRES AND WHEELS

The vehicle is equipped with tubeless, low pressure tires designed specifically for off-road use only. Rapid tire wear will occur if the vehicle is ridden on paved surfaces.

Tire Changing

The front and rear tire rims used on all models are of the 1-piece stamped steel type and have a very deep built-in ridge (**Figure 63**) to keep the tire bead seated on the rim under severe riding conditions.

A bead breaker tool and suitable tire irons are required to change the tires.

1. Remove the valve stem cap and core and deflate the tire. Do not reinstall the core at this time.
2. Lubricate the tire bead and rim flanges with a liquid dish detergent or any rubber lubricant. Press the tire sidewall/bead down to allow the liquid to run into and around the bead area. Also apply lubricant to the area where the bead breaker arm will come in contact with the tire sidewall.
3. Position the wheel into the bead breaker tool (**Figure 64**).
4. Slowly work the bead breaker, making sure the tool is up against the inside of the rim, and break the tire bead away from the rim.
5. Using your hands, press down on the tire on either side of the tool and try to break the rest of the bead free from the rim.
6. If the rest of the tire bead cannot be broken loose by hand, raise the tool, rotate the tire/rim assembly and repeat Steps 4 and 5 until the entire bead is broken loose from the rim.

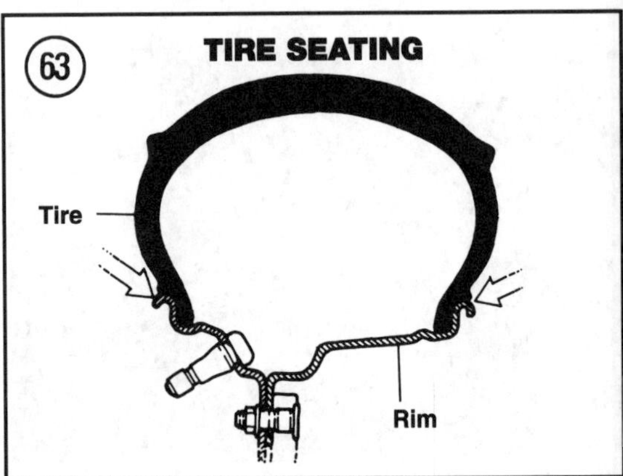

63 TIRE SEATING

64

7. Turn the wheel over and repeat to break the opposite side loose.

CAUTION
When using tire irons in the following steps, work carefully so that you don't damage the tire or rim sealing surfaces. Damage to these areas may cause an air leak.

8. Lubricate the tire bead and rim flanges as described in Step 2. Then pry the bead over the rim with 2 tire irons as shown in **Figure 65**. Take small bites with the tire irons.

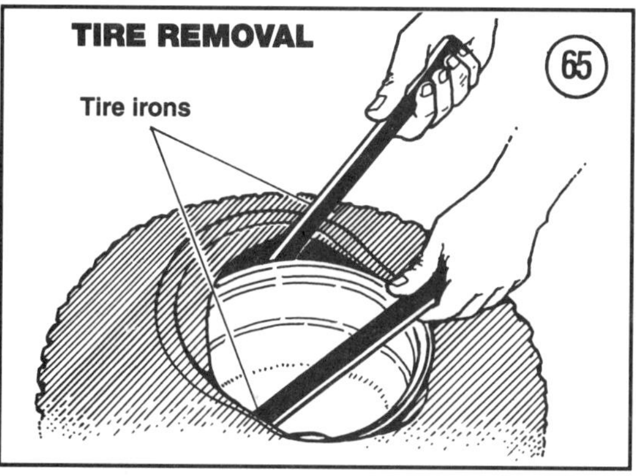

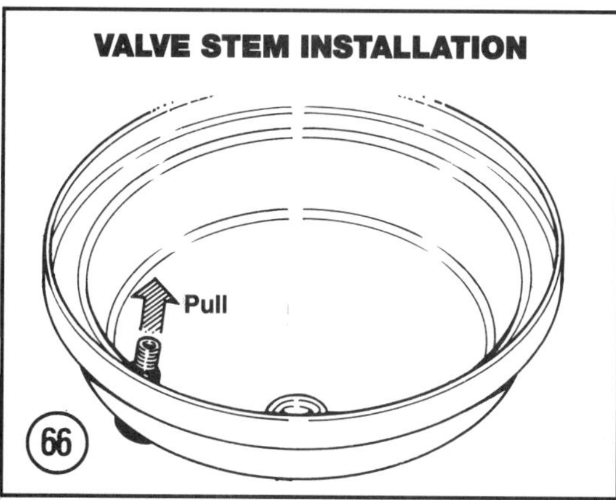

9. When the top tire bead is free, lift the second bead up into the center rim well and remove it as described in Step 8.

10. Inspect the sealing surface on both sides of the rim. If the rim has been hit it may leak air.

11. To replace the air valve, perform the following:

   a. Support the rim and pull the valve stem out of the rim. Discard the valve stem.
   b. Lubricate the new valve stem with soap and water.
   c. Pull the new valve stem into the rim, from the inside out, until it snaps in place (**Figure 66**).

NOTE
There are special tools available for installing valve stems into the rims. See your dealership or an automotive parts store.

12. Inspect the tire for cuts, tears, abrasions or any other defects.

13. Wipe the tire beads and rims free from any lubricating agent.

14. Apply clean water to the rim flanges, tire rim beads and onto the outer rim.

NOTE
Use only clean water and make sure the rim flange is clean. Clean the rim flange before wetting down the tire.

15. The tire tread on the stock front and rear tires are directional. Position the tire onto the rim so the rotation arrow on the side wall (**Figure 67**) is pointing in the direction of wheel rotation.

16. Install the tire onto the rim starting with the side opposite the valve stem. Push the first bead over the rim flange. Force the bead into the center of the rim to help installation (**Figure 68**).

17. Install the rest of the bead with tire irons.

18. Repeat to install the second bead onto the rim.

19. Install the valve stem core.

WARNING
*Do not inflate the tire past the maximum inflation pressure (for seating tires) listed in **Table 3**. Doing so can explode the tire and cause severe personal injury.*

20. Apply a tire mounting lubricant onto the tire bead and inflate the tire to the maximum tire pressure (for seating tires) listed in **Table 3**.

21. Check that the rim lines on both sides of the tire are parallel with the rim flanges as shown in **Figure 69**. If the rim flanges are not parallel, deflate the tire and break the bead. Then lubricate the tire and reinflate the tire.

NOTE

If there are air bubbles around the tire, the tire bead is leaking.

22. Deflate the tire to the operating tire pressure listed in **Table 3**.

23. Install the air valve cap.

Cold Patch Repair

The rubber plug type of repair is recommended only for an emergency repair, or until the tire can be patched correctly with the cold patch method.

Follow the manufacturer's instructions for the tire repair kit you are going to use.

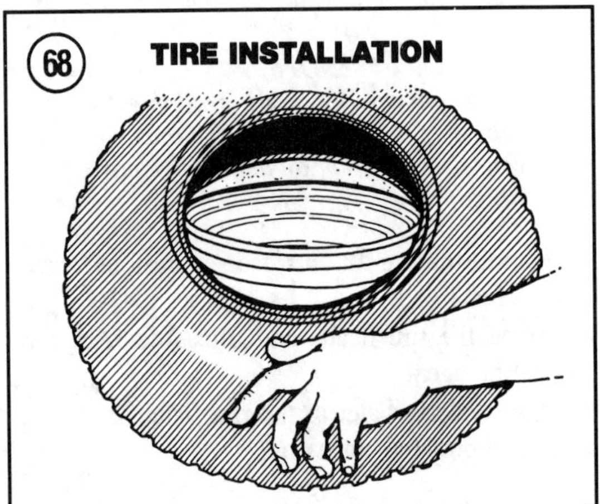

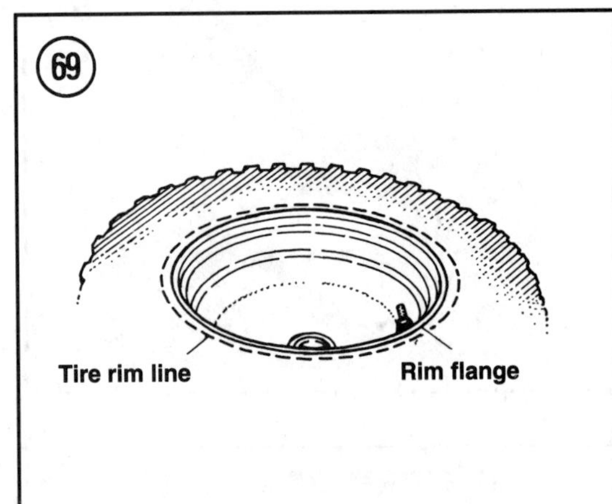

Table 1 FRONT SUSPENSION AND STEERING GENERAL SPECIFICATIONS

Item	Specification
Frame type	Steel tube
Caster angle	2.5°
Trail	15 mm (0.59 in.)
Tread (standard)	
Front	820 mm (32.28 in.)
Rear	840 mm (33.07 in.)
Toe-in	5-15 mm (0.20-0.59 in.)
Front suspension type	Double wishbone
Front shock absorber	Coil spring, oil damper
Front wheel travel	100 mm (3.94 in.)

Table 2 TIRE AND WHEEL SPECIFICATIONS

Item	Specifications
Front tire	
Type	Tubeless
Size and manufacturer	AT25 × 8-12/Dunlop KT402
Rear tire	
Type	Tubeless
Size and manufacturer	AT25 × 10-12/Dunlop KT406
Maximum rim runout (radial and lateral limit)	2.0 mm (0.08 in.)

Table 3 TIRE INFLATION PRESSURE

Year	Front psi (kPa)	Rear psi (kPa)
1993-1995	2.4-3.3	3.2-3.9 (22-27)
1996-on	3.2-3.9 (22-27)	3.2-3.9 (22-27)
Maximum tire pressure for seating tires	20 (138)	20 (138)

10

Table 4 FRONT SUSPENSION TIGHTENING TORQUES

	N•m	in.-lb.	ft.-lb.
Steering shaft bearing retainer nut	40	—	29
Upper and lower arm pivot bolt nuts	45	—	32
Front shock abosrber mounting nuts	45	—	32
Steering shaft nut	30	—	22
Steering shaft bearing block mounting bolts			
1993-1995	20	—	14
1996-on	23	—	17
Tie rod end steering shaft nut	25	—	18
Tie rod end locknuts			
1993-1995	30	—	22
1996-on	35	—	25
Steering knuckle and tie rod end nut	25	—	18
Steering knuckle and upper arm nut	25	—	18
Steering knuckle and lower arm nut			
1993-1995	35	—	25
1996-on	48	—	35
Front wheel lug nuts	55	—	40
Front axle and front wheel hub nut	130	—	95
Steering knuckle and front brake plate bolt	28	—	20
Master cylinder clamp bolts	10	88	—
Handlebar holder bolts	20	—	14

CHAPTER ELEVEN

FRONT DRIVE MECHANISM

This chapter describes repair and replacement procedures for the front drive mechanism. This includes the front axles, front differential gearcase and front drive shaft.

Table 1 lists torque specifications for the front drive mechanism assembly. **Table 1** is located at the end of the chapter.

FRONT AXLE

Figure 1 is an exploded view of the left- and right-side front axles.

Removal/Installation

1. Unbolt and remove the front guard.
2. Remove the front wheel and shock absorber as described in Chapter Ten.
3. Remove the brake drum (Chapter Thirteen).
4. Disconnect the tie rod (**Figure 2**) from the steering knuckle as described in Chapter Ten.
5. Disconnect the lower control arm (**Figure 3**) from the steering knuckle as described in Chapter Ten.
6. Remove the upper control arm from the frame as described in Chapter Ten.
7. Place several shop cloths (A, **Figure 4**) on the lower control arm so the front axle can rest on it after removal from the steering knuckle.
8. Carefully pull the steering knuckle and upper control arm (B, **Figure 4**) and disengage the front axle from the steering knuckle.
9. Rest the front axle (C, **Figure 4**) on the lower control arm.

CAUTION
When removing the front axle, be careful not to damage the rubber boot.

CAUTION
To avoid damage to the front differential seal and splines, pull the constant velocity joint straight out and off the front differential.

10. To remove the front axle, the puller jaws must be postioned against the shoulder on the inner constant-velocity joint. On some models, this shoulder is not large enough to provide sufficient contact surface for the puller. On these models, attach a hose clamp around the joint (**Figure 5**) and tighten it securely. The hose clamp provides a shoulder for the puller to contact.
11. Attach a 2-jaw puller to the backside of the constant velocity joint (**Figure 6**). Make sure the puller securely contacts the shoulder or hose clamp

CAUTION
Once the front axle set ring is released from the front differential, the front axle will easily slide out. Be sure to hold the axle while using the side hammer to avoid dropping the front axle.

12. Operate the puller to disengage the front axle set ring from the groove in the front differential (**Figure 7**) and remove the front axle assembly.

13. Repeat these steps for the other front axle if necessary.

14. Inspect the front axle(s) as described in this chapter.

15. Install the front axle by reversing these removal steps, while noting the following:

   a. Install a new set ring (A, **Figure 8**) onto the constant-velocity joint. Make sure it is properly seated in the axle groove.

   b. Lubricate the front axle splines (B, **Figure 8**) with a molybdenum disulfide grease.

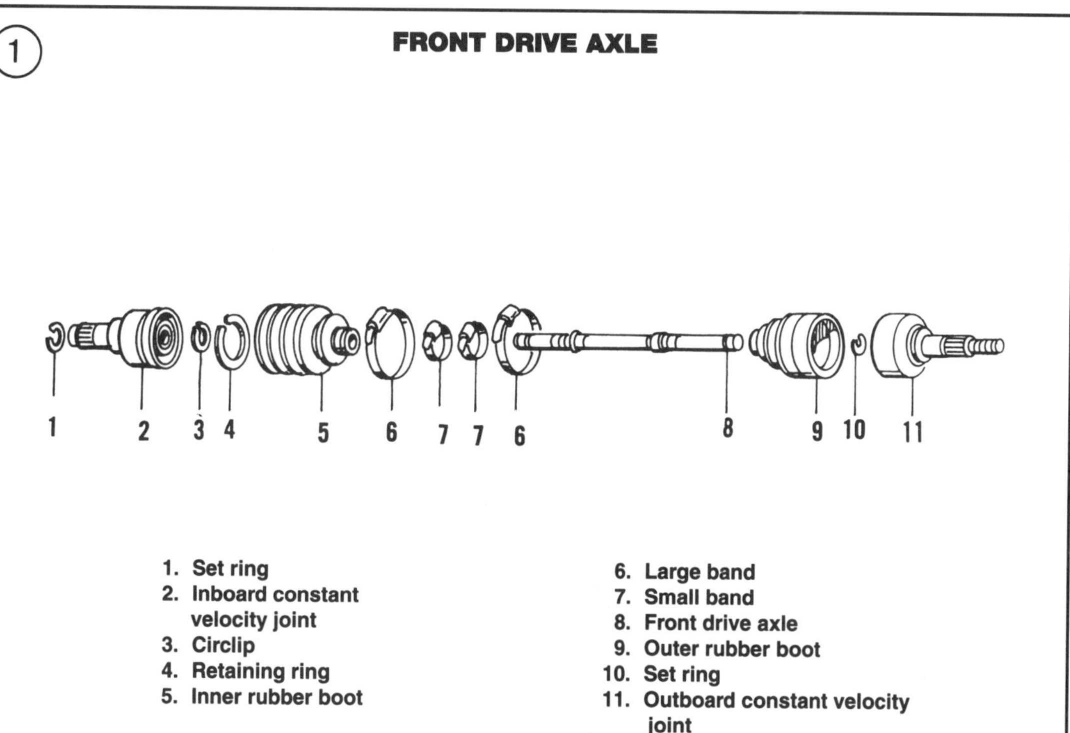

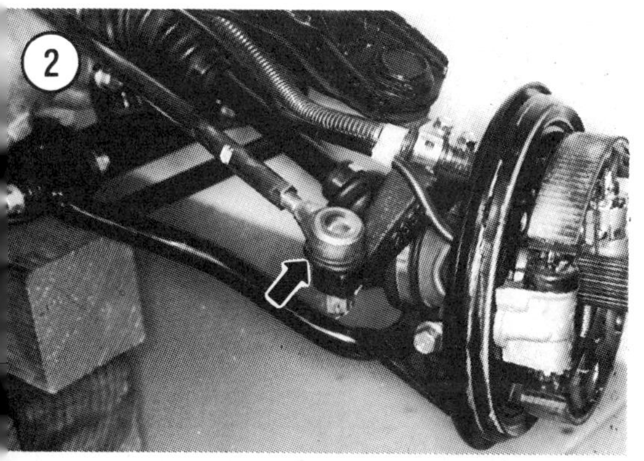

c. Lubricate the front differential seal and inner splines (**Figure 9**) with a molybdenum disulfide grease.
d. Carefully guide the front axle into the steering knuckle (**Figure 10**).
e. Install all steering and suspension components as described in Chapter Ten.
f. Install the brake drum (Chapter Thirteen).

Inspection

NOTE
The axle boots are subjected to much abuse. Damaged boots allow dirt, mud and moisture to enter the boot and contaminate the grease and damage the bearing.

1. Inspect the rubber boots (A, **Figure 11**) for wear, cuts or damage. Replace if necessary as described in this chapter.
2. Move each end of the front axle (B, **Figure 11**) in a circular motion and check the constant velocity joints for excessive wear or play.

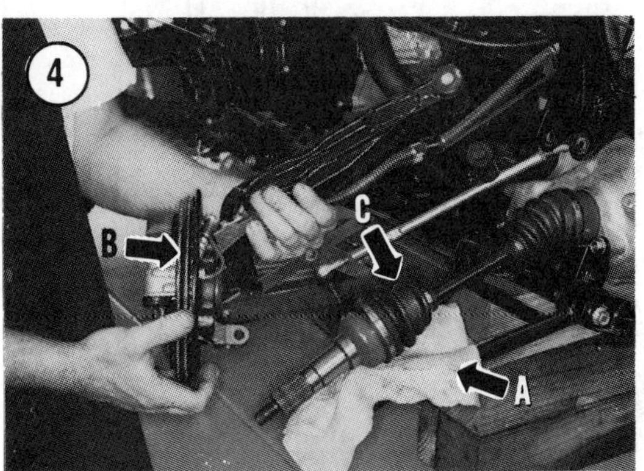

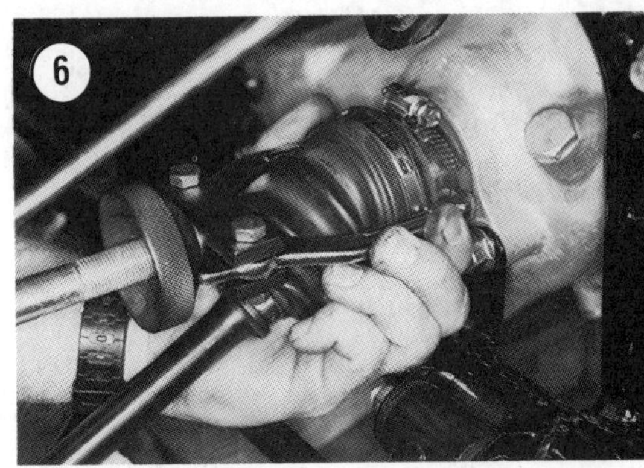

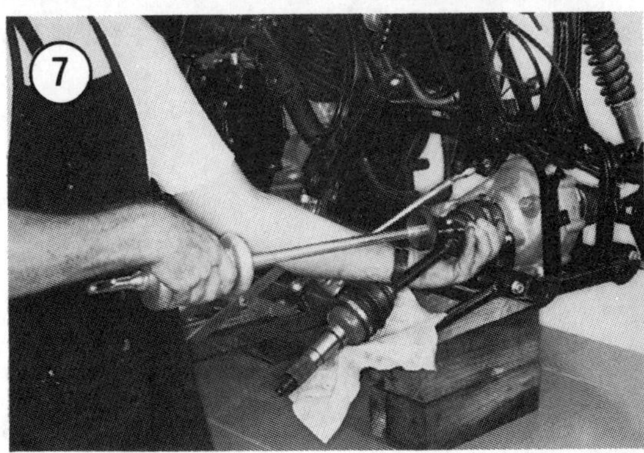

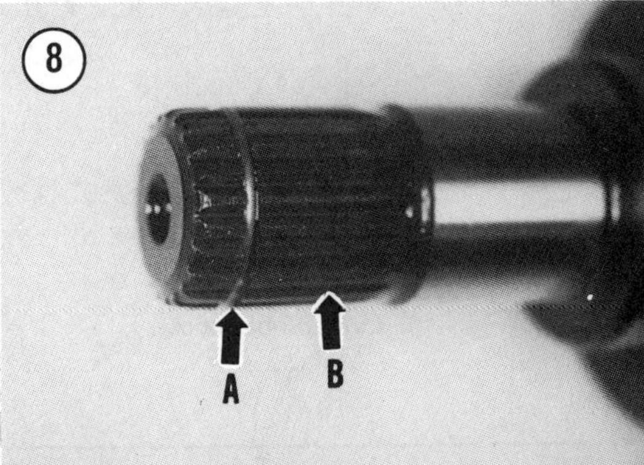

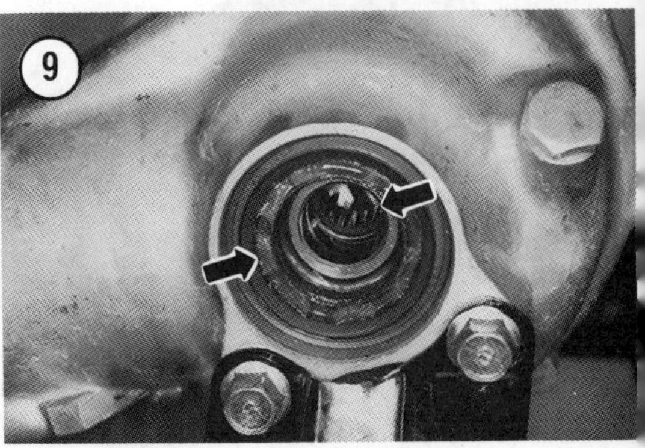

10

Front Axle Boots

Removal

The inboard or outboard constant-velocity joints are not available as replacement parts. Therefore, if either the joint or the axle is damaged, replace the axle as a unit assembly. The inboard joint can, however, be removed from the axle to allow axle boot replacement.

The front axle boot replacement kit includes both rubber boots, 4 new clamps and grease.

Refer to **Figure 1** for this procedure.

1. Remove the front axle as described in this chapter.
2. Open both inboard joint boot band clamps (**Figure 12**) with a screwdriver. Discard the clamps.
3. Carefully slide the boot (A, **Figure 13**) onto the front axle and off the inboard joint.
4. Wipe out all of the grease within the inboard joint cavity (B, **Figure 13**).
5. Remove the retaining ring (**Figure 14**) from the inboard joint.
6. Remove the inboard joint (**Figure 15**).

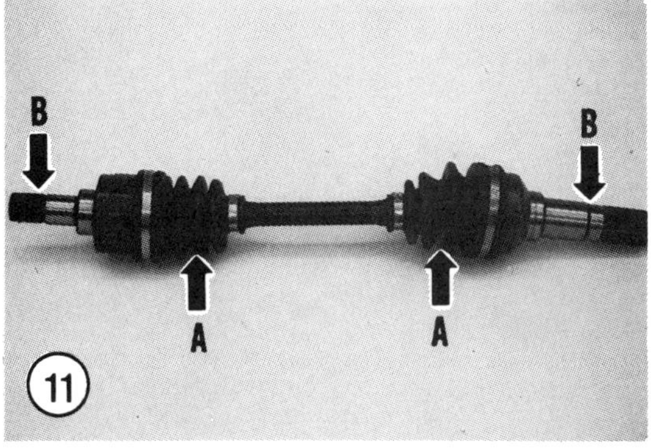

11

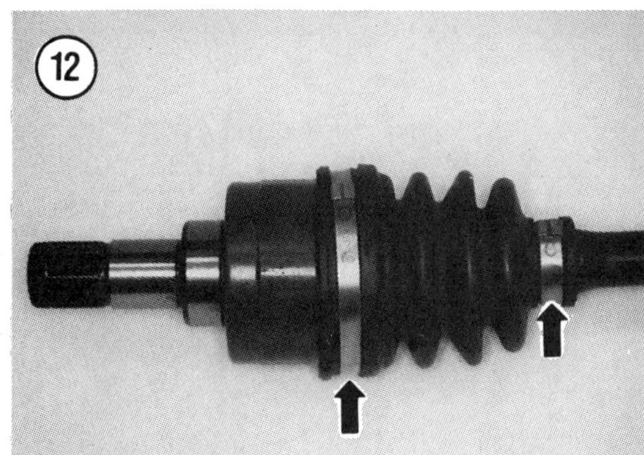

12

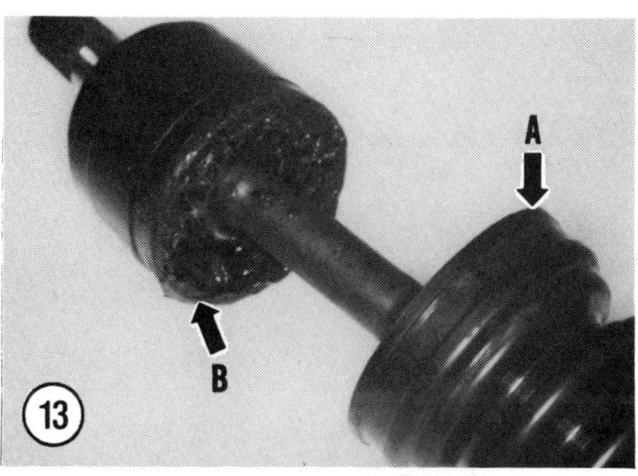

13

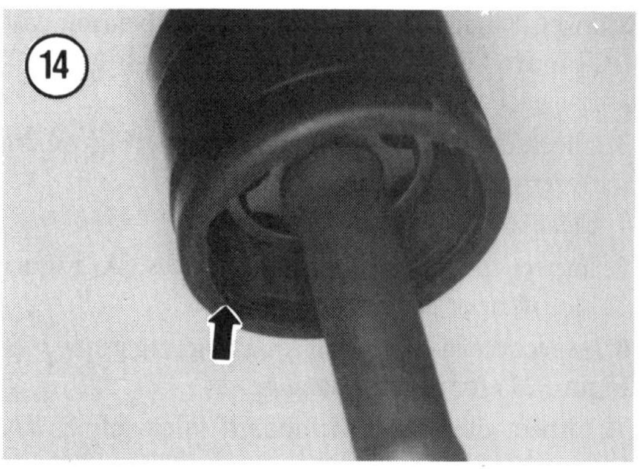

14

15

7. Remove the circlip (**Figure 16**) and slide off the bearing assembly (**Figure 17**). Be careful not to drop any of the steel balls from the bearing cage.
8. Slide the inboard boot off the front axle.

NOTE
To remove the outboard boot, continue with Step 9.

9. Open the outboard joint boot clamps (A, **Figure 18**) with a screwdriver. Discard the clamps.
10. Slide the outboard boot (B, **Figure 18**) off the front axle.
11. Inspect the front axle as described in this chapter.

Inspection

Refer to **Figure 1** for this procedure.

CAUTION
Before cleaning the rubber boots, make sure the cleaning solvent will not damage rubber products.

1. Clean the bearing assembly in solvent. Dry the bearings with compressed air or allow to air dry.
2. Inspect the steel balls (**Figure 19**), bearing case (A, **Figure 20**) and the bearing race (B, **Figure 20**) for wear.
3. Check the bearing race inner splines (**Figure 20**) for wear or damage.
4. Clean and dry the inboard joint.
5. Inspect the inboard joint ball guides (A, **Figure 21**) for wear or damage.
6. Inspect the inboard joint retaining ring groove (B, **Figure 21**) for wear or damage.
7. Inspect the axle and inboard joint splines (A, **Figure 22**) wear or damage.
8. Check the circlip groove (B, **Figure 22**) in the inboard joint shaft for severe wear or damage.
9. Inspect the inboard joint for cracks or damage.
10. Move the outboard joint axle and check for excessive play or noise (**Figure 23**).
11. Inspect the front axle for bending, wear or damage.
12. Inspect the inner end splines, the outer end splines and the front hub cotter pin hole for wear or damage.
13. Replace the front axle assembly if any of the components are excessively worn or damaged. Indi-

16

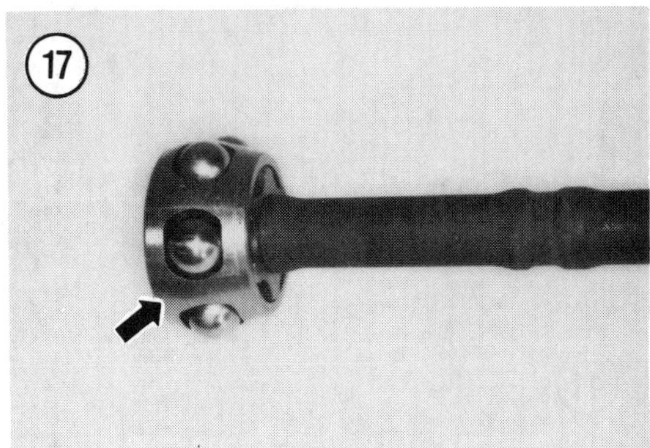
17

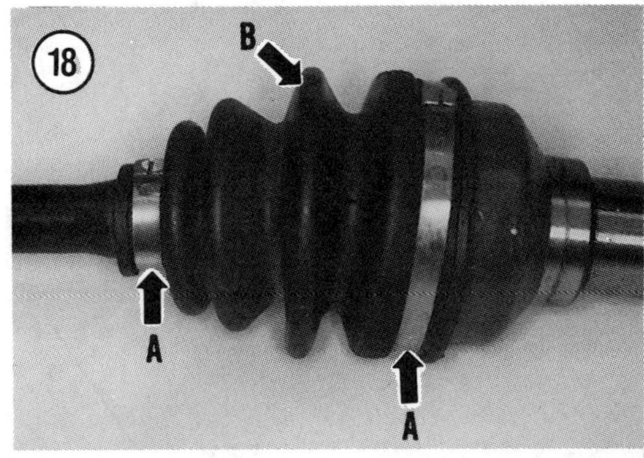

18

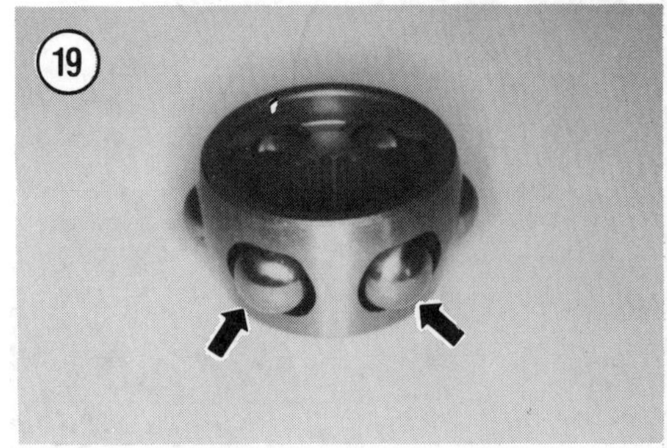
19

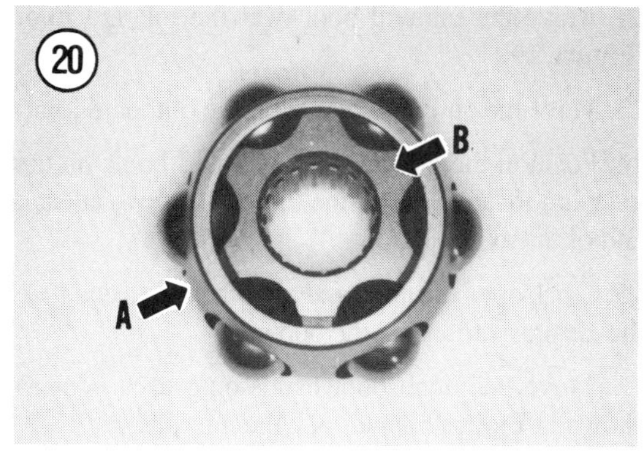

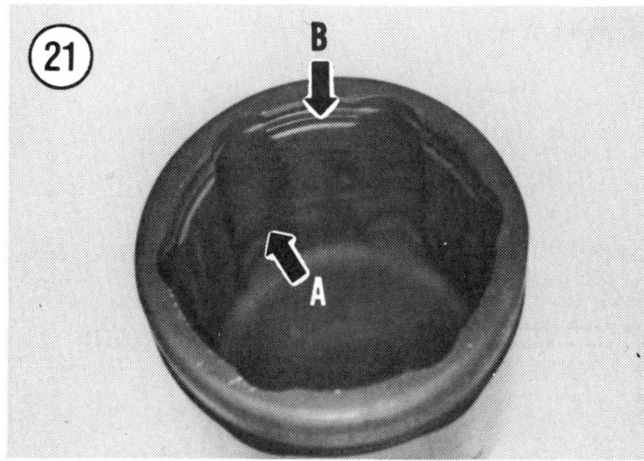

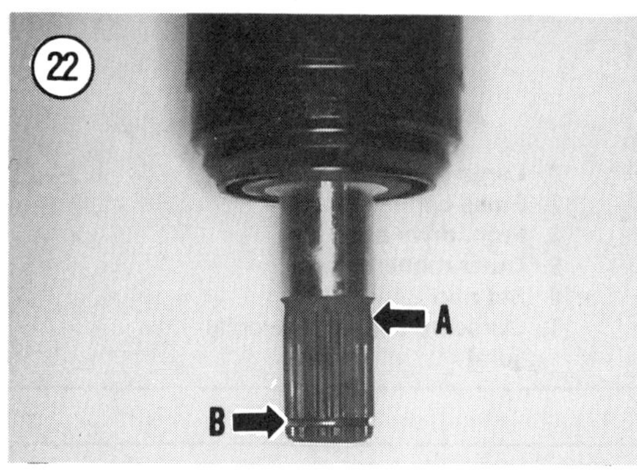

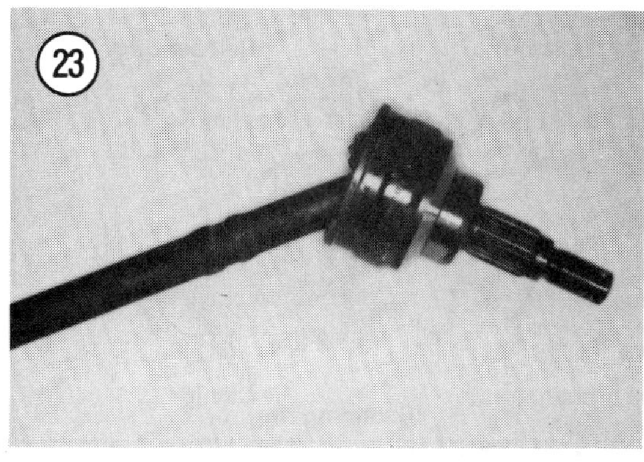

vidual replacement parts for the front axle, other than the rubber boots and clamps, are not available.

Front Axle Boots Installation

Before installing the rubber boots, note the following:

a. The inboard and outboard rubber boots are *not* symmetrical and must be installed on the correct end of the front axle.

b. A special grease is supplied with the Yamaha replacement boot kit. When grease is called for in the following steps, use this grease. If you did not buy a replacement boot kit, use molybdenum disulfide grease.

c. Do not assemble the bearing assembly until the parts are clean and dry. The bearing assembly must be dry when lubricating it.

Refer to **Figure 24** for this procedure.

1. If the outboard boot was removed, install a new boot onto the front axle. Correctly position the boot as shown in B, **Figure 18**.

2. Install 2 new small boot clamps onto the front axle.

3. Install the inboard boot and move the small boot clamp onto the boot (**Figure 25**). Do not lock the boot clamp at this time.

4. If the inboard bearing assembly (**Figure 26**) was disassembled, assemble the bearing as follows:

   a. Position the bearing race with the wide inner diameter going on first and install the race into the bearing case. Align the steel ball receptacles in both parts.

   b. Install the steel balls into their receptacles in the bearing case.

   c. Pack the bearing assembly with grease included in the boot replacement kit. Grease will help hold the steel balls in place.

5. Install the bearing—small diameter end first—onto the front axle (**Figure 17**).

6. Push the bearing assembly on until it stops, then install a new circlip (**Figure 16**) into the groove in the shaft. Make sure the circlip seats in the groove completely.

7. Apply a liberal amount of grease to the bearing assembly (**Figure 27**). Work the grease between the balls, race, and case. Check for voids and fill with grease.

8. Lubricate the inboard joint inner surface with grease.

9. Install the inboard joint over the bearing assembly and install the retaining ring. Make sure the retaining ring seats in the groove completely. Position the retaining ring so that its end gap aligns with one of the outer race projections as shown in **Figure 28**.

10. After the retaining ring is in place, fill the inboard joint cavity behind the bearing assembly with grease (B, **Figure 13**).

11. Pack each boot with grease.

12. Move the inboard boot over the inboard joint (**Figure 29**).

13. Move the outboard boot over the outboard joint.

14. Position the inboard and outboard boots on the axle and locate them in the locating groove at each end of the axle.

15. Crack open the large end of each boot to equalize the air pressure inside the boots.

16. Move the small boot bands onto each boot as shown in **Figure 30** and lock them in place.

(24)

FRONT DRIVE AXLE

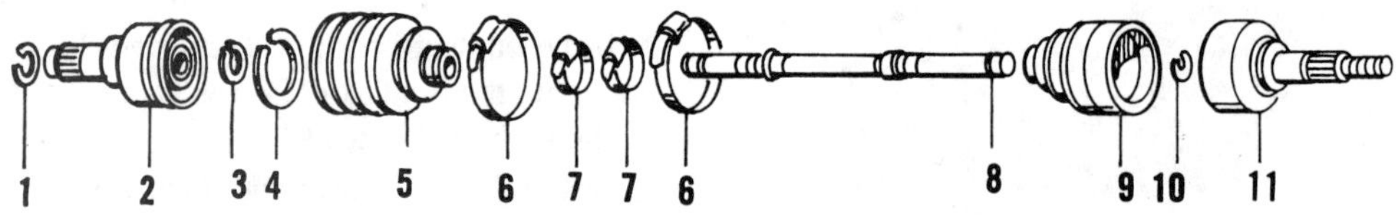

1 2 3 4 5 6 7 7 6 8 9 10 11

1. Set ring
2. Inboard constant velocity joint
3. Circlip
4. Retaining ring
5. Inner rubber boot
6. Large band
7. Small band
8. Front drive axle
9. Outer rubber boot
10. Set ring
11. Outboard constant velocity joint

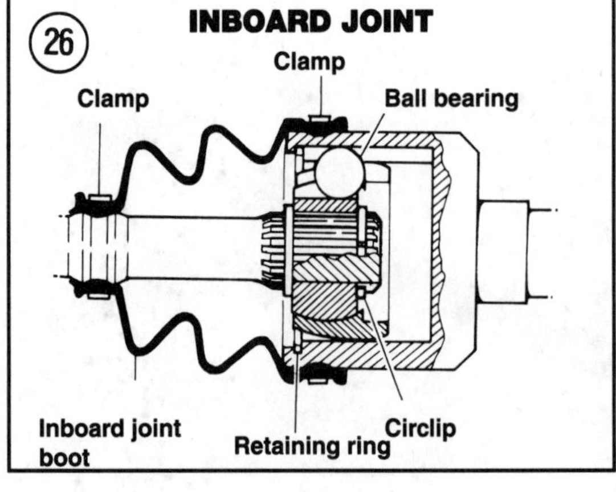

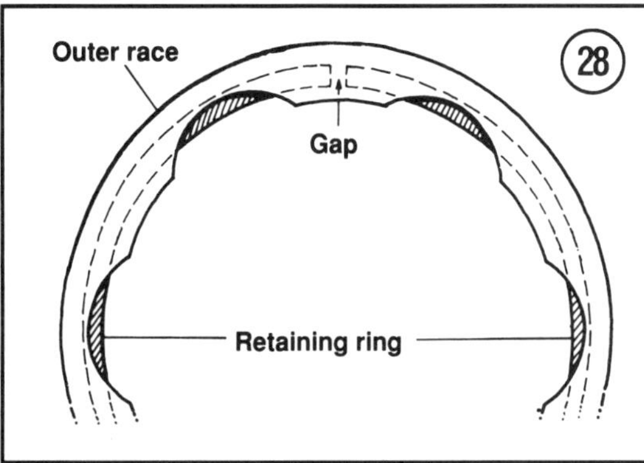

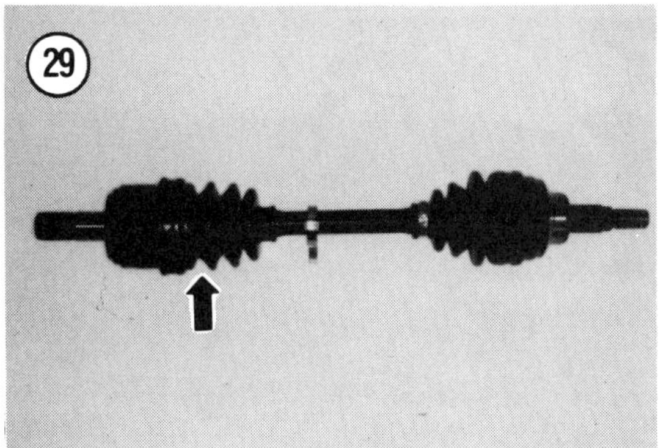

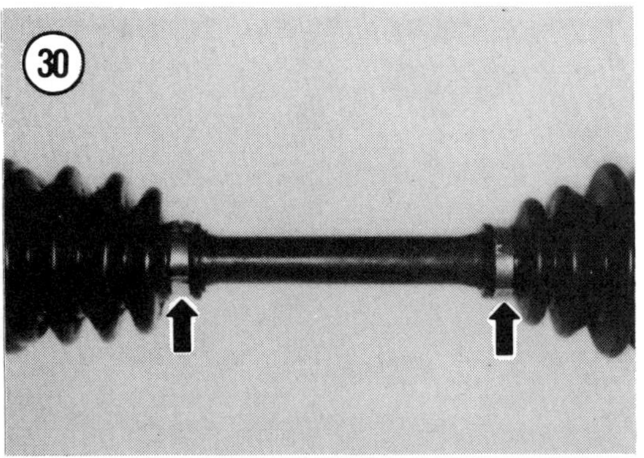

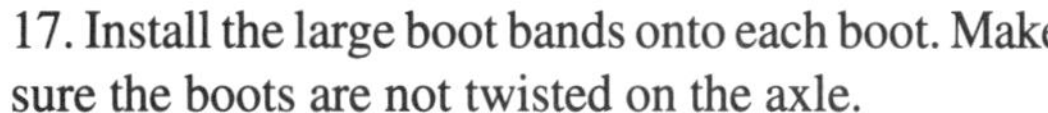

17. Install the large boot bands onto each boot. Make sure the boots are not twisted on the axle.
18. Refer to **Figure 31** and lock both large boot bands in place.
19. Apply grease to the end of the axle splines.
20. Install the front axle as described in this chapter.

FRONT DIFFERENTIAL GEARCASE

Removal

1. Unbolt and remove the front engine guard.
2. Drain the oil from the front gearcase (Chapter Three).
3. Remove the front axles as described in this chapter.
4. Tie the upper control arm assembly (**Figure 32**) to the frame.
5. Remove the oil cooler hose clamp bolt and clamp (A, **Figure 33**).
6. Remove the bolts and washers (B, **Figure 33**) securing the front section of the drive shaft protector and remove the protector (C, **Figure 33**).

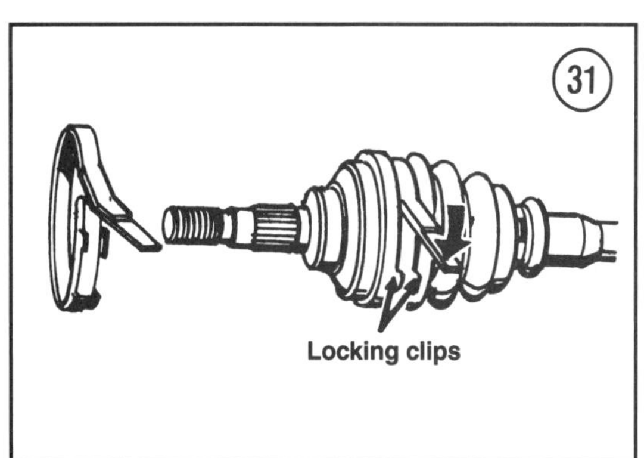

7. Remove the gearcase mounting bolts. See **Figure 34** (side bolts) and **Figure 35** (rear bolts).
8. Disconnect the vent hose from the front final gearcase.
9. Slide the rubber boot (**Figure 36**) off the front universal joint and onto the drive shaft.

NOTE
When disconnecting the drive shaft in Step 11, the spring and spring seat will fall off. Do not lose these parts.

10. Lift the gearcase up and move it forward to disengage the front universal joint (**Figure 37**) from the drive shaft, then remove the gearcase.
11. Install the gearcase by reversing these steps, while noting the following:
    a. Lubricate the shaft splines with molybdenum disulfide grease.
    b. Slide the spring seat and spring (B, **Figure 38**) onto the drive shaft.
    c. Position the gearcase into the frame and align the front drive shaft splines with the gearcase. Push the gearcase onto the drive shaft until it bottoms out.
    d. Install the side (**Figure 34**) and rear (**Figure 35**) gearcase mounting bolts and tighten finger-tight.
    e. Tighten the rear gearcase mounting bolts (**Figure 35**) as specified in **Table 1**.
    f. Tighten the side gearcase mounting bolts (**Figure 34**) as specified in **Table 1**.
    g. Slide the drive shaft rubber boot (A, **Figure 38**) back over the spring (B, **Figure 38**) and onto the front universal joint. Make sure it is correctly seated on both the drive shaft and the universal joint (**Figure 36**). This is necessary to keep moisture and dirt out of the front universal joint.
    h. Fill the front differential gearcase with the recommended type and quantity of oil as described in Chapter Three.

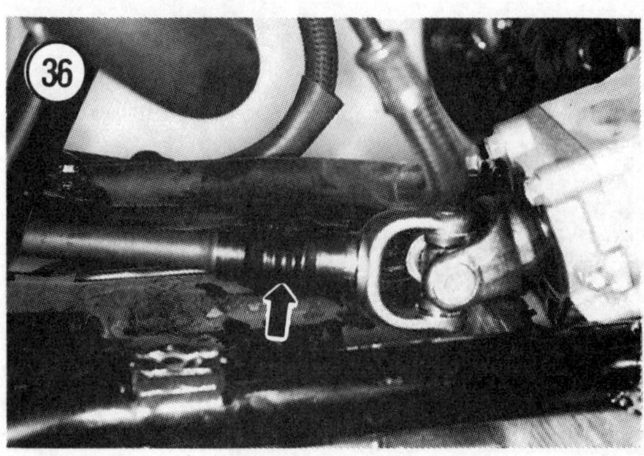

Disassembly/Inspection/Assembly

The front differential gearcase requires a number of special tools for disassembly and reassembly. The price of these tools could be more than the cost of most repairs performed at a dealership.

1. Check the entire front final drive unit for oil leakage.

2. Inspect the pinion gear splines for excessive wear or damage. If damaged, refer repair to a Yamaha dealership.

3. Rotate the drive pinion by hand. It should turn smoothly and quietly. If the rotation is rough or noisy, have the unit serviced at a Yamaha dealership.

FRONT DRIVE SHAFT

The front drive shaft (**Figure 39**) connects the front differential gearcase to the transfer gearcase.

Removal/Installation

1. Park the vehicle on a level surface and set the parking brake. Block the wheels so the vehicle will not roll in either direction.

NOTE
The front drive shaft cannot be removed without first removing either the front differential gearcase or the transfer gearcase. The front differential is the easiest component to remove, but if the transfer gearcase is also going to be removed for service, remove it instead.

2. Remove the front differential or transfer gearcase as required.

3. Remove the oil cooler hose clamp bolt and clamp (A, **Figure 33**).

4. Remove the bolts and washers (B, **Figure 33**) securing the front section of the drive shaft protector and remove the front protector (C, **Figure 33**).

5. Remove the bolts and washers securing the rear section of the drive shaft protector and remove the rear protector (**Figure 40**).

6. Pull the front drive shaft toward the front and disengage it from the transfer gearcase and remove it from the vehicle.

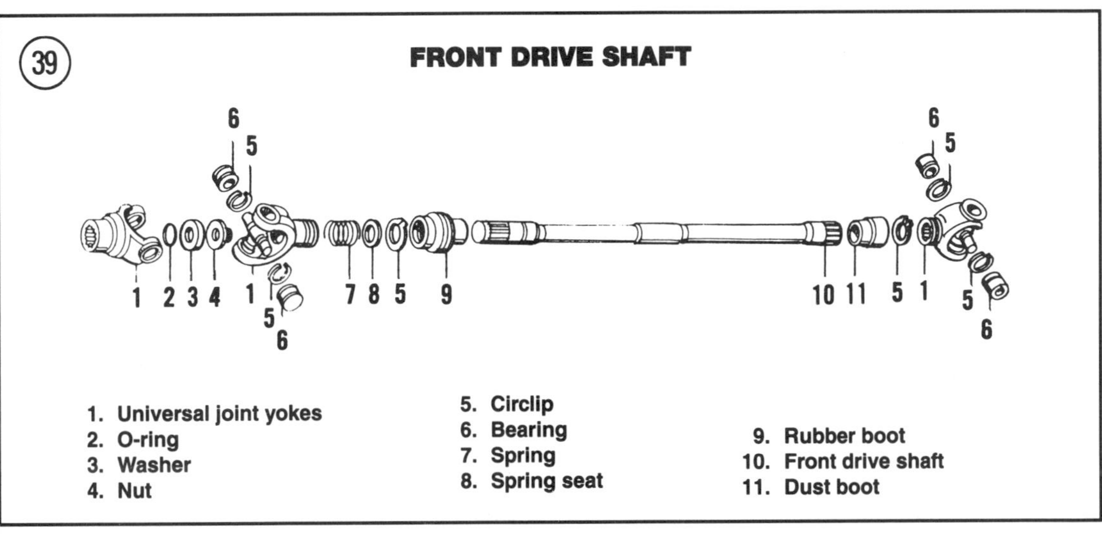

1. Universal joint yokes
2. O-ring
3. Washer
4. Nut
5. Circlip
6. Bearing
7. Spring
8. Spring seat
9. Rubber boot
10. Front drive shaft
11. Dust boot

11

7A. If the front differential is still in place, slide the drive shaft rubber boot (**Figure 36**) off the front universal joint and onto the drive shaft.

7B. If the transfer gearcase is still in place, slide the drive shaft dust boot off the rear universal joint and onto the drive shaft.

8. Remove the front drive shaft from the frame.

9. Install the front drive shaft by reversing these removal steps, while noting the following:

   a. Perform the *Inspection* procedures in this section.
   b. Lubricate the front drive shaft splines and the front and rear universal joint splines with molybdenum disulfide grease.
   c. Slide the drive shaft front rubber boot (A, **Figure 38**) back over the spring (B, **Figure 38**) and onto the front universal joint.

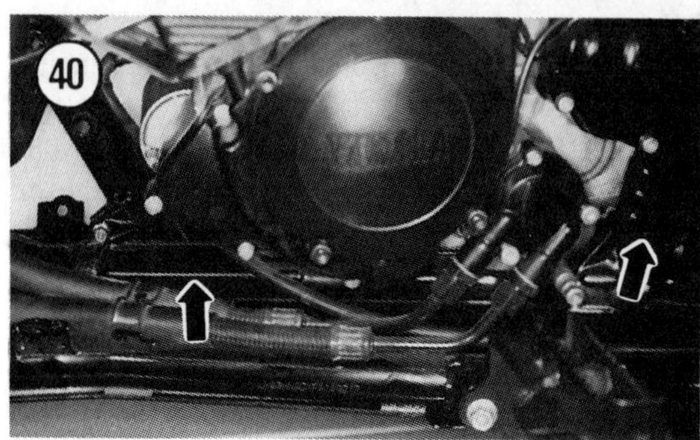

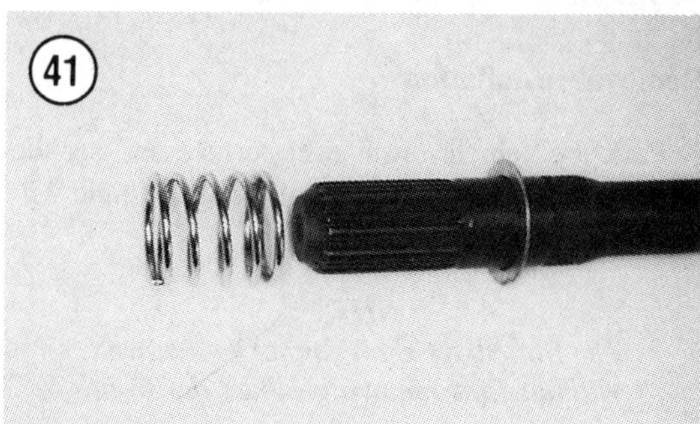

Inspection

1. Check the front drive shaft for damage or bending.
2. Remove the spring (**Figure 41**) from the front splines. Check the spring for damage or stretched coils. Replace if necessary.
3. Wipe the old grease off the drive shaft splines.
4. Inspect the splines (**Figure 41**) for excessive wear or damage. Replace the drive shaft if the splines are damaged. If the splines are damaged also, inspect the inner splines on both universal joints for wear or damage.
5. Check the spring seat (A, **Figure 42**) and circlip (B, **Figure 42**) for wear or damage. Replace either part if necessary.
6. Check the rubber boot and replace if damaged.

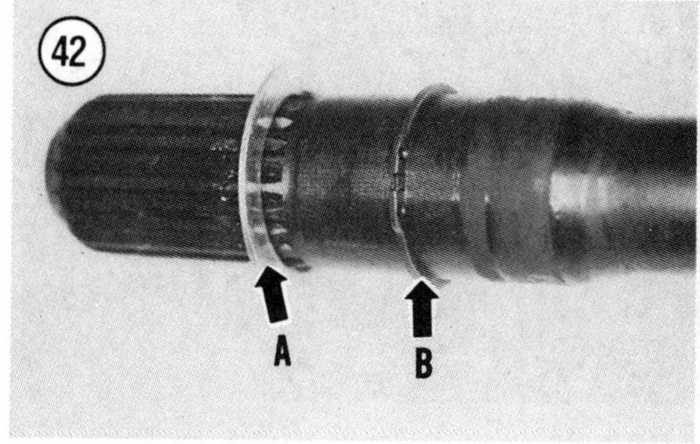

Table 1 FRONT DRIVE MECHANISM TIGHTENING TORQUES

	N•m	ft.-lb.
Gearcase mounting bolts		
Side bolts	55	40
Rear bolts	23	17

CHAPTER TWELVE

REAR SUSPENSION

This chapter provides repair and replacement procedures for the rear wheel and hub, rear suspension components. Service to the rear suspension consists of periodically checking bolt tightness, lubrication of all pivot points, swing arm bearing replacement and rear shock replacement.

Rear suspension specifications are listed in **Table 1** and torque specifications in **Table 2**. **Tables 1** and **2** are found at the end of this chapter.

NOTE
The 4-wheel drive is engaged at all times. It is not possible to shift the transfer gearcase out of 4-wheel drive. Therefore, if a service procedure requires rotating a wheel, all 4 wheels must be raised off the ground.

REAR WHEELS

Removal/Installation

1. Park the vehicle on level ground and set the parking brake. Block the front wheels so the vehicle cannot roll in either direction.

2. Identify the rear tires with an L (left side) or R (right side) mark. Refer to these marks to install the wheels on their correct side.

3. Loosen the lug nuts (**Figure 1**) securing the wheel to the hub/brake drum.

4. Raise the rear of the vehicle so that the rear wheel(s) is off the ground. Support the vehicle with safety stands or wooden blocks. Make sure they are properly placed before beginning work.

5. Remove the lug nuts and remove the rear wheel.

6. Clean the lug nuts in solvent and dry thoroughly.

7. Inspect the wheel for cracks, bending or other damage. If necessary, replace the wheel as described under *Tires and Wheels* in Chapter Ten.

8. Install the wheel onto the studs. The rotation arrow (**Figure 2**) on each tire must face forward.
9. Install the lug nuts with their tapered end (**Figure 3**) facing toward the wheel. Tighten the nuts finger-tight to center the wheel squarely against the brake drum.
10. Tighten the rear wheel lug nuts (**Figure 1**) as specified in **Table 2**.
11. After the wheel is installed completely, rotate it and apply the rear brake several times to make sure that the wheel rotates freely and that the brake is operating correctly.
12. Measure wheel runout with a dial indicator as described under *Wheel Bearings* in this chapter.

WHEEL BEARINGS

The following procedure inspects the runout of the rear wheels, hubs, rear axle and wheel bearings. The rear wheel bearings are mounted inside the final drive housing.

Inspection

1. Check that the lug nuts (**Figure 1**) are tightened to the torque specification in **Table 2**.
2. Park the vehicle on level ground and set the parking brake.
3. Raise the vehicle so all 4 wheels are off the ground. Support the vehicle with safety stands or wooden blocks. Make sure they are properly placed before beginning work.
4. Mount a dial indicator against the rim as shown in **Figure 4** to measure radial and lateral runout. Turn the tire slowly by hand and read the movement indicated on the dial indicator. See **Table 1** for runout limits. Note the following:
   a. If the runout is out of specification, first check the condition of the wheel assembly. If the wheel is bent or damaged, it may require replacement.
   b. If the wheel condition is good but the runout is out of specification, remove the wheel and check the hub assembly for damage.
   c. If the wheel and hub condition is good but the runout is excessive, remove the rear axle and check its runout as described in this chapter.
   d. If the rear axle is not bent, the rear wheel bearings are probably worn or damaged.

REAR HUB (LEFT SIDE)

Removal/Installation

1. Remove the left rear wheel as described in this chapter.
2. Remove the rubber cap (**Figure 5**) from the end of the axle.
3. Remove the rear axle nut cotter pin and discard it.

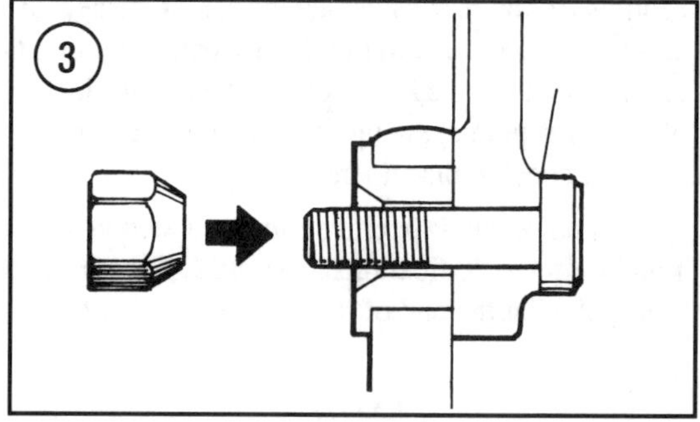

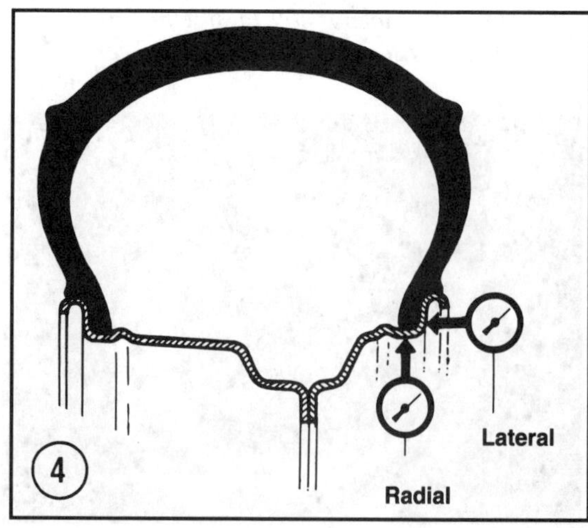

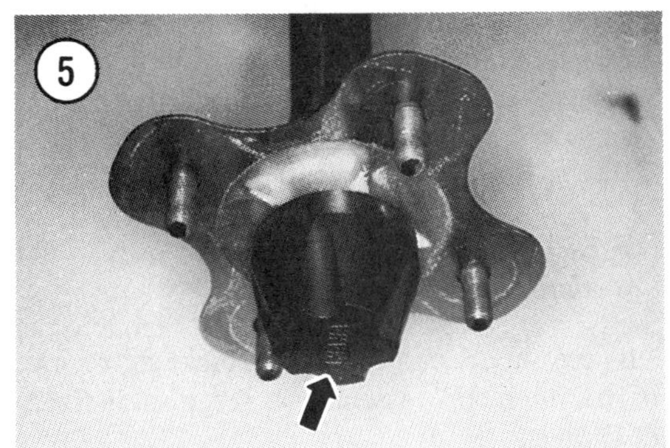

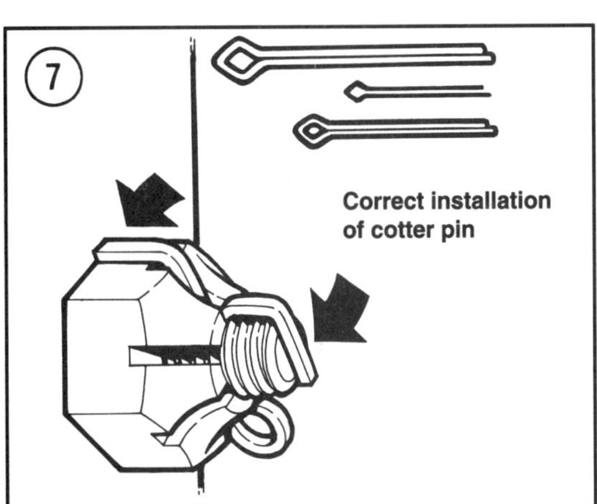

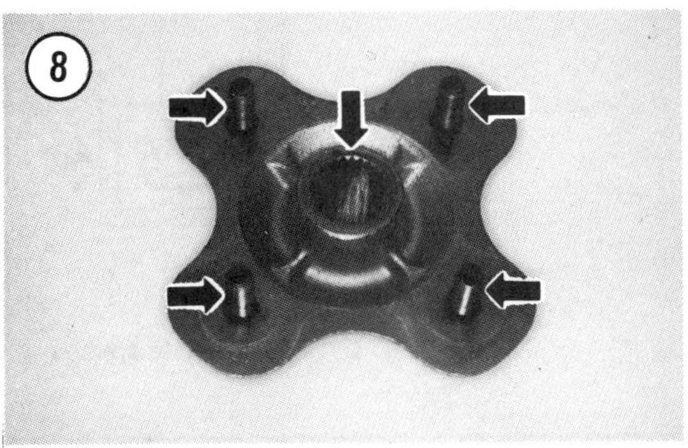

4. Remove the rear axle nut (A, **Figure 6**), washer (B, **Figure 6**) and rear hub (C, **Figure 6**).

5. Clean the rear hub and axle splines of all rust and other residue.

6. Install the rear hub onto the rear axle and push it on until it stops.

7. Install the washer and the rear axle nut.

8. Tighten the rear axle nut (A, **Figure 6**) as specified in **Table 2**.

9. Install a new cotter pin and bend the ends over completely (**Figure 7**).

Inspection

1. Inspect the hub inner splines (**Figure 8**) for wear or damage. Replace the hub if necessary.

2. Check the studs (**Figure 8**) for damaged threads. Repair minor thread damage with the appropriate size metric die. If the damage is severe, replace the hub assembly as the studs cannot be replaced separately.

3. Inspect the axle splines (**Figure 9**) for twisting or other damage.

4. Check the axle cotter pin hole. Replace the axle if the hole is damaged or excessively worn.

REAR HUB/BRAKE DRUM (RIGHT SIDE)

The right side hub is a combination rear hub and brake drum assembly. Refer to Chapter Thirteen for removal, inspection and installation procedures.

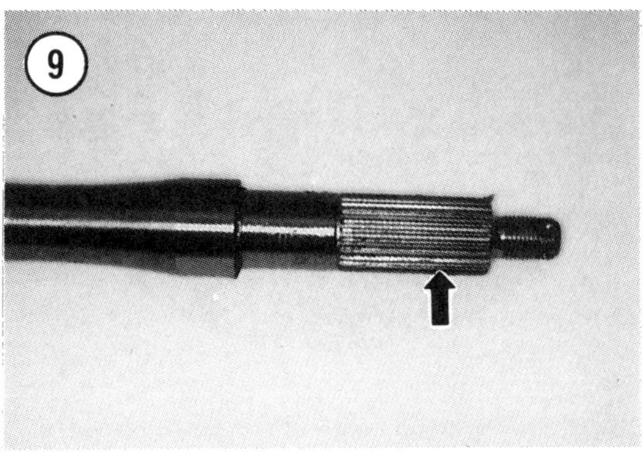

REAR AXLE

The rear axle can be removed while the final drive unit is mounted in the frame.

Refer to **Figure 10** when servicing the rear axle in this section.

Removal

1. Remove the rear wheels as described in this chapter.

2. Remove the brake drum (**Figure 11**) as described in Chapter Thirteen.

NOTE
The rear axle can be removed with the rear brake backing plate attached to the swing arm. It is removed in this procedure for clarity.

3. If necessary, release the parking brake and remove the rear drum brake assembly as described in Chapter Thirteen.

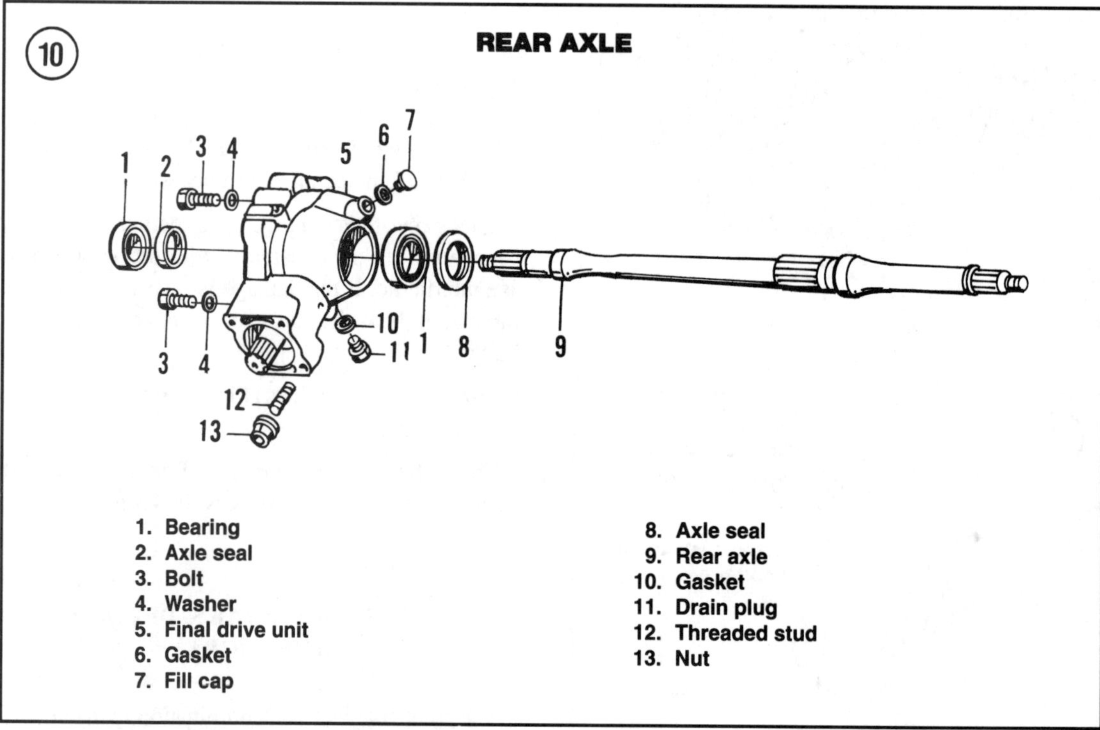

1. Bearing
2. Axle seal
3. Bolt
4. Washer
5. Final drive unit
6. Gasket
7. Fill cap
8. Axle seal
9. Rear axle
10. Gasket
11. Drain plug
12. Threaded stud
13. Nut

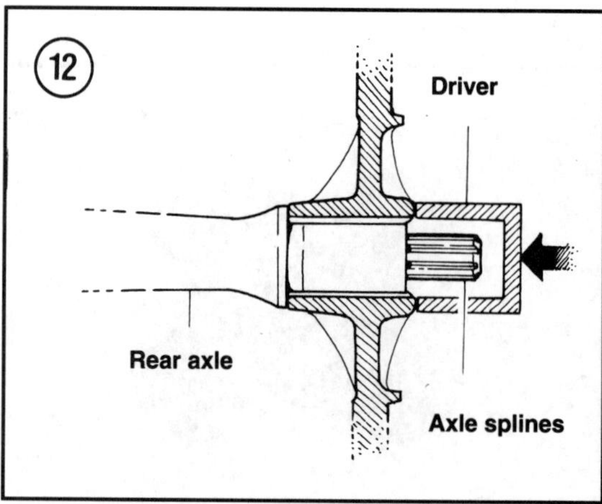

4. Make sure the vehicle is secured on a stand.

WARNING
Safety glasses must be worn when driving the axle out in the following steps.

CAUTION
When removing the rear axle, never hit directly against the axle with a hammer as this will damage the axle threads. Use a suitable piece of pipe and hammer as described in Step 5.

5. Center a piece of pipe over the right side rear axle threads and set it against the axle shoulder (**Figure 12**). Drive against the pipe with a hammer and remove the axle from the left side.

6. Inspect the final drive unit dust cover, oil seal and bearings as described in this chapter.

7. Inspect the axle as described in this chapter.

Inspection

1. Wash and dry the axle. Remove any rust and corrosion residue from the axle surfaces.

2. Inspect the axle for fatigue, fractures and other damage. Inspect the splines (A, **Figure 13**) for twisting or other damage.

3. Check the hole at each end of the axle where the cotter pin fits. Make sure there are no fractures or cracks leading out toward the end of the axle. Replace the axle if necessary.

4. Check the bearing machined surfaces (B, **Figure 13**) or scoring, cracks or other damage.

5. Measure the axle runout with a set of V-blocks and a dial indicator (**Figure 14**). If the axle runout exceeds 1.5 mm (0.06 in.), replace the axle.

WARNING
Do not attempt to straighten a bent axle. Axle failure may occur during riding and cause loss of control and severe personal injury.

6. Inspect the hub splines (**Figure 15**) and brake drum splines for excessive wear or damage. Replace the hub(s) and/or brake disc if necessary.

7. Inspect the axle seals (**Figure 16**) for wear or damage and replace if necessary.

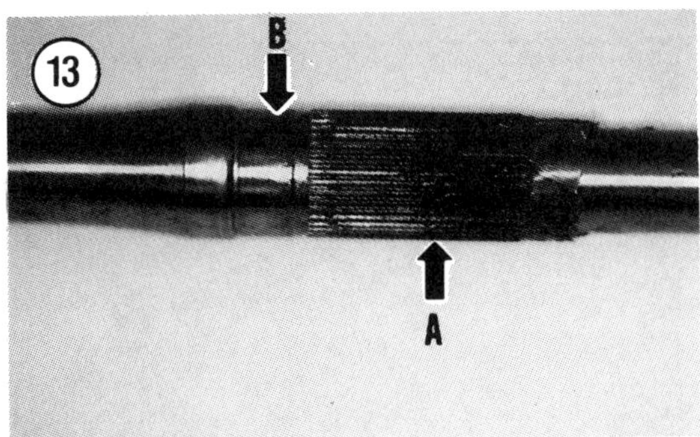

12

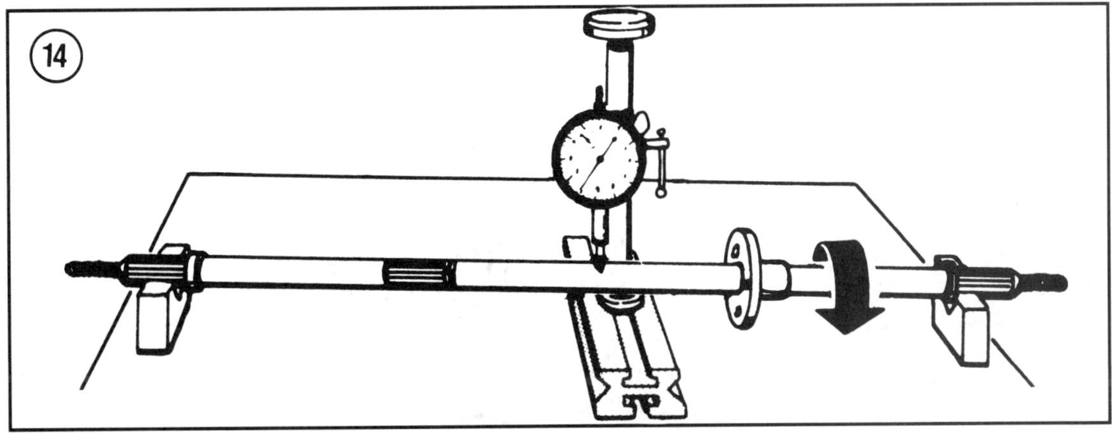

Installation

1. Apply a light coat of wheel bearing grease to the lips of the axle (**Figure 16**) and to the splines (A, **Figure 13**) on the rear axle.

CAUTION
Make sure the rear axle splines are correctly aligned with the ring gear splines in the final drive unit before exerting any force on the rear axle.

2. Working from the left-hand side, slide the rear axle (**Figure 17**) assembly into the final drive unit. Push the axle in until it stops (**Figure 18**). If necessary, drive the axle into place with the same piece of pipe (**Figure 12**) used during axle removal.
3. Install the rear brake drum (Chapter Thirteen).
4. Install the left-hand axle hub as described in this chapter.
5. Install the rear wheels as described in this chapter.

FINAL DRIVE UNIT AND SHORT DRIVE SHAFT

Removal

This procedure describes removal of the final drive unit and the short drive shaft located within the rear swing arm.

1. Remove the rear axle as described in this chapter.
2. Remove the skid plate from underneath the final drive unit.
3. Drain the final gear case oil (Chapter Three).
4. Disconnect the vent hose (**Figure 19**) from the final drive unit.

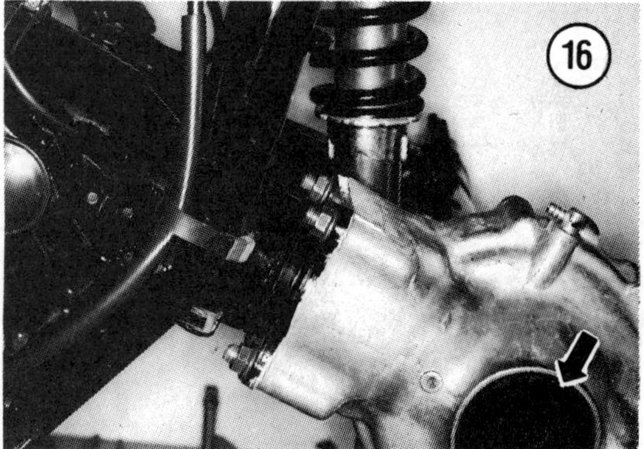

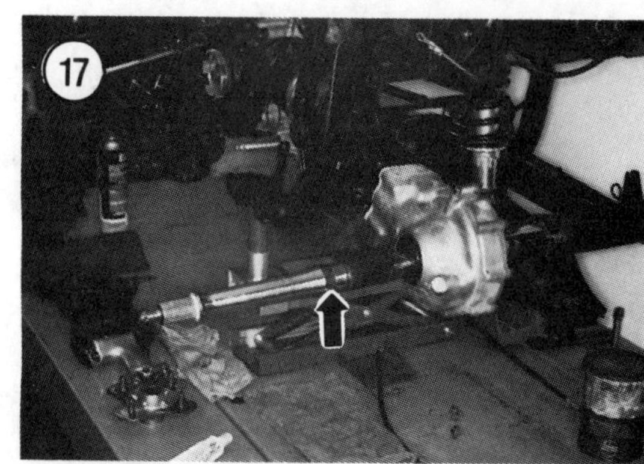

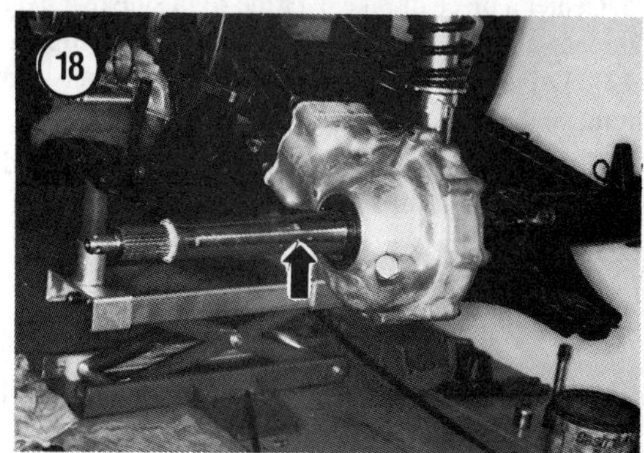

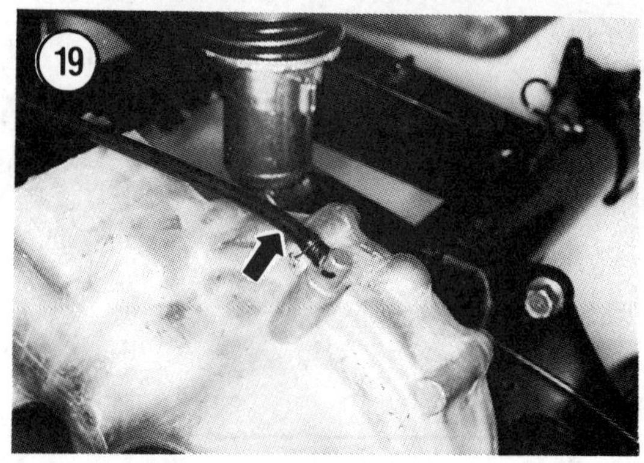

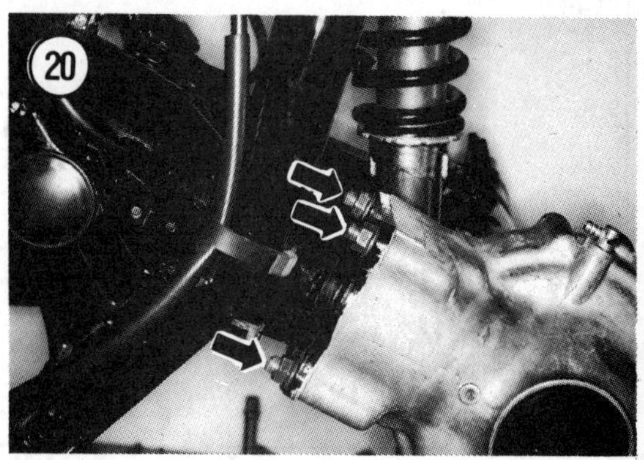

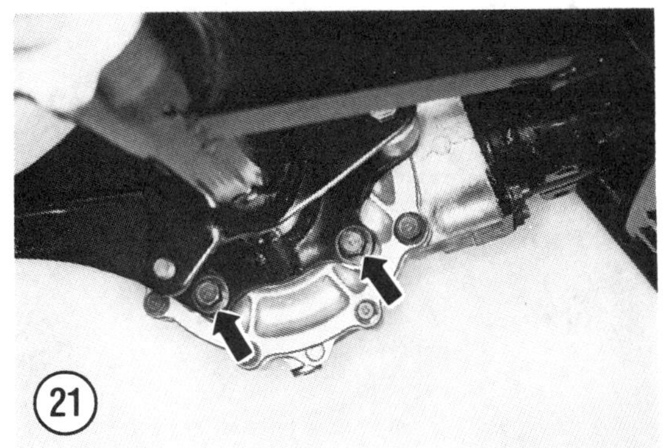
21

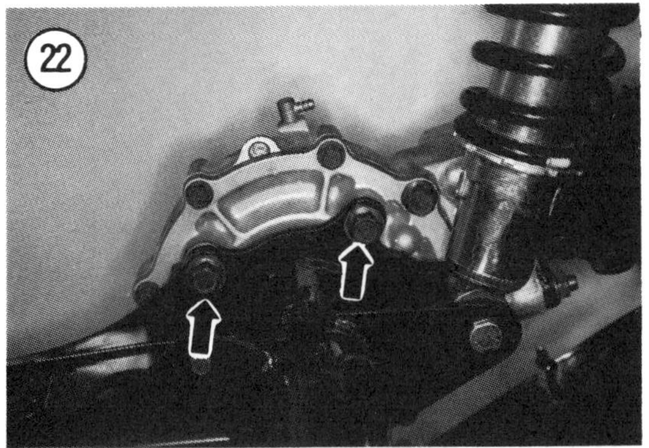
22

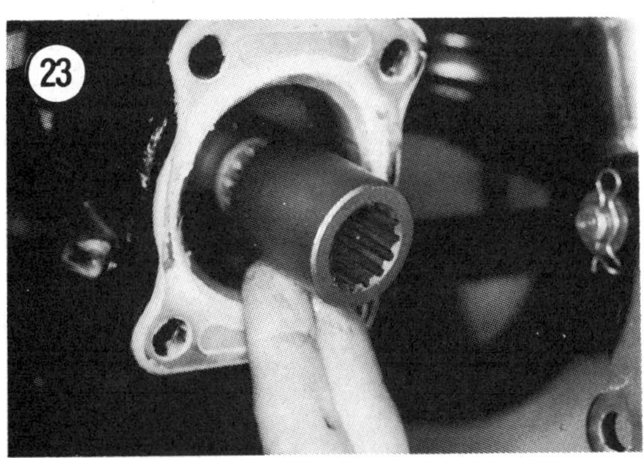
23

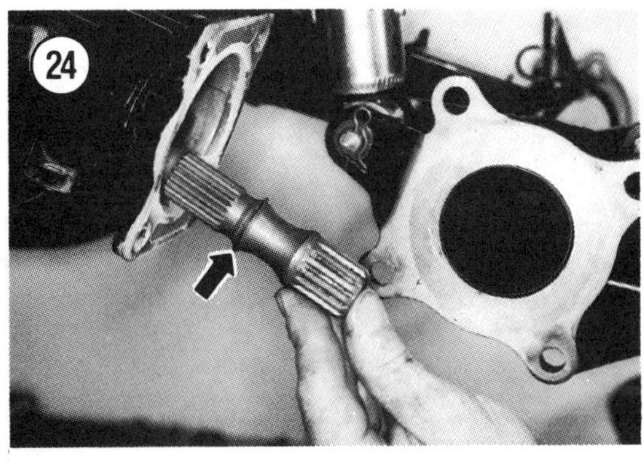
24

5. Support the final drive unit with a jack or wooden blocks.

NOTE

***Figure 20** shows 3 of the 4 nuts used to secure the final drive unit to the swing arm. Be sure to remove all 4 nuts.*

6. Loosen, the 4 nuts (**Figure 20**) securing the final drive unit to the swing arm.
7. Remove the lower (**Figure 21**) and upper (**Figure 22**) bolts securing the final drive unit to the swing arm.
8. Hold onto the final drive unit, then remove the 4 nuts (**Figure 20**) loosened in Step 5.
9. Pull the final drive unit toward the rear and away from the swing arm.
10. Remove the coupler (**Figure 23**) and the short drive shaft (**Figure 24**) from the swing arm.
11. Refer to the *Disassembly/Inspection/Assembly* procedure for further information.
12. Remove all sealer residue from the swing arm and final drive unit mating surfaces.

Installation

1. Lubricate the drive shaft and coupler spines with a lithium soap base grease.
2. Install the short drive shaft with the end containing the circlip (**Figure 24**) going in first. Align the splines and install the short drive shaft into the universal joint within the swing arm. Push it in until it stops (**Figure 23**) and hold it in this position.
3. Install the coupler onto the end of the short drive shaft (**Figure 23**).
4. Apply Yamabond No. 4, ThreeBond Liquid Gasket 1104, or RTV sealant onto the swing arm mating surfaces.
5. Partially install the 2 bottom studs of the final drive unit into the swing arm mounting holes (**Figure 25**).
6. Tip the final drive unit up, insert a screwdriver between the 2 assemblies and align the coupler with the final drive splines (**Figure 26**). Then remove the screwdriver and push the final drive unit on until it bottoms.
7. Hold the final drive unit in this position and install the 4 mounting nuts (**Figure 20**) finger-tight.
8. Install the 2 upper (**Figure 22**) and 2 lower (**Figure 21**) bolts securing the final drive unit to the swing arm. Tighten all 4 bolts finger-tight.

9. Tighten the 2 upper (**Figure 22**) and 2 lower (**Figure 21**) final drive unit bolts as specified in **Table 2**.
10. Tighten the 4 final drive unit nuts (**Figure 20**) as specified in **Table 2**.
11. Connect the vent hose (**Figure 19**) to the final drive unit. Secure the hose with its clamp.
12. Install the rear axle as described in this chapter.
13. Refill the final drive unit with lubricant.

Disassembly/Inspection/Assembly

The final drive unit requires a considerable number of Yamaha special tools for disassembly and reassembly. The price of all of these tools could be more than the cost of most repairs performed at a Yamaha dealership.

1. Check the entire unit for oil leakage, cracks or other damage.
2. Inspect the pinion gear splines (A, **Figure 27**) and the coupler splines (B, **Figure 27**) for wear or damage. Slide the coupler onto the pinion gear splines and move it back and forth. It must slide easily with no binding.
3. Check the ring gear splines (**Figure 28**) for wear or damage.
4. Inspect the studs (C, **Figure 27**) for damage. Repair minor thread damage with a metric tie, or replace the studs as described in Chapter One.
5. Check the bearing housing cover bolts (**Figure 29**) for looseness. Tighten loose bolts as specified in **Table 2**.
6. Inspect the O-ring (A, **Figure 30**) and both seals (B, **Figure 30**, typical) for wear, hardness and deterioration.
7. Turn each wheel bearing (**Figure 31**, typical) with your finger. The bearings should rotate freely with no binding or roughness.

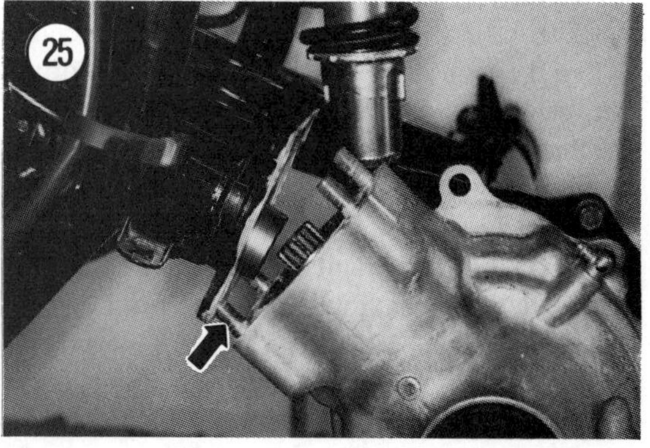

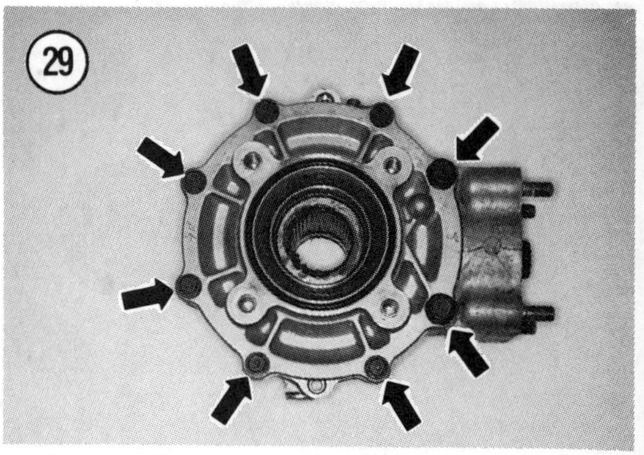

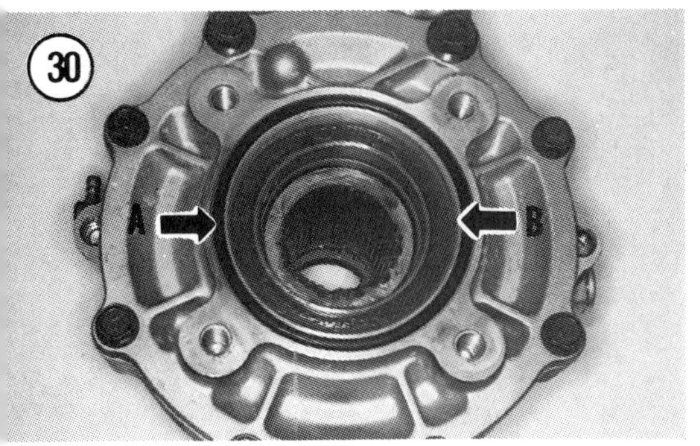

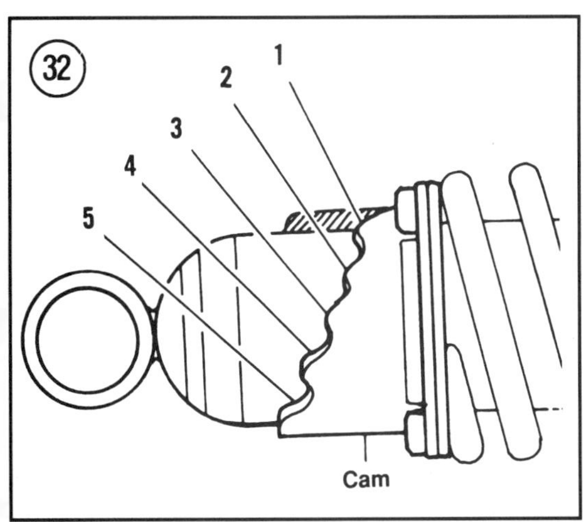

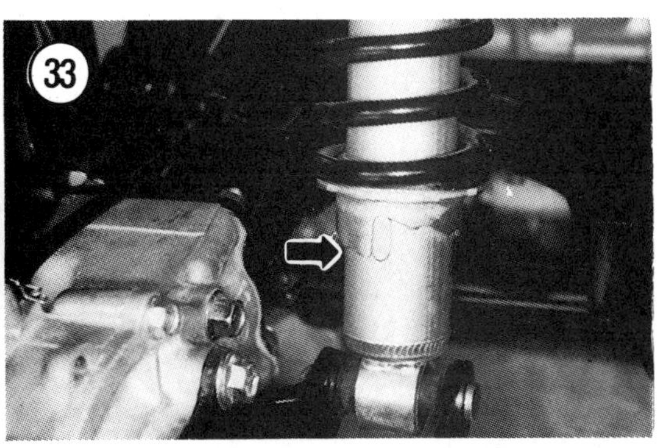

8. If any of the previous components are faulty, refer all service to a Yamaha dealership.

TIRE CHANGING AND TIRE REPAIRS

Refer to Chapter Ten for these service procedures.

SHOCK ABSORBER

All models use a single rear shock absorber and spring assembly. The stock shock absorber is a sealed unit and should not be disassembled.

Shock Spring Preload Adjustment

The rear shock absorber spring is provided with 5 preload positions (**Figure 32**). The No. 1 position is soft and the No. 5 position is hard. The spring preload can be changed by rotating the cam (**Figure 33**) at bottom of the spring. Spring preload can be changed to suit rider weight, load and riding conditions.

Shock Absorber Removal/Installation

NOTE
This procedure is shown with the final drive unit removed to show the lower mounting components. Do not remove the final drive unit for this procedure.

1. Support the vehicle with the rear wheels off the ground. Block the front wheels so the vehicle cannot roll in either direction.
2. Remove the spring clip or cotter pin (A, **Figure 34**) and washer (B, **Figure 34**) and the lower pivot pin (**Figure 35**).

3. Remove the nut and bolt securing the upper end of the shock absorber to the frame.

4. Remove the shock absorber (**Figure 36**) from the frame.

5. Remove the 2 thrust washers (**Figure 37**) from the bottom shock mount.

6. Inspect the shock absorber as described later in this section.

7. Install the shock absorber by reversing these steps while noting the following.

8. Clean the shock bolt, nut and pivot pin in solvent. Dry thoroughly.

NOTE

Use a lithium soap base grease when grease is called for in the following steps.

9. Lubricate the upper and lower shock bushings with grease.

10. Lubricate the pivot pin and upper mounting bolt with grease.

11. Lubricate the inside of both thrust washers with grease and install them onto the lower shock mount (**Figure 37**).

12. Install the shock absorber so that its spring adjuster faces down.

13. Install the upper shock bolt from the left side. Then install the nut and tighten as specified in **Table 2**.

14. Install the lower pivot pin (**Figure 35**) from the right side. Then install the washer (B, **Figure 34**) and the spring clip (A, **Figure 34**) or a new cotter pin. Bend the cotter pin arms over to lock it in place.

35

36

37

Shock Inspection

The stock shock absorber is a sealed unit and cannot be disassembled. If any part of the shock is damaged, replace the shock absorber.

1. Check the damper unit (**Figure 38**) for fluid leakage or other damage. Replace the shock if leaks are found.

WARNING

Do not attempt to disassemble the damper unit. Disassembly will release gas that is under pressure and cause possible eye injury.

38

2. Check the shock absorber bushings for deterioration, severe wear or other damage. If either is damaged, replace the shock absorber.

3. Inspect the upper mounting bolt and nut for damage.

4. Inspect the pivot pin and spring clip for severe wear or damage. Replace if necessary. If a cotter pin is used in place of the spring clip, discard the cotter pin and install a new one.

5. Replace the thrust washers (**Figure 37**) if severely worn or damaged.

SWING ARM

Bearings are pressed into both sides of the swing arm. Seals are installed on the outside of each roller bearing to prevent dirt and moisture from entering the bearings. Refer to **Figure 39** when servicing the swing arm in this section.

Swing Arm Bearing Inspection

Inspect the swing arm roller bearings periodically for excessive play, roughness or damage.

1. Remove the rear wheels as described in this chapter.

2. Remove the spring clip (A, **Figure 34**), washer (B, **Figure 34**) and lower pivot pin (**Figure 35**) securing the lower end of the shock absorber to the swing arm. Move the lower end of the shock absorber out of the way.

3. Remove the 2 thrust washers (**Figure 37**) from the lower shock mount.

NOTE
Have an assistant steady the vehicle when performing Step 4.

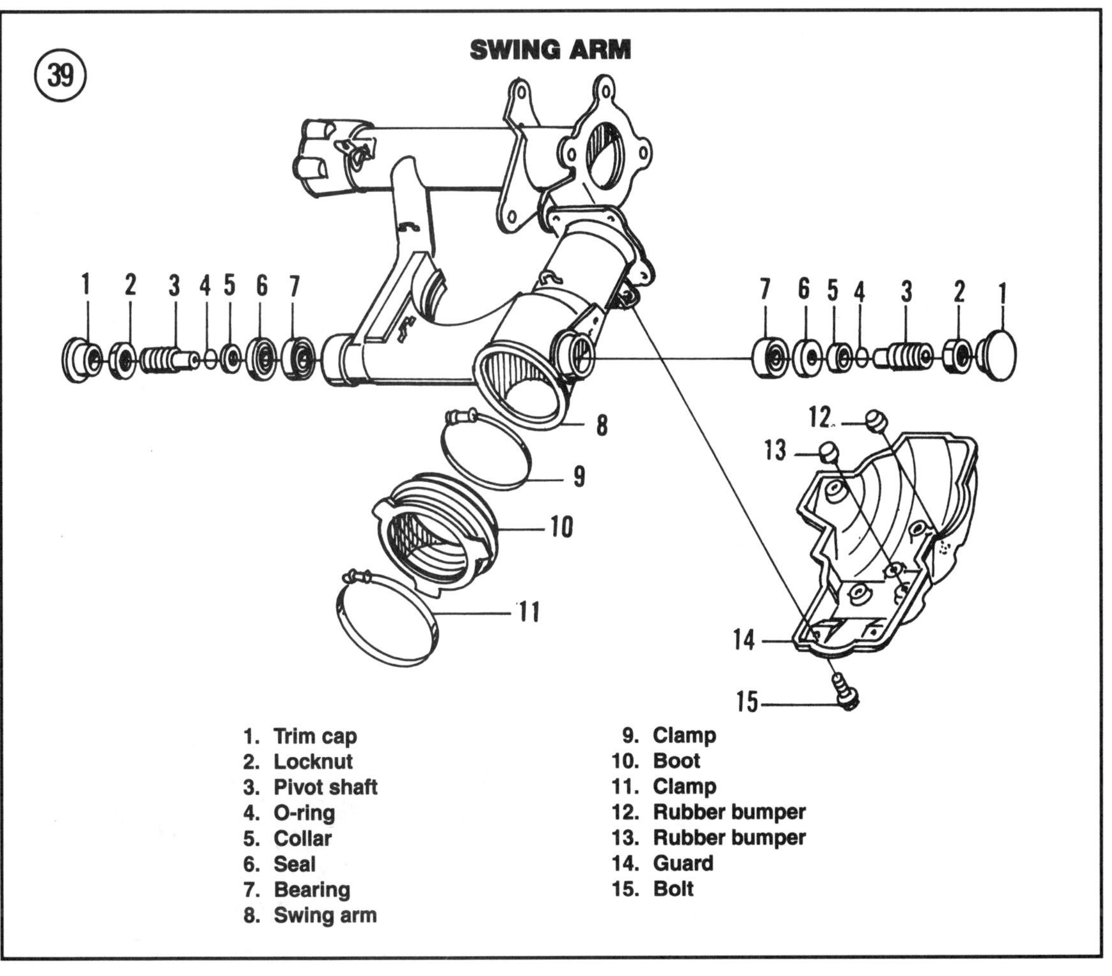

1. Trim cap
2. Locknut
3. Pivot shaft
4. O-ring
5. Collar
6. Seal
7. Bearing
8. Swing arm
9. Clamp
10. Boot
11. Clamp
12. Rubber bumper
13. Rubber bumper
14. Guard
15. Bolt

12

4. Grasp the ends of the rear axle and try to move it from side to side in a horizontal arc. There should be no noticeable side play.
5. Grasp the rear of the swing arm once again and pivot it up and down through its full travel. The swing arm should pivot smoothly without roughness or binding.
6. If play is evident and the pivot shaft on each side is tightened correctly, remove the swing arm and inspect the bearings as described in the following sections.

NOTE
Use a lithium soap base grease when grease is called for in the following steps.

7. Lubricate the pivot pin with grease.
8. Lubricate the inside of both thrust washers with grease and install them onto the lower shock mount (**Figure 37**).
9. Install the lower pivot pin (**Figure 35**) from the right side. Then install the washer (B, **Figure 34**) and the spring clip (A, **Figure 34**) or a new cotter pin. Bend the cotter pin arms over to lock it in place.

Removal

The swing arm can be removed with or without the final drive unit and rear axle installed in the swing arm. If the swing arm is going to be serviced, remove the rear axle and the final drive unit as described in this chapter.

1. Remove the rear fender (Chapter Fourteen).
2. Remove the rear axle as described in this chapter.
3. Remove the final drive unit and short drive shaft as described in this chapter.
4. Remove the brake backing plate from the swing arm (Chapter Thirteen).
5. Remove the rear shock absorber as described in this chapter.
6. Remove the clamping screws (A, **Figure 40**) on the drive shaft rubber boot.
7. Remove the cap (B, **Figure 40**) from each side of the swing arm pivot.
8. Remove the locknut (**Figure 41**) from each swing arm pivot shaft.
9. Loosen the left and right side pivot shafts (**Figure 42**). Then remove the pivot shafts, O-rings and swing arm (**Figure 43**).

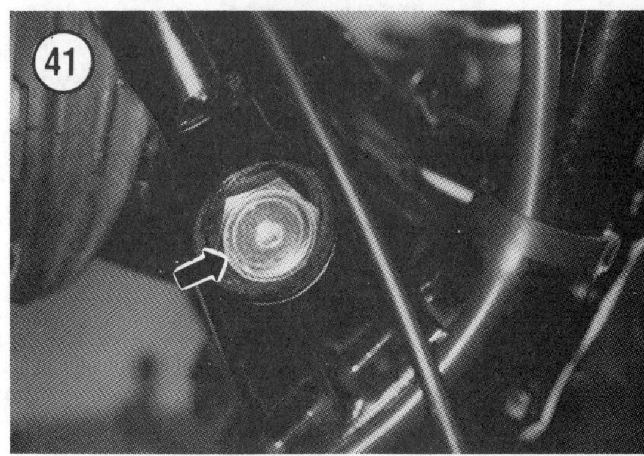

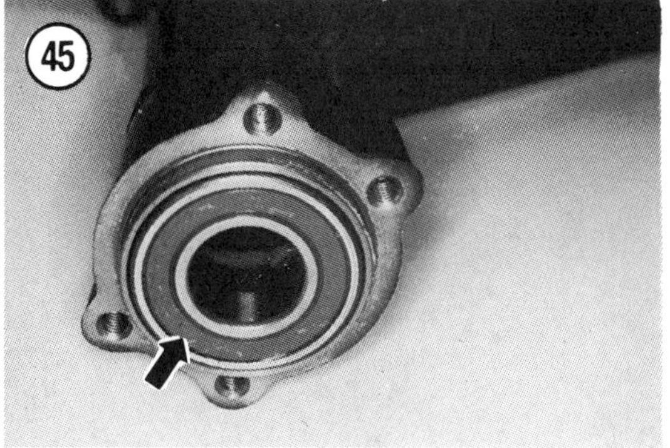

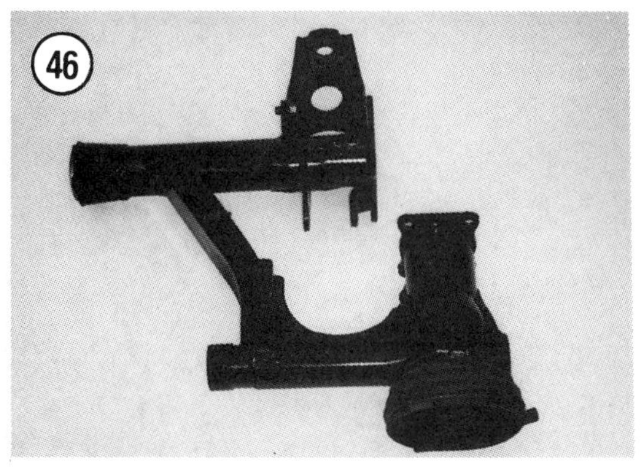

Swing Arm Inspection

1. Clean and dry all parts.
2. Check the seals for wear or damage. See A, **Figure 44**, typical.
3. Bearing wear is difficult to measure. Turn each bearing (B, **Figure 44**) with your finger. The bearings should turn without roughness or excessive play.
4. Check each pivot collar (C, **Figure 44**) for scoring, cracks or excessive wear. Replace the bearings and collars as a set.
5. Turn the rear axle ball bearing (**Figure 45**) with your finger. The bearing should turn smoothly with no roughness or excessive play.
6. Replace worn or damaged swing arm bearings or the rear axle ball bearing as described under *Bearing Replacement* in this chapter.
7. Check the swing arm (**Figure 46**) for cracks, bending or other damage. On models so equipped, check the trailer hitch for cracks or damage. Refer repair to a Yamaha dealership or welding shop.
8. Check the rubber boot (**Figure 47**) for deterioration, cracks or damage and replace if necessary.
9. Inspect the pivot shafts and locknuts (**Figure 48**) and replace if damaged.
10. Inspect the frame pivot shaft threads (**Figure 49**) for damage.

Swing Arm Bearing Replacement

Do not remove the swing arm pivot bearings and the rear axle right-hand ball bearing unless replacement is required. Replace both pivot bearings at the same time.

1. To remove the pivot bearings, perform the following:
   a. Remove the collar from the pivot shaft seal.
   b. Carefully pry the pivot shaft seal (A, **Figure 44**) out of the swing arm bore.
   c. Support the swing arm in a vise with soft jaws.
   d. Remove the bearing with a slide hammer type bearing removal tool.
   e. Repeat for the opposite collar, pivot shaft seal and bearing.
2. To remove the rear axle ball bearing, perform the following:
   a. Support the swing arm in a vise with soft jaws.
   b. Remove the bearing with a slide hammer type bearing removal tool.
   c. Repeat for the seal located behind the bearing.
3. Clean and dry the bearing bores. Remove all corrosion and rust from the bore surfaces.
4. Pack the bearings with a lithium-soap based grease prior to assembly:
5. To install the pivot bearings, perform the following:
   a. Install bearings with their manufacturer's name and size code facing out.
   b. Press in the bearing (B, **Figure 44**) until it bottoms out in the bearing bore.
   c. Press in the seal (A, **Figure 44**) until it bottoms against the bearing.
   d. Install the collar (C, **Figure 44**) into the oil seal.
6. To install the rear axle ball bearing, perform the following:
   a. Press in the oil seal—closed side facing out—into the axle bore until it bottoms.
   b. Install the bearing with its manufacturer's name and size code facing out. Press in the bearing until it bottoms.

Installation

1. Lubricate the following parts with a lithium-soap based grease:
   a. Pivot bearings and seals. Refer to B, **Figure 44**.
   b. Pivot shafts (**Figure 48**).
2. Position the swing arm into the frame and hold it in position with a small floor jack or wooden blocks.
3. Install a new O-ring (4, **Figure 39**) onto each pivot shaft.
4. Install a pivot shaft (**Figure 50**) into each side of the frame to hold the swing arm in place. Do not tighten at this time.
5. Tighten the pivot shafts and locknuts in the following order:
   a. Tighten the *right-hand* pivot shaft (**Figure 51**) as specified in **Table 2**.
   b. Install the *right-hand* locknut (**Figure 51**) and tighten the locknut to the torque specification listed in **Table 2**.

49

50

51

c. Tighten the *left-hand* pivot shaft (**Figure 42**) until it touches the collar, then tighten as specified in **Table 2**.

d. Install the *left-hand* locknut (**Figure 41**) and tighten as specified in **Table 2**.

6. Pivot the swing arm to check bearing play and tightness.

7. Install the pivot shaft caps (B, **Figure 40**).

8. Install the rear shock absorber as described in this chapter.

9. Move the drive shaft rubber boot into position (A, **Figure 40**). Make sure the clamps are positioned correctly on the rubber boot, then tighten both clamping screws securely.

10. Install the brake backing plate on the swing arm (Chapter Thirteen).

11. Install the final drive unit and short drive shaft as described in this chapter.

12. Install the rear axle as described in this chapter.

13. Install the rear fender (Chapter Fourteen).

Table 1 REAR SUSPENSION GENERAL SPECIFICATIONS

Item	Specification
Rear suspension type	Swing arm with solid rear axle
Rear wheel travel	110 mm (4.33 in.)
Rear shock absorber	
Type	Coil spring, oil damper
Travel	75 mm (2.95 in.)
Spring free length	258.8 mm (10.19 in.)
Spring installed length	221.3 mm (8.71 in.)
Spring rate	2.7 kg/mm (151.2 in.-lb.)
Rim runout (radial and axial runout limit)	2.0 mm (0.08 in.)

12

Table 2 REAR SUSPENSION TIGHTENING TORQUES

	N•m	in.-lb.	ft.-lb.
Rear wheel lug nuts	55	—	40
Rear wheel and brake drum nuts	55	—	40
Rear axle nuts	150	—	110
Swing arm and rear brake plate bolts	28	—	20
Pivot shaft and frame bolts	6	53	—
Pivot shaft locknuts	130	—	94
Rear shock absorber and frame nut	50	—	36
Final drive unit			
To drive shaft portion of swing arm nuts	23	—	17
To axle portion of swing arm bolts	45	—	33
Bearing housing mounting bolts			
8 mm bolts	23	—	17
10 mm bolts	40	—	29

CHAPTER THIRTEEN

BRAKES

This chapter describes service procedures for the front and rear brake systems.

The front brakes are actuated by the hand lever on the right side of the handlebar. The rear brake is actuated by the brake pedal and the parking brake cable is actuated by the left-hand brake lever. The parking brake is incorporated into the rear drum brake assembly.

Brake specifications are listed in **Table 1**. **Table 1** and **Table 2** are at the end of this chapter.

FRONT BRAKE DRUM

WARNING
*When working on the brake system, never blow off brake components or use compressed air. Do **not** inhale any airborne brake dust as it may contain asbestos, which can cause lung injury and cancer. As an added precaution, wear an OSHA approved filtering face mask and thoroughly wash your hands and forearms with warm water and soap after completing any brake work.*

Removal/Installation

1. Remove the front wheels (Chapter Ten).

2. Remove the front axle cotter pin, axle nut and flat washer (A, **Figure 1**).

3. Remove the front brake drum (B, **Figure 1**). If the front brake drum is tight, perform Step 4.

4. Withdraw the brake shoes away from the brake drum as follows:

   a. Remove the rubber plug (C, **Figure 1**) from the brake drum.

   b. Rotate the brake drum until the hole is adjacent to one of the wheel cylinder adjusters.

NOTE
***Figure 2** shows both wheel cylinders with the brake drum removed.*

c. Insert a slotted screwdriver into the hole (**Figure 3**) and rotate the adjuster wheel toward the center of the hub several clicks.

d. Turn the brake drum to uncover the other wheel cylinder adjuster (**Figure 2**) and repeat substep c loosen it.

e. Remove the brake drum.

NOTE
The brake drum should slide off the brake shoes after loosening both wheel cylinder adjusters. If the brake drum is still tight, contamination on the brake drum and brake shoe surfaces may be holding it in place. If the brake drum will not slide off after loosening the wheel cylinder adjusters, perform substep f.

f. Remove the brake drum with a puller as shown in **Figure 4**.

5. Replace the O-ring (A, **Figure 5**) if damaged.
6. Inspect the brake drum and brake shoes as described in this chapter.
7. Install by reversing these removal steps, while noting the following.
8. Apply high-temperature brake grease to the lips of the dust seal (B, **Figure 5**).
9. Tighten the front axle nut (A, **Figure 1**) as specified in **Table 2**.
10. Install a new cotter pin (A, **Figure 1**). Bend the cotter pin arms over to lock it (**Figure 6**).
11. Adjust the front brakes (Chapter Three).

Inspection

When measuring the brake drum in this section, compare the actual measurement to the specification

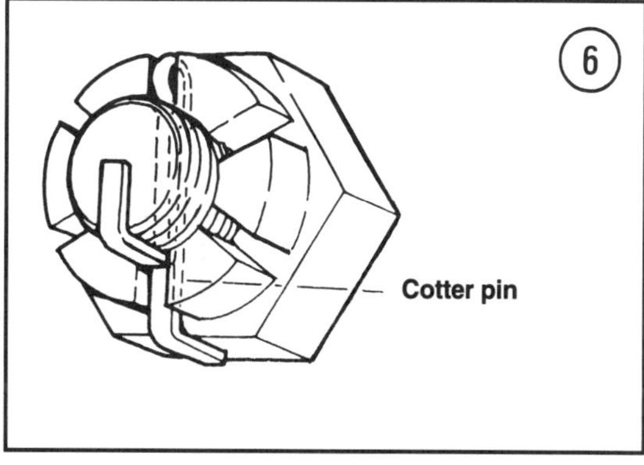

in **Table 1**. Replace the brake drum if damaged or out of specification as described in this section.

1. Check the drum surface for oil or grease and clean with a rag soaked in lacquer thinner. Then check the brake shoe linings for contamination.

NOTE

Do not clean the brake drum with any type of solvent that may leave an oil residue.

2. Clean the brake drum in a detergent solution. Then dry thoroughly to prevent rust from forming on the drum surface.

NOTE

Discard the detergent solution and wash your hands.

3. Check the drum contact surface (**Figure 7**) for scoring or other damage.
4. Measure the brake drum inside diameter (**Figure 8**) and compare to the maximum (MAX) diameter dimension cast in the brake drum (**Figure 9**), or refer to the service limit in **Table 1**.

NOTE

If the maximum specification cast on the drum differs from the service limit ***Table 1****, use the drum mark.*

5. Inspect the brake drum (A, **Figure 10**) for cracks or damage.
6. Inspect the wheel mounting studs (B, **Figure 10**) for thread damage. Repair minor damage with a metric thread die.
7. Inspect the drum splines (C, **Figure 10**) for twisting or damage.

FRONT DRUM BRAKE

The front drum brakes are actuated by hydraulic fluid and controlled by a hand lever on the front master cylinder. As the brake linings wear, the brake fluid level drops in the master cylinder reservoir and automatically adjusts for wear.

When working on hydraulic brake systems, the work area and tools must be clean. Place the parts on clean lint-free cloths and wipe all oil and other chemical residues off of the tools. Tiny particles of foreign matter and grit in the master cylinder or wheel cylinders can damage the components. If there is any doubt about your ability to correctly and safely carry out major service on the brake components, take the job to a Yamaha dealership or brake specialist.

NOTE

If you recycle your old engine oil, ***never*** *add used brake fluid to the old oil. Most oil retailers may not accept the oil if other fluids (fork oil, brake fluid, or any other type of fluids) have been combined with it.*

Consider the following when servicing the front drum brake.

1. When adding brake fluid, use only a brake fluid clearly marked DOT 3 or DOT 4 from a sealed container. Other types may cause brake failure. Try to always use the same brand name. Before intermixing brake fluid, make sure the 2 types are compatible. Some brake fluid will draw moisture which greatly reduces its ability to perform correctly. It is a good idea to purchase brake fluid in small containers and discard any small left-over quantities properly. Do not store a container of brake fluid with less than 1/4 of the fluid remaining as this small amount will draw moisture very rapidly.

CAUTION
Do not intermix silicone based (DOT 5) brake fluid as it can cause brake component damage leading to brake system failure.

CAUTION
Never reuse brake fluid (like fluid expelled during brake bleeding). Contaminated brake fluid can cause brake failure. Dispose of used brake fluid according to local, or EPA toxic waste regulations.

2. Do not allow brake fluid to contact any plastic parts or painted surfaces as damage will result.
3. Always keep the master cylinder reservoir and spare cans of brake fluid closed to prevent dust or moisture from entering. This would result in brake fluid contamination and brake problems.
4. Use only new DOT 3 or DOT 4 brake fluid to wash parts. Never clean any internal brake components with solvent or any other petroleum-base cleaners as these cleaners will destroy the rubber components.
5. Whenever any component has been removed from the brake system the system is considered *opened* and must be bled to remove air. Also, if the brake feels *spongy* this usually means air has entered the system and it must be bled. For safe brake operation, refer to *Brake Bleeding* in this chapter for complete details.

CAUTION
Never reuse brake fluid. Contaminated brake fluid can cause brake failure. Dispose of brake fluid according to local EPA regulations.

WARNING
When working on the brake system, never blow off brake components or use compressed air. Do ***not*** *inhale any airborne brake dust as it may contain asbestos, which can cause lung injury and cancer. As an added precaution, wear an OSHA approved filtering face mask and thoroughly wash your hands and forearms with warm water and soap after completing any brake work.*

FRONT BRAKE SHOE REPLACEMENT

Refer to **Figure 11** when replacing the front brake shoes.

There is no recommended mileage interval for changing the front brake shoes. Lining wear depends on riding habits and conditions.

NOTE
Service one set of brake shoes at a time. Leave the other set intact as you may need to refer to them during the procedure.

1. Remove the front brake drums as described in this chapter.
2. Measure the brake shoe lining thickness with a vernier caliper (**Figure 12**) and check against the service limit in **Table 1**. Replace the brake shoes as a set if out of specification.
3. Push the retainer and then twist the pin (**Figure 13**) to remove the retainer. Repeat for the other retainer and pin. See **Figure 14**.
4. Remove the brake shoe and spring assembly (**Figure 15**) from the backing plate and the wheel cylinders. See **Figure 16**.
5. Remove the 2 pins (A, **Figure 17**).
6. Disconnect the return springs and separate the brake shoes.

7. Inspect the return springs for damaged or stretched coils.

8. Measure the return spring free length and compare to **Table 1**. Replace the springs if out of specification or if they are unequal in length.

NOTE
Always replace both return springs at the same time.

9. Inspect the pins and retainers (**Figure 18**) and replace if worn or damaged.

10. Inspect the wheel cylinders (B, **Figure 17**) for damaged boots or leaking brake fluid. If necessary, service the wheel cylinders as described in this chapter.

11. Install the new brake shoes and attach the springs as shown in A, **Figure 16**. Make sure to offset the spring coils as shown in A, **Figure 16**.

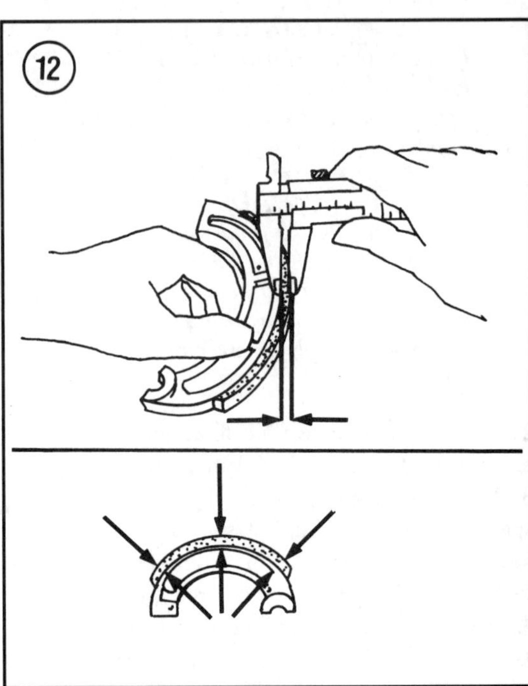

(11)

FRONT DRUM BRAKE

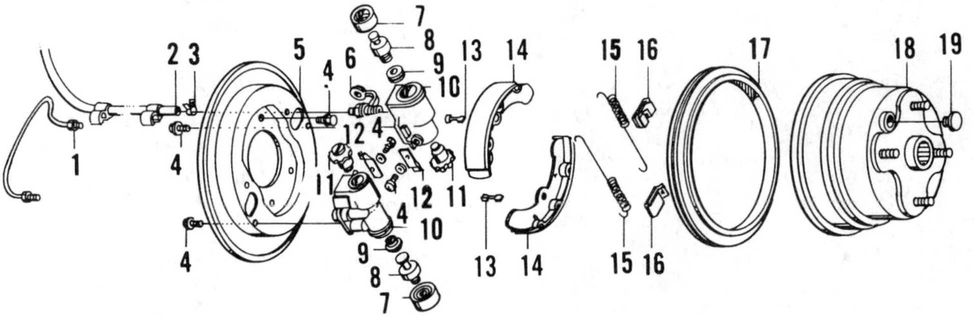

1. Brake line
2. Vent hose
3. Hose clamp
4. Bolt
5. Backing plate
6. Bleed valve
7. Dust seal
8. Piston
9. Piston cup
10. Wheel cylinder body
11. Adjuster wheel
12. Lock spring
13. Pin
14. Brake shoe
15. Return spring
16. Retainer
17. Dust seal
18. Hub/drum
19. Rubber plug

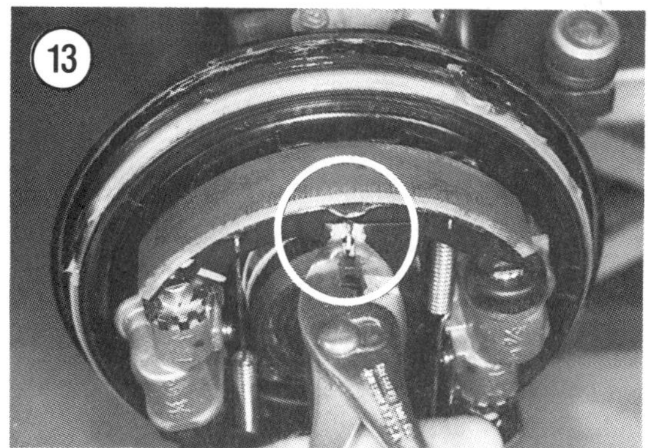

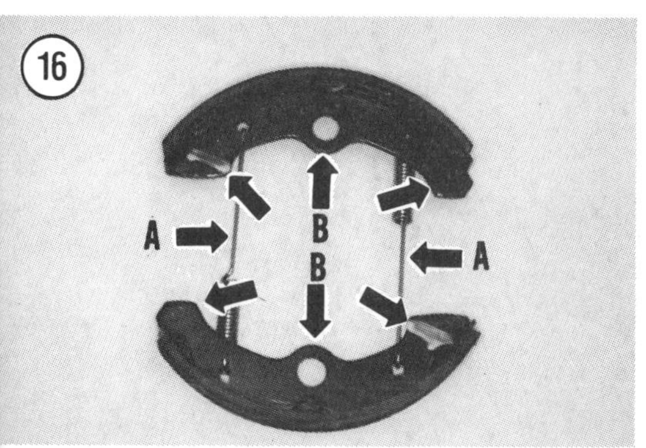

12. Lightly lubricate the points indicated in B, **Figure 16** with silicone brake grease. Do not apply to the brake shoe or brake drum braking surfaces.

CAUTION
Silicone brake grease is not the same as a silicone sealant (RTV) used on engine gaskets. Make sure the lubricant is specified for brake use. For example, Permatex Ultra Disc Brake Caliper Lube (part No. 20356) is an acceptable brake system lubricant.

WARNING
Do not apply too much grease or it may fall onto the brake linings and cause brake slippage.

13. Install the upper brake shoe into the upper wheel cylinder notches (**Figure 15**).

14. Hold the upper brake shoe in place, then pull up on the lower brake shoe and install it into the lower wheel cylinder notches (**Figure 15**). If a spring popped out of its shoe slot, reinstall it with a pair of locking pliers (**Figure 19**). Make sure both spring

13

ends are hooked into the brake shoe holes and slots (A, **Figure 20**).

15. Install the pins and retainers as follows:
    a. Insert the pins (B, **Figure 20**) into the backing plate and hook them in place.
    b. Insert a screwdriver behind the wheel cylinder to hold the pin in place (A, **Figure 21**).
    c. Install the retainer (B, **Figure 21**) and secure it with a pair of pliers (C, **Figure 21**).
    d. While holing the pin in place with the screwdriver, compress the retainer (**Figure 13**) with the pliers, then rotate the pin 90° (**Figure 13**) with the pliers to lock the pin in place.
    e. Remove the pliers and screwdriver and repeat for the other retainer and pin assembly.
    f. Make sure both retainers and pins are properly locked in place.
16. Repeat these steps to replace the brake shoes on the opposite side.
17. Install the front brake drums as described in this chapter.
18. Adjust the brake shoes (Chapter Three).

BACKING PLATE

Refer to **Figure 11** when servicing the backing plate in this section.

Removal

1. Remove the brake shoes as described in this section.
2. Disconnect the vent hose from the backing plate.
3. Remove the brake hose banjo bolt and sealing washers (A, **Figure 22**) at the back of the brake backing plate. Place the loose end of the brake hose in a thick plastic bag or container to prevent the entry of dirt and foreign matter and to prevent brake fluid from leaking out onto the suspension and brake components. Tie the brake hose up out of the way.

CAUTION
Wash brake fluid off any painted or plated surfaces immediately as it will destroy the finish. Use soapy water and rinse completely.

4. Remove the bolts (C, **Figure 17**) that hold the brake backing plate to the steering knuckle. Then remove the brake backing plate (B, **Figure 22**). A sealer is used between the steering knuckle and backing plate. If the backing plate is tight, carefully tap it with a soft faced hammer to remove it.
5. To service the wheel cylinders, refer to *Wheel Cylinders* in this chapter.
6. Perform the *Inspection* procedure in this section.

Inspection

1. Remove all sealer residue from the backing plate and steering knuckle mounting surfaces.

19

20

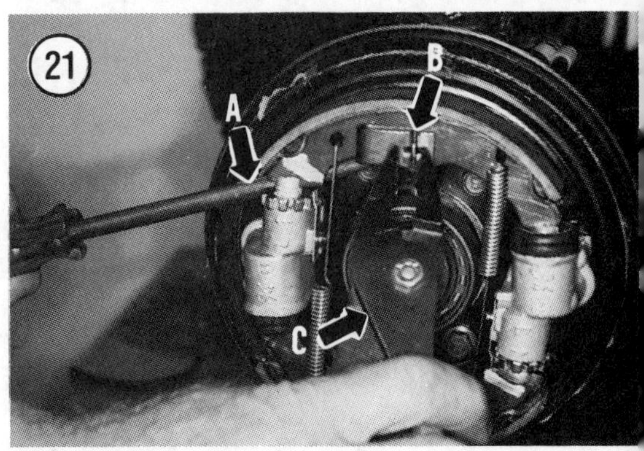

21

2. Wipe off all old grease from all of the brake panel parts.

3. Inspect the backing plate for damage.

4. Inspect the wheel cylinder brake line. If necessary, replace as described under *Wheel Cylinders* in this chapter.

Installation

1. If removed, install the wheel cylinders as described in this chapter.

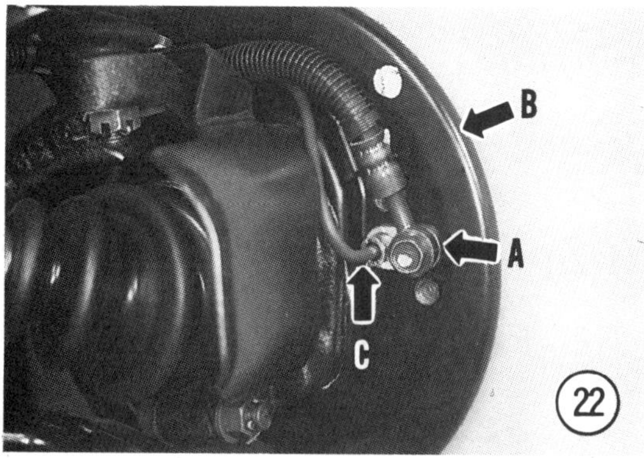

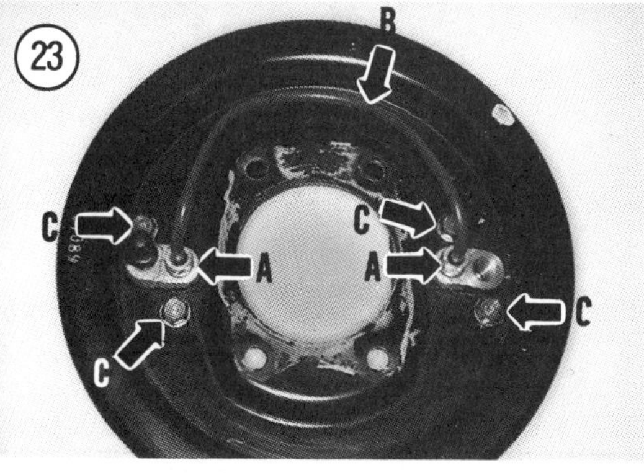

2. Apply a light coat of ThreeBond TB1104, Yamaha bond No. 1215 or equivalent gasket sealer onto the backing plate and steering knuckle mating surfaces.

3. Install the backing plate (B, **Figure 22**) onto the steering knuckle so that the wheel cylinder brake line (C, **Figure 22**) is at the top.

4. Apply a heat resistance threadlock onto each of the backing plate mounting bolts. Then install and tighten the bolts (C, **Figure 17**) as specified in **Table 2**.

5. Reconnect the brake hose with the banjo bolt (A, **Figure 22**) and 2 new sealing washers. Install a new sealing washer on each side of the brake hose. Tighten the brake hose banjo bolt as specified in **Table 2**.

6. Reconnect the vent hose and secure it with its hose clamp.

7. Install the brake shoes as described in this chapter.

8. Bleed the front brakes as described under *Brake Bleeding* in this chapter.

WHEEL CYLINDERS

Refer to **Figure 11** for this procedure.

Removal

1. Remove the brake backing plate as described in this chapter.

2. Loosen the brake line fittings (A, **Figure 23**) and remove the brake line (B, **Figure 23**).

NOTE

The wheel cylinders are unique to each side of the vehicle and are marked with a R (right side) or L (left side) and must be reinstalled on the correct side of the vehicle. Each wheel cylinder is also marked with an arrow that must point away from the center of the brake backing plate.

3. Remove the wheel cylinder mounting bolts (C, **Figure 23**) and remove the wheel cylinders (**Figure 24**).

4. If necessary, service the wheel cylinders as described in this chapter.

Wheel Cylinder Disassembly/Inspection/Assembly

Refer to **Figure 25** for this procedure.

NOTE
Replace the dust seal, piston and piston cup whenever the wheel cylinder is disassembled.

1. Remove the adjuster from the cylinder body.
2. Remove the dust cover from the cylinder body bore groove and remove the cover.
3. Pull the piston and piston cup out of the cylinder bore. Discard the piston and piston cup.
4. Inspect the cylinder bore for scratches and damage. If the cylinder body is worn or damaged, replace the wheel cylinder assembly. The body cannot be replaced separately.
5. Coat the new piston cup and piston and the cylinder bore with new DOT 3 OR DOT 4 brake fluid.
6. Install the piston into the cylinder so that the cup end goes in first. Make sure the cup does not turn inside out during installation.
7. Install a new dust cover over the piston. Make sure it is properly seated on the piston and in the cylinder body groove.
8. Apply a *light coat* of silicone brake grease to the adjuster (**Figure 26**) and install the adjuster into the wheel cylinder.

Installation

1. Install the wheel cylinders as follows:
   a. Install the wheel cylinders by referring to the L (left side) and R (right side) wheel cylinder marks. In addition, each wheel cylinder is marked with an arrow that must point away from the center of the brake backing plate when the wheel cylinder is installed.
   b. Install the wheel cylinders in their correct location on the brake backing plate (**Figure 24**).
   c. Apply a heat resistance threadlocking compound onto each of the wheel cylinder mounting bolts. Then install and tighten the bolts (C, **Figure 23**) as specified in **Table 2**.

NOTE
*Yamaha specifies to replace the wheel cylinder brake line (B, **Figure 23**) everytime it is removed.*

2. Install a new brake line (B, **Figure 23**) onto the backside of the wheel cylinders. Tighten the fittings securely.
3. Install the backing plate as described in this chapter.

FRONT MASTER CYLINDER

Refer to **Figure 27** when servicing the master cylinder in the following sections.

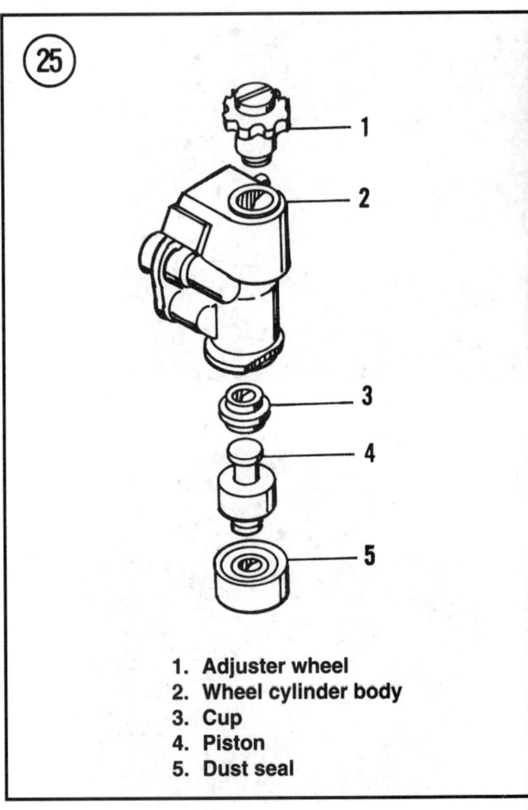

1. Adjuster wheel
2. Wheel cylinder body
3. Cup
4. Piston
5. Dust seal

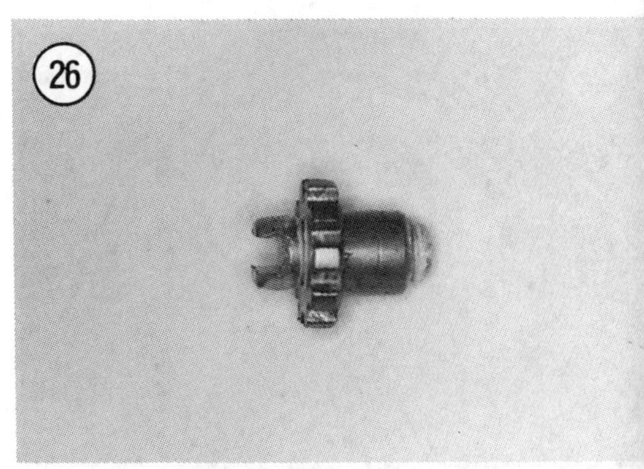

Removal/Installation

1. Park the vehicle on level ground and set the parking brake.
2. Cover the area under the master cylinder to prevent brake fluid leakage from damaging any component that it might contact.

CAUTION
If brake fluid should contact any surface, wash the area immediately with soapy water and rinse completely. Brake fluid will damage plastic, painted and plated surfaces.

3. To remove brake fluid from the reservoir:

   a. Remove the master cylinder cover screws and remove the cover (A, **Figure 28**) and diaphragm.

   b. Use a clean syringe and remove the brake fluid from the reservoir. Discard the brake fluid properly.

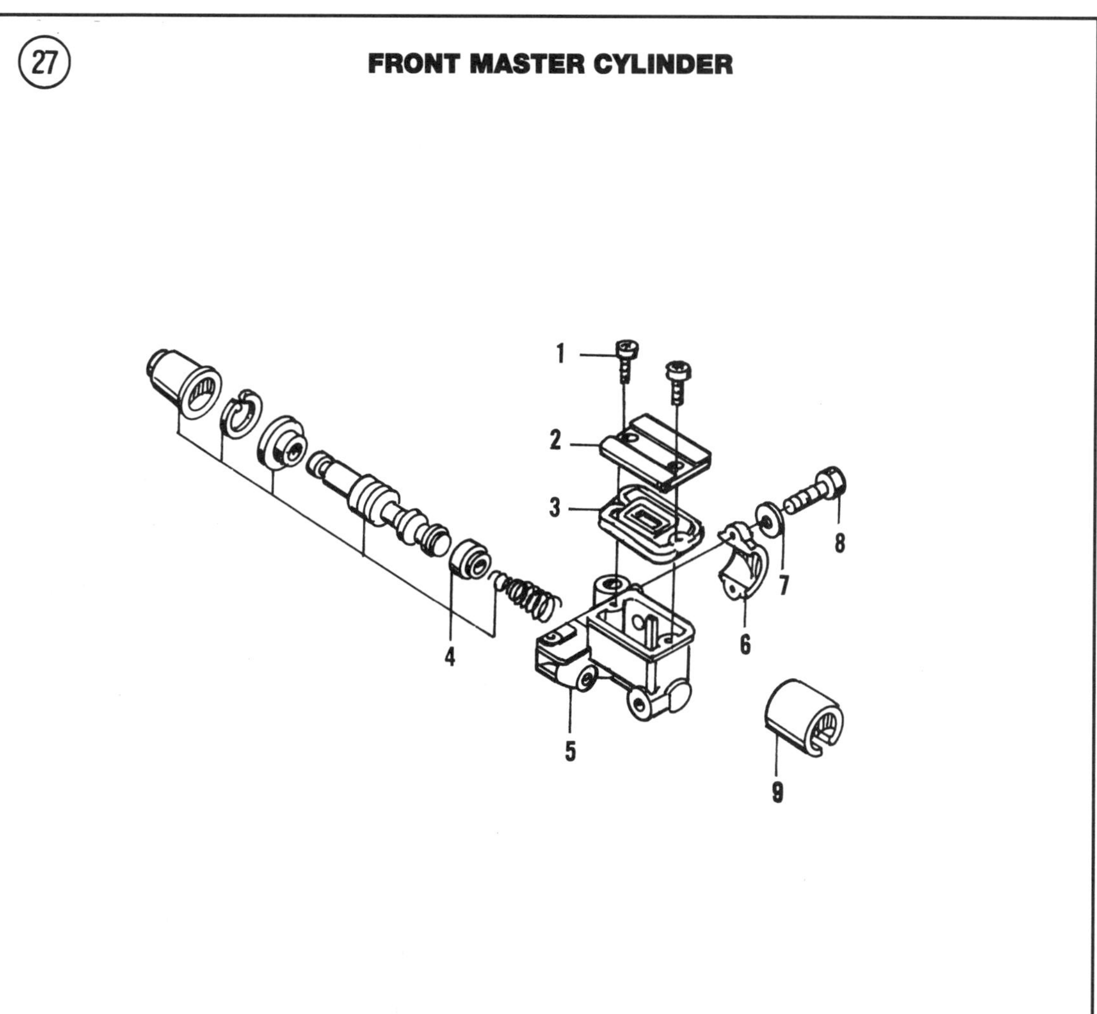

4. Pull the rubber boot (B, **Figure 28**) off the banjo bolt.

5. Remove the banjo bolt (C, **Figure 28**) and the sealing washers securing the upper brake hose to the master cylinder. Place the loose end of the brake hose in a plastic bag to prevent the entry of dirt and foreign matter and to prevent residual brake fluid from leaking out onto the frame components. Tie the brake hose to the handlebar.

6. Unbolt and remove the master cylinder and its clamp (**Figure 29**) from the master cylinder.

7. If necessary, service the master cylinder as described in this chapter.

8. Clean the handlebar, master cylinder and clamp mating surfaces.

9. Move the locating spacer and index it against the throttle lever housing. Then install the master cylinder, clamp and mounting bolts. Install the clamp with its UP mark and arrow (**Figure 29**) facing up. Then move the master cylinder and index it against the locating spacer. Tighten the bolts as specified in Table 2.

10. Install the upper brake hose onto the master cylinder, using the banjo bolt and 2 new washers. Install a washer on each side of the hose fitting. Tighten the banjo bolt as specified in **Table 2**.

11. Refill the master cylinder with DOT 3 or DOT 4 brake fluid and bleed the brake as described in this chapter.

WARNING
Do not ride the vehicle until the front brakes are working properly. Make sure the brake lever travel is not excessive and the lever does not feel spongy—both indicate that the bleeding operation needs to be repeated.

Disassembly

Refer to **Figure 27** for this procedure.

1. Remove the master cylinder as described in this chapter.

2. Unbolt and remove the hand lever and spring (**Figure 30**).

3. Remove the screws, top cover and diaphragm.

4. Pour out any brake fluid and discard it properly. *Never* reuse brake fluid.

5. Remove the rubber boot (**Figure 31**) from the end of the piston and piston bore.

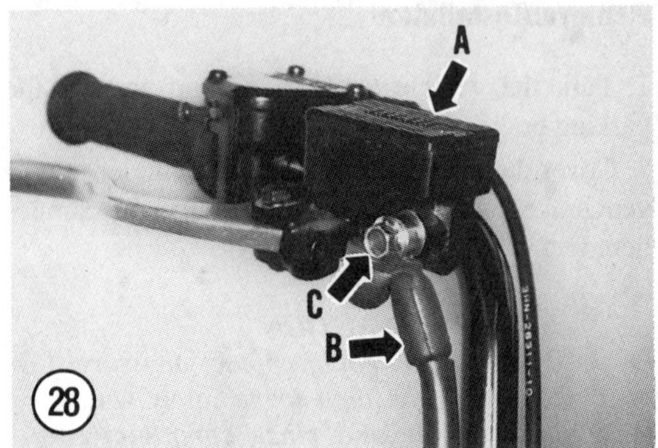

28

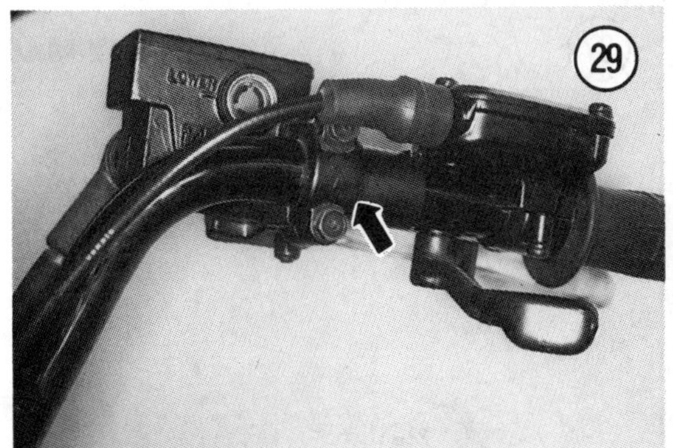
29

30

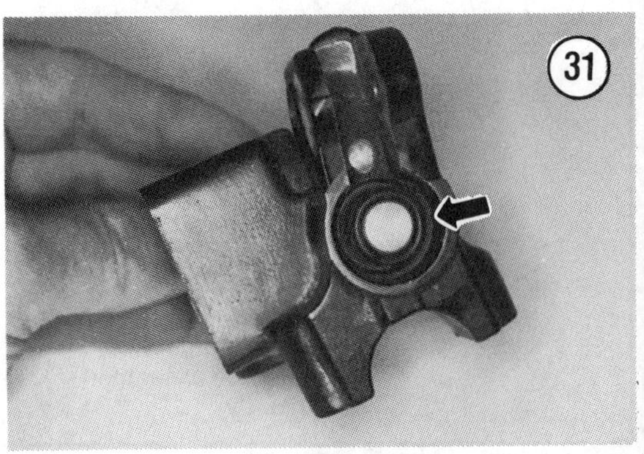
31

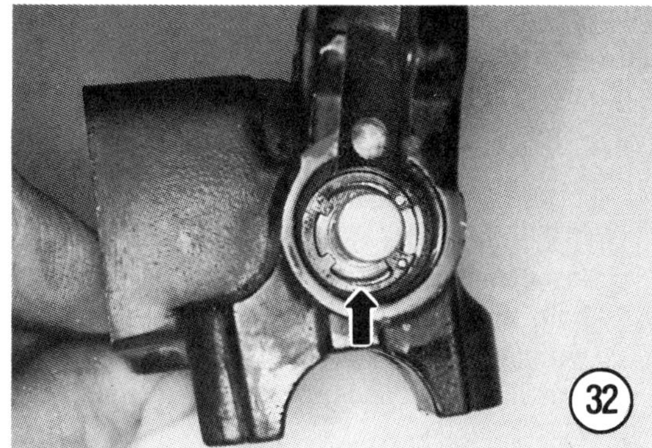
32

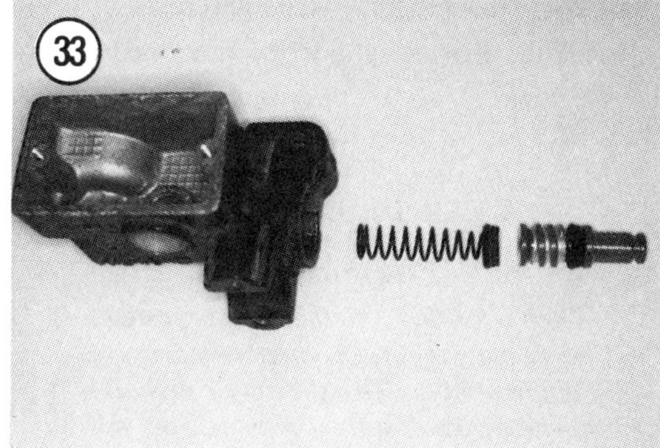
33

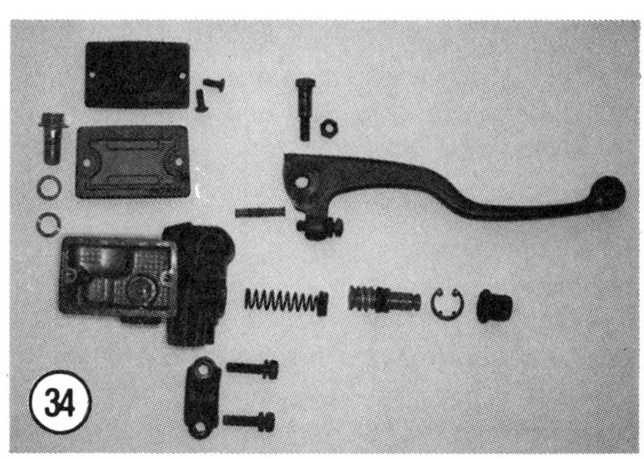
34

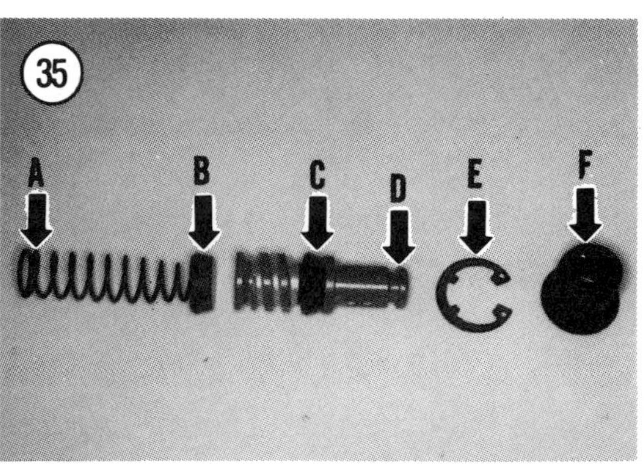

35

6. Remove the circlip (**Figure 32**) from the bore groove.

7. Remove the piston and spring assembly (**Figure 33**).

Inspection

When inspecting the master cylinder components (**Figure 34**) in this section, replace worn or damaged parts.

1. Clean the diaphragm, reservoir housing (inside) and piston assembly with new brake fluid. Place the parts on a clean lint-free cloth.

2. Inspect the piston assembly (**Figure 35**) for:
   a. Broken, distorted or collapsed piston return spring (A, **Figure 35**).
   b. Worn, cracked, damaged or swollen primary (B, **Figure 35**) and secondary cup (C, **Figure 35**).
   c. Scratched, scored or damaged piston (D, **Figure 35**).
   d. Corroded, weak or damaged circlip (E, **Figure 35**).

If any of these parts are worn or damaged, replace the piston assembly.

3. Inspect the cylinder bore (**Figure 36**) for scratches, severe wear, corrosion or other damage. Do not hone the bore to remove nicks, scratches or other damage.

4. Check for plugged supply and relief ports in the master cylinder. Clean with compressed air.

NOTE
A plugged relief port will cause the brake shoes to drag on the drum.

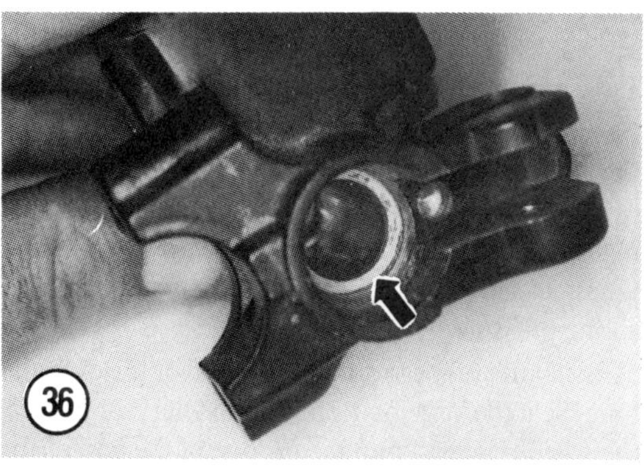
36

5. Check the entire master cylinder body for wear or damage. If damaged in any way, replace the master cylinder assembly.
6. Check the cover and diaphragm for damage and deterioration.
7. Inspect the banjo bolt threads in the master cylinder body bore for the banjo bolt. Repair minor damage with the correct size metric tap, or replace the master cylinder assembly.
8. Check the hand lever pivot holes and mounting lugs on the master cylinder body for elongation or cracks. If damaged, replace the master cylinder assembly.
9. Inspect the hand lever and pivot bolt and replace if damaged.

Assembly

1. Soak the cups and the piston assembly in new brake fluid for at least 15 minutes to make them pliable. If installing a new piston assembly, soak the new cups in brake fluid before installing them in Step 2. Coat the inside of the cylinder bore with fresh brake fluid.
2. If installing a new piston assembly, install the primary cup onto the spring as shown in B, **Figure 35**. If the new secondary cup was not installed onto the piston, install it over the piston and seat it into the piston groove as shown in C, **Figure 35**.

CAUTION
When installing the piston assembly, do not allow the cups to turn inside out as they will be damaged and allow brake fluid to leak past the cups and out of the bore.

3. Install the spring and piston assembly into the master cylinder bore in the direction shown in **Figure 33**. Check that the cups did not turn inside out.
4. Push the piston in and hold it in place, then install the circlip (**Figure 32**) into the cylinder bore groove. Install the circlip with its flat edge facing out (away from the piston). Check that the circlip is fully seated in the bore groove. Push and release the piston a few times. It should move smoothly and return under spring pressure.
5. Install the rubber boot into the end of the cylinder bore. Seat the large boot end against the circlip. Seat the small boot end into the groove in the end of the piston (**Figure 37**). Make sure it is correctly seated in the cylinder bore (**Figure 31**).
6. Install the brake lever (**Figure 30**) as follows:
   a. Lubricate the spring, adjust bolt end and piston end with silicone brake grease.
   b. Install the spring into the brake lever.
   c. Install the brake lever and bolt. Tighten the bolt, then check that the brake lever pivots with no binding or roughness. Then hold the bolt and install and tighten the nut securely.
   d. Operate the brake lever again to make sure it operates freely within the master cylinder.
7. Install the diaphragm, cover and screws.
8. Install the master cylinder as described in this chapter.

REAR DRUM BRAKE

WARNING
When working on the brake system, never blow off brake components or use compressed air. Do **not** *inhale any airborne brake dust as it may contain asbestos, which can cause lung injury and cancer. As an added precaution, wear an approved filtering face mask and thoroughly wash your hands and forearms with warm water and soap after completing any brake work.*

Rear Brake Drum Removal/Installation

Refer to **Figure 38** for this procedure.

1. Remove the right side rear wheel (Chapter Twelve).

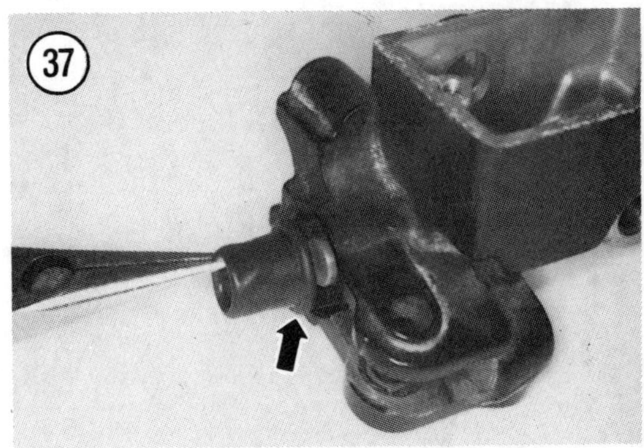

2. Remove the rear axle cotter pin, axle nut and flat washer (**Figure 39**).

3. Remove the rear brake drum (**Figure 39**). If the rear brake drum is tight, loosen the brake cable adjusters (**Figure 40**) to withdraw the brake shoes away from the brake drum. Then remove the brake drum.

NOTE

The brake drum should now slide off the brake shoes. If the brake drum is still tight, contamination on the brake drum and brake shoe surfaces may be holding it in place. If you cannot remove the brake drum after loosening the cable adjusters, use the puller shown under ***Front Brake Drum Removal/Installation*** *in this chapter.*

4. Remove the O-ring (A, **Figure 41**) and washer (B, **Figure 41**), if necessary.

5. Replace the O-ring (**Figure 41**), if damaged.

6. Inspect the brake drum, brake shoes and brake drum dust seal as described in this chapter.

(38)

REAR BRAKE DRUM

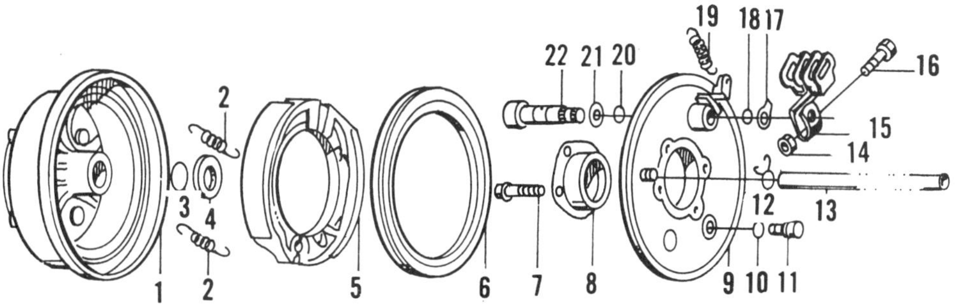

1. Brake drum
2. Return spring
3. O-ring
4. Washer
5. Brake shoes
6. Dust seal
7. Bolt
8. Retainer
9. Backing plate
10. O-ring
11. Bolt
12. Hose clamp
13. Vent hose
14. Nut
15. Cam lever
16. Bolt
17. Wear indicator plate
18. O-ring
19. Spring
20. O-ring
21. Washer
22. Camshaft

7. Install by reversing these removal steps, while noting the following.
8. If necessary, regrease the brake drum dust seal (**Figure 42**) with brake grease.
9. Tighten the rear axle nut (**Figure 39**) as specified in **Table 2**.
10. Install a new cotter pin (**Figure 39**). Bend the cotter pin arms over to lock it (**Figure 43**).
11. Adjust the rear brake (Chapter Three).

Inspection

When measuring the brake drum in this section, compare the actual measurement to the new and service limit specification in **Table 1**. Replace the brake drum if out of specification or damaged as described in this section.

1. Check the drum surface for oil or grease and clean with a rag soaked in lacquer thinner. Then check the brake shoe linings for contamination.

NOTE
Do not clean the brake drum with any type of solvent that may leave an oil residue.

2. Clean the brake drum in a detergent solution. Then dry thoroughly to prevent rust from forming on the drum surface.

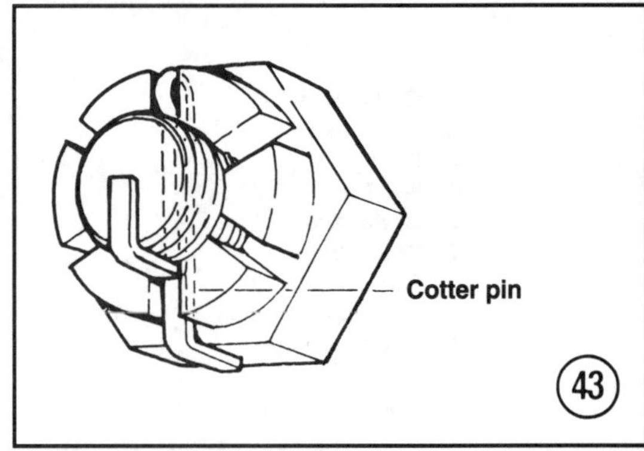

NOTE
Discard the detergent solution and wash your hands.

3. Check the drum contact surface (**Figure 44**) for scoring or other damage.
4. Measure the brake drum inside diameter (**Figure 45**) and compare to the maximum (MAX) diameter specification cast in the brake drum (**Figure 46**), or refer to the service limit in **Table 1**.

NOTE
*If the maximum diameter cast on the drum differs from the service limit in **Table 1**, use the drum mark.*

5. Inspect the brake drum (A, **Figure 47**) for cracks or damage.
6. Inspect the wheel mounting studs (B, **Figure 47**) for thread damage. Repair minor damage with a metric thread die.

7. Inspect the drum splines (C, **Figure 47**) for twisting or damage.

REAR BRAKE SHOE REPLACEMENT

Refer to **Figure 38** when replacing the rear brake shoes.

There is no recommended mileage interval for changing the rear brake shoes. Lining wear depends on riding habits and conditions.

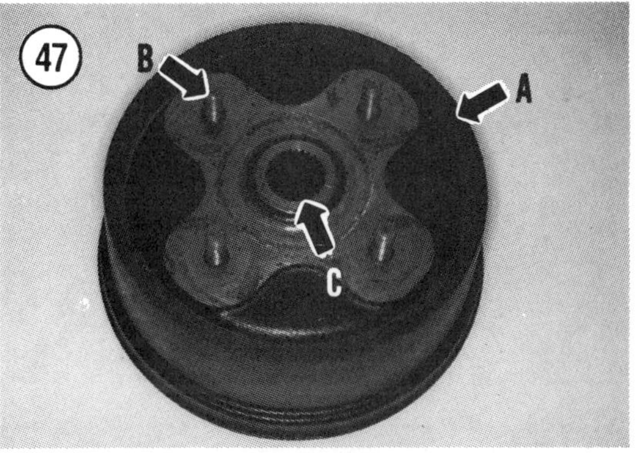

1. Remove the rear brake drum as described in this section.

2. Measure the brake shoe lining thickness with a vernier caliper (**Figure 48**) at several locations along the shoe. Check against the service limit in **Table 1**. Replace the brake shoes as a pair if the lining thickness is too thin.

NOTE
If the brake linings are in good condition and are going to be reinstalled, place a clean shop cloth on the linings to protect them from oil and grease during removal.

3. Carefully pull out on the center both brake shoes (A, **Figure 49**) into a V-formation and remove the brake shoes from the camshaft and anchor pin.

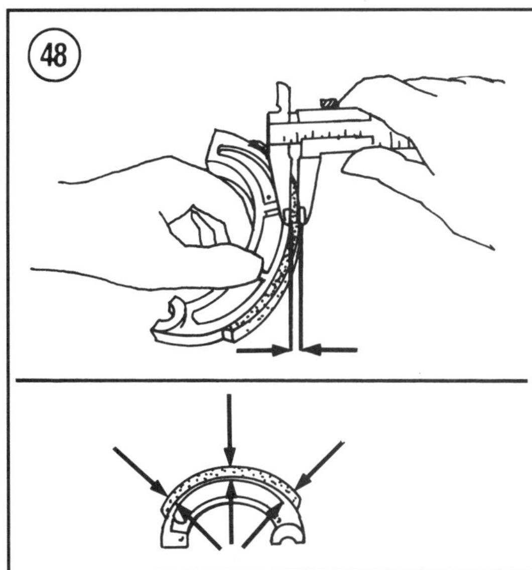

4. Disconnect the brake shoe springs (**Figure 50**) and separate the brake shoes.
5. Inspect the springs and replace if there are any bent or unequally spaced coils.

NOTE
Always replace both springs at the same time.

6. Remove old grease from the camshaft and anchor pin surfaces.
7. Apply a light coat of high-temperature brake grease onto the camshaft and anchor pin. Avoid getting any grease on the brake backing plate where the brake linings may come in contact with it.
8. Install the springs onto the brake shoes (**Figure 50**).
9. Hold the brake shoes in a V-formation with the return springs attached and snap the brake shoes into place. Make sure both brake shoes are firmly seated on the brake backing plate and are correctly seated on the camshaft and anchor pin.
10. Install the rear brake drum as described in this chapter.
11. Adjust the rear brake (Chapter Three).

BACKING PLATE

Refer to **Figure 38** when servicing the backing plate in this section.

Removal/Inspection/Seal Replacement

1. Remove the rear brake drum as described in this chapter.
2. Unscrew the brake adjusters (**Figure 40**) from the end of the rear brake rod and brake cable. Then remove the barrel and spring from the rod and cable ends. Reinstall the brake adjusters parts onto their respective rod or cable end so they don't get lost.
3. Disconnect the vent hose (**Figure 40**) from the backing plate fitting.
4. Remove the O-ring (A, **Figure 41**) and washer (B, **Figure 41**) from the axle.
5. Remove the bolts (B, **Figure 49**), washers and retainer plate securing the backing plate to the swing arm mounting flange.
6. Remove the backing plate from the rear axle.
7. Inspect the brake drum dust seal (**Figure 51**) for severe wear, damage, hardness or deterioration. If the brake drum seal is severely worn or damaged, replace it as follows:

a. If still installed, remove both brake shoes.
b. Support the brake backing place and pry the brake drum seal (**Figure 51**) out of the backing plate.
c. Clean the backing plate seal contact surface.
d. Align the new oil seal with the groove in the brake backing plate, then slowly and squarely press the dust seal into the brake backing plate.
e. Pack the seal lips with a high-temperature brake grease. Do not overgrease the seal.

8. Remove all sealer residue from the backing plate (A, **Figure 52**) and swing arm mating surfaces.

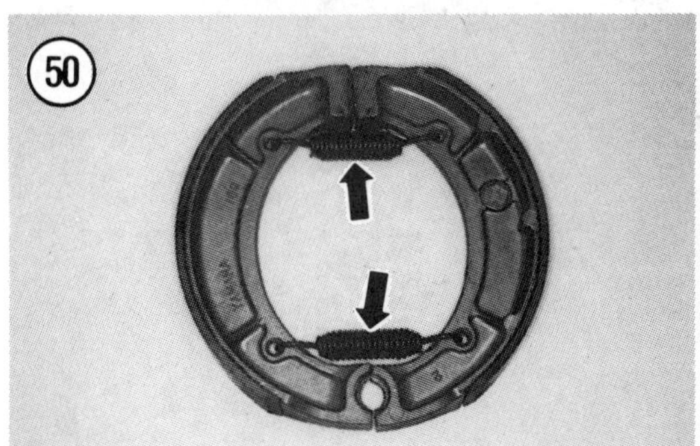

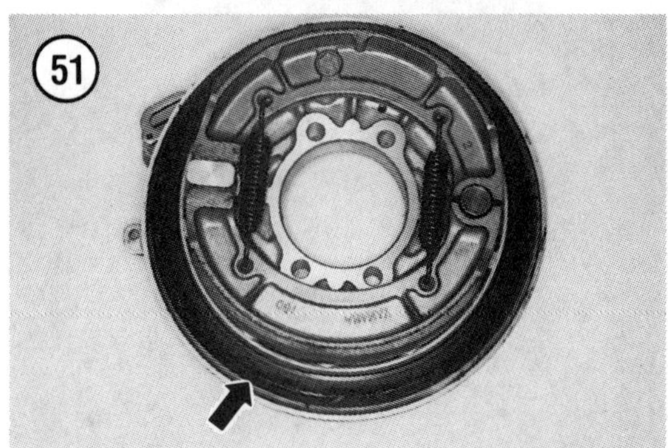

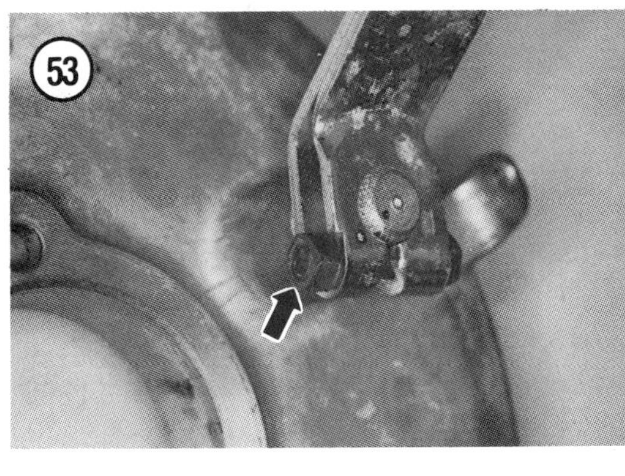

54

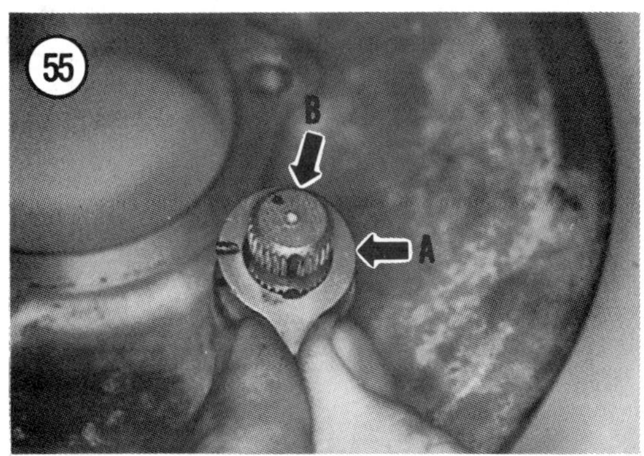

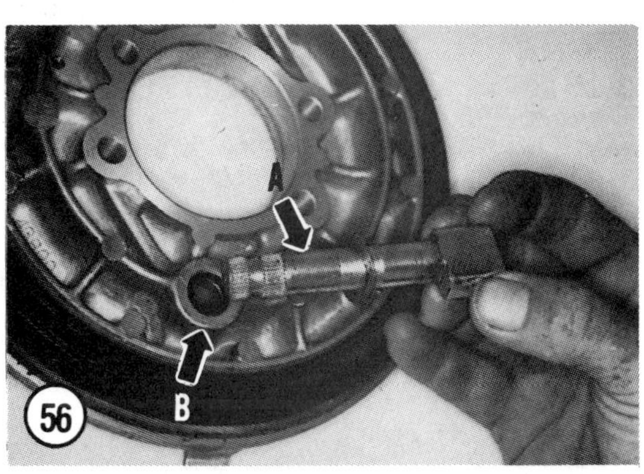

Camshaft Lever Removal/Installation

Refer to **Figure 38** for this procedure.

1. Remove the brake shoes as described in this chapter.
2. Remove the brake cam lever nut and bolt (**Figure 53**).
3. If not already marked, make punch marks on the cam and cam lever (**Figure 54**) so that they can be installed in the same position.
4. Remove the cam lever (B, **Figure 52**) and the brake wear indicator plate (A, **Figure 55**).
5. Remove the cam (B, **Figure 55**) and washer from the backing plate. See A, **Figure 56**.
6. Remove the O-ring (B, **Figure 56**) from the hole in the backing plate. Replace the O-ring if worn or damaged.
7. Remove old grease from the camshaft, anchor pin and camshaft hole.
8. Inspect the cam and replace if severely worn or damaged.
9. Inspect the cam lever and replace if severely worn or damaged.

NOTE

Use a high-temperature brake grease when grease is called for in the following steps.

10. Lubricate the O-ring with grease and install it into the cam hole groove (B, **Figure 56**).
11. Lubricate the camshaft and anchor pin with grease.
12. Install the washer onto the cam (A, **Figure 56**), then install the camshaft into the backing plate. Wipe up all excess grease around the cam and backing plate hole.

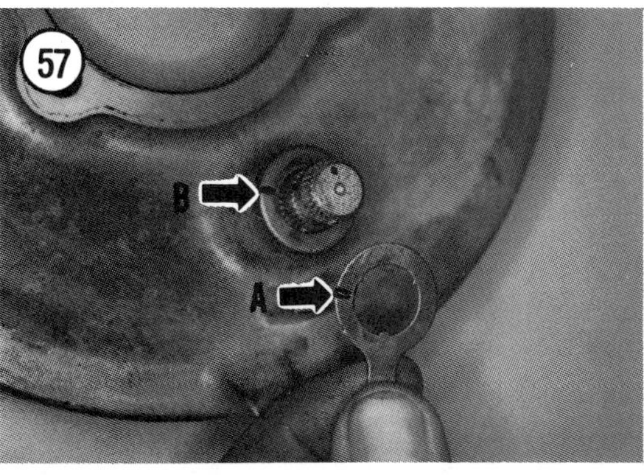

13. Turn the backing plate over.

14. Align the index mark on the wear indicator (A, **Figure 57**) with the index mark on the raised boss of the backing plate (B, **Figure 57**). Push the wear indicator down onto the cam, making sure the index marks are still aligned (**Figure 58**).

15. Align the cam index mark with the cam lever index mark (**Figure 54**) and install the cam. Push the cam lever all the way down into position.

16. Install the bolt and nut and tighten as specified in **Table 2**.

17. Move the camshaft lever by hand to make sure it moves smoothly and without any binding or roughness.

18. Install the brake shoes after installing the backing plate onto the swing arm.

Installation

1. Apply a light coat of ThreeBond TB1104, Yamaha bond No. 1215 or equivalent gasket sealer onto the backing plate (A, **Figure 52**) and swing arm mating surfaces.

2. Install the backing plate onto the swing arm so that the brake cam faces to the rear as shown in **Figure 40**.

3. Install the retainer plate and the backing plate mounting bolts (B, **Figure 49**) and tighten as specified in **Table 2**.

4. Install the washer (B, **Figure 41**) and seat it against the retainer plate.

5. Lubricate the O-ring (A, **Figure 41**) with a high-temperature brake grease and install it over the axle and seat it against the washer.

6. Connect the vent hose (**Figure 40**) onto the backing plate fitting.

7. Reconnect the rear brake pedal rod, spring, barrel and adjuster onto the cam lever's right side (A, **Figure 59**).

8. Reconnect the parking brake cable, spring, barrel and adjuster onto the cam lever's left side (B, **Figure 59**).

9. Reconnect the spring (C, **Figure 59**) between the backing plate and cam lever.

10. Install the rear brake drum as described in this chapter.

11. Adjust the rear brake (Chapter Three).

FRONT BRAKE HOSE REPLACEMENT

Replace the upper brake hose and lower brake hoses every 4 years. Replace the metal brake lines if damaged.

The front brake hoses and their fittings are shown in **Figure 60**.

1. Remove the front fender (Chapter Fourteen).

2. Remove both front wheels (Chapter Ten).

3A. Drain the brake system with a vacuum pump. Follow the pump manufacturer's instructions.

3B. To drain the brake fluid manually, perform the following:

   a. Connect a clear hose onto the brake bleeder valve. Insert the open end of the hose into a clean container (**Figure 61**).
   b. Pump the brake lever a few times, then open the bleeder valve and apply the brake lever. When the brake lever reaches the end of its travel, close the bleeder valve and release the brake lever.
   c. Repeat this step a few times to remove as much brake fluid from the system as possible.

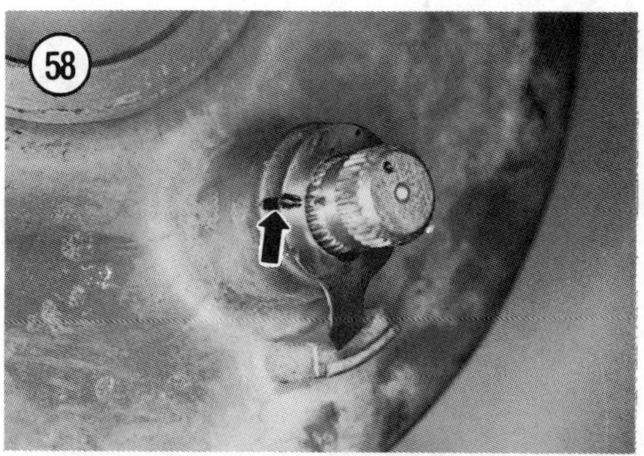

FRONT BRAKE HOSES

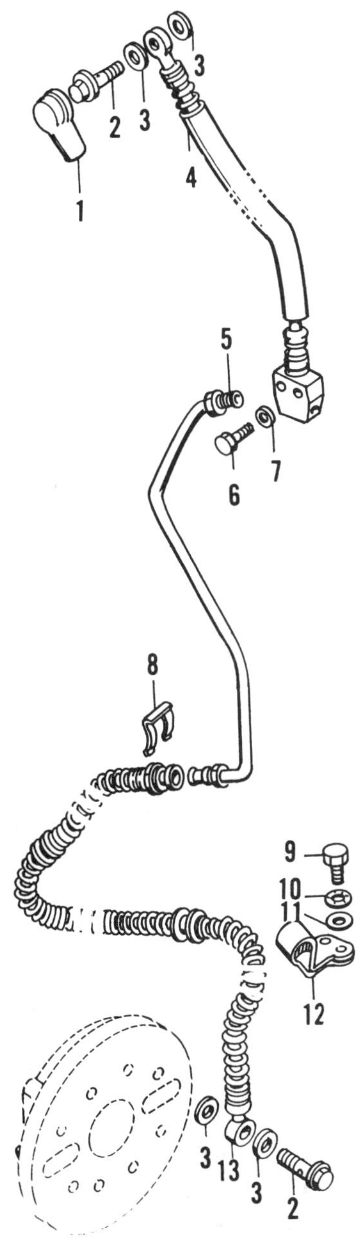

1. Rubber boot
2. Banjo bolt
3. Sealing washer
4. Upper brake hose
5. Metal brake pipe
6. Bolt
7. Washer
8. Clip
9. Bolt
10. Lockwasher
11. Washer
12. Clamp
13. Lower brake hose

13

d. When you have drained as much fluid as possible, close the bleeder valve and disconnect the hose at the valve.

4. Repeat Step 3 for the other side. Because there is now air in the brake lines, not all of the brake fluid will drain out.

NOTE
Because there will always be some residual brake fluid in the lines, be careful when disconnecting and removing the brake hoses in the following steps.

5. Unscrew and remove the master cylinder cover and diaphragm.

6. Remove the banjo bolt and sealing washers (**Figure 62**) at the back of the wheel cylinder. Hold the open hose end in a container to catch any residual brake fluid.

7. To remove the upper brake hose (4, **Figure 60**) and 3-way fitting, perform the following:

NOTE
The upper brake hose and the 3-way fitting are an assembly and cannot be separated.

a. Remove the banjo bolt and sealing washers (**Figure 63**) at the master cylinder.
b. Disconnect both brake pipe fittings (A, **Figure 64**) from the 3-way fitting at the base of the upper brake hose. Plug the ends of the brake pipes to prevent the entry of foreign matter.
c. Remove the mounting bolts (B, **Figure 64**) securing the 3-way fitting to the frame.
d. Remove the upper brake hose assembly (C, **Figure 65**) from the frame.

8. To remove the lower brake hose (13, **Figure 60**), perform the following:

NOTE
The following steps are shown with the brake backing plate removed from the steering knuckle for clarity. It is not necessary to remove the backing plate for this procedure.

a. Note the routing of the lower brake hose through the frame and the front suspension arms prior to removal of the hose. The hose must be reinstalled through the same path to avoid damage to the hose during suspension arm movement when riding.

61

62

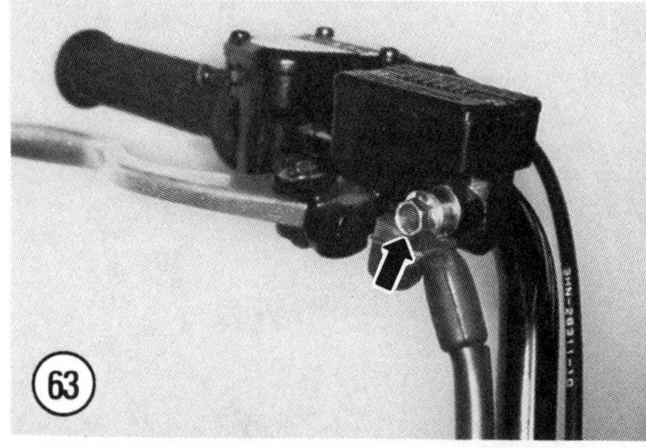
63

64

b. Disconnect the brake pipe fitting (**Figure 65**) from the fitting on the end of the lower brake hose.
c. Disconnect the clamp from the lower brake hose.
d. Remove the clip (A, **Figure 66**) securing the lower brake hose to the mounting bracket on the frame.
e. Remove the bolts, lockwasher and washers securing the hose clamp to the upper suspension arm.

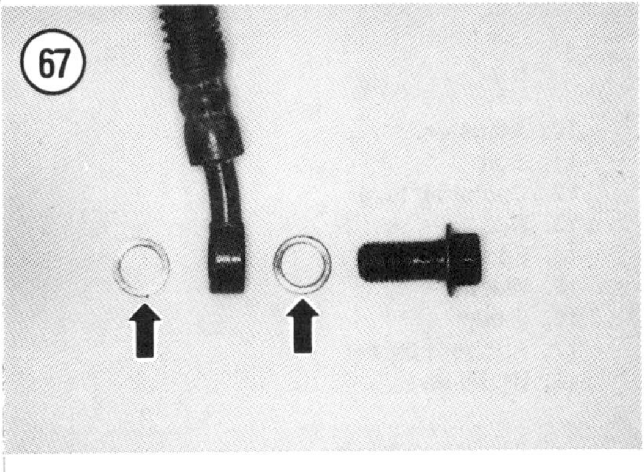

f. Remove the lower brake hose (B, **Figure 66**) from the frame and suspension arms.
g. Repeat for the other brake hose.

9. To remove the metal brake pipe (5, **Figure 60**), perform the following:
   a. Completely unscrew the brake pipe fitting(s) (A, **Figure 64**) from the 3-way fitting at the base of the upper brake hose.
   b. Completely unscrew the brake pipe fitting (**Figure 65**) from the fitting on the end of the lower brake hose. Plug the ends of the brake hose to prevent the entry of foreign matter.
   c. Remove the brake pipe(s) from the frame.
10. Inspect the brake hoses for damage or deterioration.
11. Install new brake hose(s) and metal lines in the reverse order of removal. Install new sealing washers (**Figure 67**).
12. Tighten the banjo bolts and the brake pipe fittings as specified in **Table 2**.
13. Refill the master cylinder with fresh brake fluid clearly marked DOT 3 OR DOT 4. Bleed the brake as described in this chapter.

WARNING
Do not ride the vehicle until you are sure that the brakes are operating properly.

REAR BRAKE PEDAL

Refer to **Figure 68** for the rear brake pedal and rod and the parking brake cable.

1. Remove the rear fender (Chapter Fourteen).
2. Unhook the brake pedal return spring (A, **Figure 69**) and the No. 2 select lever control cable and spring (B, **Figure 69**) from the brake pedal arm.
3. Remove the right footpeg and guard (**Figure 70**).
4. Disconnect the brake adjuster and disconnect the brake rod from the camshaft lever (**Figure 71**).
5. Disconnect the brake cable from the cable bracket (**Figure 72**).
6. Remove the E-clip and washer (**Figure 73**) securing the brake pedal to the pivot post on the frame.
7. Pull the rear brake pedal assembly off the pivot post on the frame and remove it.
8. Reverse these steps to install the rear brake pedal, while noting the following:
   a. Lubricate the brake pedal pivot post with grease.
   b. Make sure the E-clip is properly seated in the pivot post groove (**Figure 73**).

c. Adjust the rear brake as described in Chapter Three.

WARNING
Do not ride the vehicle until you are sure that the brakes are operating properly.

BRAKE BLEEDING

Bleed the front brakes if they feel spongy, after repairing a leak or replacing parts in the system or when replacing the brake fluid.

This section describes 2 techniques for bleeding the brake system. The first is with a vacuum pump, and the second is with a container and a piece of clear tubing.

1. Remove the dust cap from the bleed valve on the wheel cylinder.

2A. If using a vacuum pump, assemble the pump by following the manufacturer's instructions. Then connect the vacuum pump hose to the wheel cylinder bleed valve.

2B. If a vacuum pump is not being used, perform the following:

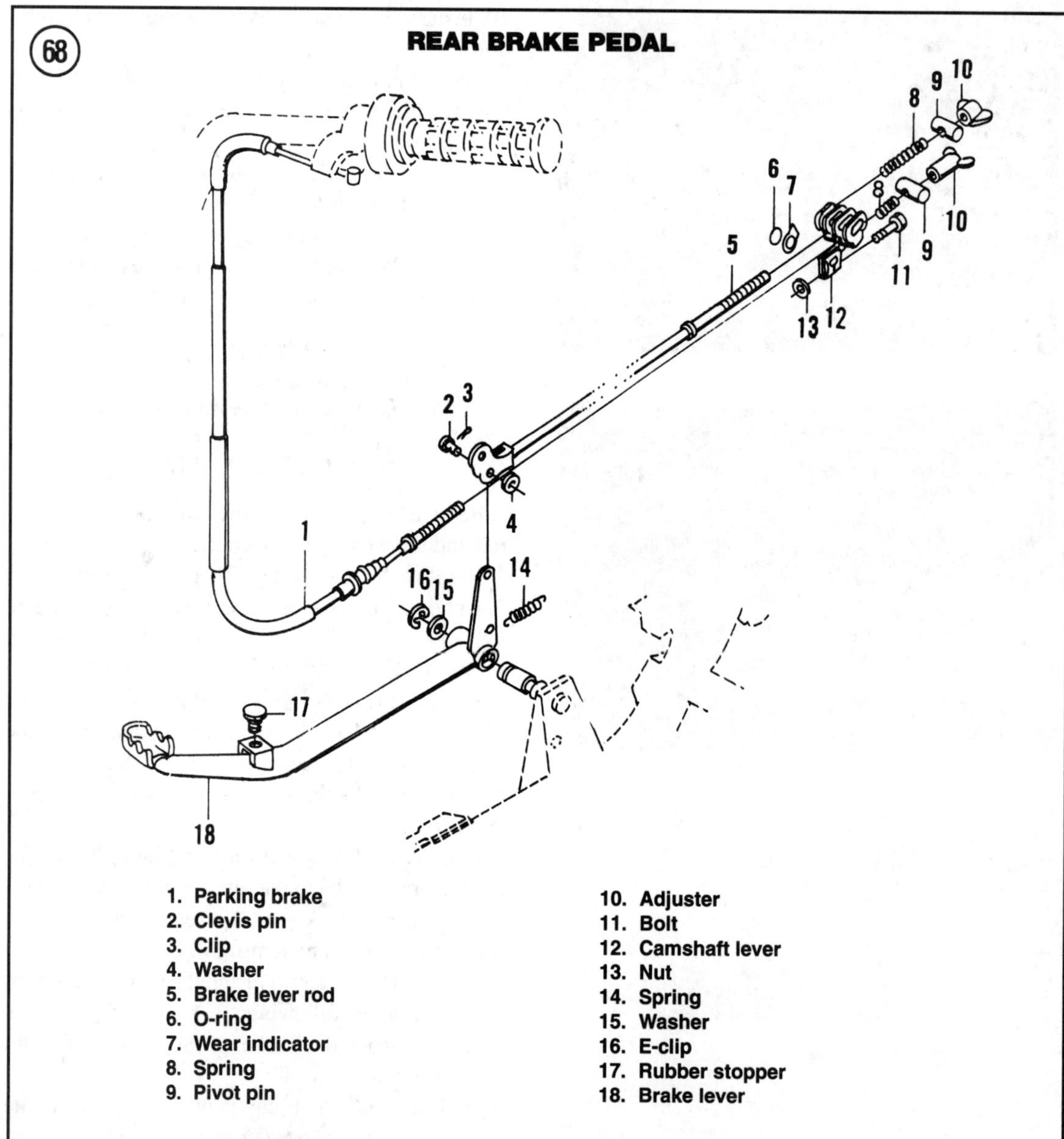

68 **REAR BRAKE PEDAL**

1. Parking brake
2. Clevis pin
3. Clip
4. Washer
5. Brake lever rod
6. O-ring
7. Wear indicator
8. Spring
9. Pivot pin
10. Adjuster
11. Bolt
12. Camshaft lever
13. Nut
14. Spring
15. Washer
16. E-clip
17. Rubber stopper
18. Brake lever

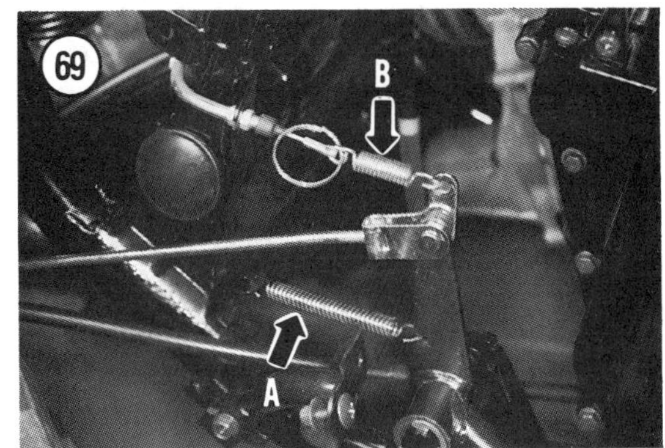

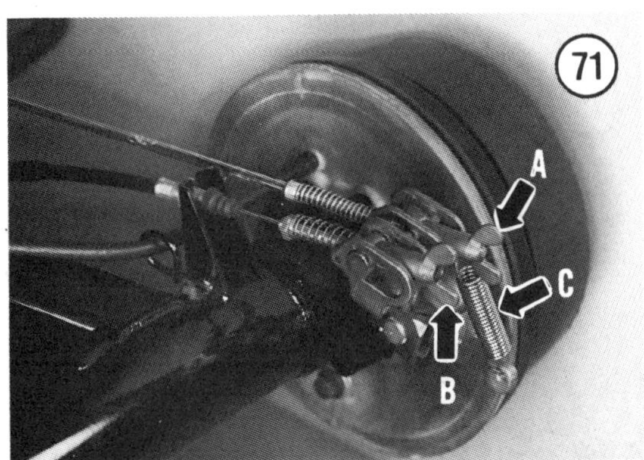

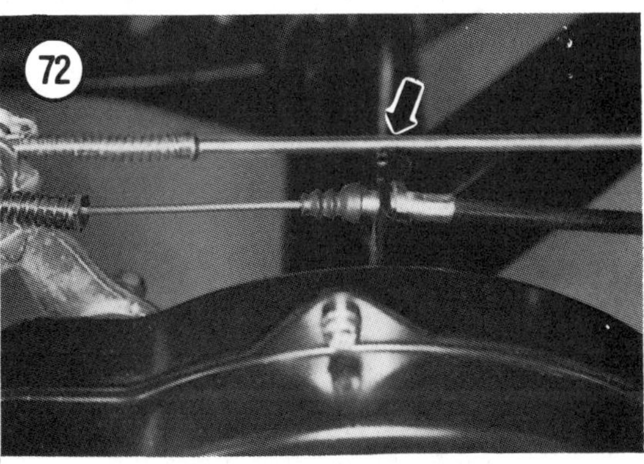

a. Connect a piece of clear tubing onto the bleed valve.

b. Insert the other end of the tube into a container partially filled with new brake fluid. Tie the tube in place so that it cannot slip out of the container. See **Figure 74**.

3. Clean the master cylinder cover of all dirt and foreign matter.

4. Turn the front wheels so that the master cylinder is level.

5. Cover the area underneath the master cylinder with a heavy cloth to protect the parts from the accidental spilling of brake fluid.

CAUTION

Wash spilled brake fluid from any plastic, painted or plated surface immediately as it will destroy the finish. Clean with soapy water and rinse completely.

6. Unscrew and remove the master cylinder top cover (A, **Figure 75**) and diaphragm.

7. Fill the master cylinder with DOT 3 or DOT 4 brake fluid.

WARNING

Use DOT 3 or DOT 4 brake fluid from a sealed container. Do not intermix different brands of fluid. Do not use a silicone base DOT 5 brake fluid as it can damage the clutch components leading to brake system failure.

NOTE

When bleeding the front brake, check the fluid level in the master cylinder often. If the reservoir runs dry, air will enter the system. If this occurs, the entire procedure must be repeated.

8A. If using a vacuum pump, perform the following:

a. Operate the vacuum pump several times to create a vacuum in the attached hose.
b. Open the bleed valve 1/4 turn to allow air and fluid to be extracted through the line. When the flow of air and fluid starts to slow down, close the bleed valve.
c. Operate the brake lever several times and release it.
d. Refill the master cylinder reservoir as necessary.
e. Repeat for the opposite brake line.
f. Repeat these steps until there is a solid feel when operating the brake lever and there are no bubbles being released from the system.

8B. If a vacuum pump is not being used, perform the following:

a. Operate the brake lever several times until resistance is felt, then hold it in its applied position. If the system was opened or drained completely, there will be no initial resistance at the brake lever.
b. Open the bleed valve 1/4 turn and allow the lever to travel to its limit, then close the bleed valve and release the brake lever.
c. Operate the brake lever several times and release it.
d. Refill the master cylinder reservoir as necessary.
e. Repeat for the opposite brake line.
f. Repeat these steps until there is a solid feel when operating the brake lever and there are no bubbles being released from the system.

NOTE

If you are flushing the system, continue with Step 9 until the fluid being drawn from the system is clean.

9. Remove the vacuum pump or container and hose from the system. Snap the bleed valve dust cap onto the bleed valve.

10. If necessary, add brake fluid to correct the level in the reservoir. It should be to the upper level line (B, **Figure 75**).

11. Install the diaphragm and cover. Tighten the screws securely.

12. Recheck the feel of the brake lever. It should be firm and offer the same resistance each time it is operated. If the lever feels spongy, check all of the hoses for leaks and bleed the system again.

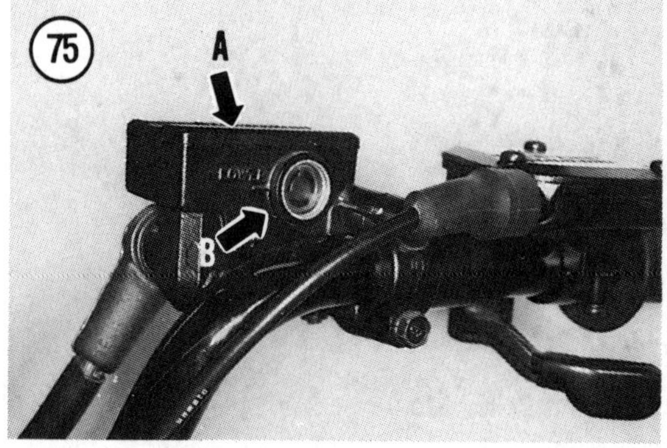

Table 1 BRAKE SPECIFICATIONS

	New mm (in.)	Service limit mm (in.)
Front drum brakes		
Brake drum inside diameter	160 (6.30)	161 (6.34)
Brake lining thickness	4.0 (0.16)	1.0 (0.04)
Brake shoe spring free length	104 (4.09)	—
Rear drum brakes		

Table 2 BRAKE TIGHTENING TORQUES

	N•m	in.-lb.	ft.-lb.
Axle nuts			
Front axle	130	—	95
Rear axle	150	—	110
Brake backing plate mounting bolts			
Front plate	28	—	20
Rear plate	30	—	22
Brake hose banjo bolts	25	—	18
Brake pipe fittings	18	—	13
Brake hose and wheel cylinder bolt	27	—	20
Caliper bleed screw	6	53	—
Master cylinder mounting bolts	10	88	—
Rear wheel and brake drum nuts	55	—	40
Rear brake cam shaft nut	9	79	—
Rear camshaft lever mounting bolt and nut	10	88	—
Wheel cylinder mounting bolt	10	88	—

CHAPTER FOURTEEN

BODY

This chapter contains removal and installation procedures for body panels, the carrier/racks and the foot rests.

It is suggested that as soon as the part is removed from the vehicle all mounting hardware (i.e. small brackets, bolts, nuts, rubber bushings, metal collars, etc.) be reinstalled onto the removed part. Yamaha makes frequent changes during the model year, so the part and the way it is attached to the frame may differ slightly from the one used in the service procedures in this chapter.

SEAT

Removal/Installation

1. Park the vehicle on level ground and set the parking brake.
2. On the left-hand side, pull the seat lever up (**Figure 1**). Then lift the rear of the seat and remove it.
3. Check the lever bracket (A, **Figure 2**) on the bottom of the seat for loose mounting fasteners or a weak return spring. Replace missing or damaged rubber dampers (B, **Figure 2**).
4. Slide the seat hook underneath the frame brace. Then push the seat down until it locks in place.

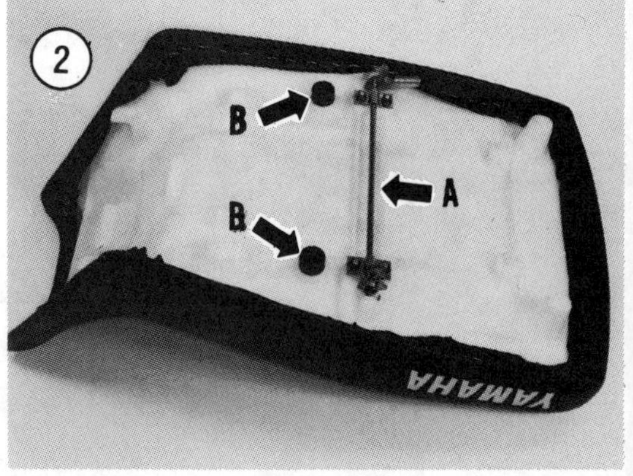

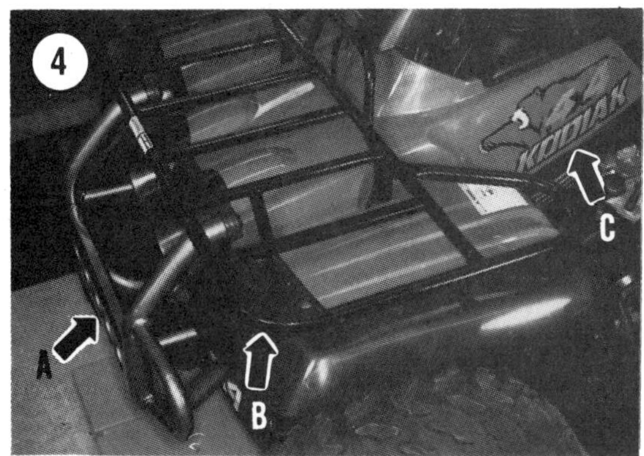

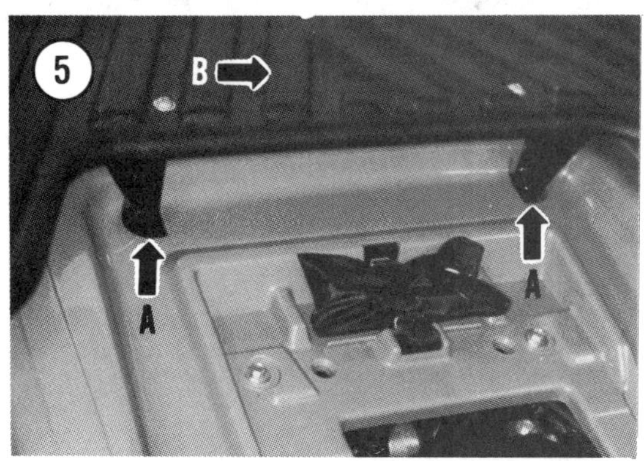

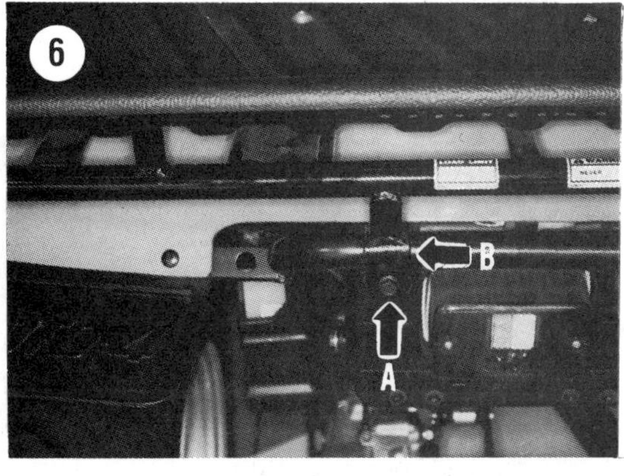

5. Check that the seat is firmly locked in place.

WARNING
Do not ride the vehicle until the seat is secured in place.

FRONT GUARD

Removal/Installation

1. Park the vehicle on level ground and set the parking brake.
2. Remove the bolts securing the front guard to the frame. See **Figure 3**, typical.
3. Remove the front guard.
4. Install by reversing these removal steps.

FRONT BUMPER

Removal/Installation

1. Park the vehicle on level ground and set the parking brake.
2. Remove the bolts securing the front bumper (A, **Figure 4**) to the frame and remove the front bumper.
3. Install by reversing these removal steps. Tighten the bolts securely.

FRONT CARRIER RACK

Removal/Installation

1. Park the vehicle on level ground and set the parking brake.
2. Remove the bolts securing the front carrier rack (B, **Figure 4**) to the frame and remove it.
3. Install by reversing these removal steps. Tighten the bolts securely.

REAR CARRIER RACK

1. Park the vehicle on level ground and set the parking brake.
2. Working under the rear fender, remove the bolts securing the front mounting brackets (A, **Figure 5**) to the frame.
3. Remove the rear clamping bolts (A, **Figure 6**) and clamp. Don't lose the protective sleeve located on the rear guard (B, **Figure 6**) under the clamps. See **Figure 7**.

4. Remove carrier/rack (B, **Figure 5**) from the rear fender and frame.

5. Install by reversing these removal steps. Refer to **Figure 8** and tighten the bolts securely.

REAR GUARD

1. Park the vehicle on level ground and set the parking brake.

2. Remove the rear carrier/rack as described in this chapter.

3. Working under the rear fender, remove the bolts (A, **Figure 9**) on each side securing the rear guard to the frame.

4. Remove rear guard (B, **Figure 9**) from the frame.

5. Install by reversing these removal steps. Tighten the bolts securely.

FUEL TANK COVER ASSEMBLY (1993-1995)

Removal/Installation

1. Park the vehicle on level ground and set the parking brake.

WARNING

Fuel vapors are present when removing the fuel tank cap. Because gasoline is an extremely flammable and explosive petroleum, perform this procedure away from all open flames (including pilot lights) and sparks. Do not smoke or allow someone who is smoking in the work area as an explosion and fire may occur. Always work in a well ventilated area. Wipe up any spills immediately.

2. Unscrew the fuel filler cap (A, **Figure 10**) and remove it and the vent tube (B, **Figure 10**).

3. Remove the fuel tank cover mounting bolts and remove the fuel tank cover (**Figure 11**).

CAUTION

The fuel tank cover locking tabs and receptacles on the front fender are small and fragile. Take care in unhooking them in the following step or they may fracture and break off.

4. Carefully pull the fuel tank cover back and unhook the locking tab on each side where it hooks on the front fender. Remove the cover (**Figure 11**).

5. Reinstall the fuel filler cap (**Figure 12**) onto the fuel tank.

6. Install by reversing these removal steps.

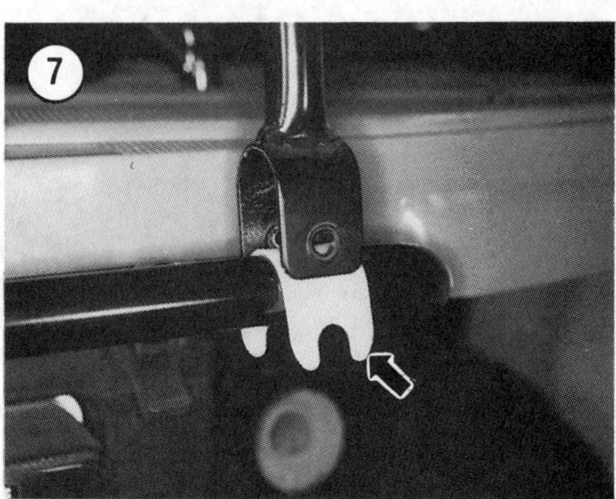

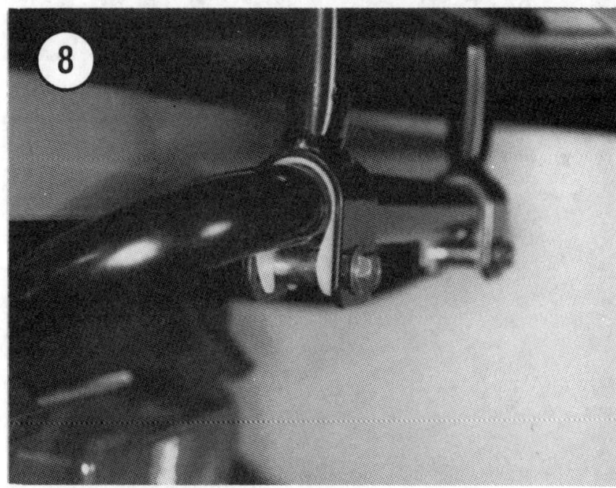

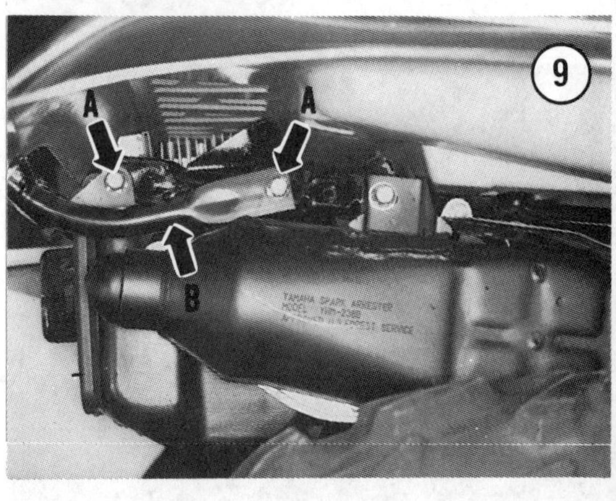

FRONT FENDER

Removal/Installation

Refer to **Figure 13** (1993-1995) or **Figure 14** (1996-on) for this procedure.

1. Park the vehicle on level ground and set the parking brake.

2. Remove the seat as described in this chapter.

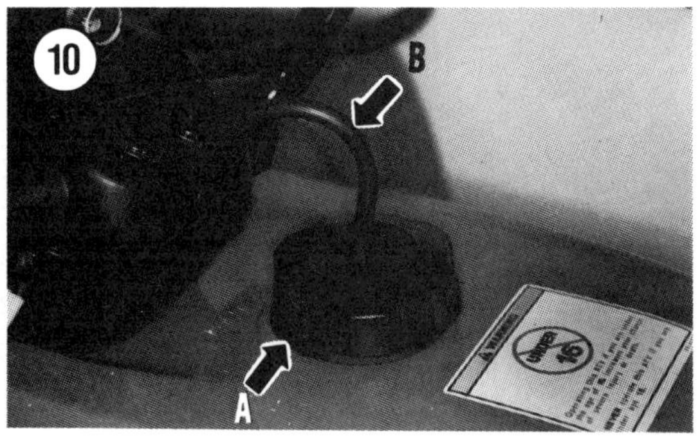

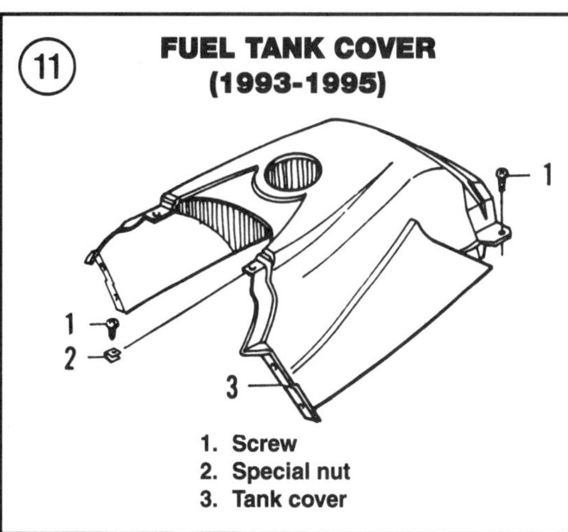

1. Screw
2. Special nut
3. Tank cover

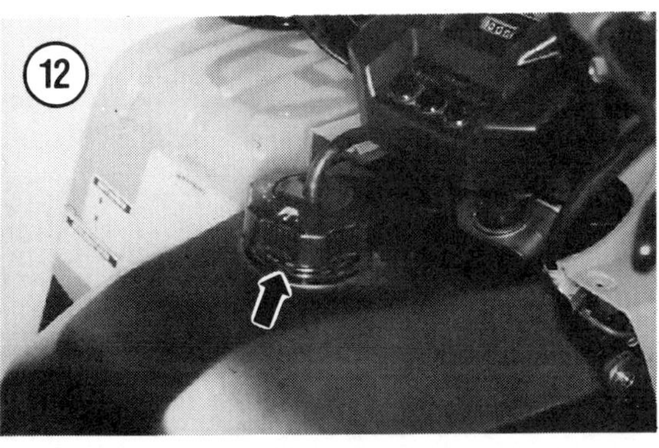

3. Remove the front carrier rack and front guard as described in this chapter.
4. On 1993-1995 models, remove the fuel tank cover as described in this chapter.
5. Working under the front fender, disconnect the headlight electrical connectors.
6. Remove the nuts and bolts securing the front fender assembly to the frame. See **Figure 13** or **Figure 14**.
7. Carefully remove the front fender (C, **Figure 4**) from the frame.

WARNING

The fender stays project away from the frame and are a dangerous protrusion. If the front fender is going to be left off for any period of time while servicing the engine, remove the fender stays to avoid either damage to yourself or the fender stays.

8. Remove the bolt securing each front fender stay and remove both fender stays.
9. Install by reversing these removal steps, while noting the following:
   a. Tighten all bolts and nuts securely. Do not overtighten as the plastic fender may fracture at the mounting hole.
   b. Make sure the headlight electrical connectors are free of corrosion. Clean off if necessary.
   c. Check the headlight operation.

REAR FENDER

Removal/Installation

Refer to **Figure 15** for this procedure.

1. Park the vehicle on level ground and set the parking brake.
2. Remove the seat as described in this chapter.
3. On 1996 and later models, remove the battery (Chapter Three).
4. Remove the rear carrier rack (A, **Figure 16**) as described in this chapter.
5. Remove the bolt/washers securing the top of the rear fender to the frame.
6. Remove the bolt on each side securing the front of the front fender to the frame.
7. Lift the rear fender partially up to make sure all fasteners are removed.

13

FRONT FENDER (1993-1995)

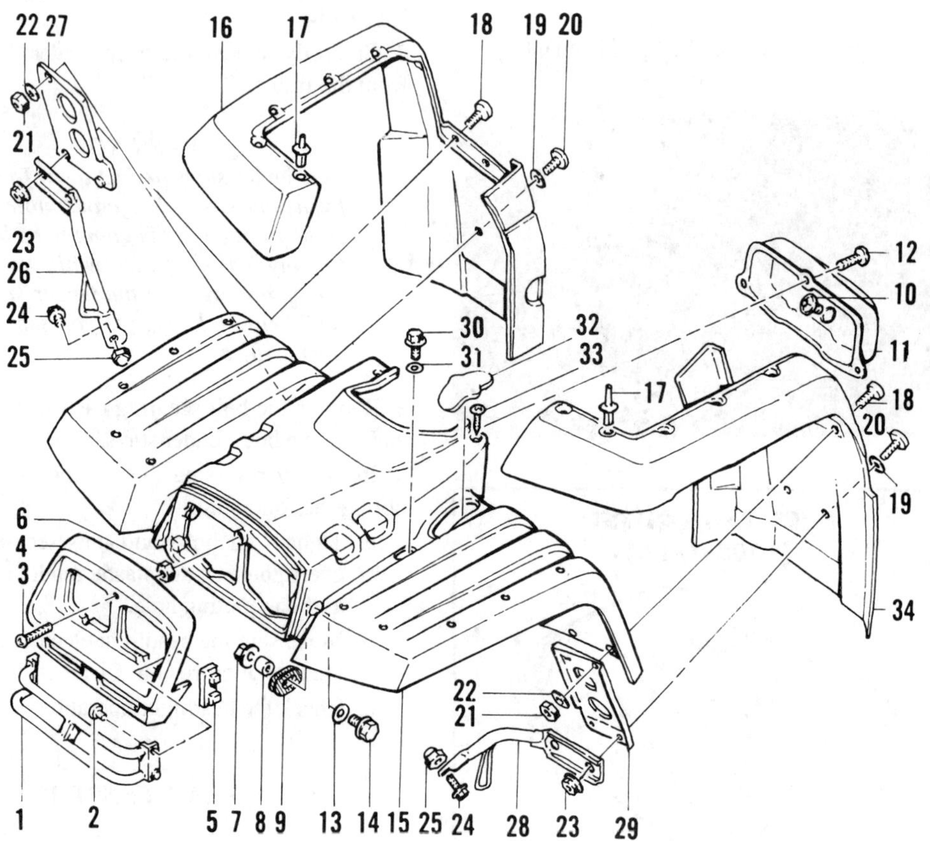

1. Headlight guard
2. Bolt
3. Bolt
4. Headlight panel
5. Special nut
6. Nut
7. Nut
8. Collar
9. Grommet
10. Screw
11. Headlight housing
12. Screw
13. Washer
14. Bolt
15. Front fender
16. Outer fender
17. Rivet
18. Screw
19. Washer
20. Screw
21. Nut
22. Washer
23. Nut
24. Bolt
25. Acorn nut
26. Fender stay
27. Flap
28. Fender stay
29. Flap
30. Bolt
31. Washer
32. Cover
33. Screw
34. Outer fender

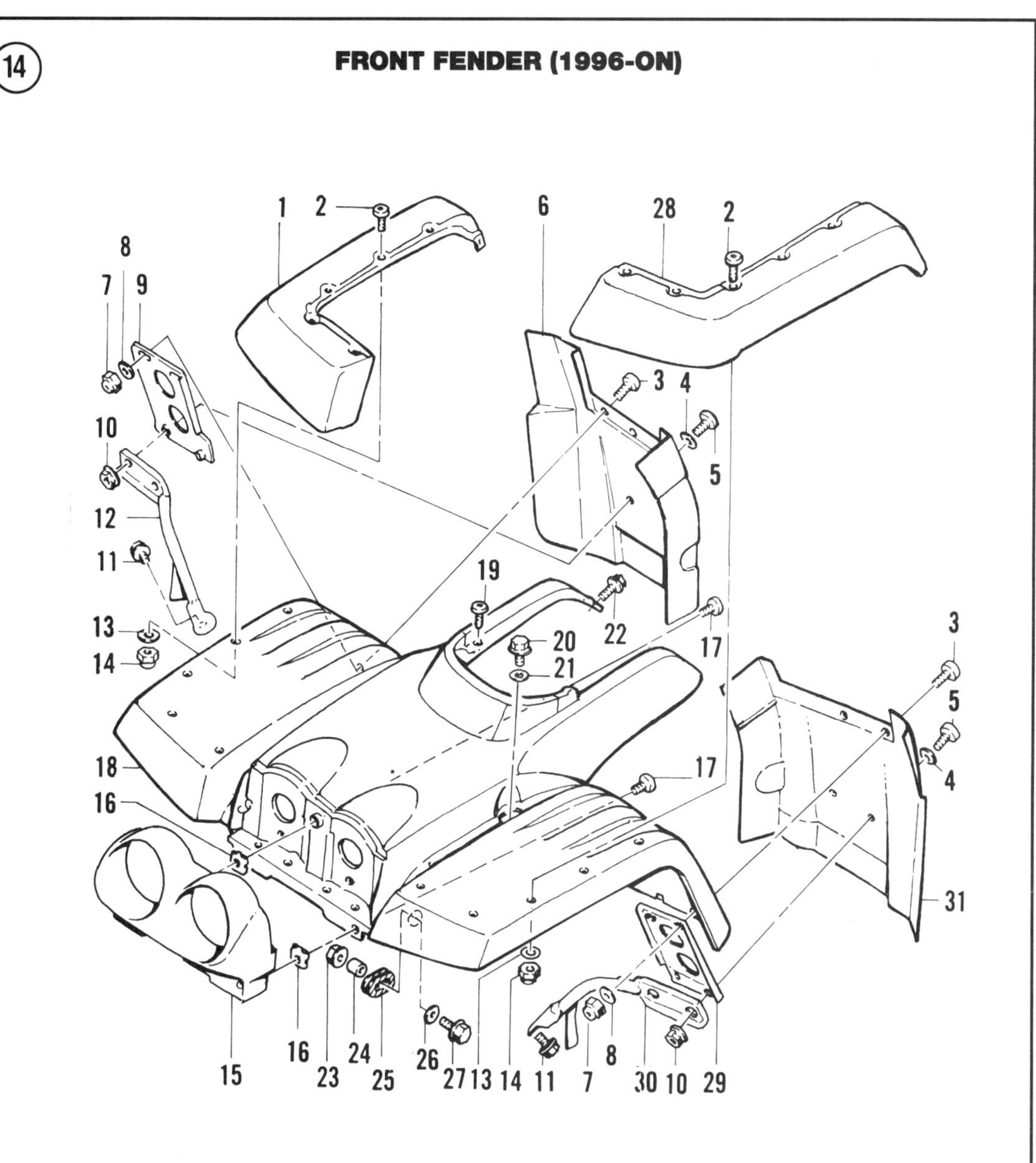

1. Outer fender
2. Screw
3. Screw
4. Washer
5. Screw
6. Flap
7. Nut
8. Washer
9. Flap
10. Nut
11. Bolt
12. Fender stay
13. Washer
14. Nut
15. Headlight panel
16. Spring nut
17. Screw
18. Front fender
19. Screw
20. Screw
21. Washer
22. Screw
23. Nut
24. Collar
25. Grommet
26. Washer
27. Bolt
28. Outer fender
29. Flap
30. Fender stay
31. Flap

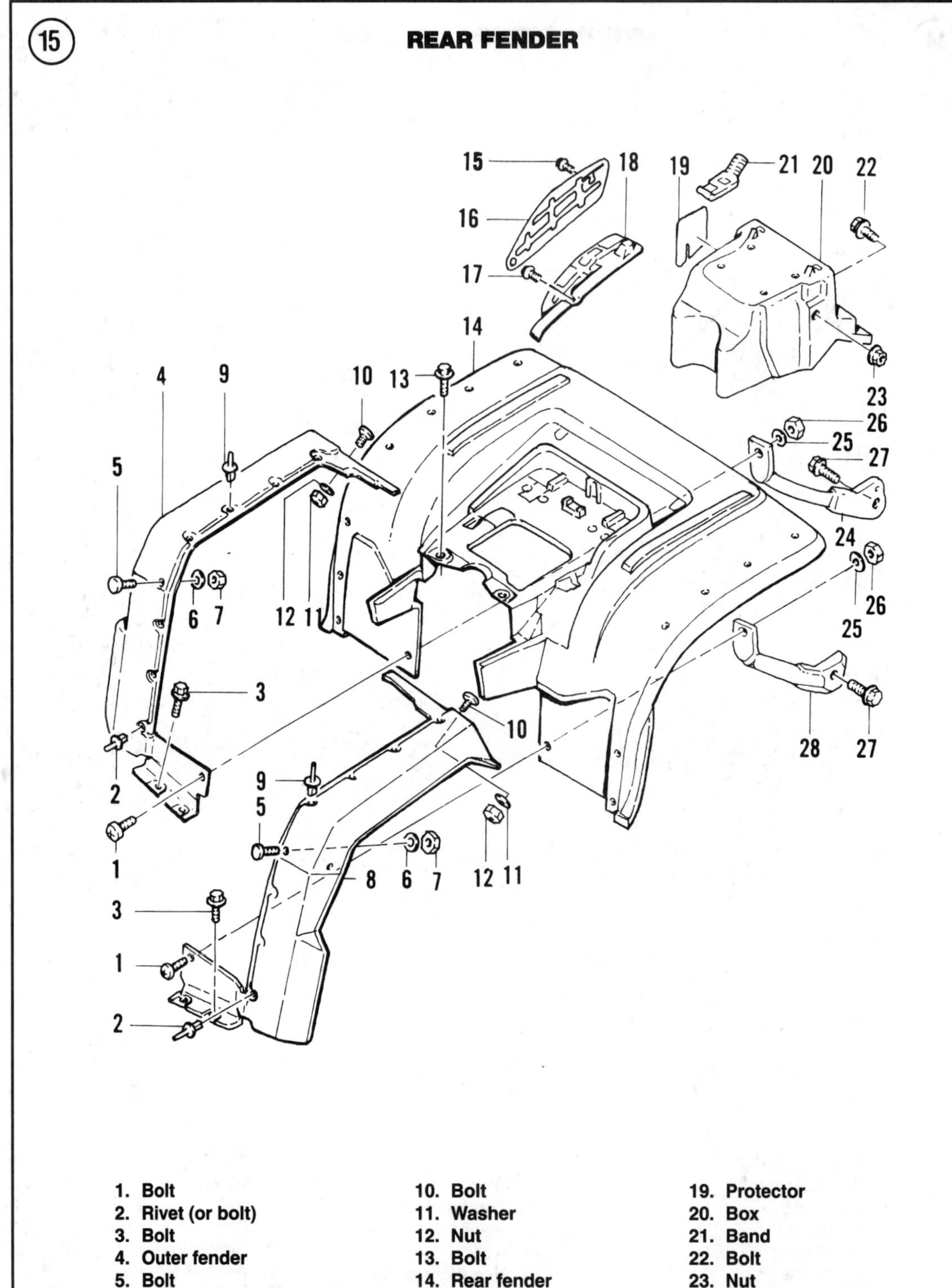

1. Bolt
2. Rivet (or bolt)
3. Bolt
4. Outer fender
5. Bolt
6. Lockwasher
7. Nut
8. Outer fender
9. Rivet
10. Bolt
11. Washer
12. Nut
13. Bolt
14. Rear fender
15. Bolt
16. Fender cover
17. Screw
18. Fender cover
19. Protector
20. Box
21. Band
22. Bolt
23. Nut
24. Fender stay
25. Washer
26. Nut
27. Bolt
28. Fender stay

8. Carefully remove the rear fender (B, **Figure 16**) from the frame.

9. Install by reversing these removal steps. Tighten all bolts securely. Do not overtighten as the plastic fender may fracture at the mounting holes.

FOOT RESTS

Removal/Installation

Refer **Figure 17** for this procedure.

1. Park the vehicle on level ground and set the parking brake.

(17)

FOOTREST ASSEMBLY

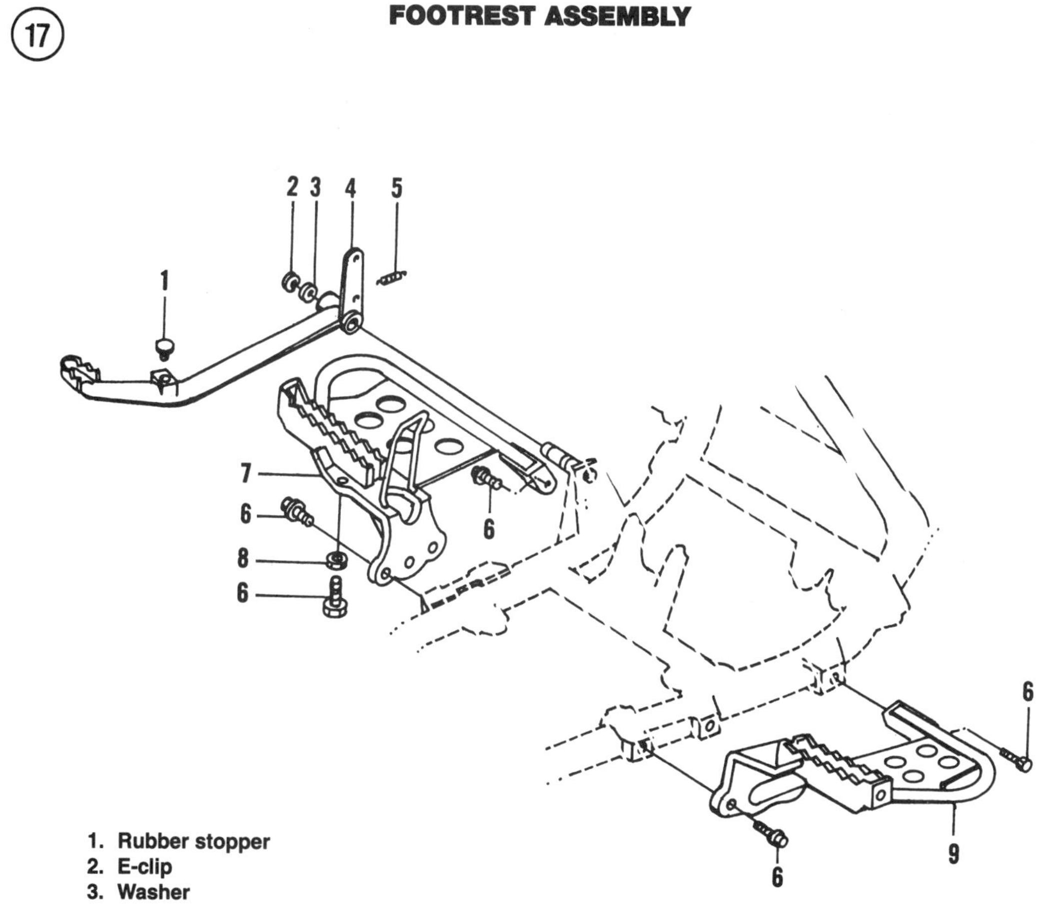

1. Rubber stopper
2. E-clip
3. Washer
4. Rear brake lever
5. Spring
6. Bolt
7. Footrest (right-hand)
8. Washer
9. Footrest (left-hand)

2A. On the left-hand side, remove the bolts (**Figure 18**) and remove the foot rest (**Figure 19**) from the frame.

2B. On the right-hand side, the rear brake pedal (A, **Figure 20**) does not have to be removed. Remove the bolts (**Figure 18**) and remove the foot rest (B, **Figure 20**) from the frame.

3. Install by reversing these removal steps. Tighten all bolts securely.

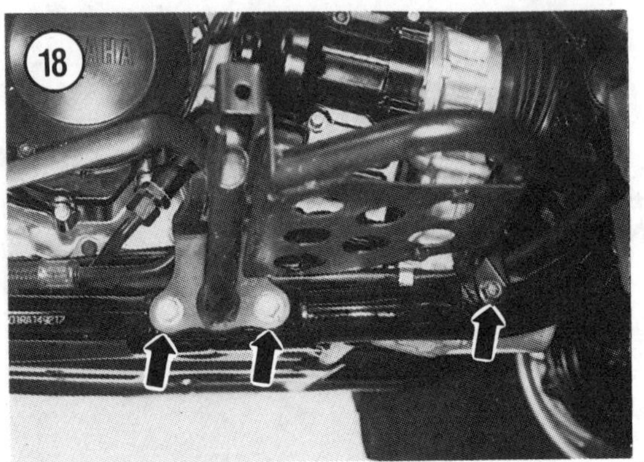
18

19

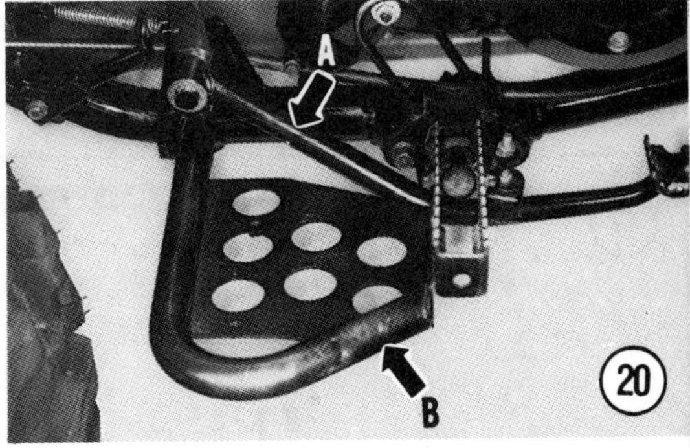

20

INDEX

S

T

U

V

W

YFM400FW

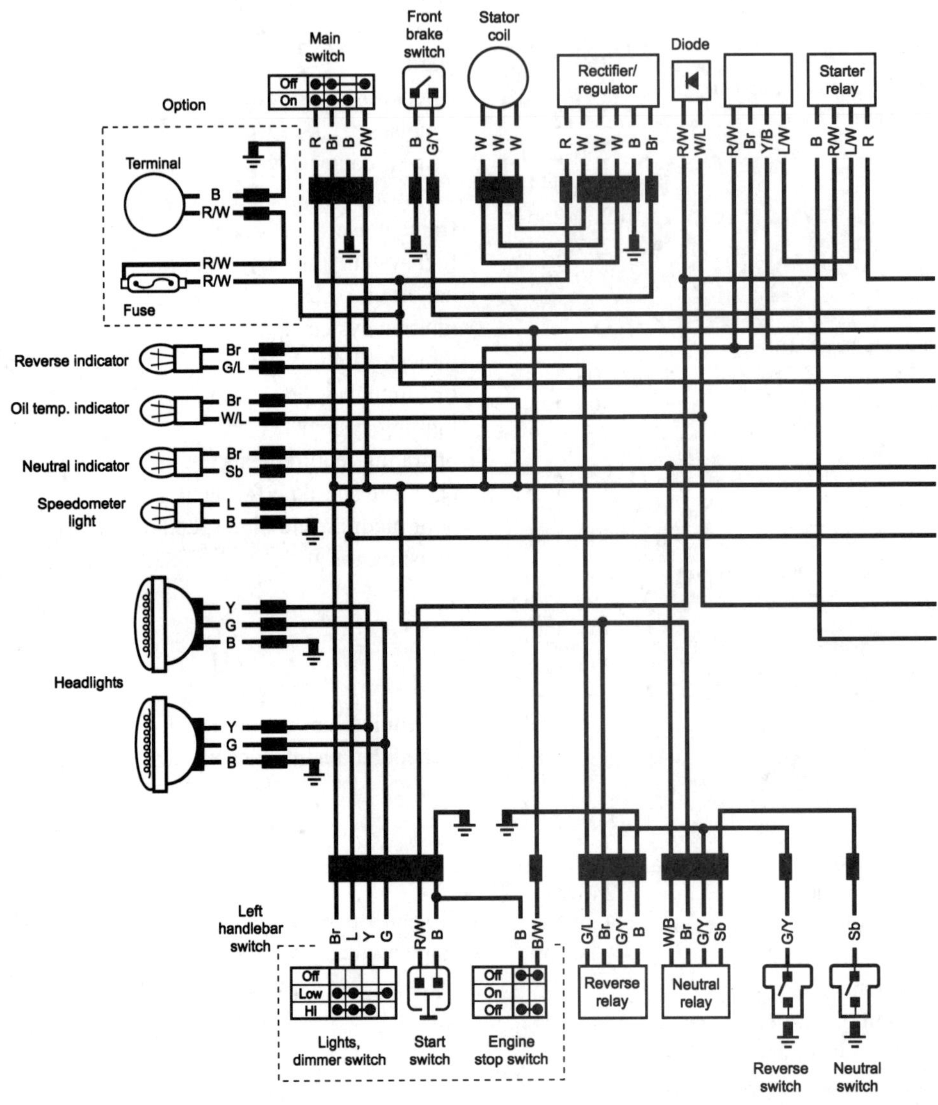

Main switch
Off
On
Front brake switch
Stator coil
Rectifier/ regulator
Diode
Starter relay
Option
Terminal
Fuse
Reverse indicator
Oil temp. indicator
Neutral indicator
Speedometer light
Headlights
Left handlebar switch
Low
Hi
Lights, dimmer switch
Start switch
Engine stop switch
Reverse relay
Neutral relay
Reverse switch
Neutral switch

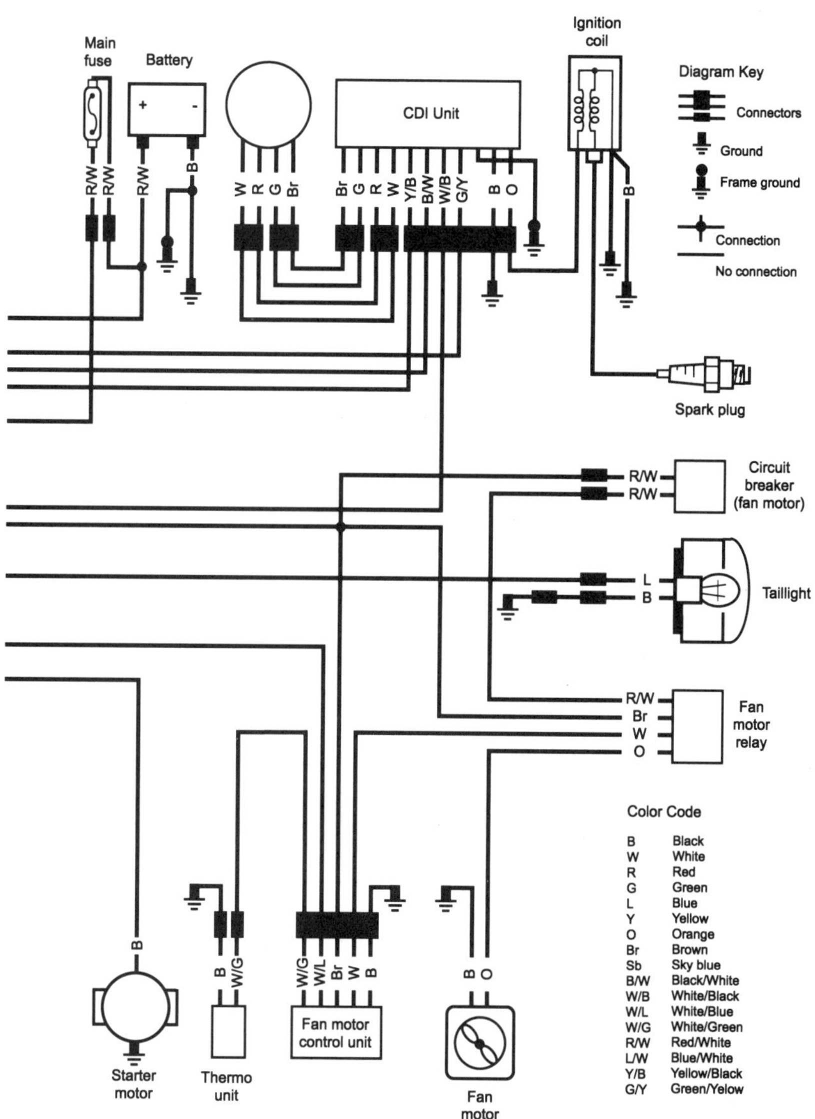
Main fuse
Battery
CDI Unit
Ignition coil
Diagram Key
Connectors
Ground
Frame ground
Connection
No connection
Spark plug
Circuit breaker (fan motor)
Taillight
Fan motor relay
Color Code
B Black
W White
R Red
G Green
L Blue
Y Yellow
O Orange
Br Brown
Sb Sky blue
B/W Black/White
W/B White/Black
W/L White/Blue
W/G White/Green
R/W Red/White
L/W Blue/White
Y/B Yellow/Black
G/Y Green/Yelow
Starter motor
Thermo unit
Fan motor control unit
Fan motor

MAINTENANCE LOG

Date	Miles	Type of Service